INTER-ETHNIC RELATIONS AND THE FUNCTIONING
OF MULTI-ETHNIC SOCIETIES

EARLY EUROPEAN RESEARCH

VOLUME 18

Series founded by Andrew Lynch and Claire McIlroy with the Australian Research Council Network for Early European Research, and now directed by The University of Western Australia Centre for Medieval and Early Modern Studies.

General Editors
Jacqueline Van Gent, University of Western Australia
Kirk Essary, University of Western Australia

Editorial Board
Tracy Adams, University of Auckland
Emilia Jamroziak, University of Leeds
Matthias Meyer, Universität Wien
Fabrizio Ricciardelli, Kent State University Florence Center
Juanita Feros Ruys, University of Sydney
Jón Viðar Sigurðsson, Universitetet i Oslo
Nicholas Terpstra, University of Toronto

Previously published volumes in this series
are listed at the back of the book.

Inter-Ethnic Relations and the Functioning of Multi-Ethnic Societies

Cohesion in Multi-Ethnic Societies in Europe
from c. 1000 to the Present, II

Edited by
PRZEMYSŁAW WISZEWSKI

BREPOLS

British Library Cataloguing in Publication Data
A catalogue record for this book is available
from the British Library

The project 'Cohesion Building of Multi-Ethnic Societies, 10th–20th c.' is financed within the framework of the National Programme of the Development of Humanities established by the Polish Ministry of Science and Higher Education and carried out in the Historical Institute of the University of Wrocław, agreement no. 12H 13 0446 82.

© 2022, Brepols Publishers n.v., Turnhout, Belgium

This is an open access publication made available under a cc by-nc 4.0 International License: <https://creativecommons.org/licenses/by-nc/4.0/>. No part of this publication may be reproduced, stored in a retrieval system, or transmitted, in any form or by any means, for commercial purposes, without the prior permission of the publisher, or as expressly permitted by law, by licence, or under terms agreed with the appropriate reprographics rights organization.

D/2022/0095/287
ISBN 978-2-503-60228-8
E-ISBN 978-2-503-60229-5
DOI 10.1484/M.EER-EB.5.131518
ISSN 2295-9254
E-ISSN 2295-9262

Printed in the EU on acid-free paper.

Table of Contents

Introduction: Inter-Ethnic Relations within Multi-Ethnic Societies
Przemysław Wiszewski — 9

Organizing Violence: Peace and War in Twelfth-Century Catalonia
Maria Bonet DONATO — 27

The Andalusian Urban Elites and the Almoravids in the Upper Border of al-Andalus during the Twelfth Century: An Example of Multi-Ethnic Coexistence
Jesús BRUFAL-SUCARRAT — 57

Shaping Identities in a Common Cultural Background: Muslims and Jews in the Medieval Portuguese Kingdom
Maria Filomena LOPES DE BARROS — 73

Ethnic and Religious Minorities and the Portuguese Military Orders as Recorded in the _Pontificia Corpora_ (Twelfth to Sixteenth Centuries)
Paula PINTO COSTA and Joana LENCART — 97

Social and Economic Relations between Sardinians and Aragonese in the Twelfth to Fifteenth Centuries
Luciano GALLINARI — 115

How to Live Together? Germans and Poles in Silesia in the Thirteenth to Fifteenth Centuries
Przemysław WISZEWSKI — 141

Between Coexistence and Persecution: Economic Activity and the Cohesion of Multi-Ethnic Societies in Cities of the Polish Territories (between the Thirteenth and the First Part of the Sixteenth Century)
Grzegorz MYŚLIWSKI — 159

Ethnic-Economic Relations within the Cities of Lublin, Zamość, and Lviv in the Sixteenth to Nineteenth Centuries
Andrzej Pleszczyński • 209

Economic and Social Aspects of Multi-Ethnic Transylvania during the Thirteenth and Fourteenth Centuries
Cosmin POPA-GORJANU • 227

The Dracula and the Others: The Multi-Ethnic Character of the Hungarian Political Elite until the Fifteenth Century
Daniel BAGI • 249

The Medical Marketplace as a Way of Communicating beyond Religion: Non-Christian Medical Practitioners in the Society of the Grand Duchy of Lithuania
Monika RAMONAITĖ • 263

Towns as Areas of Ethnic Communication and Competition: The Case of Karaites in Trakai/Troki and Vilnius/Wilno/Vilna in the Seventeenth to Twentieth Centuries
Dovilė TROSKOVAITĖ • 291

A Gift or 'Poklon dla Pana' as One of the Ways of Building Social Cohesion: The Case of the Vilnius Jewish Community in the Second Half of the Eighteenth Century
Jurgita ŠIAUČIŪNAITĖ-VERBICKIENĖ • 309

Façades of a Multi-Ethnic Empire: Presenting and Publicizing the Coronation of the 'All-Russian Emperor', Alexander III (1883)
Endre SASHALMI • 321

Polish American Parishes of the Nineteenth to Twenty-First Centuries and their Role in Shaping Polish American Identity and Status
Joanna WOJDON • 339

Concluding Remarks: Inter-Ethnic Cooperation — Fluid Networks of Everyday Practices
Przemysław WISZEWSKI • 357

Index • 363

List of Illustrations

Figures

Figure 2.1. The Almoravid Empire and its expansion. Image by the author. 59

Figure 2.2. The Almoravid Empire in al-Andalus. Image by the author. 60

Figure 2.3. NDVI image of Huahbala's *almúnya*. Source: Institut Cartogràfic i Geològic de Catalunya. 68

Figure 2.5. Detail of Muslim ashlars in Sant Ruf Absis. Image by the author. 69

Figure 2.4. Absis of Sant Ruf, and Muslim ashlars on the bottom of the wall. Image by the author. 69

Figure 10.1. First page of Vienna Illuminated Chronicle / *Chronicon Pictum Vindobonense* / *Képes Krónika*. Source: Wikimedia Commons, <https://commons.wikimedia.org/wiki/File:K%C3%A9pes_Kr%C3%B3nika_1360.jpg>. Image in the public domain. 253

Figure 15.1. Immaculate Conception Church in Panna Maria, Texas. Photo by Krzysztof Wojdon (2018). 340

Figure 15.2. Holy Trinity Church in Chicago. Photo by Krzysztof Wojdon (2014). 347

Maps and Charts

Map 1.1. The Iberian Peninsula in 1195. Source: <https://commons.wikimedia.org/wiki/File:P%C3%A9ninsule_ib%C3%A9rique_en_1195.png>. Elryck, CC BY-SA 4.0. 28

Map 2.1. The Iberian Peninsula between 1037 and 1065. Source: <https://commons.wikimedia.org/wiki/File:P%C3%A9ninsule_ib%C3%A9rique_en_1065.png>. Elryck, CC BY-SA 4.0. 58

Map 3.1. Muslims in the thirteenth, fourteenth, and fifteenth centuries. Source: Maria Filomena Lopes de Barros, *Tempos e Espaços de Mouros: A Minoria Muçulmana no Reino Português (Séculos XII a XV)* (Lisbon: Fundação Calouste Gulbenkian – Fundação para a Ciência e a Tecnologia, 2007), pp. 138, 142, and 145. 75

Map 4.1. The Iberian Five Kingdoms (14th century). Source: Julio López-Davalillo Larrea, *Atlas Historico de España y Portugal desde el Paleolítico hasta el siglo XX* (Madrid: Ed. Sintesis, 1999), p. 117. 98

Chart 4.1. The chronological distribution of the *pontificia corpora* through the centuries. 101

Map 5.1. Kingdom of Aragon: Mediterranean Expansion. Source: <https://commons.wikimedia.org/wiki/File:Reiaume_d%27Aragon_-_Expansion_en_Mediterran%C3%A8a.png>. Nicolas Eynaud, CC BY-SA 3.0. 116

Map 5.2. Crown of Aragon and Kingdom of Sardinia. Source: <https://commons.wikimedia.org/wiki/File:Reino_de_Cerdenya_en_a_Corona_d%27Arag%C3%B3 n.svg>. Willtron, CC BY-SA 3.0. 116

Map 6.1. Silesia 1294–1296. <https://commons.wikimedia.org/wiki/File:Silesia_1294-1296.svg>. CC BY-SA 2.5. 142

Map 7.1. Poland, Lithuania, and the Teutonic state at the beginning of the fifteenth century. Source: <https://commons.wikimedia.org/wiki/File:Poland,_Lithuania_and_Teutonic_state_at_the_beginning_of_the_XV_es.svg>. derivative work: Rowanwindwhistler, CC BY-SA 3.0. 160

Map 8.1. Polish-Lithuanian Commonwealth in 1764. Source: <https://commons.wikimedia.org/wiki/File:Polish-Lithuanian_Commonwealth_in_1764.PNG>. Mathiasrex, Maciej Szczepańczyk, based on layers of Halibutt, CC BY-SA 3.0. 210

Map 9.1. Administrative division of Transylvania, c. 1111–1867. Source: https://commons.wikimedia.org/wiki/File:Siebenb%C3%BCrgen_1300-1867.jpg. DietG, CC BY-SA 3.0. 228

Map 10.1. Hungary 1490. Source: <https://commons.wikimedia.org/wiki/File:Hungary_1490_(PL2018).png>. CC BY-SA 4.0. 250

Map 11.1. The Lithuanian State in the thirteenth–fifteenth centuries. Source: <https://commons.wikimedia.org/wiki/File:Lithuanian_state_in_13-15th_centuries.png>. CC BY-SA 2.5. 264

Map 14.1. Subdivisions of the Russian Empire in 1897. Source: <https://commons.wikimedia.org/wiki/File:Subdivisions_of_the_Russian_Empire_in_1897_(governorate_level,_uyezd_level_and_localities).svg>. CC BY-SA 4.0. 322

PRZEMYSŁAW WISZEWSKI

Introduction

Inter-Ethnic Relations within Multi-Ethnic Societies

The research presented in this book is the result of work undertaken by the project 'Cohesion Building of Multi-Ethnic Societies, 10th–20th c.'. It aimed to analyse the mechanisms that made it possible for different ethnic groups in the past to coexist within a single political entity.[1] The first volume resulting from this project was devoted to how communities shaped their collective memories in order to ensure the smooth operation of multi-ethnic political communities. The contributors focused on the study of written sources which described how specific ethnic groups used the past.[2] In this, the second volume of the project, the researchers take a subsidiary approach to discourse analysis to look beyond the texts; they focus primarily on activities that built a sense of cohesion within a political community that was made up of different ethnic groups.

The starting point for the research presented here is the concept of *social identity*; according to this the identity of individuals and groups is formed through social interaction. The identity that emerges in this way always has a multilayered structure as a consequence of the diverse nature of these relationships. Moreover, it is created through both social relationships and the choices made within *social relations* by individuals; these choices opened up new forms of interaction. The *identities* of group members and the groups themselves are created by integrating individuals' experiences into wider group narratives. And in turn, these group narratives shape the individual's perception of and narrative about the world.[3] Ethnic identities are based on stories about the past, but their interpretations and sometimes their shape change as ethnic identities themselves update, transform, among other things, under the influence of relations with other groups. Richard Jenkins, with reference to the

---

1 For more on the project, see Wiszewski, 'Preface: Cohesion of Multi-Ethnic Societies'.
2 Wiszewski, 'Introduction: Multi-Ethnicity and Memory'.
3 Frazer, 'Introduction: Identities in Early Medieval Britain', pp. 3–5.

Przemysław Wiszewski • (przemyslaw.wiszewski@uwr.edu.pl) is a Professor of Medieval and Early Modern History at the Historical Institute, University of Wrocław, with special interest in the medieval and early modern history of social relations, values structures within medieval societies, and regional history.

Inter-Ethnic Relations and the Functioning of Multi-Ethnic Societies: Cohesion in Multi-Ethnic Societies in Europe from c. 1000 to the Present, II, ed. by Przemysław Wiszewski, EER 18 (Turnhout: Brepols, 2022), pp. 9–25

BREPOLS ❧ PUBLISHERS   10.1484/M.EER-EB.5.132144

This is an open access chapter made available under a cc by-nc 4.0 International License.

views of Max Weber and Everett Hughes, emphasized that ethnic identities are based on a belief in a community of origin, but that the need for this belief is created by collective action arising from political causes and relating to the presence of groups composed of 'Others': 'ethnic identification arises out of and within the interaction between groups'.[4] Jenkins complemented this constructivist and dynamic approach to the nature of ethnic community by pointing to the constant updating of boundaries between ethnic communities. The definition by individuals of the specificity of their own group and its difference from other ethnic groups occurs in the context of concrete situations. In this way, the culture of an ethnic group is actualized by individuals in relation to a specific time and place. As a result, it is constantly changing.[5]

Such an approach leaves the following question unanswered: Why is it that the active community, which results from the coexistence of different ethnic groups in one political community, has sometimes led to the assimilation of multiple groups into one entity? In contrast, ethnic distinctiveness has been maintained at other times, and we observe in one political organization the parallel functioning of multiple ethnic groups working together. In doing so, it is important to differentiate relations between ethnic groups in the Middle Ages and the modern period and those that arose as a result of the transformation of multi-ethnic state organisms that had existed for hundreds of years into nation-states in the nineteenth and twentieth centuries. The latter process was the result of a cultural transformation initiated by the French Revolution, which found its political expression in the idea of the nation as a state-forming entity. In earlier eras and in multi-ethnic and multinational states until the end of the twentieth century, the acceptance of political identity (one's own participation in the political community) was not strictly linked to ethnic and cultural affiliation.[6] Only with the passage of time and under special circumstances could multiple ethnic groups have been transformed into one.[7] Which again brings us to the question posed above: Why did ethnic diversity disappear in some cases while it was maintained in others? For centuries, this has been the question faced by historians of border regions or communities subject to strong cultural and political influences from their neighbours. Initially, the concept of races/ethnic communities that were supposed to form homogeneous, complete *ethnic packages* was referred to. According to this theory, all members of an ethnic community were characterized

---

4 Jenkins, *Rethinking Ethnicity*, pp. 10–11.
5 Jenkins, *Rethinking Ethnicity*, pp. 13–14.
6 See Kappeler, *The Russian Empire*, for an attempt to cover the history of Russia as a multi-ethnic political organism, with the indication that 'in fact, the ideal of the ethnically uniform nation state first arose in the nineteenth century, and it was the source of a great deal of misery for mankind. Studying the history of multi-ethnic empires can serve to remind us that there are alternative principles with regard to the structure of states and societies' (p. 3). Reynolds, 'The Idea of a Nation as a Political Community', pp. 57–58, argued that medieval *nations* had identical main features to their modern counterparts: a belief in a common origin, customs, laws, and sometimes language. They differed from modern nations only in their lack of universality. However, this scholar referred to the situation of the inhabitants of selected western European kingdoms (Great Britain and France), neglecting the reality of the multi-ethnic monarchies of central and southern Europe.
7 Reynolds, 'The Idea of a Nation as a Political Community'.

by a specific culture, which was fully distinct from other groups. Additionally, their political activity was marked by long-standing differences. From the nineteenth century onwards, distinct physical characteristics were also attributed to ethnic communities.

Since the second half of the twentieth century, such concepts have been used less and less as a narrative framework for stories about inter-ethnic relations. They tend to appear in popular or politically motivated approaches.[8] Such conceptions of the community are more popular for the period prior to the early nineteenth century, in which ethnic issues do not play as important a role as earlier scholars have indicated. Attention is drawn, in particular, to the intermingling of cultures and languages and the inconsistent use of ethnic categories by historical sources.[9] But even this does not explain the clearly visible ethnic distinctiveness of the groups that nevertheless worked together in political communities. An example of the stability of the different cultural characteristics of ethnic groups living within a single urban community was provided by the analysis of the diet of the inhabitants of medieval and early modern Tallinn (fourteenth–sixteenth centuries). Analyses of skeletal remains have shown that people from local population groups (Estonians and Ruthenians) mainly consumed local varieties of plants and livestock (cattle). In contrast, the diet of migrants — mainly of German origin — was characterized by a significant proportion of fish and seafood. In one case, a change in diet can be noted; one individual, who was buried in St Barbara's Cemetery in Tallinn, had grown up eating a traditional diet, but then included fish in their diet later in life. Ethnic communities, while forming distinct professional groups, were therefore not fully closed. They certainly knew the patterns of behaviour that defined them, including those relating to diet. They did not reject the possibility of adopting the customs of other groups living in Tallinn. Nor did the change in diet mean acculturation — the individual in question was buried in a cemetery associated with the local community. However, this was an exceptional case. Diet — in part a derivative of economic and religious circumstances — was a stable part of the cultural characteristics which emphasized the distinctiveness of the local ethnic groups.[10] This was a distinction that had not been erased despite centuries of cooperation within the urban political community.

In order to recognize the conditions conducive to cooperation between ethnoses, it is useful to look at the circumstances which might lead to the breakdown of cooperation and the transition of the relationship into a state of conflict. This was a recurring theme throughout the 'Cohesion Building' project. Inter-ethnic conflicts, especially those with a religious basis, appear relatively frequently in the literature on medieval and modern Europe. So much so that the phenomenon of racism is highlighted as being constantly linked, in varying situations, to the history of the West. In doing so, Bethencourt clearly distinguishes it from ethnocentrism and

---

8 Harland, 'Rethinking Ethnicity and "Otherness"', pp. 114–15, writes about this kind of impact of Britain's exit from the European Union on historiographical interpretations of Britons' ethnic distinctiveness from Romans and Anglo-Saxons in Gildas's work *De Excidio*.
9 See for example Hammond, 'Ethnicity and the Writing of Medieval Scottish History'.
10 Lightfoot and others, 'The Influence of Social Status and Ethnicity on Diet', pp. 98–100.

emphasizes the element of aggression present in racism, directed against entire groups and all its members with whom the aggressors had relations.[11] In the case of Jewish historical research, the vision of an almost permanent religious-ethnic conflict in relations with Christian communities overshadows the fact that Jewish communities have for decades and indeed centuries cooperated with neighbouring Christian communities. This was accompanied by social tensions, but it was not always underpinned by anti-Semitic attitudes.[12] At the same time, it seems that the persuasive power of elite medieval Christian literature which emphasized the deep conflict between followers of Christ and Jews overshadowed the reality of social behaviour. This leads historians who study the official written sources to conclude that there was widespread anti-Semitism, though in different forms, in the Middle Ages.[13] In one of the studies presented in this volume, Monika Ramonaitė proves that the anti-Semitism evident in public narratives did not prevent the maintenance of peaceful and mutually beneficial cooperation between Christians and Jewish professionals in the early modern period. The issue of the prevalence of animosity, or of 'dormant hostility', aroused by using a variety of techniques to spread particular statements among a wide audience, mainly by members of political power structures, runs through the research carried out within the framework of this project.

This discussion of inter-ethnic relations will conclude with a volume on the relationship between the political activities of the most influential actors in society and the coexistence of ethnic groups. This collection bridges visions of the past and the future, that is, the functioning of legal orders and the use of arguments with ethnic aspects in domestic political activity. But in order to understand how politicians influence inter-ethnic relations, it is crucial to recognize the ties and dependencies that arise between different ethnic groups in a single political community. These relationships formed a proper network of dependencies that political actors used for their purposes. Therefore, this volume is crucial for understanding the political mechanisms that affected inter-ethnic cooperation, but which also created a demand for the production of new historiographical narratives or the modification of existing historiographical visions. The shift from the analysis of visions of the past (volume one) to the study of behaviour in existing multi-ethnic societies (the current volume) is intended to enable inter-ethnic relations to be set in the context of the practical demands of social life. Therefore, the main issue presented in this volume is the analysis of activities that were designed to build inter-ethnic relations. The contributors focus on the effects of the analysed events on the presence of their protagonists. The coexistence of different ethnic groups is looked at here not through the prism of theoretical analyses undertaken by the intellectual elites, but by following community members' responses to the current needs of their contemporary circumstances as recorded in the sources.

---

11 Bethencourt, *Racisms*, p. 8: 'Racism distinguishes itself from ethnocentrism in that it does not refer to a disdained or feared neighbourhood or distant community in the abstract; it generally targets groups with which the reference community is engaged'.

12 Chazan, *Medieval Stereotypes and Modern Anti-semitism*, p. 130.

13 The use of this term for the Middle Ages has recently been advocated by Soyer, *Medieval Antisemitism?*, p. 21.

The volume starts with a series of chapters focusing on the history of medieval southern Europe. The past of multi-ethnic communities living in the Iberian Peninsula is often presented mainly in the context of conflicts between cultures and/or religions. Nonetheless, members of the very diverse cultural communities who inhabited the Iberian Peninsula had to work together to achieve their political goals, even though they were aware of the differences between them.[14] Therefore, in seeking to answer the question of the mechanisms that enable ethnically divided communities to function in changing cultural and political contexts, we begin our journey with the context of events in the Iberian Peninsula. **Maria Bonet Donato** points out how, during the course of the twelfth century, the rulers of Catalonia used the political-religious conflict with neighbouring Muslim states to create a new political community. This community was to be formed by Christians, regardless of their ethnic origin, who recognized the full political domination of the Catalan rulers. Agreements between political dignitaries and military orders or other military leaders created the conditions for Christian progress against the Muslims, whereby they conquered and dominated a huge border area. The count, Ramon Berenguer IV, and his son, King Alfonso, shifted their military responsibilities in the territories to other agents, at a time when the feudal war was still the best way of expressing the power of the feudal authorities in the Catalan regions. Peace among the Christians encouraged agrarian and trade development, and the conquests consolidated this economic growth, bringing about a major qualitative advance. The protection of the inner peace within Christian society under the Catalan counts and the violence required by them towards the 'Others', the Muslims outside of Catalan society, created the possibility of building a single political society, irrespective of internal ethnic and social divisions. In this case, the sense of threat to the Catalan Christians by Muslims from the west was a factor that facilitated integration and blurred the ethnic differences of members of one religious community. The rulers' sharing of the monopoly of the use of violence with their knights strengthened the relationship of the Christian elite with the monarchy and pushed aside any differences unrelated to the idea of conquest, including those based on ethnicity.

When thinking about ethnic differences in the Iberian Peninsula, the reader usually relates them to the relationship between Christians and Muslims. Meanwhile, relations between different ethnic groups that shared the same religion have been equally important for a long time. This problem is particularly pronounced in politically Muslim-dominated areas. Individual waves of Muslims who gained political advantage through military conquest from the south had to offer some form of cooperation with co-religionists previously settled on the peninsula. The problems of these relationships were concentrated in cities and their associated rural areas. **Jesús Brufal-Succarat** shows how cooperation between the ethnically different groups of Almoravid and Andalus elites was strengthened for economic reasons; consequently the elites sought to close ranks against social changes in a society which was endangered by Christian expansion. He highlights the important role of the Andalusian medinas and their

---

14 See Barros, 'Muslims and Jews' and Echevarria, 'Does Cohabitation Produce *Convivencia?*'.

elites in defining their culture and the future of their societies despite the pressure of politically dominant Almoravids. He proves in respect of the Zaragoza elite that through their relations with the Almoravid emir, they accepted their members' participation in religious reforms, and through that, they maintained Zaragoza's territorial independence. But most of all, he focuses on the specific case of Lleida. In this district, the farthest north administrative unit of the Western Muslim world in the twelfth century, the Lleida Andalusian society and the Almoravid elite led the city and its territory to face the challenges of the Christian conquest together. The local elite strengthened their position and prevented social advancement from the lower social strata with the help of the religious figure of the *alfaqui*. Fragments of written sources visualized how the elite were enriched by their members' many properties both within the city and outside. Huahbala, the last Almoravid qadi, is a clear example of a high official who arrived in Lleida and gained many properties of substantial value. The Almoravid governor of Valencia, Ibn' Aixa, owned up to four rural properties in the south of Lleida. Their vestiges have lasted until today in the form of the place name 'Avinganya' or in the economic heritage as seen in the Trinitarian monastery of Avinganya (Seròs, Lleida). It is evident that the Almoravids followed the same pattern of social representation by owning large landed properties as the Andalusian elite did before their arrival. Without a doubt, rural properties, many of them *almúnyas*, were treated as symbols of power in al-Andalus regardless of the ethnic origin of proprietors. The evidence shows that despite the religious and cultural differences, the two groups of Muslims worked closely together to preserve the traditional arrangement of intergroup relations. Members of the economic and political elite sought to form a single, coherent group. While respecting ethnic distinctions, they developed a common language of symbols and actions to communicate their social status. Eventually, the evolution of these relationships was interrupted by the expansion of Christian political organizations. Nevertheless, the analysed examples show a model of limited acculturation to build up a politically and economically dominant stratum while maintaining ethnic differentiation, which we explore later with the example of medieval Silesian knighthood.

A tendency to strengthen the cohesion of political society despite ethnic differences was visible within Iberian kingdoms even when the military threat from their neighbours was not the dominant factor in political affairs. At that time the process covered a wider spectrum of society and was of a more complex nature. The political community included a significant number of people of a different religion who did not participate in the conquest. **Maria Filomena Lopes de Barros** draws attention to this situation when describing the realities of late medieval Portuguese society. She presents a comparative analysis of various cultural factors that reinforced ethnic identity or supported efforts to increase the homogeneity of high and late medieval Portuguese society, which consisted of Jews, Muslims, and Christians. The author points to — since the thirteenth century — the growing need for legal distinctiveness, social separateness, and public, visual distinctiveness of given ethnic groups within society. That was caused by two factors: the Church policy after the Fourth Lateran Council and the economic interests of Christian municipalities. At first, the royal authorities tried to weaken the restrictiveness of legal measures enacted to accomplish these aims, but from the middle of the fourteenth century, and especially during the next century, the Crown acted as the guardian of the separateness of Christians and ethnic/religious minorities. But the presence of legal acts that aimed to minimize the possibility of the mixing of multi-ethnic Portuguese society on different levels, from sexual life to organizing public space, suggests that at the same time, there were thriving cross-cultural contacts. Nevertheless, both conditions of ordinary life and the interests of the Crown to try to impose the same level of control over all subjects supported the introduction of Portuguese as the universal language of both official and everyday communication in the kingdom. This had a tremendous effect on the cultures of minorities and blurred sharp boundaries between ethnicities. Faced with the distinctiveness of the ethnic legal codes of minorities, the Crown decided to incorporate their elements into the common law of the kingdom. That supported, in fact, the model of a united legal society which was divided according to ethnic/religious lines. But that was possible because for centuries, despite mutual suspicions, Christian, Jews, and Muslims organized their lives and spaces according to two principles: maintaining ethnic identity according to the standards of the cultural majority and reconciling this with cultural, economic, political, and social contexts for achieving a prosperous life on the Iberian Peninsula. The various sociolinguistic and identity-linked allegiances of minorities did not prevent them from fully integrating into a given cultural context and being recognized as 'Portuguese' in the Middle Ages.

Muslims verbally expressed their double affiliation: by assuming an internal self-definition forced by Christian law, as *free Moors*, and by representing themselves in relationships with the Islamic *'umma* as *gurabā'* (foreign, sing. *garīb*). Only the hard choice between expulsion or religious assimilation ordered by King Manuel for Jews and Muslims opened the possibility for building a homogeneous Portuguese society — but which was only united in appearance. Those who chose to stay in the kingdom and convert to Christianity were not free from their ethnic identification. That was visible in the actions taken to separate New Christians (*cristãos-novos*), of Jewish or Muslim descent, from Old Christians (*cristãos-velhos*), who were the majority in the kingdom. Although seen as very important, sometimes crucial in social relations, religion did not prevent the possibility of discerning different ethnicities within one political body. The author points out the tendency for ethnic groups to remain distinct in the Kingdom of Portugal but at the same time stresses the importance of external political factors in building the persistence of these divisions.

Paula Pinto Costa and **Joana Lencart** analyse the influence of one of these forces, that is, the papacy, on the situation in the kingdom. They try to identify how the Holy See supported the role of the military orders in the relationship between the Portuguese Crown, the papacy, and ethnic minorities. They examine papal charters issued by the chancellery of the Holy See for the military orders in Portugal. They focus on the way in which the ethnic minorities were presented in the charters that describe the role played by the military orders in crusade activities in medieval Portugal. The chronology of the selected documents is wide, ranging from the twelfth to the sixteenth centuries. Without a doubt, the Holy See promoted the military orders as intermediaries between the Portuguese Crown, the papacy, and ethnic minorities. The general interest of the Holy See in relations between Christian and non-Christian actors within society increasingly accentuated the dominance of Christians over other religions. However, in papal charters, terminology change regarding non-Christian ethnicities, from generally negative, moral characteristics towards politically charged, suggests everlasting conflict between Christians and non-Christian nations. This was a conflict in which the military orders had to play important roles in cooperating with the Portuguese Crown. For that reason, the popes promoted the adaptation of their internal organization to the new challenges imposed by the monarchy. The only ethnic minorities mentioned by the papal charters are Muslims; there are no references to Jews. It seems that the papacy had not intended to spread a theological narrative focusing on the role of the Jews in history. The main subjects of these documents were political issues and territorial administration. The historical circumstances, not religious affairs, were the core framework that shaped the Holy See's policy towards the ethnic minorities as far as Portugal and the military orders were concerned. Current political circumstances have defined the specificity of the narrative that shaped Portuguese society through the activities of the chivalric orders. Antagonistic relations between Christians and Muslims were to play a dominant role in them. However, as we have seen above, multi-ethnic communities did not easily or passively submit to external political influences. They were also able to maintain their specificity against the trends suggested by the dominant political players.

Meanwhile, **Luciano Gallinari** in his chapter shows the effects of the divergence of the paths of the major political players and most of the minor actors with regard to the process of building an inclusive political community. He focuses on relations between Sardinians and Aragonese (under this term, he describes all subjects of various political bodies of the Crown of Aragon) between the twelfth and fifteenth centuries. In his analysis, he tries to demonstrate the flaws in the theses popular among contemporary historians about national foundations of prolonged conflict between both ethnic groups. He approaches the problem from a double perspective. Gallinari opens his research with the deconstruction of social and political relations at the highest political and institutional level between the Aragonese sovereigns and the judges of Arborea. He clearly explains that the conflict between them was caused by a clash of expectations about the political and social order on the island, and at first, it did not have much in common with 'national' background. Contrary to that, both sides cooperated with themselves to merge Sardinian polities within the wider context of the Crown of Aragon. This resulted in a new form of political culture and economic order for islanders that was changed once again by the wars between judges of Arborea and kings of Aragon from the mid-fourteenth until the mid-fifteenth centuries. But even during these wars the ethnic context of conflict was not commonly accepted, although the rulers of *Giudicato* tried to define this rebellion as a fight for the freedom of Sardinians. Equally interesting is his attempt to analyse the cohesion of ethnically diverse, small urban societies. He focuses his attention especially on relations between diverse ethnic communities of lower social status. To this aim, he uses the case study of the Pisan city of *Castel di Castro* and the following Catalan city of *Castell de Càller* (current Cagliari), which in the years 1323–1326 passed from Tuscan rule to Aragonese; this city was inhabited by Sardinians, Pisans, and Iberians. The processes of building social cohesion within this politically — in theory — divided society involved economic activities, social careers, marriage strategies, and political choices. All of them made *Castell de Càller* a melting pot of the three different cultures and traditions. The chapter shows how modern perspectives on the inevitable conflicts between competing nations can cover and hide much more complicated processes of social and cultural adjustments accelerated by a need for peaceful coexistence in unfavourable natural conditions and a possibility for fast economic development and political careers through cooperation with the Continent. Faced with a devastating political conflict between two aristocratic actors, the island community chose to seek cooperation between different ethnic groups to ensure economic stability. The locals were not a priori hostile towards newcomers. They treated them as one more element in the social game, entering into alliances with them or becoming embroiled in conflict with them depending on the circumstances.

The mechanisms of creating a multi-ethnic political community through policies initiated from the bottom up and diverse techniques for adaptation which were used by different social groups are discussed by **Przemysław Wiszewski**. The author focuses on social relations in late medieval Silesia (thirteenth–fifteenth century). In the thirteenth century, the relatively ethnically homogeneous, Polish-speaking community of Silesian inhabitants changed in character. To strengthen their military and economic capital, the local rulers invited migrants, who were mainly German-speaking, from the West to settle in this border region. Throughout the thirteenth and fourteenth centuries, the court elite, knights, and burghers largely adopted the German language and culture while emphasizing their connections with the region's past. At the same time, alongside this ethnic and cultural group, there was also a Polish-speaking community in some regions that used their own 'Polish' law. Wiszewski tries to answer the following question: Did the different social groups in medieval Silesia deal differently with their multi-ethnic character? Knights, townsmen, and peasants chose different strategies to cope with the heterogeneity of their groups. Knights adopted and developed German courtly culture and cooperated closely with the dukes by responding to their needs. But they also collaborated with the local Polish knights to fit into the local power structures as fast as possible. The German migrants did not assimilate with their Polish peers, but all of them were moulded by the cultural needs of the ducal courts. The urban communities evolved more slowly and gradually through the diffusion of the attractive elements of the material culture of both dominant ethnicities, under the pressure of German which was the dominant language of trade in the region of Brandenburg, Saxony, Bohemia, Moravia, and Silesia. In this context, the peasants' situation is the most obscure. After initial ethnic segregation, they disregarded ethnicity and mixed within local communities. But they often preserved elements of their ethnic cultures. In the case of smaller ethnic groups, that could lead to ethnic identification as a common differentiator of a given society even in the second half of the fourteenth century. But that rarely happened with Germans and Poles. Their practice of cohabitation seems to be purely pragmatic and brought them huge success in that external observers were not able to discern their ethnicity, nor was it acknowledged as important for their existence within the Silesian community. Ethnicity in medieval Silesia was not connected in general terms with anything distinctive in the legal order of the region. The dukes did not try to use ethnic differences as a reason for conflict or as a tool for governance over their multi-ethnic communities. In this case, the grassroots aspiration to create a single political community which preserved ethnic distinctions, but that, at the same time, was composed of social groups with a relatively coherent position irrespective of the ethnic origin of its members, was in line with the interests of the main political powers (the Silesian dukes and Czech kings).

Contrary to the situation in Silesia, the problem of multi-ethnicity of urban communities has only been solved to a limited extent in the borderlands of Latin and Orthodox Europe. **Grzegorz Myśliwski** focuses on the consequences of economic activities for inter-ethnic relations between the secular inhabitants of the main medieval cities within the Polish state between the thirteenth and fifteenth centuries. From the beginning of the analysed period, these communities were divided not only in ethnic terms but also legally. Ethnic divisions were mirrored in the spaces of the cities analysed. Ethnic groups inhabited distinct streets and districts, and that was the case not only with Jews but also other ethnicities, like Armenians (Lviv) or Italians (Kraków). These differences — both in a legal context and in everyday living conditions — did not cause conflicts by themselves. On the contrary, the starting point for analyzing the economic life of the studied communities is non-antagonistic ethnic and legal divisions in their cities. There is no evidence to indicate that their inhabitants wanted to constitute one community of a town in today's understanding of this word, a community without ethnic divisions. Hence, it should be ascertained that for most of the period under study, economic activity — extending beyond the ethnic limits — led to more and more numerous relations between members of various ethnicities in the same city. Despite conflicts, recorded in city books, these actions usually led to satisfactory results: purchases of desired goods, providing cash, employment, or support for poor people of various ethnic origins with money or a meal. It could have had a positive impact on the reception of multiple ethnicities in the city. It is striking that the most cohesive urban society was that of the city of Lviv — the most varied in terms of ethnicities living there. Generally, economic relations facilitated the crossing of ethnic barriers and, consequently, contributed to the cohesion of urban communities, especially with their Christian members. However, as regards the cities where pogroms and the expulsion of Jews took place, it may be said that the impact of the economic life on the cohesion of entire urban communities could resemble a sinusoid in shape — its gradual growth was demolished every few or several dozen years by collective, ethnic violence towards Jewish people. But the restoration of economic relations often occurred later.

The emphasis on the importance of economic cooperation as a facilitator of the cohesion of multi-ethnic groups is confirmed by **Andrzej Pleszczyński**'s study of cities from the strict borderland of Latin and Orthodox Europe in the early modern period. He compares ethnic diversity and the politics of building ethnic identities in three eastern-central European cities — Lublin, Zamość, and Lviv — between the sixteenth and the nineteenth centuries. The purpose of this comparison is to look at the evolution of the ethnic, economic, and inter-ethnic relations within these cities, in the context of external political and economic changes that occurred from the late Middle Ages until the beginning of so-called industrial epoch, which started in the region of eastern-central Europe shortly before the middle of the nineteenth century. In his conclusions, he points at a gradual decline in ethnic diversity in cities threatened by the economic and political crisis of the seventeenth century. The same crisis could easily provoke inter-ethnic conflicts within towns. Sometimes strict control over townsmen's lives by the owner prevented conflicts between ethnic groups. However, belonging to a numerous, wealthy, and privileged ethnic group was a more specific source of personal security. These large ethnic groups rarely chose to oppose each other because their members had too much to lose, and the outcome of a dispute was unpredictable. The situation of the largest city, Lviv, turns out to be particularly interesting. The city was the most ethnically diverse amongst the cities studied, and at the same time its citizens operated in the most difficult political conditions. However, cooperation between different ethnic and religious groups is much more frequent than conflicts. Apparently, it was cooperation, not conflict, that optimized the residents' profits from living in a dangerous environment, but one that gave hope for a relatively prosperous life, even if the price was to live and cooperate peacefully with 'Others'.

Cosmin Popa-Gorjanu presents a completely different strategy of how rulers divided society and how ethnic and social relations evolved in Transylvania. He deals with the evidence of relations between diverse, in terms of ethnicity, population groups in Transylvania in the thirteenth and fourteenth centuries. His essay focuses on some of the documents that shed light on specific groups and moments and which help scholars to understand the diversity and complexity of the social and economic aspects of these ethnic groups and their evolution. In this period, Transylvania was inhabited by three major ethnic groups — Romanians, Hungarians, Germans — and several others of lesser importance. One of the key questions that arises during the analysis of these ethnic groups is why Transylvania did not evolve into a melting pot. How was it possible that three major ethnic groups continued to coexist in the region despite some assimilation processes? Popa-Gorjanu describes in detail as far as possible the stratification of local society before the thirteenth century and then characterizes different groups of migrants that had settled in Transylvania from the second half of the twelfth century onwards. Various ethnic minorities were invited during the thirteenth century by the Hungarian kings and also by the noblemen and Church institutions to settle, and they enjoyed extensive economic privileges. The most peculiar was the situation of the Saxons who were partially granted special rights as a community living under royal protection in one part of Transylvania, but they were also dispersed on the estates of multiple noblemen as well as Church villages. The latter group was given special rights only within the borders of specific landed properties. Sometimes they mixed with Romanians in the same villages, but cases of acculturation and the establishment of one, cohesive, new ethnic community on this basis were extremely rare. The unevenness of the status of various ethnic and social groups suggests that mechanisms of growth favoured groups of new settlers and warriors invited by the kings and noblemen. The royal guests (*hospites*) were, in fact, the group that benefitted in the greatest measure from royal generosity and protection. The fact that they brought with them more advanced technologies and contributed to the region's economic development is indisputable. Groups of guests of different sizes received charters of privileges. They were granted suitable lands for economic activities and extensive self-administration rights, judicial autonomy, and exemptions from taxation and tolls, in exchange for providing the king with certain military services. Clearly, the information we receive from the statutory evidence creates an image of inequality within a society separated into privileged and unprivileged groups. The imbalance between the number of collective privileges preserved by royal guests' communities or the nobility and other local communities remains one of the main obstacles to assessing to what extent a mechanism for building cohesion within this society was at work in the thirteenth century.

The inter-ethnic relations in medieval Transylvania analysed by Cosmin Popa-Gorjanu led to a community permanently divided along ethnic lines. However, this model of creating a social structure from groups separated by ethnicity did not have a lasting effect on the elites of the neighbouring Kingdom of Hungary. **Daniel Bagi** sets out the consequences for the Hungarian elites of the local rulers' support for migration from western Europe to strengthen the position of the court in society. He focuses his attention on the dynamic character of foreigners' participation in the political life of the medieval Kingdom of Hungary. He acknowledges that the kingdom was from the beginning of its history populated by a multi-ethnic society. Like everywhere in the eastern-central European states, the political and ecclesiastical elites were recruited from different parts of Europe. But he stresses that during the eleventh to thirteenth centuries, ethnic identity did not play a significant role in foreigners' political activities during their stay in the kingdom. This attitude started to change after the extinction of the Arpad dynasty; a radical shift occurred during the reign of Sigismund of Luxemburg. The king himself was a foreigner, and to provide a peaceful reign, he created a new group of elites, involving new, mostly foreign people. Their ethnic composition represented both the royal political interests and its changes during the fifteenth century. The changes are identifiable, especially after the danger of Ottoman invasion increased in the second half of the fifteenth century. Accordingly, the ethnic character of the foreigners changed. Instead of nobles and aristocrats of western (Italy, Germany, Austria) or northern (Poland) origin, a new network of royal friends appeared, who came mainly from south-eastern Europe. The older elites had integrated into Hungarian society, whereas the newer elites were more separated; they were strongly connected to a specific ruler in Hungary, but their roots and future always remained in their homeland.

Daniel Bagi shows how far the general circumstances of outsiders in a community depended on the policies of the main actors (rulers), but also on their decision to stay permanently in the new environment or to maintain contact with their former homelands. He emphasizes the importance of the individual decisions by both newcomers and rulers and the variability of the political contexts which saw the emergence of new ethnic groups within the Hungarian elite. The changing nature of these forces (promoting integration into society or acculturation of local elites, striving to build a future in a new country or treating the stay in Hungary as part of a *colonial* experience) makes it impossible to look at the multi-ethnic community of medieval Hungarian elites as a permanent phenomenon, characteristic of a specific, *national* history. It was a story created by the rulers and their approach to transforming elites and subject communities to a much greater extent.

A similarly pragmatic approach to ethnic distinctiveness is emphasized by **Monika Ramonaitė** when addressing the issue of relations between Jews and Christians in the Grand Duchy of Lithuania. She focuses in her chapter on non-Christians (Jews and Karaites) who provided medical services to Christians in the Great Duchy of Lithuania during the modern era. She analyses their position within the medical marketplace as well as society's attitude towards them. This chapter aims to determine what educational and employment opportunities were available to Jewish and Karaite medical practitioners in a Christian environment. She tries to find out how important the religious aspects were while evaluating and choosing non-Christian medical services. The author concludes that within the Grand Duchy of Lithuania, Jewish medical doctors with a university degree could obtain a well-paid position and even become the personal doctors of the king. And despite popular anti-Semitism, evidence of criticism and the rejection of Jewish medical practitioners' services on religious grounds could not be found. Juridical cases of accusations of intentional harm to the health and life of a client by Jewish medical doctors were absent from the sources. Apparently, religious matters did not significantly affect the medical marketplace of the Grand Duchy of Lithuania. The most important criterion for choosing the right medical services was their availability. The Jews adjusted themselves to the medical marketplace in the Grand Duchy of Lithuania and mostly offered their services in those places where other medical practitioners were absent, or where there were very few of them.

The pragmatism of the more significant group of the subjects who formed the diverse ethnic groups, combined with the changing political circumstances, led to a situation in which the political decisions of the most important actors moderated, but did not determine, the approach of the different ethnic groups to coexistence within one complex political community. Was this approach chosen by the sheer size and political dependence of the groups analysed? After all, a ruler should not be interested in antagonizing his subjects (although, as we have seen, this is not so obvious). So, did conflicts between different ethnic groups not occur more easily in smaller communities? Face-to-face contacts which both accentuated a sense of difference and provided constant competition for key and often scarce resources may have contributed to the more frequent emergence of social tensions, especially in cities, where the fundamental problem for each inhabitant was to find their own niche in an economic ecosystem with a high degree of internal competitiveness.

While the earlier chapters observed the city as a space of political and economic interaction between different ethnic groups (Myśliwski, Pleszczyński), **Dovilė Troskovaitė** analyses selected Lithuanian cities as centres of ideological identity of competing groups of Jews who constituted a minority within a broader political community. She points out that a given city may be inhabited by a particular ethnic group different from the state's dominant society, which sees this particular territory as their own space, where they experience, express, and embed their unique identity.

The group identifies themselves with this place and sees it as their homeland, no matter its actual political belonging. In her chapter, she examines territorial arguments in the ideological struggle between Jewish groups, which led to the formation of modern nationalism in one of them — Polish Lithuanian Karaites. She argues that dominant groups had an important role in the territorialization of certain areas by the non-dominant groups, even though this territorialization is symbolic. She focuses on the case of Karaites and their relation with particular towns, those of Vilnius/Wilno/Wiln and Trakai/Troki, their role in the formation of modern national Karaite identity, their relationship to Jewish self-perception, and the role of Polish society in this process. The general questions of the chapter are these: How did an ethnic minority maintain and strengthen its identity within the network of social relations with the politically and demographically dominant ethnicities? How did Karaites manage to define and secure *their* place on Earth and save themselves from the disastrous consequences of their long-lasting failure to fit in with the political and economic interests of the dominant ethnic communities?

Thanks to the support of state authorities, for centuries, Trakai was a privileged place for Karaite settlements. They were considered to be closer to the culturally dominant political, ethnic groups than Rabbinic Jews. In return, they were allowed to remove from *their territory* — the city of Trakai — the culturally similar but much larger group of Orthodox Jews. Therefore, Trakai was perceived as a place chosen for the independent development of a unique community of Karaites that cooperated with the social milieu which consisted of the privileged members of the ethnic mosaic of the Grand Duchy of Lithuania. In Vilna, in the interwar period, the Karaites enjoyed the support of the authorities. But that did not make them a unique ethnic group. In fact, the Karaites remained one of the many ethnic communities in the mosaic of the urban community and struggled to secure their ethnic identity. That is why Vilna did not gain such a special status in the memory of the Karaites as Trakai/Troki. In Vilna, Karaites were just one among many underprivileged minorities living and cooperating with themselves and with authorities there, and that was not a fact which enabled pride in being a member of an ethnic group of particular importance for the history of a larger political community of the Grand Duchy of Lithuania or Poland.

The examples of the urban communities presented suggest that favourable conditions for cooperation did not necessarily lead to acculturation and the obliteration of the specificity of ethnic groups in cities. On the contrary, these distinctions may have been a source of competitive advantage due to specialization in a particular trade or service. Nevertheless, the combination of these distinctions with political and social status within the city usually led to tensions and periodic outbreaks of conflict. These communities where ethnicity did not determine opportunities for social advancement were, relatively speaking, free from tensions and conflict. Peaceful cooperation was also guaranteed by the great ethnic diversity of the larger communities. The exclusion of one group was a risk for all, as it could have triggered an avalanche of depredations of other minority groups. Smaller communities were easier for one ethnic group to dominate. And this could happen even when, paradoxically, it represented a minority across the state. It is striking that the process of ethnic territorialization, in this case, was largely based on the skilful use of information directed at a wider audience. Narratives oriented in this way created a vision of the past and, consequently, of the present, allowing real socio-ethnic relations to be reinterpreted and changed. Communicating with the other ethnic groups of a given society about the ethnic group's desired place in society was central to this aim. This makes it all the more worthwhile to look at how the circulation of information in multi-ethnic communities could be used to establish cooperation between groups.

Jurgita Šiaučiūnaitė-Verbickienė analyses communication between social groups understood primarily not as a means of information transfer but as a way of creating bonds and introducing new practices. Because no matter which historical period is discussed, gifts — which are the main object of analysis here — always have a pleasant and favourable effect on those who receive them. Within the context of the social structures of the eighteenth century and earlier, gifts which were meant to please or show loyalty to the recipient were a common means of maintaining good relationships and communication. They also enabled daily issues to be overcome. In this chapter which is based on the case of the Vilnius Jewish community, she draws attention to the symbolic and social meaning of these practices which have not been widely explored although they are very typical in early modern societies. The subject under analysis is the giving of gifts during the last quarter of the eighteenth century as an act of communication which bridged gaps between specific social groups within the Grand Duchy of Lithuania and in the same moment as one of the ways of building cohesion within its multi-ethnic society. The main questions discussed here concern communication strategies and the pragmatic intentions of these acts performed by the Vilnius Jewish elite: What kind of gifts did the Jewish community give, and what circle of recipients was this practice intended for? What strategies did the Vilnius kahal use in the planning of gift giving, and which aims in the context of cohesion building were meant to be achieved? Historical data shows that the Jewish communities in Vilnius and Opatów had a clear-cut gift-giving strategy and were consistent in it. They sought to maintain regular contacts with influential and useful individuals directly involved with the community and periodically gave gifts to potentially useful or generally powerful members of the public. Gifts were given year after year to a defined group of useful individuals. They were a way to improve Jewish relations with a society that was not always favourably disposed towards them. The most important element in the context of gift giving was choosing the most appropriate tactic and strategic planning of the gift-giving process. At the end of the eighteenth century, the indebted Vilnius Jewish community operated along the lines of measures that had proven to be effective, closing the gap between the dominating Christian, Lithuanian, Rus', and Polish parts of society on the one hand and the Jews on the other.

Jurgita Šiaučiūnaitė-Verbickienė, while analysing the mechanism of building relations and cooperation in a multi-ethnic community, has studied the asymmetry of these relationships. In doing so, she looks at it from the perspective of the ethnic group which had a lower political and social standing than the dominant ethnic community in wider society. The same problem of asymmetry in the arrangement of relations to strengthen the multi-ethnic community is addressed by **Endre**

Sashalmi. However, he looks at this from the point of view of the dominant ethnic group and the construction by its representatives of a model of domination over the other parts of the multi-ethnic society. He analyses the symbolic meaning of the enthronement ceremony of Tsar Alexander III (1883) based on the expression of the multi-ethnic character of his dominion. He stresses that through rituals, iconography, and legal acts, the new idea was expressed that shaped the Russian Empire until the end of its history: the cohesion of the multi-ethnic society was founded on the domination of Russian nationality. The true centre of the empire was Russia itself, and the only true subjects of the tsar were Russians. As the head of this society, the tsar was crowned by the Heavens, and he was even depicted as an intercessor or mediator between God and the people, which, in fact, he was according to the Orthodox Church. At the same time, images printed during preparation for the enthronement ceremony also emphasized the multi-ethnic character of the tsar's empire by representing various ethnic groups. But once again, this phenomenon was clearly subordinated to the principles of Russian nationalism, of which the Orthodox faith was the core element. The entire communication campaign connected with the enthronement was focused on rejecting the liberal vision of the equal or almost equal position of the various ethnicities under the emperor's rule which had previously been expressed by Alexander II. Alexander III and his retinue wanted to send a clear message: Russia was for Russians. If a given ethnic group would not acculturate and accept a new, Russian identity, it must accept its own peripheral standing in the imperial society.

The dialectical nature of the relationship between an underprivileged ethnic group and the institutions controlled by the dominant ethnic community and the political structures they direct is presented in the final chapter by **Joanna Wojdon**. She analyses the role of Polish parishes in shaping the identity and building the position of the Polish ethnic group in the United States in the second half of the nineteenth and twentieth centuries. Migrants to the United States with Polish ethnic roots formed separate parishes for religious worship very early on. They were not unique in this; the Irish and Italians had done the same before. Their own parishes for believers with Polish roots served primarily to build the cohesion of their ethnic group and to preserve their identity in a foreign society. The parish church was also the centre of the cultural and social life of the migrant community. The combination of Catholic religious worship with the cultural identity of the migrants strengthened their sense of worth in relation to their Protestant surroundings, which treated the poor Catholics coming from central Europe as an inferior social stratum. Over time, these parishes began to function as centres for the assimilation of migrants and their descendants into American society. Indeed, they were part of the American Church structure. The changing functions of these ethnic parishes point to the dialectical role of structures that bind ethnic groups together to cooperate with other groups within a multi-ethnic society. They did not block the establishment of relationships with other U.S. citizens, and over time supported the limited acculturation of parishioners. At the same time, they provided stability of culture, discipline, and social control in the face of the depredations of migrants by the privileged majority.

Works Cited

Secondary Studies

Barros, Maria Filomena Lopes de, 'Muslims and Jews in Medieval Portugal: Interaction and Negotiation (Fourteenth–Fifteenth Centuries)', in *Minorities in Contact in the Medieval Mediterranean*, ed. by Clara Almagro Vidal, Jessica Tearney-Pearce, and Luke Yarbrough, Cultural Encounters in Late Antiquity and the Middle Ages, 33 (Turnhout: Brepols, 2020), pp. 351–70

Bethencourt, Francisco, *Racisms: From the Crusades to the Twentieth Century* (Princeton, NJ: Princeton University Press, 2014)

Chazan, Robert, *Medieval Stereotypes and Modern Anti-semitism* (Berkeley: University of California Press, 1997)

Echevarria, Anna, 'Does Cohabitation Produce *Convivencia*? Relationships between Jews and Muslims in Castilian Christian Towns', in *Minorities in Contact in the Medieval Mediterranean*, ed. by Clara Almagro Vidal, Jessica Tearney-Pearce, and Luke Yarbrough, Cultural Encounters in Late Antiquity and the Middle Ages, 33 (Turnhout: Brepols, 2020), pp. 337–50

Frazer, William O., 'Introduction: Identities in Early Medieval Britain', in *Social Identity in Early Medieval Britain*, ed. by William O. Frazer and Andrew Tyrell, Studies in the Early History of Britain (London: Leicester University Press, 2000), pp. 1–22

Hammond, Matthew H., 'Ethnicity and the Writing of Medieval Scottish History', *Scottish Historical Review*, 85, no 219.1 (2006), 1–27

Harland, James M., 'Rethinking Ethnicity and "Otherness" in Early Anglo-Saxon England', in 'Comparative Studies on Medieval Europe', ed. by Walter Pohl and Andre Gingrich, special issue, *Medieval Worlds: Comparative and Interdisciplinary Studies*, 5 (2017), 113–42

Jenkins, Richard, *Rethinking Ethnicity: Arguments and Explorations*, 2nd edn (London: SAGE Publications, 2008)

Kappeler, Andreas, *The Russian Empire: A Multi-ethnic History*, trans. by Alfred Clayton (London: Routledge, 2013)

Lightfoot, Emma, Magdalena Naum, Villu Kadakas, and Erki Russow, 'The Influence of Social Status and Ethnicity on Diet in Medieval Tallin as Seen through Stable Isotope Analysis', *Estonian Journal of Archaeology*, 20.1 (2016), 81–107

Reynolds, Susan, 'The Idea of a Nation as a Political Community', in *Power and the Nation in European History*, ed. by Len Scales (Cambridge: Cambridge University Press, 2005), pp. 54–66; repr. in Susan Reynolds, *The Middle Ages without Feudalism* (London: Routledge, 2013)

Soyer, François, *Medieval Antisemitism?*, Past Imperfect (Leeds: ARC Humanities Press, 2019)

Wiszewski, Przemysław, 'Introduction: Multi-Ethnicity and Memory in Medieval and Modern Societies', in *Memories in Multi-Ethnic Societies: Cohesion in Multi-Ethnic Societies in Europe from c. 1000 to the Present, I*, ed. by Przemysław Wiszewski (Turnhout: Brepols, 2020), pp. 19–28

———, 'Preface: Cohesion of Multi-Ethnic Societies in Medieval and Early Modern Europe', in *Memories in Multi-Ethnic Societies: Cohesion in Multi-Ethnic Societies in Europe from c. 1000 to the Present, I*, ed. by Przemysław Wiszewski (Turnhout: Brepols, 2020), pp. 11–17

MARIA BONET DONATO

Organizing Violence

Peace and War in Twelfth-Century Catalonia

How can violence lead to the emergence of an ethnically or regionally diverse political community whose elites have avoided emphasizing this diversity? During the twelfth century the rulers of Catalonia used the conflict with neighbouring Muslim states to create a new political community. This community was to be formed by Christians, regardless of their origin, who recognized the leadership of the Catalan rulers. The protection of the inner peace within Christian society under the Catalan counts and the violence required by them towards the 'Others', the Muslims outside of Catalan society, created the possibility of building a single political society, irrespective of the internal territorial and social divisions. In this case, the sense of threat to the Catalan Christians by Muslims was a factor that facilitated integration and blurred the differences of members of the political community. The new political community was formed, whose elites established new forms of domination based on the progressive control of peace and war for increasing the effectiveness of the conquest of al-Andalus. Alongside the building of the new political community, new institutional and cultural discourses were created for advocating violence against Muslims who were seen as enemies given their differentiated ethnic-religious condition. The emphasis within them on ethno-religious differentiation occurred while a relative or theoretical unitary Christian society was claimed and promoted, which aimed for surpassing previous violence and internal divisions.

How Violence Was Valued and Organized in Twelfth-Century Catalonia

This chapter addresses the process of change in the definition of violence in twelfth-century Catalonia. The valorization of peace for specific groups of the community turned into the valorization of violence against a religious-ethnic group, the Muslims, which involved the conquest of their lands, their property, and even of their people. All this

> **Maria Bonet Donato** • (maria.bonet@urv.cat) is Professor of Medieval History at the Universitat Rovira i Virgili, Tarragona. Her main field is the military orders at the Crown of Aragon and the social history of medieval Catalonia.

Inter-Ethnic Relations and the Functioning of Multi-Ethnic Societies: Cohesion in Multi-Ethnic Societies in Europe from c. 1000 to the Present, II, ed. by Przemysław Wiszewski, EER 18 (Turnhout: Brepols, 2022), pp. 27–55

BREPOLS ❧ PUBLISHERS   10.1484/M.EER-EB.5.132145

This is an open access chapter made available under a cc by-nc 4.0 International License.

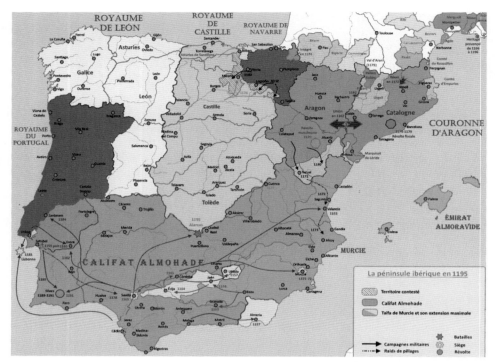

Map 1.1. The Iberian Peninsula in 1195. Source: <https://commons.wikimedia.org/wiki/File:P%C3%A9ninsule_ib%C3%A9rique_en_1195.png>. Elryck, cc by-sa 4.0.

gave rise to a military and political change of great significance that found in the new concept of peace and war important grounds for this transformation.

Violence was an essential element in defining, justifying, and exercising feudal or political power during the important changes that took place in twelfth-century Catalonia. The rejection of certain violent actions and the promotion of others led to another way of organizing war, which could at times take on a penitential character and be set in the contractual conditions of feudal relationships. The tradition of instituted peace was a notable feature of Catalonia, and the county and royal power cemented its authority through guarantees of peacekeeping.[1] This protective role contributed to its predominance in the control and management of major military events. In fact, the emerging political authority was active in the reorganization of war, at the same time as its agents became stronger or performed new roles. However, violent conflicts, local wars, and conquests were recurrent features in the warfare of those days.[2]

The needs of the time shaped the kind of war that was appropriate or possible. Foundations were being laid for the exercise of legitimate domination and legitimate

---

1 Bisson, 'The Organized Peace', and Font i Rius, 'Los inicios de la Paz y Tregua'.
2 Bonet, 'Wars in 12th Century Catalonia', pp. 164–69 and 189.

violence, something that in later periods would be administered by the state. Certain powers were becoming predominant in new power relationships, and war and peace were essential elements in dominant relationships. Cities and military orders, representing new and emerging realities, were involved in the process of defining which forms of violence were legitimate by either containing or promoting its use. In general, the rise of feudal violence has been considered by some to be the result of the decline of political power, although some authors single out the decline of public institutions. Nevertheless, negotiation, agreement, ideology, and other processes related to pacification emerged among the feudal aristocracy and under the leadership of certain political players. Peace emerged from the increasing maturity of the feudal relationship and the reorganization of the political order, although war also had a far-reaching impact. This process involved reinforcing certain political powers and functions exercised by elements of the feudal class. This occurred in a context of geopolitical changes in the feudal West that were marked by alliances and conflicts between regional powers, as well as the rise of the Church as an arbitrating and legitimizing force. Moreover, the choice of a single enemy, based on its religion and ethnicity, to some extent favoured the construction of a collective regional identity, and even an interregional one, that found its clear expression in the new forms of the political power.

The following pages explain how the reorganization of violence came about as a response to socioeconomic changes and the redefinition of political or power relationships. The main political authority, be this the count or the king, was the ultimate expression of the gradual emergence of the idea of legitimate domination that was nurtured in peace and security and justified in and by war. War together with justice, as an alternative to peace, were the axes of the power relationships. The value given to the fight against the Muslims as a sacred and important violent undertaking justified and, to certain extent, favoured the most important military developments in the second half of the twelfth century. The spiritual reward to be gained from subjecting the 'perfidious' Muslims was a metaphor for the material rewards which came with the military turn of events.

'God's Peace and War' and the Rise of Political Leadership

The pacification of the knights and lords took place over more than two centuries and gradually passed from feudal aggression within one's territory to a type of warfare pursued more often in neighbouring lands. Private war, that is, war for its own sake, gave way to war by consensus during the twelfth century. Great expeditions contributed to stabilizing the power relationships within the aristocracy, but a consensus had been reached before this, when the days and spaces in which the lords were allowed to exercise violence were restricted. The new agreement was reached or disseminated through meetings or assemblies of Peace and Truce from the eleventh century onward, and solutions were expanded and revised until the thirteenth century.[3] The concepts

---

3 Barthélemy, *L'an mil*, pp. 569–76.

of peace and truce were gradually assimilated or equated into the terminology used in these meetings. Peace was identified with the idea of security.[4]

The institution of the Peace and Truce of God was a response to the development of feudal society, and above all to the needs caused by economic growth. The increase in agrarian wealth and its growing relationship with the market and commercial expansion could not take place properly in the presence of predatory and destructive practices such as theft, kidnapping, and other forms of brutality that formed part of the way feudal powers acted in the so-called first feudal age. Pacifying solutions stopped the abuses that had existed in agrarian economies with a high degree of autarky, and may be said to have worked insofar as they provided the lords with a certain standard of living in a near-subsistence farming economy. Theft or violent action had made up for shortages, as for example when arbitrary agrarian rents were extracted. In the emerging economy, stocks or accumulated agrarian resources were essential to growth, and therefore measures to protect them had to be introduced. Furthermore, gains from conquests provided new lands or interests in other markets that reinforced economic growth. These conquests were justified by new ideas about war.

The first peace statutes were implemented by the Catalan bishops in the eleventh century and laid down conditions which did not only protect ecclesiastics and their wealth. Over time, protection was extended and included goods, activities, or groups linked to strategic productive sectors. At this time the instituted peace was confined mainly to the diocese, and proceedings against violators of the Truce of God were administered by the bishops.[5] During the twelfth century, some of these judicial responses involved or were directed by secular political authorities, usually a count or the king. Double jurisdiction and fines administered by the prelate and the count or king were introduced and imposed in the last few decades, although in the county of Urgell the count was the only one to do so.[6] He was claimed to have the grace to maintain justice in a statement that emphasized that the 'potentes' (powerful) —– were in charge of administering justice.[7] However, if the defendants did not submit to justice, then they were excommunicated and excluded from the Peace and Truce. Justice was defined as a source of power by the Count of Urgell in the preamble of the Peace and Truce provisions of 1187, with justice, backed by biblical references, invoked as the necessary condition for administering the peace.

Pacification protected expressly strategic sectors and elements of the economic renewal during the eleventh and twelfth centuries. It was frequently aimed at

---

4 Power was the protector guaranteeing peace to the protected: Lambert, 'Introduction', p. 2.

5 *Les constitucions*, ed. by Gonzalvo, no. 4 (1064), §§ III, XIV, XXIV; no 5 (1064–1066), §§ III and XVII, among others.

6 *Les constitucions*, ed. by Gonzalvo, no. 15 (1173), §§ IX, XVI; no. 17 (1188), §§ VII, XIX; and no. 18 (1192), § V. Some earlier examples, such as the Peace and Truce, led the Templars' double jurisdiction, which was at once comital and ecclesiastical, despite the rupture being a sacrilege (*Les constitucions*, ed. by Gonzalvo, no. 11 (1134)) or in 1155 when it was established that kings could judge whether the peace had been broken on the advice of archbishops and bishops (*Les constitucions*, ed. by Gonzalvo, no. 12, § XXVII).

7 *Les constitucions*, ed. by Gonzalvo, no. 16, § IX.

agricultural production, cattle farmers or peasants, and there were certain references protecting animals for agricultural work and peasants' houses.[8] In the last part of the twelfth century, certain provisions clearly defended ownership rights. Rural peace was so important that the kings Alfonso the Chaste (1162–1196), also known as Alfonso II of Aragon, and Peter the Catholic (1196–1213), also II of Aragon, collected resources in order to guarantee it, while peasant militias were created to defend it.[9]

The Prince's Leadership in War, Peace, and Law

Some of the peacekeeping solutions of the eleventh century protected markets and merchants, and punished counterfeiters.[10] In addition, from the middle of the twelfth century other provisions protected public roads, thus providing security for commercial activity to take place.[11] Sometimes it was specified that the protection was directed at merchants or passers-by circulating on the public roads, and it was explicitly related to fairs and markets by the end of the twelfth century.[12] The *Usatges of Barcelona*, understood to be legislation implemented by Count Ramon Berenguer IV (1131–1162) and inspired by Roman law, claimed that roads on land and 'sea' belonged to the 'potestas' (power), that is, the count, who would punish violators of the Peace and Truce of God on these routes.[13] Other rules or *usatges* protected commercial spaces and established royalties. They imposed the count's peace and truce on the city of Barcelona, and also on ships travelling along the Catalan coast and on the minting of coins.[14] The specific mention of the principal city in the county relates to the private or feudal notion of territory defined in the Peace and Truce that was set out by the Church and for the Church. Despite this private approach, the comital policy for political authority over peace started to protect commercial activity under its jurisdiction throughout the second half of the twelfth century by establishing peace in key places and among professional groups.

Other solutions of peace and truce were intended to preserve certain groups and individuals involved in important economic activities, as well as other people that could not defend themselves and were vulnerable to seigniorial violence. Unarmed churchmen and peasants were specifically referred to in these aforementioned solutions, as was their property, and sometimes merchants and bourgeois or other

---

8 *Les constitucions*, ed. by Gonzalvo, no. 10 (1131), §§ II–III; no. 14 (1173), §§ VI–VIII; no. 15, §§ VI–VIII; no. 16, § IV; no. 17, § VI.

9 Bisson, 'The Organized Peace', p. 291.

10 *Les constitucions*, ed. by Gonzalvo, no. 2, p. 7.

11 *Les constitucions*, ed. by Gonzalvo, no. 14 (1173), § XII; no. 15, § XI; no. 16, § II; and no. 17, § XVII.

12 *Les constitucions*, ed. by Gonzalvo, no. 16 (1187), § III; no. 18, § III; and no. 19 (1198), § IV. In England roads provided protection and peace to users in the late eleventh century: Lacey, 'Protection and Immunity', p. 83.

13 Valls Taberner, *Los Usatges de Barcelona*, p. 88, no. 62. In relation to the dating of the text, see Bonnassie, *Cataluña mil años atrás*, pp. 340–41.

14 Valls Taberner, *Los Usatges de Barcelona*, p. 88, no. 61; p. 87, no. 60; and p. 89, no. 66 respectively.

unarmed people such as widows or villagers. Those who could not defend themselves enjoyed a 'natural immunity' as did their properties because of their defencelessness.[15] Yvo de Chartres's *Panormia* defined the members of society covered by truce and measures of protection that were almost the same as those embraced by Catalan peace standards, these members being ecclesiastics, peasants, merchants, and pilgrims.[16] Moreover, the peace and protection promoted by French king Louis VII was directed at peasants and merchants in Soissons in 1155.

The peace terms were imposed on new spaces during the twelfth century, going beyond and transforming the preceding protection of ecclesiastical private spaces. In 1108, peace and truce was applied in an area with specific needs, Olèrdola, because it had been attacked by Muslims. Ten years later the pacification was implemented with regard to peasant activity encompassing an entire county, Cerdagne, by Count Ramon Berenguer III (1097–1131). His grandson, Alfonso the Chaste, applied peace measures in the county of Roussillon and in the bishopric of Elna in 1173.[17]

Political leaders extended peace measures to more general entities than just the ecclesiastical ones in the twelfth century. When in 1131 Ramon Berenguer III together with several bishops granted security guarantees, he referred to them as 'ac tractandum de comuni utilitate ipsius terre' (treating the common utility of the 'land'), although he kept the focus on goods and ecclesiastical persons.[18] In the last decades of the twelfth century, both Alfonso the Chaste and the Count of Urgell proclaimed peace and truce solutions to the extent that their political authority enabled them to do so.[19] The king stressed the 'common utility or good' in all his land, but now, for the first time, specified the dimensions of Catalonia and enforced peace and truce in all social groups. In so doing, he intended to exterminate kidnappers and thieves. In the first references to the territory, King Alfonso defined it as only referring to certain places on the borders, whereas his son asserted that the peace applied to 'all Catalonia', although Catalonia continued to be defined as 'from Salses to Lleida'.[20] The process of transition from the bishopric to the principality has been conceived as the passage from peace derived from the diocesan jurisdiction to territorial peace.[21] The peace was applied to Catalonia, the area which had traditionally developed peace and truce, and therefore excluded the Kingdom of Aragon.

Other kings enacted the peace for whole kingdoms, sometimes temporarily, as did Henry I of England as early as 1100, or Louis VII of France during his absence on the Crusade, or the general peace given by Frederick I of Germany in 1152 and

---

15 Contamine, *La guerra*, p. 343; *Les constitucions*, ed. by Gonzalvo, no. 3 (1033), p. 6; no. 4, §§ V–X; no. 5, §§ IV–XII; no. 6, §§ IV–VIII, XV; no. 12, § XVII; no. 13, § XV; no. 14, §§ IV–X; no. 15, §§ IV–IX; no. 16, §§ III–VII; no. 17, §§ II–VII.

16 Graboïs, 'De la trève de Dieu a la paix du roi', p. 586.

17 *Les constitucions*, ed. by Gonzalvo, nos. 8 (1118) and 14.

18 *Les constitucions*, ed. by Gonzalvo, no. 10.

19 *Les constitucions*, ed. by Gonzalvo, nos. 15, 16, and 17.

20 *Les constitucions*, ed. by Gonzalvo, no. 15 (1173) and no. 19 (1198).

21 *Les constitucions*, ed. by Gonzalvo, p. xxvi.

amplified in the Diet of Roncaglia in 1158. The progressive control of the peace was an instrument through which the main political power in a territory could assert itself.[22]

The *Usatges* of Ramon Berenguer IV had some provisions that were inspired by the ideas of peace and truce, with the novelty that the count, referred to as the prince and understood as the authority, legislated on the administration of peace and truce, which was taken to be a central activity of his government. The occurrence of this tradition in the legal code is reflected in some constitutions of peace and truce that were compiled at the end of this legislation.[23] Besides offering protection in certain situations, the 'prince', that is, Ramon Berenguer IV, was said to have to direct security, warfare and peace, and truce relations with foreign enemies, and especially with Muslims. This went beyond the understanding that peace and truce should protect areas and individuals. Furthermore, the legislation specified that he led the process, and all subjects in 'his land' had to comply.[24] It was also stipulated that all of them should help to maintain the peace and security that the princes conferred on Muslims on land and at sea.[25]

Another general provision on the prince's authority indicated that he should command the hosts 'with which they were to destroy Spain'. At this time, the name Spain referred to the Muslim part. The same legal code forbade the sale of arms to Muslims 'without the consent of the prince' (the count), and if anybody eventually did, he had to recover the arms or pay a heavy fine. Moreover, anyone disseminating secrets or information about a lord's cavalcade to Muslims was also subject to an equivalent fine.[26] The famous *usatge princeps namque* required all men under his authority to come to defend 'the land' if it was attacked, but also if he besieged enemies in turn.[27]

It was an early attempt at general mobilization that was invoked during the Middle Ages and later. Also, it should be noted that it was the expression of a new trend in political thought regarding the prince's leadership at the top of the community in war, peace, and law. In fact, there was some theoretical elaboration or recognition at the time by either his son or grandson. Alfonso the Chaste introduced a general statement about the prince's commitments in the preamble to an assembly of Peace and Truce: 'the prince has the power to stop war, establish the peace, and preserve

---

22 Pascua, *Guerra y pacto*, p. 26; Sabaté, 'Idees de pau', p. 17. An approach to the context, Ladero, 'Paz en la guerra', pp. 21–26.

23 Valls Taberner, *Los Usatges de Barcelona*, p. 130, no. 172; p. 132, no. 173; p. 136, no. 174.

24 Valls Taberner, *Los Usatges de Barcelona*, p. 88, no. 63, and about the enemies (*inimici*), p. 89, no. 65.

25 Valls Taberner, *Los Usatges de Barcelona*, p. 89, no. 64. Christian kings or leaders of the northern half of the Peninsula received payments or pariahs to guarantee peace to Muslims, which explains this rule.

26 Valls Taberner, *Los Usatges de Barcelona*, p. 108, no. 123.

27 Valls Taberner, *Los Usatges de Barcelona*, pp. 90–91, no. 68. Kagay, 'The National Defense Clause', pp. 57–58. According to Kagay, this rule marked the path to 'Catalonia's emergent sense of nationhood' and allowed the Catalan count to seek more power. There was no reference to people or territory, only to the 'land' subject to the authority, i.e. the count. His understanding of 'nation in arms' seems far from the meaning of the rule, in which the links between vassals and the count are paramount and the count's dominion over the 'land' is referred to.

it'.[28] In practice, the charisma of the count, Ramon Berenguer IV, was enhanced especially because of his leadership after the conquests, and he had defined himself as 'the glorious conqueror of Spain' in a donation in 1149.[29] Nevertheless, when the conquest was over the dominance of the count was transferred to the lords. Once the count established a vassal at a frontier point, 'next to Muslim land', he told the vassal that he was there in the count's place, and in the count's land.[30]

The articles of law that referred to the military authority claimed by the count contrasted with other articles related to the dynamics of feudal warfare in the same legal text, such as the ones titled 'if someone failed his lord in the hosts and rides' or 'anyone who was obliged to help his master and abandoned in battle'.[31] This was indeed the military reality; that is, the lords were actually those who used violence or defended the territories, while the count and his son, the king, as lords were able to conquer. *Usatge* 73 stated that the erection of forts, castles, and even churches was subject to authorization by the prince or count and depended on the vassal relationship. This shows how the military leadership of the emerging political power had its roots in feudal hierarchies, at least at the ideological or theoretical level.[32] It is known that the castles were the centres of military domination over the territory, and that Catalonia was full of castles at that time.[33]

Feudal violence was remedied with monetary compensation: even in the case of murder, the crime could be put right by paying a sum. The sixty ounces of gold asked for in compensation for a killing was also imposed for offences of siege, pulling the hair of a gentleman, or cutting off a limb during an assault. In these crimes, social status and the severity of the injuries modulated or reduced the amount demanded, but vengeance was still referred to as the last solution in some cases.[34] Revenge was remedied through fines under feudal law, enacted now by the comital authority, although other *usatges* granted compensation to the family of the victim, or even allowed them to pursue offenders in acts that recalled early avenging practices.[35] Justice was also envisioned as a comital activity, but despite how this was planned in the text, feudal formulas were described in the *Usatges*.

Progressive Pacification and 'Legitimate' Violence

Progressive pacification of the violent actions of the feudal class contrasted with provisions that stated that the power or highest court (i.e. the count) must correct

---

28 *Les constitucions*, ed. by Gonzalvo, nos. 15 and 20.
29 *Diplomatari de la catedral de Tortosa*, ed. by Virgili, p. 60.
30 *Els Pergamins*, ed. by Baiges and others, IV, no. 982: 'Et quod sis inde meus estandant de mea terra, de finibus scilicet Barchinone atque Tortuose et Ispanie'.
31 Valls Taberner, *Los Usatges de Barcelona*, p. 82, no. 34; p. 83, no. 37.
32 Valls Taberner, *Los Usatges de Barcelona*, p. 92, no. 73.
33 Ferrer i Mallol, 'La organización militar en Cataluña', pp. 120–23.
34 Valls Taberner, *Los Usatges de Barcelona*, pp. 74–76, nos 5–6; pp. 77–78, nos 13–15, 17–19, 21; p. 79, nos 22–23; p. 86, no. 58 — it refers to revenge.
35 Valls Taberner, *Los Usatges de Barcelona*, p. 101, nos 100–101.

criminals such as thieves, scammers, or adulterers either forcefully or by exhibiting aggressiveness. These criminals could have their feet and hands broken, their eyes removed, be locked up, and even hanged. Women could have their noses, lips, ears, or breasts cut off, and could be burned if necessary.[36] However, the power was allowed to forgive them. Violence was also part of justice. The definition of peace conditions involved the development of a system of punishment for offenders, which strengthened political entities as was the case with the bishoprics, and later with the counties and royalty during the twelfth century. In addition to excommunication, the count and his men were authorized to apply violence against those who did not respect the peace or provide compensation. In one ordinance of peace and truce this comital violence was even expressed as revenge.[37] The new model tended to surpass and supplant the manorial court.

Another solution warned that if an excommunicated person did not want to make up for any damage done, the bishop and the king's representative or provost should gather an army by recruiting one man from each hide (*mansus*) in the diocese to participate in the revenge.[38] This was regarded as so serious that those who did not join the contingent were in turn excommunicated and left room for what has been called legitimate violence, even in a territory subjected to peace and for peaceful aims. The concept of revenge justified this action, but the scope of its implementation was a jurisdictional or territorial one.

Other legal norms of the time contributed to the pacification or limitation of the lords' abuses and uncontrolled violence, and were specifically formulated in the cities through the instrument of the city charter. The towns were clearly in need of peace terms for their development. The two cities taken from the Muslims, Tortosa and Lleida, soon received these charters. They set out the conditions leading to peace that were subject to county authority and upheld by means of justice, which prevented potential retaliation or the spiralling of violence by imposing fines. The model was transferred to other places like Agramunt.[39] It was a priority to ensure order among both conquerors and Christians, and thus neutralize violence in order to maintain their unity against the subjugated Muslim population as well as to revive urban activities such as trade. It was stipulated that anyone who made threats with a knife, sword, or spear in Tortosa and Lleida was subject to a burdensome fine from the court — *curia* — and non-payment resulted in their right hand being cut off. At about the same time, the provincial council of Lleida imposed religious penalties on those who brandished weapons or caused death in cities or elsewhere.[40] In Tortosa it was also stated that fugitive Muslim slaves had to be returned to their owners in an orderly manner and without any abuses, which shows the need to maintain certain conditions in order to control the violence against the ethnic group under

---

36 Valls Taberner, *Los Usatges de Barcelona*, p. 100, nos 94–95.
37 *Les constitucions*, ed. by Gonzalvo, no. 16, §§ XI and XII.
38 *Les constitucions*, ed. by Gonzalvo, no. 17, §§ XIV and XV. In most of the dioceses of Occitania, these *militias* were organized: Bisson, 'The Organized Peace', p. 306.
39 Font Rius, *Cartas de población*, pp. 121–26, no. 75 (1149); pp. 129–32, no. 79 (1150); p. 176, no. 79 (1163).
40 *Les constitucions*, ed. by Gonzalvo, no. 12 (1155), § XVI.

Christian subjection. Measures to limit private or random violence intertwined with the establishment of a judicial system. Rules were established with a series of procedural safeguards for applying justice. However, failure to compensate for a display of violence by paying a fine was punishable by having the perpetrator's right hand cut off. Violence was used to try to stamp out violence.

Violence against the authority was specifically forbidden in these charters. It was prohibited to 'do battle' against the count. Even if in general the idea of battling referred to private combat, here it was not allowed because the count was the lord or the authority in the conquered towns. In Lleida, the two lords, the counts of Barcelona and Urgell, declared that they would defend all the inhabitants and their property 'everywhere on land or sea where they had power against all men'. The counts' right to defend exceeded the urban jurisdiction and pertained to another territorial concept where they were the main lords. In a letter of confirmation of franchises addressed to the city of Barcelona, the king ensured the safety of the city, and therefore of its people, whom he made 'free' from oppression and 'bad mores' in 1163. In 1198, Count Ermengol VIII confirmed the charter of Agramunt and added some security rules, 'tam quam in pace quam in guerra' (both in peace and in war), and specifically in trading of merchandise.[41] The *paciarii* were established as guarantees of peace in cities in the courts of Lleida in 1214, which meant the culmination of a peace process in Catalan towns, most significantly in those that had been in Muslim hands. Such was the connection between the administration of 'peace' and some city governments that the main posts in the local municipalities of Tortosa and Lleida were called *paers*, that is, *paciarii*.[42] As the example shows, peacemaking processes and other processes curtailing violence culminated in a new stage in the thirteenth century. In the early thirteenth century, as T. Bisson has explained, the maintenance of peace and the curbing of feudal violence, confirmed through services and payments, moved to regional communities.[43]

However, in the Catalan case, we want to emphasize the importance of the count, and later the king, as a key player in the provision of law, ideology, and the development of pacification, in contrast to what happened in southern France. This relates not only to the fact that he was the architect of the principal conquests of the Muslim territory, but also due to his close relationship with the city of Barcelona, the seat of the lordly and political power of his lineage. The fight against Muslims, active or latent, contributed to the need to coordinate the defence of certain regions, and thus maintain the balance or condition of peace for the inhabitants, especially of those towns and regions recently occupied. Thus, in 1188 a bull from Pope Clement III addressed to the people of Tarragona stopped some penitents from marching to Rome so that they could fight to repel the Muslim naval attacks suffered by their city, granting them the same amount of penance as if they had fought in Jerusalem.[44]

---

41 Font Rius, *Cartas de población*, pp. 173–74, no. 120, and pp. 286–88, no. 209.
42 Font i Rius, 'Orígenes del régimen municipal', pp. 316–25.
43 Bisson, 'The Organized Peace', p. 308.
44 Blanch, *Arxiepiscopologi*, I, pp. 112–13.

From Peace of God to War of God

Peace was guarded by religious condemnation, which materialized in the penalty of excommunication and was one of the common elements of repression for those who broke the terms of the peace process and the truce. The spiritual censures were strengthened and diversified and took the form of earthly punishments such as fines, judgements of God, or exile, which were already in place by the eleventh century. Christians who captured, enslaved, or killed Christians were also excommunicated. In the assembly of Peace and Truce of 1064–1066, it was specified that those who respected the Peace and Truce would be in God's grace and might even achieve forgiveness of sins, thus offering a reward instead of the punishment applied to those who breached the provisions.[45]

The penitential solution was a positive alternative to excommunication in the peace movement, and as such would be highly important in validating or singling out the crusade movement and the military expansions against the Muslim lands of al-Andalus, for instance in Catalonia. C. Erdmann stated that once the peace was protected by the Church and its maintenance was a religious obligation, the war that led to that peace had to be a service to God.[46] H. E. J. Cowdrey has also established a connection between peace and truce and the Crusade in defining the ideological conditions of the leadership of the papacy and aristocratic peace. He considers, though, that the lasting impact of peace cannot be compared with pilgrimage or holy war.[47] We understand that there are two key variables in the transition from peace of God to war for God, these being political or military leadership and the overlap of the administration of peace and war in the same person or institution, such as the count or the king. The Church's role was particularly significant, and it provided an element of alterity ideologically speaking, in the confirmation of the political leadership and in offering faithful knights from the military orders. Even so, war was the place where emerging political powers cemented their authority.

Just as conviction and reward became closely linked in the deployment of the peace movement, war and warriors were gradually defined within the new framework, which in turn contained or controlled violence. Defenceless churchmen were protected, as were peasants, but on some occasions clerics who carried weapons or committed unlawful acts were condemned.[48] Those farmers and their goods who rode in cavalcades with their lords were also outside the protection of peace.[49] From the 1060s, various provisions shaped the violence in a more precise way. In the assembly

---

45 *Les constitucions*, ed. by Gonzalvo, no. 5, § XXI.

46 Erdmann, *The Origin of the Idea of Crusade*, pp. 64–94.

47 Cowdrey, 'From the Peace of God to the First Crusade', p. 61. Contamine, *La guerra*, p. 348, notes the proximity between the peace movement and the Crusades, especially in pilgrimage vows. Also Flori, *La guerra santa*, pp. 59–98, and Barthélemy, *La chevalerie*, pp. 254–60, explain the relationship between the Truce of God and Crusades. Despite the fact, as Barthélemy points out, that Christian knighthood was not pacified, after all.

48 *Les constitucions*, ed. by Gonzalvo, no. 7 (1068), § V.

49 *Les constitucions*, ed. by Gonzalvo, no. 15, § VI, and no. 17, § VI.

of 1064, those who rode with their lords with the intention of causing damage were condemned for wreaking 'depredation or devastation' and for breaking the 'peace and truce'. The same thing happened to those who caused damage or committed other forms of misdeeds but did not submit to the authority or judgement of the Church.[50] Excommunication befell people, their goods, and even companions if they had participated in the cavalcades. Also, the sons of magnates who jeopardized the vassals of their parents were expressly condemned and were not allowed to return to the family castle or enjoy family protection.[51] Those who attacked by surprise ('aguayt') during the truce and caused the capture of the castle or deaths were subject to ecclesiastical justice.[52] Once again, the imposition of certain compensation after attacking castles by surprise during the truce was updated in the middle of the twelfth century.[53] Another provision of the assembly of 1064 offered protection for a certain period of time to those who marched on an expedition (the one called the pre-crusade of Barbastro) and according to the truce of God.[54] Similar policies were developed in the next century for the Crusaders.

The Crusaders were protected with the security of peace, but also took a qualitative leap when they were rewarded for their contribution to the holy war. This form of positive assessment of military activity against the enemies of the faith inspired a provision of peace and truce aimed at the people defending the Olèrdola castle in 1108. The inhabitants and knights who were in charge of restoring the Olèrdola castle were also protected by the peace and truce in 1108. The site had been devastated by the attacks of the Muslims or 'paganorum inimicis nominis Christi' (enemies of Christ's name), and therefore all who defended the castle and its region would benefit.[55] The defence was rewarded with a guarantee of peace, which was now granted by Count Ramon Berenguer III and the Bishop of Barcelona.

Can these factors explain the particular definition of peace and truce attributed to the early Templars before their involvement in military activity? In 1134, the Archbishop of Tarragona, a pre-eminent figure in the Church, as well as Ramon Berenguer IV along with other prelates granted safety and security to the Templars, who were under the protection and defence of God and St Peter. This protective link was a key issue, whilst military activity was only referred to in a very general way.[56] Subsequently, the Templars and the Hospitallers were subject to protection, security, and peace in perpetuity, as were other ecclesiastical people and as was expressed and repeated occasionally.[57] Later, these orders had specific military obligations

---

50 *Les constitucions*, ed. by Gonzalvo, no. 4, §§ XVIII, XXIII, XXVI, XXVII, and no. 5, § XXIII.
51 *Les constitucions*, ed. by Gonzalvo, no. 4, § XIX, and no. 5, § XXIV.
52 *Les constitucions*, ed. by Gonzalvo, no. 5, § XIX, and no. 6, § XIII.
53 Valls Taberner, *Los Usatges de Barcelona*, p. 96, no. 83.
54 *Les constitucions*, ed. by Gonzalvo, no. 4, § XVI. Flori disputes that the conquest of Barbastro was an anticipated crusade but describes religious aspects that would end up being characteristic of the Crusades; Flori, *La guerra santa*, pp. 272–75.
55 *Les constitucions*, ed. by Gonzalvo, no. 8 (1108).
56 *Les constitucions*, ed. by Gonzalvo, no. 11 (1134).
57 *Les constitucions*, ed. by Gonzalvo, no. 14, § V, no. 15, or no. 19 as examples.

ORGANIZING VIOLENCE   39

such as those concerning the defence of the frontier; however, around 1145, in the neighbouring region of Narbonne, the Templars started to charge in exchange for protecting the peasants as the Hospitallers did later in Osona.[58]

'Restorative Violence' against Muslims: Discourses and Memories

In Olèrdola there was a direct relationship between the rejection of Muslim violence, which involved destroying churches, arson, and kidnapping, and the progressive definition of another form of violence that was defensive and restorative. This understanding of violence as restorative became further entrenched and is illustrated by the fact that arsonists could exchange excommunication for a penance of one year's fighting in Muslim lands — 'Ierosolimis vel in Ispania in servitio Dei' (in Jerusalem or in Spain in the service of God) — in the second half of the twelfth century.[59] This reflects an idea of the Crusade or holy war in which the Hispanic lands in Muslim hands were identified with Jerusalem. However, defining peacekeeping or security conditions did not stop feudal war, and even some peace arrangements made certain exceptions in some of these situations. Roads or tracks were protected unless the lords of the territory were clearly involved in war.[60] The concept of war was being remodelled, and as in the case of peace and truce, the new interpretation gave birth to a new way of managing the military process.

The emergence and development of the concept of holy war dates back to the eleventh century, when aristocratic elites prospered in the areas of Aragon and Catalonia, as C. Laliena has stated. The providential character of war had already appeared in the middle of the eleventh century, as Arnau Mir de Tost put it in 1048. At this time the idea of holy war flourished, as did the idea of a just war for the liberation of Christians. These ideas shared two key components of further military developments: the union of Christians and the definition of the enemy.[61] Ecclesiastical reform provided the ideological ingredients, while the papacy led part of the process of promoting holy war. The pope favoured forming ties with major political powers while promoting other complementary focuses of ecclesiastical power, that is, the bishops, as renewed emerging authorities. Urban II addressed the main counts of Catalonia, Barcelona, Urgell, and Besalú, so they could help the Bishop of Vic in the restoration of Tarragona in 1089.[62] The spiritual benefits offered to those who participated were the remission of sins, and significantly were offered to those who wanted to go on a pilgrimage to do penance in Jerusalem or other places. A reference in the bull is worth mentioning: divine providence would guide them, and the Christians who occupied Tarragona would rise up like a wall against the Muslim neighbours. The bull is an interesting record because it contains significant items that were proclaimed by the same pope

---

58   Bisson, 'The Organized Peace', p. 300; Freedman, 'Military Orders in Osona'.
59   *Les constitucions*, ed. by Gonzalvo, no. 12, § XXVII; no. 14, § XXV, but less detailed.
60   *Les constitucions*, ed. by Gonzalvo, no. 15, § XI.
61   Laliena, 'Guerra sagrada y poder real', pp. 104–07, and on identity related to holy war ideology in eleventh-century Catalonia, Sabaté, 'Frontera peninsular e identidad', pp. 76–78.
62   Mansilla, *La documentación pontificia hasta Inocencio III*, nos 41–42.

to promote the First Crusade a few years afterwards, but this time it refers instead to the restoration of the Church and the occupation of Tarragona.[63]

Holy war was not only a discourse disseminated by the papacy, but also served as an argument in the Catalan counts' early projects, as when Count Ramon Berenguer III proposed to conquer the region of Tortosa in 1097. In his concession to the churches of the 'kingdom of Tortosa', the long introduction put forward the idea of a certain Christ-mimesis of himself as Christ-redeemer, 'who with his own blood had redeemed the Church, whose unity was attacked and destroyed by the enemies of the faith in the lands of Hispania (Spain)'. He founded the Church of the Holy Sepulchre, commanding it to be built for the redemption of the recipient, the Abbot of Sant Cugat, of men 'pro delictorum suorum poenitentia', and of himself. The count would be redeemed by his restoration of the Church in the 'taifa kingdom' of Tortosa, with the Holy Sepulchre being a symbolic element in the process. In doing so, Ramon Berenguer III echoed a formula devised by the papacy before the success of the First Crusade.[64] Another county grant issued to the Count of Pallars during the same campaign to conquer Tortosa contained almost no trace of crusade ideology. Probably the contents of the count's message depended on the interlocutor.[65] The church was a key element in achieving legitimacy for the aims pursued by the Count of Barcelona. The project to restore Tortosa is interesting because in general the Aragonese Crusaders' vocation is better known, as is Peter I in comparison with his contemporary Ramon Berenguer III.[66] Moreover, the crusade movement had greater manifestations in Aragon than in Catalonia, at least in the early part of the twelfth century.[67] Catalan comital power used the crusader discourse to promote a reorganization of the Church based on the count's interests and different from other contemporary restorative guidelines. During the first half of the twelfth century, the need to restore ecclesiastical sites became clearer, but especially those which had been outside the Christian faith for centuries, such as Tarragona, Huesca, Tortosa, and Lleida.

The documents written to restore Tarragona and Huesca emphasized that these sites had been abandoned for years or had been outside the faith for 390 or 460 years because of the 'impetus of the barbarians'. The proposed restoration of Tortosa made clear that the bishopric had been destroyed and oppressed by the pagans and, as with Huesca and Lleida, that it 'had been subject to Muslim perfidy'.[68] The restoration of the Church and the consolidation of the crusading movement were the shared goals of the count and the popes. In this sense, Ramon Berenguer IV was

---

63 Crusading was a Mediterranean-wide phenomenon at this period, Cheveddan, 'Pope Urban II', p. 34.

64 Risco, España Sagrada, XLII, pp. 279–82.

65 Els Pergamins, ed. by Baiges and others, II, no. 296. There are two mentions of the intervention of divine providence in the success of the conquest: 'ex Dei adiutatorio in omni regno Tortuose... dante Deo'.

66 Utrilla, 'Conquista, guerra santa y territorialidad en el reino de Aragón'.

67 According to Purkis, Crusading Spirituality, p. 125, this Christ-mimesis was evident in the person and actions of Peter I of Aragon, known as 'rex crucifer'.

68 Mansilla, La documentación pontificia hasta Inocencio III, no. 50; Laliena, 'Guerra sagrada y poder real', p. 110; Diplomatari de la catedral de Tortosa, ed. by Virgili, no. 13 for Tortosa and no. 19 for Lleida.

recognized for having restored three hundred churches after his conquests, as was memorialized in the dynastic written account of the *Gesta comitum Barchinone et regum Aragonie* (*Deeds of the Counts of Barcelona and Kings of Aragon*).[69] This reveals the connection of the major powers and the coexistence between the two processes of restoration and conquest. It reinforced the reform of the Church, but emerging comital power participated in or even led the process during its early stages.[70] The union between the Church and the Count of Barcelona suffered vicissitudes, as was common in other feudal power relationships. The Archbishop of Tarragona appointed a prince in 1129 to serve the Church, entrusting him instead of the count 'to exercise war in defence of Christianity' during the restoration and 'repopulation' of Tarragona. He chose a Norman prince, despite the vassal relationship that the archbishop had with the count, who had previously given him the territory of Tarragona. The task for the Norman was not just to occupy an abandoned city, but to defend Christianity.[71]

The two emerging powers, the papacy and the Count of Barcelona or leaders of similar status, intersected at the same pace, while the crusader ideals became more refined and stronger. Ramon Berenguer III showed this in his preparations for military action in the conquest of Majorca, when the pope urged him to take up the fight against Muslims.[72]

The Pisan version *Liber Maiolichinus de gestis pissanorum illustribus* tells of the Pisan-Catalan crusade that conquered Majorca (1113–1115). The pope gave the cross to the Pisans, with the purpose of ending the capture of Christians and curtailing Muslim piracy that plagued the Mediterranean coasts.[73] The Pisan source highlighted the leadership of the Count of Barcelona, referred to as the Duke of Catalans ('dux catalanensis'), also 'rector Catalanicus hostes' or hero, a term in turn used to refer to the Count of Ampurias. At the time that Count Ramon Berenguer III was establishing pacts with the Pisans to attack Majorca, he gave an assurance of safety to the Pisan people and their goods in Arles and Saint Gilles in 1113.[74] In the same way that conditions of peace and security had favoured the consolidation of regional and local trade, the agreements for peace and security granted to some allies benefitted the progressive commercial hegemony of the Christian allies in the western Mediterranean. In turn, peace among Christians was accompanied by the covenants made in the war against Muslims. This shows how peace and security conditions favoured efficient war, or at least were accounted for in this way. A decade later, agreements between Genoa and the Count of Barcelona led to Genoese commercial traffic coming under comital

---

69 *Gesta comitum Barchinone*, ed. by Cingolani, pp. 102–03.
70 The donation by the Count of Barcelona, Ramon Berenguer II, to Saint Peter and the pope placed the count under pontifical dependence through the possible restoration of the site: Archivo Histórico Archidiocesano de Tarragona, *Llibre de la corretja*, no. 1 (1090).
71 Font Rius, *Cartas de población*, pp. 87–89, no. 51.
72 Bishko, 'The Spanish and Portuguese Reconquest', p. 406.
73 *Liber Maiolichinus*, rev. by Pierazzo.
74 *Tractats i negociacions diplomàtiques*, ed. by Ferrer i Mallol and Riu i Riu, pp. 162–63, and no. 37, pp. 289–92.

protection and the inclusion of Barcelona on the sea routes to Muslim Spain, and they also manifested support for a possible war against Muslims.[75]

In 1092 there was an unsuccessful attempt by the Christians to conquer Tortosa, which has been associated with the failure of Castile to conquer Valencia. Despite the parsimony of the sources, the military enterprise had a Pisan-Genovese fleet, and the Count of Barcelona, Berenguer Ramon II, and King Sancho Ramírez of Aragon collaborated, each aspiring to take the town for himself.[76]

However, the *Liber* tells of a confusing episode in which the Pisans attacked and caused terror 'by mistake' on the Blanes coast, thinking that they had reached the coast of Majorca, eventually realizing that the people were 'Christians and Catalans'.[77] This is the first known reference to the Catalans, and it is significant because it is evidence of the appearance of the collective identity of Christian groups to counter a common enemy: the Muslims. Not surprisingly, Christians and Catalans are mentioned together in the same way. Interestingly, in another part of the poem, the count accused the Muslims of depopulating the coast of Blanes, due to a fear of attacks. In addition, Ramon Berenguer III stressed the aforementioned argument for the restoration of the Church. He described atrocities, such as killing monks and priests, that Muslims had committed inside churches that were later abandoned.[78] The story has clearly been reworked in an attempt to hide or justify the pillage committed by the Pisans before they became allies with the 'Catalans', and especially in the interests of the count, who finally joined them.[79] It seems difficult to believe that the Pisans completely lost their way. It also seems unlikely that churches in an unimportant place north of Barcelona were abandoned due to Muslim attacks as is described by the count. The story has been rewritten with crusaders' arguments that paint the Catalan ally as a hero or a military leader, even if he did not take part in the expansion in Tarragona around the same time. On the other hand, the explanation of the abandonment of the temples and their becoming overgrown with trees and bushes in Blanes is close to that offered by Orderic Vitalis on the abandonment of others in Tarragona before the restoration, and it seems a commonplace in restoration discourses.[80]

Papal bulls preceded and accompanied the processes of conquest. Callixtus II exhorted all bishops, kings, counts, and princes to fight Muslims in 1123, equating those involved in the peninsular conquests with the defenders of the crusader states in terms of prerogatives and spiritual benefits.[81] He explicitly referred to the release

---

75 *Tractats i negociacions diplomàtiques*, ed. by Ferrer i Mallol and Riu i Riu, no. 41: 'et quod Ianuensis populus quiete habeat transitum [...] per comite [...] terram ad faciendam pacem et guerram cum voluerit sarracenis'.

76 *Tractats i negociacions diplomàtiques*, ed. by Ferrer i Mallol and Riu i Riu, p. 160.

77 *Liber Maiolichinus*, verses 245–50.

78 *Liber Maiolichinus*, verses 285–90.

79 We agree that there was no previous agreement between Pisa and Barcelona for this expedition to conquer Majorca, as M. Teresa Ferrer i Mallol argues: *Tractats i negociacions diplomàtiques*, ed. by Ferrer i Mallol and Riu i Riu, p. 162.

80 *The Ecclesiastical History of Orderic Vitalis*, ed. and trans. by Chibnall, p. 402.

81 Flórez, *España Sagrada*, XXV, pp. 223–24. Ayala, 'Religiosidad militar y cancillería regia', pp. 48–49.

ORGANIZING VIOLENCE   43

of the churches from the oppression of the heathen, and he said that 'the sons of God are dead by the oppression of the pagans'. He also nominated Oleguer, the archbishop of Tarragona and bishop of Barcelona, as his delegate or 'legatus' of holy war in the peninsular lands. The papacy also participated by re-establishing the reformed episcopal sees in the subsequent conquests. However, Oleguer had no role in the expansion process, something contradicted by the stories narrated in the hagiographic tradition, which probably tried to erase the ineffectiveness of the purported contribution of the Church.[82]

Shortly before the conquest of Tortosa, another bull was published in favour of the military campaign that would be led by Ramon Berenguer IV.[83] The pontiff also encouraged the participation of soldiers in these expeditions. In 1152, Eugene III urged the faithful to follow the Count of Barcelona, once again assuring spiritual benefits equal to those enjoyed by fighters in the Holy Land.[84] A year later, Anastasius IV backed the leadership of the Count of Barcelona, telling the faithful to follow Ramon Berenguer IV and insisting on the need 'to attack the infidels and enemies of the cross [...] to defend the Christian faith and the whole Church'. He also identified Eastern and Western Crusades, and specifically referred to the benefits promised by the first Crusade propagator, Urban II.[85] The pontifical push coincided with 'the purpose of spreading the faith and defending Christianity' or even 'of oppressing or devastating Muslims' expressed by the leaders of the Catalan conquest. These types of statements were repeated in documents issued before or during military campaigns, such as the conquest of Tortosa and Lerida, and in other contemporary records, clearly in those addressed to the military orders.[86]

The new political forms coincided with the renewal in historical memory, as happened with the *Deeds of the Counts of Barcelona* that was an important piece in the construction of political memory, probably compiled in the 1180s by monks from Ripoll.[87] Its narrative paid attention to the comital lineage, established dynastic legitimacy, and celebrated Ramon Berenguer IV as the restorer of Count Guifré the Hairy's county. In this sense, the text stressed a legitimate dynastic descendancy from Guifré, who was portrayed as the heroic founder of the anti-Muslim cause.[88] Besides, the members of the lineage were recognized as successful fighters against Muslims in this dynastic account. This distinguished feature was applied to Ramon Berenguer III, who was described as 'the one always victorious against Muslims' and

---

82   Aurell, 'Esclavage et croisade'. Mc Crank, 'Saint and Hero', notes that Oleguer was revered as a hero, while acknowledging the lack of military evidence.

83   Bishko, 'The Spanish and Portuguese Reconquest', p. 410 (22 June 1148).

84   *Colección de documentos inéditos*, ed. by de Bofarull, no. 128, pp. 314–15.

85   *Colección de documentos inéditos*, ed. by de Bofarull, no. 133, pp. 320–21: 'ad expugnationem infidelium et inimicorum crucis Christi viriliter [...] pro defensione Christiane fidei et tocius sancte ecclesie'.

86   The count referred to the Hospitallers in 1150, Archivo Histórico Nacional, Saint John's Order, folder 686, n. 2. Another reference in *Cartulaire general*, ed. by Delaville le Roulx, pp. 621–22, or also in 1157, *Colección de documentos inéditos*, ed. by de Bofarull, no. 94, pp. 243–45.

87   Cingolani, 'Seguir les vestígies dels antecessors'. *Gesta comitum Barchinone*, ed. by Cingolani, p. 14.

88   *Gesta comitum Barchinone*, ed. by Cingolani, pp. 68–69.

also to his son, who 'attacked bravely twenty thousand Muslims' with only fifty-two knights, after inspiring King Alfonso VII to conquer Almeria.[89] This specific military role, highlighted in the chronicle, was in line with the prince's role as the leader in the fighting against the Muslims that was claimed in the *Usatges*. However, the members of the lineage were presented with a special charisma in the *Deeds*, because they were heroic and brave fighters who opposed the main enemies of the faith, the Muslims. In addition, they were reported as the most committed against the Muslims among the Spanish Christian kings.[90]

Agreements for War against Muslims and for Peace

The comital leadership prospered under the redefinition of peace and war. The agreements of the Catalan counts, especially between the Count of Barcelona and mercantile cities, kings, and other Christian political leaders, were essential in order to carry out military enterprises or establish peace. The pacts between the Catalans and other Christian powers are beyond the scope and purpose of this study, but they were the framework and, in part, the reason for the process of affirming comital power and reinforcing unity against a common enemy, the Muslims. Nevertheless, it is fundamental to highlight the importance of comital influence in Provence and the links between the Count of Barcelona and the Italian states which have been magnificently explained by P. Benito Monclús and M. T. Ferrer Mallol.[91]

The approach to crusade ideology by the Count of Barcelona, Ramon Berenguer IV, was intentionally set out in the solution he imposed to settle the issue of the rights of the Order of the Temple in the Kingdom of Aragon in 1143 after a series of fruitless negotiations.[92] The count stated that he would 'defend the Western Church in Hispanic lands, by attacking, reducing, and oppressing Muslims; he would also exalt faith and the religion of Western Christendom by following the example of the Templars defending the Eastern Church'. This last point shows how he was taking the baton from the institution that had been the heir of the Kingdom of Aragon thanks to its crusading role, thus remaining close to the main 'crusader' King Alfonso I of Aragon. There was also a discourse of 'Otherness' or complementarity between the Hispanic lands and the Eastern lands. Furthermore, he specified that the Templars had renounced the constitution of a 'militie Christi in Ispaniis adversus mauros' (knighthood of Christ in Spain against the Moors). This argument was linked to his

---

89 *Gesta comitum Barchinone*, ed. by Cingolani, pp. 98–99, 100–102.
90 This also referred to King Alfonso the Chaste, *Gesta comitum Barchinone*, ed. by Cingolani, pp. 122–23.
91 Benito Monclús, 'L'expansió territorial ultrapirenenca'; Ferrer i Mallol, 'Les relacions del comtat de Barcelona i de la Corona catalanaragonesa'.
92 *Colección de documentos inéditos*, ed. by de Bofarull, no. 43, pp. 93–99. The explanation of this comital imposition and lack of agreement contrasts with what is generally found in the bibliography, Bonet, 'Historiografía e investigación', p. 65. However, Forey, *The Templars in the Corona of Aragon*, p. 23, had already observed that there was no evidence of renunciation of the Templars, but it must have been made in a separate document.

insistence 'ad exercendum officium milicie in regione Ispanie' (to fulfil the obligation to fight in Spain) against the Saracens in a penitential formula. He did this in honour of his father, whom he stated had died as a Templar. This reference claims him to be the heir of somebody who joined the order at the end of his life, and for this reason he was apparently free of any personal interest before the King of Aragon's will was settled. The association of Ramon Berenguer III with the Temple was almost certainly forged by his son.[93] The comital discourse reinforced and legitimized his dual heritage as a son of a Templar and a political leader. Furthermore, he established a dynastic and ideological bridge between the Temple and the count, allowing the matter of the will to be settled, bolstering the figure and person of the Count of Barcelona, and also legitimizing him as a prince of Aragon.

In the solution applied to the Templars by Ramon Berenguer IV, they were called on to be involved in the conquests, especially in the military occupation of new lands. Later on, the count and his son the king established military orders to occupy conquered lands, following his resolution of 1143. The count gave a fifth of the lands conquered from the Muslims to the Templars, and later a tenth to the Hospitallers.[94] This was to promote their assistance in these conquests and in occupying regions. He also wanted the Templars to attack Muslims, and this explains why he gave them a fifth from the expeditions. The count agreed not to make 'peace and truces' with the enemy without asking the Templars' advice. Also, in 1146, Ramon Berenguer IV confirmed the Templars' right to 'obtain' or capture Muslims during their service in al-Andalus, thus boosting his role in capturing Muslims, which was a strategy to harass the enemy.[95] At that time, this was mostly a statement of intent because the Templars' real military potential was weaker than he expected. In the aforementioned document, the 'Otherness' pursued by the count shows how these knights, specialized in fighting but also members of the Church, were ideal or maybe idealized to contribute to later comital conquests and regal ones.

The process of forging links and loyalties, undertaken by the count and the king together with other emerging powers to obtain military contingents for great military enterprises, was a key element in achieving victories.[96] It further conditioned the distribution of power after the conquests in the middle of the twelfth century. Taking Tortosa as an example, in 1136 Ramon Berenguer IV established a vassal agreement with William of Montpellier, who obtained Tortosa in fee as well as castles, and in return promised to join the count in peace and war according to his will.[97] Then, in 1146 Ramon Berenguer IV made an agreement with Genoa, while another agreement

---

93 Miret i Sans, *Les cases de Templers i Hospitalers*, p. 23, suggested that the document in which Ramon Berenguer III was linked to the Temple was false. The son's responsibility in the probable falsification is explained in Bonet, 'Historiografía e investigación', p. 61.

94 *Colección de documentos inéditos*, ed. by de Bofarull, no. 94, pp. 243–45, and, *Els Pergamins*, ed. by Baiges and others, IV, no. 1028.

95 *Col·lecció diplomàtica*, ed. by Sarobe, no. 12.

96 Bonet, 'Wars in 12th Century Catalonia', pp. 180–83.

97 *Colección de documentos inéditos*, ed. by de Bofarull, no. 22.

to conquer Almeria was made with the Castilian king.[98] The Genoese took the conquest of Tortosa as an episode in a very ambitious programme, which had at its vertices Almeria, Tortosa, and finally the Balearic Islands, but they recognized the leadership of the Count of Barcelona by saying that they would not attack any place, city or castle, without his consent. Commercial accords of great importance for Genoa are referred to in one of two records kept about agreements between the Count of Barcelona and the Genoese to conquer Tortosa and the Balearics. Genoa obtained tax-free trade from the Rhone to the west and access to a third of the cities that the count might conquer, and a neighbourhood district with a corn exchange. The fact that the Genoese wanted to acquire a presence in these cities shows that their main objective was to establish colonial bases in the western Mediterranean. The need for leadership in political and trading matters led to pacts for war and trade. These agreements guaranteed the effectiveness of these prominent leaders, united powerful groups, and also foreshadowed the division of power and political or economic functions in the conquered regions.[99] The document of the agreement with Genoa was sworn to by important figures like the Counts of Urgell, Ampurias, and Roussillon, as well as the retinue of the Count of Barcelona, and it featured members of the aristocracy. The consensus for conquest and the commitments in favour of Genoa were obtained by Ramon Berenguer IV, just as he had managed with the Templars, and it shows how he exercised clear leadership in the preparation of war and, the most important issue, the status quo after it.

In the same year another agreement was concluded with the seneschal, Guillem Ramon de Moncada, who was given 'lordship of Tortosa in the form of a third of the revenues of the city and territory'.[100] Moncada's rights to the Balearic Islands were settled in the agreement, and it was his grandson and great-grandson who died during James I's expedition, undoing the pact, but at the same time showing how seriously these pacts were taken. Furthermore, by incorporating Moncada, the count established similar conditions to those of the Genoese for someone in his own circle. The fact that both were granted Tortosa and the Balearics as well as a third of the revenues indicates a comital strategy to give equal weight to the principal vassal of his court.

The Count of Barcelona set another vassal agreement with the Count of Urgell for the subsequent conquest of Lleida in May 1148, before embarking on the conquest of Tortosa. Both facts and projects were related. The division of Lleida gave a third part to the Count of Urgell as a vassal, and a fifth of the two remaining thirds retained by the Count of Barcelona went to the Templars. Ramon Berenguer IV gave the castle of Ascó, in Muslim lands, to the Count of Urgell, as a reward for benefits given to

---

98 *Colección de documentos inéditos*, ed. by de Bofarull, no. 144, pp. 337–39, and no. 141, pp. 332–34, and updated edition in *Tractats i negociacions diplomàtiques*, ed. by Ferrer i Mallol and Riu i Riu, no. 52, pp. 314–18; no. 51, pp. 309–13.

99 *Tractats i negociacions diplomàtiques*, ed. by Ferrer i Mallol and Riu i Riu, no. 51, pp. 309–13. In the other agreement about the Genoese presence in the conquered lands, it would be a third, including both fortresses and cities.

100 *Colección de documentos inéditos*, ed. by de Bofarull, no. 51.

the Templars.[101] There would be a castellan chosen by the Count of Barcelona. The castellan would have to go on campaigns against Muslims if the Count of Urgell did not fulfil his obligation to do so, and the Count of Barcelona would have the right to stay there. This example shows how vassalage agreements were modelled by the principal leader, Ramon Berenguer IV, who took Ascó as a strategic location and with a formula to ensure the effectiveness of his delegate, be it a prominent vassal or a mere castellan who represented him.

Other donations anticipated conquests, such as when Arnal Berenguer received Siurana in 1146. Bertrà Castellet, among others, participated in this enterprise and was awarded with the castellany for his efforts.[102] The conquest of Siurana, a rural Muslim district, was the last to be directed by the count, and it opened up the possibility of conquering other sites, such as Miravet and Ascó in 1153–1154. All these main strongholds were located in a region between the two Muslim cities conquered before. The comital strategy was to take out the most important places first, starting with the main Muslim town, Tortosa. The donation of Ascó to the Count of Urgell was made on condition that he assisted in the conquest by attacking from inland positions, should the conquest of Lleida occur before that of Tortosa. The Count of Barcelona told him that he should make 'pacem et guerram sarracenis et christianis' (peace and war for both Christians and Muslims), as a duty to his lord. This phrase went beyond the traditional formulas in documents of vassalage in which the vassal pledged to help defend and go to war on behalf of his master. However, in the case of the Count of Urgell, he was being assigned a responsibility attributed to the Count of Barcelona according to the law. Despite the fact that power was delegated, this reflected his weakness as principal commander. The right of making peace and war was clearly expressed as a key issue in the political system.

The Count of Barcelona financed important aspects of military deployment with pariahs. Ironically, he defined pariahs as the result of the peace established with Muslims, but understood in the frame of a vassal relationship.[103] For instance, the Count of Barcelona promised the Count of Urgell two thousand morabetinos of pariahs until Lleida was conquered, and granted two thousand morabetinos to the Hospitallers to erect a fortress in a strategic place, Amposta, after conquering the neighbouring town of Tortosa plus one thousand annually from pariahs.

Despite the strengthening of the figure of Count Ramon Berenguer IV in the organization, conquest, and later distribution of the Muslim kingdom of Tortosa, the Genoese version in *De Captione Almerie et Tortuose* offers a different narrative which needs to be taken as a suggestive counterpoint. There was no such comital dominance in the conquest, as comes to light in the situations described therein. The title of Cafaro's chronicle — Consul of Genoa before 1147 and expeditionary — shows how the Genoese naval actions of 1147 and 1148 were related, and indeed the Count of

---

101 *Colección de documentos inéditos*, ed. by de Bofarull, no. 54, pp. 126–29.
102 *Colección de documentos inéditos*, ed. by de Bofarull, no. 50, pp. 112–13.
103 *Colección de documentos inéditos*, ed. by de Bofarull, no. 20, pp. 47–48, 'decimum de ipsis pariis Ispanie que a modo inde exierint comite nominatim per ipsam pacem ad fevum'.

Barcelona participated in both of them. Cafaro tells us that the count came to Almeria with fifty-three men, while Alfonso VII of Castile, called the emperor, had no more than four hundred knights and an infantry of one thousand.[104] After returning from Almeria, the Genoese spent the winter in Barcelona with their families, where they stocked up for subsequent conquests, in line with previous agreements with the count.

The aforementioned account of the siege of Tortosa referred to three contingents located on three flanks: one was made up of half of the Genoese warriors with 'some warriors from the count', another with the count and William of Montpellier, and the third of Englishmen, Templars, and other foreigners. The story highlights the courage and strength of the Genoese, but also an uncontrolled episode in which they acted 'sine consilio consulum et ceterorum' (without the advice of consuls and others), showing that the Genoese were not under the military command of the count. It is also suggested that the Count of Barcelona was left with twenty knights for lack of resources and the 'Ianuenses namque viri audacissimi […] iuraverunt quod a Tortosa non recederant' (Genoese, the bravest men, swore not to withdraw from Tortosa).[105] Although the count was really diminished in this account, the prior agreement was upheld: a third of the conquered land for the 'audacious' and two-thirds for the count.

From the middle of the twelfth century and onwards, the King of Castile, also called the 'Emperor of Spain', Alfonso VII and his son Alfonso VIII, drew up various treaties with the Count of Barcelona, and later his son, the King of Aragon, sharing future land gains in Muslim countries. They also divided up the Kingdom of Navarre.[106] Indeed, the imperial idea was related to the submission of al-Andalus in a few records from the chancellery of Alfonso VII.[107] This is not the place to explain the complexity of the balance of power in the Peninsula, although it is worth pointing out that a common strategy defined common enemies, in reference to not only Muslim lands but also Navarre. The agreements resulted in attacks on Navarre by both neighbouring leaders, which were interspersed in time with other attacks on al-Andalus. Already in 1139, Ramon Berenguer IV, acting as Prince of Aragon, and Alfonso VII agreed to share any lands acquired from the King of Pamplona, Sancho, proportionately; one-third for the emperor and two for the count.[108] They also made a pact not to make truces or settlements without consulting each other. The agreement between the two political leaders also led in 1141 to the recognition of Ramon Berenguer IV as vassal of the Castilian king, and in 1151 to the well-known treaty of Tudillén. This was made to achieve peace. The text was headed with the three key expressions of the process:

---

104 Caffarus, *De Captione*, ed. by Ubieto Arteta, p. 24. The difference between the two armies is striking, but in any case it reflects some precariousness in the comital contribution.

105 Caffarus, *De Captione*, ed. by Ubieto Arteta, p. 34. This account is far from the official image offered by the *Gesta comitum Barchinone*, ed. by Cingolani, pp. 102–03. The chronicle claims the unbelievable presence of two hundred thousand warriors gathered by the count with Genoese support.

106 Cantera Montenegro, 'Los tratados de paz y la delimitación', pp. 401–10; Estepa, 'El reinado de Alfonso VIII', pp. 214–15.

107 Ayala, 'Religiosidad militar y cancillería regia', p. 61.

108 *Colección de documentos inéditos*, ed. by de Bofarull, no. 28, pp. 64–65.

ORGANIZING VIOLENCE   49

peace, strong vassal relations, and lasting covenants.[109] The treaty solved to some extent the issue of Navarre, thus leaving the Count of Barcelona subject to vassalage to the Castilian king, again. This bond was mentioned in other pacts on spaces to conquer, but with some interesting specifications. When conquering the city of Valencia and its lands and Denia, the count was linked to the Castilian king based on earlier bonds between Navarre and Castile. However, if Ramon Berenguer IV could conquer the city of Murcia, he would be considered a vassal in just the same way as had happened with Zaragoza. If the Castilian king did not help the Count of Barcelona for justified reasons, the count would gain full domination of Valencia. Degrees of interdependence were drawn up, based largely on past agreements, but also foreshadowing greater degrees of independence from the leader of Barcelona in certain cases.

The papacy had promoted the holy war and spoken in favour of peace among Christian dignitaries. Eugene III encouraged the Count of Barcelona and the 'Duke' of Pamplona to achieve peace, because 'war had caused harm to the Church and hit the poor hard', in accordance with the peace discourse. He asked Ramon Berenguer IV to reform the peace in God's honour and for the tranquillity of the Christian people under the count's government, but he also reminded him to act against the enemies of the cross of Christ.[110] The count's mission was to bring peace to the Christians and fight against the Muslims, with the support of the bishops and backed up by the pope. Adrian IV demanded that the Archbishops of Tarragona and Narbonne intervene against those who opposed the count and those who favoured the Muslims.[111]

The military leadership of Ramon Berenguer IV is evident because of the continuity of war under his command. He fought against Navarre, and later he participated with Sancho IV and Alfonso VII in Almeria in 1147; a year later he conquered Tortosa, then Lleida in 1149. Next, in 1150, he attacked resistant nobles in Occitania; he resumed attacks against Navarre in 1151, and won Miravet and Siurana in 1153. However, he did not experience only victories, as his own lands were attacked when Sancho IV of Navarre moved against Zaragoza in 1156. Despite the arrival of the Almohads, the military career of his son also demonstrated a similar continuity. He conquered the Teruel region (1169–1171), launched attacks against Almohads, and even tried to conquer Valencia (1172), as well as participating in the conquest of Cuenca (1177) and the Occitan war. Both father and son participated in attacks led by Castile, but there was no help from the Castilians in the Catalan or Aragonese conquests. It is possible to attribute this unbalanced relationship to the vassalage of the count and his son to the Castilian king, which, on the other hand, is far from the image given in the comital chronicle.

After the conquest, it was necessary to strengthen the frontier because of pressure from the Almohads. Political power achieved this by establishing and expanding the domain of the military orders, among them the Templars and Hospitallers. However, the military orders were also used for political-military purposes by the monarchs

---

109 *Colección de documentos inéditos*, ed. by de Bofarull, no. 62, pp. 168–74: 'vera pax et firma conveniencia et perpetua concordia'.
110 *Colección de documentos inéditos*, ed. by de Bofarull, no. 131, pp. 318–19.
111 *Colección de documentos inéditos*, ed. by de Bofarull, no. 129, pp. 315–16.

of Aragon and Navarre fighting on the western border of Aragon. Therefore, they were given lands in order to mark the kings' positions in the border areas of their kingdoms, these lands being finally set out in a peace treaty in 1149.[112] Military orders were mainly the instruments of the emerging political powers who patronized them, and they returned this favour above and beyond their crusader duties.

The military orders became lords of the southern frontier of Catalonia thanks to land granted by the count and the king. The formation of commanderies there mostly took the place of earlier donations to other lords that were involved in the occupation and defence of the region but who had failed.[113] Other military orders were added to strengthen the defences in the gains made in the Teruel region and also the Ebro valley by Alfonso the Chaste, who promoted a model of militarization of extensive border regions with Muslim lands mainly under the orders' domain. This programme was developed by the monarch in the last three decades of the twelfth century, and these institutions were his indisputable agents. It went further than his father's policy had in Catalonia. A parallel process was developing in southern Castilian lands granted to military orders by the monarchy.[114] The king outlined a specific military mission for the orders, already established in the frontier lands of the Crown of Aragon. He ordered them to attack the Muslims, round them up and establish truces with them, when he set up the orders of the Alhambra and Alcala, or when he gave Villel and Alcañiz to the Order of Calatrava.[115] The characteristic elements of war in this region as defined by the king were the defence and control of the territories and the organization of peace and war, which took place from fortified sites near the border. In so doing he was delocalizing his military responsibility, despite having led the conquest, in accordance with the main formula for conducting military activity in the territories. In other areas, King Alfonso also chose to strengthen his presence at sites through the development of castellanies or the appearance of castle-guards under his authority, as he did in Montblanc and la Riba (1176–1178).[116]

Military control of the Catalan lands remained in the hands of the lords, as can be clearly seen in the enfeoffments that were given in the territory of Tarragona by the three main lords. They specified the military obligations of vassals, who were often required to fortify the place that they had been granted, and they also affirmed fidelities in a time marked by feudal war. This was the reality of war in the territories.[117] The importance and autonomy of the lords explains why the Count of Urgell refused to construct fortifications in an area in 1132, and even promised to remove the one he had built, even though he had been rewarded with a payment.[118] This contrasts with the measures of control and intervention in the fortifications by the count specified in the *Usatges*.

---

112 Forey, *The Templars in the Corona of Aragon*, pp. 7, 37, and 44.
113 Bonet, 'Las dependencias personales y las prestaciones económicas', pp. 460–62.
114 Ruiz Gómez, *Los orígenes de las órdenes militares*, from p. 121.
115 *Alfonso II. Rey de Aragón*, ed. by Sánchez Casabón, pp. 375–76, 599–601.
116 *Alfonso II. Rey de Aragón*, ed. by Sánchez Casabón, pp. 288–90; *Diplomatari de Santa Maria de Poblet*, ed. by Altisent, no. 571, pp. 418–19.
117 Bonet, 'Las dependencias personales y las prestaciones económicas', pp. 444–46.
118 *Diplomatari de Santa Maria de Poblet*, ed. by Altisent, no. 79, p. 81.

Epilogue

Socioeconomic changes demanded and gave rise to new forms of domination. Agricultural, commercial, and urban developments forced conditions of peace, but war was better organized and more effective, therefore contributing to economic growth which in turn strengthened the emerging political powers. The county or royal authority and the main Church authorities defined which violence was legitimate from the eleventh century and during the twelfth century, thus directing the administration of peace and the deployment of large military enterprises. Excommunication and penance legitimized repression and the use of violence. In addition, violence administered in the name of justice and peace remained a tool for new forms of domination. Moreover, restorative violence against a religious-ethnic group, the Muslims, was justified and boosted thanks to new discourses and memories that ended in the conquest of their lands and properties.

Agreements between political dignitaries and military orders or other military leaders created the conditions for Christian progress against the Muslims whereby they conquered and dominated huge frontiers. The count, Ramon Berenguer IV, and his son, King Alfonso, shifted their military responsibilities in the territories to other agents, while feudal war was still the highest expression of the feudal authorities in the Catalan regions. However, the emergence of the county or royal role in peace and war in the twelfth century reached its full expression in the thirteenth century.

Peace among the Christians encouraged agrarian and trade development, and the conquests consolidated this economic growth, bringing about a major qualitative advance. In the end, the protection of the Christians and the violence required towards the 'Others', the Muslims, meant a different valorization and organization of that violence which also gave rise to a qualitative improvement in local economies and a distinctive, new definition of political power.

Works Cited

Manuscripts and Archival Sources

Archivo Histórico Archidiocesano de Tarragona, *Llibre de la corretja*, no. 1
Archivo Histórico Nacional, Military Orders, Saint John's Order, folder 686

Primary Sources

Alfonso II. Rey de Aragón, Conde de Barcelona y Marqués de Provenza: Documentos (1162–1196), ed. by Ana Isabel Sánchez Casabón (Zaragoza: Institución 'Fernando el Católico', 1995)
Blanch, Josep, *Arxiepiscopologi de la Santa Església metropolitana i primada de Tarragona*, 2 vols (Tarragona: Excma. Diputació Provincial de Tarragona, 1985)

Caffarus, *De Captione Almerie et Tortuose*, ed. by Antonio Ubieto Arteta (Valencia: Anúbar, 1973)

Cartulaire général de l'Ordre des Hospitaliers de Saint Jean de Jérusalem (1100–1310), ed. by Joseph Delaville le Roulx, vol. I (Paris: Leroux, 1894)

Colección de documentos inéditos de la Corona de Aragón, ed. by Próspero de Bofarull, vol. IV (Barcelona: Archivo General de la Corona de Aragon, 1849)

Col·lecció diplomàtica de la Casa del Temple de Gardeny (1070–1200), ed. by Ramon Sarobe (Barcelona: Fundació Noguera, 1998)

Les constitucions de pau i treva de Catalunya (segles XI–XIII), ed. by Gener Gonzalvo i Bou (Barcelona: Generalitat de Catalunya, Departament de Justícia, 1994)

Diplomatari de la catedral de Tortosa (1062–1193), ed. by Antoni Virgili (Barcelona: Fundació Noguera, 1997)

Diplomatari de Santa Maria de Poblet: Anys 960–1177, ed. by Agustí Altisent (Poblet: Abadia de Poblet, Departament de Cultura de la Generalitat de Catalunya, 1993)

The Ecclesiastical History of Orderic Vitalis, ed. and trans. by Marjorie Chibnall, vol. VI (Oxford: Oxford University Press, 1978)

Flórez, Enrique, *España Sagrada*, XXV: *Contiene las memorias antiguas eclesiásticas de la Santa Iglesia de Tarragona* (Madrid: Antonio Marin, 1770)

Font Rius, José María, *Cartas de población y franquicia de Cataluña*, I: *Introducción, diplomatario, presentación monográfico-local e índices* (Madrid: Consejo Superior de Investigaciones Científicas, 1969)

Gesta comitum Barchinone et regum Aragonie, ed. by Stefano M. Cingolani (Santa Coloma de Queralt: Obrador Edèndum, 2012)

Liber maiolichinus de gestis Pisanorum illustribus, ed. by Carlo Calisse (Rome: Istituto Storico Italiano, 1904), <https://archive.org/details/libermaiolichinooenrigoog>

Liber Maiolichinus de gestis pissanorum illustribus, on-line edition revised by Elna Pierazzo <https://web.archive.org/web/20090203234051/http://dante.di.unipi.it/ricerca/html/lbm.html> [accessed 11 May 2022]

Els Pergamins de l'Arxiu Comtal de Barcelona, de Ramon Berenguer II a Ramon Berenguer IV, ed. by Ignasi Baiges and others, vols I–IV (Barcelona: Fundació Noguera, 2010)

Risco, Manuel, *España Sagrada*, XLII: *Contiene las antigüedades civiles y eclesiásticas de las ciudades de Dertosa, Egara y Emporias con los documentos concernientes a los asuntos que tratan* (Madrid: imprenta de la viuda de D. Joaquín de Ibarra, 1801)

Tractats i negociacions diplomàtiques de Catalunya i de la Corona catalanoaragonesa a l'edat mitjana, ed. by Maria Teresa Ferrer i Mallol and Manuel Riu i Riu (Barcelona: Institut d'Estudis Catalans, 2009), vol. I

Valls Taberner, Fernando, *Los Usatges de Barcelona: Estudios, comentarios y edición bilingüe del texto* (Barcelona: Promociones publicaciones universitarias, 1984)

Secondary Studies

Aurell, Martin, 'Esclavage et croisade dans la "Vie et miracles" de l'évêque Oleguer (1137) de Barcelona', in *Les sociétés méridionales à l'âge féodal: Espagne, Italie et sud de la France, X^e–XIIIe s. Hommage à Pierre Bonnassie*, ed. by Hélène Débax (Toulouse: CNRS, Université de Toulouse-Le Mirail, 1999), pp. 87–91

Ayala, Carlos de, 'Religiosidad militar y cancillería regia: El discurso sobre la guerra santa en el reinado de Alfonso VII (1135–1157)', in *Cister e as ordens militares na Idade Media: Guerra, Igreja e Vida Religiosa*, ed. by José Alburquerque and Carlos de Ayala (Tomar: Instituto Politécnico de Tomar, 2015), pp. 47–72

Barthélemy, Dominique, *L'an mil et la paix de Dieu: La France chrétienne et féodale 980–1080* (Paris: Librairie Arthème Fayard, 1999)

———, *La chevalerie: De la Germanie antique à la France du XIIᵉ siècle* (Paris: Librairie Arthème Fayard, 2007)

Benito Monclús, Pere, 'L'expansió territorial ultrapirenenca de Barcelona i de la Corona d'Aragó: Guerra, política i diplomàcia (1067–1213)', in *Tractats i negociacions diplomàtiques de Catalunya i de la Corona catalanoaragonesa a l'Edat Mitjana*, vol. I.1, ed. by María Teresa Ferrer i Mallol and Manuel Riu i Riu (Barcelona: Institut d'Estudis Catalans, 2009), pp. 130–50

Bishko, Charles, 'The Spanish and Portuguese Reconquest (1095–1492)', in *A History of the Crusades*, III: *The Fourteenth and Fifteenth Centuries*, ed. by Harry W. Hazard (Madison: University of Wisconsin Press, 1975), pp. 396–456

Bisson, Thomas N., 'The Organized Peace in Southern France and Catalonia ca. 1140–ca. 1233', *American Historical Review*, 82.2 (1977), 290–311

Bonet, Maria, 'Las dependencias personales y las prestaciones económicas en la expansión feudal en la Cataluña Nueva (siglo XII)', *Hispania*, 66 (223) (2006), 425–81

———, 'Historiografía e investigación sobre el Temple en la Corona de Aragón', in *Milites Templi*, ed. by Sonia Merli (Perugia: Volumnia Editrice, 2008), pp. 39–86

———, 'Wars in 12ᵗʰ Century Catalonia: Aristocracy and Politacal Leadership', *Imago Temporis: Medium Aevum*, 9 (2015), 163–89

Bonnassie, Pierre, *Cataluña mil años atrás (siglos X–XI)* (Barcelona: Editorial Península, 1988)

Cantera Montenegro, Margarita, 'Los tratados de paz y la delimitación de las fronteres en la Corona de Castilla, siglos XII–XIII', in *Guerra y paz en la edad media*, ed. by Ana Arranz Guzmán, M. Pilar Rábade, and Óscar Vilarroel (Madrid: Sílex, 2013), pp. 401–21

Chevedden, Paul E., 'Pope Urban II and the Ideology of the Crusades', in *The Crusader World*, ed. by Adrian J. Boas (New York: Routledge, 2016), pp. 7–53

Cingolani, Stefano M., 'Seguir les vestígies dels antecessors: Llinatge. Reialesa i historiografia a Catalunya des de Ramon Berenguer IV a Pere II (1131–1285)', *Anuario de Estudios Medievales*, 36.1 (2006), 201–40

Contamine, Philippe, *La guerra en la Edad Media* (Barcelona: Labor, 1984)

Cowdrey, H. E. J., 'From the Peace of God to the First Crusade', in *La primera cruzada, novecientos años después: El concilio de Clermont y los orígenes del movimiento cruzado*, ed. by Luis García-Guijarro (Castellón: Castelló d'Impesssió, 1997), pp. 51–61

Erdmann, Carl, *The Origin of the Idea of Crusade* (Princeton, NJ: Princeton University Press, 1977)

Estepa, Carlos, 'El reinado de Alfonso VIII: Los horizontes peninsulares', in *Las Navas de Tolosa (1212–2012): Miradas cruzadas*, ed. by Patrice Cressier and Vicente Salvatierra (Jaén: Universidad de Jaén, 2014), pp. 211–20

Ferrer i Mallol, Maria Teresa, 'La organización militar en Cataluña en la Edad Media', *Revista de Historia Militar*, 45 (2001), 119–222

——, 'Les relacions del comtat de Barcelona i de la Corona catalonaragonesa amb els estats italians en els segles XI–XII', in *Tractats i negociacions diplomàtiques de Catalunya i de la Corona catalanoaragonesa a l'Edat Mitjana*, vol. 1.1, ed. by María Teresa Ferrer i Mallol and Manuel Riu i Riu (Barcelona: Institut d'Estudis Catalans, 2009), pp. 151–245

Flori, Jean, *La guerra santa: La formación de la idea de cruzada en el Occidente cristiano* (Madrid: Trotta, 2003)

Font i Rius, Josep Maria, 'Los inicios de la Paz y Tregua en Cataluña', in *Estudios jurídicos en honor del profesor Octavio Pérez-Vitoria* (Barcelona: J. M. Bosch Editor, 1983), I, pp. 235–50

——, 'Orígenes del régimen municipal de Cataluña', in Josep Maria Font i Rius, *Estudis sobre els drets i institucions locals a la Catalunya Medieval* (Barcelona: Publicacions i Edicions de la Universitat de Barcelona, 1985), pp. 281–560

Forey, Alan J., *The Templars in the Corona of Aragon* (Oxford: Oxford University Press, 1973)

Freedman, Paul, 'Military Orders in Osona during the Twelfth and Thirteenth Centuries', *Acta historica et archaeologica mediaevalia*, 3 (1982), 55–69

Graboïs, Aryeh, 'De la treve de Dieu a la paix du roi: Étude sur les transformations du mouvement de la paix au XIIe siècle', in *Mélanges offerts à René Crozet à l'occasion de son soixante-dixième anniversaire par ses amis, ses collègues, ses élèves et les membres du C.E.S.C.M.*, ed. by Pierre Gallois and Jean-Yves Riou (Poitiers: Société d'études médiévales, 1966), pp. 585–96

Kagay, Donald, 'The National Defense Clause and the Emergence of the Catalan State', in Donald Kagay, *Government and Society in the Medieval Crown of Aragon* (Aldershot: Ashgate, 2007), pp. 57–97

Lacey, Helen, 'Protection and Immunity in Later Medieval England', in *Peace and Protection in the Middle Ages*, ed. by T. B. Lambert and David Rollason (Durham: Durham University Press, 2009), pp. 78–96

Ladero, Miguel Ángel, 'Paz en la guerra: Procedimientos medievales', in *Guerra y paz en la edad media*, ed. by Ana Arranz Guzmán, M. Pilar Rábade, and Óscar Vilarroel (Madrid: Sílex, 2013), pp. 15–40

Laliena, Carlos, 'Guerra sagrada y poder real en Aragón y Navarra', in *Guerre, pouvoir et idéologies dans l'Espagne chrétienne aux alentours de l'an mil: Actes du Colloque international organisé par le Centre d'Etudes Supérieures de Civilisation Médiévale, Poitiers-Angoulême (26, 27 et 28 septembre 2002)*, ed. by Thomas Deswarte and Philippe Sénac (Turnhout: Brepols, 2005), pp. 97–112

Lambert, T. B., 'Introduction. Some Approaches to Peace and Protection', in *Peace and Protection in the Middle Ages*, ed. by T. B. Lambert and David Rollason (Durham: Durham University Press, 2009), pp. 1–16

Mansilla, Demetrio, *La documentación pontificia hasta Inocencio III (965–1216)* (Rome: Instituto Español de Estudios Eclesiásticos, 1955)

Mc Crank, Lawrence J., 'Saint and Hero: Oleguer of Barcelona', *Butlletí Arqueològic*, 19–20 (1997–1998), pp. 245–56

Miret i Sans, Joaquim, *Les cases de Templers i Hospitalers en Catalunya* (Barcelona: Imprenta de la Casa Provincial de Caritat, 1910)

Pascua, Esther, *Guerra y pacto en el siglo XII: La consolidación de un sistema de reinos en Europa Occidental* (Madrid: Consejo Superior de Investigaciones Científicas, 1996)

Purkis, William J., *Crusading Spirituality in the Holy Land and Iberia c. 1095–c. 1187* (Woodbridge: Boydell, 2008)

Ruiz Gómez, Francisco, *Los orígenes de las órdenes militares y la repoblación de los territorios de la Mancha (1150–1250)* (Madrid: Consejo Superior de Investigaciones Científicas, 2003)

Sabaté, Flocel, 'Frontera peninsular e identidad (siglos XII–XIII)', in *Las Cinco Villas aragonesas en la Europa de los siglos XII y XIII*, ed. by Esteban Sarasa (Zaragoza: Institución Fernando el Católico, 2007), pp. 47–94

——, 'Idees de pau a l'edat mitjana', in *Idees de pau a l'edat mitjana: Reunió científica. XIII Curs d'Estiu Comtat d'Urgell, celebrat a Balaguer els dies 2, 3 i 4 de juliol de 2008*, ed. by Flocel Sabaté (Lleida: Pagès, 2010), pp. 1–36

Utrilla, Juan, 'Conquista, guerra santa y territorialidad en el reino de Aragón: Hacia la construcción de un nuevo orden feudal 1064–1194', in *Las Cinco Villas aragonesas en la Europa de los siglos XII y XIII*, ed. by Esteban Sarasa (Zaragoza: Institución Fernando el Católico, 2007), pp. 95–127

JESÚS BRUFAL-SUCARRAT

The Andalusian Urban Elites and the Almoravids in the Upper Border of al-Andalus during the Twelfth Century

An Example of Multi-Ethnic Coexistence

In the previous chapter, Maria Bonet Donato pointed out how the rulers of Catalonia in the twelfth century created a cohesive Christian political community by intersecting the ethnic differences between its members. In this chapter, I propose a change of perspective; I will look at a similar process which took place in the community of al-Andalus during the eleventh and twelfth centuries.

Introduction

The aim of this chapter is to show how Andalusians and Almoravids interacted from the last years of the eleventh century until the first half of the twelfth century in the Andalusian district of Lleida. Data extracted from the Latin and Arabic written sources facilitate the study of urban elites made up of Almoravids and Andalusians. These two ethnic groups coexisted in the same political body.

The Andalusian institutional context in the twelfth century was its incorporation into the Almoravid Emirate, which was governed from Marrakech. In the Ebro valley, which was the north-east frontier of al-Andalus, Almoravid society was visible through its spiritual and military elite, the Banū Lamtuna. They were Muslims who came from sub-Saharan African areas and had an ideology based on a radical interpretation of the Quran. Their integration with the Andalusians of the Ebro valley was not intensive. They governed the main medinas, but their low number implied coexisted with the Andalusian local elite, well identified in urban areas like the medinas of Lleida, Tortosa, and Zaragoza.

Jesús Brufal-Sucarrat • (jesus.brufal@uab.cat) is Serra Húnter Fellow and Professor of Medieval Archaeology at the Autonomous University of Barcelona. His research is focused on the early and high medieval history of Catalonia, especially the period of Muslim domination.

Inter-Ethnic Relations and the Functioning of Multi-Ethnic Societies: Cohesion in Multi-Ethnic Societies in Europe from c. 1000 to the Present, II, ed. by Przemysław Wiszewski, EER 18 (Turnhout: Brepols, 2022), pp. 57–72

BREPOLS ❧ PUBLISHERS   10.1484/M.EER-EB.5.132146

This is an open access chapter made available under a cc by-nc 4.0 International License.

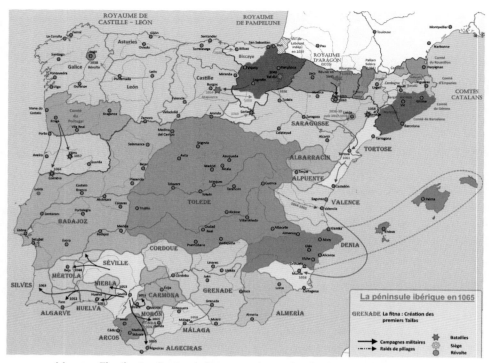

Map 2.1. The Iberian Peninsula between 1037 and 1065. Source: <https://commons.wikimedia.org/wiki/File:P%C3%A9ninsule_ib%C3%A9rique_en_1065.png>.

However, the Almoravids developed strategies of power; the ways in which their power was represented were similar to the methods employed by the Andalusian elite and that had been previously rejected by the Almoravids themselves. At the same time, the Almoravids attacked and marginalized the Andalusian Christians, who were well represented in the rural areas and had coexisted with the Andalusian Muslims in the Ebro valley since the eighth century.

Historical Context: Eleventh–Twelfth Centuries

The study of the Andalusian urban society and its identities in the territorial context of the Ebro valley in the twelfth century requires us to go back to the end of the eleventh century to understand the institutional complexity of the phase of the collapse of the Andalusian taifas (principalities) and the social conflict given the fear of regression of the border and the payment of abusive taxes decreed by the ruling lineages. In this historical context, the accentuation of opposing social movements

Figure 2.1. The Almoravid Empire and its expansion. Image by the author.

and rejection of the idea of taifa should be emphasized;[1] this was mainly driven by the religious sectors of society.[2] The *fuqahā* (Muslim jurists specializing in religious law) are the most visible social group in the course of the eleventh century, who adopted a dual position in the new political context: on the one hand, most of the *fuqahā* opposed the new taifa system,[3] and on the other, minority groups offered collaboration and put their training at the service of new princes of the taifas.[4] The adverse relations of these two groups is exerted on the Andalusian population, through an influence that progressively assumes a shape of ideas contrary to the political status of the taifas. The history of eleventh-century Andalusian society suggests different responses to the changing political circumstances. The situation on the borders of al-Andalus with the Christian kingdoms was increasingly tense. The territorial regression and the fear of the periods of war provoke a steady approach by the majority of society towards the most extreme religious groups.[5] Thus, in the 1080s and 1090s, Andalusian embassies came to Marrakech, where they asked for help from the Almoravid emir Yūsuf.[6]

The distress of the Andalusian border society was exploited by supporters of the Almoravids. Once the latter's positions in the western Maghreb were consolidated, the Almoravids' territorial aspirations towards the Iberian Peninsula took shape, especially after the requests for help led by the *fuqahā* and by al-Mutamīn, the king of the taifa of Seville. The penetration from the south was certainly easy and convenient, although the conquest took time. The difficult situation that al-Andalus was going through favoured the Almoravids, with their orthodox discourse of Islam

---

1   The direct opposition to the taifa kingdoms comes from the hands of literary authors close to the Caliphate of Cordoba. Turki, 'L'enseignement politique et la théorie du califat d'Ibn Hazm'; Antuña, *Abenhayán de Córdoba y su obra histórica*; Antuña, 'Ibn Hayyān de Córdoba y su Historia de la España musulmana'.
2   Clément, *Pouvoir et Légitimité en Espagne Musulmane*, p. 83.
3   Clément, *Pouvoir et Légitimité en Espagne Musulmane*, pp. 105–06.
4   Wasserstein, *The Rise and Fall of the Party-Kings*, p. 149.
5   Dozy, *Scriptorum arabum loci de Abbadidis*, p. 188.
6   Dozy, *Scriptorum arabum loci de Abbadidis*, p. 201; Lagardere, *Les Almorávides jusqu'au règne de Yusuf B. Tasfin*, pp. 102–03.

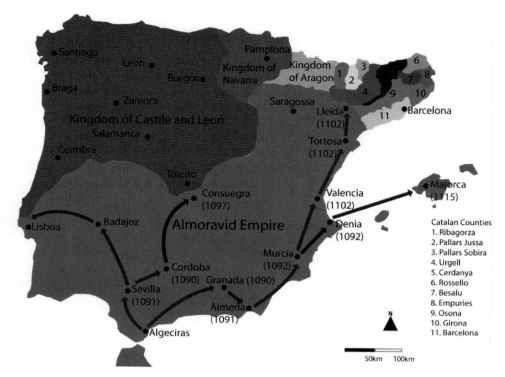

Figure 2.2. The Almoravid Empire in al-Andalus. Image by the author.

and their military force, when they went to settle on the Andalusian peninsular domains. However, there were continuous problems with the consolidation of the area under the Almoravids' authority. The case of Valencia was the most expensive and insistent. In fact, until its conquest in 1102, the districts of the Ebro valley were not incorporated by Abū Muḥammad ʿAbd Allāh ibn Fātima, who seized Alpont, Albarracín, Tortosa, and Lleida (Figure 2.1).

The situation in Zaragoza is certainly special if we compare it with the rest of the Andalusian territories. Once ibn Fātima had consolidated his control over the territory, he started his incursion from the Levante towards the upper border of al-Andalus. The taifa prince of Zaragoza, al-Mustaʿīn, sent an embassy to the city of Marrakech to negotiate directly with the emir Yūsuf ibn Tasfīn. In exchange for paying tribute to the emir and his children and after signing a friendship treaty, the ruler of Zaragoza retained his status as prince of taifa independent from the Almoravid emirate. That is why ibn Fātima failed to complete his endeavours to conquer the main city in the east parts of al-Andalus.

This political context resulted in the search for an alternative capital of the Almoravids' territories to the old one in Zaragoza. For the Almoravids, the real danger was the Kingdom of Castile and its rulers who had conquered Andalusian territory in the centre of the Iberian Peninsula. In addition, it must be considered that the Andalusian districts of Tortosa and Lleida were at that time immersed in a serious economic crisis due to the military defeats of the eleventh century. They effectively lost much of their territories due to the military advance of the Christian rulers of Urgell and Barcelona counties (Figure 2.2).[7]

In this context, the city of Valencia emerges as a true and safe capital. After its rulers' territorial hegemony was consolidated in the eleventh century, the city became the capital of an independent taifa. For the Almoravids, focusing territorial organization efforts around the capital in the *Sharq al-Andalus* (Eastern Iberian Peninsula) was a guarantee of having a strong place positioned far from the dangers of the border. Securing their centre of government here, they were able to face more directly and more effectively aggressive movements on the border with the Kingdom of Castile. Thus, the social perception of the new administrative and territorial organization turned to the south (Valencia) and not towards the north (Zaragoza) as before.

Changes in the positioning of the central places of power in our period of interest resulted in a shift in the role played by other districts within the Almoravids' territory. For the first time, Lleida and Tortosa were considered to be two second-line Andalusian districts, away from the political and institutional turmoil of al-Andalus and pressures by Christian counties immersed in a phase of full territorial expansion. The initial expansion of the Almoravids towards the districts of the Ebro valley was limited to the occupation of the territories that maintained the ancient taifas of Tortosa and Lleida; they could not reconquer their lost territories, which were now in the hands of the counties of Urgell and Barcelona, and the Kingdom of Aragon. In addition, in the year 1105, three years after their arrival in the Lleida district, the Almoravids lost Balaguer, the second city of the region. The absence of effective military interventions and a clear policy of colonizing rural space to recover lost territory was thus demonstrated. On the one hand, these factors suggest the low military strength of the Almoravids in the territory of the Ebro valley. But on the other, their presence here for almost half a century shows that there were other actors who defended and united these northern spaces of Western Islam against the Christian expansion.

The Andalusian City and Urban Society: The Case of Lleida

The urban world of the upper frontier was in the twelfth century one of the keys to understanding the Andalusian social and political context. To know who were the social groups who made decisions within urban society, we will analyse a specific case of the city of Lleida. For this aim it is convenient to start with the Andalusian *ulama* from Lleida in the twelfth century.

The *ulama*, the true guardians of legitimizing discourse, as a group consisted of people from the Lleida territory. They were the elite of the local population who had obtained this position through their knowledge of theology and law; they

---

7 Brufal, *El món rural i urbà en la Lleida islàmica*, pp. 231–33.

highlighted the strength of the Andalusian society in the Islamic world. To be more specific, the social origin of *ulama* was no longer from a low or medium strata of society, as we can see in the eleventh century. On the contrary, since the last decade of the eleventh century and during the course of the twelfth century, the *ulama* came from the urban social elite of the city of Lleida,[8] like Muḥammad ibn Aḥmad ibn Ammar ibn Muḥammad at-Tuǧibī himself, and also Abū ʿAbd Allāh Muḥammad, both descendants of the Arab lineage of the Tujibids. This social change was connected with the arrival of the Almoravids, whose very visible leadership — the tribe of the Banū Lamtuna — was a hermetic group that led the new ruling elite of al-Andalus. The Almoravids' opposition to the social ascent of local inhabitants to a position of *ulama* was a consequence of the social control exercised by the Almoravid military elite.

Apart from the *ulama*, the urban society of Lleida was formed from family groups that possessed a large number of urban and rural properties.[9] In fact, there were many individuals who owned a large part of the peri-urban space of the city of Lleida together with properties situated in the rural territory and integrated into their family assets. These owners and their possessions are known from the Latin documentation of conquest and the survival of the specific anthroponymy in the territory.[10] The sources also corroborate the trend of a polarization of society into rigidly separated social segments, whose elite controls a significant part of territory and probably, as a part of its territory, its natural resources (basically water).

The Latin documents of the first half of the twelfth century already incorporated the names of owners from Lleida and their urban and rural properties that we associate with the urban elite of Lleida. Avinazalon is an Andalusian estate owner from Lleida who held land near the city, specifically in the small territory of Fontanet.[11] Subsequently, various Latin documents record the intramural properties of Lleida, as well as, from the exterior 'omnem hereditatem quam Iachob sarracenus habuit unquam vel tenuit in civitatem Lerida vel in tota Yspania' (all heritage, which belonged ever to Jacob Saracen or which [he] had in the city of Leida or in all Spain),[12] 'omnem hereditatem quam Avialiez sarracenus habuit unquam vel tenuit in civitate Lerida vel in tota Yspania' (all heritage, which belonged ever to Avialiez Saracen or which [he] had in the city of Leida or in all Spain).[13] Both references correspond to documents from 1146, when Lleida had not yet been conquered, a fact that puts us before distributions of patrimonies that belonged to Muslims who still lived in Lleida, as is the case of

---

8 Lleida Ulemas: Abū-l-Walīd Yaḥyā ibn Muḥammad al-Umawīibn Qabrūq (d. 1114), Abū ʿAbd Allāh Muḥammad ibn Aḥmad ibn' Ammar ibn Muḥammad at-Tuǧibī al-Laridī (d. 1125), Abū al-Hassan ʿAli ibn' Abd Allāh ibn Muḥammad al-Tuǧibī al-Waʿīz, Abū Isaac Ibrahīm ibn Muʿad al-Qadī, Abū ʿAbd Allāh Muḥammad ibn Yūs-uf ibn Firrūḥ al-Ǧudamī, Abū-r-Rabī Sulaymān ibn Yūsuf ibn ʿAwwam al-Anṣārī ibn ʿAwwam.

9 Brufal, 'Les almunias du district musulman de Lérida'.

10 Brufal, *El món rural i urbà en la Lleida islàmica*, pp. 243–45.

11 Miret i Sans, *Les cases de Templers i Hospitalers*, p. 76.

12 *Diplomatari de Santa Maria de Poblet*, ed. by Altisent, pp. 103–04 (doc. 106).

13 *Diplomatari de Santa Maria de Poblet*, ed. by Altisent, p. 104 (doc. 107).

THE ANDALUSIAN URBAN ELITES AND THE ALMORAVIDS   63

Avialiez. Flocel Sabaté has clearly pointed out the circumstance that here reflects the conquerors' knowledge of life in Lleida, including the names of their leaders.[14]

The Latin documents include more examples which refer to owners from Lleida. In 1147 Guerau de Jorba and his wife Saurina gave Ferran and his wife Ermessèn 'turrem que fuit de Pichato Mauro, cum omnibus suis terminis et pertinenciis quas unquam habuit vel habere debet, usque in flumen Sigor et quomodo vadunt ipsos terms in circuitu' (the court, which belonged to Pichato the Muslim, with all its borders and extensions, which ever belonged or should belong to [the court], until the River Sigor and in whatever manner go these borders around).[15] This property is located in the vicinity of Alcarràs, near the *acequia* (communal watercourse) that carries the name of the town. This was a rich and fertile territory for the practice of agriculture and livestock.

In August 1148 Ramon Berenguer IV gave Arnau de Montpaó

> infra muros Ilerde ipsum capudmanssum of Azmed Alsaraguzi, cum suis domibus integre et cum omnibus suis tenedonibus ac pertinentiis que sibi pertinent vel pertinere debent in omnibus locis infra Ilerdam et de foris, ut abeas eas per me.
>
>> (a fief/property that belonged to Azmed Alsaraguzi within the walls of Leida with all its houses and with all its privileges and extensions, which belonged or should belong to it everywhere between Leida and the courts, as they were left to me.)[16]

This remarkable donation included the *castrum* of *Avifarau*, currently known as the small territory of Vinfaró, a geographical area that stands out for a high hill on which archaeological remains of the Islamic period are located.

The Latin documentation from 1149 allows us to identify more hereditary possessions of the social elite of Lleida. Firstly, an Almoravid owner who possessed

> illas casas in Lerida of Avincohona Alfachi [...] simul cum omni tenedone, et pertinenciis earum que sibi pertinent vel pertinere debent in omnibus locis tam infra civitatem quam de foris.
>
>> (these houses in Leida which belonged to Avincohona Alfachi [...] with all their privileges and extensions, which belonged or should belong to them in all places within the city and in courts.)[17]

A second example from the same year, which goes in the same direction as the previous one, qualifies the possessions as 'illas casas in Lerida de Aben Hahaul, cum omnibus tenedonibus et pertinenciis suis, quas habet infras Ilerdam et de foris in hareditate propria et francha' (these houses in Leida which belonged to Aben Hahaul with all their privileges and extensions, which [he] had within the city and from courts as

---

14 Sabaté, *Història de Lleida*, p. 278.
15 *Diplomatari de Santa Maria de Poblet*, ed. by Altisent, p. 109 (doc. 115).
16 *Diplomatari de Santa Maria de Poblet*, ed. by Altisent, p. 109 (doc. 115).
17 *Col·lecció diplomàtica*, ed. by Sarobe, p. 113 (doc. 23).

true and hereditary possession).[18] Similarly, urban and rural properties stand out in the following document recording property donations:

> dono tibi Pontio de Sancta Fide in termino of Ilerda ipsam turrem of Avincidel ubi stabat Mocudriina, cum decem pariliatas de alaudio in Segrian, quantum decem parilios de bobus possint laborare de uno anno in alio; et dono tibi ipsos molendinos qui sunt in termino predicte turris. Adiungo etiam huic dono duos mansos intus civitatem Ilerde, unum qui fuit de alchadio Avimaat et alium qui fuit of Avipelag.

> > (I give you, Ponto de Sancta Fide, within the borders of Leida, this court of Avincidel, where stays Mocudriina, with ten plowlands from free land property in Segrian, which ten ploughlands a man can plough with oxen one year to another, and I give you these mills, which are within borders of the court. I add to this gift two hides within the town of Leida, one which belonged to judge Avimaat and one which belonged to Avipelag.)[19]

What conclusions should we draw from these examples from 1149? It is worth mentioning the numerous possessions that belonged to Avincohona, who held the position of *faqīh* and whose properties were both inside and outside the city. Avimaat, who held the position of qadi, also possessed remarkable properties in Lleida itself. Aben Hahaul owned properties inside and outside the city, but without specifying their locations. Avincidel was a landowner too in the meaning we defined above. It is also remarkable that Avipelag was an owner of the village named Vimpèlec (settlement located in the municipality of la Portella), and had an *almúnya* (an orchard) in the vicinity of Alguaire and in the vicinity of Torregrossa, as well as houses within the city of Lleida. Certainly, urban possessions indicate that Andalusian and Almoravid elites resided in the urban world and that since the twelfth century the city was synonymous with power and sovereignty over the territory itself. In this sense, documents have been preserved in which a Muslim was mentioned as an owner of houses within the city of Lleida. The social prestige of residing in the city and the urban business were sufficient to identify such families as the Andalusian elite: 'ego Ermengaudus, comes Urgellensis, facio hunc cartam donationis vobis Ramon de Anglerola de unas casas in Lerita cum sua hereditate qui fuerunt de Aicifona' (I Ermengaudus, *comes* of Urgell, prepare this document of gift for you, Ramon of Anglerola, [a gift of] a home in Leida with its heritage which belonged to Aicifona).[20] The distributions of properties which belonged earlier to Muslims from Lleida continued in 1150, as is clear in the Latin documents. The donations that reached us continue to describe large properties, which combine urban and village farms that had belonged to Muslims residing in Lleida. From this year there are two documents of special interest for our study. The first refers to urban properties of a man from Lleida named Aisam whose houses are located 'devant la porta de la ciutat

---

18 *Col·lecció diplomàtica*, ed. by Sarobe, p. 114 (doc. 24).
19 *Diplomatari de Santa Maria de Poblet*, ed. by Altisent, p. 112 (doc. 119).
20 *Col·lecció diplomàtica*, ed. by Sarobe, p. 114 (doc. 25).

THE ANDALUSIAN URBAN ELITES AND THE ALMORAVIDS   65

de Lleyda envers' (in front of the gate of the city of Leida towards [the gate]).[21] This precise location refers to the Magdalena neighbourhood, an area that developed with fervour from the second half of the tenth century and was consolidated in the eleventh century. Archaeological evidence confirms that it was an economically active neighbourhood due to the presence of merchants, and precisely because of this, in the twelfth century and as the dates progress towards the conquest of the year 1149, it was a prosperous neighbourhood.[22]

The second document from 1150 also provides data on an Andalusian owner, named Avigalifa, who only owned urban properties in Lleida: 'ipsas domes Ilerda que fuerunt de Avigalifa, cum omnibus tenedonibus et pertinenciis suis quas habent in omnibus' (These houses [in] Leida which belonged to Avigalifa, with all their hereditary properties and extensions, which [he] had in all [of them]).[23] A year later, in 1151, another document reveals more owners of houses built in the city of Lleida: 'ipsas casas de Almorre' (these houses of Almorre).[24]

In a donation granted by Ramon Berenguer IV in the year 1152 in the vicinity of Corbins, 'donamus vobis III parellades de alod in una nostra torre que vocant Algebelli […] est namque ipsa torre in terminum de Corbins, in locum que vocant a Vall Porcar' (We give you three ploughlands from free land in [the land estate of] our tower, which is called Algebelli […]. This tower is within the borders of Corbins, in the place called Vall Porcar). In this fragment the name *torre* needs to be highlighted as a word synonymous with a rural *almúnya*, a type of Andalusian settlement which belonged to the urban elite or rural landowners.[25] In the same document, in the boundaries of the property, the term *torre* was repeated, referring to another property related to the Lleida elite:

> Et affrontat de una parte ipso alod quod donamus vobis sive ipsa turre in alod de Arnal Rufaca, de alia in terminum de Lerida, de IIIᵃ in flumen Segre, de IIIIᵃ affrontat in ipsa torre que vocant Gardia qui est contra Corbins.
>
> (And it stands from the one side in free land which we give you and the tower of Arnal Rufaca, from the other side in the borders of Lleida, from the third side in the River Segre, from the fourth side in the tower called Gardia which is opposite Corbins.)[26]

Logically, as these Latin documents were issued years after the date of the conquest of Lleida, it is increasingly difficult to study and follow the configuration of Andalusian properties because of the feudal distributions and subsequent purchases and sales of lands that originally were part of an Andalusian hereditary complex. Despite everything, in a document from 1153 the lands of Fontanet of a Muslim named Portel

---

21 *Col·lecció diplomàtica*, ed. by Sarobe, pp. 116–17 (doc. 25).
22 Loriente and Oliver, *L'antic Portal de Magdalena*.
23 *Col·lecció diplomàtica*, ed. by Sarobe, p. 119 (doc. 29).
24 *Diplomatari de la catedral de Tortosa*, ed. by Virgili, p. 78 (doc. 29).
25 Eritja, *De l'almunia a la turris*; Brufal, *L'espai rural i urbà del districte de Lleida*.
26 *Col·lecció diplomàtica*, ed. by Sarobe, pp. 132–33 (doc. 41).

were noted, which were given to the Templar House of Gardeny. The interesting fact is that the initial property consisted of an urban-rustic estate, offered by Count Ermengol VI d'Urgell,

> ad faciendas omnes voluntates vestras, videlicet duas petias de terra que sunt in Fontaneto inter terras Militie, que dedit mihi comes Urgelli et fuerunt hereditatis sarraceni qui vocatur Portel.

> > (for making all that you want, that is, two parts from the lands which lay in Fontanet within lands of the military order, which the *comes* of Urgell gave to me and which belonged before to the hereditary estate of a Saracen called Portel.)[27]

In a document from 1155, the Temple also received the land of *Fontaneto* near to *Sicoris flumen* and another piece of land with the tower that stood there. This property belonged to the Muslim Avincrep.[28] In the same year we obtain more data from a written text referring to urban properties that consisted of 'ipsas meas mansions in Lerida que fuerunt de illo mauro Avizurata' (these houses of mine in Leida, which belonged to this Muslim Avizurata).[29] In this case the use of the plural in reference to urban houses is remarkable, a fact that clearly reflects the high social status of the owner.

In a document from 1158, ten years after the conquest, Berenguer d'Uliola divides his patrimony and grants a piece of land to the Templars of Gardeny that had belonged to the Muslim Agph: 'donamus [...] peciam terre quam habemus in Fontaneto per donum domini nostri Raimundi, comitis Barchinone, que terra fuit cuiusdam sarraceni nomine Agph' (We give [...] a part of land, which we have in Fontanet as a gift from our lord Raimundus, *comes* of Barcelona. The land belonged previously to one Saracen named Agph).[30] In 1159 the memory of the properties of the Muslims who had inhabited the Andalusian Lleida was still alive, as in the sentence 'unum campum de terra en la roal quod fuit of Zaida, moro' (one field from the land *en la roal* which belonged to Zaido the Muslim).[31]

In this historical context, further from the conquest of Lleida, Andalusian properties were fragmenting into small properties, which is symptomatic of the change in population and of a different vision for the territory. Even later, in 1168, we find a donation of an *almúnya* (court/orchard) in the Llitera and in Alpiconcel: 'dono et concedo [...] ipsa mea almunia que est in Litera [...] ipsa mea almunia que vocatur Alpichonzel' (I give [...] this my court, which is in Lleida [...] this my court which is called Alpiconcel).[32] It is important to note that in 1168 the names given to the places by the Andalusians remained in use although in this case we have no references about the extent of the property, nor about the name of the former owner.

---

27 *Col·lecció diplomàtica*, ed. by Sarobe, p. 141 (doc. 50).
28 *Col·lecció diplomàtica*, ed. by Sarobe, pp. 157–58 (doc. 63).
29 *Diplomatari de la catedral de Tortosa*, ed. by Virgili, pp. 107–08 (doc. 57).
30 *Col·lecció diplomàtica*, ed. by Sarobe, pp. 177–78 (doc. 80).
31 *Col·lecció diplomàtica*, ed. by Sarobe, pp. 186–87 (doc. 89).
32 *Diplomatari de Santa Maria de Poblet*, ed. by Altisent, p. 260 (doc. 338).

The content of the Latin texts before and after the conquest of the city of Lleida and its territory recorded the names of a large group of individuals who had accumulated numerous urban and rural properties as their heritage. These men are identified as the social elite of this territory. They were visible in urban spaces, such as Lleida, but also in the rural landscape through large land properties of the *almúnya* type. Thanks to their ownership of the *almúnyas*, they and their families had practically controlled the rural space since the taifa period.

The Andalusian elite lived side by side with the Almoravids whose numerical superiority was seen in the army and in religious and jurisprudence positions. However, their mutual family relations in the north-eastern territories of al-Andalus were possible, since the names of the *ulama* installed in Lleida came from Andalusian lineages, although their *nisbas* are of Arab origin like the Banū Tujīb. On the other hand, the etymological study of the proper names or the names of the Andalusian families that are listed in the Latin documents and Latinized is more complex. Despite this, the Latin texts recorded a network of a Muslim urban elite, which was acknowledged by the Christians. The possessions of these Muslims in the Lleida territory were widely recognized, and therefore we can identify through the properties' names the Andalusian and Almoravid elites' presence in the urban and rural landscape.

Huahbala, Last Qadi of Lleida and Great Urban and Rural Owner

Of all the characters found in the Latin documents, the most important is Huahbala, the Almoravid qadi of Lleida. We know his name and position from a document issued in 1154 where he was mentioned in donations made by Ponç, the scribe, to Bernat, chaplain: 'supradictus honor de illo Alchadi de Lerida nomine Hualballa' (abovementioned position of al-qadi of Lleida called Huahbala).[33] He was the most senior representative of the city on issues relating to justice and religion who was named just before the city fell into the hands of the Christians.

We know more about this man, once again thanks to the Latin documents. In a charter from 1152, Ramon Berenguer IV gave to the abbot Duran and to the friars of the monastery of Sant Ruf a place that belonged to Huahbala to build a church, home of the future canon friars of Sant Ruf de Lleida:

> illam videlicet cortatam que fuit de illo mauro Huahbala, sicut habetur et continetur ab oriente usque ad terram comitis Palariensis et sicut inde venitur usque ad veterem alveum Sicoris, preter illam insulam quam dedi Bernardo Sabasio, a meridie in ipso torrente qui descendit in Sicorim, ab occidente in terram Berengarii de Turre Rubea.
>
> > (truly this clearing which belonged to the Muslim Huahbala, as it stretches from the east until the land of the *comes* Palariensis and from there it comes

---

33 *Col·lecció diplomàtica*, ed. by Sarobe, pp. 93–94 (doc. 44).

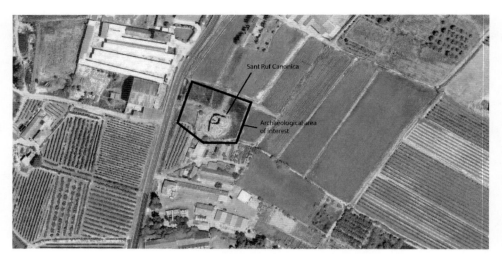

Figure 2.3. NDVI image of Huahbala's *almúnya*. Source: Institut Cartogràfic i Geològic de Catalunya.

until the old riverbed of Segre, save the island I gave to Bernardus Sabasius, then [it neighbours] from the south to the Torrente [River] which flows into the Segre [River], and from the west [it is adjacent to] the land of Berengarius of Turre Rubea.)[34]

According to the delimitations described in the text, the extent of the old property of Huahbala was considerable, amounting to over the 380 hectares (since the Torrent and the Segre Rivers formed its boundaries, and then the Grealó, Marimon, and Granyena lands were mentioned that already had an owner as the result of the earlier distribution of the property of defeated Muslims). The properties do not end with the ones we have mentioned. In another document dated 1149, the donations of some 'casas in Lerida de Vahbola mauro cum omnibus suis tenedonibus et pertinenciis que illi pertinent in omnibus locis infra Ylerdam et extra' (houses in Lleida owned by Vahbola the Muslim with all its privileges and extensions, which belonged to them in all places within and outside of Lleida).[35] According to Pere Balañà and Dolors Bramon, the name Vahbola refers to Huahbala himself. The change in the name's orthography is a result of the Latinization process of Arabic names (Figure 2.3).

Huahbala's property corresponds to a stately *almúnya*. Currently the exact location of the residence is unknown. Despite this, there are two elements that indicate a possible and suitable geographical space to build the structures for the *almúnya*. On the one hand, the NDVI map of soils and vegetation indicates the land that today occupies the building of the canon friars of Sant Ruf as the only one that does not have any traces

---

34 *Col·lecció diplomàtica*, ed. by Sarobe, pp. 132–33 (doc. 41).
35 *Diplomatari de la catedral de Tortosa*, ed. by Virgili, p. 62 (doc. 17).

THE ANDALUSIAN URBAN ELITES AND THE ALMORAVIDS   69

Figure 2.4. Absis of Sant Ruf, and Muslim ashlars on the bottom of the wall. Image by the author.

Figure 2.5. Detail of Muslim ashlars in Sant Ruf Absis. Image by the author.

of vegetation. This idiosyncrasy is related to the existence of material structures in the subsoil, as in the case of archaeological sites. On the other hand, remains of *almúnya* structures might be identified as large Andalusian-manufactured stone rigs that were reused at the base of the apse of the canons of Sant Ruf church. After the Christian conquest, Andalusian stonework using stone ashlar was not widely known to Christian stonecutters. Hence the explanation of the reuse of these stone rigs, which denoted the nobility of a building's owner, to build this Christian sacred space. It seems now that part of the base of the central apse of the Sant Ruf church was built with material from *expolia* from the former residence of the Muslim Huahbala (Figures 2.4 and 2.5).

Without doubt, Huahbala was a very important character in the Islamic Lleida of the twelfth century. He held the position of the most important qadi in the territory. This placed him in a top position in the district. He lived in Lleida, and the documents contain traces of him as the owner of numerous properties, both within and outside the city of Lleida. It is certainly a clear example of a landowner residing in the city. Although we do not know from when he became qadi, we can say that he responds perfectly to the profile of a member of the urban elite, whose land estate was very extensive and signalled their social position.

In addition, as the main qadi, he must have been related to the Almoravid elite and thus connected with their discourse of reform and religious orthodoxy. However, the pattern of building his social status that he follows is typical for an Andalusian great landowner model that was created in the tenth century and consolidated in the eleventh century in the context of the taifa kingdoms. The *fuqahā*, the biggest critics of the fiscal policies of the taifa rulers and, in turn, the main propagators of the Almoravid reform, validated his arrival to recover the purest Islam. But Huahbala did not fit with the reformist spirit, and probably in the Andalusian territory this model is repeated, perhaps especially in the border areas with Christianity, because they are spaces far from the territories under the strongest influence of the Almoravid discourse.

Conclusions

To conclude, I continue to highlight the important role of Andalusian medinas and their elites in defining their own destiny and culture despite pressure from the politically dominant Almoravids. I demonstrated that, using the example of the change of regional capitals from Zaragoza to Valencia, the Zaragoza elite in relations with the Almoravid emir accepted its members' participation in religious reform but maintained Zaragoza's territorial independence. Finally, I have focused on the specific case of Lleida. In this district, the farthest north administrative unit of the Western Muslim world in the twelfth century, the Lleida Andalusian society and the Almoravid elite led the city and its territory together against the challenges of the Christian conquest. The local elites strengthened its ranks and prevented social advancement from lower social strata with the help of the religious figure of the *alfaqui*. Fragments of written sources visualized how the elite were enriched with the many properties its members owned both within the city and outside. Huahbala, the last Almoravid qadi, is a clear example of a high official who arrived in Lleida and had many properties of substantial value. The Almoravid governor of Valencia, Ibn 'Ganiya, owned up to four rural properties in the south of Lleida. Their vestiges have lasted until today in the form of the place name 'Avinganya' or in the heritage as seen in the Trinitarian monastery of Avinganya (Seròs, Lleida). It is evident that the Almoravids followed the same pattern of social representation by owning large land properties as the Andalusian elite did before their arrival. Without a doubt, rural properties, many of them *almúnyas*, were treated as symbols of power in the upper border of al-Andalus regardless of the ethnic origin of the proprietors. The Andalusian urban elite and the Almoravid elites used the same economic and social patterns despite their different ideological and ethnic origins.

In short, both social groups coexisted and cooperated in the management and enjoyment of Andalusian power in the upper border of al-Andalus but by excluding the population from the management of power.

Works Cited

Primary Sources

Col·lecció diplomàtica de la Casa del Temple de Gardeny (1070–1200), ed. by Ramon Sarobe (Barcelona: Fundació Noguera, 1998)

Diplomatari de la catedral de Tortosa (1062–1193), ed. by Antoni Virgili (Barcelona: Fundació Noguera, 1998)

Diplomatari de Santa Maria de Poblet: Anys 960–1177, ed. by Agustí Altisent (Barcelona: Abadia de Poblet, Departament de Cultura de la Generalitat de Catalunya, 1993)

Secondary Studies

Antuña, Melchor, *Abenhayán de Córdoba y su obra histórica: Discurso leido en la solemne distribucion de premios, presida por S. A. R. Infanta Doña Paz de Borbon, que tuvo lugar el dia 14 de Diciembre de 1924 en el Real Colegio de Alfonso XII de El Escorial* (Madrid: Imprenta del Real Monasterio de El Escorial, 1925)

——, 'Ibn Hayyān de Córdoba y su Historia de la España musulmana', *Cuadernos de Historia de España*, 4 (1946), 5–72

Brufal, Jesús, 'Les almunias du district musulman de Lérida (xie–xiie siècles)', in *Terroirs d'Al-Andalus et du Maghreb (viiie–xve siècle): Peuplements, ressources et sainteté*, ed. by Élise Voguet and Sophie Gilotte (Saint-Denis: Éditions Bouchène, 2015), pp. 141–70

——, *L'espai rural i urbà del districte de Lleida (segles xi–xii): Espais de secà meridionals* (Lleida, Universitat de Lleida, 2008), <http://hdl.handle.net/10803/8190>

——, *El món rural i urbà en la Lleida islàmica (segles xi–xii): Lleida i l'est del districte. El pla del Mascançà i Castelldans* (Lleida: Pagès Editors, 2013)

Clément, Françoise, *Pouvoir et Légitimité en Espagne Musulmane à l'époque des Taifas (v^e/xie siècle)* (Paris: L'Harmattan, 1997)

Dozy, Reinhart, *Scriptorum arabum loci de Abbadidis*, vol. ii (Leyden, 1852)

Eritja, Xavier, *De l'almunia a la turris: Organització de l'espai a la regió de Lleida (segles XI–XIII)* (Lleida: Edicions i Publicacions de la Universitat de Lleida, 1998)

Lagardere, Vincent, *Les Almorávides jusqu'au règne de Yusuf B. Tasfin (1039–1106)* (Paris: L'Harmattan, 1989)

Loriente, Ana, and Anna Oliver, *L'antic Portal de Magdalena* (Lleida: Edicions i Publicacions de la Universitat de Lleida, 1993)

Miret i Sans, Joaquim, *Les cases de Templers y Hospitalers en Catalunya* (Barcelona: Imprenta de la Casa Provincial de Caritat, 1910)

Sabaté, Flocel, *Història de Lleida: Alta edat mitjana* (Lleida: Pagès Editors, 2003)

Turki, Abdel Magid, 'L'enseignement politique et la théorie du califat d'Ibn Hazm', in *Théologiens et juristas de l'Espagne musulmane* (Paris: Maisonneuve & Larose, 1982), pp. 69–99

Wasserstein, David, *The Rise and Fall of the Party-Kings: Politics and Society in Islamic Spain, 1002–1086* (Princeton: Princeton University Press, 1985)

MARIA FILOMENA LOPES DE BARROS

Shaping Identities in a Common Cultural Background

Muslims and Jews in the Medieval Portuguese Kingdom

In the previous chapters, the processes that led to the building of cohesive multi-ethnic societies, though dominated by one particular religion, were identified. How was such a community built when the political society included simultaneously in one kingdom significant groups of Christians, Muslims, and Jews? Was it possible to combine two trends: to create a homogeneous political community and to emphasize the distinctiveness of the ethnic and religious groups that made it up? The legal, political, and cultural changes which took place between the thirteenth and fifteenth centuries in Portugal make it possible to present the conditions which made such actions possible.

Introduction

The Christian conquest of the Portuguese territory (completed by the mid-thirteenth century) incorporated Jewish and Muslim ethnic-religious minorities. Legitimized by the Christian powers, the institutions known as *comunas* (communes) provided a legal framework for Jews and Muslims,[1] with their own magistrates (the *rabi* and the *alcaide* respectively) and their confessional law — albeit subject to the general law of the kingdom. The *comunas*, then, constituted a vehicle for the expression of these minorities' identities and, at the political level, for their ability to negotiate. Not all Jews and Muslims, however, were included in the communal apparatus: while every commune was communitarian in its nature, not all communities could be identified with communes. Other groups, either small in numbers or consisting

---

1 The word *comunas* comes from the Latin root. In Castile, Aragon and Navarre, on the other hand, those legitimized communities are called *aljama*, from the Arabic root *al-ğāmaʿa*.

Maria Filomena Lopes de Barros • was a Professor of Medieval History and Islamic Studies at the Universidade de Évora, Terragona. Her main interest was in the history of Muslim communities during medieval and early modern times on the Iberian Peninsula.

Inter-Ethnic Relations and the Functioning of Multi-Ethnic Societies: Cohesion in Multi-Ethnic Societies in Europe from c. 1000 to the Present, II, ed. by Przemysław Wiszewski, EER 18 (Turnhout: Brepols, 2022), pp. 73–96

BREPOLS ❧ PUBLISHERS   10.1484/M.EER-EB.5.132147

This is an open access chapter made available under a cc by-nc 4.0 International License.

of isolated family units, were present in the territory as well. It was a mutable reality, which was very dependent on the chronology considered.

The ethnogeneses of these two minorities are distinct. The Muslims were the remainders of the former majority — the warring enemy of the Christian conquerors — whereas the Jews were already an established minority in al-Andalus who, ever since the first stages of the Christian conquest, were utilized in the tasks of colonization and cultural mediation. In Portugal, we see an asymmetry in the documentation as far as the two formative processes are concerned. The legitimization of Muslim communes can be dated back to 1170, when the first Portuguese king granted a *carta de foral* (settlement charter) to the *mouros forros* (free Moors) of Lisbon, Almada, Palmela, and Alcácer. For the Jews, no known document gives us evidence of any initial pact with Christian powers, in contrast to what we see in the other Iberian kingdoms.[2] For both groups, however, the end of their existential cycle in Portugal came on 5 December 1496, when King Manuel I published his *Edict of Expulsion/ Assimilation* of the two minorities. The alternative — either a forced conversion to Christianity or a departure from the kingdom (with a deadline in October 1497) — configures a new society, apparently homogeneous and supposedly cleansed of all confessional beliefs other than that of the majority.

Different rhythms and requirements in the process of conquest resulted in a clear differentiation between the institutionalized settlements of both minorities: Jewish communes were spread throughout the whole kingdom, while their Muslim counterparts were restricted to a region in the south that was limited by the Tagus River basin (see Map 3.1). From a demographic perspective, in fact, the Jews were substantially more numerous than the Muslims, at least when we consider the late Middle Ages — with a few exceptions in some urban centres in the Algarve, such as Silves and Loulé. The constant expulsions and persecutions inflicted on Jews all over Europe resulted in the migratory movement of these groups into the Iberian Peninsula. In the case of the Portuguese territory, this phenomenon is expressed above all in two key moments, involving the Crowns of Castile and Aragon: the 1391 persecutions and the 1492 expulsion.[3] Thus, Maria José Tavares identified a fivefold increase in the number of Jewish communities, going from around thirty to 150 in the period from the end of the fourteenth century to the expulsion/forced conversion decree of 1496.[4] In contrast, the Muslim communes decreased in number during the same period, albeit at a much slower pace.[5]

The ways in which these minorities organized their internal structures display some disparities, too, which reveal the social and political asymmetries between the two communities.[6] With the Jews, there is a primordial connection to the king,

---

2   For some of these pacts, see Baer, *A History of Jews in Christian Spain*, pp. 80–88.
3   On the mobility of Castilian Jews in the Portuguese kingdom, and its reflection on onomastics, see Tavares, 'Judeus de Castela em Portugal'.
4   Tavares, 'Linhas de Força da História', p. 450.
5   Barros, *Tempos e Espaços de Mouros*, pp. 135–52.
6   For a comparison of the two minorities' administrative and judicial structures, see Tavares, 'Judeus e Mouros no Portugal'.

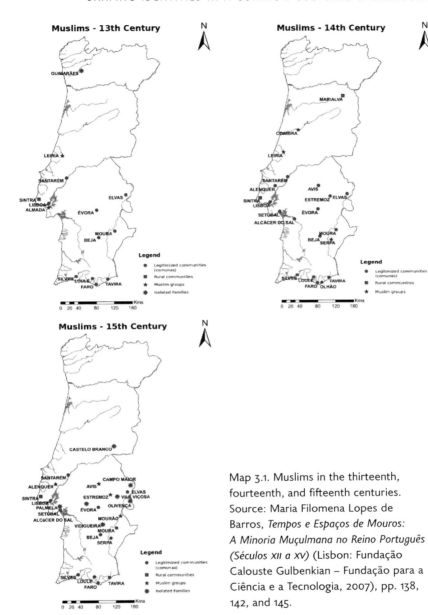

Map 3.1. Muslims in the thirteenth, fourteenth, and fifteenth centuries. Source: Maria Filomena Lopes de Barros, *Tempos e Espaços de Mouros: A Minoria Muçulmana no Reino Português (Séculos XII a XV)* (Lisbon: Fundação Calouste Gulbenkian – Fundação para a Ciência e a Tecnologia, 2007), pp. 138, 142, and 145.

through the figure of the chief rabbi, a Jew in the court who enjoyed the monarch's complete trust, generally his physician, his rent collector, or the administrator of the kingdom's finances, either as 'almoxarife mor do reino' or as the kingdom's chief treasurer (*tesoureiro mor do reino*) — although this post was abolished in 1463.[7] Until that time, however, the Jews in the kingdom were subject to the absolute authority of the chief rabbi wherever judicial appeals were concerned. In contrast, there was no corresponding figure in the Muslim community (although the *chief alcalde* position does emerge in other peninsular kingdoms),[8] so that the mandatory appeals and complaints were referred to the central Christian tribunals, reinforcing the sway of the majority's values and law.[9]

Defining Boundaries, Limiting the 'Other'

The gradual affirmation of a *respublica christiana* under the aegis of the papacy necessarily implied a growing delimitation of the boundaries which separated the various religious groups: Christian-Latin ethnocentrism is defined, also, in opposition to the alterity of Jews and Muslims. One of the themes pervading the whole of canon law reflects, in fact, the existing anxiety over interconfessional contacts, consequently seeking to strictly separate the various communities. Such a delimitation was, nonetheless, defined in terms of an asymmetry which the Church fully assumed, through the ideological construction of a hierarchy of faiths: at the social and symbolic levels, the ethno-religious minorities were subordinated to Christians, just as their public behaviour had to progressively follow a public expression of Christianity.

In this way, through a discourse aimed first at Jews and later extended to Muslims as well, a norm was established according to which the members of either minority would be barred from holding any form of power over Christians and were forbidden to hold public office or to possess Christian slaves. Both rules date back to the councils of the Visigothic period, as far as people of the Jewish faith were concerned.[10] The interdiction is expressed in canon 69 of the Fourth Lateran Council (1215) — justified by the absurdity of allowing someone who 'blasphemes against Christ' to hold any power over Christians ('Quum sit nimis absurdum, ut blasphemus Christi in Christianos vim potestatis exerceat') — while the second is set out in canon 26 of the Third Lateran Council (1179).[11]

The subordination of the 'Other' would necessarily have to be reflected in a public space which was intended to be Christianized, among other things, in terms

---

7 Tavares, 'Linhas de Força da História', p. 449. On this position, see also Tavares, *Os Judeus em Portugal*, I, pp. 115–18; Ferro, *Os Judeus em Portugal*, pp. 52–53.
8 Soyer, *The Persecution of the Jews and Muslims*, p. 40. Cf. for Castile, Echevarría Arsuaga, 'De Cadí a Alcalde mayor'.
9 Barros, 'Les musulmans portugais'.
10 Cf. Ferreira, *Estatuto Jurídico de Judeus*, pp. 90–91.
11 Cf. Ferreira, *Estatuto Jurídico de Judeus*, p. 142; Gregorius IX, *Decretalium compilatio*, bk v, tit. VI, chap. II.

of sensory perceptions and behaviour. The Fourth Lateran Council (in its canon 68) determines that Jews would be forbidden to show themselves 'during Holy Week and on Easter Sunday' (the justification being that, on those days, they show off their best clothes and mock the Christians), and also to dance 'causing outrage to the Redeemer':[12] they must keep the doors and windows of their homes shut on Good Friday.[13] This compulsory behaviour rests on another idea: keeping Jews invisible on a day on which their deicidal nature (from the Catholic doctrinal perspective) stands out starkly. Paradoxically, the same canon from that council advocates for their visibility in the public space (the same also held true for Muslims), calling for visual markers that can immediately identify their 'Otherness'.

It is argued that, 'in certain provinces', Jews and Muslims can be told apart from Christians by their attire, but in other places there is much confusion. For this reason, and 'by mistake', Christians engage in union with Jewish or Muslim women, and men from the minorities do the same with Christian women. In order to avoid these reprehensible unions (*dampnate commixitionis*), it is decided that 'throughout the whole province of the Christians, and all the time', such persons, whether men or women, should be publicly differentiated from Christians by their garments, adding 'for we read that this was ordained to them by Moses'.[14]

In their quest to promote the homogenization of Christian public spaces, canon law also sought to regulate what people could hear as well as see. At the Council of Vienne (1311–1312), canon 25 urges the prohibition of the Muslims' calls to prayer (*adhān*),[15] due to the public nature of those invocations, which of course were made aloud and thus affected Muslims as well as Christians.[16]

Other measures necessarily addressed this definition of boundaries among confessional groups, bearing witness to the Church's anxiety over contacts between Christians and individuals from other faiths. Among the most pressing issues was in fact that of cohabitation: Christians were forbidden to live under the same roof as Jews and Muslims, while Christian women were barred from wet-nursing Jewish children (or Muslim, by analogy), just as Jewish women were barred from caring for Christian children.[17] Following the diverse regulations inserted in the *Decretales* on this subject, it was pointed out that 'a continuous and easy conversation, coupled with frequent familiarity' subjects the simpler souls to the superstition and perfidy

---

12 Ferreira, *Estatuto Jurídico de Judeus*, p. 146.
13 Gregorius IX, *Decretalium compilatio*, bk v, tit. VI, chap. IV.
14 Ferreira, *Estatuto Jurídico de Judeus*, p. 146; Gregorius IX, *Decretalium compilatio*, bk v, tit. VI, chap. XV.
15 Another aspect dealt with is the prohibition of peregrination to the tombs of their saints.
16 'Sacerdotes eorum Zazabala vulgariter nuncupati, in templis seu Mesquitis suis, ad quae iidem Sarraceni conveniunt, ut ibidem adorant perfidum Machometum, diebus singulis, certis horis in loco aliquo eminenti eiusdem Machometi nomem, Christianitas et Sarracenis audientibus, alta voce invocant et extollunt, ac ibidem verba quaedam in illius honorem publice profitentur', Fernandéz y González, *Estado social y político*, doc. LXII, p. 376. The ruling is found in the *Clementinas* (1317), a compilation ordered by Clement V, to collect all the canons resulting from the Council of Vienne: Ferreira, *Estatuto Jurídico de Judeus*, p. 162.
17 Ferreira, *Estatuto Jurídico de Judeus*, p. 142 (Third Lateran Council) and p. 161 (*Decretals*).

of Jews.[18] In other places there was a more negative ideological discourse in the construction of alterity — implicating both minorities, but levelled primarily at the followers of Moses. The Jews had, thus, condemned themselves to perpetual servitude, through their own involvement in Christ's crucifixion; and these people who in that way condemned the Redeemer and who were, 'with such great mercy', received in Christianity, show their lack of gratitude towards Christians. As the common proverb goes, they behave as 'a mouse in the sack, a serpent in the bosom, fire in the chest' (mus in pera, serpens in gremio, et ignis in sinu),[19] and in this way they justified the danger of conviviality and therefore its prohibition.[20]

Space, Time, and Body

The Church's ideological discourse was necessarily reflected in the structuring of a society which was bent on a progressive affirmation of Western Christianity. The appropriation made, by both minorities, of verbal and symbolic systems, as well as attitudes and behaviour, in common with the majority, is met by a discourse which objectifies them, gradually making way for a Christian ethnocentrism. In this sense, the limitations imposed on the living conditions of Muslims and Jews, especially when their interaction with the Christian majority is considered, became progressively established within time and space. In fact, religion — in its dimension of social functionality — implies a definition of *Christianitas* which evolves into a process of *ecclesialization*, that is, a situation where 'all modes of individual religious conduct were conditioned, bounded, and configured by socially institutionalized systems of words, symbols, attitudes, and actions'.[21] Naturally, such a process also implies a movement towards the legitimation of social institutions, through the Church's power to confer ontological status, as a cosmic and sacred mark of reference.

This construction of alterity on the part of the Church (especially evident in the case of the Jews) provided an ideological discourse that fits the demands of popular representatives within the context of economic, social, and political competition with the minorities. The *infidel* emerged as a psychologically efficient concept, and so it was often put to use in the institutional framework of the Portuguese Cortes (parliament).[22] It is those representatives who, during the Elvas Cortes of 1361, asked King Pedro I (1357–1367) for the spatial separation of the Moors and Jews; they argued citing the fact that these live 'mingled among Christians' and do 'things which cause scandal and disgust among Christians'. The monarch ruled that, 'in large towns' and in other places counting more than ten households, separate space should be allotted for the minorities to settle down,[23] in a ruling later turned into a general ordinance

---

18 Gregorius IX, *Decretalium compilatio*, bk v, tit. VI, chap. VIII.
19 On the papacy's use of that proverb, see Rist, *Popes and Jews*, p. 264.
20 Gregorius IX, *Decretalium compilatio*, bk v, tit. VI, chap. XIII.
21 Garcia de Cortázar, 'La "Civitas Dei"', p. 276.
22 For a general view, see Coelho, 'Le discours sur les minorités religieuses'.
23 *Cortes Portuguesas: Reinado de D. Pedro I*, ed. by Marques and Dias, art. 40°, p. 52.

of the kingdom.[24] It is beyond doubt that the Moorish and Jewish quarters existed beforehand, which expressed an urban materialization of confessional identities: we have proof of their previous existence in the kingdom's main urban centres. What constituted a change, pointing irrevocably to the sociological evolution of Western *Christianitas*, is the compulsory nature of this segregation which, by giving rise to the formation of new boroughs, reveals an ever more hierarchical and compartmentalized perception of ethno-religious communities.

Once again, popular representatives were the most fervent supporters of enforcing this rule of spatial segregation and control of physical space — an issue which would be taken up repeatedly in the aftermath of the Cortes held in Elvas. In the Cortes of Coimbra, in 1390, the king was asked to rule that 'Jews should live inside their *judiarias* (Jewish quarters) and the Moors in their outskirts, notwithstanding any privileges they might be entitled to'. The monarch assented to this, adding that, wherever such boroughs did not already exist, they should be 'set apart' by the local judges and aldermen.[25] In the Cortes of Santarém-Leiria, held in 1433, it is proposed that municipalities be authorized to create new *judiarias* and to change the location of the existing ones, so that Jews would not dwell among Christians, nor would their quarters occupy the best areas of cities and towns. Demagogical discourse emphasizes an alleged asymmetry in the use of space, stating that *judiarias* were located 'in the best places [...] while Christians live in the worst, so that the latter were the object of some indignities by these Jews'. Psychological persuasion also made use, of course, of ideological assumptions: for the first time in this context, we see a reference to the sin which, from the perspective of *Christianitas*, the conviviality among members of the two creeds necessarily entailed. In a way, the king's reply got around the municipalities' proposal, by postponing its enforcement and decreeing that, for the time being, the situation should not undergo modification.[26] The insistence on this subject goes even further, as far as the municipal jurisdiction was concerned. In the Santarém Cortes of 1468, a petition was made against the royal permits which allowed Jews to live, either temporarily or permanently, with Christians;[27] another petition was submitted against the purchase of houses outside the Jewish quarters, in the Cortes of Coimbra-Évora, in 1472–1473.[28] In both cases, however, total acquiescence was denied by the king.

Control of space, therefore, became one of the main priorities of municipal representatives, constituting a common goal which generated an ever more demanding discourse. From the imposition of segregated neighbourhoods, it moves on to the requirement that the Moors and Jews will actually live there, in an absolute manner. It even risked meddling in the Crown's rights, by requesting that the Jews be stripped of the privileges which allowed them to surpass these constraints. In fact, the Jews,

---

24 *Ordenações Afonsinas*, ed. by Albuquerque, II, tit. CXII, p. 535.
25 Arquivo Histórico da Câmara Municipal de Lisboa, *Livro Primeiro de Cortes*, fol. 66.
26 Sousa, 'As Cortes de Leiria-Santarém de 1433', p. 122.
27 Sousa, *As Cortes Medievais Portuguesas*, p. 376, item 2.
28 Sousa, *As Cortes Medievais Portuguesas*, p. 423, item 159.

even more than the Muslims, would be the target of the municipalities' intentions, which shows the greater social and economic assets of the Jewish communities (and its greater demographic weight, especially after 1391), which directly projected them as an element set in competition with the Christian majority.

These rulings were progressively expanded. In 1366, King Pedro I forbade Christian women from entering on their own the *mouraria* (Moorish quarter) of Lisbon and defined the paths they must follow to go around it. He sets apart, however, the *judiarias*, where Christian women could go, provided they were accompanied by two Christian men if they were married, or one if they were widows. Any Jew or Moor who received a Christian woman in his home would be punished by death. These laws were justified by the denunciation, made by some *homens-bons* (honourable citizens), that Christian women, 'through the deceit and tricks of the Devil', committed fornication — 'pecado de fornizio' — with men of other faiths. It was specified that such infractions occurred in the boroughs of those minorities ('on the outskirts where the Moors live, and in the *judiarias* where the Jews live').[29]

This formulation, which once again refers back to canon law, contains as a specific element the repudiation of interfaith contact in its most intimate form: that of mixed sexual intercourse which, as S. Barton points out, is the cause of a special collective anxiety that imposes itself gradually during the twelfth and thirteenth centuries throughout Christian Iberia.[30] This is directly mirrored in the laws of the kingdom: the *Ordenações Afonsinas* established the prohibition of carnal intercourse between a Jew or a Moor and a Christian woman, or inversely of a Christian man with a Jewish or Moorish woman, invoking the need to keep the *Law of God*, in a direct reference to canon 68 of the Fourth Lateran Council. The corresponding penalty would be the harshest — death — with exceptions being made in those cases where the woman was forced, or did not know that her partner belonged to one of the minorities, in which cases she would suffer no penalty at all.[31]

Other elements are present in the 1366 diploma mentioned above: the ruling that any member of the minorities caught outside his own quarter after sundown would be flogged, 'with public announcement throughout the city'; the closing-up of the *judiaria*, through the compulsory closure of some of its gates.[32] These measures, which

---

29 *Cortes Portuguesas: Reinado de D. Pedro I*, ed. by Marques and Dias, pp. 534–35.
30 This anxiety over interfaith sexuality, deriving from a complex set of factors, is due in particular to the universalist doctrine of ecclesiastical sovereignty, promoted by the reformist popes after the second half of the eleventh century. However, for Muslims and Jews alike, these restrictions constituted, at the same time, a vital mechanism which allowed them to preserve the very stability of their communities. Barton, *Conquerors, Brides and Concubines*, pp. 72–75. See also, on this subject for the Crown of Aragón, Nirenberg, *Communities of Violence* (ch. 5, 'Sex and Violence between Majority and Minorities', pp. 127–65).
31 *Ordenações Afonsinas*, ed. by Albuquerque, V, tit. XXV, pp. 94–95. As shown by Luís Miguel Duarte, 'Um luxo para um país pobre?', in the Portuguese Kingdom the extreme measure of death seems to have been rarely applied, possibly due to the country's demographic needs. Among the few cases properly recorded, however, two Muslims stand out. One is accused of having had sex with another Muslim man, while the other is accused of having raped a Christian woman.
32 *Cortes Portuguesas: Reinado de D. Pedro I*, ed. by Marques and Dias, pp. 534–35.

only applied to the city of Lisbon, seem to have been progressively extended — or ratified — under King João I (1385–1433) to the whole of the kingdom, through a general ordinance which imposed the closing of the Jewish and Moorish quarters' gates when the bells of the Angelus were rung.[33]

It is this same canon 68 of the Fourth Lateran Council that extended throughout Europe the obligation, imposed on the Jews, to wear distinctive signs and badges. Such an obligation is also applied, in the Iberian Peninsula, to the Muslims, added in this case to the differentiation of garments or, as we see in Castile and Aragon, of beards and hairstyles.[34] As early as March 1218, on the orders of King Henry IV (an eleven-year-old child at the time), the English Jews were coerced into wearing on their chests, over their outer garments, two badges in the shape of white rectangles — the first instance, in Europe, of the adoption of such measures.[35] In the Portuguese kingdom, the process turns out to be longer and more complex, seemingly due to the monarch's extended reluctance against the imposition of badges on his Jewish subjects. Ecclesiastical authorities, again and again, questioned the kings on this issue, accusing them of not following the norm — both King Afonso III (1249–1279) and King Dinis (1279–1325).[36] It is only with Afonso IV (1325–1357) that the mandatory character of this practice is mentioned,[37] that is, more than a century after it was stipulated by the Fourth Lateran Council.

Nevertheless, this measure seems to have been slow to take root, possibly due to resistance from the communities themselves — judging from the discourse of the popular representatives in the Cortes. On the other hand, the privilege of exemption from wearing the badge became a royal prerogative, which the king did not relinquish.[38] The urban elites repeatedly expressed their discontent over this state of affairs, becoming the staunchest supporters of a canon law whose ideology, as stated above, widely coincides with their own interests of competition and hegemony in the face of the two minorities. The popular reasoning is invoked, in 1391, by King João I in order to alter the law 'because he was told by some among his people, in the Cortes', that most of the Jews in their estates wore very small badges, of various shapes, badly sewn or placed so low that they could not be seen, often covered up, so that they could not be told apart from Christians, 'which brought great peril and damage to the people'. Faced with this line of reasoning, the king ordered the placement of red hexagonal badges 'on the chest, above the stomach, as large as the king's round seal', in a visible position over their outer garments. The penalty imposed on anyone who failed to wear the badge or in any way to observe this disposition would be the loss of their clothes, added to imprisonment.[39]

---

33 *Ordenações Afonsinas*, ed. by Albuquerque, II, tit. LXII, p. 356.
34 For Castile, see Ladero Quesada, 'Los Mudejares de Castilla', pp. 62–65; for Aragon, see Ferrer i Mallol, *Els Sarraïns de la Corona Catalano Aragonesa*, pp. 41–60.
35 Tolan, 'The First Imposition of a Badge on European Jews'.
36 Cf. Ferreira, *Estatuto Jurídico de Judeus*, pp. 247–48.
37 Ferro, *Os Judeus em Portugal*, p. 65.
38 Cf. Ferro, *Os Judeus em Portugal*, pp. 65–66; Tavares, *Os Judeus em Portugal*, II, table 9, pp. 780–828.
39 *Ordenações Afonsinas*, ed. by Albuquerque, II, tit. LXXXVI, pp. 499–501.

The issue of differentiation in clothing assumed a distinct configuration when it came to the Muslim minority. For medieval society, the most visible and tangible symbol of interfaith boundaries was projected on the body itself, through the choice of clothing. In this visual and symbolic mode of communication, the presence of codes and the almost immediate correspondence between referent and sign identify and materialize a hierarchization advocated by canon law and enhanced by ordinary law. However, while for the Jewish community we are dealing with the humiliating imposition of exterior signs, in the case of the Muslims the question seems to be rooted in the parameters of identity, which were made evident in the so-called *traje de mouros* (Moorish garments). In that sense, anyway, the various discourses on this issue bring forward several actors: where Jews are concerned, popular representatives, ecclesiastical hierarchies, and the king are involved; Muslims, in turn, establish a direct dialogue with the monarch, acting as the negotiators of their own exteriorization of identity.

Again, it would be during the reign of Afonso IV that this measure seems to take hold, alongside the mandatory badges for Jews.[40] But we will have to wait for the next king, Pedro I, to see the negotiations on these complex problems begin to be recorded in written sources.[41] On 18 February 1359, a letter by the monarch answered the requests of the Muslims of Moura (Alentejo) against those measures which, as they say, date specifically from that reign: the obligation to wear *aljubas* (short vests) with sleeves two palms wide, which stopped them from working. The king ruled that the sleeves could be made narrower, while confirming the obligation to wear *aljubas* or *albornozes* (long mantles), made with fabric which varied according to the owner's social status, and with chest-high badges (*quartos diante nos peitos*). Another concession, though, is made in this norm: they were authorized to take off these mantles when they reached their workplace, in the rural area of the outskirts of Moura, and while they laboured there.[42]

The purpose of these rulings on Moors and Jews was to ensure that these groups were visibly identifiable. Accordingly, the king expressly confirmed that, when moving around to and from the rural lands — when encounters with Christians were most likely — Muslims were obliged to wear their specific attire. As mentioned in this particular ordinance, they would also exhibit identifying signs (the *quartos diante nos peitos*), which would only be mentioned again in a later period. The negotiation on sleeve width is of great significance, even more so as it will appear again in later decrees, showing us a legislation that increasingly enforced a constructed and projected image of alterity. In fact, it constitutes a vector of inhibition in the body's relationship to the world around it. It is enough to condition and impose different gestural expressions

---

40 The mention appears in a poem by the troubadour Afonso Giraldes, in praise of Afonso IV, saying that the king had forced every Jew to wear a badge, and every Muslim an *almexia*, an outer tunic ('e fez a todos os judeus | trazer sinaes divisados | e os mouros almexias | que os pudessem conhecer') — cf. Macedo, 'Os sinais da infâmia', § 29.
41 On this issue, see Macedo, 'Os sinais da infâmia'; Barros, *Tempos e Espaços de Mouros*, pp. 182–94.
42 *Chancelarias Portuguesas: D. Pedro I*, ed. by Marques, doc. 360, p. 143.

SHAPING IDENTITIES IN A COMMON CULTURAL BACKGROUND 83

and postures in everyday activities — even more apparent when side by side with Christians — due, among other things, to the issue of access to objects.

While we have no concrete evidence that the *almexias, albornozes,* or *aljubas* mentioned already corresponded to the group's specific dress styles, we can infer this connotation from the Arabic origin of the terms and by comparison with garments worn in the Islamic period. Anyway, this perception would be taken up by the minority itself in Portugal, in later negotiations with the Crown. Muslims would invoke their own ways and the parallelism with the *Terra de Mouros* (Land of the Moors) against the new rulings which imply the changes in clothing, as well as the conflicts they generate.

In 1436, King Duarte (1433–1438) acted as a mediator between the Muslims of Lisbon and the city's *alcaide-pequeno* (a Christian official), who had forbidden them to wear *albornozes*, against their ways and customs, as they said; they had always worn them, and furthermore those garments were 'worn and customary in the Land of the Moors'. The monarch ruled in their favour because, as he said, those clothes were totally different from the Christians and had always been worn by them.[43] This text, included in the *Ordenações Afonsinas,* served as the foundation for the general law issued by Afonso V (1438–1481), applied to all free Moors — *mouros forros* — in the kingdom, specifying the mandatory garments for the members of this minority: *aljubas* with *aljubetes,* as had always been their use, but with sleeves wide enough 'for them to rotate in each an *alda* for measuring cloth';[44] the *albornozes* should be closed and sewn, with their scapulars; when they wore *balandraus* (long coats) or hoods, they should also wear scapulars on the back, as had always been their use. Any infraction would be punished, as in the case of Jews, by loss of the garments and imprisonment.[45]

This ordinance insisted on, and reiterated, the external character of these capes, implicitly projecting the canonical rules of Islam, by decreeing that clothes should not have a tight fit which would show the body's contour. This is particularly evident in those wide tunics, namely the *aljuba,* the *balandrau,* and the *albornoz.* And while the first of the three coincides with the garment worn by Christians,[46] the tendency towards discrimination and subordination of the Muslim minority would remain: it was reflected in the exaggerated width of the sleeves, a deliberate manipulation of the garments which conferred identity to these Muslims.

The general trend in this period, in fact, points to a progressive hiding of the bodies of Jews and Muslims inside closed garments — as this ordinance mentions, specifically, regarding the *albornozes.* The Moors of Lisbon once more complained to Afonso IV about this fact, in 1454, saying that, contrary to their custom, they were forced to wear their capes all sewn up and closed on the front, which made them too

---

43 *Ordenações Afonsinas,* ed. by Albuquerque, II, tit. CIII, pp. 536–38.
44 One *alda* or *alna* probably amounted to 66 cm: Barroca, 'Medidas-Padrão Medievais Portuguesas', pp. 54–55.
45 *Ordenações Afonsinas,* ed. by Albuquerque, II, tit. CIII, pp. 538–39.
46 Cf. Marques, 'O traje', fig. 31.

heavy to work in. The king conceded that the capes might be open on the front, with their 'hooded hats' (*capelos de capuz*).[47] This state of affairs, however, was revised by his successor, King João II (1481–1495), responding to the intervention of the people's representatives in the Cortes of Évora-Viana de Alvito in 1482. 'The people think', these procurators maintained, that the Moors and Jews, as well as their women, should in the matter of clothes and badges 'go about as they used to of old', allowing them to be recognized by the public. Furthermore, they decry the Jews' external signs of wealth (adding what seems to be the main point in their argument: 'the worst part is that they are royal rent collectors'), invoking 'the damnable dissolution among Jews, Moors, and Christians both in living and in the clothes they wear'. This expression directly translated the 'dampnate commixitionis' from canon 68 of the Fourth Lateran Council, in what seems to constitute a premeditated quote. Whatever it may be, the monarch reiterated, among other dispositions, that the Jews and Muslims close up their outer clothes — in the first case, with the distinctive badge already mentioned, and in the second instance, with a red moon placed on their shoulders if they choose to keep them open.[48] Alterity is finally forced to yield to the control of expression through clothing which, despite protests by the Muslims, would eventually impose itself in the last quarter of the fifteenth century, under pressure from the municipal oligarchies.

Finally, and adding to the gradual process of 'Christianization' of space — in the corporal and physical delimitation of alterity which entailed the progressive closing-up of clothing and of boroughs — the popular representatives would demand, too, the uniformization of time. In the Cortes held in Coimbra in 1390, they referred directly to canon 28 of the Council of Vienne, quoting 'the Holy Church's ordinance' which forbade Muslims to make their calls to prayer (*adhān*). Thus, they requested that it should be forbidden in the kingdom, since the invocation of *Mafamede* (*Mahound*) amounted to *blasphemy* against God — a request to which the king gave his consent.[49] The interdiction against the muezzin's call to prayer completed, at the end of the fourteenth century, a cycle which had begun with the conquest of the territory. In the southern urban centres of the Portuguese kingdom, where Muslim communes were concentrated, time would at last be punctuated by the bells of churches. While this represents an undeniable loss for the identity of those communities, it also implies a homogenization of perception, aligning Muslims with the general parameters of the urban *universitas*. Some municipalities even attempted to go farther, trying to impose on Muslims the observance of Sundays and holy days, but they were prevented from doing this by the king's intervention.[50]

---

47 Lisbon, Arquivo Nacional da Torre do Tombo (hereafter, TT), *Chancery of King Afonso V*, book 10, fol. 119ᵛ.

48 Lisbon, TT, *Núcleo Antigo*, nº 118, fols 172ᵛ–173.

49 Arquivo Histórico da Câmara Municipal de Lisboa, *Livro Primeiro de Cortes*, art. 17, fol. 68ᵛ. On this measure, see Constable, 'Regulating Religious Noise'.

50 Cf. Barros, *Tempos e Espaços de Mouros*, pp. 316–19.

Between Cultures

The ideological and legislative construction of alterity's frontiers, which grew ever more restrictive — in the Portuguese kingdom as in its counterparts in Western Christendom — did not deter, on the one hand, a continuous political negotiation between Christian powers and the Jewish and Muslim communes. On the other hand, there was constant tension between the pragmatism of day-to-day life and the strict legislative discourse, which was frequently sidelined by the specific contexts of life. From the cultural perspective, in the broadest sense, the continual relations between the majority and the minorities can be seen as heterogeneous and hierarchical, but at the same time they were mutual, although unequal.[51] This leads to a cumulative process of identity shaping. Implicitly, the political negotiation among these groups implies a cultural negotiation — working beneath the surface and taking more time — between the dominant Latin-Christian culture and the Arab-Islamic and Hebrew-Jewish minority cultures.

In this asymmetric process, the affirmation of a Christianized domination of space and time, coupled with systems of words, symbols, attitudes, and actions, necessarily implies an acculturation of the minority communities. Linguistic expression, to start with, enforced uniformity in the cultural patterns of the Portuguese kingdom, bringing together both the Christian population, as a whole, and the Jewish and Muslim populations. One specific moment symbolically marked this process: the prohibition of the use of Arabic and Hebrew in notarial documents, decreed sometime before 1415 by King João I.[52] This measure conveyed, more than any idea of an alleged *intolerance*, an attitude of control on the part of the royal administration, imposing on its offenders the highest penalty: death.[53] The monarch was eager to change procedures so as to gain total control over the notarial establishment, turning what had been an elective position into one by royal appointment, accompanied by payment of the corresponding rent. In fact, it was during this reign, in 1402 to be exact, that the rent paid by the notary of Lisbon's Muslim commune became compulsory (the commune had been exempt until that date). There is mention of the need for Christian, Jewish, and Muslim notaries to make that payment.[54]

At a later period, under Afonso V, this legislation was taken up again, with corrections. The king, considering his predecessor's law to be 'too hateful' and out of proportion with the infraction, decreed that the death penalty should only be applied to any notary who used Arabic or Hebrew with an evil intention; if not, he would only lose his office and undergo a public flogging.[55] These changes in the legislation

---

51 On the application of these concepts to a later context, see Barreto, 'A aculturação portuguesa'.
52 This law is from before 1415, the date of the conquest of Ceuta, since João I calls himself only 'King of Portugal and the Algarve'.
53 *Ordenações Afonsinas*, ed. by Albuquerque, II, tit. CXVI, pp. 557–58.
54 Barros, *Tempos e Espaços de Mouros*, p. 361.
55 *Ordenações Afonsinas*, ed. by Albuquerque, II, tit. CXVI, pp. 557–58.

reveal that its spirit had already been taken in,[56] making it unnecessary to resort to the death penalty in such absolute terms. In fact, two documents from the second half of the fifteenth century illustrate this gradual transformation of the communes' internal output. Both were written in Portuguese, and they share the same typology: they are marriage contracts (*tasmiya*, in Arabic, *kettubá*, in Hebrew) from the same space, the city of Lisbon.

The oldest of the two, dated 29 May 1473, implements the nuptial agreement made between Azmede Cabeças and Fotaima, the latter represented by her legal proxy (*wālī*) — her maternal uncle Caçome, from Coina.[57] The *kettubá* — celebrated, according to the document itself, on '15 Tevet 5243' / January 1483[58] — between Josep Crespim and Rica, a widow, lays down not only the agreement made by the consorts but also the act of the wedding itself.[59] Both documents are written in the homes of the grooms' parents (respectively Adela Cabeças, in the Moorish quarter, and Jacob Crespim, in the Old Jewish Quarter), where the ceremonies were held. Both utilized some terms of their own, in Arabic and Hebrew, and mentioned the laws of their respective communities ('the law of the Moors and the law of the Jews'). Finally, both documents were written by the notaries of their respective communes, who stamped them with their seals of validation — in the first case, the Christian Fernão Vasques, in the second case the Jew Yuda Barceloní.

As mentioned by Burns, speaking of a different context in space and time, notarial culture was insidious and pervasive. 'Any window on its activities, its acculturative impact on both societies, and its function as a bridge between them merits attention.'[60] In fact, the concrete example of these two diplomas illustrates this acculturation process. The writing style employed involved a protocol which in formal terms is shared with other notarial documents issued in the kingdom, using similar scripts and abbreviations — which is especially significant in the *kettubá*, since it is the work of a Jewish notary. The normality of the language is disturbed, however, by the words and expressions which provided links to a specific expression of identity. The *tasmiya*, in fact, guarantees the validity of the document, even in the absence of 'some word(s) from the law of the Moors [...] due to the said letter being written in *aljamia*'.[61] In the body of the text, which fully observes the precepts of Islamic law,[62]

---

56 Nevertheless, there are exceptions to this rule, sanctioned by the king's power. Thus, a royal diploma from 1488 mentions a Muslim scribe in Loulé (Algarve) who is in charge of writing marriage contracts in Arabic (*as cartas das arras aravigas*): Lisbon, TT, *Chancery of King João II*, book 15, fol. 86[r-v].

57 Barros, *Tempos e Espaços de Mouros*, pp. 559–64.

58 The Hebrew and Christian dates do not agree. This is, nonetheless, the formula inscribed in the document.

59 Cf. Barros, 'A *kettubá* in Portuguese'.

60 Burns, *Jews in the Notarial Culture*, p. 25.

61 *Aljamia* is the process of transcribing one language using the characters of another (e.g. Hebrew or Arabic written in the Roman alphabet, or Portuguese/Castilian/Catalan written in Arabic or Hebrew characters). In this specific case, however, *aljamiado* refers to Portuguese.

62 The declaration of offer (*īğāb*) on the part of the man (Azmede Cabeças) and the acceptance (*qabūl*) by the woman's representatives (because she was a minor) — her mother, Zoaira, and her *wālī*, Caçome of Coina — in the presence of enough witnesses (Ale Çoleima, *alcaide* of the commune, Mafamede de Avis, Azmede Puxare, Brafeme Robalo, Mafamede Cordeiro, Azmede Pacheco, and others).

SHAPING IDENTITIES IN A COMMON CULTURAL BACKGROUND   87

one word only is given in Arabic: *alfadia* (*al-hadiyyya*), the bridegroom's wedding present. The *kettubá*, in turn, utilizes more words in Hebrew,[63] since its author is himself a Jew. The document's typology — presented only, unlike the preceding one, as a *carta de arras* (marriage contract) — is expressed in two languages: 'carta de arras and wedding, which is called quetuba', at the beginning of the diploma; 'carta de arras and quetuba', at the end.

The internal output of these communities is scarce. The 1496 *Edict of Expulsion/Assimilation* necessarily defines a collective memory whose archive has been stripped of the documentation of the Jewish and Muslim communes — thought to be, if not ideologically disturbing, at least conspicuous and unneeded. Nevertheless, another diploma from the same Jewish commune of Lisbon, dating from October 1485, confirms the internalization of this notarial culture expressed in Portuguese. This is the language utilized to record the transaction of a communal property, under the authority of the respective rabbi and representatives, written and sealed by the notary Abraão Manuel, whose seal bears his name inscribed in Hebrew.[64] The vitality of Jewish notaries, for that matter, is in sharp contrast with the near non-existence of their Muslim counterparts who, throughout the fifteenth century at least, were replaced in their posts by Christians. Muslim scribes, nevertheless, remained in the service of the commune, working as a sort of minor notaries.

The ample evidence which comes to us from Jewish notaries, in contrast to the absence of their Muslim counterparts, bears clear witness to the different cultural allegiances of the members of this minority. As far as the fifteenth century is concerned, identifications, made exclusively in Hebrew[65] or in Portuguese,[66] are joined also by mixed formulas,[67] the ones which in fact better express the borderline existence of these communities. In parallel, the same reality is apparent in a signature by Lisbon's Muslim notary, Yūsuf b. Ibrahīm b. Yūsuf Al-Laḥmī (late fourteenth – early fifteenth centuries), a licentiate in the Moors' law, whose first name is transliterated in Portuguese as *Juffiz*, over which he writes the corresponding Arabic version (Yūsuf), which complements his full identification, in Arabic, with the first name already mentioned, the *nasab* (b. Ibrahīm b. Yūsuf), and the tribal *nīsba* (Al-Laḥmī).

This signature, in fact, is contained in a diploma, written in Portuguese as well, which illustrates the output of the legal experts of Lisbon's Muslim commune throughout

---

63 For the date ('three days into the month of Tebet'), in the word *quidesim* (*quidushin* — matrimony), in the formula read by the groom when accepting the bride as his wife, subsequently translated to Portuguese ('tu serás para mim apartada por mulher com este anell como lei de Moisés e Israel'), and in the word *azemeqte* (*asmakta*) inserted in the guarantee clauses.

64 Oliveira, 'A colecção de pergaminhos', pp. 47–79.

65 David Negro, notary of the Lisbon commune in 1445, inscribes his first name, in Hebrew, inside the sign: Tavares, *Os Judeus em Portugal*, II, p. 710. This is similar to the case of the above-mentioned Abraão Manuel.

66 José Cohen, notary of the same commune in 1466, places at the centre of the sign his name, *Jussepe*, and, on its right-hand side his surname, *Coffem*: Tavares, *Os Judeus em Portugal*, II, p. 712.

67 Salomón Benafaçam, a scribe in the Moura commune, places inside his sign a line with his first name in Hebrew and, underneath, his surname, *Benafaçom*, in Portuguese: Tavares, *Os Judeus em Portugal*, II, p. 720.

the whole medieval period: that of Maliki Islamic law (*fiqh*). In effect, the mode of tax collection applied by the monarch to the kingdom's Muslims is structured, from its formative years, along the lines of Islamic law. The royal charters determined the payment of the *alfitra* (*al-fitra*), the *azaque/azoque* (*al-zakāt*), and the *ğizya*, the latter listed as a capitation but not called by this name. The king would establish the application and updates to this tax with the help of Lisbon's Muslim legal experts. This attitude, assumed since the days of the conquest, directly forces those experts to command the language of the majority and to translate their own linguistic codes.

The expression of this factor of identity, for the minority, as well as of usefulness, for the Crown, is present throughout the whole medieval period. One of the most representative documents, dating from the reign of João I, is concerned with the systematization of taxes and services to which the kingdom's Muslims are liable. Its validation fell to the aforementioned Yūsuf b. Ibrahīm b. Yūsuf Al-Laḥmī who, to that effect, signed the diploma 'by his own hand, writing his name in Portuguese and in Arabic too'. This same monarch, for that matter, charged some Muslims from the commune with drawing up a list of the rules of Islamic inheritance law (*'ilm al-farā'iḍ*), by which the king gains the status of beneficiary, becoming a legitimate heir of past Islamic rulers. This line of action was expanded under King Afonso V who, seeing as doubtful ('imperfect and very obscure') the previous declaration, orders the *alcaide* (magistrate) of the Lisbon commune to gather 'the learned Moors who know their law' from that city in order to correct and amend it. The end result, which is much extended and complete, was published in the so-called *Ordenações Afonsinas* (the general law of the land), with the meaningful title *De como El Rey deve herdar dos mouros forros moradores em seu Reino e senhorio* (How the King should inherit from the free Moors living in his kingdom and estate).[68]

A more specific phenomenon is that of double cultural adscription, which is particularly visible in the Jewish community. Portuguese, just like other national tongues, undergoes a 'hebraification' when it is transliterated into Hebrew script.[69] In fact, among the sixty or so books handwritten in Hebrew and copied in the Portuguese kingdom from the end of the thirteenth century to the end of the fifteenth (at least in libraries located outside Portugal),[70] there is a Jewish-Portuguese corpus comprising seven manuscripts (in addition to one in Castilian-Hebrew),[71] covering technical and

---

68 *Ordenações Afonsinas*, ed. by Albuquerque, II, tit. XXVIII, pp. 222–42. For all these elements, see Barros, *Tempos e Espaços de Mouros*, chap. 3, pp. 421–32.
69 Strolovitch, 'Old Portuguese in Hebrew Script', p. 30. From a linguistic viewpoint, this author argues: 'The adaptation of Hebrew script for writing medieval Portuguese should be viewed, like most orthographies, as a synthesis of influences: neither derivative of the Roman-letter "target" nor dependent upon the conventions of the Hebrew-letter "matrix"' (p. 34).
70 These manuscripts are found in public and university libraries and private collections around the world, with greater incidence on Oxford (11 volumes), Parma (7 volumes), London (6 volumes), New York (6 volumes), Paris (5 volumes), Jerusalem (4 volumes), Zurich (4 volumes), Cambridge (3 volumes), and the Vatican (3 volumes). Only fourteen biblical, Talmudic, and scientific fragments are in Portuguese libraries and archives: Moita, 'O Livro Hebraico Português', I, p. 69. On the last topic, see Moita, 'Manuscritos hebraicos em Portugal'.
71 *O Tesoro de los Proves* (*Thesaurus pauperum*), by Pedro Hispano: Moita, 'O Livro Hebraico Português', II, n° 79, pp. 372–74.

SHAPING IDENTITIES IN A COMMON CULTURAL BACKGROUND   89

scientific topics (astrology/astronomy,[72] medicine,[73] and the technique of paints[74])
and instructions for the *Haggadah*.[75]

Exceptionally — when compared to the other Iberian kingdoms — so far we
have no record of any similar written output by Portuguese Muslims. *Aljamia* only
appears in the sixteenth century, in the specific context of the expansion to Morocco.[76]
Another paradigm, that of Arabic written in Latin script, can, however, be found
sporadically, in media other than parchment or paper. A stone embedded in the castle
of Alandroal (Alentejo), possibly from the late thirteenth century, bears the motto
of the kings of Granada (La GALIB ILLA ALLA), followed by its translation (God
is and God will be, the one he chooses will be the winner) and by the identification
of the man responsible for building the fortress, 'the Moor Calvo'.[77]

Within Cultures

Adherence to a common language, either using the same script — as we can see in
the notarial culture, and probably in everyday life too, of the late Middle Ages — or
resorting to 'hebraification' (in the absence of medieval reports of an 'arabization'),
does not do justice to the cultural identity of these minorities. For their cosmogonic
and religious expression, both Hebrew (and Aramaic) and Arabic, as sacred and
liturgical languages, are inseparable from these groups' unique expression. The same
is true of the feeling of belonging to a supranational community with which contact
is made, necessarily, through a common language.

This is especially evident in the case of Muslims. Their insertion in the *'umma*
implies constant dialogue with spaces and peoples under Islamic power (*dār al-Islām*),
a fact which the Portuguese king sometimes uses to his own advantage. In 1347, in the

---

72 *Livro cunprido en os juizos das estrelas*, by Ali aben Ragel (Torres Vedras, 1411): Moita, 'O Livro
    Hebraico Português', II, nº 9, pp. 51–54; *De Magia*, by Juan Gil de Burgos (Portugal, *c.* 1400–1425):
    Moita, 'O Livro Hebraico Português', II, nº 40, pp. 217–20; one *Miscelânea astrológica* (*Sefer lada'at
    haye ha-molad* — Portugal, 1451–1497), with texts in Hebrew, includes an original text, written in
    Portuguese using Hebrew characters, by Moisés of Leiria, physician and chief Rabbi to king João I:
    Moita, 'O Livro Hebraico Português', II, nº 43, pp. 226–29.

73 *Necessário*, by Samuel Esperel (Portugal, 1450–1497), copied by the doctor José Catalan: Moita,
    'O Livro Hebraico Português', II, nº 10, pp. 55–58; fragments with the translation of *Magna Chirurgia*,
    by Guy de Chauliac (Portugal, 1451–1497): Moita, 'O Livro Hebraico Português', II, nº 41, pp. 221–22.

74 A compilation copied in Loulé, in 1462, includes, among other texts in Hebrew, the *Livro de como
    se fazem as cores das tintas* (Book on How the Colours of Paints Are Made): Moita, 'O Livro
    Hebraico Português', II, nº 11, pp. 59–66. On this work, see Strolovitch, 'O libro de Komo', pp. 213–23
    (*aljamiado*) and pp. 224–36 (English translation).

75 Moita, 'O Livro Hebraico Português', II, nº 42, pp. 223–25. D. Strolovitch refers to the existence of two
    different fragments, which Tiago Moita sees as being parts of the same manuscript; cf. Strolovitch,
    'Old Portuguese in Hebrew Script', pp. 31–32.

76 Cf. Lopes, *Textos em Aljamia Portuguesa*. The term *al-aǧamīa* is of Arab origin and designates what
    is non-Arab, *foreign*. In the Iberian Peninsula, it is applied mostly to the transcription of the national
    language using Arabic script, although the opposite is possible as well.

77 Barroca, *Epigrafia medieval Portuguesa*, II, pp. 1109–13.

context of a war with Castile, Afonso IV sends his chief equerry, the Muslim Master Ali, to the Marinid sultan of Fez, with a proposal for a treaty of alliance — which the latter will turn down, alleging a truce with the Castilian monarch. In 1391, in a similar context of war, King João I sends forth his servant, Mafamede de Avis, to the Kingdom of Granada, to deliver to the sultan two captive Moors native to that land. He does not, however, specify the mission's ultimate goal — possibly an alliance proposal, like before.[78] At a later time, in 1454, a letter written in Arabic from the Muslims of Lisbon to the Mamluk sultan Īnāl (857/1453–865/1461) mentions the dispatch of two emissaries from the same commune, the *faqīh*/s Abū al-'Abbās b. Aḥmad b. Muḥammad al-Ru'aynī and Abū 'Abd Allāh Muḥammad b. Aḥmad al-Wandāǧī, as instructed by King Afonso V.[79] In addition, this proficiency in Arabic was also put to use in the royal service with North Africa: we know of two letters, from 1468 and 1504, sent respectively by King João II and King Manuel (1495–1521) to the inhabitants of Azemmour (Morocco), both of them translated from Portuguese by Muḥammad b. Qāsim al-Ru'aynī, *ḫaṭīb* from the Lisbon commune.[80]

The issue of proficiency in Arabic and Hebrew seems to be restricted to the elites of both communities,[81] although we lack the elements to prove, in a conclusive way, this very likely conjecture. The Arabic language, in fact, characterized the early stages of integration into the Portuguese kingdom of both Muslims and Jews, since the latter too were immersed in the prevailing culture of al-Andalus;[82] Arabic was gradually replaced by the tongue of the majority. In spite of all this, everyday life was liturgically punctuated by both Arabic and Hebrew, as was the knowledge and divulgation of written outputs of religious character, in keeping with the principles of their respective bodies of confessional law.

In the aforementioned set of Hebrew manuscripts copied in Portugal, we find a vast majority of biblical codices (47 per cent of the total), complemented by biblical commentaries (5 per cent of the total) and dictionaries and treatises on grammar (3 per cent of the total), both indispensable to the interpretation of the Holy Book. Prayer books (including the *siddurim*, represented by seven manuscripts, a *maḥzor*, and a *Haggadah de Pesaḥ*) represent the same proportion as science books (medicine and astrology/astronomy), with 15 per cent of the total. A significant share (10 per cent of the total) goes to items of Halachic literature, containing the works on Jewish law that were more widely spread in the peninsular context.[83] This general

---

78 Barros, 'Os Láparos', pp. 325–26.
79 Barros, 'The Muslim Minority', pp. 32–33.
80 Barros, 'The Muslim Minority', pp. 31–32.
81 Hebrew is the language used in a letter sent by Guedaliah Ibn Yahia Negro (1436–1487), physician and astrologer to Afonso V, to Isaac Abravanel (1437–1508), a counsellor to the same king, describing the Battle of Toro, which took place on 11 March 1476: Steinhardt, 'Um documento hebraico'.
82 As, for exemple, the arabized name of a Jew from Coimbra, Habīb Allāh: cf. Gomes, *A comunidade judaica*, doc. 9, pp. 66–67.
83 Moita, 'O Livro Hebraico Português', I, pp. 74–81. The disappearance of a significant portion of these manuscripts accounts for the absence of copies from the Talmud, which must have been abundant, given its centrality to the studies and everyday life of Jews: Moita, 'O Livro Hebraico Português', I, p. 75. See also, on this issue, Tavares, 'Manuscrito hebraico e aramaico em Lisboa' and Tavares,

trend is reinforced with the introduction of printing, in which Hebrew typography played a major role. In fact, from the thirty or so texts printed in Portugal from 1487 to 1500, fifteen volumes were published in Hebrew, meaning almost half of the known output.[84] Like manuscripts before them, the corpus of Portuguese incunabula in Hebrew is essentially made up of religious works, highlighted by a large number of biblical books and their commentaries, followed by Halachic texts and liturgical books[85] — printing crystalizes the sacred discourse.

No equivalent survey work has yet been carried out for the Muslim minority,[86] but it is likely that this community and its linguistic code were not involved in the first period of printing in Portugal. Other evidence, however, points to a diffusion of Islamic law in Arabic,[87] in parallel with Halachic law, even though we lack copies made in the Portuguese territory. In effect, a manuscript of the *Kitāb al-qudā'bi-Qūrṭuba* (*History of the Judges of Cordova*), by Muḥammad Al-Ḥušanī (d. 971), currently in the Bodleian Library of Oxford, contains an indication of ownership which registers three owners: the celebrated Ibn Baṭṭuta, Umār b. Aḥmad b. Yūsuf al-Maqdisī, who identifies himself as coming from Portugal (*bi arḍ Burtuqāl*), and finally his son Ibrāhīm b. 'Umār b. Aḥmad, *al-faqīh*, called Sugraṭ (*šahīr bi Ṣugrat*), who is the owner of the manuscript in the year 875 AH (1470).[88] The circulation and copy of law treatises employed in training the *fuqahā'* (sing. *faqīh*), analysed by K. Miller in the case of Aragon's Muslim communities,[89] must hence have followed a similar course all throughout the Iberian Peninsula. In the Portuguese kingdom, for that matter, the already mentioned production of Islamic inheritance law in Portuguese, during the fifteenth century, wholly mirrors the Maliki norm, which prevailed in the western Mediterranean. Other elements confirm this view, namely the nickname *faqīh*, which appears solely in Arabic (in the manuscript mentioned above, as in the letter sent by Lisbon's Muslims to the Mamluk sultan Īnāl) — a mark of identity, a word that functioned only in the internal context and in their relations with the *'umma*. In the national tongue, the Christian powers translate the term either by 'a licentiate in the

---

'Manuscritos hebraicos na Torre do Tombo'.

84 Moita, 'O Livro Hebraico Português', I, p. 125. Portuguese Hebrew typography was active for nearly a decade at the end of the fifteenth century, from 1487 to 1497, in three distinct workshops in the country's central and southern regions — specifically in the cites of Faro, Lisbon, and Leiria. The active periods of the different workshops rarely overlapped, with the exception of those located in Leiria and Faro, which probably worked in parallel in 1496 and 1497: Moita, 'O Livro Hebraico Português', I, p. 127.

85 Moita, 'O Livro Hebraico Português', I, pp. 133–34.

86 The work by Sidarus, *World Survey of Islamic Manuscripts*, does not include any internal criticism allowing us to identify the places where these manuscripts were copied and considers only the Portuguese context.

87 The circulation of law manuals in the peninsular context is made also by translation into the national language, e.g. in Castilian, or in *aljamiado*; cf., for example, Abboud-Haggar, 'Las *Leyes de Moros*' and Abboud-Haggar, *El Tratado Jurídico*.

88 The manuscript was copied in the year 695 of the Hegira (1296), by 'Abd 'Allāh b. Muḥammad b. Alī Al-Lawātī: Ribera, *História de los Jueces*, p. xliv.

89 Miller, *Guardians of Islam*.

Moors' law' (as can be seen in the survey of Islamic taxation, validated by the notary of Lisbon, Yūsuf b. Ibrāhīm b. Yūsuf Al-Laḥmī) or by 'men of letters who know their law' (a phrase employed in the normative rulings of inheritance law).

In another medium, nevertheless, Arabic and Hebrew fulfil their role as sacred languages, expressing an identity that has not been stained by the society of the majority. Carved in stone, the religious referents of both minorities are recovered — either in the universe of the dead, with the tombstones from their cemeteries, or in the foundational inscriptions of their religious buildings.[90] In the latter instance, they are documented in Hebrew only,[91] in the case, for example, of the epigraphs on the foundation of the New Synagogue of Lisbon and of the Monchique Synagogue in Porto. The first was the work of Rabbi Jehudah, the son of Gedalyah, having been completed in the year 5067 (1307); the second, from the fourteenth century, was founded by Rabbi Jehudah ben Maner, with Joseph ben Arieh acting as the overseer of the respective works.[92] Either way, it is in this liturgical immersion that, through the mother tongues, one recovers, beyond the referents of the time, the Arab-Islamic and Hebrew onomastics — which in archival documentation are normalized, following the parameters set by the majority. The sphere of what is sacred is the only one with no room for contamination.

The various sociolinguistic and identity-linked allegiances of the Muslims and Jews configure a specificity that fully inserts them in a given cultural and territorial context — in the case at hand, whatever it meant to be 'Portuguese' in the Middle Ages. Muslims, for that matter, verbally expressed this double affiliation: by assuming an internal self-definition conveyed by Christian power and law, as *mouros forros* (free Moors), and by living a relationship which bound them to the Islamic *'umma* as *gurabā'* (foreign, sing. *garīb*).[93] The expulsion/religious assimilation of these minorities by King Manuel, the only political measure taken in Iberia involving both communities at once,[94] created a new sociological reality, which was only homogeneous in appearance. This homogeneity is symbolically materialized in the Crown's great undertaking, the Hospital de Todos os Santos (All Saints Hospital), built in Lisbon. Its construction would employ the material memory whose disappearance was desired — the tombstones of the city's Muslim and Jewish cemeteries, donated by the king for the construction of the hospital, with all tombstone inscriptions conveniently hidden.[95] The walls of the hospital, just like society itself, are only apparently uniform. Be it as it may, the forced Christianity of those who remain in the kingdom will give rise to

---

90 For a survey of these inscriptions, see Barroca, *Epigrafia medieval Portuguesa*, III, pp. 53–84 (Arabic epigraphy) and pp. 85–94 (Hebrew epigraphy).

91 Only in the Great Mosque of Lisbon has an ablution basin been found which bears an inscription in Kufic characters: Barroca, *Epigrafia medieval Portuguesa*, III, pp. 69–70.

92 Barroca, *Epigrafia medieval Portuguesa*, III, pp. 87–88 and 89–90.

93 Cf. Barros, 'The Muslim Minority', pp. 27–31.

94 In the remaining Iberian kingdoms, the forced conversion of Jews and Muslims is dealt with separately.

95 Barros, *Tempos e Espaços de Mouros*, p. 607.

new sociological boundaries: those which separate New Christians (*cristãos-novos*), of Jewish or Muslim descent, from Old Christians (*cristãos-velhos*), the majority in the kingdom. The Inquisition and the statutes of cleanliness of blood would guarantee that those boundaries would remain in place.

Works Cited

Manuscripts and Archival Sources

Arquivo Histórico da Câmara Municipal de Lisboa, *Livro Primeiro de Cortes*
Lisbon, Arquivo Nacional da Torre do Tombo, *Chancery of King Afonso V*, book 10
Lisbon, Arquivo Nacional da Torre do Tombo, *Chancery of King João II*, book 15
Lisbon, Arquivo Nacional da Torre do Tombo, *Núcleo Antigo*, n°118

Primary Sources

Chancelarias Portuguesas: D. Pedro I (1357–1367), ed. by A. H. de Oliveira Marques (Lisbon: Instituto Nacional de Investigação Científica, 1984)
Cortes Portuguesas: Reinado de D. Pedro I (1357–1367), ed. by A. H. de Oliveira Marques and Nuno José Pizarro Dias (Lisbon: Instituto Nacional de Investigação Científica, 1986)
Gregorius IX, *Decretalium compilatio*, I IntraText Edition CT: <http://www.intratext.com/ixt/lato833/_INDEX.HTM> [accessed 17 August 2017]
Oliveira, José Augusto da Cunha Freitas de, 'A colecção de pergaminhos do Arquivo Histórico Municipal de Almada', *Anais de Almada*, 7–8 (2006), 47–79
Ordenações Afonsinas, ed. by Martim Albuquerque, 5 vols (Lisbon: Fundação Calouste Gulbenkian, 1984)
Ribera, Julián, *História de los Jueces de Córdoba por AlJoxaní* (Madrid: Imprenta Ibérica – E. Maestre, 1914)
Strolovitch, Devon L., 'O libro de Komo se fazen as Kores das tintas todas (Transliteration)', in *The Materials of the Image*, ed. by Luís Urbano Afonso (Lisbon: Cátedra de Estudos Sefarditas 'Alberto Benveniste', 2010), pp. 213–23 (*aljamiado*) and pp. 224–36 (English translation)

Secondary Studies

Abboud-Haggar, Soha, 'Las *Leyes de Moros* son el libro de *Al-Tafrī*'', *Cuadernos de Historia del Derecho*, 4 (1997), 163–201
——, *El Tratado Jurídico de Al-Tafrī' Ibn Al-Ğallāb: Manuscrito aljamiado de Almonacid de la Sierra*, 2 vols (Zaragoza: Institución 'Fernando El Católico', 1999)
Baer, Yitzhack, *A History of Jews in Christian Spain*, vol. 1 (Illinois: Vader Books, 2001)
Barreto, Luís Filipe, 'A aculturação portuguesa na expansão e o luso-tropicalismo', in *Portugal: Percursos de interculturalidade*, 1: *Raízes e estrutura*, ed. by Mário Ferreira Lages and Artur Teodoro de Matos (Lisbon: Alto Comissariado para a Imigração e Minorias Étnicas (ACIME), 2008), pp. 478–503

Barroca, Mário, 'Medidas-Padrão Medievais Portuguesas', *Revista da Faculdade de Letras: História*, 2nd Ser., 9 (1992), 53–85

Barroca, Mário Jorge, *Epigrafia medieval Portuguesa (862–1422)*, 3 vols (Lisbon: Fundação Calouste Gulbenkian – Fundação para a Ciência e a Tecnologia, 2000)

Barros, Maria Filomena Lopes de, 'A *kettubá* in Portuguese from the Jews of Lisbon (15th century)', *Hamsa: Journal of Judaic and Islamic Studies*, 4 (2018), 33–45, <https://doi.org/10.4000/hamsa.514>

——, 'Os Láparos: Uma família muçulmana da elite comunal olisiponense', in *Lisboa Medieval: Os rostos da Cidade*, ed. by Luís Krus, Luís Filipe Oliveira, and João Luís Fontes (Lisbon: Livros Horizonte, 2007), pp. 322–44

——, 'The Muslim Minority in the Portuguese Kingdom (1170–1496): Identity and Writing', *eJournal of Portuguese History (e-JPH)*, 13.2 (2015), 18–33, <https://www.brown.edu/Departments/Portuguese_Brazilian_Studies/ejph/html/issue26/pdf/v13n2a02.pdf>

——, 'Les musulmans portugais: La justice entre la normativité chrétienne et la normativité islamique', in *Religious Cohabitation in European Towns (10th–15th Centuries) / La cohabitation religieuse dans les villes Européennes, x[e]–xve siècles*, ed. by J. V. Tolan and S. Boissellier (Turnhout: Brepols, 2014), pp. 207–22

——, *Tempos e Espaços de Mouros: A Minoria Muçulmana no Reino Português (Séculos XII a XV)* (Lisbon: Fundação Calouste Gulbenkian – Fundação para a Ciência e a Tecnologia, 2007)

Barton, Simon, *Conquerors, Brides and Concubines: Interfaith Relations and Social Power in Medieval Iberia* (Philadelphia: University of Pennsylvania Press, 2015)

Burns, Robert I., *Jews in the Notarial Culture: Latinate Wills in Mediterranean Spain, 1250–1350* (Berkeley: University of California Press, 1996)

Coelho, Maria Helena da Cruz, 'Le discours sur les minorités religieuses aux Cortes portugaises du Moyen Âge', *Parliaments, Estates and Representations*, 31 (2011), 1–16

Constable, Olivia R., 'Regulating Religious Noise: The Council of Vienne, the Mosque Call and Muslim Pilgrimage in the Late Medieval Mediterranean World', *Medieval Encounters*, 16 (2010), 64–95

Duarte, Luís Miguel, 'Um luxo para um país pobre? A pena de morte no Portugal Medievo', *Clio & Crimen*, 4 (2007), 63–94, <https://repositorio-aberto.up.pt/handle/10216/56088>

Echevarría Arsuaga, Ana, 'De Cadí a Alcalde mayor: La élite judicial mudéjar en el siglo XV (II)', *Al-Qanṭara*, 24.2 (2003), 273–90

Fernandéz y González, Francisco, *Estado social y político de los mudejares de Castilla, considerados en si mismos y respecto de la civilización española* (Madrid: Hipérion, 1985; 1st edn: Madrid, 1865)

Ferreira, Joaquim de Assunção, *Estatuto Jurídico de Judeus e Mouros na Idade Média Portuguesa* (Lisbon: Universidade Católica Editora, 2006)

Ferrer i Mallol, Maria Teresa, *Els Sarraïns de la Corona Catalano Aragonesa en el Segle XIV: Segregació i Discriminació* (Barcelona: CSIC, 1987)

Ferro, Maria José, *Os Judeus em Portugal no Século XIV* (Lisbon: Guimarães & Cª Editores, 1979)

Garcia de Cortázar, José Angél, 'La "Civitas Dei": La ciudad como centro de vida religiosa en el siglo XIII', in *El Mundo Urbano en la Castilla del Siglo XIII*, vol. I, ed. by M. González Jiménez (Sevilla: Ayuntamiento de Ciudad Real – Fundación El Monte, 2006), pp. 275–301

Gomes, Saul António, *A comunidade judaica de Coimbra medieval* (Coimbra: Inatel, 2003)

Ladero Quesada, Miguel Angel, 'Los Mudejares de Castilla en la Baja Edad Media', in *Los Mudejares de Castilla y otros Estudios de Historia Medieval Andaluza* (Granada: Universidad de Granada, 1989), pp. 11–132

Lopes, David, *Textos em Aljamia Portuguesa: Estudo filológico e Histórico*, new edn (Lisbon: Imprensa Nacional, 1940)

Macedo, José Rivair de, 'Os sinais da infâmia e o vestuário dos mouros em Portugal nos séculos XIV e XV', *Bulletin du centre d'études médiévales d'Auxerre | BUCEMA*, Hors-série, n° 2/2008: *Le Moyen Âge vu d'ailleurs*, <https://journals.openedition.org/cem/9852>

Marques, A. H. de Oliveira, 'O traje', in *A Sociedade Medieval Portuguesa*, 3rd edn (Lisbon: Livraria Sá da Costa, 1974), pp. 23–62

Miller, Kathryn A., *Guardians of Islam: Religious Authority and Muslim Communities of Late Medieval Spain* (New York: Columbia University Press, 2008)

Moita, Tiago, 'O Livro Hebraico Português na Idade Média: Do Sefer He- Aruk de Seia (1284–1285) aos manuscritos tardo-medievais da 'Escola de Lisboa' e aos primeiros incunábulos', 2 vols (unpublished doctoral Thesis, University of Lisbon, 2017)

——, 'Manuscritos hebraicos em Portugal', *Medievalista online*, 11 (July-December 2017), <https://doi.org/10.4000/medievalista.1350>

Nirenberg, David, *Communities of Violence: Persecution of the Minorities in the Middle Ages* (Princeton, NJ: Princeton University Press, 1998)

Rist, Rebecca, *Popes and Jews (1095–1291)* (Oxford: Oxford University Press, 2016)

Sidarus, Adel Yousef, *World Survey of Islamic Manuscripts*, II: *Portugal* (London: Al-Furqān – Islamic Heritage Foundation, 1993)

Sousa, Armindo de, 'As Cortes de Leiria-Santarém de 1433', *Estudos Medievais*, 2 (1982), 71–224

——, *As Cortes Medievais Portuguesas (1385–1490)*, vol. II (Lisbon: Instituto Nacional de Investigação Científica – Centro de História da Universidade de Lisboa, 1990)

Soyer, François, *The Persecution of the Jews and Muslims of Portugal* (Leiden: Brill, 2007)

Steinhardt, Inácio, 'Um documento hebraico sobre a Batalha de Toro', *Cadernos de Estudos Sefarditas*, 5 (2005), 115–34

Strolovitch, Devon L., 'Old Portuguese in Hebrew Script: Beyond "O livro de como se fazem as cores"', in *The Materials of the Image*, ed. by Luís Urbano Afonso (Lisbon: Cátedra de Estudos Sefarditas 'Alberto Benveniste', 2010), pp. 30–43

Tavares, Augusto, 'Manuscrito hebraico e aramaico em Lisboa', *Didaskalia*, 8 (1978), 187–94

——, 'Manuscritos hebraicos na Torre do Tombo', *Didaskalia*, 11 (1981), 379–92

Tavares, Maria José Ferro, 'Judeus de Castela em Portugal no final da Idade Média: Onomástica familiar e mobilidade', *Sefarad*, 74.1 (2014), 89–144

——, 'Judeus e Mouros no Portugal dos Séculos XIV e XV (Tentativa de estudo comparativo)', *Revista de História Económica e Social*, 9 (1982), 75–89

———, *Os Judeus em Portugal no Século xv*, vol. I (Lisbon: Universidade Nova de Lisboa, 1982)

———, *Os Judeus em Portugal no Século xv*, vol. II (Lisbon: Instituto Nacional de Investigação Científica, 1984)

———, 'Linhas de Força da História dos Judeus em Portugal das origens à atualidade', *Espacio, Tiempo y Forma*, 3rd Ser., 6 (1993), 447–74

Tolan, John, 'The First Imposition of a Badge on European Jews: The English Royal Mandate of 1218', in *The Character of Christian–Muslim Encounter*, ed. by Douglas Pratt, Jon Hoover, John Davies, and John A. Chesworth (Leiden: Brill, 2015), pp. 145–66

PAULA PINTO COSTA AND JOANA LENCART

Ethnic and Religious Minorities and the Portuguese Military Orders as Recorded in the *Pontificia Corpora* (Twelfth to Sixteenth Centuries)

In the previous chapter, Filomena Barros proved that in high and late medieval Portugal the activities of external institutions modified long-established processes for building a cohesive multi-ethnic society. Here, we intend to look at the problem from a slightly different angle, that is, reconciling the interests of Portuguese actors of social life, their local traditions, and legal norms with the influence of the external institutions on the shape of a multi-ethnic society. For this purpose, we identify references about ethnicity and religious minorities in papal charters issued for Portuguese military orders during the high and late Middle Ages. This presents the evidence for the influence of the military orders on the relationship between the Portuguese Crown and the papacy. In their charters, the popes focused only on one minority: Muslims. The presence of the Jews and their role in the Portuguese history were omitted. The main subjects of these documents were political issues and territorial administration. The current political affairs were the core framework that shaped the Holy See's policy towards the ethnic minorities in Portugal and defined the specificity of the narrative which shaped Portuguese society through the activities of the chivalric orders. Antagonistic relations between Christians and Muslims were to play a dominant role, despite obvious instances of long-term cooperation.

Paula Pinto Costa • (ppinto@letras.up.pt) is Associate Professor of Medieval History in the Faculty of Arts and Humanities of the University of Porto (FLUP) and a Researcher at CITCEM (Transdisciplinary Culture, Space, and Memory Research Centre). Her main research areas are medieval history and the military orders, especially the Hospitallers and Templars.

Joana Lencart • (jlencart@letras.up.pt) is a PhD from the University of Porto and researcher at CITCEM (Transdisciplinary Culture, Space, and Memory Research Centre). Her main research areas are medieval history and the military orders, especially the Templars and the Order of Christ.

Inter-Ethnic Relations and the Functioning of Multi-Ethnic Societies: Cohesion in Multi-Ethnic Societies in Europe from c. 1000 to the Present, II, ed. by Przemysław Wiszewski, EER 18 (Turnhout: Brepols, 2022), pp. 97–114

BREPOLS ❧ PUBLISHERS   10.1484/M.EER-EB.5.132148

This is an open access chapter made available under a cc by-nc 4.0 International License.

Map 4.1. The Iberian Five Kingdoms (14th century). Source: Julio López-Davalillo Larrea, *Atlas Historico de España y Portugal desde el Paleolítico hasta el siglo XX* (Madrid: Ed. Sintesis, 1999), p. 117.

Introduction

The aim of this chapter is to study how the military orders influenced relations between the papacy and the Portuguese Crown on the issue of ethnic minorities.[1] It is possible that this topic may be confused with the study of papal bulls concerning the crusades; these have already been discussed by historians.[2] Our approach is to examine the documentary sources, more precisely the *pontificia corpora*. However, we have to acknowledge that these sources provide only a partial view of the relationship between the papacy and the Portuguese Crown. A similar approach was undertaken in a book published in 2015 which focused on this topic — ethnic minorities — through studying the chancery, chronicle, literary, and doctrinal sources.[3] Nevertheless, this study is innovative, given the gaps in the research about the military orders and

---

1 For an overview on this theme, see Barros, 'Ethno-Religious Minorities'.
2 Dinis, 'Antecedentes da expansão ultramarina portuguesa' and Fonseca, Pimenta, and Costa, 'The Papacy and the Crusades in xv[th] Century Portugal'.
3 Ayala Martínez and Fernandes, eds, *Cristãos contra muçulmanos*.

ethnic minorities. The area and period of study is the Portuguese kingdom between the twelfth and the sixteenth centuries. The chronological delimitations of the study reflect the formation of the kingdom in the first half of the twelfth century in the context of the Iberian reconquest, and the Turkish threat in the late Middle Ages, particularly in the sixteenth century, combined with the role played by the knights of the Order of St John in the Mediterranean wars.

This chapter aims to assess how committed the military orders were to this agenda and to identify how the Holy See took account of the ethnic minorities in these political scenarios. Given that the military orders had been settled in Portugal since the twelfth century, it is difficult to explain why there are so many papal documents which lack any reference to the friars, even when the topic was the Crusades. This silence raises some questions about the aims of the military orders. So, we can ask some key questions. Did the papacy believe that the Portuguese monarchy would have other resources to fight the Muslims without the direct commitment of the military orders? Was there anyone who was able to match the skills of these institutions and the goals achieved by the friars, who also benefited from the same kind of protection granted by the papal documents sent to Portugal (the crusaders themselves, such as those who fought in Lisbon in 1147, Silves in 1189, and Alcácer do Sal in 1217)? Or, did the popes consider the Portuguese kings their main point of contact and expected them to motivate the friars to fight in the war? Both the second and third hypotheses seem to be key points for the discussion.

Sources and Literature

There were three criteria on which we based our selection of the documents: documents produced by the Holy See, which mentioned both the military orders and the ethnic minorities. Some of them were not specifically addressed to the Portuguese military orders, although they also had an impact in Portugal. This means, for example, that we have to take into account those papal diplomas which were addressed to the Order of Calatrava (this means Avis, its Portuguese branch). The leading collection of manuscripts is deposited in the Portuguese National Archive (Torre do Tombo, Lisbon).[4] The main collections that gather together printed *pontificia* documents are the *Bullarium Ordinis Militiae de Calatrava, Bulário Português, Corpo Diplomatico Portuguez, Monumenta Henricina*, and *Descobrimentos Portugueses*.[5]

As we know, there is a large collection of papal diplomas relating to Portugal which were edited as part of the commemoration in the twentieth century of the Portuguese discoveries; this is because the overseas expansion received backing from several papal bulls. Almost all of them concerned the Crusades and the participation of the kingdom in those expeditions, considering it as part of the territorial reconquest achieved from the twelfth to mid-thirteenth centuries.

---

4 Lisbon, Arquivo Nacional da Torre do Tombo (hereafter, TT), *Coleção Especial, Bulas.*
5 See all citations in the Works Cited.

Although the military orders had an important role in the reconquest, given their typical profile and aims, many papal documents exhorted the Crusades without making any reference to these orders.

Until now, there have not been many historiographical studies on relations between the military orders and ethnic minorities, although the Muslims and Jews had a special role in Iberian medieval history, where the military orders were strongly established. Indeed, it is only in the last two decades that some important research on these topics has been undertaken, and it is noteworthy that these were the works published by Filomena Barros and Clara Almagro Vidal. The first author was an expert on minority communities in Portugal, and we want to draw attention to the first paper she wrote on the Order of Avis and the Muslims.[6] The case of rural Aragon was also studied with a similar scope at the end of the twentieth century.[7] Less than a decade later, in the beginning of the twenty-first century, a paper about the information that circled from Rhodes to Iberia, relating the Turks,[8] should be highlighted, along with a second one that summarized some papal documents, with respect to the normative rules of the Orders, which points out only a few elements about the minorities.[9] The more recent approaches demonstrate a deep interest in these issues. The essays from Clara Almagro Vidal, regarding religious minorities and the military orders in Castile, enhance the state of knowledge.[10] Also, for the Iberian Peninsula, we can point to two other papers about the interaction between the military orders and ethnic minorities. One, by Philippe Josserand, emphasized the so-called peaceful contacts between Christians and Muslims,[11] and the second one, by Juan Rebollo Bote, underlines the role of Islamic continuity in the territory of Extremadura administrated by the military orders.[12] On the other hand, we can also mention a paper based on the Arabic sources,[13] and finally all the research results achieved within the project 'Cohesion Building of Multi-Ethnic Societies, 10th–21st Century'.[14]

Although without focusing on the ethnic minorities, Dias Dinis in 1962 considered three clearly different groups, in terms of both the subject and chronology, of papal documents which concerned the Portuguese monarchy, in the period between 1179 and 1411. The first group of papal documents were letters that praised and supported the Portuguese reconquest of lands seized from Muslim control (1179–1234); the

---

6 Barros, 'A Ordem de Avis e a minoria muçulmana'.
7 Gerrard, 'Opposing Identity'.
8 Lázaro, '"Novas do Turco sam viindas per via de Rodes"'.
9 Ferreira, 'A documentação pontifícia'.
10 Almagro Vidal, 'La Orden de Calatrava y la minoría mudéjar'; Almagro Vidal, 'Religious Minorities' Identity'; Almagro Vidal, 'Moros al servicio de la órdenes militares'.
11 Josserand, 'En péninsule Ibérique et par-delà'.
12 Rebollo Bote, 'De andalusíes a mudéjares'.
13 Lewis, 'Friend or Foe'.
14 Barros, 'Assy como he devudo aos Reyx Mouros em seus Regnos e Senhorios'; Costa, 'Between Portugal and Latin East'; Costa and Pimenta, 'Multiethnic Portuguese Society'.

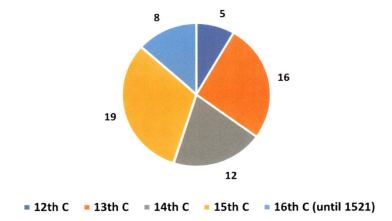

Chart 4.1. The chronological distribution of the *pontificia corpora* through the centuries.

second comprised the letters about the Crusades which gave spiritual support to the Portuguese who fought in the Holy Land, as well as to those who subsidized these actions, granting the subsequent indulgences (1234–1341); and the third encompassed the letters for the Crusades against the Moors of Granada and Morocco for fighters involved in both offensive and defensive war by granting some ecclesiastical income to the realm (1341–1411). Accepting the applicability of this previous approach, we extended the chronological framework until the end of the reign of Manuel I in 1521. Extending the analysis to the sixteenth century enables us to take into consideration the Turkish threat, which was an important issue for both the papacy and the Western monarchies. Manuel I (1495–1521) had expressed the desire to be the King of Jerusalem, in the first decade of the sixteenth century, which was evidence of Portuguese involvement in this symbolic Mediterranean context.[15]

The chronological distribution of the documents shows a particular concentration in the fifteenth century, a phenomenon which is confirmed by the figures for the first two decades of the sixteenth century. This spread of documents throughout the Middle Ages shows that it would not be desirable to narrow the study of minorities to the period of the reconquest. After the mid-thirteenth century, when the territorial reconquest of Portugal came to an end, many aspects of life continued just as they had before. The Arabic communities remained established in the realm, and they were accepted by the monarchy. Compelling reasons, like their well-established settlement and their involvement in economic activity, could explain the permanence of these ethnic groups in late medieval Portugal.

---

15 Costa, *D. Manuel I*, pp. 175–79.

The Focal Points of Charters' Narrative

The analysis of the *pontificia corpora* is complex, as scholars have acknowledged; we can assess it according to the themes the documents cover. Analysing the sixty selected papal bulls, we find out that half of them concern the funding of war using income from tithes (17 bulls) and heritage issues (12). Usually the military orders were exempt from tithes, because they constantly exposed their people and lands to the so-called enemies of the Christian faith, as clearly argued in a document from 1341.[16] On the other hand, when we used 'heritage' as a label to classify the documents, we can highlight the papal protection granted to the churches built in the conquered places; this occurred several times between the twelfth and the fifteenth centuries.[17]

A second group, which includes almost all of the second half of the sixty selected documents, covers a wider range of matters. Among them, the most important one concerns the friars' obligations to fight in the war (6). Indeed, this question arose within the context of the advance of the Ottomans into Europe during the fifteenth and sixteenth centuries. Probably, the greater distance from this enemy, the decrease of the income from the fourteenth century from the land they rented out, and the failed attempts to dominate the eastern Mediterranean, which had been getting worse since the second half of the thirteenth century, explain why the Western kingdoms were reluctant to get involved in this war. Bearing in mind this context, in February 1456, the pope asked D. Álvaro, bishop of Silves and apostolic nuncio in Portugal, to compel the four military orders to fight the Turks in the Mediterranean.[18] The same point was revisited a couple of months later, when Prince Henry, the governor of the Order of Christ, was encouraged to do the same.[19] The Order of St John had a particular perspective, because its main conventual headquarters were located on the island of Rhodes. These circumstances demanded great challenges on the political and cultural border of Europe. In order to try to achieve a solution, Leo X persuaded some Christian princes to fight the Turks in the Mediterranean to aid the Master of the Hospitallers.[20] During the second decade of the sixteenth century, the Turkish threat intensified, and the pope insisted that the Portuguese king should, on the one hand, motivate the Hospitallers to defend Rhodes and, on the other hand, fund the Mediterranean war.[21] There is a similar number of grants where the pope gave indulgences to those who had died fighting the Muslims or the Turks.[22] For instance, Nuno Fernandes Tinoco,

---

16 *Monumenta Henricina*, I, doc. 86, pp. 194–99.
17 *Monumenta Henricina*, I, doc. 11, pp. 25–26 ([1186–1187].01.30), doc. 15, p. 32 (1196.08.08), doc. 20, pp. 40–41, doc. 21, pp. 41–42 (1217.01.21), doc. 23, pp. 43–44 (1217.02.10); *Monumenta Henricina*, VIII, doc. 1, pp. 1–4 (1443.01.09).
18 *Monumenta Henricina*, XII, doc. 113, pp. 212–15 (1456.02.15).
19 *Monumenta Henricina*, XIII, doc. 20, pp. 27–29 (1456.08).
20 *Corpo Diplomatico Portuguez*, I, pp. 306–07 (1515.01.05).
21 *Corpo Diplomatico Portuguez*, I, p. 476 (1517.07.05), and XI, pp. 224–25 (1520.05.01), pp. 234–35 (1520.06.03), respectively.
22 Muslims: *Bullarium Ordinis Militiae de Calatrava*, p. 73 (1240.06.02); *Monumenta Henricina*, VII, doc. 228, pp. 336–37 (1442.12.19). Turks: *Monumenta Henricina*, XII, doc. 64, pp. 123–29 (1455.05.15).

ETHNIC AND RELIGIOUS MINORITIES AND THE PORTUGUESE MILITARY ORDERS   103

a knight of St James, was granted an indulgence if he died in the maritime war against the Saracens. In the same document, the aforementioned friar was authorized to take prisoners and to convert them into slaves, confiscating their assets.[23]

We can see from our sources that the Holy See also focused on the main question from a spiritual point of view as well as adding some jurisdictional privileges. For example, the Order of Christ was granted spiritual jurisdiction in Africa (between Cape *Bojador* and *Não*, Guinea and India),[24] as well as some prayers[25] and the administration of some sacraments. It is quite interesting to observe the royal decision, supported by the papal bull, to baptize slaves, African people, and Muslims in the church devoted to Our Lady of Conception ('Nossa Senhora da Conceição') in Lisbon, property of the Order of Christ.[26] These kinds of measures reveal the demand to be included, at least of some minorities, which contributed to social peace and cohesion.

As well as the spiritual objectives, the Holy See was also interested in the more material involvement of the military orders in the funding of military activities using their own income (4 documents).[27] Also in this category, we can see papal (5)[28] and royal (4)[29] policies in their attempts to be involved in the administration of these institutions. By accepting the role of the military orders as intermediaries between the Portuguese Crown, the papacy, and ethnic minorities, the Holy See therefore promoted the reform of their internal organization by trying to get them to adapt to the new challenges imposed by the monarchy.

Finally, there is a third group composed of only four diplomas which are about the war; these provided exemptions to those who participated in a special mission. These bulls can also enlighten us about the status of these wars.[30] The wars against Christians, Muslims, and other enemies of the kingdom were accepted at the same level by this kind of rhetoric, including in the fifteenth century.[31] It is significant that at three different points in the thirteenth century, the pope granted the same privileges to several different missions. This occurred in 1218, when a bull matched the defence of the Holy Land with the rebuilding of the castle of Alcácer, by guaranteeing the same privileges to those who participated in these two different campaigns.[32] In turn, the defence of the Holy Land

---

23 *Monumenta Henricina*, XII, doc. 87, pp. 168–71 (1455?.08.26).

24 *Monumenta Henricina*, XII, doc. 140, pp. 289–92 (1456.03.13).

25 Lisbon, TT, *Ordem de Avis / Convento de S. Bento de Avis*, nº 31 (1492.08.26).

26 *Corpo Diplomatico Portuguez*, XI, pp. 76–78 (1513.08.07); pp. 113–14 (1516.01.10).

27 *Monumenta Henricina*, I, doc. 77, pp. 166–67 (1330.07.01); *Monumenta Henricina*, I, doc. 99, p. 236 (1345.05.22); *Monumenta Henricina*, XII, doc. 117, pp. 229–33 (1456.02.16); *Monumenta Henricina*, XIII, doc. 5, pp. 6–7 (1456.07.07).

28 Lisbon, TT, *Coleção Especial*, cx. 1, nº 3 ([1159–1181]); *Bulário Português*, doc. 24, pp. 26–30 (1198.07.15), doc. 41, p. 55 (1199.04.28), doc. 201, pp. 357–58 (1214.05.20); *Monumenta Henricina*, VII, doc. 43, pp. 58–60 (1440.02.20).

29 *Monumenta Henricina*, I, doc. 61 (Latin version) and doc. 62 (Portuguese translation), pp. 97–119 (1319.03.14); *Monumenta Henricina*, II, doc. 148, p. 303 (1418.10.08), doc. 180, pp. 368–69 (1420.20.25); *Monumenta Henricina*, V, doc. 30, pp. 69–72 (1434.09.09).

30 *Monumenta Henricina*, I, doc. 29, pp. 54–55 (1218.01.26).

31 *Monumenta Henricina*, I, doc. 147, pp. 336–37 (1411.03.20).

32 *Monumenta Henricina*, I, doc. 28, pp. 52–54 (1218.01.12).

was treated, in 1229, as the fight against the unfaithful,[33] and, in 1274, as the defence of the Christian faith against the Saracens of Africa.[34] All these examples reflect the context of the reconquest and are very significant. This means that to reinforce the motivation to fight in this Iberian war, the Holy See had to recognize it as one of the major objectives; therefore it was compared with the defence of the Holy Land.

The comparison between such diverse historical scenarios reoccurs later in the Middle Ages. As we will explain later on, the military orders were obliged to build convents in Africa in the mid-fifteenth century. They did not appreciate this obligation and so they tried to avoid fulfilling it. In 1464, the military orders argued that their mission was to defend Portugal against the unfaithful under the control of the Portuguese king and not to fight against the unfaithful in African territory.[35] There was a great deal at stake. What was indeed relevant was the war inside the realm, because it supported the political border. A similar situation occurred in Castile, when Pope Celestine III had exempted Diego López de Haro from his vow of crusade just because he was involved in military duties 'contra barbariem paganorum, qui nuper Yspaniarum limites occuparunt' (against the barbarity of pagans, who recently occupied the frontier of Spain).[36]

The Military Orders and Ethnic Minorities

All the military orders were recorded in papal documents in relation to ethnic and religious minorities. The majority of these diplomas were addressed to the military orders as a whole, although each one of them was mentioned separately. The Order of Christ was the main target as it was referred to in twenty-two diplomas. This number can be increased if we add twelve more bulls that mention the Templars, the former institution whose heritage was used to create the Order of Christ (1319). In a practical sense, Avis (15 documents) and Calatrava (12) represented a single institution, because the first is a branch of the latter. Just two documents refer to Calatrava and Avis at the same time. The Orders of St John and St James were each mentioned in twenty bulls. The case of St John is unique, as its headquarters were in Rhodes where the Turkish threat was particularly serious and permanent. The case of St James can be explained by its prominent role in the Iberian reconquest. Finally, three bulls were addressed as a whole to the Teutonic Knights, and the Orders of St John, Christ, St James, and Calatrava, and only two other diplomas to the military orders in general.

If we analyse the content of the *pontificia corpora* in greater depth, we realize how these documents deal with ethnic minorities. In order to undertake this exercise, we have to identify the terminology used — the nouns and the value judgements — as they were employed in the texts. The most common expressions used to designate these minorities

---

33 *Monumenta Henricina*, I, doc. 34, pp. 59–60 (1229.10.14).

34 *Monumenta Henricina*, I, doc. 54, pp. 83–84 (1274.08.06).

35 *Monumenta Henricina*, XIV, doc. 133, pp. 309–14 (1464.09.16).

36 Ayala Martínez, 'El Reino de León y la Guerra Santa', especially p. 205.

were 'sarracenorum' (25 documents), followed by 'inimicis nominis christiani' or 'inimicis crucis Christi', or 'inimicis fidei' (enemies of Christ's name, of Christ's cross, of faith, 13 documents). We can add terms like 'infidelium' (unfaithful, 12 documents), 'turcorum' (9), 'agarenos' (children of Hagar, i.e. pagans, 6 documents), and finally 'paganorum' (3).

On the other hand, when we examine the value judgements made in these documents, we find that these diplomas use a wide range of terms. We can assemble those into three different groups of concepts: perfidy, tyranny, and impious nation. With regard to 'perfidy', the most commonly used label, we may say that it was linked to diverse minorities, like 'perfidos agarenos',[37] 'perfidorum infidelium',[38] 'perfidi sarraceni',[39] and 'perfidissimi turchi'.[40] In turn, with regard to the word 'tyranny', the papal bulls contain expressions like 'magni turcarum tyranni'[41] and 'tyrannide sarracenorum'.[42] Lastly, for 'nation', we considered that it transmits a certain value judgement because the documents associated it with a people who did not have the same religious beliefs, as is shown by the following expressions: 'barbararum nationum et infidelium' (nation of barbarians and infidels),[43] and 'sarracenorum natio et impia christiani nominis inimica' (nation of Saracens and impious enemy of Christ's name).[44] According to H. Nicholson, the Islamic people considered the military orders to be 'terrible enemies, who should be given no quarter'.[45]

It is possible to add to the interpretation of the documents through undertaking an analysis based on these terms and concepts. Given that our study covers such a long period of time between the twelfth and the sixteenth centuries, it is very important to be aware that the terminology used to refer to ethnic minorities in the *pontificia corpora* seems to have undergone several changes during this period. In the twelfth and thirteenth centuries, the concepts were 'sarracenos' or 'sarracenorum';[46] 'inimicis nominis christiani'[47] or 'inimicis crucis Christi'[48] or 'inimicorum Christi';[49] 'infidelium'[50] and 'paganorum'.[51] In the fourteenth century, more specifically in

---

37 *Monumenta Henricina*, I, doc. 86, pp. 194–99 (1341.04.30), doc. 105, pp. 248–50 (1375.04.02).
38 *Monumenta Henricina*, VII, doc. 43, pp. 58–60 (1440.02.20).
39 *Monumenta Henricina*, I, doc. 61, pp. 97–110 (1319.03.14).
40 *Corpo Diplomatico Portuguez*, I, pp. 18–24 (1501.10.23).
41 *Corpo Diplomatico Portuguez*, I, pp. 306–07 (1515.01.05).
42 *Monumenta Henricina*, XV, doc. 34, pp. 49–50 (1472.08.12).
43 *Corpo Diplomatico Portuguez*, I, pp. 61–75 (1505.07.12).
44 *Monumenta Henricina*, I, doc. 61, pp. 97–110 (1319.03.14).
45 Nicholson, *Images of the Military Orders*, p. 183.
46 *Monumenta Henricina*, I, doc. 11, pp. 25–26 ([1186–1187].01.30), doc. 15, p. 32 (1196.08.08), doc. 20, pp. 40–41 (1217.01.18), doc. 21, pp. 41–42 (1217.01.21), doc. 23, pp. 43–44 (1217.02.10), doc. 24, pp. 44–45 (1217.02.10); *Bullarium Ordinis Militiae de Calatrava*, p. 73 (1240.06.02); Ferreira, *Memórias e notícias*, pp. 825–26 (1265.06.08); *Monumenta Henricina*, I, doc. 54, pp. 83–84 (1274.08.06), doc. 56, pp. 86–87 (1275.11.12).
47 *Monumenta Henricina*, I, doc. 28, pp. 52–54 (1218.01.12), doc. 34, pp. 59–60 (1229.10.14), doc. 54, pp. 83–84 (1274.08.06), doc. 56, pp. 86–87 (1275.11.12).
48 Lisbon, TT, *Coleção Especial*, cx. 1, n° 3 ([1159–1181].02]).
49 *Bulário Português*, doc. 24, pp. 26–30 (1198.07.15).
50 *Monumenta Henricina*, I, doc. 34, pp. 59–60 (1229.10.14), doc. 54, pp. 83–84 (1274.08.06).
51 Lisbon, TT, *Coleção Especial*, cx. 1, n° 3 ([1159–1181].02]); *Bulário Português*, doc. 24, pp. 26–30 (1198.07.15); *Bullarium Ordinis Militiae de Calatrava*, pp. 115–16 (1259.02.12).

106   PAULA PINTO COSTA AND JOANA LENCART

Table 4.1. Different actions by the Military Orders towards ethnic minorities referred in the *pontificia corpora* (twelfth to sixteenth centuries).

Action	Quotation	Primary Source
Against	'paganorum **contra** christianos'	Lisbon, TT, *Coleção Especial*, cx. 1, nº 3
Redeem	'Captivos **evadentes servitutem sarraceniam**'	*Bulário Português*, doc. 201, pp. 357–58.
Release	'sarracenorum manibus **liberantes**'	*Monumenta Henricina*, I, doc. 15, p. 32, doc. 23, pp. 43–44; *Bulário Português*, doc. 24, pp. 26–30
Defend	'paganorum **defensare**'	*Bulário Português*, doc. 24, pp. 26–30
Expel	'**expugnandum** inimicos nominis christiani'	*Monumenta Henricina*, I, doc. 28, pp. 52–54
Exterminate	'ad desolacionem et **exterminium** perfidorum infidelium'	*Monumenta Henricina*, VII, doc. 43, pp. 58–60.
	'ac **exterminium** hostium eorundem'	*Monumenta Henricina*, I, doc. 86, pp. 194–99.
Repress and smash	'ad **reprimendum** et **conterendum** infidelium'	*Monumenta Henricina*, **XII, doc. 113, pp. 212–15.**
Offend	'**propulsandum** impugnationes contumelias et ofensas'	*Descobrimentos Portugueses*, I, doc. 135, pp. 150–54; doc. 141, pp. 160–65.
Oppose	'et vallium fidei inexterminabile adversus incursus infidelium hostium **opponantur**'	*Monumenta Henricina*, I, doc. 61.
Fight	'novam militiam **pugilum** christi religiose viventium'	*Monumenta Henricina*, I, doc. 61.

* Only one example is given for each expression.

1319, new words were introduced, namely 'perfidy' ('perfidi sarraceni') and 'nation' ('sarracenorum natio et impia christiani nominis inimica').[52] In the fifteenth century, in particular in 1472, another term appears in these documents: 'tyranny' ('tyrannide sarracenorum').[53] It is not easy to explain this variation in concepts. Indeed, at the beginning, in the twelfth and thirteenth centuries, the ethnic minorities were not identified with pejorative adjectives; to refer them the papal chancery used their names. The papal bull of the foundation of the Order of Christ, enacted in 1319, introduced the adjective *perfidious*, and from this moment on, it was used to classify different types of ethnic minorities. From the fourteenth century onwards, the ethnic minorities became more identified with a *nation*, in a pejorative sense associated with a political background.

The documents that we selected, issued by the Holy See, also reveal different actions and attitudes taken by the Military Orders towards the ethnic minorities.

---

52   *Monumenta Henricina*, I, doc. 61 and doc. 62 (Portuguese version), pp. 97–119.
53   *Monumenta Henricina*, XV, doc. 34, pp. 49–50.

Some of them evoked the liberation of the Christians, while others instigated the fight against the unfaithful. Therefore, these *pontificia corpora* mention a multiplicity of actions, as shown in Table 4.1. Besides stimulating activity against unfaithful people, the Holy See was also worried about Christians who might cooperate with the *infidelium*, threatening such people with the penalty of excommunication.[54]

The hostility which the Holy See displayed was justified either by the distinct religious beliefs or by the political positions held by the popes and kings. Within these articulations of power, the pope assumed above all a political role. In contrast, people who inhabited areas where coexistence was normal would have distinct behaviour when facing 'Otherness'. The challenges of daily life compelled mutual collaboration.[55] But the *pontificia corpora* do not focus on this perspective, because the pope preached a standard discourse without being aware of the complexity of Portuguese society.

Our analysis of the *pontificia corpora* can be enriched by the identification of the geographical place-names mentioned in these papal bulls. Indeed, they refer to a wide range of places, which can be sorted out in four groups. The first was the Holy Land; the second, Portugal, Algarve, Spain, and Granada; the third, Benamarim, Africa, and Guinea; and finally, Rhodes and Constantinople. This means from the neighbourhood within the Iberian sphere and the realm of Benamarim and Granada to the distant Turks who were spread all over the eastern Mediterranean. From Ceuta on (1415) the focus moves from the ethnic minorities in Portugal to those in Africa, and a little bit later to those in Constantinople and Rhodes. Contrary to that, according to Paul Cobb, Islamic writers did not recognize in their texts separate areas of conflict, because they saw it as a 'global Frankish assault on Islam'.[56]

Different scenarios correspond to different enemies: from *sarracenorum* to *turcorum*. The first bull we can find out in our documentary sources which refers to the Turks dates to 1455.[57] It is quite interesting to study the impact that this change had on the level of tolerance or intolerance upon ethnic minorities in Portugal. In order to evaluate the level of tolerance of Portuguese medieval society, we can not narrow our investigation to the *pontificia corpora* alone. We must include other kind of sources, like royal diplomas, normative texts, sermons, and religious literature, which we will study further later in the project 'Cohesion Building of Multi-Ethnic societies, 10th–21st Century'. We should emphasize that, according to Fernão Lopes, a Portuguese royal chronicler from the fifteenth century, Lisbon was a city where a huge variety of foreign people including Africans, Muslims, and Jews might meet.[58]

---

54 A bull from March 1175 urged the Iberian kings to fight against Almohads and threatened the excommunication of Christians who collaborated with the Saracens (Ayala Martínez, 'El Reino de León y la Guerra Santa', p. 186).

55 González Jiménez, 'La cruzada ad partes africanas'.

56 Cobb, *The Race for Paradise*, p. 156.

57 *Monumenta Henricina*, XII, doc. 64, pp. 123–29 (1455.05.15).

58 Lopes, *Cronica de D. Fernando*, p. 7.

The Military Orders and the Aims of Popes and Kings

From the perspective of the *pontificia corpora*, we can still analyse the aims of the papacy and the Crown which had three key strands that are highly indicative of the fifteenth-century political situation: collaboration during the war, the administration of the military orders, and building convents in Africa with the support of the knights. Regarding the collaboration during the war, 1411 is a symbolic moment as Pope John XXIII gave permission to the military orders to collaborate with the Crown in the war against Christians, Muslims, and other enemies of the Portuguese kingdom, for political and economic reasons.[59] It is worthwhile underlining the recognition of these three distinct groups, including the Christians, at the same level; the unique common element was that they were enemies of the Portuguese kingdom.

In regard to the administration of the military orders, there are also some relevant achievements. King João I intended to give the governance of the Portuguese military orders to his sons, after he had sought permission from the Holy See. Therefore, in 1418 the governance of the Order of St James was given to Prince John, using the argument that this Order would provide some income for the war against the unfaithful.[60] In 1420 the administration of the Order of Christ was given to Prince Henry,[61] and, in 1434, the Order of Avis was handed to Prince Fernando.[62] Hence, these military orders remained linked to the royal family, although the perpetual annexation bull of these three Orders to the Crown would only be enacted in 1551.[63]

The third key moment regards the construction of the convents in Africa by the military orders. This obligation yielded several objections from the friars. In 1456, Pope Callixtus III compelled the four military orders to build convents in Africa.[64] However, eight years later, in 1464, Pope Paul II revoked the previous obligation, accepting the arguments presented by the military orders. The Orders clearly explained their reasons: they could not finance these African matters, which were only useful to the Portuguese king, and not to the Orders themselves; the military orders already supported the sons of the kings; and many noblemen and *milites* considered that life in Africa was unseemly and so they did not encourage anyone to take the habit in any military order.[65] Indeed, the goals of the pope and the king were different from those of the military orders. Keeping these episodes in mind, we can highlight 1456 as a key year. On 15 February, Pope Callixtus III demanded that Álvaro, bishop of Silves and apostolic nuncio in Portugal, order the Orders of Christ, Avis, St James, and St John to fight against the Turks,

---

59 *Monumenta Henricina*, I, doc. 147, pp. 336–37.
60 *Monumenta Henricina*, II, doc. 148, p. 303.
61 *Monumenta Henricina*, II, doc. 180, pp. 368–69.
62 *Monumenta Henricina*, V, doc. 30, pp. 69–72.
63 *Corpo Diplomatico Portuguez*, VII, pp. 90–100.
64 *Monumenta Henricina*, XII, doc. 116, pp. 225–29.
65 *Monumenta Henricina*, XIV, doc. 133, pp. 309–14.

under the penalty of excommunication and deprivation of offices and benefices possessed by the friars.[66] On the same day the pope compelled the four military orders to build convents in Africa.[67] On the following day, the pope asked Álvaro, bishop of Silves, to evaluate the tithe to be applied to the crusade against the Turks, authorizing him to urge its payment to the Order of Christ, Avis, and other Orders in general.[68] On 7 July, Callixtus III decided that those who did not accomplish the visitation of the churches in their jurisdictional area must give the respective income to fund the war against the Turk as a means of redemption.[69] In August, the same pope urged Prince Henry to cooperate with the Holy See in the struggle against the Turks.[70] In this context, the war and the tithes were the main concerns for both the pope and the king, because the Mediterranean threat was becoming so serious.

After reading Gomes Eanes de Zurara, another Portuguese royal chronicler from the fifteenth century, who wrote the recollection about Ceuta, it seems that the masters of the military orders, among other prestigious people, were not involved in the attack on that African city.[71] But, as we know, this reflects just the way the author wanted to tell the story as well as the royal strategy, as it was the king himself who approved the text.

In the sixteenth century, the Turks were a new common challenge shared by the papacy, the monarchy, and the Order of St John, above all the other similar institutions. The eastern Mediterranean military situation was too difficult. In 1515, Pope Leo X requested that the Portuguese king fight against the Turks, because the Order of St John at Rhodes had asked them to;[72] and, in 1517, considering the permanent Turkish threat, the same pope demanded that the Portuguese king compel the Portuguese Hospitallers to participate in the defence of Rhodes, as the island was at risk of being besieged.[73] The Portuguese friars had to be ordered to participate in the distant Mediterranean war. The pope used King Manuel I as a special intermediary as he was the main authority in Portugal, even above the vow of obedience that the friars owed to the pope. The close relationship with some of these friars would be crucial for accomplishing those objectives.

If we change the perspective from war to the spiritual approach, it seems that it was only from the mid-fifteenth century onwards that some spiritual concerns had arisen around the themes discussed in this chapter. We can give some examples. In 1456, Callixtus III granted to the Order of Christ the spiritual jurisdiction of all the overseas territories.[74] In 1492, the pope asked the master of Avis for some prayers to

---

66 *Monumenta Henricina*, XII, doc. 113, pp. 212–15.
67 *Monumenta Henricina*, XII, doc. 116, pp. 225–29.
68 *Monumenta Henricina*, XII, doc. 117, pp. 229–33.
69 *Monumenta Henricina*, XIII, doc. 5, pp. 6–7.
70 *Monumenta Henricina*, XIII, doc. 20, pp. 27–29.
71 Duarte, *Ceuta 1415*, p. 43.
72 *Corpo Diplomatico Portuguez*, I, pp. 306–07 (1515.01.05).
73 *Corpo Diplomatico Portuguez*, I, p. 476 (1517.07.05).
74 *Monumenta Henricina*, XII, doc. 137, pp. 286–88 (1456.03.13).

benefit his aspiration of dominance over the Turks.[75] And, in 1513, the pope, answering a royal request, authorized the baptism of *niger* people and Muslims in a church of the Order of Christ at Lisbon (*Nossa Senhora da Conceição*).[76] This kind of measure has contributed to the social conscientiousness about the so-called 'Other'. Bearing in mind these three examples, we should underline, at the same time, a different approach to the Turks, whom we can call the new enemy, and to the Muslims, the so-called old enemy, on a par with the African people, who became much more common in Lisbon in the sixteenth century.

The *Pontificia Corpora* and Other Narrative Sources

The *pontificia corpora* may have influenced other narratives such as sermons, literary texts (like *trovadores*, e.g., a kind of medieval poetry[77]), and other kinds of religious literature, and may also have contributed towards shaping royal political opinions, favouring different behaviours towards ethnic minorities in Portugal.

In the fifteenth century, the Battle of Ourique (1139), a hard-fought clash between King Afonso Henriques and the Muslims, was rediscovered and reinvented. Soon after 1139, the year of the conflict, the aforementioned Afonso updated his status, entitling himself King of Portugal instead of count of the territory.[78] In the fifteenth century, all the narratives on this subject added a sacred dimension to this ancient military episode, supporting the basis of the concept of nationality. So, on the one hand, the sense of a Portuguese nation emerged from the confrontation with 'Otherness' (e.g. the Muslims in Ourique), and, on the other, the same 'Otherness' was used as a legitimation of royal power during this period. In this sense, the Muslims were both an enemy and a crucial element which gave an advantage to the Portuguese kingdom since its origin was a key component to its future political development.

Also in the fifteenth century, the royal chronicler Gomes Eanes de Zurara reproduced a sermon that had been preached in a small village, Lagos, located in the southern limit of the kingdom. Precisely on the eve of the conquest of Ceuta (1415), Friar João de Xira pronounced an enthusiastic speech, the so-called *Sermão de Lagos*, encouraging those fighting against the enemies of the faith.[79] He even threatened those who did not fight with death.

In the third decade of the fifteenth century, the Portuguese monarchy had a particular dilemma to resolve. It had to be decided if the king were to fight, or not, the war against the Muslims of Benamarim.[80] The advice of Infant João provided a new perspective, as evidenced by the following words:

---

75 Lisbon, TT, *Ordem de Avis / Convento de S. Bento de Avis*, nº 31 (1492.08.06).
76 *Corpo Diplomatico Portuguez*, XI, pp. 76–78 (1513.08.07).
77 Oliveira, 'A Cruzada e o Ultramar'.
78 Buescu, 'A memória das origens'; Cintra, 'Sobre a formação e evolução'.
79 'Inimigos da nossa santa Fé católica', Zurara, *Crónica da Tomada de Ceuta*, cap. LII.
80 *Descobrimentos Portugueses*, I, doc. 286, pp. 352–60.

If God could hear their claims, we should not boldly make such a war, either against the Muslims, or against the Jews, who are the worst people in the world. [...] We are not sure if the war against the Muslims could be interpreted as a way to serve God, because we have never heard or saw that Our Lord, the Apostles, or the Church Doctors had ordered the war against the unfaithful. [...] They wanted to convert them by preaching and miracles.[81]

Conclusions

The papal documents do not confirm the aforementioned peaceful coexistence. As a result of the analysis of the specific terms used in the papal charters, the most common image of the society was a disruptive one. In fact, the medieval world of powers was organized on a dual scheme — ourselves and the other; the good and the bad — a Manichean approach which aimed at the dominance of an opponent.

Given that the key aim of this essay is to study how the military orders were involved in the relationship between the Portuguese Crown and the papacy in relation to ethnic minorities, we can highlight, in our conclusion, the final remarks achieved by this research. The chronology of the selected documents has a wide range, from the twelfth to sixteenth centuries. In the documents of the *pontificia corpora*, the only ethnic minorities mentioned are Muslims; there are no references to the Jews, although they had an important role in Northern African trade, as well as in international trade. It seems that the papacy had not developed a theological narrative through the *pontificia corpora*, which had the territorial administration and the political issues as the main goals. The focus was indeed on the territorial domain (the Holy Land, Iberia, Africa, Constantinople, and Rhodes) and not on religious perspectives. The historical circumstances, and not religious affairs, were the core framework that shaped the Holy See's policy towards ethnic minorities.

Other profound aspects, such as identity, communication, and symbolic representation, should be considered, but these papal documents did not support the analysis of such aspects. For instance, language would be one of the most important elements of ethnic identity, as well as the urban ghettos (*mourarias* and *judiarias*, special living quarters for Muslims and Jews according to the royal law), clothing, weapons, or hairstyles. As an earlier study demonstrated, the friars would have had major difficulty in understanding and being understood by the Arabic peoples.[82] Another question that needs further research is that of whether the Iberian Muslims identified themselves more with the people from Iberia or with those in Northern Africa. But it is not possible to answer all of these complex questions using only the *pontificia corpora*. There are therefore possibilities for further research on these aspects of daily life.

81 'e se Deus ouvyse os seus rogos não deviamos ousadamente cometer tal guerra, e nom digo tam somente contra mouros, mas ainda contra judeus que som a mais roym gente do mundo [...]; Ainda guerra dos mouros nom somos certos se he serviço de Deus, porque eu nom vy nem ouvy que Noso Senhor nem algum dos seus apostolos nem doctores da Igreja mandassem que guerreasem infieis mas antes per pregação e milagres os mandou converter', *Descobrimentos Portugueses*, I, doc. 286, p. 354.
82 Forey, 'Literacy and Learning in the Military Orders', p. 200.

Works Cited

Manuscripts and Archival Sources

Lisbon, Arquivo Nacional da Torre do Tombo, *Coleção Especial, Bulas*
Lisbon, Arquivo Nacional da Torre do Tombo, *Ordem de Avis / Convento de S. Bento de Avis*

Primary Sources

Bulário Português, ed. by Avelino de Jesus da Costa and Maria Alegria F. Marques (Coimbra: Instituto Nacional de Investigação Científica / Centro de História da Sociedade e da Cultura da Universidade de Coimbra, 1989)
Bullarium Ordinis Militiae de Calatrava, ed. by D. Ignacio Jose Ortega y Cotes, D. Juan Francisco Alvarez de Baquedano, and D. Pedro de Ortega Zuñiga y Aranda (Madrid: Typographia de Antonio Marin, 1761)
Corpo Diplomatico Portuguez contendo os actos e relações políticas e diplomaticas de Portugal com as várias potências do mundo desde o século XVI até os nossos dias, 15 vols (Lisbon: Tipographia da Academia Real das Sciencias, 1862–1932)
Descobrimentos Portugueses, ed. by João Martins da Silva Marques, 5 vols (Lisbon: Instituto Nacional de Investigação Científica, 1988)
Ferreira, Alexandre, *Memórias e notícias da célebre Ordem Militar dos Templários* (Lisbon: Officina de Joseph António da Sylva, 1735)
Monumenta Henricina, 15 vols (Coimbra: Comissão Executiva do V Centenário da Morte do Infante D. Henrique, 1960–1974)
Zurara, Gomes Eanes de, *Crónica da Tomada de Ceuta*, introduction and edition by Reis Brasil (Mem Martins: Publicações Europa-América, 1992)

Secondary Studies

Almagro Vidal, Clara, 'Moros al servicio de la órdenes militares en el reino de Castilla: Algunas reflexiones', in *Actas del XIII Simposio Internacional de Mudejarismo* (Teruel: Centro de Estudios Mudéjares, 2017), pp. 191–200 [available at <https://www. academia.edu/35280104/Moros_al_servicio_de_las_órdenes_militares_en_el_ reino_de_Castilla_Algunas_reflexiones>]
——, 'La Orden de Calatrava y la minoría mudéjar', in *As Ordens Militares: Freires, guerreiros, cavaleiros*, ed. by Isabel Cristina Ferreira Fernandes, vol. II (Palmela: GesOS / Câmara Municipal de Palmela, 2012), pp. 617–30 [available at <http:// www.academia.edu/3556275/La_Orden_de_Calatrava_y_la_minor%C3%ADa_ mudéjar>]
——, 'Religious Minorities' Identity and Application of the Law: A First Approximation to the Lands of Military Orders in Castile', in *Law and Religious Minorities in Medieval Societies: Between Theory and Praxis*, ed. by Ana Echevarria, Juan Pedro Monferrer-Sala, and John Tolan (Turnhout: Brepols, 2016), pp. 197–210 [available at <https://halshs. archives-ouvertes.fr/halshs-01730396/document>]

Ayala Martínez, Carlos de, 'El Reino de León y la Guerra Santa: Las estrategias ideológicas (1157–1230)', in *Cristãos contra muçulmanos na Idade Média Peninsular: Bases ideológicas e doutrinais de um confronto (sécs. x–xiv)*, ed. by Carlos de Ayala Martínez and Isabel Cristina F. Fernandes (Madrid: Edições Colibri / Universidad Autonoma de Madrid, 2015), pp. 173–211

Ayala Martínez, Carlos de, and Isabel Cristina F. Fernandes, eds, *Cristãos contra muçulmanos na Idade Média Peninsular: Bases ideológicas e doutrinais de um confronto (sécs. x–xiv)* (Madrid: Edições Colibri / Universidad Autonoma de Madrid, 2015)

Barros, Filomena, 'Assy como he devudo aos Reyx Mouros em seus Regnos e Senhorios: La fiscalidad regia dos mudéjares en el reino portugués', unpublished paper presented at the 'International Medieval Meeting', Lleida, 26 June 2018)

——, 'A Ordem de Avis e a minoria muçulmana', in *Ordens Militares: Guerra, Religião e Poder*, ed. by Isabel Cristina Fernandes, vol. II (Lisbon: Edições Colibri / Câmara Municipal de Palmela, 1999), pp. 167–73

Barros, Maria Filomena Lopes de, 'Ethno-Religious Minorities', in *The Historiography of Medieval Portugal, c. 1950–c. 2010: A Collective Book and a Collaborative Project*, ed. by José Mattoso, Maria de Lurdes Rosa, Bernardo Vasconcelos e Sousa, and Maria João Branco (Lisbon: Instituto de Estudos Medievais da Universidade Nova de Lisboa, 2011), pp. 571–89

Buescu, Ana Isabel, 'A memória das origens: Ourique e a fundação do reino (sécs. xv–xviii)', in *Memória e Poder: Ensaios de História Cultural (sécs. xv–xviii)* (Lisbon: Ed. Cosmos, 2000), pp. 11–28

Cintra, Luís Filipe Lindley, 'Sobre a formação e evolução da lenda de Ourique (até à Crónica de 1419)', *Revista da Faculdade de Letras de Lisboa*, 3rd Ser., 23.1 (1957), 168–215

Cobb, Paul M., *The Race for Paradise: An Islamic History of the Crusades* (Oxford: Oxford University Press, 2014)

Costa, João Paulo Oliveira e, *D. Manuel I* (Rio de Mouros: Círculo de Leitores, 2005)

Costa, Paula Pinto, 'Between Portugal and Latin East: How Did the Military Orders Deal with the Multiethnic Challenge in the Medieval Times?', unpublished paper presented at the 'International Medieval Meeting', Lleida, 27 June 2018)

Costa, Paula Pinto, and Maria Cristina Pimenta, 'Multiethnic Portuguese Society in the Realm of John I (1385–1433): From the Administrative Practices to the Royal Official Narrative', paper presented at the International Medieval Congress, 4 July 2017, University of Leeds (submitted for publication)

Dinis, A. J. Dias, 'Antecedentes da expansão ultramarina portuguesa: Os diplomas pontifícios dos séculos xii a xv', *Revista Portuguesa de História*, 10 (1962), 1–118

Duarte, Luís Miguel, *Ceuta 1415: Seiscentos anos depois* (Lisbon: Livros Horizonte, 2015)

Ferreira, Maria Isabel Rodrigues, 'A documentação pontifícia: Fonte para o estudo da normativa das Ordens Militares', in *As Ordens Militares e de Cavalaria na construção do mundo ocidental*, ed. by Isabel Cristina Fernandes (Palmela: Edições Colibri/Câmara Municipal de Palmela, 2005), pp. 35–67

Fonseca, Luís Adão, Cristina Pimenta, and Paula Pinto Costa, 'The Papacy and the Crusades in xv[th] Century Portugal', in *La Papauté et les Croisades: Actes du VIIe congress de la Society for the Study of the Crusades and the Latin East / The Papacy and the Crusades: Proceedings of the VIIth Conference of the Society for the Study of the Crusades and the Latin East*, ed. by Michel Balard, Crusades, Subsidia, 3 (Farnham: Ashgate, 2011), pp. 141–54

Forey, Alan, 'Literacy and Learning in the Military Orders during the Twelfth and Thirteenth Centuries', in *The Military Orders: Welfare and Warfare*, ed. by Helen Nicholson, vol. II (Aldershot: Ashgate, 1998), pp. 185–206

Gerrard, Christopher, 'Opposing Identity: Muslims, Christians and the Military Orders in Rural Aragon', *Medieval Archaeology*, 43 (1999), 143–60, <https://doi.org/10.5284/1000320>

González Jiménez, Manuel, 'La cruzada ad partes africanas: Alfonso X el del fecho de Allende', in *Cristianos y musulmanes en la Península Ibérica: La guerra, la frontera y la convivencia*, ed. by Juan Ignacio Ruiz de la Peña (Ávila: Fundación Sánchez Albornoz, 2009), no. 3

Josserand, Philippe, 'En péninsule Ibérique et par-delà: Les ordres militaires face à l'Autre à la lumière de quelques contacts réputés pacifiques', in *Cristãos contra muçulmanos na Idade Média Peninsular: Bases ideológicas e doutrinais de um confronto (sécs. X–XIV)*, ed. by Carlos de Ayala Martínez and Isabel Cristina F. Fernandes (Madrid: Edições Colibri / Universidad Autonoma de Madrid, 2015), pp. 231–46

Lázaro, António, '"Novas do Turco sam viindas per via de Rodes": Algumas notas sobre a circulação de informação no princípio do séc. XVI', in *As Ordens Militares e de Cavalaria na construção do mundo occidental*, ed. by Isabel Cristina Fernandes (Palmela: Edições Colibri/Câmara Municipal de Palmela, 2005), pp. 383–411

Lewis, Kevin James, 'Friend or Foe: Islamic Views of the Military Orders in the Latin East as Drawn from Arabic Sources', in *The Military Orders*, VI.1: *Culture and Conflict in the Mediterranean World*, ed. by Jochen Schenk and Mike Carr (Abingdon: Routledge, 2017), pp. 20–29

Lopes, Fernão, *Crónica de D. Fernando* (Lisboa: Imprensa Nacional Casa da Moeda, 2004)

Nicholson, Helen, *Images of the Military Orders, 1128–1298: Spiritual, Secular, Romantic* (Leicester: University of Leicester, 1989)

Oliveira, Luís Filipe, 'A Cruzada e o Ultramar: Dos trovadores ao conde de Barcelos', in *Cristãos contra muçulmanos na Idade Média Peninsular: Bases ideológicas e doutrinais de um confronto (sécs. X–XIV)*, ed. by Carlos de Ayala Martínez and Isabel Cristina F. Fernandes (Madrid: Edições Colibri / Universidad Autonoma de Madrid, 2015), pp. 355–67

Rebollo Bote, Juan, 'De andalusíes a mudéjares: Continuidad musulmana en la Extremadura de las Órdenes Militares; From Andalusian Muslims to Mudejars: Islamic Continuty in the Extremadura of Military Orders', in *Las Órdenes Militares en Extremadura* (Garrovillas de Alconétar: Federación Extremadura Histórica, 2015), pp. 153–75; available at <http://www.academia.edu/26041851/De_andalus%C3%ADes_a_mudéjares_Continuidad_musulmana_en_la_Extremadura_de_las_Órdenes_Militares_From_andalusian_muslims_to_mudejars_islamic_continuty_in_the_Extremadura_of_Military_Orders>

LUCIANO GALLINARI

Social and Economic Relations between Sardinians and Aragonese in the Twelfth to Fifteenth Centuries

This chapter focuses on relations between Sardinians and the Aragonese (with this term we indicate all subjects of the various political bodies within of the Crown of Aragon) between the twelfth and fifteenth centuries and the new common identity they produced through different but connected activities, which strengthened the relationships between their ethnic groups within the new common political community. We will try to analyse this delicate issue from two different points of view.

The first examines the initial peaceful relationships and the subsequent conflict at the highest political and institutional level between the Aragonese sovereigns and the judges of Arborea. In these initial relations, we find confirmation that identities are also constructed through the choices made by some 'individuals [that] opened up new forms of interaction' as well as through the integration of 'individuals' experiences into wider group narratives'.[1] This occurred in the mid-twelfth century when dynastic relations began between Judge Barisone I of Arborea (1146–1185/1186) and the family of the Counts of Barcelona who had become Kings of Aragon at that time. It also happened with the case of Judge Hugh II of Arborea (1321–1335) who immediately tried to insert his dynasty and his polity into the new institutional and cultural *container*, that is, the *Regnum Sardiniae et Corsicae*.[2] Thus he helped to ensure over thirty years of peaceful relations between the *Giudicato* and the *Regnum*.

---

1 Wiszewski, 'Introduction: Inter-Ethnic Relations within Multi-Ethnic Societies', in this volume.
2 The *Regnum Sardiniae et Corsicae* was created by Pope Boniface VIII and enfeoffed to James II of Aragon in 1297. See, among many others, Arribas Palau, *La conquista de Cerdeña*; Salavert y Roca, 'Un nuevo documento'; Cadeddu, 'Giacomo II d'Aragona e la conquista'; Cadeddu, 'L'espansione catalano-aragonese nel Mediterraneo'; Sanna, 'Papa Giovanni XXII, Giacomo II d'Aragona e la questione del Regnum Sardinie et Corsice'; and Sanna, 'La Sardegna, il Papato e le dinamiche delle espansioni mediterranee'.

> **Luciano Gallinari** • (luciano.gallinari@isem.cnr.it) is a researcher at the Istituto di Storia dell'Europa Mediterranea of the National Research Council of Italy. He has published on medieval history and Byzantine history.

Inter-Ethnic Relations and the Functioning of Multi-Ethnic Societies: Cohesion in Multi-Ethnic Societies in Europe from c. 1000 to the Present, II, ed. by Przemysław Wiszewski, EER 18 (Turnhout: Brepols, 2022), pp. 115–140

BREPOLS ☙ PUBLISHERS

10.1484/M.EER-EB.5.132149

This is an open access chapter made available under a cc by-nc 4.0 International License.

Map 5.1. Kingdom of Aragon: Mediterranean Expansion. Source: <https://commons.wikimedia.org/wiki/File:Reiaume_d%27Aragon_-_Expansion_en_Mediterran%C3%A8a.png>. Nicolas Eynaud, CC BY-SA 3.0.

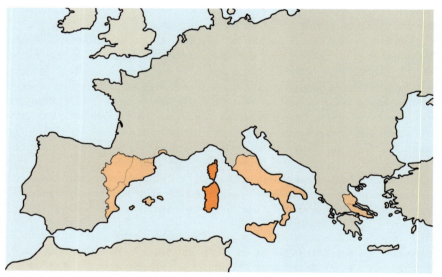

Map 5.2. Crown of Aragon and Kingdom of Sardinia. Source: <https://commons.wikimedia.org/wiki/File:Reino_de_Cerdenya_en_a_Corona_d%27Arag%C3%B3 n.svg>. Willtron, CC BY-SA 3.0.

These interactions changed abruptly from the mid-fourteenth century when several sources show the development of an ethnic identity on the island, a concept that, on the basis of appropriately interpolated narratives of the past, aims to oppose, even militarily: individuals, families (Judge Marianus IV of Arborea (1347–1375) and his brother John), and even entire societies (the *Giudicato* and the *Regnum*). Since the beginning of the twentieth century, this second period (1353–1420) had been the subject of analysis that is characterized by nationalistic and identitarian overtones, which belonged and continue to belong today more to the historiography than to the history of that period. Moreover, these overtones are the result of fairly free interpretations of the available sources, and the models of feudal and vassal bonds.[3]

The second point of view is that of the cohesion of ethnically diverse, small societies analysed from the perspective of the lower social strata that are efficiently reflected in urban contexts, where a most remarkable propensity for cooperation can be observed. And to this end we will focus on the case study of the Pisan city of *Castel di Castro* (1215–1326) and the following Catalan city of *Castell de Càller* (both are the historical centre of the present-day city of Cagliari), which after 1326 passed from Tuscan rule to Aragonese. From this point onwards, some very interesting processes of social coexistence took place between the Aragonese, Pisans, and Sardinians, which gave *Castell de Càller* the characteristics of a melting pot of different cultures and traditions through a horizontal integration and interconnections of different ethnic identities with diverse beliefs. This, over time, created a new Sardinian multilayered social identity in the fifteenth century and then in the modern era too. This is very well demonstrated by the unfortunately limited notarial sources from the capital of the *Regnum*, which show how its urban society gravitated towards a growing cohesion between the Sardinian and Aragonese *Nationes*, even shortly after the end of the long-drawn-out military struggle mentioned above.

The limited size of the case study analysed, the result of both the small number of available sources and the reduced geographical area, makes it possible to create a methodologically interesting and stimulating examination of one of the central themes of this miscellaneous volume, which is the meta-textual analysis of the different activities that led to the construction of the sense of a unique community within political and institutional bodies composed of different ethnic groups.

A Social Cohesion of Two Dynasties

Aragonese Kings and Arborea Judges in the Twelfth Century

In the mid-twelfth century, Sardinia was divided into four polities called *Iudicati* — Arborea, Calari, Gallura, and Logudoro (or Torres) — which appeared together for the first time in a document issued by Pope Gregory VII in 1073.[4] They emerged from the fragmentation of the institutional development of the Byzantine *Provincia Sardiniae* that we can define as Archontate/*Iudicatus* of Sardinia by the titles of archon/*iudex* of its supreme rulers mentioned in Byzantine and papal sources between the ninth and tenth centuries.[5]

In 1157 Judge Barisone I of Arborea married Agalbors, daughter of Ponç de Cervera, viscount of Bas, and Princess Almodis, sister of Ramon Berenguer IV, count

---

3 See for instance Sedda, ed., *Sanluri 1409*, and note 36 below.
4 *Das Register Gregors VII*, pp. 46–47. The most recent historiographical reference work on the medieval history of Sardinia is Metcalfe, Fernández-Aceves, and Muresu, eds, *The Making of Medieval Sardinia*.
5 Sardinia was reintegrated into the Roman Empire in 554. See Gallinari, 'The *Iudex Sardiniae* and the *Archon Sardanias*', pp. 215–35, and the references contained therein.

of Barcelona, prince of Aragon and Tortosa, and marquis of Provence. Through this initiative, this judge opened up new forms of interaction between Sardinians and the Aragonese: perhaps since then human and cultural migrations started from the Iberian Peninsula to the *Giudicato* of Arborea (and vice versa?).[6] This marriage led Agalbors's brothers and *fideles* to become landowners and officials of *Curadorias*, the *Giudicato*'s administrative districts, undermining members of traditional local families and creating social tensions that would erupt in a more violent way after Judge Barisone I's death in 1185/1186.

Perhaps between October 1157 and 14–15 August 1158 Barisone I replied to Ramon Berenguer IV's repeated requests for information on the possible participation of Pisa in a military expedition to conquer Majorca and the Balearic archipelago. He wrote that he had discussed on it with the Archbishop of Pisa, Villano, when he was in Sardinia as Apostolic Legate and added that he had urged the consuls and senators of Pisa to unanimously agree with Ramon Berenguer on the Majorcan enterprise. Regardless of the content, the judge underlined with particular emphasis precisely the familiarity and friendship between them, which made him an *adnexus* to the Catalan count:

> Raimundo, Dei gratia comiti Barchinone, principi Aragonum, Tortose et Provincie marchioni illustri, amico et affini precipuo. P[arason] Dei nutu Arvorensis rex et iudex […]. Vobis et uestre celsitudini amicicia et affinitate unanimiter et indissolubiliter adnexus uester sum prorsus et omnia pro uoto uestro euenire cupimus.[7]

> (To Ramon, by the grace of God Count of Barcelona, Prince of Aragon, Tortosa and illustrious Marquis of Provence, friend and excellent relative. Barisone by God's will, king and judge of Arborea […]. I am completely, unanimously, and indissolubly united with you and your majesty by friendship and kinship, and I desire that everything will be done according to your desires.)

The vocabulary used by the judge is of special interest. Although he defines himself as 'Arvorensis rex et iudex', in addressing the Iberian ruler, Barisone I reveals the disparities in their political importance. It is not only the term *celsitudo* which indicates

---

6 Artizzu, 'Penetrazione catalana in Sardegna nel secolo XII' and Petrucci, 'Cagliari nel Trecento', pp. 29–30. The start of these important contacts with the Catalan (and later Aragonese) world, which led to the settlement on the island of important Iberian families, was wanted by the Arborea judge to counter the growing power of the Commune of Pisa in the rest of the island. This attitude is well reflected in the animated dispute with the Commune of Genoa at the imperial court of Frederick I Barbarossa for dominion over Sardinia between 1164 and 1165. See Pistarino, 'Genova e la Sardegna nel secolo XII'; Pistarino, 'Genova e la Sardegna'; and Seche, 'L'incoronazione di Barisone'. The Tuscan Commune was present in Sardinia from the beginning of the eleventh century when, in collaboration with Genoa, it drove from the island the lord of Denia (near Valencia), who had made a brief conquest of a part of the island in 1015–1016. See, among others, Zedda, 'Bisanzio, l'Islam e i giudicati'; Zedda and Pinna, 'La nascita dei giudicati'; Gallinari, 'Reflections on Byzantine Sardinia'; and Metcalfe, 'Muslim Contacts with Sardinia'.
7 *Colección de documentos inéditos del Archivo General de la Corona de Aragón*, IV, doc. CLI, pp. 305–06.

the sovereignty of Ramon Berenguer, corroborated by the presence of the title of *princeps*, but also the desire that everything would be done according to Ramon's wishes, as if he was some kind of feudal lord, institutionally superior to the judge.[8]

About twenty years later on 8 October 1186, Agalbors, who was now widowed, undertook to settle Barisone I of Arborea's debts to the Commune of Genoa for the coronation as King of Sardinia by Emperor Frederick I Barbarossa in 1164, and asked King Alfonso I of Aragon's help in recovering the *Arborensem regnum* from the hands of Peter I, son of her husband's first marriage, who had succeeded to the throne.[9] Agalbors defined herself as *Arboree regina*, and qualified as 'king' her nephew Ponç or Poncet, son of Hug de Cervera, viscount of Bas and brother of Agalbursa, another designated heir, who — according to the traditional historiography — ruled under the dynastic name of Hughes in *condominium* with Peter I, and embodied a direct link between the *Giudicato* of Arborea and the Kingdom of Aragon.[10] On 30 November 1186 King Alfonso I of Aragon stood as a guarantor for his niece Agalbors with the Commune of Genoa since he was committed to helping her to recover the *Giudicato* of Arborea which had fallen into Pisa's sphere of influence on the initiative of Peter I.[11]

Although this was a clash between 'political' groups, the very fact that thirty years after its arrival in Sardinia the 'Catalan' community aspired to the throne of the *Giudicato* is a clear confirmation of the social cohesion and political fusion that had been created at the top of the *Giudicato* of Arborea's society between the indigenous Sardinian elites and the foreign, Aragonese aristocracy. Moreover, these family ties between the new judges and the dynasty of the Counts/Kings of Aragon left significant marks in the historical memory of the kings of Aragon, who repeatedly recalled them at the turn of the thirteenth century and the fourteenth century. In that period, Aragonese dynasts were organizing the practical fulfilment of the *Regnum Sardiniae et Corsicae*.

This investiture is a real watershed in the history of Sardinia, because from then on the institutional structure of the island changed in a very profound way. The deeds of the Aragonese kings which were done in the name of the Aragonese–Sardinian cohesion created a political, social, and institutional configuration for many centuries: for example, the feudal structure that disappeared from the island only in the first half of the nineteenth century.

---

8 Seche, 'L'incoronazione di Barisone'.

9 'The imperial nomination as king of Sardinia allowed Barisone I to feel himself and be considered a *pleno iure* king, the only case in the centuries-old history of Sardinian *Giudicati*, along with that of Heinz of Hohenstaufen son of the emperor Frederick II, who had the same title in 1238 after marrying the *iudicissa* of Torres Adelasia'. See Gallinari, 'Feelings and Political Discourses', p. 13.

10 *Codice Diplomatico della Sardegna*, pp. 256–57. Recent studies being carried out by Giuseppe Seche offer more than a hint at limiting the traditional claim of the simultaneous power sharing (*condominium*) between the two rulers.

11 Sánchez Casabón, *Alfonso II Rey de Aragón*, pp. 575–76. The management of the Arborea 'dossier' by Genoa was intertwined not only with the inveterate problem of the Ligurian Commune's relations with Pisa, but also with the relatively new problem of the growing economic and political power of the kings of Aragon, who were actively contending with the Genoese for control of the entire Occitan area.

The Aragonese Kings and Arborea Judges in the Thirteenth–Fifteenth Centuries

Between 1297 and 1323, there were many contacts between the Aragonese kings and the Arborea judges. The former were eager to have the economic and logistical support of Arborea's rulers for a successful military conquest of the part of Sardinian territory held by the Commune of Pisa. The sources show that the Aragonese kings stressed the bonds of kinship between them and the judges, arranged marriages between the main island rulers and important noble Iberian families,[12] and granted noble and chivalrous titles to the judges' sons.[13] Some of these events examined in more detail shed light on the crucial process carried out by the Aragonese kings, in order to facilitate the inclusion and assimilation of the judges of Arborea and their House within the highest social strata of the entire Crown of Aragon.

On 3 April 1328 *Donnikellu* (Prince, in Sardinian) Peter, son of Judge Hugh II of Arborea, was knighted by the new King of Aragon, Alfonso IV. This event is particularly significant for at least three key reasons: (1) the young heir to the *Giudicato* had made the explicit request for knighthood; (2) he was appointed by a king during the important enthronement ceremony; and (3) he was the second of the eighteen new knights personally created by the monarch.[14] This confirmed the policy of inclusion of the Arborea dynasts in the Iberian aristocracy desired by the Aragonese sovereigns and not only them. It was also desired by Judge Hugh of Arborea himself. It should be noted that the first of these knights was Pere de Exerica, the natural son of King James II of Aragon and therefore half-brother of King Alfonso IV himself, and that Pere married Bonaventura of Arborea, one of Judge Hugh II's daughters, thus becoming brother-in-law of the future judges Peter (III) and Marianus (IV). Four years later, on 15 December 1332, King Alfonso IV informed Hugh II of Arborea of his intention to knight another his sons, Marianus, on the occasion of the young *donnikellu's* wedding.[15]

Two other important elements must be taken into account to grasp the extent of the policy of social, political, and economic cohesion between the two dynasties of the kings of Aragon and the judges of Arborea. The first is the policy of marriages extended to all the legitimate children of Hugh II. Apart from Bonaventura, another daughter of Hugh II, Maria, married Galceran de Rocabertí, brother of Timbors de

---

12   On 20 March 1293 King James II proposed to knight personally the son of Judge Mariano III of Arborea, if his father agreed; then he planned a possible marriage of the judge or his son with the daughter of the *Infanta* of Greece, who was 'of noble birth and great lineage'. Archivo de la Corona de Aragón (hereafter, ACA), *Cancillería*, reg. 252, fols 51^v–52, doc. 10, pp. 11–12.

13   We have pointed out several times the almost total absence of the *Militia* in the *Giudicati* societies, with some exceptions that concerned, however, knights coming from the Italian Peninsula or the Crown of Aragon. The absence of the *Militia* had important repercussions in the structure of the *Giudicati* armies: see Fois, 'L'organizzazione militare nel Giudicato d'Arborea'; Gallinari, 'Guglielmo III di Narbona'; Gallinari, 'Una società senza cavalleria?'; and Garau, *Mariano IV d'Arborea e la guerra*.

14   Muntaner, 'Crònica', p. 936, and *Diplomatario aragonés de Ugone II de Arborea*, doc. 194, pp. 241–42.

15   *Diplomatario aragonés de Ugone II de Arborea*, doc. 319, pp. 387–88.

Rocabertí, since 1336 wife of the future judge Marianus IV. John of Arborea married in 1337 Sibilla de Moncada, a member of another illustrious and powerful family of the Catalan nobility.

The second element is Marianus and John's stay at the court of the King of Aragon from 1331: the two *donnikkellos* arrived there at the age of ten–twelve years for their education. Some scholars supposed that during his long stay in Catalonia, from where he would leave for Sardinia only in 1342, Marianus IV took inspiration for the political and institutional management of the *Giudicato* of Arborea, which he led from 1347.[16]

John of Arborea and the Facilitation of Inclusion

One of the most interesting figures for analysing the social and economic cohesion between Aragonese and Sardinians is John of Arborea. This is because of his double, institutional position as a direct vassal of King Peter IV of Aragon, for some feudal concessions of territories/lands, and simultaneously as a *naturalis*, that is, a subject of the judge of Arborea. John tried to reconcile his dual role, but this was increasingly difficult after his brother Marianus became judge of Arborea in 1347. The sources clearly show that since the 1340s John was particularly appreciated by King Peter IV of Aragon. He enjoyed the sovereign's favour and trust, and consequently he obtained a series of rewards that considerably improved his economic and social status. A significant example was his nomination as lord of Monteacuto and Bosa made before the summer of 1338, when he returned to Sardinia with his new family.[17] The sources show that John was abundantly rewarded by King Peter IV as his zealous supporter.

He gained other, equally important, concessions which made him perhaps the most important royal vassal on the island, whose dominion could compete with that of the judge of Arborea himself. From a letter written on 12 August 1343 by the Aragonese governor general Guillem de Cervelló to King Peter IV, who asked him to export certain quantities of wheat, barley, and oats from Sardinia, we know that John of Arborea had had a special authorization for the trade in cereals, which he then gave to his brother, Judge Peter III.[18] This was a very important privilege, given the very valuable nature — not only economically but also strategically — of the goods he could trade.

---

16 Casula, *La Sardegna aragonese*, I: *La Corona d'Aragona*, pp. 232–34.
17 Monteacuto and other territories belonging to the former *Giudicato* of Logudoro constituted, at least from the beginning of the fourteenth century, a sort of prerogative of the sons of the judges of Arborea. In May 1331, Hugh II of Arborea assigned them to each of his two cadet sons, the *donnikkellos* Marianus (the future judge) and John. The castles of Goceano and Marmilla were assigned to the former, and the castles of Monteacuto and Barumele to the latter. Both assignments consisted of the relative pertinences of castles. These assignments were done *in feudum honoratum ad imperpetuum*. The judge's document was confirmed by King Alfonso IV of Aragon on 7 April 1332. After 3 April 1336, the new king Peter IV of Aragon confirmed to John of Arborea the title of Lord of Monteacuto, while on 11 September 1339 he granted to Marianus the title of Count of Goceano and Lord of Marmilla. For more details, see Soddu, 'Forme di decentramento del potere', pp. 45–50.
18 *Carte reali diplomatiche di Pietro IV il Cerimonioso* (hereafter, *CRD di Pietro IV*), pp. 87–88.

As further confirmation of this royal favour, between 1347 and November 1349 King Peter IV of Aragon granted John of Arborea the power to receive in his name the barony and the castle owned by the Doria barons, the most bitter enemy of the Crown in Sardinia. He was also responsible for starting a trial against the Dorias who had remained rebels against royal authority. However, in April 1346, news had spread in Sardinia of the death of the nobleman Galeotto Doria, lord of Castelgenovese (today Castelsardo), who in his will had appointed John of Arborea as guardian of his universal heir who, at the same time, was also his son-in-law.[19] Some documents seem to show very clearly how the Lord of Monteacuto tried to a certain extent to keep the balance in his political play with both more powerful parties.[20]

Finally, in the conflict between the King of Aragon and the judge of Arborea, John chose to support the Aragonese. His political and institutional choices seem to have been confirmed after his imprisonment by his brother, Judge Marianus IV, in November 1349. He was never released again, despite numerous requests by the king.[21] In this context, the testimony of Pere de Moncada, brother of Sibilla de Moncada, wife of John, is interesting. It was issued in August 1353 during the trial initiated by the royal officers against Judge Marianus IV, for his rebellion. The witness reported that, according to Sibilla, it would have been sufficient for John to have agreed with the judge to move against the King of Aragon to be released two years earlier.

We should not forget that this testimony was issued for a political trial against the judge of Arborea, and that it would report Sibilla de Moncada's interpretation of this conflict between the two brothers. She would therefore have had every interest in further discrediting her brother-in-law Marianus IV.

It was in the mid-fourteenth century that Marianus IV decided to begin the armed rebellion against the King of Aragon, because he resented the lack of rewards for all the political, logistical, economic, and military aid given to the kings of Aragon by his father and himself. The judge had previously expressed his interest in expanding his dominion in the direction of the towns of Alghero, Bosa, and in the region of Gallura. Except for the first city, which remained in royal hands from 1353 onwards, the other two possessions were confirmed and granted *ex novo* by the Aragonese sovereign to Marianus's brother.

At that point, the judge believed that there would be no possibility of either expanding his territorial possessions or improving his status, as had been promised

---

19 *CRD di Pietro IV*, doc. 266, p. 125.
20 *CRD di Pietro IV*, doc. 335, pp. 170–71.
21 John's double legal status — he was both a *Giudicato* subject and a direct vassal of the King of Aragon for his possessions of Bosa, Planargia, and Gallura — created a political and institutional conflict between him and his brother that was based on the very delicate theme of the judge's *iurisdictio* over each subject. The judge had the 'merum et mixtum imperium and the gladii potestas', that is, the faculty to investigate, torture, and punish every single person in the *Giudicato*. From this point of view, according to Marianus IV, the numerous requests for the liberation of his brother made by Bernat de Cabrera, royal lieutenant in Sardinia, violated the judge's *iurisdictio*, which was based on customs that dated back to a period for which there was no human memory of the opposite state. On the *iurisdictio*, see Fabbrini, '"Auctoritas", "Potestas" "Iurisdictio" in diritto romano', p. 492, n. 2, p. 493, n. 3, and p. 497; Ullmann, *Law and Politics in the Middle Ages*, p. 34; Mayali, 'De la juris auctoritas a la legis potestas', p. 131; and Caravale, *Ordinamenti giuridici dell'Europa medievale*, p. 524.

to his father Hugh II in the bull of enfeoffment of the *Giudicato* of Arborea. He felt he was supposed to be content to be considered a royal vassal like the others in the *Regnum*. That caused him to start his armed insurrection against King Peter IV of Aragon. In reality, if we look at it from a detached perspective, we must note that the House of Aragon granted various improvements in the legal and social status of the judges, as well as expansions of their area of influence, as we have already mentioned above. In the early 1340s, King Peter IV's attitude changed — because based on a precise political calculation he wanted to weaken the House of Arborea — and he created a competition between the brothers for royal favours. However, the king seems to have placed greater trust in John, possibly because of suspicions about Marianus's loyalty to him.

There is also one scholar who sees in the difficult relationship between Marianus IV and his brother

> l'apogeo e al tempo stesso la degenerazione di un fenomeno istituzionale radicato nella tradizione consuetudinaria dei regni giudicali [...] quello della condivisione e della frammentazione del potere e del territorio. Una 'fragilità costituzionale' alla quale Mariano oppone e impone una più moderna visione unificatrice ed accentratrice.[22]

> (the apogee and at the same time the degeneration of an institutional phenomenon rooted in the customary tradition of the Giudicati kingdoms [...] that of the sharing and fragmentation of power and territory. A 'constitutional fragility' to which Marianus opposes and imposes a more modern unifying and centralizing vision.)

The Social Cohesion between the Aragonese, Pisan, and Sardinian Institutions

Inside the Regnum Sardiniae et Corsicae: Thirteenth–Fourteenth Centuries

After having devoted our attention to what was happening at the top of Sardinian society, especially having focused on the political actions undertaken by the Aragonese sovereigns who sought to integrate the House of Arborea into the *Regnum*, now let us consider what occurred at the same time in the lower strata of that polity. Let us start with the situation of coexistence and social cohesion between Sardinians and the Pisans, the direct holders of one third of the island between 1297 (creation of the *Regnum*) and 1323 (start of the Aragonese conquest of the island).[23]

---

22 Soddu, 'Forme di decentramento del potere', p. 51. This scholar has recently returned to the subject of the nature of the power of the Sardinian *Iudices*: Soddu, 'Il potere regio nella Sardegna giudicale'.

23 On the commercial relations between Sardinia and the Crown of Aragon before the conquest of the island, see Soldani, *I mercanti catalani e la Corona d'Aragona in Sardegna*, with the references to the previous bibliography and historiography on this issue.

More than thirty years ago, when describing the so-called Pisan Sardinia, Sandro Petrucci pointed out that there was a small inter-regional trade in which the inhabitants of Sardinian origin also had a certain role. These people conducted commercial distribution of various products within the island, among different urban centres, and between these and the castles under the Tuscan Commune's authority. In addition, as regards the capital of the area ruled by Pisa, that is, *Castel di Castro*, there were Sardinians who resided in the so-called *Appendici* (i.e. the suburbs of *Castel di Castro*) and were integrated with the Tuscans to the point that they participated in their commercial activities on the island.[24]

The sources also show that there was a close cohesion between Tuscan migrants and Sardinian inhabitants. The latter were welcomed into the Pisan economic system on the island, and not only in *Castel di Castro*. These close relations were also found in the reverse direction. As a matter of fact, the basis for the jurisdictional activity of the city's *Castellani* was created both by the *Breve* of Pisan origin and also by the *Carta Loci*, called in Sardinian *Carta de Logu*, that is, a sort of civil and criminal code, of the former *Giudicato* of Calari which was conquered in 1257–1258 by Pisa allied to the other three Sardinian *Giudicati*. Most likely the *Carta* had been revised and adapted to apply to those territories now legally under the dominion of the Tuscan Commune.[25]

In this regard, a further demonstration of how much this cohesion of Sardinian and Tuscan legal tradition continued during the following years of the Aragonese dominion is given by Iberian sources. They attest that in the 1340s Sardinians were judged according to the local *Carta* about fifteen years after Pisa's political authority had almost totally disappeared from the *Regnum*.[26]

Civic and economic close relations between indigenous Sardinians and foreigners can be observed at the beginning of the fourteenth century. Among Sardinians who owned landed property some of them were called 'habitatores' (inhabitants), that is, native residents of *Castel di Castro*, while others were 'burgenses' (townsmen), that is, descendants of Pisa's citizens born on the island or in the city itself. These two categories of islanders living side by side were the result of the phenomenon of the urbanization of Sardinia in the second half of the thirteenth century. They seem to have been craftsmen who did not have a particularly high turnover, who had had professional relationships with Pisan merchants since the end of the thirteenth century. Sources

---

24 Petrucci, 'Aspetti della distribuzione commerciale in Sardegna', pp. 623–35. The *Appendici* were three quarters located on the slopes of the hill where the *Castel di Castro* itself stood. They were called *Bagnaria* (or *Lapola*), *Stampace*, and *Villanova*. We will return to them in more detail. A miscellaneous volume on the foundation of the settlement of *Castel di Castro* di Cagliari was published in 2015; see Zedda, ed., '1215–2015'.

25 *Statuti inediti della città di Pisa dal XII al XIV secolo*, II, p. 88; Fascetti, 'Aspetti dell'influenza e del dominio pisani in Sardegna nel Medio Evo', p. 32.

26 It was King Peter IV of Aragon himself who on 1 March 1342 ordered Guillem de Cervelló, governor of Sardinia, to judge, according to Sardinian custom and the *Carta* of Sardinians, Margiano de Pullo, inhabitant of the territory of Palma, and all the others accused of the death of Gregorio Regí. If the governor had already done otherwise by imposing fines, he would have had to revoke the provisions adopted. See *CRD di Pietro IV*, doc. 155, pp. 70–71.

also inform about the presence of Genoese, Neapolitans, Sicilians, and Umbrians in *Castel di Castro*. There were also merchants of Iberian origin, such as Catalans but especially Majorcans, who were often very closely related to representatives of the most important Pisan families in the Sardinian city. Iberian shipowners also operated in the city, and from 1301 a consul of the Catalans appointed by the *Consellers* of Barcelona was active there.[27]

Before the Aragonese military expedition, which began in 1323, several memorials and reports written mainly by clergymen suggested political strategies for the control of the island to the Iberian sovereign, and expressed the support and expectations of large sectors of Sardinian society — clergymen, nobles, and plebians — for a transfer of the island to the effective control of the Iberian Crown. These are very intriguing sources for their pragmatic purpose and the way they narrated events and situations within the island in relation to elites who held authority in Sardinia. These were the judges of Arborea but also the noble families of Italian origin such as Doria, Malaspina, and Gherardesca. The specific information these sources contain requires very careful analysis, since it is all too evident that these narratives were biased and served as *captationes benevolentiae regis* for their authors. Their attitude of open support for the Crown of Aragon was based on the fact that the Aragonese king was the feudal holder of the *Regnum* on behalf of the Apostolic See.

There is, however, one exception which is the letter written in 1303, or in years immediately close to that date, by the Dominican friar Federico de Fulgineo, the judge of Arborea's former confessor, who proposed to the king a more delicate political operation. In fact, he suggested to him a solution that would promote social cohesion between the migrating Iberians and the islanders. Even if he appears to act in favour of the Aragonese dynasty in Sardinia, he also supported the House of Arborea, by proposing almost covertly a prominent political role on the island for Judge Hugh II. For this purpose, his observations about the island people are noteworthy. Sardinians were presented in very negative terms as a sort of scattered flock ('Sunt enim modo Sardi velut oues non habentes pastorem'), and as rebels against the law and Aragonese king: 'volendo suo domino naturali tam optimo contra iura resistere' ([they] wanted to resist their natural and best lord against the law). They could not be governed by local elders because of widespread envy and their inexperience unless they were acting on behalf of an external authority. Therefore, Fulgineo made two recommendations to King James II: (1) to appoint 'homo aliquis prudens' (one wise man) — in all likelihood, the judge of Arborea himself — who would be able to mediate between Sardinians and their new feudal lord, and (2) to not deploy from the beginning a great war equipment that would have frightened islanders, although the friar believed it was useful to instil fear of war in them.[28]

---

27 D'Arienzo, 'Una nota sui consolati catalani in Sardegna nel secolo xɪv'; Batlle, 'Noticias sobre los negocios de mercaderes'; Cadeddu, 'Neri Moxeriffo, console dei catalani'.

28 Salavert y Roca, *Cerdeña y la expansión mediterranea*, doc. 55, pp. 76–77, [25 June 25, 1303?. Pisa]: 'populus ille Sardicus tot iam annorum curiculis insultibus conquassatus […] me nuper fuisse confessorem iudicis Arboree et ab eo beneficia mee conditionis paruitatem excedentiam recepisse, quare in Sardinia diutius conuersatus, extimo quedam ut regia maiestas vestra facilius et commodius

126   LUCIANO GALLINARI

Although the author presented an interesting picture of the early fourteenth-century Sardinian society, Fulgineo's narrative proposes a negative biased version of the political situation on the island and is not very reliable. We cannot neglect the fact that many people, such as Fulgineo himself, offered their services and expertise to the new *dominus* when it became clear that the Crown of Aragon would have undertaken the *Regnum*'s conquest. As soon as *Infant* Alfonso arrived at Sardinia he focused on the siege of the Pisan city of *Villa di Chiesa*, today's Iglesias. As the head of the Aragonese army he used in some of his initiatives both Sardinians and Pisans and other Tuscans, who were politically aligned with the Iberians. It is interesting to note that some of these Sardinians supporting the Aragonese ruler had offices given by the Commune of Pisa in the southern territories of the island, and held old *Giudicato* titles: they were 'armentari' (a kind of administrator), 'maiores, iudices de facto'. In addition, they owned property in *Castel di Castro* and were rewarded by the *Infant* Alfonso with feudal possessions in the surrounding area of the Pisan capital that he planned to conquer immediately after *Villa di Chiesa*.[29]

In addition to some Sardinians who immediately sided with the Aragonese and helped them in various ways with their conquest of Sardinia, the sources also show that many Sardinians who resided in the *Appendici* of *Castel di Castro* — mostly in the district of *Stampace* — formed an alliance with Pisan citizens resident in the *Castle* itself, who were engaged in defending themselves from the Aragonese landings. The Iberians, according to the *Memoria de las cosas que han aconteçido en el reino de Cerdeña*, took up position *al puerto de Cállar* (in the harbour of *Castel di Castro*), and both Pisans' and Sardinians' reaction against intruders was ready and effective: 'la gente del castillo et apéndicçes [...] fizieron muy grande estrago en la gente d'ellas' (the inhabitants of the *Castle* and the *Appendici* [...] made a great massacre among the people of them [the Aragonese galleys]).[30]

---

dictam insulam consequatur. [...] et quamuis inter eos sint quidam principaliores in quos respicit populus vniuersus, tamen illi inexperientia et invidia operante nequeunt dictum populum Sardicum sine diuisionibus et emulationibus gubernare. [...] Quamuis ergo bonum sit bellorum timorem eis ingerere, tamen puto quod in principio non esset melius magno apparatu armarum eos amplius deterrere, quia credunt quod si bello soiugauerunt aut se de Sardinia expellendos aut se omnes necis gladio morituros. Set optimus modus esset si predictos principaliores posset aliquis homo prudens, qui hoc sagaciter ageret per blanditias et pacis promissiones alicere, quia reliquus populus illo fertur quo hii principaliores eos deducunt'. About the dating of this letter: Casula, *La Storia di Sardegna*, p. 135, seems to be in favour of a period close to 1323, when the Kingdom of Sardinia and Corsica's conquest was undertaken.

29   Gonnario Camboli was captain of the village (*villa*) of Decimo and other localities in March 1324: ACA, *Cancillería, Secretorum*, reg. 396, fol. 118ᵛ (1324, marzo 12). He had previously been an *armentarius* of the village of Gippi: ACA, *Cancillería, Secretorum*, reg. 396, fol. 93ʳ (1323, gennaio 20). He owned two *alberchs* in the Street (*Ruga*) of the Elephant, one with seven attics and a shop, one in the Municipal Street (*Ruga*), and one and the half of another in the Merchants' Street (*Ruga*). Conde y Delgado de Molina and Aragó Cabañas, *Castell de Càller*, Text I, annotations 377, 505, 578, and 592, pp. 76, 87, 93, and 95; Text II, annotation 56, p. 117. Petrucci, 'Cagliari nel Trecento', p. 91.

30   The *Memoria de las cosas*. It is an anonymous chronicle of real and legendary events that occurred between 1005 and 1479 that is a quite difficult to assess accurately. Probably it was composed at the end of the fifteenth century in *Castell de Càller* compiling previous documentary and narrative

At that point, however, the *Infant* Alfonso would send a fleet of thirty other galleys that landed at the church of Santa Maria de Portu Gruttis, so-called because it stood in the former eastern Roman necropolis of *Karales*. Also on this second occasion, the collaboration between the Pisan inhabitants of the *Castle* and the Sardinians and other 'nationes' residing in the *Appendici* would have worked:

> Los de castillo de Cáller, viendo la tal cosa, comunicar[ro]n con los de los apéndiçes et hordenaron todos juntos, axì a pie como a cavallo, de dalle un salto.

> > (The inhabitants of *Castel di Castro,* seeing this, contacted those of the *Appendici* and ordered all to make an attack together, those on foot as well as those on horseback.)[31]

This chronicle is one of the few produced in Sardinia, and it is believed that it was composed in *Castell de Càller* in the fifteenth century based on documents that may have been collected from the former archives of the *Giudicato* of Arborea and the Marquisate of Oristano, its institutional successor, between 1420 and 1478. This hypothesis seems plausible because the historical narrative carried out by this source reveals a clear pro-Arborea character, by cleverly manipulating the real course of events and creating a kind of Sardinian ethnic identity in order to highlight two issues: (1) the elaboration of a historical 'discourse' on the presumed kingship of the judges of Arborea resulting from dynastic links with the Royal House of Navarre since the mid-eleventh century, and (2) the House of Arborea's decisive role in the Aragonese conquest of Sardinia.

Regarding issue (1) the *Memoria de las cosas* and Juan Francisco Fara, the most important Sardinian historian of the modern era, report a legend or popular tradition — with some slight variations — on an anonymous princess of Navarre. According to the *Memoria* she was exiled by her father since she had a love affair with an important knight of the kingdom. Instead, according to Fara, she was kidnapped without her father's knowledge, and brought by a storm to Ogliastra, on the eastern coast of Sardinia, in the mid-eleventh century. The woman was used by both sources to establish a kin relationship between the Arborea's rulers and the Navarrese royal family through her transfer to the area of Cape San Marco in the western coast near Tharros, the then capital of the *Giudicato* of Arborea.[32]

---

sources from Sardinia, Italy, and Catalonia of different ages and origins. Our oldest copy was written in Castilian perhaps between 1570 and 1585. It appears to be a text characterized by an interesting set of popular legends, behind which it shows a para-literary tradition also relevant from a historical-political point of view.

31 *Memoria de las cosas*, pp. 33–35.

32 Gallinari, 'Identity-Making Discourses', pp. 324–28. The *Memoria* does not mention explicitly the wedding between the princess and the judge of Arborea, but it does report that, for some time, she 'lived on the island of Sardinia'. The chronicle retains further explicit traces of the ties between the Princess of Navarre and the judges of Arborea, as a brief but meaningful reference to the escape of the inhabitants of Santa Igia — capital of the *Giudicato* of Calari, destroyed by Pisans in 1257–1258 — to the lands of the judge of Arborea 'that were entirely populated by the descendants of Navarre'. See *Memoria de las cosas*, pp. 4–8.

On the other hand, regarding issue (2) we can stress that we have some reservations about the presumed importance of Judge Hugh II of Arborea who was described by the *Memoria* as the main logistical and political support inside the island for the Iberians as he had a basic role in the foundation of the first Aragonese settlement in Sardinia, namely the fortress of *Bonaria*, from where the Iberians began to attack *Castel di Castro*. Personally we have some doubts about this narrative of events, since there is no evidence of the role of Hugh II as the founder of *Bonaria* in Iberian chronicles, although their authors extensively mentioned the judge of Arborea and his help in the Aragonese military operations.[33]

The clash between the kings of Aragon and the City of Pisa ended with the victory of the Iberian Crown that succeeded the Pisan Commune in the direct control of two thirds of Sardinia. Regardless, the *Appendici* of the new Aragonese city of *Castell de Càller* continued to be the place of daily cohabitation and coexistence between Iberians, Sardinians, and Italians. It was only in the years around the mid-fourteenth century in conjunction with the beginning of Judge Marianus IV of Arborea's rebellion that the sources recorded a growing number of episodes of violence between members of various ethnicities, which indicate an increase in quarrels and insubordination against the city and royal authority. The phenomenon became more worrying for the Crown when the civic unrest became connected with the Arborea uprising, and it received support from some prominent inhabitants of the *Appendice* of Stampace.[34] This put in serious danger the cohesion of the society of the Aragonese city, because the situation of open war that continued during the government of Marianus IV (d. 1375) and his son Hugh III (d. 1383) also involved the Pisans still present throughout the south of the island.

A special mention should be made of the *Appendice* of Villanova located to the east of the *Castle*, a welcoming spot for many Sardinians coming from the villages of the *Campidano* plain and from the area of the ponds and salt pans that surrounded the capital of the *Regnum*. It was a popular location for Sardinians to migrate to, especially in the years immediately before and during the armed rebellion of Marianus IV of Arborea. During the war unfortified settlements located on flatlands were extremely unsafe. In these years the sources show several cases of islanders who sided with and remained loyal to the King of Aragon. Thanks to their new political alliance and to some links with powerful people of the *Regnum* such as the family of Carrós, they were able to consolidate their economic and social position and move to the *Appendice* of Villanova between the 1340s and 1350s. Here they are attested as merchants, shopkeepers, and officials in charge of controlling the sector of the provisioning of cereals for the capital. That was a task of great difficulty because of the war brought by the judge of Arborea. Assignments like these reveal the trust that Aragonese authorities had in these people.

---

33 Gallinari, 'An Important Political Discourse Pro-Judicate of Arborea', pp. 71–72.

34 Petrucci, 'Cagliari nel Trecento', p. 500, reports that seventeen inhabitants of *Stampace* are known in 1353 to have joined the anti-Aragonese rebellion, while for the second insurrection of 1364–1365 only three of them are attested. He also points out that almost all the known rebels of *Stampace* were Sardinians.

All sources, together with others from the Aragonese Archives, show that during the last years of the long reign of King Peter IV (1336–1387), the judges' propaganda did not convince all the islanders to fight against the Aragonese. Many of the peoples living in the *Giudicato* and the *Regnum*'s territories did not accept the war against the Iberians and moved consciously to *Castell de Càller*. The number of these migrants reached such a level in 1379 that it was necessary to reserve one-third of *Castell de Càller*'s customs revenues to keep them alive.[35] Financial documents show how the Aragonese sovereign ordered that the incomes of the duties from the salt pans of *Castell de Càller* were to be used to support these Sardinians who gave up the equalization of their legal status to that of Catalans and Aragonese, the two founding *nationes* of the Crown itself. Moreover, he assigned to them or even to their widows some pensions to allow a decorous survival within the city or in its immediate surroundings.[36]

Inside the Giudicato *of Arborea: Fourteenth–Fifteenth Centuries*

In the previous section we reflected on the internal situation of the *Regnum* and the difficulties for a peaceful coexistence and subsequent cohesion of Sardinian-Aragonese society. Now we will look at the internal situation of the *Giudicato* of Arborea between the fourteenth century and the first decades of the fifteenth century. In this case the difficulties for the historian are greater because of the scarcity of the sources produced in the small Sardinian 'state', some of which are preserved as copies contained in sources kept outside the island. In fact, we have to use almost exclusively documents produced outside Sardinia, especially texts written by the Aragonese, which makes situation a little more complicated.

What is striking in the centuries-old history of the *Giudicato* of Arborea is that in both the internal and external sources a specific family or an aristocratic or oligarchic group — with the names of its members — that was able to somehow compete with judges of Arborea's power was never mentioned. Their dynasty maintained its position through various changes and genealogical grafts, perhaps from 1073,[37] almost until 1420, when the small Sardinian polity disappeared. And this is an element that should certainly be taken into account when trying to draw a picture of the economic

---

35 Anatra, 'Dall'unificazione aragonese ai Savoia', p. 273.

36 See the cases of Rayner Pisquella, a native of Bosa who moved to the *Appendice* of *Stampace* (28 March 1380), or Giovanni de Querqui, who was able to enjoy the properties owned in Alghero as if he were of Catalan or Aragonese nationality: 'ac si essetis de nacione Cathalanorum vel Aragonensium genitus seu productus' (8 April 1380): ACA, *Cancillería, Sardiniae*, reg. 1046, fols 41^r–42^r and 105^r–106^r.

37 The archon/judge of Arborea is known from three seals, two of which were initially dated to the eleventh century: that of Zerkis (Ζερκις ἄρχων Αρβορέας), and Ο[ρ]ζόκορ, who was presumably Orzokor I of Zori identified as the *giudice* Torbennios, who is known from early twelfth-century sources. See Zucca, 'Zerkis, iudex arborensis', pp. 1109–11; *Il Condaghe di Santa Maria di Bonarcado*, p. 35; Zucca, 'Il castello di Laconi e le origini del Giudicato d'Arborea', p. 125; Spanu and Zucca, *I sigilli bizantini della Sardenia*, pp. 31 and 145–46; Spanu and others, 'L'Arcontato d'Arborea tra Islam ed eredità bizantina', p. 529. See also the more recent considerations by Muresu, *La moneta 'indicatore'*, pp. 356–59.

and social life of the *Giudicato* and medieval Sardinia, because this small local 'state' and its society appears undoubtedly cohesive in the sources at least until the 1380s. Afterwards, the documents allow us to see in the time span of about forty years several strong social and political upheavals of the *Giudicato* society, which was tired of forced coexistence with the Aragonese in the narrow geographical area of the island.

The definition of a cohesive society applied to the *Giudicato* of Arborea needs some explanation. To do this, we intend to use the data that also comes from the reading of a precious source, which is extremely rich in information about the interior of the *Giudicato* society between the twelfth and early thirteenth centuries: the *Condaghe di Santa Maria di Bonarcado*. Although the monastic register described a lengthy interval, it does not show any personage capable of competing with the power of the judges' dynasty, whose members are the protagonists of the life of Arborea not only because they sit on the *Giudicato* throne, but also because their family in the broadest meaning of the term controlled the main public offices (*curadores, armentarios, mayores*, etc.). The only other protagonists of the life of the *Giudicato* are the high officials of the Church: archbishops, bishops, and abbots.

It should be noted that the dynasty of judges remained practically unchallenged in the management of power for almost the entire period between 1321 (when Hugh II ascended to the *Giudicato* throne) and 1410 (stipulation of the *Capitulationes* of St Martin, which sanctioned the return to royal obedience of a third of the *Giudicato*'s territory, including its capital Oristano). In fact, even in three moments of serious internal trouble the sources do not allow us to identify individuals or families belonging to the *Giudicato* oligarchy that tried to counteract or deprive the official dynasty of its power. The sources' authors were always very general in indicating the existence of groups opposing the *Giudicato*'s rulers and their politics, which from the mid-1350s was aimed solely at the direct clash with the kings of Aragon.

A careful analysis of the sources coming mostly from the Iberian Peninsula, but in some cases also from Arborea, allows us to understand that in the second half of the fourteenth century and the very first years of the *Quattrocento* the political and social cohesion within the *Giudicato* of Arborea was obtained through a harsh exercise of authority by rulers such as Marianus IV and his son Hugh III.[38] But once the position of the rulers was challenged by their subjects, the Sardinians, it was not easy to return to the old ways of exercising power. That applies even to Brancaleone Doria, count of Monteleone and husband of Leonor of Arborea, daughter of Marianus IV, who

---

38 There are documents and testimonies that prove that Marianus IV ordered his officers in charge of recruiting foreign Sardinians to the *Giudicato* to mutilate and even kill those who refused to join the Arborea army. As an example, see the letter of Marianus IV, issued on 29 September [1353] and fallen into the hands of the Catalans, in which the judge ordered Azzo da Modena and Cino de Sori to verify how many armed people were available in each village of the former *Giudicato* of Calari, and in the event that the inhabitants of those villages had tried to drive them away, as had happened before, they should have condemned them immediately to the gallows, so that without hesitation these people would take sides with him, and not capture them and bring them to Oristano. *CRD di Pietro IV*, doc. 425, p. 218. On the death of Hugh III, see Putzulu, 'L'assasinio di Ugone III d'Arborea' and Tanda, 'La tragica morte del giudice Ugone III d'Arborea', pp. 91–115.

ruled the *Giudicato* on behalf of his wife and his son, Judge Marianus V, from 1390 until 1407, when the last member of the Doria Bas House was killed, a gesture that allowed the definitive removal of the Doria family from the *Giudicato*'s political scene.[39]

It is striking that the sources did not mention conspiracies or rebellions organized by elites of *Giudicato* society against Judge Marianus IV, while attesting three episodes of conspiracies or rebellion that happened consecutively during the government of Hugh III (1375–1383), the regency of Leonor of Arborea (1383–1392?), and finally during Brancaleone Doria's *de facto* government (1390–1407). These upheavals are actually three attempted coups against the judges which had different outcomes. The first ended with the murder of Judge Hugh III and his little daughter and heir in 1383. The second was an initiative led by an indefinite *populus Sardinie* which declared himself ready to return to royal obedience under some conditions.[40] The third attempt to get rid of the judges occurred in 1410 a few months after the defeat suffered by the *Giudicato* army in the Battle of Sanluri on 30 June 1409.

The most interesting aspect of these three attempts to subvert the political order established in the *Giudicato* of Arborea is that they show Sardinians' hostility towards the local dynasty of the judges, openly displayed by at least the subjects of Oristano, the *Giudicato*'s capital, and the immediate surroundings. These three attempted coups represent two concepts: (1) the emergence at the surface of states of mind characterized by *animosity* or *dormant hostility* which were the result of a set of actions and discourses carried out mainly by the rulers of the *Giudicato* in the second half of the fourteenth century, and (2) a significant denial of many historiographical interpretations on the entire fourteenth- and fifteenth-century history of the *Giudicato* that has been interpreted in nationalistic terms as a relentless war between the *Sardinian nation* and the *Catalan nation*.[41] It is evident that the clash between the rulers and the society had much deeper social and economic roots and was independent of the dominant ethnicity within the *Giudicato* society.

The Social and Economic Cohesion between Sardinians and Aragonese in the Fifteenth and Sixteenth Centuries

Despite all the facts cited so far regarding the social and economic coexistence and cohesion between Sardinians and Iberians during the fourteenth century, we must stress the persistence of the open hostility between the *Giudicato* and the *Regnum* that hindered a fusion of Sardinians and Iberians both in the small island polity and in the Sardinian territory directly subject to the King of Aragon (*Regnum*). The prolonged political, institutional, and military conflict made the situation on the island completely

---

39 Gallinari, 'Nuovi dati su Mariano V sovrano di Arborea'; Gallinari, 'Nuevas hipótesis sobre la relación familiar'.

40 ACA, *Cancillería, Secretorum*, reg. 1295, fols 80ʳ–81ᵛ [13 May 1385. Girona].

41 For the last use and interpretation in nationalist and identitarian terms of the political, economic, and sociocultural effects of the clash between the Aragonese and the Sardinians, see Gallinari, 'La batalla de Sanluri'.

unstable until at least 1420, when King Alfonso V of Aragon bought the rights to the Arborea from William II, viscount of Narbonne, the last judge who had tried to maintain his possessions despite the secession of a third of the historical territory of the *Giudicato*, which in 1410 was transformed into the Marquisate of Oristano. The story of Leonardo Cubello, its ruler, can also be seen as paradigmatic for the search for personal and dynastic cohesion, since he became the founder of a new House equated at his request with the barons of the Crown of Aragon.[42]

In the time span 1410–1420 some notables of the former *Giudicato* and its new capital, Sassari, obtained important institutional and political roles on the island, together with titles and assignments from King Alfonso V of Aragon to ensure their social insertion within the new institutional structure, the *Regnum*, which now included all of Sardinia.[43] From that moment on, a relatively peaceful period began between the Aragonese and the Sardinians. And that applied both to those living in the territory of the former *Giudicato* and those who, although residing outside it, had joined the Arborea's cause and had opposed the return of Iberian authority for longer. It was a difficult and slow process because the relationships based on mutual trust had been undermined by many decades of bloody war.[44]

Now we would like to focus on a few cases of coexistence and social inclusion in *Castell de Càller*, between the third decade of the fifteenth century and the beginning of the next century, observed through the last wills. This type of document is a rich source of data which is very useful for reconstructing a variety of personal and social relationships. The period covered by these sources partly overlaps with the long time span of internal peace that the island enjoyed for almost sixty years from 1420 to 1478. Once again, the attention is focused on the city because it relies on sources which are not numerous but are very informative for the subject of this book and have been scrupulously analysed by researchers.[45] The results of their work offer extremely stimulating data, since they point in the direction of a cohesion between the two *nationes* — the Sardinian and the Aragonese — in the broadest sense used in this chapter. A cohesion which, in fact, advanced faster than has been suggested by historians until recently.

An important element for understanding the difference between this city and other regions of the island subject to the authority of the judges of Arborea is that *Castell de Càller*, although it had been attacked several times by the judges' army

---

42 Gallinari, 'Guglielmo III di Narbona'; Sini, 'Elia de Palmas'; Sini, 'Reflections on the Socio-political and Cultural Transmissions', pp. 101–16; Gallinari, 'The Catalans in Sardinia and the Transformation of Sardinians'.

43 On the city of Sassari, see at least Mattone and Tangheroni, eds, *Economia, società, istituzioni a Sassari nel Medioevo e nell'età moderna*; Gallinari, 'Sassari', pp. 357–63; Simbula and Soddu, 'Gli spazi dell'identità cittadina tra signori'; Soddu, 'Le subordinazioni delle città comunali'.

44 Gallinari, 'Ethnic Identity in Medieval Sardinia'.

45 See among others Olla Repetto, 'La donna cagliaritana tra '400 e '600'; Oliva, 'Cagliari catalana nel Quattrocento'; Martí Sentañes, 'El poder urbano en clave identitaria'; Oliva, 'Mobilità sociale, ceti cittadini e potere regio nella Cagliari catalana'; Guia Marín, 'La construcción de un espacio político' and the bibliography contined therein; and Meloni, 'Society and Identity in Fifteenth-Century Cagliari Testaments'.

during the long war, was never conquered after 1326. In that year it was entirely repopulated by exclusively Iberian people, while Sardinians, Pisans, and foreigners were expelled and resided in the *Appendici*.[46] As has been pointed out by the scholar who has recently dedicated herself to the analysis of the fusion between Sardinians and Iberians, some sources examined in recent years show 'a slow integration process' and the revival of the attractiveness of this city not only for 'new inhabitants from the Crown's mainland kingdoms', but also for Sardinian villagers.[47] This city seems to have been attractive partly as a result of the end of the wars with the *Giudicato* of Arborea, and also by the situation of the peninsular territories of the Crown, where the consequences of the Catalan civil war (1462–1472) were experienced.[48]

With regard to the inclusion and cohesion between Sardinians and Aragonese, a paradigmatic person is Masedo Meli, a merchant of Sardinian origin. He was one of the few entrepreneurs documented by sources who achieved a good social position in the trade of Sardinian products even outside the island, in Iberian cities such as Barcelona and Valencia.[49] He is also an interesting figure because he retained an awareness of his origins. Although he resided in the *Appendice* of Villanova he was originally from the village of Laconi, which received a donation from him for the restoration of a chapel built by his father in the parish church of the village.

With regard to the social cohesion between Aragonese and Sardinians, perhaps the most interesting fact that emerges from recent research is that the testaments seem to confirm what has already been supposed in recent studies, namely that

> during the fifteenth century, the ethnic and spatial division between Sardinians, residents in the appendici, and Catalans living in Castello, was not clear as had been believed for a long time, and despite the royal regulation that established precise boundaries, the barriers were not rigid, and permitted frequent exchanges and contacts. Therefore, an osmosis of cultures, and a mixture of modes of existence, were frequent.[50]

Previous studies have highlighted the case of the *cirurgicus* Rafael Aguilar, originally from Barcelona but resident in the *Appendice* of Lapola, who named as his universal heir the maidservant from whom he had a daughter, thus demonstrating that he felt an integral part of the social reality in which he lived.[51] Another exemplary case is that of the *Stampace* merchant Julià Scamado, whose social rise was achieved thanks to his economic position and his friendships that allowed him to obtain permission to reside in the *Castle* itself and marry a Catalan woman.[52]

---

46 Conde y Delgado de Molina and Aragó Cabañas, *Castell de Càller*; Petrucci, 'Cagliari nel Trecento'.
47 Meloni, 'Society and Identity in Fifteenth-Century Cagliari Testaments', p. 91.
48 Anatra, 'Cagliari e il suo territorio'.
49 On the commercial relations between Sardinia and Valencia, see the recent work of Seche, 'Il carteggio mercantile Dessì-Navarro', and the references therein.
50 Meloni, 'Society and Identity in Fifteenth-Century Cagliari Testaments', pp. 94–95.
51 Archivio di Stato di Cagliari, Atti notarili, Tappa di Cagliari, Atti sciolti, notary Pietro Baster, vol. 45, fol. 14^{r-v}, pp. 286–89.
52 Meloni, 'Society and Identity in Fifteenth-Century Cagliari Testaments', p. 96.

Before concluding this description there is another aspect of the role of melting pot played by *Castell de Càller* in the fifteenth century that we want to highlight. Funeral rites and the religious legacies arranged by the deceased show how the high level of fusion between the Sardinian people of the *Appendici* and the Aragonese occurred.[53] The cohesion of men of island and Iberian origin did not mean the total acculturation of Sardinians. The process can take the opposite direction, widening scope for cultural practices specific to the Sardinians, as in the case of the devotion to Our Lady of Bonaria, whose cult was born in Catalan *Castell de Càller* and who today is the patron saint of Sardinia. A perfect example of coexistence of both ethnicities is the fact that the cult of the Virgin Mary of Montserrat did not eliminate the worship of Sardinian martyrs; this cult was brought to the island at the end of the Middle Ages during the *Giudicati* Age (eleventh–fifteenth centuries).[54]

Finally, research has shown that this merger between ethnicities took place more quickly in the lower strata of society than among elites but later spread to the upper strata. After a period of relative peace lasting about half a century, there was the last blaze of rebellion that seemed to be related to the wars of the previous century because of the political and identitarian way the name 'Arborea' was used as an agglutinative of indigenous identities. It happened for the last time in 1478, during the military clash between Leonardo de Alagón — the last Marquis of Oristano and a distant descendant of the judges — and Nicolàs Carròs of Arborea, viceroy of Sardinia. The Sardinians rose up, shouting the former *Giudicato*'s name, and experienced the last defeat which marked the definitive disappearance of the Marquisate of Oristano and the final demise of Sardinian rebellions, but not of the evocative power of the name *Arborea*.[55]

Conclusions

The multiple ways in which the sources can be read and analysed enable us to overcome many misconceptions and stereotypes that have developed over many decades about relations between the Aragonese and Sardinians. These are still a negative feature of the historiography of medieval Sardinia that continues to interpret the island's history within the context of categories such as nationalism.[56] All attempts at interpretation using strict definitions of identity in relation to 'Others' show more and more clearly

---

53 An example is the request of all those who made a will, whether they lived in the *Castle* or in the *Appendici* of the city, to celebrate as 'a *post mortem* ritual, the *trentenari de san Amador*, a series of 33 masses celebrated for 33 consecutive days after death, accompanied by a ritual number of candles. This custom, highly widespread in Catalonia, Majorca, and to a certain extent throughout the Iberian peninsula, appears to have become, in the mid-fifteenth century, common heritage for all the city's inhabitants'. Meloni, 'Society and Identity in Fifteenth-Century Cagliari Testaments', p. 99.

54 Meloni, *Il santuario della Madonna di Bonaria*; Coroneo, 'Il culto dei martiri locali Saturnino'.

55 Sini, 'Reflections on the Socio-political and Cultural Transmissions'.

56 See as an example the survival of these historiographic stereotypes mentioned in the recent miscellaneous volume Hobart, ed., *A Companion to Sardinian History*.

their fragility when new documentary and narrative sources offer a more articulated vision of cohesion and coexistence rather than a rigid nationalistic opposition, as we have tried to propose so far.

The analysis of the sources we have mentioned in this chapter, in addition to those we have been studying for several years now in an attempt to reconstruct the history and relations between Sardinia and the Iberian world in the broadest sense of the term, leads us to evaluate a hypothesis that we had already formulated with much less supporting evidence thirteen years ago in our second doctoral thesis. Today, a fortiori, thanks to a careful reading of the published sources and the discovery of further unpublished documents, we can reiterate with even more data that what has been presented as a nationalistic clash between Sardinians and the Aragonese was a purely political and institutional confrontation pursued by some judges of Arborea, from the mid-fourteenth century onwards. And in order to rally the Sardinian people against the 'invader', they made extensive use of nationalistic and identity-based discourse. In so doing, they acted in perfect synchrony with many other European dynasties with an extremely prestigious past and a princely status, who were hostile towards the feudal ties that made strong bonds with their sovereigns.

Why did the judges do it? Because they were the ones who had the most to lose from the increasing inclusion of the Arborea and Sardinian society within the *Regnum*.

In this perspective, Marianus IV, his children Hugh III and Leonor, and later Brancaleone Doria, although they had very different human and political personalities, rejected militarily their new social identity that was born from the encounter with Aragonese society, unlike the rest of the middle and lower social strata of the island who showed much greater ease in merging with the 'Other'.

This provides a better understanding of why, despite the long war between islanders and the Aragonese (1353–1420, though not continuously), during the fifteenth century, especially in *Castell de Càller*, the coexistence and the creation of a new Sardinian-Aragonese society proceeded, notwithstanding the new insurrection by the Marquises of Oristano, which ended in 1478 and temporarily slowed down the process of consolidation that accelerated again at the beginning of the sixteenth century.

Works Cited

Manuscripts and Archival Sources

Archivio di Stato di Cagliari, Atti notarili, Tappa di Cagliari, Atti sciolti, notary Pietro Baster, vol. 45, fol. 14^{r-v}, ed. by Gabriella Olla Repetto, 'Notai sardi del secolo XV: Pietro Baster', in *Studi storici e giuridici in onore di Antonio Era* (Padova: Cedam, 1963), pp. 269–98

Archivo de la Corona de Aragón, *Cancillería, Cancillería, Sardiniae, Cancillería, Secretorum* in Vicente Salavert y Roca, *Cerdeña y la expansión mediterranea*, vol. II (Madrid: Consejo Superior de Investigaciones Científicas, 1956)

Colección de documentos inéditos del Archivo General de la Corona de Aragón, ed. by Próspero de Bofarull y Mascaró, vol. IV (Barcelona: D. José Eusebio Monfort, 1849)

Primary Sources

Carte reali diplomatiche di Pietro IV il Cerimonioso, re d'Aragona, riguardanti l'Italia, ed. by Luisa D'Arienzo (Padova: CEDAM, 1970)

Codice Diplomatico della Sardegna, ed. by Pasquale Tola, presentation by Alberto Boscolo, introduction by Francesco Cesare Casula (Sassari: Carlo Delfino editore, 1984)

Il Condaghe di Santa Maria di Bonarcado, ed. by Maurizio Virdis (Cagliari: CUEC, 2002)

Diplomatario aragonés de Ugone II de Arborea, ed. by Rafael Conde y Delgado de Molina (Sassari: Fondazione Banco di Sardegna, 2005)

Memoria de las cosas que han aconteçido en algunas partes del reino de Cerdeña, ed. by Paolo Maninchedda (Cagliari: CUEC, 2000)

Muntaner, Ramon, 'Crònica', in *Les quatre grans cròniques*, ed. by Ferran Soldevila (Barcelona: Editorial Selecta, 1971), pp. 664–1000

Das Register Gregors VII, I: Buch I–IV, ed. by E. Caspar, Monumenta Germaniae Historica: Epistolae selectae, 2 (Berlin, 1920)

Sánchez Casabón, Ana Isabel, *Alfonso II Rey de Aragón, Conde de Barcelona y Marqués de Provenza: Documentos (1162–1196)* (Zaragoza: Institución 'Fernando el Católico', 1995)

Statuti inediti della città di Pisa dal XII al XIV secolo raccolti e illustrati per cura del prof. F. Bonaini (Florence: Vieusseux, 1854–1857)

Secondary Studies

Anatra, Bruno, 'Cagliari e il suo territorio', in *La società sarda in età spagnola*, ed. by Francesco Manconi, vol. 1 (Cagliari: Consiglio regionale della Sardegna, 2003), pp. 48–55

——, 'Dall'unificazione aragonese ai Savoia', in John Day, Bruno Anatra, and Lucetta Scaraffia, *La Sardegna medioevale e moderna*, vol. x of *Storia d'Italia*, ed. by Giuseppe Galasso (Turin: UTET, 1984), pp. 189–663

Arribas Palau, Antonio, *La conquista de Cerdeña por Jaime II de Aragón* (Barcelona: Instituto Espanol de Estudios Mediterraneos, 1952)

Artizzu, Francesco, 'Penetrazione catalana in Sardegna nel secolo XII', in *Pisani e catalani nella Sardegna medioevale*, ed. by Francesco Artizzu (Padova: CEDAM, 1973), pp. 9–23

Batlle, Carmen, 'Noticias sobre los negocios de mercaderes de Barcelona en Cerdena hacia 1300', in *La Sardegna nel mondo mediterraneo: Atti del primo Convegno internazionale di studi geografico-storici (Sassari, 7–9 aprile 1978)*, II: *Gli aspetti storici*, ed. by Manlio Brigaglia (Sassari: Gallizzi, 1981), pp. 277–89

Cadeddu, Maria Eugenia, 'L'espansione catalano-aragonese nel Mediterraneo: Riflessi nella storiografia iberica contemporanea', in *Quel mar che la terra inghirlanda: Studi mediterranei in ricordo di Marco Tangheroni*, ed. by Franco Cardini and Maria Luisa Ceccarelli Lemut (Rome: Pacini editore, 2007), pp. 149–55

——, 'Giacomo II d'Aragona e la conquista del regno di Sardegna e Corsica', in 'Corona d'Aragona e Mediterraneo: Strategie d'espansione, migrazioni e commerci', ed. by Maria Eugenia Cadeddu, special issue, *Medioevo: Saggi e rassegne*, 20 (1995), 251–316

——, 'Neri Moxeriffo, console dei catalani a Castel di Castro nel 1320', *Anuario de Estudios Medievales*, 28 (1999), 197–206

Caravale, Mario, *Ordinamenti giuridici dell'Europa medievale* (Bologna: Il Mulino, 1994)

Casula, Francesco Cesare, *La Sardegna aragonese*, 1: *La Corona d'Aragona* (Sassari: Chiarella, 1990)

———, *La Storia di Sardegna* (Sassari: Carlo Delfino, 1994)

Conde y Delgado de Molina, Rafael, and Antonio M. Aragó Cabañas, *Castell de Càller: Cagliari Catalano aragonese* (Cagliari: Istituto sui rapporti italo-iberici del CNR, 1984)

Coroneo, Roberto, 'Il culto dei martiri locali Saturnino, Antioco e Gavino nella Sardegna giudicale', *Mélanges de l'École Française de Rome. Moyen Âge*, 118.11 (2006), 5–16

D'Arienzo, Luisa, 'Una nota sui consolati catalani in Sardegna nel secolo XIV', *Anuario de Estudios Medievales*, 10 (1980), 593–610

Fabbrini, Fabrizio, '"Auctoritas", "Potestas" "Iurisdictio" in diritto romano', *Apollinaris: Commentarius instituti utriusque iuris*, 51.1–2 (1978), 492–561

Fascetti, Bianca, 'Aspetti dell'influenza e del dominio pisani in Sardegna nel Medio Evo: II. Condizioni economiche e sociali', *Bollettino storico Pisano*, 10 (1941), 1–72

Fois, Graziano, 'L'organizzazione militare nel Giudicato d'Arborea', *Medioevo: Saggi e rassegne*, 13 (1988), 35–51

Gallinari, Luciano, 'La batalla de Sanluri: Un pretexto para una nueva interpretación nacionalista e identitaria de la historia medieval sarda', *Aragón en la Edad Media*, 32 (2021), 147–85

———, 'The Catalans in Sardinia and the Transformation of Sardinians into a Political Minority (12th–15th Centuries)', *Journal of Medieval History*, 45.3 (2019), 347–59

———, 'Ethnic Identity in Medieval Sardinia: Rethinking and Reflecting on 14th and 15th Century Examples', in *Perverse Identities: Identities in Conflict*, ed. by Flocel Sabaté (Bern: Peter Lang Publishers, 2015), pp. 81–117

———, 'Feelings and Political Discourses in the Giudicati Sardinia (11th–13th Centuries)', in *International Medieval Meeting, Lleida, 2017* (York: ARC Humanities Press, forthcoming)

———, 'Guglielmo III di Narbona, ultimo sovrano d'Arborea, e la guerra dei Cent'anni', *Medioevo: Saggi e rassegne*, 18 (1993), 91–121

———, 'Identity-Making Discourses in the Kingdom of Sardinia and Corsica and the Giudicato of Arborea', in *Identity in the Middle Ages*, ed. by Flocel Sabaté i Curull (York: Arc Humanities Press, 2021), pp. 309–28

———, 'An Important Political Discourse Pro-Judicate of Arborea Drawn up in the Capital of the Catalan-Aragonese Regnum Sardinie et Corsice (14th–15th c.)', in *Centri di potere nel Mediterraneo occidentale dal Medioevo alla fine dell'Antico Regime*, ed. by Lluis J. Guia Marin, Maria Grazia Rosaria Mele, and Giovanni Serreli (Milan: Franco Angeli, 2018), pp. 65–73

———, 'The *Iudex Sardiniae* and the *Archon Sardanias* between the Sixth and the Eleventh Century', in *The Making of Medieval Sardinia*, ed. by Alex Metcalfe, Hervin Fernández-Aceves, and Marco Muresu (Leiden: Brill, 2021), pp. 204–39

———, 'Nuevas hipótesis sobre la relación familiar entre Brancaleone Doria y el futuro juez de Arborea Mariano V en las fuentes de finales del siglo XIV', *RiMe: Rivista dell'Istituto di Storia dell'Europa Mediterranea*, 11.1 (December 2013), 191–232, <https://doi.org/10.7410/1081>

———, 'Nuovi dati su Mariano V sovrano di Arborea', *Medioevo: Saggi e rassegne*, 21 (1996), 127–46

————, 'Reflections on Byzantine Sardinia between Seventh and Eleventh Centuries in the Light of Recent Historiographical Proposals', in *Ricordando Alberto Boscolo: Bilanci e prospettive storiografiche*, ed. by Maria Giuseppina Meloni, Anna Maria Oliva, and Olivetta Schena (Rome: Viella, 2015), pp. 83–107

————, 'Sassari: Da capitale giudicale a città regia', in *El món urbà a la corona d'Aragó del 1137 als decrets de Nova Planta: XVII Congrés de Història de la Corona d'Aragó*, III: *Barcelona-Lleida, 2000* (Barcelona: Universitat de Barcelona, 2003), pp. 357–63

————, 'Una società senza cavalleria? Il Giudicato di Arborea e la Corona d'Aragona tra XIV e XV secolo', *Anuario de Estudios Medievales*, 33.2 (2003), 849–79

Garau, Andrea, *Mariano IV d'Arborea e la guerra nel Medioevo in Sardegna* (Cagliari: Condaghes, 2017)

Guia Marín, Lluis, 'La construcción de un espacio político: Cagliari y sus apéndices', in *Mediterraneo e città: Discipline a confronto*, ed. by Lluis Guia Marín, Maria Grazia Mele, and Giovanni Serreli (Milan: Franco Angeli, 2018), pp. 31–48

Hobart, Michelle, ed., *A Companion to Sardinian History* (Leiden: Brill, 2017)

Manconi, Francesco '"De no poderse desmembrar de la Corona de Aragón": Sardegna e Paesi catalani, un vincolo lungo quattro secoli', *Archivio Sardo: Rivista di studi storici e sociali*, n.s., 1 (1999), 25–47

Martí Sentañes, Esther, 'El poder urbano en clave identitaria: Notas sobre las oligarquías catalano-aragonesas a través del Llibre Verd de Cagliari', in *Sardegna e Catalogna officinae di identità: Riflessioni storiografiche e prospettive di ricerca. Studi in memoria di Roberto Coroneo*, ed. by Alessandra Cioppi (Cagliari: CNR-ISEM, 2013), pp. 387–431

Mattone, Antonello, and Marco Tangheroni, eds, *Economia, società, istituzioni a Sassari nel Medioevo e nell'età moderna* (Cagliari: Edes, 1986)

Mayali, Laurent, 'De la juris auctoritas a la legis potestas: Aux origines de l'état de droit dans la science juridique medievale', in *Droits savants et pratiques françaises du pouvoir (XIᵉ–XVᵉ siècles)*, ed. by Jacques Krynen and Albert Rigaudière (Bordeaux: Université de Bordeaux, 1992), pp. 129–49

Meloni, Maria Giuseppina, *Il santuario della Madonna di Bonaria: Origini e diffusione di un culto* (Rome: Viella, 2011)

————, 'Society and Identity in Fifteenth-Century Cagliari Testaments', in *Sardinia from the Middle Ages to Contemporaneity: A Case Study of a Mediterranean Island Identity Profile*, ed. by Luciano Gallinari (Bern: Peter Lang, 2018), pp. 89–100

Metcalfe, Alex, 'Muslim Contacts with Sardinia: From Fatimid Ifriqiya to Mujāhid of Dénia', in *The Making of Medieval Sardinia*, ed. by Alex Metcalfe, Hervin Fernández-Aceves, and Marco Muresu (Leiden: Brill, 2021), pp. 250–60

Metcalfe, Alex, Hervin Fernández-Aceves, and Marco Muresu, eds, *The Making of Medieval Sardinia* (Leiden: Brill, 2021)

Muresu, Marco, *La moneta 'indicatore' dell'assetto insediativo della Sardegna bizantina (secoli VI–XI)* (Perugia: Morlacchi, 2018)

Oliva, Anna Maria, 'Cagliari catalana nel Quattrocento: Società, memoria, identità', in *Élites urbane e organizzazione sociale in area mediterranea tra tardo Medioevo e prima Età moderna*, ed. by Maria Giuseppina Meloni (Cagliari: CNR-ISEM, 2011), pp. 91–133

——, 'Mobilità sociale, ceti cittadini e potere regio nella Cagliari catalana', in *La mobilità sociale nel Medioevo italiano*, I, ed. by Lorenzo Tanzini and Sergio Tognetti (Rome: Viella, 2016), pp. 153–80

Olla Repetto, Gabriella, 'La donna cagliaritana tra '400 e '600', *Medioevo: Saggi e rassegne*, 11 (1986), 171–207

Petrucci, Sandro, 'Aspetti della distribuzione commerciale in Sardegna: Secoli XII–XIV', in *Mercati e consumi: Organizzazione e qualificazione del commercio in Italia dal XII al XX secolo, I Convegno Nazionale di Storia del commercio in Italia, Reggio Emilia, 6–7 giugno 1984* (Bologna: Analici, 1986), pp. 623–35

——, 'Cagliari nel Trecento: Politica, istituzioni, economia e società. Dalla conquista aragonese alla guerra tra Arborea ed Aragona (1323–1365)' (unpublished doctoral thesis, University of Sassari, 2006)

Pistarino, Geo, 'Genova e la Sardegna: Due mondi a confronto', in *La storia dei Genovesi: Atti del Convegno di studi sui ceti dirigenti nelle istituzioni della Repubblica di Genova*, IV (Genova: Brigati, 1984), pp. 191–236

——, 'Genova e la Sardegna nel secolo XII', in *La Sardegna nel mondo mediterraneo: Atti del primo Convegno internazionale di studi geografico-storici, Sassari, 7–9 aprile 1978*, II: *Gli aspetti storici*, ed. by Manlio Brigaglia (Sassari: Gallizzi, 1981), pp. 33–125

Putzulu, Evandro, 'L'assassinio di Ugone III d'Arborea e la pretesa congiura aragonese', *Anuario de Estudios Medievales*, 2 (1965), 333–57

Salavert y Roca, Vicente, *Cerdeña y la expansión mediterranea*, vol. II (Madrid: Consejo Superior de Investigaciones Científicas, 1956)

——, 'Un nuevo documento para la historia de Cerdeña', in *Studi storici in onore di Francesco Loddo Canepa*, vol. II (Florence: Sansoni Editore, 1959), pp. 301–12

Sanna, Mauro G., 'Papa Giovanni XXII, Giacomo II d'Aragona e la questione del Regnum Sardinie et Corsice', in *Tra diritto e storia: Studi in onore di Luigi Berlinguer promossi dalle Università di Siena e di Sassari*, ed. by Luigi Berlinguer, vol. II (Rubbettino: Soveria Mannelli, 2008), pp. 737–52

——, 'La Sardegna, il Papato e le dinamiche delle espansioni mediterranee', in *La Sardegna nel Mediterraneo tardomedievale*, ed. by Pinuccia Franca Simbula and Alessandro Soddu (Trieste: CERM, 2013), pp. 103–21

Seche, Giuseppe, 'Il carteggio mercantile Dessì-Navarro: Una fonte per le relazioni commerciali tra Valenza e la Sardegna nella seconda metà del Quattrocento', in *Commercio, finanza e guerra nella Sardegna tardomedievale*, ed. by Olivetta Schena and Sergio Tognetti (Rome: Viella, 2017), pp. 197–233

——, 'L'incoronazione di Barisone a "re di Sardegna" in due fonti contemporanee: Gli Annales genovesi e gli Annales Pisani', *RiMe: Rivista dell'Istituto di Storia dell'Europa Mediterranea*, 4 (June 2010), 73–93, <https://rime.cnr.it/index.php/rime/article/view/415>

Sedda, Franciscu, ed., *Sanluri 1409: La Battaglia per la Libertà della Sardegna* (Cagliari: Arkadia, 2019)

Simbula, Pinuccia F., and Alessandro Soddu, 'Gli spazi dell'identità cittadina tra signori e Corona nella Sardegna medievale', in *Identità cittadine e aggregazioni sociali in Italia, secoli XI–XV: Convegno di studio (Trieste, 28–30 giugno 2010)*, ed. by Miriam Davide (Trieste: CERM, 2012), pp. 135–73

Sini, Giovanni, 'Elia de Palmas: La professione di diplomatico ecclesiastico durante un periodo di mutamento a cavallo tra XIV e XV secolo', *RiMe: Rivista dell'Istituto di Storia dell'Europa Mediterranea*, 12 (June 2014), 107–36, <https://doi.org/10.7410/1107>

——, 'Reflections on the Socio-political and Cultural Transmissions at the End of the *Giudicato* of Arborea: Identity-Based Resistance and (Re)construction of Historic Memory?', in *Sardinia from the Middle Ages to Contemporaneity: A Case Study of a Mediterranean Island Identity Profile*, ed. by Luciano Gallinari (Bern: Peter Lang, 2018), pp. 101–16

Soddu, Alessandro, 'Forme di decentramento del potere nell'Arborea trecentesca: *Donnikellos, apanages* e *majorìa de pane*', *Bollettino di Studi Sardi*, 1 June 2008, pp. 39–71

——, 'Il potere regio nella Sardegna giudicale', in *Linguaggi e rappresentazioni del potere nella Sardegna medievale*, ed. by Alessandro Soddu (Rome: Carocci, 2020), pp. 13–88

——, 'Le subordinazioni delle città comunali. Un caso sardo: Sassari e la Corona d'Aragona (XIV secolo)', in *Le subordinazioni delle città comunali a poteri maggiori in Italia dagli inizi del secolo XIV all'ancien régime: Risultati scientifici della ricerca*, ed. by Miriam Davide (Trieste: CERM, 2014), pp. 69–110

Soldani, Maria Elisa, *I mercanti catalani e la Corona d'Aragona in Sardegna: Profitti e potere negli anni della conquista* (Rome: Viella, 2017)

Spanu, Pier Giorgio Ignazio, P. Fois, R. Zanella, and Raimondo Zucca, 'L'Arcontato d'Arborea tra Islam ed eredità bizantina', in *Tharros Felix*, vol. V, ed. by Attilio Mastino, Pier Giorgio Spanu, and Raimondo Zucca (Rome: Carocci, 2013), pp. 515–36

Spanu, Pier Giorgio, and Raimondo Zucca, *I sigilli bizantini della Sardenia* (Rome: Carocci, 2004)

Tanda, Renata, 'La tragica morte del giudice Ugone III d'Arborea alla luce di nuove fonti documentarie', in *Miscellanea di studi medoevale sardo-catalani* (Cagliari: Istituto sui rapporti italo-iberici del CNR, 1981), pp. 91–115

Ullmann, Walter, *Law and Politics in the Middle Ages: An Introduction to the Sources of Medieval Political Ideas* (London: Hodder and Stoughton, 1975)

Zedda, Corrado, ed., '1215–2015: Ottocento anni dalla fondazione del Castello di Castro di Cagliari', special issue, *RiMe: Rivista dell'Istituto di Storia dell'Europa Mediterranea*, 15.2 (December 2015), <https://rime.cnr.it/index.php/rime/issue/view/11>

——, 'Bisanzio, l'Islam e i giudicati: La Sardegna e il mondo mediterraneo tra VII e XI secolo', *Archivio Storico Giuridico Sardo di Sassari*, n.s., 10 (2006), 39–112

Zedda, Corrado, and Raimondo Pinna, 'La nascita dei giudicati: Una proposta per lo scioglimento di un enigma storiografico', *Archivio Storico Giuridico Sardo di Sassari*, 12 (2007), 27–118

Zucca, Raimondo, 'Il castello di Laconi e le origini del Giudicato d'Arborea', in *La civiltà giudicale in Sardegna nei secoli XI–XIII: Fonti e documenti scritti. Atti del Convegno nazionale (Sassari-Usini, 16–18 marzo 2001)* (Sassari: Associazione Condaghe S. Pietro di Silki, 2002), pp. 115–26

——, 'Zerkis, iudex arborensis', in *Giudicato d'Arborea e Marchesato di Oristano: Proiezioni mediterranee e aspetti di storia locale*, ed. by Giampaolo Mele, 2 vols (Oristano: ISTAR, 2000), pp. 1103–12

PRZEMYSŁAW WISZEWSKI

How to Live Together?

Germans and Poles in Silesia in the Thirteenth to Fifteenth Centuries

The authors of the previous chapters which characterize how the medieval societies of the Iberian Peninsula and Sardinia functioned emphasized the presence of two contradictory trends. On the one hand, their daily existence required cooperation and the crossing of ethnic and religious borders without causing conflicts. On the other hand, the interference of external institutions, mainly of a religious but also political nature, led to the sharpening of ethnic differences and aroused distrust between ethnic groups. The solution to this contradiction were the royal authorities' attempts to build homogeneous communities, which gradually eliminated ethnic differences. In the case of central Europe, we can observe similar phenomena. Here, however, the religious separateness of ethnic groups has not always played such an important role as in the case of southern Europe. Language and culture were very often the basis for ethnic distinctiveness. The history of Silesia provides a classic example of building relationships between both culturally (Germans and Poles) and religiously (Christians and Jews) distinct ethnic groups in the course of daily, intense contacts.

Introduction: Various Lives, Different Laws

Borderlands are the chosen fields for studying multi-ethnic societies, especially relations between multi-ethnicity and the social cohesion of political communities.[1]

---

[1] The problem is important not only for historians but even more for contemporary political studies and sociologists, not to mention interested parties. A good example of a study which uses the methodology of social sciences, and which focuses on changes within large social groups with a 'nation' and 'nationalism' as focal points of analysis, is the book by Smith and others, *Nation-building*

Przemysław Wiszewski • (przemyslaw.wiszewski@uwr.edu.pl) is a Professor of Medieval and Early Modern History at the Historical Institute, University of Wrocław, with special interest in the medieval and early modern history of social relations, values structures within medieval societies, and regional history.

Inter-Ethnic Relations and the Functioning of Multi-Ethnic Societies: Cohesion in Multi-Ethnic Societies in Europe from c. 1000 to the Present, II, ed. by Przemysław Wiszewski, EER 18 (Turnhout: Brepols, 2022), pp. 141–158

BREPOLS ❧ PUBLISHERS   10.1484/M.EER-EB.5.132150

This is an open access chapter made available under a cc by-nc 4.0 International License.

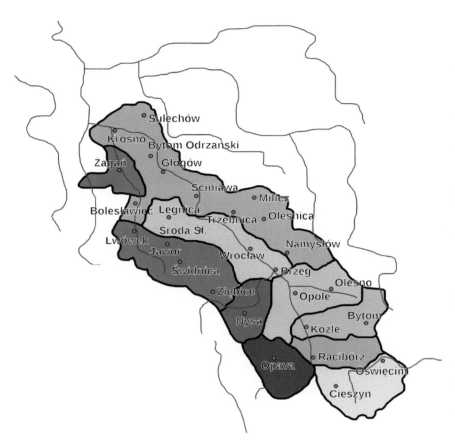

Map 6.1. Silesia 1294–1296. <https://commons.wikimedia.org/wiki/File:Silesia_1294-1296.svg>. CC BY-SA 2.5.

In central Europe, especially between the twelfth and the fourteenth centuries, there were huge waves of migrations from west to east and south-east; migrants might become locals and then they themselves might look suspiciously at other migrants, or they might cooperate or quarrel in order to ensure a better present and future for their communities.[2] Silesia is one such example of an area where huge ethnic changes took place and where various ethnicities lived together, often separated

---

in the Post-Soviet Borderlands. The authors clearly stress the growing importance of nationalism in post-Soviet countries, but by focusing on a higher level of political discourses they omit the realities of cohabitation within the multi-ethnic successor states.

2 Berend, Urbańczyk, and Wiszewski, *Central Europe in the High Middle Ages*, pp. 464–68, 471. Unluckily, the problem remained untouched in the newest synthesis by Curta, *Eastern Europe in the Middle Ages (500–1300)*.

by social status. The uniqueness of the region's history is based on the fact that the ethnically charged animosities between Christian inhabitants were not documented in the Middle Ages, when the biggest ethnic changes and, strongly related to them, social shifts appeared. Under which circumstances was it possible for communities to live in harmony?

Discussion about the role of ethnic issues in the history of Silesia has so far been determined by nationalist discourses of the nineteenth and twentieth centuries.[3] German historians, for example, focused on the *true* roots of the German culture of Silesia. Polish medievalists mainly researched the *Polish* past of Silesia (with various chronological limits) and the origin of the *separation* of the Silesians from the Polish national community. Perhaps the best examples of these types of discourses were two monographs of the history of Silesia, published during the interwar period: the German version edited by Hermann Aubin, and the Polish issued under the direction of Stanisław Kutrzeba.[4] Both syntheses were written by splendid historians of the time, like Hermann Aubin and Dagobert Frey or Władysław Semkowicz and Jan Podlacha. But clearly the German narrative was prepared from a colonialist perspective and the Polish story fitted with the nationalistic vision of Great Poland in which all of Silesia historically was and should be Polish. Both syntheses were and are popular among general readers and specialists despite the fact that during the last two decades more balanced syntheses of Silesian history have been published in the Czech Republic and Poland.[5] Conceptual frameworks for these newest works more or less refer to the first two of the three models of writing about medieval (east) central Europe discerned by Piotr Górecki: (1) emphasizing the relocation of processes — social, economic, cultural, etc. — in time which had already occurred in the West, and/or (2) the diffusion of elements of high-level order of the Western civilization to the East. The third model — acknowledging civilizations or cultures as incomparable and different — was not present in the entirety of historical writing about Silesia.[6] But no matter which model was applied, long after the end of World War II, historians too often implemented the concept of the modern nations (Czech, Germans, Poles) living in a unitarian state within the debate about the medieval history of the region.[7] This despite the fact that they studied social phenomena originating between the twelfth and the fifteenth centuries, when the organization of Silesian society was

---

3 See for a general outline of contemporary historiographical debates about the high medieval migration — especially German migration — into central and east-central Europe, Piskorski, ed., *Historiographical Approaches to Medieval Colonization of East Central Europe* and Piskorski, 'The Medieval Colonization of Central Europe'.

4 Aubin, ed., *Von der Urzeit bis zum Jahre 1526* (1st edn, Breslau 1938; the last, 6th, unchanged issue of the same edition was printed in 2000 by Thorbecke Verlag); and Kutrzeba and Semkowicz, eds, *Historia Śląska* (1st edn, Kraków 1933–1939; 2nd, unchanged edn, Kraków 2013).

5 Czapliński and others, *Historia Śląska*; Wrzesiński, ed., *Dolny Śląsk*; Jirásek, ed., *Slezsko v dějinách českého státu*.

6 See reflections by Górecki, 'Ambiguous Beginnings', pp. 197–98.

7 Even Thomas Wünsch does not avoid the trap, and in his inspiring book modelled closely on the principles of 'entangled history', he focuses on general communities of 'Czech', 'Germans', 'Poles', 'Russians' as intertwined social groups living in political entities — states; see Wünsch, *Deutsche und Slawen*.

dominated by polycentric structures, and when multifaceted relationships between social groups were differentiated in terms of the law.[8]

But even if we give up using terms like *nation* and *state* in the modern sense of the words, it cannot be denied that problems indicated by the research — a cohabitation of German- and Polish-speaking knights, clergymen, townspeople, and peasants — played an important role in the history of medieval Silesian society. Between the last quarter of the twelfth century and the middle of the fourteenth century, the arrival in Silesia of a large number of German-speaking migrants from the empire led to a great cultural change. The language of the newcomers — German — started to dominate communication between the residents of the Odra region in various moments and in varying degrees of intensity depending on the localities. The change appeared during a period of three hundred years, the thirteenth–fifteenth centuries, between the time when the dukes of the Piast dynasty started a broad economic reconstruction of their lands (so-called *Landesausbau*, starting in the last quarter of the twelfth century) and the emergence of Silesia as one province under the rule of the kings of Bohemia (the second half of the fifteenth century). The ethno-cultural change was determined by the large-scale foundation of towns and villages according to western European legal models, which began in the second half of the thirteenth century with a significant participation of the settlers from the empire. Over the decades, they had formed the elite which controlled both secular power and the legal systems, as well as wealth in local communities, especially in urban areas. At the same time, they maintained their own specific culture supported by obeying laws which had been written down, principally in German, from the second half of the thirteenth century onwards. As a result, German became the second official language — in parallel with Latin used in more solemn occasions — in written communication between Silesians.[9] Although Polish-speaking families lived without doubt in Silesian towns and villages until the end of the medieval period, their presence in sources recorded since the fourteenth century is rare. Or to be more precise: the authors of the available sources from the middle of the thirteenth century onwards did not clearly discern between German and Polish inhabitants. Ethnic differences appeared accidentally in the description of local customs, in the names of various ethnic origins, or when someone claimed to be obedient to 'German' or 'Polish law'. The latter problem has to be put in context. All knights, townspeople, and peasants were subjected in their towns and villages to local versions of traditional, Polish law or to a new, so-called 'German law'. But for a local group of Silesians, being put under the 'German' or 'Polish law' didn't mean that its members altogether became tied to that given ethnic culture. On the other hand, both the ethnic name of the law and the conscious use

---

8 See Piskorski, Jaworski, and Hackmann, eds, *Deutsche Ostforschung und polnische Westforschung*.
9 A collection concerning the towns' foundation based on German law in Poland was published recently: Mühle, ed., *Rechtsstadtgründungen*, containing articles on Silesia by Mateusz Goliński, Stanisław Rosik, and Rościsław Żerelik. For a review of studies, see Młynarska-Kaletynowa, 'O procesach lokacyjnych miast w Europie Środkowo-Wschodniej'. For a more general picture of the use of vernacular languages in the written cultures of medieval central Europe, see Adamska, 'Intersections'.

of the name by contemporary authors and legislators supported knowledge about ethnic differences within the society of the region.

Ethnicity as a concept and the implications of differences based on the past clearly had an impact on the social lives of medieval Silesians. Ethnicity could be, but was not necessarily, connected with social standing. Germans and Poles during the thirteenth century formed apparently separate communities within one social group, but later on they created mixed social and legal communities of knights, townspeople, and peasants who very often lived according to the same local laws. In such situations, how did they deal with ethnic differences within their *own* social groups? Of course, we have to differentiate between narrative and legal descriptions of social relations and relations themselves. And we have to accept that sometimes it is impossible to discern between these two dimensions in texts. Acknowledging these limitations, as an ultimate aim I will be trying to resolve if various social groups in medieval Silesia built different strategies of peaceful cohabitation or if they adapted a common matrix imposed in a given moment by law ordered by the rulers. In other words — did Silesians organize themselves into a multi-ethnic society, or did they just follow the law set out by the Silesian dukes for the sake of building a wealthy community of subjects paying their dues to the rulers?

From Segregation to Mixing Ethnicities: Peasants

Although *hospites* from various western European regions had appeared in Silesia from the middle of the twelfth century, for the first time in 1202 a clear message was issued about the organization of a settlement of groups of German settlers next to local Poles. The Duke of Silesia, Henryk I the Bearded, gave liberties to German settlers living on the estate of the Cistercian abbey Lubiąż 'separated from Poles' ('Theutonicis in possessionibus eorum segregatim a Polonibus habitantibus').[10] The separation of two categories of peasants was clearly undertaken for economic reasons — Germans were freed from all dues owed to the duke, but Poles were bound to pay their traditional services. It seems the decision was made by the duke to separate these two types of peasants. In the charter of his father, Bolesław I the Tall, for the same abbey, issued in 1175, the dual acceptance of permitting German peasants who had been invited by the abbey to settle was only mentioned. Apparently their special economic status troubled the duke who decided to clearly delimitate those who were entitled to the special liberties of Germans and those who should pay traditional, 'Polish' dues.[11] But even if the ethnic denominators used in the charter were mentioned to define a community of law rather than of culture and language, observers of the contemporary Silesian community clearly discerned newcomers and local dwellers in everyday activities. Peter, abbot of the Cistercian abbey in Henryków (Heinrichau), wrote his chronicle of the cloister's landed property in the

---

10   *Schlesisches Urkundenbuch*, I, no. 177.
11   See Wiszewski, 'The Multi-ethnic Character of Medieval Silesian Society', pp. 176–77.

146   PRZEMYSŁAW WISZEWSKI

second half of the thirteenth century (*The Henryków Book*), in which he consciously distinguished between instances when he recalled the histories of Czech, German, or Polish settlers or relations between them.

Especially in the case of German newcomers, he stressed the novelty of both people and their habits, but a novelty that easily can turn into a local custom. He focused on this changing status of German migrants when writing about a certain landowner who let Germans settle near the abbey in order to harm the monks' peace. The German settlers' women danced in the cloister's orchard, and the abbot was afraid that these dances would in time become customs which were impossible to change.[12] The fragment of the sources which has been most commented on by historians recalled a simple story that has become an iconic example of Silesian mixed ethnicities and the assimilation of newcomers. In a certain village close to the Cistercian cloister lived the former duke's servant, a Czech called Bogwal (Boguchwał). He married a peasant woman, and once when she ground wheat seeds with a quern he asked her to rest and let him grind. This in itself is not unusual, but the most notable fact is that he — a Czech servant of a Silesian duke — spoke to his wife in Polish. And after this incident, his neighbours called him 'Boguchwał Brukał', which meant 'Boguchwał the Grinder' in Polish.[13] Moreover there is the fact that the story, which contains Boguchwał's request in the form of the first Polish sentence ever written down, was recalled by a German abbot, the author of the *Henryków Book*. And he was not surprised or curious that a Czech spoke Polish — the language of his wife, apparently. He accepted Boguchwał's assimilation as normal, which explains why he shared his predecessors' certainty that the Germans' new cultural *habitus* of peasants can easily and fast turn into local custom. For him, as natural as the differences between ethnically based laws (German and Polish) was the process of the constant and peaceful domestication of different ethnic groups and cultures. Perhaps this attitude originated from the fact that he, who was of German origin, understood and spoke or at least was able to repeat Polish sentences and was very familiar with intricacies of both German and Polish laws that influenced the economic policy of the abbey. His knowledge of the mechanisms for transferring legal information within Polish peasants' society was deep enough to secure and defend the abbey's property before the ducal court.[14]

Apparently, during the thirteenth century cultural and ethnic differences between Czech, Germans, and Poles in village communities were noted in sources. Some settlements were intended to be inhabited by only one ethnicity — or by a community of one type of *ethnic* law (German or Polish). The question of their ethnic identity should be treated carefully: as in tribes, not all members of such a society in a particular moment accepted ethnic identity; the narrative was blurred with grey areas of identities. We can find this feature in Bohemia and Hungary.[15] The

---

12   *Liber fundationis*, ed. and trans. by Grodecki, I. 4, p. 124.
13   Górecki, *A Local Society in Transition*, pp. 139–40.
14   Górecki, 'Communities of Legal Memory', pp. 133, 140–46.
15   See the chapter by Cosmin Popa-Gorjanu in this book.

question is how the idea of ethnic separateness was implemented and how long it was possible to maintain this model in the context of assimilation processes which apparently strongly influenced the social and economic realities of thirteenth-century Silesia. How did the theoretically stable structure of Silesia react to changes in the ethnic composition of specific settlements? The answer to these questions is related to the pace of economic, social, and anthropogenic changes in the various parts of the region. Where the land was previously relatively densely populated by Polish peasants, few new villages were created by the invited migrants. More often in the first half of the thirteenth century, the existing communities were reformed, merged into larger settlements, their dues standardized and sometimes diminished without major changes in the ethnic character, as was the case of the villages of the so-called 'ligota, lhota'. In the second half of the thirteenth century, previous settlements were re-established according to a new legal system, which was called the 'German law'. This could mean the introduction of a new social elite to the village, specialists in implementing the new norms of 'German law' into the lives of the existing residents. These specialists — reeves (Germ. *Voigt*, Pol. *wójt*), but also certain groups of new settlers — came from the German countries or were the descendants of migrants from the West.[16] The domination of legal norms expressed in German and the introduction, as a social and economic elite of village communities, of people who used German in everyday life started the process of cultural change, in which the villages' residents transitioned from a Polish-speaking to a German-speaking culture during the fourteenth century. In settlements where in the thirteenth-century colonization of previously uncultivated land occurred, the ethnic change took place at a different pace. The foothills and forest areas in the south of the region were inhabited by migrants from German countries or local people brought in by specialists settling new inhabitants in villages governed by 'German law'. As a result, the majority of new villages — mainly on the border with the Kingdom of Bohemia — were from the beginning dominated by the German-speaking culture. But there were many mixed solutions of changes in the legal status and cultural life of the village, especially where the modernization of the economy was slower and villages organized according to the traditional 'Polish law' continued to function. This was the situation especially on the border with the Polish Kingdom — in the north (Oleśnica principality) and in the south-east (Upper Silesian principalities) of the region. In 1358 the Bishop of Wrocław sold to the dukes of Oleśnica his castellany of Milicz. Among dozens of villages mentioned in the charter only a few bore names which originated from German; the majority were apparently Polish. At the same time, a special type of ducal court operated at the castle in Milicz for those living under the Polish law.[17] Close to the town of Środa Śląska (Neumarkt), which was the major source of the Silesian type of German law for towns called 'Neumarkterrecht'

---

16   See the recent state of research and detailed analysis of the thirteenth-century change in rural settlement of the basin of the middle and upper Oława River by Adamska, *Wieś – miasteczko – miasto*, pp. 90–158.

17   Jaworski, Ruchniewicz, and Wiszewski, *Kraina stawów?*, pp. 75–76.

(the law of Neumarkt/Środa Śląska), in the middle of the fourteenth century the majority of villages still bore Polish names and contemporary sources did not mention that they were reformed according to German law. More importantly, the population of these villages was mixed from an ethnic point of view, or at least their inhabitants spoke both German and Polish. In 1386 the village Jenkowice (Jenkvitz) was populated by peasants who had German names (Margerithe Rotynne, Hannos Richter, Petir Swarcz, Michel Ehrbeth, Nitsche Schuwort), Polish names (Petzo Golambke, Bartke Golambke, Andreas Krykil, Jone Krotky), and a few with names of uncertain ethnic origin (Mathis Sirhin, Andirs Schirpicz).[18] The village was not unique in the area, and the ethnic mixing of the population was visible in sources in the seventeenth–eighteenth centuries.[19]

Over time, village communities all over Silesia became multi-ethnic in character, but with different ratios of various ethnicities. It is difficult to accurately trace the dynamics of this process. The fact remains, however, that, on the one hand, there were many examples of mixed, German-Polish village communities, whilst on the other hand the judiciary books of villages and charters issued in cases involving peasants were written during the fourteenth and fifteenth centuries in German or — more rarely — in Latin.[20] At the same moment the custom for characterizing rural communities by ethnicity or forcing neighbouring communities to maintain ethnic separateness disappeared from the sources. Simply, the thirteenth-century sources suggest that the connection between the legal codes and the ethnic character of the Silesian rural population disappeared during this century. The laws maintained their traditional, ethnic names, but from the middle of the thirteenth century they were applied to entire communities without ethnic discrimination. Ethnic groups were not privileged or discriminated against in the legal norms of the region.

Migration and the Pressure of Prestige: Dukes and Knights

Although the peasants were the most numerous group among the Western migrants to Silesia and they were the earliest, two other social groups are much more visible in the sources: knights and townspeople. German knights had been increasingly migrating to the courts of the Silesian dukes since the middle of the thirteenth century. At first, they were invited by the sons of Henryk II the Pious (d. 1241), when they fought between 1248 and 1253 for their heritage. The oldest of the brothers, Bolesław II Rogatka, was the first who believed that the presence of German knights at his court would guarantee him a military advantage over his brothers and in consequence the political success of a host. He was determined enough to give in 1248 part of his land to an archbishop of Magdeburg in return for sending knights to Silesia. Nowadays

---

18 Archiwum Państwowe we Wrocławiu, Rep. 67, Repertorium, No. 588.

19 See Nowosielska-Sobel, Tyszkiewicz, and Wiszewski, *Między panem, opatem a … autostradą*, pp. 127–32.

20 See the judiciary book of the Benedictine nuns' abbey of Legnica, fifteenth–sixteenth century, Archiwum Państwowe we Wrocławiu, Księstwo Legnickie, No. 479.

historians believe that his enthusiastic support for the newcomers caused the rebellion of Polish knights in 1251 against the duke. But this hypothesis is supported only by the fact that the German knights present up to this date at the duke's court and in his documents as witnesses disappeared after 1254 from his charters and that their disappearance started when he lost the struggle against his younger brothers, Henryk III and Konrad. Proponents of the rebellion hypothesis speculated that the Polish knights supported the younger brothers. And once he was defeated, Bolesław was forced to cooperate with his younger brother Henryk III, and he had to exclude the German knights from court and give back offices to local knights.[21] But not one contemporary author mentioned such an ethnically based rebellion. If we look closely at the sequence of events, it seems much more probable that the decisive factor for the change in the ethnic character of the elite at Bolesław's court was the simple fact that the duke was defeated in 1251 by the coalition of his brothers and the duke of the neighbouring Greater Poland (Przemysł I). When he lost the war, he was not able to pay his German mercenaries enough to stop them from fleeing his court. Perhaps they assessed his chances for further political success more realistically than the duke? But — once again — nobody mentioned rebellion against the duke, even the authors of the sources that supported the idea of the decisive valour of the German migrants for the development of Silesia (*Silesian Polish Chronicle*) or depicted the duke as incapable of ruling the land (*Chronicle of Polish Dukes*).

But although many of those first arrivals left Silesia after collecting payments and military spoils, the number of noble migrants staying there more permanently remained relatively stable throughout the second half of the thirteenth and the first half of the fourteenth centuries. The number of migrating knights was much higher in comparison with other parts of the Piasts' realm. The reason for the growing number of German knightly migrants at Silesian ducal courts was at least twofold. First, thanks to the previously implemented economic reform, the Silesian dukes' lands generated much larger income than landed properties in the other Piast territories, and that level of income allowed the Silesian Piasts to hire or invite a larger number of foreigners than their relatives could afford.[22] Second, the dukes wanted them for military and prestige reasons. Since the middle of the thirteenth century, the Silesian dukes had competed very aggressively, politically and militarily, with each other and with Wrocław's bishop. To build and strengthen their advantage in the political landscape of the region, they wanted German knights at their courts. Throughout thirteenth-century Europe, German knightly virtues were respected and

---

21 Jurek, *Obce rycerstwo na Śląsku*, p. 150; Jurek, 'Abstructores castrorum'.
22 The Silesian duke Henryk I's fight for prestige and political dominance in Poland was a major stimulus for the developing economy in the first half of the thirteenth century. His policy became a model of interdependent relations developed by his ancestors, continuing economic reforms to strengthen military power which enabled the conquerors to gather more land and sources of income. Their political horizon was much narrower than Henryk's and so were their possibilities to intensify the economies of their duchies. Facing growing financial needs, they started giving their land to knights instead of coins (first half of the fourteenth century), but that soon caused another financial crisis and a major drop in the political and social positions of the dukes. Wiszewski, 'Politics and Change'.

the knightly culture of the German courts was imitated among the magnates of the central European states. No wonder that the Silesian dukes who had a vast network of German relatives and political friends that supported German knightly culture (especially in Přemyslid Bohemia) tried to follow the habit with the help of knightly guests.[23] As a result, the dukes created, from the last quarter of the thirteenth century, the conditions conducive to the gradual adoption of the German language and knightly culture as a standard for all Silesian knights, including Poles or migrants from Roman countries, Czech, and Hungary.[24]

But the dukes of Silesia, first and foremost, represented themselves as the descendants of the earliest historical rulers of Poland, and they were proud of being part of the Piast dynasty. They cherished the memory of their lineage in the chronicles, and their political ambitions throughout the whole of the thirteenth century were to dominate the other Polish regions and — at the end of the century — to gain the royal crown of the Kingdom of Poland. Their roots, contemporary politics, and planned future bound them together with Polish tradition until the end of the Middle Ages. Even their internal policy was strongly related to a tradition of Piast rulership with a decisive position of a *just* — in the meaning of a Polish political tradition — ruler within a society and sustaining Polish hereditary law for the local knights.[25] But since the middle of the thirteenth century they unanimously blended these traditions with elements of the Western, mostly German, courtly culture. It is enough to remind ourselves here that one of the most powerful dukes of Wrocław, Henryk IV Probus (1257/1258–1290), is believed to be a poet, and two of the poems supposedly authored by him are contained in *Codex Manesse* together with a miniature presenting him as the winner of a knightly tournament receiving a wreath from the hands of a lady.[26] The Duke of Jawor, Henryk I (1292/1296–1346), commissioned the wall paintings in his fortified residence in Siedlęcin which portray the Lancelot cycle.[27] In the second half of the fourteenth century, good knowledge of German was required for every respectable Silesian duke. Bolesław II Rogatka of Legnica, the first one who invited German knights to Silesia, was ridiculed in the *Chronicle of Polish Dukes* because he spoke very poor German. This lack of linguistic abilities was linked by the author of the work with the duke's general characteristics: a lack of dignity in the same measure as his buffoonery.[28]

---

23 See Iwańczak, 'Höfische Kultur und ritterliche Lebensformen', pp. 283–85.

24 Jurek, 'Die Migration deutscher Ritter nach Polen'; Jurek, 'Vom Rittertum zum Adel'.

25 Constructed through the centuries, the ideal Piast ruler was changeable, but since the twelfth century it comprised quite a stable list of general virtues: piety (care for his Church as a community), justice (ruling within bonds of tradition), independence but cooperation (making decisions independently but after taking advice of the elites), love of homeland and local customs; see Wiszewski, *Domus Bolezlai*, pp. 525–37, and for the Silesian version of the model, with stronger emphasis on justice and piety, Górecki, 'The Paradox of Piast Power'.

26 Lubos, *Geschichte der Literatur Schlesiens*, p. 44; Witkowski, 'Die Ritterkultur an den Höfen der schlesischen Piasten'; Witkowski, 'Książę i dama na turnieju'.

27 Witkowski, *Szlachetna a wielce żałosna opowieść*.

28 *Kronika książąt polskich*, ed. by Węclewski, pp. 497–98.

Living on the edge of two ethnic cultures, German and Polish, and having subjects of various ethnic origins, the Silesian Piast dukes never raised ethnicity or any kind of ethnic characteristics of their foes as an issue or subject of contempt. Their *habitus* embodied the perfect mix of local traditions with Western fashions blended together by modernizing efforts, to such a degree that nowadays, it is hard to separate *German* and *Polish* aspects of Silesian courtly culture. The dukes supported the blending of cultures by refusing to build a system of law based on ethnic identity. True, they applied the rules of feudal law at first to migrant knights, but properties handed over by dukes as fiefs to them soon became possessed by Silesians of various ethnic origins, both Polish and German, who bought them without changing their legal character. The dukes changed themselves and the culture surrounding them for communicative reasons. They needed allies and powerful armies during their never-ending struggles and feuds with their kin. And because the founders of the line, Władysław II the Exile, Bolesław I the Tall, and Henryk I the Bearded, built their position on close relations with the Reich's aristocracy, their descendants naturally looked at Western countries as a promising source of additional power, of both political and military resources. But the rulers had to create friendly conditions for possible allies and military aid. The success of this policy changed courtly culture in the second half of the thirteenth century and then transformed the ducal family. The fusion of German and Polish elements in the administrative and ideological dimensions of the Piast rulership in Silesia was strong enough to prevent members of the dynasty from using ethnic issues as matters of internal policy. They did not introduce ethnic exclusivity of common laws. On the contrary, they consciously invited their subjects of various ethnic origin to participate in the implementation of new, *German* laws. And they accepted when the German knights came into possession of landed properties on *Polish* law. Even if some of them were better acquainted with the new cultural patterns than the others, all of them were united by the policy of accumulating power through strengthening cultural bonds with both locals and migrants, without losing the support of any one of the ethnic groups.[29]

Law and Diffusion of Culture: Townspeople

The formation of the ethnic composition of urban societies in Silesia was in line with the policy of the dukes and the activities of the knights. Since the beginnings of Western-style towns in Silesia in the early years of the thirteenth century, they were

---

29 Not one of the medieval Silesian dukes claimed to have supremacy over any one ethnicity living on Silesian ground with the exception of the Jews. For the latter, the Piast rulers played the role of well-paid protectors against Christian Silesians. For centuries, the Piast dukes had maintained a balance between the interests of the ducal treasury and the consequences of popular beliefs about the strangeness of the Jews. This balance was broken in the middle of the fifteenth century by the Czech king's policy. The Jews were persecuted, robbed, and expelled from all the major towns of Silesia by the direct order of the king (1453–1455, Wiszewski, 'The Multi-ethnic Character of Medieval Silesian Society', pp. 174–75).

organized according to the 'German law'. Although such a law differentiated between towns, it was based on sets of fundamental laws that were expressed in German from the end of the thirteenth century and transferred from town to town as requested by dukes (mostly) — the founders of these towns. According to the historiographic models constructed using written sources after the 1990s, the political elites of these newly founded towns, merchants and craftsmen, usually came from abroad. Groups of local inhabitants were characterized as of insignificant social status or at least unnoticeable in sources, especially in pre-town settlements which existed in the places where new towns were created. Recent archaeological research in Wrocław has demonstrated that the development of urban life in Silesia was gradual but relatively fast in terms of the material culture. The *early city* populated by Slavic inhabitants was enriched in the second quarter of the thirteenth century with a colony of 'guests' (1226). 'German law of towns' was officially declared for the city in the charter of 1261, although, according to other sources, Duke Bolesław II Rogatka organized the new city right after the Mongol invasion (1242).[30] At first, two cultures — of the Western type which characterized the new town of migrants and that of local character — prospered side by side, clearly separated. But gradually during the thirteenth century the Western type of material culture replaced traditional, Slavic elements of everyday life. In the middle of the thirteenth century, both communities — of new and old traditions — were separated but lived within the recognized boundary of the city. In 1261 Dukes Henryk III and Władysław issued a privilege for the townspeople of Wrocław which reorganized the community and gave the common 'ius civitatis Maydeburgensis' (*sic!*) (law of Magdeburg city) to all inhabitants of the territory within the borders of the city. Previously to this moment different communities of different legal standing lived 'ante civitatem infra fossata prime locationis' (outside the city, within the limits of the first town).[31] The meaning of this fragment has often been discussed, and different hypotheses have been proposed with regard to the differences between the limits of the first and the second *location* of the city.[32] No matter which will be the outcome of these discussions, the cohabitation of inhabitants living for at least several decades according to various codes of laws was evident. In 1261 the ducal power suppressed this state of ambiguity and forced one type of law on all townspeople. And around this time the Western type of material culture dominated and superseded local traditions.[33]

Were the changes in material culture relevant to the ethnic composition of the urban community? One charter of Duke Henryk III for the town of Brzeg suggests that at least in the middle of the thirteenth century the ethnic duality of townspeople was clearly discernible. Duke Henryk III permitted in 1250 the foundation of the new town in Brzeg; its inhabitants were to be ruled according to the German law: 'Polonus

---

30 Mühle, *Breslau — Geschichte einer europäischen Metropole*, pp. 29–46; *Schlesisches Urkundenbuch*, II, no. 229 (1242).

31 *Schlesisches Urkundenbuch*, III, no. 373, p. 242.

32 Rozpędowski, 'Breslau zur Zeit der ersten Lokation', pp. 132–34.

33 See the latest synthesis of the largest excavations in decades on the outskirts of the medieval city of Wrocław, Piekalski and Wachowski, eds, *Rytm rozwoju miasta na kulturowym pograniczu*.

vel cuiuscumque ydiomatis homo liber domum ibi habens ius Theotonicum paciatur' (Pole and free man of any other language will live under the German law).[34] And as the duke stated the multi-ethnic character of the town, he also stressed the equal status of its inhabitants in the law and thus his disinterest in the ethnic dimensions of townspeople's lives. The economy was of primary importance to him and his contemporary rulers, and for the state of his treasury, ethnic cohabitation which resulted in the social and economic development of the newly founded towns was much more important than differences between 'people of various languages'.[35] In recent years both archaeologists and historians supported the hypothesis of a straightforward acculturation of local inhabitants in Silesian towns. They claimed that the economic success of a Western type of town blocked the development of a Slavic version of early cities. At first, the dukes both gave privileges for migrants and supported traditional, locally functioning market centres. But the latter soon became less profitable than the towns created according to 'German law', and that caused the abandonment by the dukes of political support for the model of cultural and legal duality of city life in the region. But they also suggested that the *demographic base* for the newly founded town consisted first and foremost of Germans. And that *Westernization* of local life was in fact a result of the adaptation of migrants to local circumstances.[36] But both the charter of 1250 quoted above and the gradual change of material culture in the city of Wrocław suggest a more complicated process. Both groups — Poles and migrants, mostly Germans — lived according to the laws dictated by the ducal power. Forcing upon all townspeople various, local types of 'German law' resulted in the gradual alignment of the cultures of all inhabitants within the city walls. Both migrants and local inhabitants changed their lifestyles, but the dominant legal language, the material culture of high-status residents, and the pressure of the ducal courts' knightly culture on the urban social elites, who were mostly German-speaking families in origin, determined the vector of changes towards a specific, Silesian culture of German language and various other ethnic features.

The latest archaeological research shows us more clearly that the local population's culture had a strong presence, even in the largest towns during the thirteenth century, and was only weakened over time. But — just like the case of the knights — there were no ethnic disputes between Silesian burghers regardless of the cultural changes and the participation of various ethnic groups in these urban communities. This rule was not applied to the Jews, who officially were under the direct protection of the dukes, but mixed economic and religious issues periodically caused outbreaks of violence against them from the middle of the fourteenth century onwards. This only served to emphasize that for townspeople in Silesia, only the Jews were stigmatized as 'Others'. Germans, Poles, Walloons — all ethnicities who were predominantly Christian and were accepted as 'us' — were all people who lived under the same law and pledged allegiance to the same lord. There was no possibility that animosity

---

34 *Schlesisches Urkundenbuch*, II, no. 409, p. 257.
35 See Wiszewski, 'Politics and Change'.
36 Piekalski and Wachowski, 'Dynamika przemian osadniczych i kulturowych', p. 1117.

154 PRZEMYSŁAW WISZEWSKI

between people of different language backgrounds would turn into actual acts of violence. Apparently, the cultural influence of the ducal courts and the network of common laws with ethnic denominators but without ethnic exclusivity saved Silesia from ethnic conflicts on a larger scale. That is the hypothesis built upon the observations of the use of terminology in the judicial sources and the facts of economic and social life. But how did Silesians define inter-ethnic relations within their social groups?

Conclusion: Silesian Pragmatism of Multi-Ethnicity

Let's return to the initial question — did different social groups in medieval Silesia deal differently with their multi-ethnic character? The answer, as often, is not straightforward. On the one hand, yes, knights, townspeople, and peasants chose different strategies to cope with the heterogeneity of their groups. German knights who were migrants cooperated closely with the dukes by responding to their needs. But they also collaborated with local Polish knights to as fast as possible fit into the local system of power and participate in it. German migrants did not assimilate with their Polish peers, but all of them were moulded by the cultural needs of the ducal courts. The urban communities evolved more slowly and gradually through the diffusion of attractive elements of the material culture of both dominant ethnicities, under pressure from German as the dominant language of trade in the region of Brandenburg, Saxony, Bohemia, Moravia, and Silesia. The peasants' situation looks the most obscure in this context. After initial ethnic segregation, they disregarded ethnicity and mixed within their local communities. But they often preserved elements of their ethnic cultures. In the case of smaller ethnic groups, that could lead to ethnic identification as a common differentiator of a given society even in the second half of the fourteenth century.[37] But that rarely happened to Germans and Poles. Their practices of cohabitation seem to be purely pragmatic and brought them huge success in that their ethnicity was not discernible by external observers, nor was it acknowledged as important for their existence within the Silesian community.

On the other hand, the most decisive factor for maintaining peace in Silesia despite the ethnic diversity was without doubt the pragmatic use of legal codes. Despite their ethnic origins and names from the middle of the thirteenth century, the law codes were applied to specific communities without regard for their ethnic identity. Ethnicity in medieval Silesia was not connected in general terms with anything distinctive in the legal system of the region. And the dukes did not try to use ethnic differences as sources of conflict and tools of governance of their multi-ethnic societies. Why? That is a question about the political culture of the region that needs to be answered in a separate paper.

---

37 Piotr of Byczyna in his *Chronicle of Polish Dukes* mentioned the battle between certain ducal knights and peasants of two villages, 'Ianckow atque Wirbin' (today: Janików i Wierzbno) 'where Romans were settled' (ubi moriantur Gallici), *Kronika książąt polskich*, ed. by Węclewski, p. 514.

Works Cited

Manuscripts and Archival Sources

Archiwum Państwowe we Wrocławiu (State Archive Wrocław), collections: Rep. 67; Księstwo Legnickie (Principality of Legnica)

Primary Sources

Kronika książąt polskich, ed. by Zygmunt Węclewski, in *Monumenta Poloniae Historica*, vol. III (Lwów: Polska Akademia Umiejętności, 1878)

Liber fundationis claustri sancte Marie Virginis in Heinrichow czyli Księga Henrykowska, ed. and trans. by Roman Grodecki (Wrocław: Muzeum Archidiecezjalne we Wrocławiu, 1991)

Schlesisches Urkundenbuch, vol. I, ed. by Heinrich Appelt (Cologne: Verlag Hermann Böhlaus Nachf., 1963–71)

Schlesisches Urkundenbuch, vol. II, ed. by Wienfried Irgang (Cologne: Böhlau, 1977)

Schlesisches Urkundenbuch, vol. III, ed. by Wienfried Irgang (Cologne: Böhlau, 1984)

Secondary Studies

Adamska, Anna, 'Intersections: Medieval East Central Europe from the Perspective of Literacy and Communication', in *Medieval East Central Europe in a Comparative Perspective: From Frontier Zones to Lands in Focus*, ed. by Gerhard Jaritz and Kathlin Szende (London: Routledge, 2016), pp. 223–38

Adamska, Dagmara, *Wieś – miasteczko – miasto: Średniowieczne osadnictwo w dorzeczu górnej i środkowej Oławy* (Łomianki: LTW, 2019)

Aubin, Hermann, ed., *Von der Urzeit bis zum Jahre 1526*, vol. I of *Geschichte Schlesiens*, ed. by the Historischen Kommission für Schlesien under the direction of Hermann Aubin (Breslau: Verlag Priebatschs Buchhandlung, 1938)

Berend, Nora, Przemysław Urbańczyk, and Przemysław Wiszewski, *Central Europe in the High Middle Ages: Bohemia, Hungary and Poland, c. 900–c. 1300* (Cambridge: Cambridge University Press, 2013)

Curta, Florin, *Eastern Europe in the Middle Ages (500–1300)*, Brill's Companions to European History, 19 (Leiden: Brill, 2019)

Czapliński, Marek, Elżbieta Kaszuba, Gabriela Wąs, and Rościsław Żerelik, *Historia Śląska* (Wrocław: Wydawnictwo Uniwersytetu Wrocławskiego, 2002; 2nd edn, 2007)

Górecki, Piotr, 'Ambiguous Beginnings: East Central Europe in the Making, 950–1200', in *European Transformations: The Long Twelfth Century*, ed. by Thomas F. X. Noble and John Van Engen (Notre Dame: University of Notre Dame Press, 2012), pp. 194–228

——, 'Communities of Legal Memory in Medieval Poland (c. 1200–1240)', *Journal of Medieval History*, 24.2 (1998), 127–54

——, *A Local Society in Transition: The 'Henryków Book' and Related Sources*, Studies and Texts, 155 (Toronto: Pontifical Institute of Mediaeval Studies, 2007)

—, 'The Paradox of Piast Power: A Contemporary Observer in His Context', *Viator*, 49.2 (2018), 137–68

Iwańczak, Wojciech, 'Höfische Kultur und ritterliche Lebensformen in Polen vor dem Hintergrund der europäischen Entwicklung', in *Das Reich und Polen: Parallelen, Interaktionen und Formen der Akkulturation im hohen und späten Mittelalter*, ed. by Thomas Wünsch, with the assistance of Alexander Patschovsky, Vorträge und Forschungen, 59 (Ostfildern: Thorbecke, 2003), pp. 277–98

Jaworski, Paweł, Małgorzata Ruchniewicz, and Przemysław Wiszewski, *Kraina stawów? Dzieje Milicza i okolic (do 1945 r.)*, Historia obok: Studia z dziejów lokalnych / History Next To: Local Past Studies, 16 (Kraków: Księgarnia Akademicka, 2019)

Jirásek, Zdeněk, ed., *Slezsko v dějinách českého státu*, vols I–II (Prague: Nakladatelství Lidové Noviny, 2012)

Jurek, Tomasz, 'Abstructores castrorum: Przyczynek do dziejów społecznych i politycznych Śląska w połowie XIII wieku', in *Narodziny Rzeczypospolitej: Studium z dziejów średniowiecza i czasów wczesnonowożytnych*, ed. by Waldemar Bukowski and Tomasz Jurek (Kraków: Wydawnictwo Towarzystwa Naukowego Societas Vistulana, 2012), II, pp. 767–86

—, 'Die Migration deutscher Ritter nach Polen', in *Das Reich und Polen: Parallelen, Interaktionen und Formen der Akkulturation im hohen und späten Mittelalter*, ed. by Thomas Wünsch, with the assistance of Alexander Patschovsky, Vorträge und Forschungen, 59 (Ostfildern: Thorbecke, 2003), pp. 243–76

—, *Obce rycerstwo na Śląsku do połowy XIV w.* (Poznań: Wydawnictwo PTPN, 1996)

—, 'Vom Rittertum zum Adel: Zur Herausbildung des Adelsstandes im mittelalterlichen Schlesien', in *Adel in Schlesien*, I: *Herrschaft – Kultur – Selbstdarstellung*, ed. by Jan Harasimowicz and Matthias Weber (Munich: Oldenbourg Wissenschaftsverlag, 2010), pp. 61–67

Kutrzeba, Stanisław, and Władysław Semkowicz, eds, *Historia Śląska od najdawniejszych czasów do roku 1400*, vols I–III (Kraków: Polska Akademia Umiejętności, 1933–1939)

Lubos, Arno, *Geschichte der Literatur Schlesiens* (Munich: Bergstadtverlag, 1960), vol. I

Młynarska-Kaletynowa, Marta, 'O procesach lokacyjnych miast w Europie Środkowo-Wschodniej', in *Procesy lokacyjne miast w Europie środkowo-wschodniej: Materiały z konferencji międzynarodowej w Lądku Zdroju, 28th–29th October, 2002*, ed. by Cezary Buśko, Mateusz Goliński, and Barbara Krukiewicz, Acta Universitatis Wratislaviensis, 2985 (Wrocław: Wydawnictwo Uniwersytetu Wrocławskiego, 2006), pp. 9–17

Mühle, Eduard, *Breslau — Geschichte einer europäischen Metropole* (Cologne: Böhlau, 2015)

—, ed., *Rechtsstadtgründungen im mittelalterlichen Polen*, Städteforschung, A 81 (Cologne: Böhlau, 2011)

Nowosielska-Sobel, Joanna, Jakub Tyszkiewicz, and Przemysław Wiszewski, *Między panem, opatem a ... autostradą: Dzieje gminy Kostomłoty*, Historia obok: Studia z dziejów lokalnych / History Next To: Local Past Studies, 12 (Wrocław: Instytut Historyczny Uniwersytetu Wrocławskiego, 2019)

Piekalski, Jerzy, and Krzysztof Wachowski, 'Dynamika przemian osadniczych i kulturowych: Zakończenie', in *Rytm rozwoju miasta na kulturowym pograniczu: Studium strefy placu Nowy Targ we Wrocławiu*, ed. by Jerzy Piekalski and Krzysztof Wachowski, vol. II, Wratislavia Antiqua, 23.2 (Wrocław: Instytut Archeologii Uniwersytetu Wrocławskiego, 2018), pp. 1113–18

————, eds, *Rytm rozwoju miasta na kulturowym pograniczu: Studium strefy placu Nowy Targ we Wrocławiu*, vols I–II, Wratislavia Antiqua, 23.1–2 (Wrocław: Instytut Archeologii Uniwersytetu Wrocławskiego, 2018)

Piskorski, Jan M., ed., *Historiographical Approaches to Medieval Colonization of East Central Europe: A Comparative Analysis against the Background of Other European Inter-ethnic Colonization Processes in the Middle Ages*, East European Monographs, 611 (New York: Boulder, 2002)

————, 'The Medieval Colonization of Central Europe as a Problem of World History and Historiography', *German History*, 22.3 (July 2004), 323–43, <https://doi.org/10.1191/0266355403gh313oa>

Piskorski, Jan M., Rudolf Jaworski, and Jürgenn Hackmann, eds, *Deutsche Ostforschung und polnische Westforschung im Spannungsfeld von Wissenschaft und Politik: Disziplinen im Vergleich* (Osnabrück: Fibre, 2002)

Rozpędowski, Jerzy, 'Breslau zur Zeit der ersten Lokation', in *Rechtsstadtgründungen im mittelalterlichen Polen*, ed. by Eduard Mühle, Städteforschung, A 81 (Cologne: Böhlau, 2011), pp. 127–38

Smith, Graham, Vivien Law, Andrew Wilson, Anette Bohr, and Edward Allworth, *Nation-building in the Post-Soviet Borderlands: The Politics of National Identities* (Cambridge: Cambridge University Press, 1998)

Wiszewski, Przemysław, *Domus Bolezlai: Values and Social Identity in Dynastic Traditions of Medieval Poland (c. 966–1138)*, East Central and Eastern Europe in the Middle Ages, 450–1450, 9 (Leiden: Brill, 2010)

————, 'The Multi-ethnic Character of Medieval Silesian Society and its Influence on the Region's Cohesion (12ᵗʰ–15ᵗʰ Centuries)', in *The Long Formation of the Region Silesia (c. 1000–1526)*, ed. by Przemysław Wiszewski, Cuius regio? Ideological and Territorial Cohesion of the Historical Region of Silesia (c. 1000–2000), 1 (Wrocław: Publishing House Wydawnictwo eBooki.com.pl, 2013), pp. 167–92, Open Access copy at <https://www.bibliotekacyfrowa.pl/dlibra/publication/46981/edition/49790/>

————, 'Politics and Change: The Silesian Dukes and the Transformation of the Land in the Thirteenth and Fourteenth Centuries', in *Landscapes and Societies in Medieval Europe East of the Elbe: Interactions between Environmental Settings and Cultural Transformations*, ed. by Sunhild Kleingärtner, Timothy P. Newfield, Sébastien Rossignol, and Donat Wehner, Papers in Mediaeval Studies, 23 (Toronto: Pontifical Institute of Mediaeval Studies, 2013), pp. 183–203

Witkowski, Jacek, 'Książę i dama na turnieju: Przejawy obyczajowości turniejowej w sztuce śląskiego średniowiecza', *Quart: Kwartalnik Instytutu Historii Sztuki Uniwersytetu Wrocławskiego*, 15.1 (2010), 3–17

————, 'Die Ritterkultur an den Höfen der schlesischen Piasten', in *King John of Luxembourg (1269–1346) and the Art of his Era: Proceedings of the International Conference, Prague, September 16–20, 1996*, ed. by Klára Benešovská (Prague: KLP – Koniasch Latin Press, 1998), pp. 201–05

————, *Szlachetna a wielce żałosna opowieść o Panu Lancelocie z Jeziora: Dekoracja malarska wielkiej sali wieży mieszkalnej w Siedlęcinie*, Acta Universitatis Wratislaviensis, 2291, Historia Sztuki, 15 (Wrocław: Wydawnictwo Uniwersytetu Wrocławskiego, 2001)

Wrzesiński, Wojciech, ed., *Dolny Śląsk: Monografia historyczna* (Wrocław: Wydawnictwo Uniwersytetu Wrocławskiego, 2006)

Wünsch, Thomas, *Deutsche und Slawen im Mittelalter: Beziehungen zu Tschechen, Polen, Südslawen und Russen* (Munich: R. Oldenbourg Verlag, 2008)

GRZEGORZ MYŚLIWSKI

Between Coexistence and Persecution

Economic Activity and the Cohesion of Multi-Ethnic Societies in Cities of the Polish Territories (between the Thirteenth and the First Part of the Sixteenth Century)

In the earlier chapters, the authors focused on inter-ethnic relations, which are primarily related to political and social changes as well as the implementation and making of law. However, societal life and societal relations have always been intertwined with economic issues.[1] Moreover, economy is regarded as an important component of societal life.[2] This is relevant to every community, both in the countryside and in cities. The important issue for research is an influence of economic activity on social relations including inter-ethnic relationships. This is particularly relevant to the larger cities which attracted many foreigners who settled permanently: merchants, retail traders, entrepreneurs, and versatile craftsmen.

1. Preliminary Remarks: An Overview of the Subject

The following study will assess the consequences of economic activities for inter-ethnic relations within the secular society of inhabitants of the main cities in the historically understood Polish territories. The geographic scope of these territories needs to be explained for unfamiliar readers. As a result of the frequent border changes of the lands controlled by the Polish kings in the Middle Ages, the term *Polish territories* does not always correspond to the territory of the united Polish land or feudal principalities governed by the Polish rulers (1138–1314). In accordance with the practice of Polish historiography,

---

1 Weber, *Economy and Society*, p. 339.
2 According to Aron J. Gurevich, 'Economic activity is a component part of social practice, of the interactions between man and his environment and of man's creative action on this environment. It reflects the vital preoccupations of a society' (Gurevich, *Categories of Medieval Culture*, p. 212).

Grzegorz Myśliwski • (g.mysliwski@uw.edu.pl) is Professor of Medieval History at the University of Warsaw. His main field is the history of medieval and early modern towns in central Europe.

Inter-Ethnic Relations and the Functioning of Multi-Ethnic Societies: Cohesion in Multi-Ethnic Societies in Europe from c. 1000 to the Present, II, ed. by Przemysław Wiszewski, EER 18 (Turnhout: Brepols, 2022), pp. 159–207
BREPOLS ❧ PUBLISHERS   10.1484/M.EER-EB.5.132151
This is an open access chapter made available under a cc by-nc 4.0 International License.

Map 7.1. Poland, Lithuania, and the Teutonic state at the beginning of the fifteenth century. Source: <https://commons.wikimedia.org/wiki/File:Poland,_Lithuania_and_Teutonic_state_at_the_beginning_of_the_XV_es.svg>. derivative work: Rowanwindwhistler, CC BY-SA 3.0.

Polish territories also means regions that at some point ended up outside of the Polish border:[3] Silesia (between 1327 and 1339, it was part of the Kingdom of Bohemia)[4] and some regions annexed by the Teutonic Order — Chełmno land (outside of Poland between 1226 and 1466) and Eastern Pomerania (1309–1466).[5] This term is seldom used to describe the territory of Western Pomerania due to its short affiliation with or dependence on the Polish state (*c.* 967–1005, 1122–1181).[6] However, close relations with the adjacent Polish lands in the medieval period (especially with Greater Poland) enable us to include the western part of Pomerania in the following study, which will expand our comparative base.

We will concentrate our attention on the biggest centres in the main regions of the historically understood Polish territories: Kraków (including the suburban salt

---

3   See Gawlas, ed., *Ziemie polskie wobec Zachodu* and Gawlas, 'Introduction' and English summaries of the remaining texts that contribute to this book (pp. 441–48). See also Manikowska, 'Religijność miejska', p. 11.
4   Hołubowicz and Maleczyński, *Historia Śląska*, pp. 544–61; Hoensch, *Geschichte Böhmens*, p. 118.
5   Biskup and Labuda, *Dzieje zakonu krzyżackiego w Prusach*, pp. 140–43, 255–58, 409–17.
6   Ślaski and Zientara, *Historia Pomorza*, pp. 69–70.

mine centres in Bochnia and Wieliczka — Lesser Poland), Wrocław (Silesia), Lviv (located in Red Ruthenia — incorporated into the Kingdom of Poland in 1340),[7] Poznań (Greater Poland), Płock (Masovia), Gdańsk (Eastern Pomerania), and Szczecin (Western Pomerania). Hence, we are omitting Warsaw (it only reached the same level as Płock in the fifteenth century) and Toruń, because the ethnic history of the nearby port city, Gdańsk, is far more complex.

Though the history of each of these centres has been described in syntheses, the level of research on the local ethnic relations and economic history varies. This is mainly due to different levels of preservation of the primary sources (council and bench court books, city statutes). There are extensive sources for Wrocław, Kraków, Płock, Poznań, and Gdańsk. There are significantly fewer sources preserved for Lviv and, for the period after 1350, for Szczecin.[8] Nonetheless, it is worth attempting to compare the influence of economic issues on the level of cohesion in the heterogenous communities in these cities, with different histories and often changing political affiliations.

The issue of ethnic relations is not a new topic in the historiography of Poland (and other lands related to the historically understood Polish territories). However, this issue has rarely been viewed synthetically, leaving aside on this occasion either all of Pomerania or only its western part.[9] This absence is partially compensated by the existence of more detailed publications. Separate texts have been dedicated to Jews,[10] Italians,[11] Armenians,[12] and Walloons.[13] Naturally, due to the incorporation of Red Ruthenia (with Lviv) into the Kingdom of Poland, the Ruthenians became another important national group living in the Polish territory. Many studies have been published on the topics of their activity, status, and demography, although these were mostly marginal compared with publications on wider issues.[14]

---

7 Knoll, *The Rise of the Polish Monarchy*, pp. 121–77; Wyrozumski, *Kazimierz Wielki*, pp. 71–101.
8 Badecki, 'Zaginione księgi średniowiecznego Lwowa', pp. 520–23; Piskorski, *Miasta księstwa szczecińskiego*, pp. 8–9.
9 Ptaśnik, *Miasta i mieszczaństwo*, pp. 301–57, and Bogucka and Samsonowicz, *Dzieje miast*, pp. 265–70, respectively.
10 Particularly Brann, *Geschichte der Juden in Schlesien*, I; Charewiczowa, *Ograniczenia gospodarcze*, pp. 25–37; Grodecki, 'Dzieje Żydów'; Wyrozumska, 'Wstęp' (1995); Ziątkowski, *Dzieje Żydów*; Guldon, 'Skupiska żydowskie'; Fijałkowski, 'Początki obecności'; Zaremska, *Żydzi w średniowiecznej Europie Środkowej*; Janeczek, 'Żydzi i Ormianie'; Zaremska, *Żydzi w średniowiecznej Polsce*. See also Kapral, 'Legal Regulation', pp. 223–26; Kozubska-Andrusiv, '... propter disparitatem linguae et religionis pares ipsis non esse ...', pp. 61–64.
11 Ptaśnik, *Kultura włoska*; Sapori, 'Gli Italiani in Polonia'; Hryszko, *Januensis, ergo mercator?*.
12 Balzer, *Sądownictwo ormiańskie*; Charewiczowa, *Ograniczenia gospodarcze*, pp. 15–25; Bardach, 'Ormianie na ziemiach dawnej Polski'; Stopka, *Ormianie w Polsce dawnej*; Stopka, 'Kultura religijna Ormian'; Janeczek, 'Żydzi i Ormianie'; see also Wyrozumska, 'Wstęp' (2003); Kozubska-Andrusiv, '... propter disparitatem linguae et religionis pares ipsis non esse ...', pp. 54–57.
13 Zientara, 'Walloons in Silesia'; Goliński, *Socjotopografia późnośredniowiecznego Wrocławia*, pp. 187–219; Słoń, 'Początki osady walońskiej'.
14 Isaevič and others, eds, *Історія Львова u tr'och tomach*; see Charewiczowa, *Ograniczenia gospodarcze*, pp. 5–15; Janeczek, 'Exceptis schismaticis'. See also Kapral, 'Legal Regulation', pp. 215–19; Kozubska-Andrusiv, '... propter disparitatem linguae et religionis pares ipsis non esse ...', pp. 58–60.

2. Outline of Ethnic Transitions in the Polish Territories

In the Middle Ages (until the turn of the fifteenth and sixteenth century) the general population of the historically understood Polish territories never constituted a monolith in ethnic, as well as religious, terms.[15] In the initial period (tenth–twelfth centuries) it was the local and tribal consciousness that dominated among the Slavic autochthones. We should also include foreigners, such as the Normans, who even migrated to these territories during the conquests of the subsequent Polish territories by Mieszko I (967–991).[16] As a consequence of that ruler's baptism (966) and the creation of a Church structure and organization, there was an influx of clergy from Bohemia and Italy, but especially from Germany.[17] The timing of the first Jewish settlement is a totally different issue. In the light of the latest research, the oldest commune was founded in Kraków before 1028;[18] however, we are not certain how much earlier this took place. It appears to be certain that in the tenth century Bohemians inhabited this city, given that Kraków primarily belonged to the land of the Czech Přemyslids (until 990).[19]

Larger centres in the Polish territories at that time, such as Kraków, but also the Pomeranian cities (Wolin, Szczecin, Kołobrzeg, Gdańsk), participated in long-distance trade. Consequently, foreigners also arrived: Varangians of the Rus' and Eastern Slavs (Ruthenians) in Kraków, and Scandinavians, Ruthenians,[20] Germans, and Frisians in the Pomeranian towns.[21] It is supposed that in the tenth and eleventh centuries, Jews migrated to Gdańsk to trade in slaves.[22] Basing his interpretations on the oldest Polish chronicle, *Cronicae et gesta ducum sive principum Polonorum* (written by an anonymous author called Gallus) P. Fijałkowski put forward the view that Jews were practising this trade in Płock in the second half of the eleventh century.[23] However, it is difficult to determine if any permanent settlement of these foreigners (except for Normans and Cracow Jews) took place in these Slavic centres before the twelfth century. There were occasional newcomers from more distant lands who remained in Poland, such as the knight Hugo Butyr from the County of Holland (twelfth century).[24] The establishment of the Polish national consciousness dates back to the twelfth–thirteenth centuries.[25]

---

15 A general outline was described by B. Zientara in a synthesis by Ihnatowicz, Mączak, and Zientara, *Społeczeństwo polskie*, pp. 193–204; see also Janeczek, 'Ethnische Gruppenbildungen'.
16 Buko, *Archeologia*, pp. 350–54.
17 Geremek, 'Migracje i kontakty kulturowe', pp. 16–24.
18 Zaremska, *Żydzi w średniowiecznej Europie Środkowej*, p. 74; Zaremska, *Żydzi w średniowiecznej Polsce*, pp. 81, 331–37.
19 Wyrozumski, *Dzieje Krakowa*, p. 79.
20 Nazmi, *Commercial Relations between Arabs and Slavs*, p. 173.
21 Zbierski and Jasiński, 'Gdańsk', p. 225; Leciejewicz and Rębkowski, 'Uwagi końcowe', pp. 305, 309.
22 Echt, *Die Geschichte der Juden*, p. 13.
23 Fijałkowski, 'Początki obecności', p. 171.
24 Powierski, 'Hugo Butyr'.
25 Ihnatowicz, Mączak, and Zientara, *Społeczeństwo polskie*, pp. 208–10; Modzelewski, *Chłopi*, pp. 271–78; an overview of numerous studies on this topic was described by Gawlas, 'Stan badań', pp. 149–93; see a summary in English, Gawlas, 'Stan badań', p. 194.

Apart from such factors as the linguistic community, the tradition of dependency on the eternally ruling Piast dynasty (*domini naturales*), and, possibly, memories of selected historical events, another crucial factor which stimulated the development of a sense of identity was a significant influx of foreigners — colonizers and settlers. The majority of them came from different parts of the Holy Roman Empire.[26] However, it is worth noting that the Polish national consciousness did not exist in the Pomeranian territories. Instead, Slavic (*Sclavi*) and regional consciousness prevailed.[27] Apart from migrants from Germany, it is worth mentioning the Walloons, though significantly fewer in number, who settled in Silesia, and Prussians, who had migrated from their homeland to Masovia and Eastern Pomerania.[28]

The thirteenth century also marked the beginning of the foundation of new towns (*in cruda radice*) or the re-establishment of old ones under the German law (the versions included the Magdeburg, Lubeck, Środa in Silesia, and Chełmno law).[29] In the case of the biggest cities, it led to the accession to power and dominance by the Germans. Sometimes the officials who gathered the colonizers and organized the foundation of a city according to the new law obtained from the feudal ruler a ban on the local population that prohibited them from coming to the territory of the newly incorporated town (Kraków, 1257).[30] In other cases, a part of the native population was gradually included in the municipal community (Szczecin).[31] As time passed, the numbers of Germans rose considerably and became dominant in many centres. This situation was maintained until around the fifteenth century, although in the fourteenth century the ethnic composition of some Polish cities became more diverse.

The late medieval period, especially from the unification of part of the Polish land by Władysław I the Elbow-high and the restitution of the Kingdom of Poland in 1320, can be characterized by the petrification of ethnonational identity, but also with a further diversification of the ethnic structures, especially in urban communities. Starting from 1306, merchants and traders began to come to Poland from Italy — first the Genoese, then Florentines, Venetians, as well as migrants from the less influential urban centres of the Apennine Peninsula.[32] There were also further waves of German newcomers, especially from wealthy and expansive Nuremberg. The *terminus ab quo* of their influx was the year 1365 when Casimir the Great granted them the privilege of free passage through his land to the Rus' for a period of twenty years.[33] However, they only began to appear in Kraków in slightly higher numbers from the beginning of

---

26 A summary of the studies on this topic: Goliński, 'Wokół problematyki', p. 33.

27 Piskorski, *Miasta księstwa szczecińskiego*, pp. 170–72.

28 Zientara, 'Walloons in Silesia'; Okulicz-Kozaryn, *Dzieje Prusów*, pp. 491–95.

29 From the extensive literature, see Bogucka and Samsonowicz, *Dzieje miast*, pp. 45–88.

30 Ptaśnik, *Miasta i mieszczaństwo*, p. 293; Wyrozumski, *Dzieje Krakowa*, pp. 160–74, particularly p. 172. See more recently Goliński, 'Wokół problematyki', pp. 22, 25.

31 Piskorski, *Miasta księstwa szczecińskiego*, pp. 170–71.

32 Ptaśnik, *Kultura włoska*, pp. 18–19; Sapori, *Le marchand italien*, p. lix; Małowist, *Wschód a Zachód Europyw*, pp. 188–89.

33 Ptaśnik, 'Studya nad patrycyatem', p. 25; von Stromer, 'Nürnberger Unternehmer', p. 644.

164   GRZEGORZ MYŚLIWSKI

the fifteenth century.[34] They settled there permanently, gaining a very important role in the economic life of the city and the whole Kingdom of Poland, as well as — from the end of the fourteenth century — Wrocław, which belonged to the Kingdom of Bohemia.[35] Small numbers of Hungarians, Lithuanians, and Bohemians began to appear in the capital of the Polish state.[36]

The conquest of Red Ruthenia by Casimir the Great resulted in the inclusion of Ruthenians, Armenians, as well as Muslim Tatars, and possibly members of other ethnic communities, into the Polish state (see section 3). The fifteenth century and the beginning of the modern era were to be times of tumultuous changes, in terms of both the sense of identity and ethnic relations.

Other identities began to crystalize in the Polish territories which remained outside of the borders of the Kingdom of Poland. The process of the development of regional Silesian identity was established in the cities and towns of Silesia.[37] Meanwhile, in the politically distinct Masovia, the process of development of a separate Masovian nation also started (though it stopped in the sixteenth century after the definite incorporation of this region into the Kingdom of Poland).[38]

However, conflicts between Germans (who had been intensively Polonizing since around the second part of the fifteenth century) and Jews broke out in some centres. But overall in the period until the fourteenth century, the situation of the Jewish people appeared to be relatively advantageous. They were given numerous privileges, which regulated their status and guaranteed protection. These were first granted by the Duke of Szczecin Pomerania, Barnim I, in 1261 (see section 3). Not long after, the very advantageous charter of Jewish Liberties was issued in Kalisz by the Duke of Greater Poland, Bolesław the Pious (1264).[39] Supposedly, it applied to Jewish people in all the cities of this region, including Poznań.[40] In Silesia, a privilege granting protection to the Jews was issued slightly later by Henryk IV Probus (1285), and in the next decade by rulers of the Duchy of Świdnica and Głogów.[41] During the reign of Casimir III the Great in Poland (1333–1370), the ruler issued three Jewish privileges — in 1334, 1364, and 1367. As much as the 1367 document applied to Lesser Poland and Red Ruthenia,[42] the previous two privileges were traditionally considered by historians to encompass the whole of Poland.[43] But, as H. Zaremska has recently proven, the first privilege applied

---

34 Kutrzeba, *Handel Krakowa*, pp. 88–90.
35 From the extensive literature, see Scholz-Babisch, 'Oberdeutscher Handel', pp. 58–59, 62, 66–67, 69; von Stromer, *Die Nürnberger Handelsgesellschafft*, pp. 11, 21, 32, 36, 70, 72; von Stromer, 'Nürnberg–Breslauer Wirtschaftsbeziehungen'; Myśliwski, *Wrocław w przestrzeni*, pp. 412–48.
36 Wyrozumski, *Dzieje Krakowa*, pp. 318, 331, 347.
37 Manikowska, 'Świadomość regionalna'.
38 Samsonowicz, 'Przesłanki tworzenia się narodu'.
39 Grodecki, 'Dzieje Żydów', pp. 641–65; Zaremska, 'Statut Bolesława Pobożnego dla Żydów'. Cf. Zaremska, *Żydzi w średniowiecznej Polsce*, pp. 116–29.
40 Gąsiorowski, 'Ludność Poznania', p. 267.
41 Brann, *Geschichte der Juden in Schlesien*, I, pp. 15, 17; Bobowski, 'Ze studiów', p. 7.
42 Grodecki, 'Dzieje Żydów', p. 664.
43 Kozubska-Andrusiv, '… propter disparitatem linguae et religionis pares ipsis non esse …', p. 62.

BETWEEN COEXISTENCE AND PERSECUTION 165

exclusively to Jews living in Greater Poland.[44] Consequently, only the privilege issued by Casimir III the Great in 1364 could be applied to all the Jews inhabiting the territory of the Kingdom of Poland. Casimir III's successors were less favourably inclined towards the Polish Jews.[45] Władysław II Jagiełło (1386–1434) issued a privilege only for the Jews from the area of Lviv.[46] His eldest son, Władysław III, did not do anything on this matter. On the other hand, at the beginning of his reign, Casimir IV Jagiellon (1447–1492) validated the Casimir documents (among them one of suspect authenticity).[47] However, under pressure from the nobility and Catholic clergy (led by Cardinal Zbigniew Oleśnicki), he revoked them in 1454.

Despite providing plenty of privileges for the Jews, pogroms and expulsions occurred in the fourteenth and fifteenth centuries in Western Pomerania, Silesia, and some cities of the united Kingdom of Poland (Wrocław, Kraków, Poznań; see section 4). The King of Bohemia, Władysław the Posthumous, issued an edict regarding Silesia (on the request of the urban middle-class), which forced Jews to leave Wrocław (1455).[48] In Kraków, the municipalities forced members of the Jewish commune to leave Kraków Old Town and relocate to the other part of the Krakow agglomerate, called Kazimierz (1495).[49] It is worth noting that in the sixteenth century Sigismund I the Old (1506–1548) and his successors issued plenty of documents for royal cities and towns, which, as a result, forbade Jews from residing in these centres ('de non tolerandis Judaeis').[50] But none of these charters concerned any of the cities under study (on the limits imposed on Jewish economic activity, see below, section 7). In Wrocław, Kraków, and Poznań, the history of Jewish–Christian relations resembled the shape of a sine wave, with a dramatic break in its continuity (see sections 3, 9).

At the same time, an important and complex process of the Polonization of the townspeople ensued in some of the centres under consideration (Kraków, Lviv, Poznań, and Płock), which is what I describe below (see section 4).

---

44 Zaremska, *Żydzi w średniowiecznej Polsce*, pp. 145–46.

45 Zaremska, *Żydzi w średniowiecznej Polsce*, pp. 144, 159.

46 Zaremska, *Żydzi w średniowiecznej Polsce*, p. 149.

47 A detailed analysis of the documents and the process of their confirmation, Zaremska, *Żydzi w średniowiecznej Polsce*, pp. 159–71.

48 Wendt, *Schlesien und der Orient*, p. 123; Goerlitz, *Verfassung, Verwaltung und Recht*, p. 120. Despite that, Jews were coming to Wrocław after 1455 to attend fairs (Ziątkowski, *Dzieje Żydów*, p. 17).

49 Wyrozumski, *Dzieje Krakowa*, p. 330; Zaremska, *Żydzi w średniowiecznej Polsce*, pp. 493–504. B. Wyrozumska does not share this view, arguing that the continued economic activity of Jews in the territory of Kraków after 1495 can be supported by sources (Wyrozumska, 'Wstęp' (1995), p. 9; see *Żydzi w średniowiecznym Krakowie*, ed. by Wyrozumska, nos 907–1179), whereas M. Starzyński is of the opinion that a part of the Jewish community and its authorities moved out to Kazimierz (Starzyński, 'Najstarszy dokument hebrajski', p. 196).

50 Guldon, 'Skupiska żydowskie', p. 21. Kamianets-Podilskyi received this privilege the earliest — in 1447 (Guldon, 'Skupiska żydowskie', p. 21). However, it turned out to be ineffective; hence it had to be renewed in the second part of the fifteenth and in the sixteenth century.

3. The Ethnic Composition of the Main Polish Cities (Thirteenth–Fifteenth Centuries)

The starting point for presenting the ethnic composition of cities and towns in the Kingdom of Poland (including Gdańsk) is a table prepared by H. Samsonowicz.[51] This historian also included smaller centres of the main historic regions of Poland, which I have not taken into consideration. The chart, however, relates only to the fifteenth century and does not include Szczecin, which at the time had been outside of the borders of the Polish state for a long time back. Hence, using Samsonowicz's conclusions as a basis, I propose my own, simplified chart (see Appendix 1). It collectively depicts the ethnic composition of the urban centres under consideration between the thirteenth and first half of the sixteenth centuries. Because the table does not contain the dynamics of ethnic changes for such a long period, it is mainly supposed to serve as an aid, to be used alongside reading the ethnic history of these cities. I would also like to point out that the chart, as well as the rest of the essay, does not include clergy, whose numbers in these cities are estimated to have been from 1 per cent to possibly even 10 per cent.[52]

We should start with the centres of the southern part of the broadly understood Polish territories, which were connected through a major trade route, running from the Netherlands and Cologne to Red Ruthenia (*Hohe Strasse*)[53] — Wrocław, Kraków, and Lviv. The Slavic and Polish population was dominant in Wrocław before the thirteenth century, though national consciousness might not have been developed yet. It is generally accepted that the Jewish commune was founded here in the twelfth century.[54] Despite a few attempts to remove the Jews from the city (1226, 1317 or 1319)[55] and *pogroms* (1348, 1351, 1360, 1420, 1453),[56] the commune lasted until the final pogrom and expulsion from the city in 1455 (see above, section 2). Walloons settled in Wrocław in the second part of the twelfth century.[57] They were a Romance-speaking people that inhabited the territories of modern-day Belgium (at the time, the County of Flanders and partially the Holy Roman Empire). In the thirteenth century, their number slightly increased in Wrocław, due to the arrival of highly qualified weavers.[58]

---

51 Bogucka and Samsonowicz, *Dzieje miast*, p. 266.
52 Wiesiołowski, 'Środowiska kościelne i kultura', pp. 279–83; Maleczyński, 'Dzieje Wrocławia', pp. 86, 206; Bogucka and Samsonowicz, *Dzieje miast*, p. 161; Wiesiołowski, 'Kultura i społeczeństwo', p. 319; Myśliwski, 'Kościół katolicki', pp. 241–44.
53 Bruns and Weczerka, *Hansische Handelstrassen*, pp. 467–70, 539–48, 550–52, 568–70, 681–90; Myśliwski, *Wrocław w przestrzeni*, pp. 75–80.
54 Bobowski, 'Ze studiów', p. 5; Ziątkowski, *Dzieje Żydów*, p. 9.
55 Brann, *Geschichte der Juden in Schlesien*, I, p. 38; Bobowski, 'Ze studiów', p. 8; Goliński, 'Wrocław', p. 140.
56 From among many studies, see Brann, *Geschichte der Juden in Schlesien*, II, pp. 52, 62–64; Brann, *Geschichte der Juden in Schlesien*, III, pp. 96–97; Brann, *Geschichte der Juden in Schlesien*, IV, pp. 123–25, 131; Heck, 'Wrocław', pp. 58, 70; Bobowski, 'Ze studiów', pp. 7–8; Ziątkowski, *Dzieje Żydów*, pp. 12, 16; Goliński, 'Wrocław', pp. 156, 189; Zaremska, 'Zmowa śląskich Żydów'.
57 Székely, 'Wallons et Italiens', pp. 22–23; Zientara, 'Walloons in Silesia', pp. 132–34; Słoń, 'Początki osady walońskiej'.
58 Zientara, 'Walloons in Silesia', pp. 135–36.

BETWEEN COEXISTENCE AND PERSECUTION   167

However, the main breakthrough in ethnic relations was the granting of three urban charters (*c.* 1230, 1241/1242, 1261),[59] which resulted in an influx of Germans and, in effect, their dominance within urban life. As a result of this reorganization of the city, a Walloonian settlement was incorporated into the city and its inhabitants were later subjected to gradual Germanization.[60] It is also worth mentioning the one Italian, Antonio Ricci from Florence, a wealthy and enterprising person, who arrived at Wrocław around 1410 and died circa 1443/1444.[61] The Polish population significantly fell in numbers over the centuries, although at the beginning of the sixteenth century a number of Poles continued to live in this centre of Silesia.[62]

Kraków was an even more ethnically diverse city. As I have already written, before the thirteenth century it was inhabited by Bohemians, Poles, and Jews. It is possible that later the Walloons began to settle down here.[63] As a consequence of the granting of two urban charters (1228, 1257), Germans also began to live in Kraków as well. Their next wave came at the beginning of the fifteenth century (see above, section 2). Italians started to migrate to Kraków from the beginning of the fourteenth century (1306), with the Genoese coming first. Armenians began to arrive in the 1370s, though they only started to settle there permanently in the fifteenth century.[64] In the same century, the situation of Jewish people started to decline (pogroms in 1407, 1455, 1464, 1477, and 1494),[65] which ended in their exile (see above, section 2).

Lviv, founded in the 1240s,[66] was for a few decades inhabited exclusively by the native Ruthenian population. In that same century, Germans started to arrive from Lesser Poland and Silesia, as well as from Moldovan and Transylvanian cities.[67] It is often concluded that as early as in the Ruthenian period (before 1340), this centre was populated also by Armenians.[68] However, they were only first mentioned in the document issued by the Polish king Casimir III the Great in 1356, who granted the

---

59 From extensive literature: Maleczyński, 'Dzieje Wrocławia', p. 74; Goerlitz, *Verfassung, Verwaltung und Recht*, pp. 15, 19; Młynarska-Kaletynowa, *Wrocław w XII–XIII wieku*, pp. 8, 101, 125, 130, 158, 168; Goliński, 'Wrocław', pp. 100–101; Buśko, 'Wrocław u progu lokacji', pp. 177, 193–94.

60 Zientara, 'Walloons in Silesia', p. 136.

61 See particularly: Ptaśnik, *Kultura włoska*, pp. 36–38, 74, 76–77, 79–82, 85, 134–37, 146–51; Sapori, 'Gli Italiani in Polonia', pp. 156, 159; Székely, 'Wallons et Italiens', pp. 36–37, 51, 56; Myśliwski, *Wrocław w przestrzeni*, pp. 463–64, 470–71, 476–85, 487–90, 493–95.

62 At that time, they were mentioned by Barthel Stein in his description of Wrocław (*Bartłomieja Steina renesansowe opisanie Wrocławia*, ed. by Żerelik, cap. 13, p. 108; cap. 17, p. 111). About the locations of sermons in Polish in the fifteenth century, see Goliński, *Socjotopografia późnośredniowiecznego Wrocławia*, p. 234.

63 Zientara, 'Walloons in Silesia', p. 137.

64 Wyrozumska, 'Wstęp' (2003), p. 7.

65 Wyrozumski, *Dzieje Krakowa*, pp. 326–28, 330; Zaremska, *Żydzi w średniowiecznej Polsce*, pp. 456–77.

66 Isaevič and others, eds, Історія Львова u tr'och tomach, p. 7.

67 Isaevič and others, eds, Історія Львова u tr'och tomach, p. 78.

68 Papée, *Historja miasta Lwowa*, p. 25; Kozubska-Andrusiv, '… propter disparitatem linguae et religionis pares ipsis non esse …', p. 55.

168 GRZEGORZ MYŚLIWSKI

Magdeburg law to the city.[69] The same remark can be applied to the Jews.[70] The charter mentioned Tatars and unspecified Saracens ('dicte naciones [...] Saracenorum, Thartharorum') too — presumably Muslims who differed from Tatars — who were also inhabitants of Lviv.[71] In the Middle Ages, the area was also populated by a small group of Karaims, a nation of Turkish descent, members of which were followers of non-Rabbinic Judaism.[72] The incorporation of Lviv into the Kingdom of Poland brought a slow influx of the Polish population, which intensified during the fifteenth century.[73] It is generally assumed that in the first part of that century Italians started to migrate to this city — particularly citizens of the Republic of Genoa, who had been living previously in Genoa's largest colonial city within the Black Sea basin, Caffa.[74] However, one has to remark that as early as the fourteenth century, some 'Gallici' (Italians?) were mentioned here, but their place of origin was not defined.[75] It is likely that they resided in Lviv permanently. This is also the period in which Jacob the Greek is recorded, similarly with no mention of his place of origin.[76] It is worth noting that none of the cities under study were as ethnically and religiously diverse as Lviv.

The communities of the previously discussed cities situated in the south from *Hohe Strasse* — both in the lowlands (Greater Poland and Masovia), as well as in Pomerania — were significantly less diverse than Lviv, Kraków, or even Wrocław. Poznań, until its reorganization according to the German law in 1253, was populated mainly by Poles. In the same year as the new legal order of the city was introduced an influx of Germans arrived. Jews, who were present in other cities of Greater Poland (Kalisz, Gniezno) in the second part of the twelfth century,[77] seem to have appeared in Poznań relatively late. Although it has been suggested that they had already settled down there in the second part of the thirteenth century, undisputable traces of their presence can only be dated back as late as the second part of the fourteenth century.[78] Similar to Wrocław and

---

69 Balzer, *Sądownictwo ormiańskie*, pp. 5–8, 16; Kozubska-Andrusiv, '... propter disparitatem linguae et religionis pares ipsis non esse ...', p. 53. For a discussion of Ukrainian historians on the topic of this document and the German law in Lviv, see Kapral, 'Legal Regulation', pp. 214–15.

70 Kapral, 'Legal Regulation', p. 223.

71 *Privilegia civitatis Leopoliensis (XIV–XVIII saec.)*, ed. by Kapral, no. 1, p. 28. This issue has not been resolved so far, though different hypotheses were put forward regarding the identification of *Saracenorum*. They were thought to be Arab merchants (Czołowski, 'Lwów za ruskich czasów', p. 806; Isaevič and others, eds, Історія Львова u tr'och tomach, p. 88) or 'Suroż people', merchants from an important trading centre in Crimea — Suraż/Sudak/Soldai (Czołowski, 'Lwów za ruskich czasów', p. 806). It was mainly supposed to be Byzantine Greeks and Italians (Tichomirov, *Drevnjaja Moskva*, p. 153), due to the commercial importance of this town (Tichomirov, *Drevnjaja Moskva*, pp. 92–93; Sacharov, *Goroda severo–vostočnoj Rusi*, p. 153; Lane, *Venice*, p. 129). Oswald Balzer suggested that a comma should be placed between these two terms — consequently Tatars should be treated as an explanation of the general term 'Saraceni' (Balzer, *Sądownictwo ormiańskie*, p. 6).

72 Janeczek, 'Ethnische Gruppenbildungen', p. 427.

73 Jakowenko, *Historia Ukrainy*, p. 116; Isaevič and others, eds, Історія Львова u tr'och tomach, p. 78.

74 Charewiczowa, *Handel średniowiecznego Lwowa*, pp. 51–52.

75 *Najstarsza księga miejska (1382–1389)*, ed. by Czołowski, nos 608, 679, 709.

76 *Najstarsza księga miejska (1382–1389)*, ed. by Czołowski, no. 17.

77 Grodecki, 'Dzieje Żydów', p. 639; Zaremska, *Żydzi w średniowiecznej Polsce*, p. 114.

78 Gąsiorowski, 'Ludność Poznania', p. 267; Guldon, 'Skupiska żydowskie', p. 22.

BETWEEN COEXISTENCE AND PERSECUTION   169

Kraków, the presence of Jews in Poznań intertwined with different scales of pogroms (1367, 1369, 1399, 1434, 1447, 1453, 1464).[79] Despite the particularly catastrophic pogrom of 1464, the Jews continued to reside and conduct economic activity here. At least until *c*. 1536, when the situation became strained again but did not escalate into a pogrom or expulsion,[80] no further oppression towards the Jews occurred in this city. The fifteenth century also turned out to be essential for the history of ethnic relations in Poznań for different reasons. Around at least 1432, merchants from Nuremberg began to come (and partially settle) there.[81] Small groups of Italians (Genoese) and Armenians from distant Lviv arrived by the end of the century.[82] The limited migration of individual Bohemians and Ruthenians into Poznań was of little importance.[83]

The ethnic structure of Płock, the main city of the Masovian region for nearly the whole Middle Ages, looks far less diverse. The Polish population was dominant, although from the document of the first reorganization of this city (1237) we learn that it was previously populated by the Jews ('puteum Judeorum').[84] The archaeological evidence suggests that the Jewish community continued to reside there throughout the fourteenth century.[85] More definite written sources provide detail about the period from 1425 onwards.[86] In that century, the Jews were mentioned as taxpayers to the ruler, a duke ('census nostros ducales').[87] However, according to S. M. Szacherska, at the end of the Middle Ages, their numbers in Płock were minimal,[88] in contrast to other Masovian cities.[89] Their numbers probably started to rise in the first quarter of the sixteenth century. The proximity of the Teutonic Order and the next attempt to reorganized the city under German law (*c*. 1300)[90] caused an influx of German settlers. It is likely that Bohemians also lived here (the Duchy of Płock for a time constituted a fief of the Kingdom of Bohemia).[91] Despite the abovementioned facts, in the second part of the fifteenth century, the Płock townspeople seemed to be nearly entirely Polish. This was partly due to the settlement of the local nobility, who wanted to directly participate in the development of trade on the Vistula River with Toruń and Gdańsk.[92] In the late Middle Ages and the early modern era, many

---

79 Gąsiorowski, 'Ludność Poznania', p. 267; Wiesiołowski, *Socjotopografia późnośredniowiecznego Poznania*, p. 117; Rudzińska, 'Żydzi w późnośredniowiecznym Poznaniu', pp. 358–59.

80 Koczy, *Handel Poznania*, p. 272.

81 Schenk, *Nürnberg und Prag*, p. 82; Simsch, 'Die Handelsbeziehungen', p. 140.

82 Koczy, *Handel Poznania*, pp. 41, 263–64; Hryszko, *Januensis, ergo mercator?*, p. 128.

83 Wiesiołowski, *Socjotopografia późnośredniowiecznego Poznania*, p. 116.

84 Grodecki, 'Dzieje Żydów', p. 624; Fijałkowski, 'Początki obecności', p. 171. T. Żebrowski assumed that there were few Jews in Płock at the time (Żebrowski, 'Stolica książąt', p. 107).

85 Fijałkowski, 'Początki obecności', pp. 185–86.

86 Fijałkowski, 'Początki obecności', p. 173.

87 *Zbiór dokumentów*, I, ed. by Szacherska, no. 198 (1474), p. 284.

88 Szacherska, 'Złoty wiek miasta', p. 137.

89 Guldon, 'Skupiska żydowskie', pp. 23–24; Fijałkowski, 'Początki obecności', pp. 172–75.

90 Żebrowski, 'Stolica książąt', p. 100.

91 Żebrowski, 'Stolica książąt', p. 107. About the relationships with the Bohemian state, see more recently Suchodolska, 'Dzieje polityczne', pp. 243–45.

92 Szacherska, 'Złoty wiek miasta', pp. 132–33. The nobility tightened the relationship with this town in the fourteenth century (so Żebrowski, 'Stolica książąt', p. 107).

migrants from outside of the city and region came to Masovia, including Płock,[93] although it is hard to determine who settled there for good. One foreigner was an Austrian, Johann Alantesse from Vienna, an apothecary who in the first half of the sixteenth century became burgomaster and was granted a noble title by Holy Roman Emperor Charles V.[94]

At the end of this overview, we should mention two Baltic port cities — Szczecin and Gdańsk. The first centre was dominated by the Slavic population for a long time. But before the urban charter was granted, migrants from Germany established their enclave here (circa the middle of the twelfth century).[95] From the year 1237, Szczecin Slavs were under the urban jurisdiction, which can serve as proof of the reorganization of the city according to German law.[96] It also confirms that local Slavs were part of the new urban community. Later on, they resided in the Chyżyn district, though mainly in suburban hamlets.[97] Their proportion decreased during the thirteenth and fourteenth centuries. It came as the result of an influx of migrants from Germany (most often from Westphalia and the Rhineland — 30 per cent).[98] On the other hand, in a bench court book, there is a mention of a Slavic woman who carried a German name ('Mechtilda slavica pistrix') and two traders described by the Latin name of 'Polonus'.[99] But these are exceptions to the rule. The thirteenth century is thought to be the beginning of the Jewish population's arrival.[100] It can also be proven through the decision of Duke Barnim I of Pomerania who in 1261 issued a privilege for his capital, and Jews who resided in it were given a status that corresponded with the Magdeburg law regulations.[101] In the light of the previous research, the situation of the Jews in Szczecin appears to be favourable throughout the fourteenth century. Not only did they live within the walls, but they also had numerous property transactions, while some individuals became city councillors.[102] Some of them, such as Jordan, made a

---

93 Myśliwski, *Człowiek średniowiecza*, pp. 186–89.

94 Szacherska, 'Złoty wiek miasta', p. 136. Granting nobility, see *Zbiór dokumentów*, II, ed. by Szacherska, no. 378 (1530), pp. 146–49.

95 Piskorski, *Miasta księstwa szczecińskiego*, p. 165.

96 Piskorski, *Miasta księstwa szczecińskiego*, p. 170. About the basic documents for the reorganization of Szczecin according to German law from 1237 and 1243, see Lesiński, 'Rozdrobnienie feudalne', pp. 64, 91.

97 Piskorski, *Miasta księstwa szczecińskiego*, p. 172.

98 Lesiński, 'Rozdrobnienie feudalne', p. 128. About the mechanisms for an increase in the immigrant population and their descendants, see Piskorski, *Miasta księstwa szczecińskiego*, pp. 173–74.

99 *Das älteste Stettiner Stadtbuch*, ed. by Wehrmann, no. 659 (1312), p. 70; no. 327 (1309), p. 43; no. 1808 (1346), p. 169. At the time, the term *Polonus* could mean either a Pole or a resident of Greater Poland — the area neighbouring Western Pomerania (Ihnatowicz, Mączak, and Zientara, *Społeczeństwo polskie*, p. 209), or (less often) a Silesian (Małowist, 'Le développement des rapports économiques', p. 1020; for other examples, see Myśliwski, *Wrocław w przestrzeni*, p. 241).

100 Ślaski and Zientara, *Historia Pomorza*, p. 250.

101 Lesiński, 'Rozdrobnienie feudalne', p. 129. 'Donauimus insuper memoratis burgensibus et eorum hanc prerogativam successoribus, ut omnes iudei in ciuitate sepedicta Stetin manentes aut ubicumque in terra nostra manentes teneantur seruare in omnibus iura, que iudei in ciuitate Magdeborch manentes obseruant' (*Pommersches Urkundenbuch*, ed. by Prümers, no. 708, p. 86).

102 Lesiński, 'Rozdrobnienie feudalne', p. 129; Piskorski, *Miasta księstwa szczecińskiego*, p. 174.

BETWEEN COEXISTENCE AND PERSECUTION   171

fortune.[103] Due to the lack of sources, we are not certain what their subsequent fate was when Jews were expelled from many of the cities of the Hanseatic League in Germany.[104] Because Duke Casimir III of Pomerania renewed Barnim I's privilege of 1261 in the year 1371, it is assumed that the Jews were still resident in Szczecin.[105]

Despite an influx of foreign merchants to Gdańsk (see above, section 1), the permanent population of the centre consisted up to a point in time only of Slavs — Pomeranians.[106] However, similarly to Szczecin, Germans began to settle in Gdańsk at the turn of the thirteenth century.[107] Somewhat later, they occupied the previously existing district called *Stare Miasto* (Old Town) and transformed it into a city under German (Lubeck) law between 1257 and 1263.[108] From that time, they began to dominate Gdańsk. The ethnic composition of this city was made more diverse by Prussians, who, because of their fear of the Teutonic Order's repressions on their native territory or for commercial reasons, migrated to this port centre in the thirteenth century.[109] The composition of the city's population is correctly conveyed in the document of the Duke of Pomerelia, Mestwin II, dated circa 1271, which described the population of all parts of Gdańsk as a conglomerate of Germans, Prussians, and Pomeranians ('burgensibus Theutonicis sepedicte civitatis Gedanensis, Prutenis quoque et nostris quibusdam specialiter fidelibus Pomeranis').[110] An important fact is that the Polish national consciousness did not exist in Eastern Pomerania; instead, the population had a strong ethno-regional consciousness.[111] In the late Middle Ages, the dominant Germans defined themselves as 'Prussians', which came as a result of their sense of belonging to the state and region of the Teutonic Order.[112]

After the Teutonic Order's invasion, and the following destruction of the German commune in 1308 as well as an incorporation of the whole of Eastern Pomerania into the state of the Teutonic Order (1309),[113] the Germans, who came from various regions of the Holy Roman Empire, became more important. The *Rechtestadt* (today: Główne Miasto/Main Town) was founded in 1342 by Teutonic knights under German (Chełmno) law and became a new centre of Gdańsk. It was dominated by Germans — 'Prussians'. It is worth underlining that in this main part of the Gdańsk agglomeration the Baltic Prussians (not Germans) constituted 1 per cent of the whole population in the second half of the fourteenth century.[114] A small influx of Slavic immigrants (Pomeranians, Poles) occurred at the same time. The destroyed

---

103 Piskorski, *Miasta księstwa szczecińskiego*, p. 174.
104 Lokers, '"Men bedervet erer ok nicht"?', pp. 115, 117, 119, 121–25.
105 Ślaski and Zientara, *Historia Pomorza*, p. 251.
106 Zbierski and Jasiński, 'Gdańsk', pp. 100, 102, 227.
107 Zbierski and Jasiński, 'Gdańsk', pp. 111–12.
108 Zbierski and Jasiński, 'Gdańsk', p. 277.
109 Okulicz-Kozaryn, *Dzieje Prusów*, pp. 491–95.
110 *Pommerellisches Urkundenbuch*, ed. by Perlbach, no. 250, p. 204. About this document, see Zbierski and Jasiński, 'Gdańsk', pp. 229, 287.
111 Małłek, 'Powstanie poczucia', pp. 244–51.
112 Biskup, 'Pod panowaniem krzyżackim', pp. 386–87.
113 Zbierski and Jasiński, 'Gdańsk', pp. 323–24.
114 Biskup, 'Pod panowaniem krzyżackim', p. 386.

Altstadt (Stare Miasto/Old Town) in 1308 recovered gradually in the course of the fourteenth century as a craft centre, which was dominated by Germans.

On the other hand, the Slavic population, Pomeranians and Poles, at that time inhabited the *Altstadt* (Old Town) and suburban Osiek (*Hackelwerk*).[115] They also made up 6 per cent of the population of another member of the Gdańsk agglomeration — the Young Town (*Jungstadt*), founded in 1380 by the Teutonic Knights.[116] In contrast to the previously discussed cities, late medieval Gdańsk under the Teutonic Order's rule was never inhabited by Jews. This was because of the ban on their entry and settlement in the Teutonic Order's territory, issued by the Grand Master of the Teutonic Knights, Siegfried von Feuchtwangen, in 1309.[117] The situation did not change during the Kingdom of Poland's successful attempts to reincorporate Gdańsk. On the request of the inhabitants of Gdańsk, who were keen on the incorporation, King Casimir IV had to guarantee that, for example, Jews would not be allowed to gain urban citizenship in Gdańsk (1454).[118] Three years later, the ruler extended this prohibition to the privilege of residing in the city and trading — this was to be permitted (in practice, refused) exclusively by the city council.

At the same time, these bans also applied to all the other groups, either national or chosen on other criteria, among which were, as directly mentioned, Nurembergers, 'Lombards' (*Lumbarth*), Englishmen, Dutchmen, and Flemings.[119] In the light of the historiography, we know that Nurembergers could operate (and reside permanently) in Gdańsk.[120] It is certain that English traders lived there periodically.[121] Dutchmen also migrated to Gdańsk, due to the rapid and dynamic development of the city's trade with the Netherlands.[122] However, nothing is known about the 'Lombards'. Generally, this term is associated with Italians, although in England the term was also used to describe Jews.[123] In the case of Gdańsk, the Jews were listed separately in a document from 1457, so the term 'Lombards' did not refer to them. On the other hand, nothing is known about the presence of Italians in this Baltic port and its surrounding areas. Hence the creation of the list of groups, whose settlement and activity were supposed to depend on the decision of the Gdańsk city council, was of preventative nature. But

---

115 Biskup, 'Pod panowaniem krzyżackim', pp. 348, 350.

116 Biskup, 'Pod panowaniem krzyżackim', pp. 361, 385.

117 Lokers, '"Men bedervet erer ok nicht"?', p. 112.

118 Echt, *Die Geschichte der Juden*, p. 14.

119 'keyn Nuremberger, Lumbarth, Engelseher, Hullandir, Flamigk, Jude, adir welcherley weszens fremden wsz reichen unde landen eyn iderman ist' (*Acten der Stände Preussens*, IV, ed. by Toeppen, no. 367, p. 559). S. Echt writes about it (Echt, *Die Geschichte der Juden*, p. 14).

120 Von Stromer, 'Wirtschaft unter den Luxemburgen', p. 98; Kellenbenz, 'Gewerbe und Handel', p. 180; Orłowska, 'Zwei Brüder — zwei Städte', pp. 103–06.

121 Biskup, 'Pod panowaniem krzyżackim', pp. 384, 408–09. The subject of controversy within the field is whether the Englishmen owned their trading post (an enclave) in Gdańsk. M. M. Postan was not certain about its existence (Postan, 'Economic and Political Relations of England and the Hanse', p. 150). Ph. Dollinger was convinced it existed, with a break in its activity between 1420 and 1428 (Dollinger, *Die Hanse*, pp. 250, 397).

122 Samsonowicz, 'Handel zagraniczny Gdańska', pp. 288–89, 291, 292–302.

123 Székely, 'Wallons et Italiens', p. 34.

fifteenth-century Gdańsk was also inhabited by Scandinavians (especially Swedes) and Scots.[124] By the end of this century, approximately 10 per cent of the population could have been Polish.[125]

4. The Issue of the Polonization of the Urban Population (the Fourteenth to the First Half of the Sixteenth Century)

An overview of the chosen cities based on the ethnic relations that existed in them would not be complete if we ignored the issue of so-called Polonization. This term conveys the process by which the Polish population gained an advantage in cities and towns in the Polish kingdom in the late medieval and early modern periods.[126] The process did not occur in Szczecin in the period under study (Poles were not present there) or in Wrocław (where they only constituted a small community of little importance; see above, section 3). Meanwhile in Gdańsk, it only began to occur after 1466. In other cities of the Kingdom of Poland, the influx of the Polish population and the change of the ethnic structure of the cities took place during the fifteenth century and at the beginning of the sixteenth.

There were various reasons for immigration and migration; for example, Poles migrated to Kraków both for its attractiveness as the capital of the state and for its university.[127] It is important to stress that there were not only external, but also internal causes of Polonization. Some wealthy German merchants wanted to receive noble titles, which is also a well-known tendency in other countries (for example, this is how Wrocław patricians acted as well).[128] Receiving a noble title enabled the merchant to become a member of the political elite of contemporary Poland. The first examples of the granting of noble titles to German merchants date back to the fourteenth century. One such example is the chief entrepreneur of Krakow and the Kingdom of Poland — Niklas Wirsing-Wierzynek (died in 1360), who received the Łagoda coat of arms.[129] But the question of whether the ennobled merchant of German descent began to feel Polish because of it remains unanswered. The same question can be applied to the descendants of the ennobled merchants and traders, such as Mikołaj Serafin (of the Nieczuja coat of arms), born in the Kraków suburb Wieliczka, son or grandson of an Italian who once arrived here.[130]

---

124 Biskup, 'Pod panowaniem krzyżackim', pp. 384, 613; Samsonowicz, 'La diversité ethnique', p. 13.
125 Samsonowicz, 'La diversité ethnique', p. 8.
126 Ptaśnik, *Miasta i mieszczaństwo*, pp. 312–31; Bogucka and Samsonowicz, *Dzieje miast*, p. 266.
127 Ptaśnik, *Miasta i mieszczaństwo*, p. 321.
128 Manikowska, 'Średniowieczne miasta–państwa', pp. 273, 342; Manikowska, 'Religijność miejska', p. 29. On granting nobility titles to Wrocław merchants, see e.g. Heck, 'Struktura społeczna', p. 68; von Witzendorff-Rehdiger, 'Herkunft und Verbleib Breslauer Ratsfamilien im Mittelalter', pp. 121–25, 132–33.
129 Lichończak, 'Najstarsze dzieje', p. 45.
130 Ptaśnik, 'Studya nad patrycyatem', pp. 17–20; Bukowski, Płóciennik, and Skolimowska, 'Wstęp', pp. xxiv–xxv.

174   GRZEGORZ MYŚLIWSKI

A relevant indication of Polonization was a gradual replacement of the German language by Latin and Polish in urban sources. Latin played an important, though not dominant, role in the oldest city book of Poznań (1398–1433)[131] and the later ones, especially from 1470.[132] Its domination in the oldest court book of Płock (1489–1517) is indisputable.[133] Meanwhile in Kraków, the process of the replacement of the German language took much longer, because it only finished in the course of the first half of the sixteenth century.[134]

A separate field of research is the ethnic structure of the guilds and urban governments. The data such as Polish-sounding names and last names are less unambiguous in their significance than the language that was used in the sources. In spite of that, historians undertake research that aims to identify Polish names and last names and, consequently, formulate their conclusions. Hence, they are of the opinion that craft guilds in Poznań were composed mainly of Poles, though newer research indicates the complexity of this issue in the fifteenth century.[135] On the other hand, in Płock, the Polish character of such guilds is quite indisputable. A gradual increase of Polish-sounding names of craft guild masters can be seen in the sources from Kraków.[136] However, the dominance of masters carrying Polish names can only be affirmed for the 1530s. Similar processes occurred in Lviv, where at the beginning of the sixteenth century Poles (including Polonized Germans) made up most of the population.[137]

Leaving aside the individual motives for Polonization, such as the economic calculation, these changes occurred as a result of the pressure of external circumstances. Townsmen operated in the land of Poles, who predominated in villages and small towns, and constituted the socio-political elite of the country. A more complex issue is the interpretation of conversion to Catholicism within an ethnic context. There are examples of the conversion of Armenians in Lviv ('der getawte Ormenige', 'der cristene Ormenige'), characterized by K. Stopka.[138] According to this historian, the change of faith was perceived by other Armenians as equal to a change of nationality.[139] A different approach to conversion existed among Jews who converted to Catholicism in Kraków ('Iudaeus baptisatus, neophitus, conversus, fonte baptismatis regeneratus'), which was described in detail by H. Zaremska.[140] Individual examples can also be found in

---

131 Warschauer, 'Einleitung', pp. 125–26.
132 Gąsiorowski, 'Ludność Poznania', pp. 251–52.
133 Poppe, 'Wstęp', p. viii.
134 Ptaśnik, *Miasta i mieszczaństwo*, p. 318.
135 See comments on the topic of the name criterion in Wiesiołowski, *Socjotopografia późnośredniowiecznego Poznania*, p. 112, and Wyrozumski, *Dzieje Krakowa*, p. 321. Comments by J. Tandecki and K. Górski (Tandecki, 'Rozkwit', pp. 204–05).
136 Ptaśnik, *Miasta i mieszczaństwo*, pp. 316–17.
137 Ptaśnik, *Miasta i mieszczaństwo*, pp. 316–17; Jakowenko, *Historia Ukrainy*, p. 116; Isaevič and others, eds, *Історія Львова u tr'och tomach*, p. 78.
138 *Księga ławnicza miejska (1441–1448)*, ed. by Czołowski and Jaworski, nos 277, 560; Stopka, 'Kultura religijna Ormian', pp. 248–51; see also Janeczek, 'Żydzi i Ormianie', p. 295.
139 Stopka, 'Kultura religijna Ormian', p. 248.
140 Zaremska, *Żydzi w średniowiecznej Polsce*, pp. 435–55.

Poznań ('der getawffte Jude')[141] and Wrocław ('der getawfte Jude', 'baptisatus').[142] The question arises, can these conversions be classified as a manifestation of Polonization in the cities of the Kingdom of Poland, whereas in Wrocław of Germanization? What was the ethnic identity of Johannes Reieh, who testified in the council court in Lviv in 1479, the son of Jerzy, a Jewish convert from Wrocław?[143] As Zaremska has proved, the motives of Krakow's converts were utilitarian — they wanted to make their life and work conditions better and, in the case of younger Jews — to enable them to study at the local university.[144] Conversion to Catholicism was an absolute condition in order to receive urban citizenship.[145] However, it does not appear that conversion to Catholicism was also a form of Polonization. Jews — followers of Judaism — still considered the converts to be their compatriots, although they viewed them as living in sin.[146] It was also because the followers of Catholicism were not only Poles, but also Germans, who ruled the larger cities in the Kingdom of Poland for a long time. Moreover, there is no data about the converts who declared their ethnic identity had changed. Perhaps an exception to that rule was Jacob, a convert who participated in the pogrom of Krakow's Jews in 1407, of whom he was a descendant (*sic!*).[147] Meanwhile, Christians, despite the change of faith and adoption of new, non-Jewish names, remembered the Jewish heritage of their new co-religionists. But they gradually started to treat converts as members of the urban community,[148] which was — probably — crucial for neophytes. It seems that similar conclusions can be applied to Jewish converts in Wrocław.

5. An Ethnic Division of Labour?

The question arises of how this ethnic structure in these cities was reflected in economic life and the division of labour. Due to the dominance of the Germans in most of these urban centres for most of the period under study, it is not important to consider in which economic sectors the prevalent nation were engaged, but what the fields of economic interest of other ethnic communities were. The Germans constituted not only the patriciate but also the majority of the urban middle-class, the urban strata whose members practised various crafts. They were not only actively working in long-distance trade and finance, but also prevailed in retail trade and

---

141 *Stadtbuch von Posen*, ed. by Warschauer, no. 577 (1432), p. 207.
142 Archiwum Państwowe we Wrocławiu, *Lib.exc.sign.*, vol. 27, p. 67 (1428); vol. 31, p. 93 (1436); *Akta radzieckie poznańskie*, 1, ed. by Kaczmarczyk, no. 448 (1450), p. 161.
143 Myśliwski, *Wrocław w przestrzeni*, p. 110.
144 Zaremska, *Żydzi w średniowiecznej Polsce*, pp. 436, 438, 442–44, 454. During the pogrom in 1407, children were forcefully baptized and the adults who were not killed begged to be baptized in order to survive (Zaremska, *Żydzi w średniowiecznej Polsce*, pp. 437–38).
145 Ptaśnik, *Miasta i mieszczaństwo*, p. 295.
146 Janeczek, 'Żydzi i Ormianie', p. 279.
147 Zaremska, *Żydzi w średniowiecznej Polsce*, p. 438.
148 Zaremska, *Żydzi w średniowiecznej Polsce*, p. 443.

craft, estate investment, and other particular fields, such as maritime transport in port cities (Gdańsk, Szczecin).

Another wide range of economic activities, although not so wide as that of the Germans, was practised by the Jews. They mainly engaged in craft and retail trade, because the majority of members of the Jewish communities were not wealthy. Only rich Jews engaged in long-distance trade until they were driven out mainly by Germans — due to the pressure of the ethnically distinct competition and legal limitations (see below, section 7), not to mention the persecution. Poznań, in which the Jews conducted trade in multiple directions (Gdańsk, Germany, Northern Italy, Turkey) as late as in the first part of the sixteenth century,[149] is treated as an exception among the cities under study. But it seems that some restrictions were imposed on them as well (see below, section 7). Many Jews in other cities focused on credit activity. It refers not only to rich Jews but also, as B. Wyrozumska has shown for Kraków, to less wealthy Jews.[150]

Migrants from Italy, whose numbers in the Polish territories were small, but who were wealthy and enterprising, mostly invested in long-distance trade and mining. Being limited to the cities that are considered here, it is good to give the example of salt mines in Wieliczka and Bochnia near Kraków, which they held on lease from Polish kings.[151] Apart from managing salt mining, they also organized the trade of the product. Some Italians, such as the above-mentioned Ricci in Wrocław, were also purchasing annuities and investing in the fishery.[152] Others were also eager to take customs stations on lease and purchase land outside of the cities.[153] We should also *pro forma* mention a certain contribution of Italians to the textile industry of the Kraków agglomeration, which can be indirectly deduced from granting urban citizenship of the city (Kazimierz satellite town, to be exact) to three weavers from Florence.[154]

Armenians, mainly resident in Lviv (and other cities of Red Ruthenia) and in significantly smaller numbers in Kraków, and an even smaller community in Poznań by the end of the Middle Ages, specialized in long-distance trade, especially with the East.[155] They operated in the property market (Lviv,[156] Kraków[157]). Armenians from Lviv were also active in craft. In the late Middle Ages, they specialized in textile production (cloth, linen, cotton manufacture, perhaps also silk), as well as the production of luxury red-dyed shoes.[158] We are also familiar with separate examples

---

149 Abt, 'Ludność Poznania', p. 448; Rudzińska, 'Żydzi w późnośredniowiecznym Poznaniu', p. 356.

150 Wyrozumska, 'Wstęp' (1995), p. 8.

151 Ptaśnik, *Kultura włoska*, pp. 18–19, 38, 49–53, 57–58, 71–77, 79–81, 108; Székely, 'Wallons et Italiens', pp. 36–37; Kedar, *Merchants in Crisis*, p. 46; Sowina, 'The Relations of the Town', pp. 228–32.

152 Myśliwski, *Wrocław w przestrzeni*, p. 493.

153 Hryszko, *Januensis, ergo mercator?*, pp. 66, 69.

154 See *Italia mercatoria apud Polonos*, ed. by Ptaśnik, no. 81 (1394), p. 87.

155 Czołowski, 'Lwów za ruskich czasów', p. 806; Bardach, 'Ormianie na ziemiach dawnej Polski', p. 114; Stopka, *Ormianie w Polsce dawnej*, pp. 45–47; Kozubska-Andrusiv, '... propter disparitatem linguae et religionis pares ipsis non esse ...', p. 55.

156 Lesnikov, 'L'vovskoe kupečestvo', p. 41.

157 *Ormianie w średniowiecznym Krakowie*, ed. by Wyrozumska, for example, no. 13.

158 Stopka, *Ormianie w Polsce dawnej*, p. 50.

of Armenians in Kraków who specialized in other fields: a goldsmith (a member of a guild),[159] and a coppersmith (*cuprifaber*).[160] In the fourteenth century, Armenians managed the royal mint in Lviv.[161] It is difficult to conclude whether the entries in the sources about Armenian debts and liabilities — for example, the merchant Tayczadin[162] — confirm their involvement in credit activity or simply resulted from their trading on credit. Armenians also played an important role in relations between merchants of different nationalities, where they operated as interpreters.[163]

As I have written before, Walloons specialized in cloth production. B. Zientara suspected that among the Walloons there were merchants-wholesalers.[164] We can speculate that his assumption derives from the known activity and mobility of the Flemish merchants, who traded in cloth from Flanders in the 'old Europe' until the end of the thirteenth century.[165] Apart from that, the presence of merchants is confirmed in Walloonian communities in the German territory.[166] Although Zientara's hypothesis, supported by M. Słoń, is logical and probable, evidence of the trading activity of the Walloons on the Polish territories is missing.

Other migrant ethnic communities were not so important in the economy of these cities due to their very small numbers. We should *pro forma* mention goldsmiths in Kraków — a Bohemian, Ruthenian, and Lithuanian.[167] Perhaps the importance of Englishmen in Gdańsk was somewhat higher (see above, section 4). It is not known what kinds of work Prussians could carry out in Gdańsk (see above, sections 2, 3).

After the re-establishment of these centres according to German law, all autochthonous Slavic nations — Poles, Pomeranians, and Ruthenians — lost their basic significance in economic life. But the situation varied between the cities of the Kingdom of Poland and outside of its borders. In Kraków, although Poles constituted the largest part of the population even in the fourteenth century (5000 compared with a total of 12,500–15,000 inhabitants),[168] they were second to Germans in terms of economic importance and, in certain fields, also behind the Italians and the Jews. Despite that, the Polish population retained its relevance in some fields of craft. In the first half of the fifteenth century, Poles were prevalent in pottery production, the retail trade ('tendlatores'), and the salt trade (salt traders — 'prasoł').[169] At the turn of the fourteenth and fifteenth century, they formed a Polish guild of shoemakers

---

159 Wyrozumski, *Dzieje Krakowa*, p. 347.

160 Wyrozumska, 'Wstęp' (2003), p. 7.

161 Stopka, *Ormianie w Polsce dawnej*, p. 53.

162 It concerns Tayczadin's liabilities and debts described in his will from 1376 and transcribed under the year of 1388 (Lesnikov, 'L'vovskoe kupečestvo', p. 40; for the will, see *Najstarsza księga miejska (1382–1389)*, ed. by Czołowski, pp. 93–95).

163 Papée, *Historja miasta Lwowa*, pp. 88–89; Ptaśnik, *Miasta i mieszczaństwo*, p. 256; Janeczek, 'Tłumacz lwowski'.

164 Zientara, 'Walloons in Silesia', p. 137.

165 Małowist, *Studia z dziejów rzemiosła*, p. 38; Cipolla, *Before Industrial Revolution*, p. 201.

166 Słoń, 'Początki osady walońskiej', p. 12.

167 Wyrozumski, *Dzieje Krakowa*, p. 347.

168 Wyrozumski, *Dzieje Krakowa*, pp. 315, 318.

169 Wyrozumski, *Dzieje Krakowa*, p. 322.

(until 1405), separate from the corresponding German one.[170] Poles were also active as tailors and goldsmiths.[171]

It seems that ethnic Poles were more important for the economy of Poznań, and especially Płock. Regarding the capital of Greater Poland, there is a common view about their dominant role in the economic life of the late Middle Ages.[172] They were said to outnumber, both in numbers and in terms of their significance, the Germans and the Jews in trade (the Polish nature of the patriciate was supposed to be proof of it; see above, section 4) and in the field of finance.[173] However, in the light of the preserved sources, throughout most of the fifteenth century, Germans still played a significant role here. The key role of Poles is more visible in fifteenth-century Płock. Meanwhile in Lviv, the most ethnically diverse city, they were becoming more significant during the fifteenth century until they achieved the leading position in the course of the first three decades of the sixteenth century (see above, section 4).

A separate case is the participation of Poles in long-distance trade before around the middle of the fifteenth century — did they play any role in it at all? As much as that happened particularly in Płock,[174] but also Poznań, historians used to have some doubts about their activity in this field in Kraków. Experts in research of this city's trade had doubts as to whether two Slavic last names were held by Polish merchants, or perhaps by Bohemians.[175] It is also worth remembering the character of Peter Potrzeba ('Peter Pottrzebe', 'Peter Potrzeba'), an unquestionably Polish merchant from Kraków, who traded with Silesia in the 1430s.[176] In spite of this, until the time of the advanced Polonization of the patriciate, Poles played a small role in the long-range trade of their cities, with a possible exception of Płock and Poznań. They had more relevance in this field as long-distance carters.

Meanwhile, Ruthenians in Lviv were gradually pushed to the margins of economic life and restricted to their own district. They occupied themselves with crafts such as goldsmithing and retail trade.[177] Occasionally they provided credit.[178] Similarly as in Kraków (until a certain point in time), there were not many autochthonous merchants that have been mentioned in the sources.[179] The economic mobilization of Ruthenians occurred only in the first part of the sixteenth century.[180]

---

170 Wyrozumski, *Dzieje Krakowa*, pp. 322, 333–34, 343.

171 Wyrozumski, *Dzieje Krakowa*, p. 322.

172 Gąsiorowski, 'Ludność Poznania', pp. 251–52.

173 Bogucka and Samsonowicz, *Dzieje miast*, p. 266.

174 Szacherska, 'Złoty wiek miasta', pp. 132–34.

175 Kutrzeba and Ptaśnik, 'Dzieje handlu', p. 127.

176 Archiwum Państwowe we Wrocławiu, *Lib.exc.sign.*, vol. 28, p. 115 (1431); vol. 31, p. 140 (1437). For his trip in the merchant convoy from Kraków to Wrocław, see Myśliwski, *Wrocław w przestrzeni*, pp. 305–06.

177 *Najstarsza księga miejska (1382–1389)*, ed. by Czołowski, for example, nos 112, 171.

178 *Najstarsza księga miejska (1382–1389)*, ed. by Czołowski, for example, no. 430; *Księga ławnicza miejska (1441–1448)*, ed. by Czołowski and Jaworski, no. 292.

179 Kiryk, 'Związki Lwowa z Krakowem', pp. 19–20.

180 Kapral, 'Legal Regulation', p. 216; Kozubska-Andrusiv, '… propter disparitatem linguae et religionis pares ipsis non esse …', p. 59.

The role and relevance of Slavic autochthones in cities outside of the Kingdom of Poland's borders were mediocre. They practised as auxiliaries and workers of a lower rank. In Wrocław, Poles served as carters — participants of long-distance trade.[181] While residing in the territory of Wrocław's *Nowy Targ* (New Market),[182] they were certainly engaged in some craft activities, in compliance with the economic tradition of this part of the Silesian city. In Szczecin, Pomeranians were involved with fishery and agriculture; they were also possibly porters who formed a guild (1316).[183] In Gdańsk (specifically in the suburban *Osiek*), Pomeranians worked also in fishing and were specialized in collecting amber for local crafts and trade.[184] It is known that in the first half of the fifteenth century Poles worked as anchor manufacturers and porters in the shipyards (*Lastadia/Łasztownia*) and were part of ship crews.[185] An influx of Poles from villages to Gdańsk occurred during the fifteenth century, and some of them became members of the middle-class stratum.

In summary, it can be said that, as much as Germans, Jews, and Italians achieved high relevance in the field of production and services (on different levels), Walloons were definitely active in the field of production, Armenians in the services sector, Poles in services (by the end of the studied period) and production on a more mediocre level, and Ruthenians in services.

6. The Typology of Inter-Ethnic Economic Relations

Based on the overview above, we can conclude that the re-establishment of the abovementioned cities according to German law, the further legal regulations defining the status of various nations and their possibilities of activity as well as immigration, and the much later process of Polonization all had made an impact on division of labour based on ethnic criteria. However, ethnic criteria does not explain fully the division of labour; hence we can only discuss its ethnic circumstances with certain reservations. The borders between respective areas of the economy did not always match the ethnic divisions inside the urban communities. The previously discussed scope of the economic activity of members of the respective ethnicities allows us to describe the inter-ethnic economic relations established within the borders of the same city. In my opinion a division of these relations into three groups is justified.

First, I would like to discuss the issue of relations between members of different ethnic groups working in the same field. I want to answer the question of what prevailed in these relations — cooperation or competition? Perhaps, there was a lack of contact between members of various ethnic groups and in consequence performing their tasks separately was dominant? This category of relations includes

---

181 Petry, *Die Popplau*, p. 72.
182 Goliński, *Socjotopografia późnośredniowiecznego Wrocławia*, pp. 214, 234.
183 Lesiński, 'Rozdrobnienie feudalne', pp. 85–86.
184 Biskup, 'Pod panowaniem krzyżackim', pp. 350, 391.
185 Biskup, 'Pod panowaniem krzyżackim', pp. 386, 501.

the employer–employee relationship, because, despite the different statuses of both sides, we are dealing with activity in the same field of economy and, additionally, permanent contact between its participants.

A common trait of the second group of inter-ethnic economic relations is the supplier–client relationship. It would depend on the delivery of some product or service to the representative of one of the nations by a member of another. This relation stemmed from the supply/demand relationship on a market limited to only one centre. We will focus on the relationships in two areas: trade (seller–buyer, with the inclusion of intermediaries), and credit (lender/creditor – credit recipient/debtor).

The third group of interactions consists of the activities generally associated with social history and the history of culture (including religiosity and mentality). It represents charity (alms, founding and subsidizing hospitals) and the founding of church buildings. These activities had an impact on the cohesion of diverse urban communities through support for the poor and sick, and the sponsoring of the building of churches. Among economic effects of these relationships were not only direct donations of money but also financial transfers. Alms in the form of money meant releasing new funds for circulation, as otherwise they would have been frozen (in the best case — deposited in a bank account). The poor, after receiving the money, spent the alms on basic products, contributing to the stimulation of trade and some branches of craft (for example, textile production). In hospitals, the establishment of which resulted from the Christian *caritas* and the founders' desire to receive salvation,[186] not only did they cure diseases, but they also hosted very different people in need (see below, section 8).

On the other hand, the donation of funds for the building of churches and other sacral establishments between the thirteenth and fifteenth centuries were huge economic operations with various, also economic, effects, which provoke interesting discussions among historians. Due to the large number of studies on charity and religious foundations, as well as, on the other hand, the lack of certain detailed data for the historically understood Polish territories, we will limit ourselves to outlining the issue and posing hypotheses concerning its impact on the level of cohesion among communities within the chosen cities.

7. Compatriots, Partners, and Competitors

It has already been affirmed before that the medieval burgher was a collectivist being,[187] willingly organized into craft and merchant guilds. The question arises, whether these organizations were ethnically homogeneous or mixed in ethnic terms. Generally, we can presume that, due to the dominance of Germans in all of these cities, the craft

---

186 Słoń, *Szpitale średniowiecznego Wrocławia*, pp. 6–7; Reinhard, *Lebensformen Europas*, p. 165.
187 Rabinowič, *Życie codzienne*, p. 43; Cipolla, *Before Industrial Revolution*, p. 79; Wiesiołowski, *Socjotopografia późnośredniowiecznego Poznania*, p. 63; Manikowska, 'Średniowieczne miasta–państwa', p. 323.

guilds were ethnically quite uniform for a long while. Moreover, in Lviv, only the dominant German population (later Polish) had the right to found craft guilds. It was forbidden for Armenians.[188] In terms of the Ruthenians, it is difficult to confirm whether they ever formed craft guilds, since the existence of such organized craft guilds in medieval Rus' is a controversial topic.[189]

In other cities of the historically understood Polish territories, the members of the craft guilds were most often craftsmen of two nationalities (Kraków, Poznań), rarely other.[190] Meanwhile, merchant guilds that started their existence in all these centres between 1310 and 1489[191] were not eager to accept people of other backgrounds than German. Only in the case of the Płock guild, founded the latest of all, can we debate whether it had any German members, apart from Poles.

When it comes to companies established by partners from the same city, it is worth remembering that merchants in the Polish territories usually preferred to work individually than in partnerships.[192] There were more companies in Wrocław and Gdańsk than in the other above-mentioned cities. Not much data has been preserved about Szczecin.[193] Partnerships founded within the same city were made up of people who shared the same ethnic identity. This was typical for the Germans (everywhere), Italians and Armenians in Lviv, and the Jews in Poznań.[194] There is only one exception to the rule known to me, which is the company of two citizens of Wrocław — Antonio Ricci from Florence and German Johannes Banke. Whether the custom stations wielded jointly in Lviv by a Genoese, Cristoforo of San Remo, with a Pole, and the burgher of Lviv, Mikołaj Stradowski,[195] resulted from the earlier foundation of the company or simply the division of work and profit between two independent renters, it is difficult to decide.

As we can see, the ethnic communities were not prone to join with representatives of other nations within economic institutions from the same cities. Therefore, competition arose in the same field, which sometimes led to conflict. The first conflict between the ethnically homogeneous economic institutions took place rather early,

---

88 Bardach, 'Ormianie na ziemiach dawnej Polski', p. 114.

89 In Russian-Soviet historiography there was a strong tendency to seek to prove the existence of merchant guilds (see Rabinowič, *Życie codzienne*, pp. 38–39; Tichomirov, *Rosja*, pp. 77–80). However, in Veliky Novgorod, there were no guilds (Janin, 'Znaczienije otkrytija', pp. 19–20).

90 Wyrozumski, *Dzieje Krakowa*, pp. 334, 347; Wiesiołowski, *Socjotopografia późnośredniowiecznego Poznania*, pp. 115–16.

91 See, among others, Markgraf, 'Zur Geschichte des Breslauer Kaufhauses', pp. 277–80; Kutrzeba and Ptaśnik, 'Dzieje handlu', pp. 131, 133; Charewiczowa, *Handel średniowiecznego Lwowa*, p. 49; Koczy, *Handel Poznania*, p. 279; Goerlitz, *Verfassung, Verwaltung und Recht*, p. 11; Żebrowski, 'Stolica książąt', p. 105; Szacherska, 'Złoty wiek miasta', p. 138; Bogucka and Samsonowicz, *Dzieje miast*, p. 237; Piskorski, *Miasta księstwa szczecińskiego*, p. 134; Goliński, 'Wrocław', p. 150; Czaja, *Grupy rządzące*, pp. 77, 85; Myśliwski, *Wrocław w przestrzeni*, pp. 140–48.

92 Kutrzeba, *Handel Krakowa*, pp. 156–57; Charewiczowa, *Handel średniowiecznego Lwowa*, p. 27; Koczy, *Handel Poznania*, p. 280.

93 Piskorski, *Miasta księstwa szczecińskiego*, pp. 135, 138.

94 Koczy, *Handel Poznania*, p. 280.

95 Hryszko, *Januensis, ergo mercator?*, p. 69.

at the beginning of the fourteenth century in Wrocław. Local German butchers complained to the city authorities about the guild of Jewish butchers, claiming they were harming the former's interests.[196] But there are not many analogous examples in these cities. In Kraków, at the outset of King Casimir III the Great's rule (1333), butchers (Germans) pressured the Jewish community to limit the number of Jewish butchers to six, and they also enforced limits in terms of retail sales.[197] In 1494, they forced the Jewish community to have no more than four butchers working for it.[198] In Lviv, there was an ongoing conflict concerning the ownership of two profitable Armenian stalls selling meat situated opposite the Dominican Corpus Christi Church.[199] They used to sell goat meat at the stalls, which first belonged to the Armenian *wójt*, and from 1469 to the Armenian commune. In 1510, the butchers demanded restrictions on their Armenian competitors' retail trade.[200] In this case, the butchers' claims failed. It seems there were no more serious inter-ethnic conflicts in the field of the wholesale trade.

Conflicts testified in urban books were of an individual, not collective, nature. Hence, we can say that for the majority of the late Middle Ages the activity of different *ethnos* in the same economic field led to the petrification of ethnic divisions without confrontational consequences. However, Wrocław was an exception to this rule. The city's magistrate prohibited Jewish retail sales of cloth (1302) and attempted to forbid Jewish butchers from selling meat to Christian clients.[201] In some of the remaining centres under study (Lviv, Kraków, Płock) the situation of trading minorities only changed for the worse in the fourth quarter of the fifteenth century. The urban authorities, which were Polonized to some extent, consisting of merchants, started at the time to impose restrictions and to suppress both long-distance and retail trade of the Jewish co-residents. In 1480, the authorities of Lviv forbade them from trading in textiles.[202] But the conflict continued.[203] The Jews managed to achieve a relaxation of this ban in 1493.[204] At the beginning of the sixteenth century, the King of Poland, Alexander Jagiellon, indebted to them, indirectly annulled all the

---

196 Myśliwski, 'Retail Trade in Wrocław', p. 282.

197 Wyrozumska, 'Nieznany dokument Kazimierza Wielkiego', pp. 191, 193. The edition of this document: Wyrozumska, 'Nieznany dokument Kazimierza Wielkiego', p. 194.

198 *Żydzi w średniowiecznym Krakowie*, ed. by Wyrozumska, no. 871, p. 186; on this agreement: Wyrozumska, 'Czy Jan Olbracht', pp. 10–11.

199 Stopka, *Ormianie w Polsce dawnej*, p. 48.

200 Charewiczowa, *Ograniczenia gospodarcze*, p. 18.

201 Grodecki, 'Dzieje Żydów', pp. 680–81. R. Grodecki expressed an opinion that the ban had already been imposed in 1315, a proof of which would be the legal notice of Wrocław councillors for the municipal authorities of Głogów in Silesia (Grodecki, 'Dzieje Żydów', p. 681). However, in the mentioned source (*Breslauer Urkundenbuch*, ed. by Korn, no. 100, p. 92) it was clearly written that the conflict is ongoing and when it is finished, the residents of Wrocław will inform the Głogów councillors about it ('noveritis, quod Judei non debent carnes vendere Christianis et adhuc nostri concives cum Judeis invicem questionibus multimodis contendunt, [...] sed si terminatum fuerit, vobis scire dabimus consequenter').

202 Kozubska-Andrusiv, '... propter disparitatem linguae et religionis pares ipsis non esse ...', p. 63.

203 Charewiczowa, *Ograniczenia gospodarcze*, p. 26; Zaremska, *Żydzi w średniowiecznej Polsce*, p. 211.

204 Charewiczowa, *Ograniczenia gospodarcze*, p. 30.

restrictions. However, the Lviv councillors strove to restore the *status quo ante* and in 1521 received a privilege from King Sigismund I the Old, who limited the Jewish trade in the city to selected products.[205] Only later was there legislation which was slightly less restrictive than the royal legislation, but that is outside of the time limits of this chapter.[206] It is worth noticing that, even if the Polonized patriciate and city council members of Lviv reluctantly accepted the commercial activity of Armenians, then apart from the incidental impeding of life or judicial persecution of one of the Armenian merchants (which in fact ended fatally),[207] they did not decide to impose legal restrictions on the Armenian trade.

Meanwhile, restrictions on the commercial activity of the Jews also took place in other cities. Not much later than in Lviv the city council of Kraków imposed severe limitations on Jewish retail sales (1485).[208] With some exceptions Jewish trade was forbidden altogether, as well as brokering in connections between the Jewish and Christian populations. This was a prelude to the expulsion of (the larger part of?) the Jewish people to outside the walls of Old Kraków a few years later (see above, section 2). In the early modern period, similar events took place in Płock. In 1521 and 1523, King Sigismund I the Old restricted the Jewish trade law, allowing them to conduct only wholesale trade of selected products (cloth, linen, oriental spices) on the weekly markets.[209] The latter document tightened the restrictions, allowing Jews of Płock to trade only in stores.[210] It is worth pointing out that in this document, the king claimed that similar limitations were in force in other cities of the Kingdom of Poland, including, among others, Kraków, Lviv, and Poznań.[211] In 1537, King Sigismund I the Old forbade the Jews of Płock from public trading and limited it to their houses.[212]

Inter-ethnic relations between **employer and employee** occurred within companies, as it seems, a bit more frequently. As an example, we can mention the salt mines near Kraków. Formally, the King of Poland was their owner but, for this chapter, a far more important aspect are the renters, who hired a lot of people. Generally, the role of *żupnik* (the renter of a salt mine) was granted to Italians or their descendants (see above, section 4). The mining company employed a large labour force,[213] the majority of which were non-Italians. Similar to the mines in Silesia, local peasants — Poles — were hired for simple jobs. Meanwhile, higher positions were filled by Germans

---

205 Kozubska-Andrusiv, '… propter disparitatem linguae et religionis pares ipsis non esse …', p. 63.

206 On this topic, see Kapral, 'Legal Regulation', pp. 225–26.

207 Specifically: Stopka, 'Kultura religijna Ormian', pp. 268–70; cf. Kapral, 'Legal Regulation', p. 221; Kozubska-Andrusiv, '… propter disparitatem linguae et religionis pares ipsis non esse …', p. 56.

208 Bogucka and Samsonowicz, *Dzieje miast*, p. 106; Wyrozumski, *Dzieje Krakowa*, p. 329; Wyrozumska, 'Czy Jan Olbracht', p. 7; Zaremska, *Żydzi w średniowiecznej Polsce*, pp. 208–09; Starzyński, 'Najstarszy dokument hebrajski', pp. 190–91.

209 Szacherska, 'Złoty wiek miasta', p. 137; Fijałkowski, 'Początki obecności', p. 184.

210 *Zbiór dokumentów*, II, ed. by Szacherska, no. 347, pp. 101–02.

211 'sed forisabunt in cameris […] secuti eciam [in] civitatitbus nostris Cracoviensis, Leopoliensis, Lublinensis et Poznaniensis id ipsum observatur' (*Zbiór dokumentów*, II, ed. by Szacherska, no 347, p. 102).

212 *Zbiór dokumentów*, II, ed. by Szacherska, no. 424, pp. 222–23; no. 434, p. 231.

213 Wyrozumski, *Państwowa gospodarka solna*, pp. 81–84, 94, 99, 101–02, 109–10.

(for example, a deputy of *żupnik* Serafin was a German — the Kraków councillor Peter Grazer).[214] Connections between the employer and employee were sometimes confrontational. Calls for a strike (1393),[215] as well as tensions caused by delayed payments, are both known to have happened.[216] However, no riots took place in the Polish territories for such reasons. Additionally, nothing is known about whether the tensions transformed into a more permanent resentment on ethnic grounds (Polish employees – Italian employer), although brief discontent occurred because there were consequential reasons for it. Inter-ethnic contact within the same company occurred elsewhere as well (Poles working for Germans in the Gdańsk Łasztownia; see above, section 5).

Relations between merchants, entrepreneurs, and carters were of a slightly different nature, as they were appointed to not only the transit of goods, but also the execution of transactions.[217] Sometimes these tasks were carried out by Poles on the commission of Germans — not only in Wrocław (see above, section 5) but also in Kraków.[218] Perhaps also in Lviv, Poles worked in this field on the commission of Armenians, although the nationality of coachmen is not confirmed.[219] To sum up, we have no confirmation of conflicts among participants of this kind of economic game. Nonetheless, these relations (commissioner–carter) did not have a serious impact on the cohesion or disintegration of urban communities.

8. Providers and Clients

For most of the period under study, trade connected people rather than divided, also in ethnic terms. The number of townspeople of the chosen cities rose in the later Middle Ages. It was especially due to the fact that, with the exception of Wrocław, the Black Death epidemic only affected the population of Polish territories on a small scale and only locally due to its scarce density.[220] Hence the number of buyers and consumers was increasing, as was the demand for goods and services, supplied by manufacturers (often directly), retailers, and wholesalers. Without a doubt, economic

---

214 Starzyński, *Krakowa rada miejska*, pp. 266–67.

215 Wyrozumski, *Państwowa gospodarka solna*, p. 103.

216 *Korespondencja żupnika krakowskiego*, ed. by Bukowski, Płóciennik, and Skolimowska, no. 8, pp. 38–39; no. 15, pp. 58–59; no. 23, pp. 88–89; no. 29, pp. 110–11; no. 34, pp. 134–35; no. 36, pp. 140–43.

217 Kutrzeba, *Handel Krakowa*, p. 157; Koczy, *Handel Poznania*, pp. 280–81.

218 Kalfas-Piotrowska, 'Stosunki handlowe', p. 246.

219 Ł. Charewiczowa recalls the admonitions of the Lviv archbishop for the Catholics not to work for Armenians, even as carters (Charewiczowa, *Ograniczenia gospodarcze*, p. 18). If the profession of a carter was not recalled only to evoke a bigger effect, but because of the criticized practice, then it would mean that this profession could be practised by both Poles and Germans. In the simultaneously released paper, this scholar concluded that carters stemmed generally from suburban areas (*podgrodzie*) (Charewiczowa, *Handel średniowiecznego Lwowa*, p. 22), so they must have been also Ruthenians.

220 Samsonowicz, *Późne średniowiecze*, pp. 87, 90; Wenta, 'List Awinioński', pp. 277–80; Wójcik, 'Klęski elementarne', p. 34.

BETWEEN COEXISTENCE AND PERSECUTION 185

development growth was also reflected in the growth of more and more numerous connections and relationships in the provider–client relationship. Did it also occur between representatives of different ethnicities in the same cities?

The late Middle Ages is regarded as a time of economic development for most of the studied cities. Wrocław is somewhat of an exception since its economic history took different shapes from the 1420s. Suburban agriculture was in recession (until *c.* 1480), but long-distance trade developed successfully (until *c.* 1459).[221] However, in the juridical municipal books of these cities, there are not many references to commercial transactions in the merchant–buyer and craftsman–buyer relationships in detail. Sources more frequently inform us about trade with foreign merchants than transactions made by residents of the same centres, regardless of their different ethnic backgrounds. Certainly, as S. Kutrzeba thought, it had not been customary to include often such trade transactions in municipal books.[222] What is worse, only a few accounting books (or rather excerpts from them) are preserved from the cities under study.

On the other hand, the lack of large quantities of such references in the official municipal books can suggest that there were not many conflicts in this field. However, certain restrictions imposed on the trade of Jewish merchants in plenty of these centres discussed (as well as Jewish butchers in Wrocław and Kraków) and Armenians in Lviv (see above, section 7) clearly depict the multi-ethnic commercial transactions within the same cities. Italian renters of the Kraków salt mines (see above, section 7) sold this product to probably all ethnic groups within the city. We know about cases of selling foreign goods to local Germans and Poles by Armenians from Kraków,[223] as well as a purchase from a German, made jointly by a Pole and an Armenian, residents of Kraków.[224] The Jews of this city sometimes sold various goods to Poles and Germans.[225] However, it was rare for them to buy from local Poles.[226] In Wrocław, apart from the listed restrictions that prove the existence of multi-ethnic trade, we can presume that in the twelfth–thirteenth centuries Jewish merchants were selling foreign goods to local residents: Germans and Poles. Moreover, Walloon weavers sold their goods to both Poles and Germans, but predominantly to wealthier German burghers. The only Italian resident there permanently, Ricci, both bought and sold various goods from and to German townsmen (sometimes through an Italian intermediary).[227]

---

221 Maleczyński, 'Dzieje Wrocławia', p. 87; Hoffmann, *Land, Liberties and Lordship*, pp. 273, 274, 282, 284, 319–20, 326; Myśliwski, *Wrocław w przestrzeni*, p. 502.

222 Kutrzeba, *Handel Krakowa*, p. 85.

223 *Ormianie w średniowiecznym Krakowie*, ed. by Wyrozumska, nos 54, 83, 88 (Germans), and nos 98, 124 (Poles).

224 *Ormianie w średniowiecznym Krakowie*, ed. by Wyrozumska, no. 123.

225 *Żydzi w średniowiecznym Krakowie*, ed. by Wyrozumska, for example, nos 236, 743 (Poles), and nos 108, 153, 801 (Germans).

226 *Żydzi w średniowiecznym Krakowie*, ed. by Wyrozumska, nos 1092, 1136.

227 *Italia mercatoria apud Polonos*, ed. by Ptaśnik, no. 50 (1428), pp. 34–35; Archiwum Państwowe we Wrocławiu, *Lib.exc.sign.*, vol. 31, p. 92 (1436).

The previously described trade restrictions imposed on the Jewish population (e.g. in Lviv, Kraków, and Poznań) clearly testify to the provider–client relationship with local Christians, especially with the dominant *ethnos* in each city (see above, section 7). The trade between Christians of various origins, also in the example of Armenians in Lviv, was already described above (sections 5, 7). Let me add a handful of information about the trade of Italians who settled in this city. It is known that in the 1440s some of them owned market stalls. They conducted retail trade, likely selling goods to all nationalities.[228] Purchases made by Lviv Italians from local Jews and Germans have also been confirmed.[229] We are also familiar with examples from fifteenth-century Poznań, where the settled Italian merchants purchased goods from local Germans,[230] but also sold the wares to Poles.[231] In Gdańsk, Pomeranian fishermen sold fish and amber to Germans (to other nationalities too?), since they had permission to collect the latter (see above, section 5). As regards Szczecin and trade with Slavs, we can presume the same *ex silentio*, because the preserved source (a bench court book) does not contain any direct information about trade. To sum up, it is worth underlining that the previously mentioned conflicts and restrictions (see above, section 7) were not inspired by clients of merchants and craftsmen of different origins but by their competitors.

The problem of relations between **lenders and debtors** looks a bit different. In spite of the Church bans on lending with interest, this kind of activity played a big role in the economy of the late Middle Ages.[232] Loans were lent not only by the Jews, since the prohibition on usury never applied to them, but also Christians — both laymen and ecclesiastical institutions. The case was similar in the Polish territories, where, as H. Samsonowicz concluded, lending on interest was widely practised in the period between the fifteenth and sixteenth centuries — by merchants, rentiers, shipowners, and mining entrepreneurs.[233] In Kraków, the German burghers used to grant credit to Italians and Jews.[234] Meanwhile, local Jews made loans to Germans and Poles.[235] In the same city, Italians sporadically lent money to Germans, and Poles to Armenians.[236] In Lviv, where there were significantly fewer preserved sources than in Kraków, credit activity was conducted quite commonly. Limiting ourselves to two published municipal books — a council one encompassing the years 1382–1389 and a bench court one from 1441–1448 — we can confirm lending money

---

228 *Księga ławnicza miejska (1441–1448)*, ed. by Czołowski and Jaworski, nos 1337, 1667.
229 *Księga ławnicza miejska (1441–1448)*, ed. by Czołowski and Jaworski, no. 90 (Jews) and no. 297 (Germans).
230 *Akta radzieckie poznańskie*, ii, ed. by Kaczmarczyk, no. 1626, p. 303; *Akta radzieckie poznańskie*, iii, ed. by Kaczmarczyk, no. 1925, pp. 32–33.
231 *Akta radzieckie poznańskie*, ii, ed. by Kaczmarczyk, no. 1679, pp. 338–39; *Akta radzieckie poznańskie*, iii, ed. by Kaczmarczyk, no. 1959, p. 47.
232 Kuske, 'Die Entstehung', pp. 73, 123; Postan, 'Credit in Medieval Trade'.
233 Samsonowicz, 'L'économie de l'Europe du Centre-Est', p. 634.
234 *Italia mercatoria apud Polonos*, ed. by Ptaśnik, no. 77, p. 83 (1439); *Żydzi w średniowiecznym Krakowie*, ed. by Wyrozumska, for example, nos 110, 245, 507, 708.
235 *Żydzi w średniowiecznym Krakowie*, ed. by Wyrozumska, for example, nos 103, 228, 415, 418, 570, 759 (Germans) and nos 397, 631, 653, 715, 726, 776, 780 (Poles).
236 *Italia mercatoria apud Polonos*, ed. by Ptaśnik, nos 7, 17; *Żydzi w średniowiecznym Krakowie*, ed. by Wyrozumska, nos 74, 80, respectively.

BETWEEN COEXISTENCE AND PERSECUTION   187

between representatives of many nationalities. The Jews lent to Germans, Italians, Armenians, and Ruthenians.[237] Germans granted credit to Armenians, Ruthenians, and, very rarely, Italians.[238] Ruthenians sporadically granted loans to Armenians and Germans.[239] Italians were another nationality that granted credits.[240] In the first half of the fifteenth century, Poles were rarely mentioned as lenders who granted credit to Armenians and Ruthenians.[241] There are also some exceptional cases, such as a Greek lending money to an Armenian,[242] and an Italian to a Muslim of an unspecified ethnic background ('Bubackr den Bessermenen').[243]

In Wrocław, the Jews lent to Germans.[244] A famous lender of the Wrocław burghers in the fifteenth century was Abraham of Opole, who permanently resided in that city.[245] Financial operations were also run by Antonio Ricci. He granted loans to Germans in Wrocław,[246] as well as borrowing money from the local burghers.[247] In terms of Poznań, J. Rudzińska assumed that local Jews granted money loans mainly to the local nobility and sporadically to merchants from Nuremberg.[248] The influx of Nurembergers caused merchants from Poznań to take loans from them.[249] However, from the preserved sources we can deduce that credit activity was also carried out by the citizens of Poznań. Local Jews granted credit to Germans and Poles.[250] We can also observe less frequent examples of money loans granted by Poles to a local Italian and a Jew.[251] In the Polonized Płock of the fifteenth–sixteenth century, transactions were mainly made by Poles within their own community. But it is also known that a Jewish banker with the name of Mushka lived here from at least 1448.[252] We have no

---

237 *Najstarsza księga miejska (1382–1389)*, ed. by Czołowski, no. 75, and *Księga ławnicza miejska (1441–1448)*, ed. by Czołowski and Jaworski, for example nos 90, 1441, 1765a (Germans); *Najstarsza księga miejska (1382–1389)*, ed. by Czołowski, no. 74 (Italians) and no. 709 (Armenians); *Księga ławnicza miejska (1441–1448)*, ed. by Czołowski and Jaworski, no. 80 (Ruthenians).

238 *Najstarsza księga miejska (1382–1389)*, ed. by Czołowski, no. 447, and *Księga ławnicza miejska (1441–1448)*, ed. by Czołowski and Jaworski, nos 115, 620, 825 (Armenians); *Księga ławnicza miejska (1441–1448)*, ed. by Czołowski and Jaworski, nos 903, 1611 (Ruthenians) and no. 981 (Italians).

239 *Najstarsza księga miejska (1382–1389)*, ed. by Czołowski, no. 430 (Armenians); *Księga ławnicza miejska (1441–1448)*, ed. by Czołowski and Jaworski, no. 292 (Germans).

240 *Księga ławnicza miejska (1441–1448)*, ed. by Czołowski and Jaworski, no. 666.

241 *Księga ławnicza miejska (1441–1448)*, ed. by Czołowski and Jaworski, nos 493, 1311 (Armenians) and nos 1535, 2435 (Ruthenians).

242 *Najstarsza księga miejska (1382–1389)*, ed. by Czołowski, no. 17.

243 *Księga ławnicza miejska (1441–1448)*, ed. by Czołowski and Jaworski, no. 1374.

244 E.g. Archiwum Państwowe we Wrocławiu, *L.Nud.*, p. 196 (1366); *Lib.exc.sign.*, vol. 36, p. 217 (1445), vol. 38, p. 230 (1451).

245 Goliński, *Wrocławskie spisy*, pp. 55–58, 60–61.

246 'Mittheilungen aus Breslauer Signaturbüchern', ed. by Stobbe, pp. 350, 352; Archiwum Państwowe we Wrocławiu, *Lib. exc. sign.*, vol. 31, p. 92 (1436).

247 Archiwum Państwowe we Wrocławiu, *Lib.exc.sign.*, vol. 31, p. 153 (1437); vol. 32, p. 116 (1439).

248 Rudzińska, 'Żydzi w późnośredniowiecznym Poznaniu', pp. 352–56.

249 Simsch, 'Die Handelsbeziehungen', p. 146.

250 *Akta radzieckie poznańskie*, I, ed. by Kaczmarczyk, no. 19, p. 7; no. 249, p. 93; no. 505, p. 180; no. 650, p. 231 (Germans); no. 346, p. 130; no. 412, pp. 150–51; no. 487, p. 174; no. 535, p. 190 (Poles).

251 *Akta radzieckie poznańskie*, II, ed. by Kaczmarczyk, no. 1623, pp. 299–301, and no. 1742, p. 394, respectively.

252 Fijałkowski, 'Początki obecności', p. 173.

knowledge of his clients, though it seems to be self-evident that he must also have given credit to the Płock burghers — Poles. In the light of the preserved source, credit was granted to a Pole by one of the few local Jews at the beginning of the sixteenth century.[253] Without doubt, moneylending at interest created ties between members of different ethnic communities, who inhabited the same centres.

B. Wyrozumska has already pointed out the conflictual nature of these relations.[254] As confirmation, we can use the memorial of the city council of Kraków from 1369 (which at the time consisted of Germans) to King Casimir III the Great, which was regularly discussed in historiography because of the mention of the 'dominacionem Judeorum' in the city.[255] More exactly, the councillors faulted Jews for the escape of a few burghers from the city due to a number of granted and undischarged loans. In two cases Jewish creditors were accused of using false bonds. Other charges that appeared consisted of receiving stolen goods and hiding thieves. Finally, indirectly expressing discontent towards the ruler, they uttered a complaint about his military requirements, for the fulfilment of which the burghers had to borrow money from the Jews. R. Grodecki viewed this memorial as a confirmation of the townspeople's growing resentment towards the local Jews.[256] However, we ought to keep in mind that not all references in the municipal books resulted from conflicts between the creditors and debtors who were insolvent or unwilling to pay off loans. Many of them were being noted down to perpetuate a credit contract or to certify the promise of debtors to pay off debts by the agreed instalments. In my opinion, in the period of economic development of the cities analysed, credit activity tended to connect rather than to divide people, because granting loans frequently must have meant mutually beneficial cooperation.

9. Benefactors and Founders

In the research conducted hitherto, attention has been drawn to the fact that within the historically understood Polish territories a lot of funds were spent on the support of institutions for social assistance by both individual burghers and city authorities.[257] In Kraków and Poznań, such expenses made up 2 per cent of the cities' budgets.[258] Based on the last wills of townsmen from Kraków and Gdańsk, as well as other towns not taken into my consideration in this study (Lublin, Chojnice), H. Samsonowicz deduced that in burghers' wills large amounts of money were allocated to devotional purposes, including supporting the poor.[259]

---

253 *Księga ławnicza miasta Płocka*, ed. by Poppe, no. 276 (1507), p. 141.
254 Wyrozumska, 'Czy Jan Olbracht', p. 7.
255 *Żydzi w średniowiecznym Krakowie*, ed. by Wyrozumska, no. 48, pp. 30–31. The text of the memorial has already been discussed (see Grodecki, 'Dzieje Żydów', pp. 685–90; Zaremska, *Żydzi w średniowiecznej Polsce*, pp. 153, 184–85).
256 Grodecki, 'Dzieje Żydów', pp. 685–86.
257 Bogucka and Samsonowicz, *Dzieje miast*, p. 156.
258 Bogucka and Samsonowicz, *Dzieje miast*, pp. 176–77.
259 Bogucka and Samsonowicz, *Dzieje miast*, pp. 242–43.

century	for devotional purposes	percentage for poor
thirteenth	32.9%	46.0%
fourteenth	37.9%	62.2%
fifteenth (until 1475)	25.4%	25.6%
1475 – mid–sixteenth	43.0%	32.2%

Analogous calculations for the remaining cities under study are not known to me, although we know that philanthropic activity commonly occurred in all urban communities.

Let us begin with an issue of alms, the form of which varied. For example, the poor in Wrocław were supported not only with money, but also food (like herring),[260] cloth,[261] and shoes.[262] This was done, similarly to the great Italian and German companies, by including a write-off on the poor in the books of accounts.[263] Burghers were giving away their money to the needy in their last wills.[264] Sometimes they shared food with them, as Wrocław burgher Mikołaj von Kattwitz who paid for two meals a week for everyone out of a horde of two hundred to three hundred beggars in the mid-fourteenth century.[265] This kind of support did not necessarily apply to people of the same nationality. In Kraków, the Catholic municipal authorities comprised of Germans were also allocating alms to poor Jewish converts.[266] Did the same occur in other cities, where Germans and Armenian Catholics lived together? Could Catholic alms apply to Christians of a different confession and nationality (Armenians and Orthodox Ruthenians)? I am not in possession of such data, either from the literature or primary sources. However, the ethnic extent of charity could also be noticed in the division into wealthier benefactors and poor in the given city. Here we should also include the suburban poor, who, according to C. M. Cipolla, were attracted to the cities because they were inhabited by wealthy benefactors.[267] We can then assume that in Kraków, Wrocław, Poznań, and Płock, eleemosynary activity must have encompassed a part of the Polish population (in Szczecin, Slavic), usually much less wealthy than German merchants and craftsmen.

Were hospitals able to integrate the different ethnicities? A hospital was a religious foundation and a place of religious practice.[268] And that could mean that in the cities

---

260 Petry, *Die Popplau*, p. 59.
261 Archiwum Państwowe we Wrocławiu, *Klose*, vol. 27, p. 2 (1368, 1380). *Bartłomieja Steina renesansowe opisanie Wrocławia*, ed. by Żerelik, cap. 28, p. 117. For Kraków, see *Żydzi w średniowiecznym Krakowie*, ed. by Wyrozumska, no 133; for Poznań, see Wiesiołowski, 'Życie codzienne ludności', p. 288.
262 Archiwum Państwowe we Wrocławiu, *Lib. scab.*, vol. 8, p. 143 (1397); vol. 9, p. 139 (1401).
263 On the charitative donations, see, among others, Sapori, 'Storia interna della compagnia mercantile', p. 672; Irsigler, 'Kaufmannsmentalität', p. 59; as regards Wrocław, see Petry, *Die Popplau*, p. 59.
264 For Gdańsk: Możejko, *Rozrachunek*, pp. 56, 58, 61, 64, 72, 73, 77.
265 Heck and Maleczyńska, *Historia Śląska*, p. 174.
266 *Żydzi w średniowiecznym Krakowie*, ed. by Wyrozumska, nos 124, 133, 212, 240.
267 Cipolla, *Before Industrial Revolution*, p. 12.
268 Słoń, *Szpitale średniowiecznego Wrocławia*, pp. 6–7.

under study Catholic hospitals accepted only co-religionists. The Jewish community in Krakow had its own hospital, like the Armenian community in Lviv.[269] Generally, it can be said that hospitals were occupied not only by the poor, sick, decrepit, and old, but also by healthy, though very poor people, as well as orphans, pilgrims, and other travellers.[270] Hospitals were mainly founded by ecclesiastical institutions,[271] sometimes by rulers (Płock, Kraków, Wieliczka near Kraków, Lviv, Gdańsk),[272] as well as city authorities.[273]

However, a striking fact is that the establishment of hospitals by the city council was a rare event in these towns. According to the results of comparative research by M. Słoń, municipal authorities from cities of Germany and central Europe seldom played a decisive role in founding hospitals (Wrocław, Lviv is less certain).[274] However, this list of exceptions should be supplemented. It is worth recalling the foundation of the Holy Cross Church in Bochnia near Kraków by the city council in 1357, even though the relevant document was preserved only in a later translation.[275] As late as the fifteenth century burghers were more often interested in founding specialist hospitals: a leprosarium for women as well as children and school hospitals in Wrocław,[276] and in Poznań hospitals for the pupils of local schools and a separate one for lepers.[277] In Gdańsk, the oldest hospital — Holy Spirit Hospital (founded by the Teutonic Order in 1333) — was placed under the administration of municipal authorities in 1382.[278] P. Simson did not rule out that the Saint George Hospital (from 1355) could have been founded by the burghers' brotherhood dedicated to this saint.[279] It is worth recalling K. Stopka's research conclusions which revealed the activity of two Armenian hospitals in Lviv and their financial maintenance by the Armenian commune.[280]

---

269 Wyrozumska, 'Czy Jan Olbracht', p. 10; Stopka, 'Kultura religijna Ormian', p. 243.

270 Piskorski, *Miasta księstwa szczecińskiego*, p. 194.

271 Bogucka and Samsonowicz, *Dzieje miast*, p. 280.

272 Nowowiejski, *Płock*, p. 535; Wyrozumski, *Państwowa gospodarka solna*, p. 163; Wyrozumski, *Dzieje Krakowa*, pp. 452–53; Słoń, 'Szpitale lwowskie', pp. 222, 224. In Gdańsk, four out of six hospitals operating until the end of the fourteenth century were certainly founded by the Teutonic Order and one by the members of secular clergy, but it was soon taken over by the monastic authorities (Simson, *Geschichte der Stadt Danzig*, pp. 79–80, 114).

273 Generally, see Bogucka and Samsonowicz, *Dzieje miast*, p. 280.

274 Słoń, 'Szpital jako centrum', pp. 372–73. However, earlier, in the case of the Lviv hospitals, he suggested a royal initiative in founding both hospitals (Słoń, 'Szpitale lwowskie', pp. 222, 224). See also remarks by J. M. Piskorski who assigned a decisive initiative to the burghers (city authorities, individual persons) in relation to the Western Pomeranian cities, although without giving specific examples (Piskorski, *Miasta księstwa szczecińskiego*, p. 195).

275 *Kodeks dyplomatyczny Małopolski*, III, ed. by Piekosiński, no. 716, pp. 110–11.

276 Słoń, *Szpitale średniowiecznego Wrocławia*, pp. 213–15 (the Eleven Thousand Companions' Hospital), 223 (Holy Sepulchre Hospital for children), 240 (St Jerome's Hospital), 248 (St John the Baptist Hospital), and 265–66 (a big St Barbara Hospital).

277 Wiesiołowski, 'Życie codzienne ludności', p. 290 — for students (St Gertrude Hospital) and lepers (Holy Cross Hospital).

278 Simson, *Geschichte der Stadt Danzig*, p. 90.

279 Simson, *Geschichte der Stadt Danzig*, p. 90.

280 Stopka, 'Kultura religijna Ormian', p. 243.

BETWEEN COEXISTENCE AND PERSECUTION   191

In Polish historiography, the issue of the founding of hospitals, apart from M. Słoń's studies, has been treated as a marginal topic. Hence it is not always certain who the founder of the hospital was. Supposedly, there is also a lack of sources in terms of their origins.[281] As in the case of the alms, here we should also presume that in the cities ruled by the German patriciate, the range of benefits encompassed not only their compatriots but also Polish Catholics and converts (Jews, Armenians). Among the donations transferred frequently to the hospitals, we should note the money transfers from the Kraków Jew (a non-convert) Michał Baruch for the Saint Hedwig Hospital in this city.[282] Their source was rent in money from his private home. Another example of a charitable initiative, carried out by the member of a minority ethnic group on behalf of a majority, was transferring four miners from the salt mine in Bochnia near Kraków to the miners' Holy Cross Church in the same city to serve this sacred institution.[283] It was done by a citizen of Kraków, the Genoese Goffredo Fattinante, in his last will of 1393.[284] His deed as the mine leaseholder and Italian could have elicited a positive reaction in the community of workers, which mainly consisted of Poles.

A separate issue is the founding of churches and monasteries by burghers in their cities. Their activity in this field began to appear in the Polish territories under study as late as in the fourteenth century.[285] They could have done it not only for religious reasons, but also for other causes.[286] In the studied cities, whether the municipal authorities partook in these foundations varied, as it depended on the given city's financial circumstances. Sometimes city councils were capable of financing the construction of entire churches (Wrocław, Szczecin, Kraków[287]), occasionally in cooperation with the bishop (Gdańsk).[288] In other centres, the patriciate's share was modest (Poznań)[289] or did not occur at all (Płock),[290] apart from the more numerous funding of chapels and altars. The wealthiest individual residents of cities could afford to finance some parts of the locally important sacral buildings. A rich German immigrant, Beringer, supposedly financed the construction of the Saint James Church in Szczecin (twelfth century).[291]

---

281 For example, in the case of Płock and St Valentine's Hospital (see Nowowiejski, *Płock*, pp. 524–25). Also on the topic of the genesis of St Katherine's Hospital — the first mention comes from 1490 (*Zbiór dokumentów*, I, ed. by Szacherska, no. 251, pp. 346–47) — nothing is known.

282 *Żydzi w średniowiecznym Krakowie*, ed. by Wyrozumska, nos 523, 533, 539.

283 *Italia mercatoria apud Polonos*, ed. by Ptaśnik, no. 6, p. 6. Generally on this topic: Ptaśnik, *Kultura włoska*, p. 62.

284 On Fattinante, see Ptaśnik, *Kultura włoska*, pp. 19, 57–64; Sowina, 'The Relations of the Town', pp. 228–32.

285 Arszyński, 'Wprowadzenie', p. 21.

286 I describe points of view in the historiograpy (Myśliwski, 'Kościół katolicki', pp. 260–62). The remarks by J. Wiesiołowski are particularly valuable (Wiesiołowski, 'Kultura i społeczeństwo', p. 314).

287 Maleczyński, 'Dzieje Wrocławia', p. 184; Lesiński, 'Rozdrobnienie feudalne', p. 103; and Arszyński, 'Wprowadzenie', p. 21, respectively.

288 Biskup, 'Pod panowaniem krzyżackim', p. 455.

289 Wiesiołowski, 'Kultura i społeczeństwo', p. 316.

290 The assumption of A. J. Nowowiejski that St Bartholomew's Church was built by the city council contradicts the quoted document from 1356 (see Nowowiejski, *Płock*, pp. 147–54).

291 Chłopocka, Leciejewicz, and Wieczorowski, 'Okres wczesnofeudalny do roku 1237', p. 55; Mroczko and Arszyński, eds, *Architektura gotycka w Polsce*, II, p. 222.

The famous entrepreneur and royal advisor Niklas Wirsing the elder (Wierzynek) co-financed the building of the presbytery of Saint Mary's Basilica in Kraków.[292] In the fifteenth century, a Lviv patrician, Peter Stecher, financially supported the construction of a part of the Catholic Cathedral of the Assumption of the Blessed Virgin,[293] while his fellow-citizen Mikołaj Czech financed a part of the building of the Church of the Dominican Order (Corpus Christi), not to mention the multiple altars.[294]

The financing of the churches or their parts by the urban authorities and individual burghers is important and relevant for the main issue of this chapter. Through strengthening the Catholic cult by the relevant community in each city, the religious divisions between the city residents were solidified. It had to be particularly significant in religiously and ethnically diverse Lviv. The subsidization of Catholic temples by the burghers must have integrated the Catholics of various origins — Germans, Poles, as well as Armenian and Jewish converts. But in some instances, founding the churches strengthened the ethnic divisions within the same denomination. Hence Beringer's foundation in Szczecin was to consolidate incoming Germans (vs. local Slavs), similarly to St Catherine's Church in Gdańsk that was founded by immigrants from Lübeck (first half of the thirteenth century).[295]

Conclusions

Let us try finally to answer the basic question of whether economic activity impacted on the cohesion of multi-ethnic communities in the given cities. From the beginning of the analysed period, these communities were divided not only in ethnic terms, but also legally, due to

1) a limited social scope of the urban citizenship, which could only be granted to wealthier people, not only Germans and then Poles, but also Italians in Kraków and Wrocław (see above, sections 5, 9), Armenians and Ruthenians in Lviv,[296] as well as Jews in Szczecin (but not in the Kingdom of Poland);[297]

2) privileges integrating the given ethnic group (Germans by urban charters, including reorganization of the city according to German law; ethno-religious privileges related to Jews and Armenians); and

3) clauses including a ban on the immigration of a given ethnic group to the city under German law (Poles in Kraków; see above, section 2).

---

292 Wyrozumski, *Dzieje Krakowa*, p. 282; Mroczko and Arszyński, eds, *Architektura gotycka w Polsce*, II, p. 124; Manikowska, 'Religijność miejska', p. 27.

293 Papée, *Historja miasta Lwowa*, p. 56. Cf. Mroczko and Arszyński, eds, *Architektura gotycka w Polsce*, II, p. 145.

294 Trajdos, 'Dobroczyńcy', p. 245.

295 Zbierski and Jasiński, 'Gdańsk', pp. 276–77.

296 Gierszewski, *Obywatele*, p. 76.

297 Piskorski, *Miasta księstwa szczecińskiego*, p. 174; Zaremska, *Żydzi w średniowiecznej Polsce*, p. 443. See also Gierszewski, *Obywatele*, p. 42.

Ethnic divisions were mirrored in the spaces of the analysed cities. Ethnic groups inhabited distinct streets and districts, as was the case of Lviv's socio-topography,[298] or the distribution of the Jewish population there and in other cities under study (apart from Gdańsk). The presumption was expressed that the Italian merchants inhabited houses close to one another in Kraków.[299]

These differences — in legal status and in everyday life conditions — did not cause conflicts by themselves. Contrary to that, the starting points for responding to the issue in the title of this chapter are non-antagonistic ethnic and legal divisions in the studied centres. One must realize that there is no evidence to indicate that their inhabitants wanted to constitute one community of a town in today's understanding of this word, a community without ethnic divisions. Hence, it should be ascertained that, for the majority of the studied period, economic activity — extending beyond the ethnic limits — led to the formation of more and more numerous relations between members of various ethnicities in the same city.

In spite of conflicts, recorded in city books, these actions usually led to satisfactory results — purchases of desired goods, providing cash, employment, or support for people of various ethnic descent with money or a meal. It could have had a positive impact on the reception of various ethnicities in the city. In regard to the statement of the confrontational consequences of moneylending at interest, it seems to be true only in part. Not all source references to credits resulted from conflicts. Credit transactions were being perpetuated in city books also *pro memoria*, to assure the debt's repayment, at the same time accepting councillors and lower judges as witnesses to the credit agreement. After all, legal sources, even in the cities in which they were preserved in higher numbers, in all likelihood do not reflect all credit (and other?) relations between multi-ethnic residents of the same centre. A portion of the transactions was most likely conducted individually and privately. It is possible that sometimes they were not noted down.[300] On the other hand, the fact that, for example, in Kraków Italians most likely did not lend money to Armenians was not a result of mutual resentment. The latter simply must have not turned to Italians for loans.

The statement about the positive impact of economic life on the cohesion of municipal communities can be applied to the vast circle of Christian townspeople for the majority of the considered period. However, for a complete solution to the issue in the title, it is fundamental to assess the role that economic factors played in the repression of the Jewish population by the German (later Polonized) townspeople of Kraków, Poznań, and also — only German — in Wrocław. Historians who have examined the resentment and repression of the European Jews between the eleventh and fifteenth centuries often point to various causes like extraordinary circumstances (Great Famine, Black Death)[301] and extra-economic factors. These include, in general,

---

298 Czołowski, 'Lwów za ruskich czasów', p. 786; Janeczek, 'Ulice etniczne'.
299 Sowina, 'The Relations of the Town', pp. 230–31.
300 As noted by a historian of a German company, in the fifteenth century, also in the Polish territories, many credit contracts were made only orally (von Stromer, *Die Nürnberger Handelsgesellschafft*, p. 77).
301 For example, Jordan, *The Great Famine*, p. 113; Rörig, *Die europäische Stadt*, p. 81; Lokers, '"Men bedervet erer ok nicht"?', p. 117.

resentment of 'the other', magnified by an increase in the size of the Jewish population (migration), accusations of causing an epidemic, poisoning wells, ritual murders, desecrating sacramental wafers, and founding secret societies.[302] Another crucial factor is instrumental, political exploitation of the resentment towards Jews and pogroms by the city authorities and monarchs.[303] Economic causes are highlighted much less frequently.[304] Supposedly, it results from the fact that sociocultural and political causes are more intriguing as objects of research than simple emotions arising from economic factors: envy towards resourceful, wealthy, and prosperous people, resentment and hatred towards Jewish creditors, as well as desire for another person's material goods, which could have been satisfied only during collective repressions of the Jews (not only the ones who were well-off). An assessment of the relevance of economic causes, also in comparison to sociocultural and political motives, is often constricted because of their frequent entanglement.

In the broadly understood Polish territories, many of these stereotypes or other rumours of different kinds (e.g. the story of an attack by the Jews on a priest who was on his way to give the last rites) were propagated and widespread.[305] On the other hand, the statement by clergyman, lawyer, and president of University of Krakow Stanisław of Skarbimierz that Christians should not do any harm to Jews ('Decens est igitur ut christianus Judeo nullam inferet iniuriam')[306] could have been shared by many only during the stabilization period.

Resentment, whether from the higher clergy, preachers, or the nobility, towards the privileges of the Jewish population coincided with the weakened internal position of the Polish monarchs after the death of King Casimir III the Great (1370) or conflicts between royal authority and magnates as was the case during the rule of King Casimir IV Jagiellon (1440–1492).[307] Undoubtedly, natural disasters, such as fires and epidemics, served as catalysts of hatred in some situations. They led to emotional outbreaks and transgressions of moral codes of the oppressors. But pogroms were not always preceded by disasters. It cannot be ruled out that repressions towards Jews outside of the borders of the Kingdom of Poland, like in the Holy Roman Empire (also in Wrocław, 1439), began to appear as a pattern and encouragement to annihilate the 'Other' in the Polish territories. The townspeople there could have possessed knowledge of what was occurring outside of the border through the foreign connections and tales of Jewish fugitives who were coming to

---

302 For example, Rutkowska-Płachcińska, 'Dżuma', pp. 92–93; Delumeau, *La Peur*, pp. 287–91; Zaremska, *Żydzi w średniowiecznej Europie Środkowej*, pp. 115, 116; Reinhard, *Lebensformen Europas*, p. 335; Lokers, '"Men bedervet erer ok nicht"?', p. 124.

303 For example, von Stromer, 'Der kaiserliche Kaufmann', p. 64; Lokers, '"Men bedervet erer ok nicht"?', p. 124.

304 For example, Delumeau, *La Peur*, pp. 274–75; Gurevich, 'Kupiec', p. 314.

305 In general, see Ihnatowicz, Mączak, and Zientara, *Społeczeństwo polskie*, pp. 201–02; in more detail: Grodecki, 'Dzieje Żydów', pp. 683–84; Zaremska, 'Zmowa śląskich Żydów'; Zaremska, *Żydzi w średniowiecznej Polsce*, pp. 456 ff.

306 Wyrozumska, 'Czy Jan Olbracht', p. 11.

307 See Zaremska, *Żydzi w średniowiecznej Polsce*, pp. 159–71.

the cities of the Kingdom of Poland. A consequent rise in their number in some cities (received unwillingly) could have also had an impact on the deterioration of relations between the Catholic townspeople (German, later also Polish) and Jewish communes. Jewish migrations, both mandatory (from abroad) and voluntary (within the Kingdom of Poland) meant an increase in the number of businessmen of different descent who also became economic competitors of the natives. Without negating the role of ideological and political factors, I think the resentment towards Jews for economic reasons always played a bigger or smaller role in pogroms and expulsions during the researched period, whether it was in Wrocław or Kraków, but also Poznań, where the Jews were not expelled. Lviv was a positive exception to this rule. Neither a pogrom nor an expulsion of the Jewish population occurred here in the period under study. This was even despite the fact that two catastrophic fires took place here (1381, 1527)[308] after reorganizing this city according to German law and the influx of the Jewish population into Red Ruthenia in the fifteenth century.[309] Even if we assume that Jews in Lviv did not have the same economic importance as, for example, in Kraków, something had to be decisive for the fact that all the remaining factors and conditions did not cause physical violence. It is also plausible that ethnic and religious diversity in Lviv caused a thorough familiarization of townspeople with multi-ethnicity. Simply, here, variety was the norm. All of this was relieving the potential thoughts about getting rid of 'the stranger'. Because of that, in Lviv the economic competition escalated and trade conflicts took place (see above, section 7, they culminated in legal restrictions on trade, applying also to Armenians), but no collective violence was directed against ethnic minorities.

Summa summarum, the title issue of the chapter cannot be unequivocally solved because of the diverse ethnic situation in each of the studied centres. Generally, economic relations facilitated the crossing of ethnic barriers and, consequently, contributed to cohesion of urban communities. This particularly relates to their Christian members. However, as regards the cities where pogroms and expulsions of the Jews took place, it may be said that the impact of the economic life on the cohesion of entire urban communities could resemble a sinusoid in shape — its gradual growth was demolished every few or several dozen years by collective, ethnic violence towards the Jewish people. A restoration of economic relations often occurred later. However, in Wrocław, the sinusoid-shaped coexistence ended in a definite catastrophe in the middle of the fifteenth century. In the cities of the Kingdom of Poland, cohesion was impaired for good from the end of the fifteenth century due to the imposition of restrictions on Jewish trade in many cities, and in Lviv also on Armenians.

The most consolidated cities were either the ones in which the economic activity was conducted by many ethnic communities, such as Lviv, or those where the ethnic structure was nearly homogeneous, based on major supremacy in numbers — Germans (in Gdańsk) or Poles (in Płock).

---

308 Papée, *Historja miasta Lwowa*, pp. 54, 68; Zhuk, 'The Architecture of Lviv', p. 102.
309 Bogucka and Samsonowicz, *Dzieje miast*, p. 158; Kozubska-Andrusiv, '... propter disparitatem linguae et religionis pares ipsis non esse ...', p. 62.

196 GRZEGORZ MYŚLIWSKI

Appendix 1

The Settled Ethnic Communities/Nations in Selected Towns in the Polish Areas between the Thirteenth Century and the First Half of the Sixteenth

town	Slavs – Poles	Slavs – Pomeranians	Slavs – Ruthenians	Slavs – Bohemians	Germans	Jews	Italians	Walloons	Armenians	Tatars	others
Wrocław	X				X	X	X	X	–	–	–
Kraków	X			X	X	X	X	X	X	–	Lithuanians, Hungarians
Lwów	X		X		X	X	X		X	X	Saraceni
Poznań	X		X	X	X	X	X		X		
Płock	X			X	X	X					
Szczecin		X			X	X					
Gdańsk	X	X			X						Prussians

Works Cited

Manuscripts and Archival Sources

Archiwum Państwowe we Wrocławiu (Wrocław, State Archive)
Klose = Zbiór Klosego, vol. 27
Lib.exc.sign. = Libri excessuum et signaturarum, vols 27, 28, 31, 32, 36, 38
Lib. scab. = Libri scabinorum, vol. 8
L.Nud. = Laurentius Nudus

Primary Sources

Acten der Stände Preussens unter der Herrschaft des deutschen Ordens, vol. IV, ed. by Max
   Toeppen (Leipzig: Duncker und Humblot, 1884)
Akta radzieckie poznańskie, I: *1434–1470*, ed. by Kazimierz Kaczmarczyk (Poznań: PTPN,
   1925)
Akta radzieckie poznańskie, II: *1470–1501*, ed. by Kazimierz Kaczmarczyk (Poznań: PTPN,
   1931)
Akta radzieckie poznańskie, III: *1502–1506*, ed. by Kazimierz Kaczmarczyk (Poznań: PTPN,
   1948)
Das älteste Stettiner Stadtbuch (1305–1352), ed. by Martin Wehrmann (Stettin: Herrcke und
   Lebeling, 1921)
*Bartłomieja Steina renesansowe opisanie Wrocławia / Die Beschreibung der Stadt Breslau
   der Renaissancezeit durch Bartholomäus Stein*, ed. by Rościsław Żerelik (Wrocław:
   Arboretum, 1995)
Breslauer Urkundenbuch, ed. by Georg Korn (Breslau: Verlalg von W. G. Korn, 1870)
Italia mercatoria apud Polonos saeculo XV ineunte, ed. by Jan Ptaśnik (Rome: Loescher, 1910)
Kodeks dyplomatyczny Małopolski, vol. III, ed. by Franciszek Piekosiński (Kraków:
   Akademia Umiejętności, 1887)
Korespondencja żupnika krakowskiego Mikołaja Serafina z lat 1437–1459, ed. by Waldemar
   Bukowski, Tomasz Płóciennik, and Anna Skolimowska (Kraków: Wydawnictwo TN
   Societas Vistulana, 2006)
Księga ławnicza miasta Płocka (1489–1517), ed. by Danuta Poppe (Warsaw: TN Płockie,
   1995)
Księga ławnicza miejska (1441–1448), ed. by Aleksander Czołowski and Franciszek
   Jaworski, Pomniki dziejowe Lwowa z Archiwum miasta, 4 (Lwów: Gmina Król. Stoł.
   Miasta Lwowa, 1921)
'Mittheilungen aus Breslauer Signaturbüchern', ed. by Otto Stobbe, *Zeitschrift des Vereins
   für Geschichte und Alterthum Schlesiens*, 6.2 (1865), 335–56
Najstarsza księga miejska (1382–1389), ed. by Aleksander Czołowski, Pomniki dziejowe
   miasta Lwowa, 1 (Lwów: Gmina Król. Stoł. Miasta Lwowa, 1892)
Ormianie w średniowiecznym Krakowie: Wypisy źródłowe, ed. by Bożenna Wyrozumska
   (Kraków: Towarzystwo Miłośników Historii i Zabytków Krakowa, 2003)
Pommerellisches Urkundenbuch, ed. by Max Perlbach (Danzig: Westpreussischen
   Geschichtsverein, 1882)

Pommersches Urkundenbuch, II: *1254–1286*, ed. by Rodgero Prümers (Stettin: Königlich Preussisches Staatsarchiv für die Provinz Pommern Stettin, 1881)

Privilegia civitatis Leopoliensis (XIV–XVIII saec.), ed. by Myron Kapral (Lviv: MGKO 'Dokumental'na skarbnicâ L'vova', 1998)

Stadtbuch von Posen, ed. by Adolf Warschauer (Posen: Eigenthum der Gesellschaft, 1892)

Zbiór dokumentów i listów miasta Płocka, I: *1065–1495*, ed. by Stella M. Szacherska (Warsaw: PAN, 1975)

Zbiór dokumentów i listów miasta Płocka, II: *1495–1586*, ed. by Stella M. Szacherska (Warsaw: PAN, 1987)

Żydzi w średniowiecznym Krakowie: Wypisy źródłowe z ksiąg miejskich krakowskich / The Jews in Mediaeval Cracow: Selected Records from Cracow Municipal Books, ed. by Bożenna Wyrozumska (Kraków: Polska Akademia Umiejętności, 1995)

Secondary Studies

Abt, Stefan, 'Ludność Poznania w XVI i pierwszej połowie XVII wieku', in *Dzieje Poznania*, vol. I, ed. by Jerzy Topolski (Warsaw: PWN, 1988), pp. 424–54

Arszyński, Marian, 'Wprowadzenie', in *Architektura gotycka w Polsce*, vol. I, ed. by Teresa Mroczko and Marian Arszyński (Warsaw: Instytut Sztuki PAN, 1995), pp. 15–22

Badecki, Karol, 'Zaginione księgi średniowiecznego Lwowa', *Kwartalnik Historyczny*, 41 (1927), 519–79

Balzer, Oswald, *Sądownictwo ormiańskie w średniowiecznym Lwowie* (Lwów: Towarzystwo dla Popierania Nauki Polskiej, 1909)

Bardach, Juliusz, 'Ormianie na ziemiach dawnej Polski: Przegląd badań', *Kwartalnik Historyczny*, 90.1 (1983), 109–18

Biskup, Marian, 'Pod panowaniem krzyżackim — od 1308 r. do 1454 r.', in *Historia Gdańska*, vol. I, ed. by Edmund Cieślak (Gdańsk: Wydawnictwo Morskie, 1985), pp. 338–627

Biskup, Marian, and Gerard Labuda, *Dzieje zakonu krzyżackiego w Prusach: Gospodarka – społeczeństwo – państwo – ideologia* (Gdańsk: Wydawnictwo Morskie, 1986)

Bobowski, Kazimierz, 'Ze studiów nad prześladowaniami i pogromami Żydów na Śląsku w dobie średniowiecza', *Śląski Kwartalnik Historyczny Sobótka*, 44.1 (1989), 5–11

Bogucka, Maria, and Henryk Samsonowicz, *Dzieje miast i mieszczaństwa w Polsce przedrozbiorowej* (Wrocław: Zakład Narodowy im. Ossolińskich, 1986)

Brann, Marcus, *Geschichte der Juden in Schlesien*, vol. I (Breslau: Wilhelm Jacobson, 1896)

——, *Geschichte der Juden in Schlesien*, vol. II (Breslau: Wilhelm Jacobson, 1897)

——, *Geschichte der Juden in Schlesien*, vol. III (Breslau: Wilhelm Jacobson, 1901)

——, *Geschichte der Juden in Schlesien*, vol. IV (Breslau: Wilhelm Jacobson, 1907)

Bruns, Friedrich, and Hugo Weczerka, *Hansische Handelstrassen: Textband* (Böhlau: Weimar 1967)

Buko, Andrzej, *Archeologia Polski wczesnośredniowiecznej* (Warsaw: Wydawnictwo Trio, 2005)

Bukowski, Waldemar, Tomasz Płóciennik, and Anna Skolimowska, 'Wstęp', in *Korespondencja żupnika krakowskiego Mikołaja Serafina z lat 1437–1459*, ed. by Waldemar Bukowski, Tomasz Płóciennik, and Anna Skolimowska (Kraków: Wydawnictwo Towarzystwa Naukowego Societas Vistulana, 2006), pp. v–lxi

Buśko, Cezary, 'Wrocław u progu lokacji', in *Wschodnia strefa Starego Miasta we Wrocławiu w XII–XIV wieku: Badania na placu Nowy Targ*, ed. by Cezary Buśko (Wrocław: Uniwerystet Wrocławski Instytut Archeologii, 2005), pp. 177–94

Charewiczowa, Łucja, *Handel średniowiecznego Lwowa* (Lwów: Zakład Narodowy im. Ossolińskich, 1925)

——, *Ograniczenia gospodarcze nacyj schizmatyckich i Żydów we Lwowie w XV i XVI wieku* (Lwów: Zakład Narodowy im. Ossolińskich, 1925)

Chłopocka, Helena, Lech Leciejewicz, and Tadeusz Wieczorowski, 'Okres wczesnofeudalny do roku 1237', in *Historia Szczecina*, vol. II, ed. by Gerard Labuda (Szczecin: PWN, 1985), pp. 15–59

Cipolla, Carlo M., *Before Industrial Revolution: European Society and Economy (1000–1700)* (New York: W. W. Norton, 1994)

Czaja, Roman, *Grupy rządzące w miastach nadbałtyckich w średniowieczu* (Toruń: UMK, 2008)

Czołowski, Aleksander, 'Lwów za ruskich czasów', *Kwartalnik Historyczny*, 5 (1891), 779–812

Delumeau, Jean, *La Peur en Occident (XIVe–XVIIIe siècles): Une cité assiégée* (Paris: Librairie Arthème Fayard, 1978)

Dollinger, Philippe, *Die Hanse*, rev. by Henn von Volker and Jörn Nils (Stuttgart: Alfred Kröner Verlag, 2012)

Echt, Samuel, *Die Geschichte der Juden in Danzig* (Leer: Rautenberg, 1972)

Fijałkowski, P., 'Początki obecności Żydów na Mazowszu (do 1526 r.)', *Kwartalnik Historii Żydów / Jewish History Quarterly*, 198 (2001), 169–93

Gawlas, Sławomir, 'Introduction', in *Studia nad rozwojem średniowiecznej Europy*, ed. by Sławomir Gawlas (Warsaw: Wydawnictwo DiG, 2006), pp. 429–40

——, 'Stan badań nad polską świadomością narodową w średniowieczu', in *Państwo, naród, stany w świadomości wieków średnich*, ed. by Aleksander Gieysztor and Sławomir Gawlas (Warsaw: PWN, 1990), pp. 149–94

——, ed., *Ziemie polskie wobec Zachodu: Studia nad rozwojem średniowiecznej Europy* (Warsaw: Wydawnictwo DiG, 2006)

Gąsiorowski, Antoni, 'Ludność Poznania od połowy XIII do XV wieku', in *Dzieje Poznania*, vol. I, ed. by Jerzy Topolski (Warsaw: PWN, 1988), pp. 245–68

Geremek, Bronisław, 'Migracje i kontakty kulturowe', in *Kultura Polski średniowiecznej X–XIII w.*, ed. by Jerzy Dowiat (Warsaw: PIW, 1985), pp. 16–25

Gierszewski, Stanisław, *Obywatele miast Polski przedrozbiorowej: Studium źródłoznawcze* (Warsaw: PWN, 1973)

Goerlitz, Theodor, *Verfassung, Verwaltung und Recht der Stadt Breslau*, I: *Mittelalter* (Würzburg: Holzner Verlag, 1962)

Goliński, Mateusz, *Socjotopografia późnośredniowiecznego Wrocławia (przestrzeń – podatnicy – rzemiosło)* (Wrocław: Wydawnictwo Uniwersytetu Wrocławskiego, 1997)

——, 'Wokół problematyki formowania się stanu mieszczańskiego w Polsce', in *Studia z historii społecznej*, ed. by Mateusz Goliński and Stanisław Rosik, Scripta historica medievalia, 2 (Wrocław: Chronicon, 2012), pp. 7–76

——, 'Wrocław od połowy XIII do początków XVI wieku', in Cezary Buśko, Mateusz Goliński, Michał Kaczmarek, and Leszek Ziątkowski, *Historia Wrocławia: Od pradziejów do końca czasów habsburskich*, vol. I (Wrocław: Wydawnictwo Dolnośląskie, 2001), pp. 96–222

————, *Wrocławskie spisy zastawów, długów i mienia żydowskiego z 1453 roku: Studium z historii kredytu i kultury materialnej* (Wrocław: Wydawnictwo Uniwersytetu Wrocławskiego, 2006)

Grodecki, Roman, 'Dzieje Żydów na ziemiach polskich do końca xiv wieku', in Roman Grodecki, *Polska piastowska*, ed. by Jerzy Wyrozumski (Warsaw: PWN, 1969), pp. 595–702

Guldon, Zenon, 'Skupiska żydowskie w miastach polskich xv–xvi wieku', in *Żydzi i judaizm we współczesnych badaniach polskich*, vol. ii, ed. by Krzysztof Pilarczyk and Stefan Gąsiorowski (Kraków: PAU, 2000), pp. 13–25

Gurevich, Aron J., *Categories of Medieval Culture*, trans. by G. L. Campbell (London: Routledge & and Kegan Paul, 1985)

————, 'Kupiec', in *Człowiek średniowiecza*, ed. by Jacques Le Goff, trans. by M. Radożycka-Paoletti (Warsaw: Volumen, Marabut, 1996), pp. 303–51

Heck, Roman, 'Wrocław w latach 1241–1526', in *Wrocław, jego dzieje i kultura*, ed. by Zygmunt Świechowski (Warsaw: Arkady, 1978), pp. 56–76

————, 'Struktura społeczna średniowiecznego Wrocławia na przełomie xiv/xv w.', *Sobótka*, 7 (1952), 57–94

Heck, Roman, and Ewa Maleczyńska, *Historia Śląska*, vol. i.2 (Wrocław: Zakład Narodowy im. Ossolińskich, 1961)

Hoensch, Jörg, *Geschichte Böhmens: Von der slavischen Landnahme bis zur Gegenwart* (Munich: Beck, 1997)

Hoffmann, Richard, *Land, Liberties and Lordship in a Late Medieval Countryside: Agrarian Structure and Change in the Duchy of Wrocław* (Philadelphia: University of Pennsylvania Press, 1988)

Hołubowicz, Władysław, and Karol Maleczyński, *Historia Śląska*, vol. i.1 (Wrocław: Zakład Narodowy im. Ossolińskich, 1960)

Hryszko, Rafał, *Januensis, ergo mercator? Działalność gospodarcza Genueńczyków w ziemi lwowskiej na tle kontaktów Polski z czarnomorskimi koloniami Genui w xv wieku* (Kraków: TW 'Historia Iagellonica', 2012)

Ihnatowicz, Ireneusz, Antoni Mączak, and Benedykt Zientara, *Społeczeństwo polskie od x do xx wieku* (Warsaw: Książka i Wiedza, 1979)

Irsigler, Franz, 'Kaufmannsmentalität im Mittelalter', in *Mentalität und Alltag im Spätmittelalter*, ed. by Cord Meckseper and Werner Goez (Göttingen: Vandenhoeck & Ruprecht, 1985), pp. 53–75

Isaevič, Jaroslav, and others, eds, *Історія Львова у тр'ох tomach*, i: *1256–1772*, ed. by Jaroslav Isajewicz (Lviv: Centr Evropii, 2006)

Jakowenko, Natalia, *Historia Ukrainy od czasów najdawniejszych do końca xviii wieku*, trans. by Ola Hnatiuk and Katarzyna Kotyńska (Lublin: Wydawnictwo Naukowe PWN, 2000)

Janeczek, Andrzej, 'Ethnische Gruppenbildungen im spätmittelalterlichen Polen', in *Das Reich und Polen: Parallelen, Interaktionen und Formen der Akkulturation im hohen und späten Mittelalter*, ed. by Thomas Wünsch, with the assistance of Alexander Patschovsky, Vorträge und Forschungen, 59 (Ostfildern: Thorbecke, 2003), pp. 401–46

————, 'Exceptis schismaticis: Upośledzenie Rusinów w przywilejach prawa niemieckiego Władysława Jagiełły', *Przegląd Historyczny*, 75.3 (1984), 527–42

———, 'Tłumacz lwowski: Z zagadnień komunikacji językowej w wieloetnicznym mieście późnego średniowiecza', in *Gospodarka, społeczeństwo, kultura w dziejach nowożytnych: Studia ofiarowane Pani Profesor Marii Boguckiej*, ed. by Andrzej Karpiński, Edward Opaliński, and Tomasz Wiślicz (Warsaw: IH PAN, 2010), pp. 203–22

———, 'Ulice etniczne w miastach Rusi Czerwonej w XIV–XVI wieku', *Kwartalnik Historii Kultury Materialnej*, 47.1–2 (1999), 135–37

———, 'Żydzi i Ormianie — dwie gminy religijno–prawne w krajobrazie etnicznym późnośredniowiecznej Polski', in *Animarum cultura: Studia nad kulturą religijną na ziemiach polskich w średniowieczu*, vol. I, ed. by Halina Manikowska and Wojciech Brojer (Warsaw: IH PAN, 2008), pp. 271–98

Janin, Valentin L., 'Znaczienije otkrytija bieriestianych gramot dla izuczienija tiecziestwiennoj istorii', in *Berestânye gramoty: 50 let otkrytiâ i izučeniâ: materialy meždunarodnoj konferencii Velikij Novgorod, 24–27 sentâbrâ 2001 g.* (Moscow: INDRIK, 2003), pp. 15–23

Jordan, William Ch., *The Great Famine: Northern Europe in the Early Fourteenth Century* (Princeton, NJ: Princeton University Press, 1998

Kalfas-Piotrowska, Stefania, 'Stosunki handlowe polsko–śląskie za Kazimierza Wielkiego', *Roczniki Towarzystwa Przyjaciół Nauk na Śląsku*, 5 (1936), 227–79

Kapral, Myron, 'Legal Regulation and National (Ethnic) Differentiation in Lviv, 1350–1600', in *On the Frontier of Latin Europe: Integration and Segregation in Red Ruthenia*, ed. by Thomas Wünsch and Andrzej Janeczek (Warsaw: IAiE PAN, University of Constance, 2004), pp. 211–28

Kedar, Beniamin Z., *Merchants in Crisis: Genoese and Venetian Men of Affairs and the Fourteenth-Century Depression* (New Haven: Yale University Press, 1976)

Kellenbenz, Hermann, 'Gewerbe und Handel am Ausgang des Mittelalters', in *Nürnberg — Geschichte einer europäischen Stadt*, ed. by Gerhard Pfeiffer (Munich: Beck, 1971), pp. 176–86

Kiryk, Feliks, 'Związki Lwowa z Krakowem w późnym średniowieczu', in *Lwów: Miasto, społeczeństwo, kultura*, vol. II, ed. by Henryk W. Żaliński and Kazimierz Karolczak (Kraków: Wydawnictwo Naukowe WSP, 1998), pp. 9–39

Knoll, Paul W., *The Rise of the Polish Monarchy: Piast Poland in East Central Europe, 1320–1370* (Chicago: University of Chicago Press, 1972)

Koczy, Leon, *Handel Poznania do połowy XVI w.* (Poznań: PTPN, 1930)

Kozubska-Andrusiv, Olha., '… propter disparitatem linguae et religionis pares ipsis non esse …: Minority Communities in Medieval and Early Modern Lviv', in *Segregation – Integration – Assimilation: Religious and Ethnic Groups in the Medieval Towns of Central and Eastern Europe*, ed. Derek Keene, Balazs Nagy, and Katalin Szende (Farnham: Ashgate, 2009), pp. 51–66

Kuske, Bruno, 'Die Entstehung der Kreditwirtschaft und des Kapitalverkehrs', in Bruno Kuske, *Köln, der Rhein und das Reich: Beiträge aus fünf Jahrzehnten wirtschaftgeschichtlicher Forschung* (Cologne: Böhlau, 1956), pp. 48–137

Kutrzeba, Stanisław, *Handel Krakowa w wiekach średnich na tle stosunków handlowych Polski* (Kraków: Akademia Umiejętności, 1902)

Kutrzeba, Stanisław, and Jan Ptaśnik, 'Dzieje handlu i kupiectwa krakowskiego w wiekach średnich', *Rocznik Krakowski*, 14 (1910), 1–146

202 GRZEGORZ MYŚLIWSKI

Lane, Federic C., *Venice: A Maritime Republic* (Baltimore: Johns Hopkins University Press, 1973)

Leciejewicz, Lech, and Marian Rębkowski, 'Uwagi końcowe: Początki Kołobrzegu w świetle rozpoznania archeologicznego', in *Kołobrzeg: Wczesne miasto nad Bałtykiem*, ed. by Lech Leciejewicz and Marian Rębkowski (Warsaw: Fundacja na Rzecz Nauki Polskiej, 2007), pp. 299–317

Lesiński, Henryk, 'Rozdrobnienie feudalne (1278–1478)', in *Dzieje Szczecina*, vol. II, ed. by Gerard Labuda (Warsaw: PWN, 1985), pp. 61–194

Lesnikov, Michail P., 'L'vovskoe kupečestvo i ego torgovye svjazi v XIV veke', in *Problemy ekonomičeskogo i političeskovo razvitija stran Evropy*, ed. by Viktor F. Semenov (Moscow: Moskovskij Gosudarstvennyj Pedagogiceskij Institut, 1964), pp. 38–54

Lichończak, Grażyna, 'Najstarsze dzieje rodziny Wierzynków w Krakowie', *Krzysztofory*, 8 (1981), 38–55

Lokers, Jan, '"Men bederdet erer ok nicht"? Juden in Hansestädten: Probleme und Perspektiven der Forschung', in *Am Rande der Hanse*, ed. by Klaus Krüger, Andreas Ranft, and Stephan Selzer, Hansische Studien, 22 (Trier: Porta Alba Verlag, 2012), pp. 105–33

Maleczyński, Karol, 'Dzieje Wrocławia od czasów najdawniejszych do roku 1618', in Wacław Długoborski, Józef Gierowski, and Karol Maleczyński, *Dzieje Wrocławia do roku 1807* (Warsaw: PWN, 1958), pp. 11–336

Małłek, Janusz, 'Powstanie poczucia krajowej odrębności w Prusach i jej rozwój w XV i XVI wieku', in *Państwo, naród, stany w świadomości wieków średnich*, ed. by Aleksander Gieysztor and Sławomir Gawlas (Warsaw: PWN, 1990), pp. 244–52

Małowist, Marian, 'Le développement des rapports économiques entre la Flandre la Pologne et les pays limitrophes du XIIIe au XIVe siècle', *Revue belge de Philologie et d'Histoire*, 10.4 (1931), 1013–65

——, *Studia z dziejów rzemiosła w okresie feudalizmu w zachodniej Europie w XIV–XV wieku* (Warsaw: PWN, 1954)

——, *Wschód a Zachód Europyw XIII–XVI wieku: Konfrontacja struktur społeczno-gospodarczych* (Warsaw: PWN, 1973)

Manikowska, Halina, 'Religijność miejska', in *Ecclesia et civitas: Kościół i życie religijne w mieście średniowiecznym*, ed. by Halina Manikowska and Hanna Zaremska (Warsaw: IH PAN, 2002), pp. 11–34

——, 'Średniowieczne miasta–państwa na Półwyspie Apenińskim', in *Rozkwit średniowiecznej Europy*, ed. by Henryk Samsonowicz (Warsaw: Wydawnictwo Bellona, 2001), pp. 250–377

——, 'Świadomość regionalna na Śląsku w późnym średniowieczu', in *Państwo, naród, stany w świadomości wieków średnich*, ed. by Aleksander Gieysztor and Sławomir Gawlas (Warsaw: PWN, 1990), pp. 253–67

Markgraf, Hermann, 'Zur Geschichte des Breslauer Kaufhauses', *Zeitschrift des Vereins für Geschichte und Alterthum Schlesiens*, 22 (1888), 249–80

Młynarska-Kaletynowa, Marta, *Wrocław w XII–XIII wieku: Przemiany społeczne i osadnicze* (Wrocław: Zakład Narodowy im. Ossolińskich, 1986)

Modzelewski, Karol, *Chłopi w monarchii wczesnopiastowskiej* (Wrocław: Zakład Narodowy im. Ossolińskich, 1987)

Możejko, Beata, *Rozrachunek z życiem doczesnym: Gdańskie testamenty mieszczańskie z XV i początku XVI wieku* (Gdańsk: Wydawnictwo Uniwersytetu Gdańskiego, 2010)

Mroczko, Teresa, and Marian Arszyński, eds, *Architektura gotycka w Polsce*, vol. II, ed. by Andrzej Włodarek (Warsaw: Instytut Sztuki PAN, 1995)

Myśliwski, Grzegorz, *Człowiek średniowiecza wobec czasu i przestrzeni (Mazowsze od XII do połowy XVI wieku)* (Warsaw: Krupski i Ska, 1999)

———, 'Kościół katolicki a miasta między Odrą a górnym Bugiem i Pełtwią (połowa XIII–XVI w.): Stymulator czy przeszkoda ich rozwoju gospodarczego?', in *Ecclesia et civitas: Kościół i życie religijne w mieście średniowiecznym*, ed. by Halina Manikowska and Hanna Zaremska (Warsaw: IH PAN, 2002), pp. 235–67

———, 'Retail Trade in Wrocław between around the Mid-Thirteenth and the Fifteenth Century', in *Il commercio al minuto: Domanda e offerta tra economia formale e informale. Secc. XIII–XVIII / Retail Trade: Supply and Demand in the Formal and Informal Economy from the 13th to the 18th Century*, ed. by Giampiero Nigro (Florence: Firenze University Press, 2015), pp. 277–94

———, *Wrocław w przestrzeni gospodarczej Europy XIII–XV wiek. centrum czy peryferie?* (Wrocław: Wydawnictwo Uniwersytetu Wrocławskiego, 2009)

Nazmi, Ahmed, *Commercial Relations between Arabs and Slavs (9th–11th centuries)* (Warsaw: Wydawnictwo Akademickie Dialog, 1998)

Nowowiejski, Antoni J., *Płock: Monografja historyczna* (Płock: Rosiński, 1917)

Okulicz-Kozaryn, Łucja, *Dzieje Prusów* (Wrocław: Leopoldinum, 1997)

Orłowska, Anna P., 'Zwei Brüder — zwei Städte: Die Nürnberger Gebrüder Geier in Danzig', in *Es geht um die Menschen: Beiträge zur Wirtschafts- und Sozialgeschichte des Mittelalters für Gerhard Fouquet zum 60. Geburtstag*, ed. by Harm von Seggern and Gabriel Zeilinger (Frankfurt am Main: Peter Lang, 2012), pp. 103–09

Papée, Fryderyk, *Historja miasta Lwowa w zarysie* (Lwów: Książnica Polska, 1924)

Petry, Ludwig, *Die Popplau: Eine schlesische Kaufmannsfamilie des 15. und 16. Jahrhunderts* (Breslau: M & H. Marcus, 1935)

Piskorski, Jan M., *Miasta księstwa szczecińskiego do połowy XIV wieku* (Warsaw: PWN, 1987)

Poppe, Danuta, 'Wstęp', in *Księga ławnicza miasta Płocka (1489–1517)*, ed. by Danuta Poppe (Płock: TNP, 1995), pp. i–xx

Postan, Michael M., 'Credit in Medieval Trade', in *Medieval Trade and Finance* (Cambridge: Cambridge University Press, 1973), pp. 1–27

———, 'Economic and Political Relations of England and the Hanse from 1400 to 1475', in *Studies in the English Trade in the Fifteenth Century* (London: George Routledge and Sons, 1933), pp. 91–153

Powierski, Jan, 'Hugo Butyr: Fragment stosunków polsko–niderlandzkich w XII w.', *Zapiski Historyczne*, 37.2 (1972), 9–44

Ptaśnik, Jan, *Kultura włoska wieków średnich w Polsce* (Warsaw: PWN, 1959)

———, *Miasta i mieszczaństwo w dawnej Polsce* (Kraków: PAU, 1934)

———, 'Studya nad patrycyatem krakowskim wieków średnich', *Rocznik Krakowski*, 16 (1914), 1–90

Rabinowič, Michail, *Życie codzienne w ruskim i rosyjskim mieście feudalnym*, trans. by Wiktor Dłuski (Warsaw: PIW, 1985)

Reinhard, Wolfgang, *Lebensformen Europas: Eine historische Kulturanthropologie* (Munich: C. H. Beck, 2006)

Rörig, Fritz, *Die europäische Stadt im Mittelalter und die Kultur des Bürgertums im Mittelalter* (Göttingen: Vandenhoeck & Ruprecht, 1955)

Rudzińska, Jolanta, 'Żydzi w późnośredniowiecznym Poznaniu', in *Civitas Posnaniensis: Studia z dziejów średniowiecznego Poznania*, ed. by Zofia Kurnatowska and Tomasz Jurek (Poznań: Wydawnictwo PTPN, 2005), pp. 345–60

Rutkowska-Płachcińska, Anna, 'Dżuma w Europie Zachodniej w XIV w. – straty demograficzne i skutki psychiczne', *Przegląd Historyczny*, 69.1 (1978), 75–102

Sacharov, Anatolij M., *Goroda severo–vostočnoj Rusi XIV–XV vekov* (Moscow: Moskovskij uni., 1959)

Samsonowicz, Henryk, 'La diversité ethnique au Moyen Âge: Le cas polonais', *Acta Poloniae Historica*, 71 (1995), 5–16

——, 'L'économie de l'Europe du Centre-Est du Haut Moyen Âge au XVIᵉ siècle', in *Histoire de l'Europe du Centre-Est* (Paris: Presses Universitaires de France, 2004), pp. 621–41

——, 'Handel zagraniczny Gdańska w drugiej połowie XV wieku (rejonizacja handlu na podstawie ksiąg cła palowego)', *Przegląd Historyczny*, 47.2 (1956), 283–352

——, *Późne średniowiecze miast nadbałtyckich: Studia nad dziejami Hanzy nad Bałtykiem w XIV–XV w.* (Warsaw: PWN, 1968)

——, 'Przesłanki tworzenia się narodu mazowieckiego na przełomie XV i XVI wieku', in *Narody: Jak powstawały i jak wybijały się na niepodległość? Profesorowi Tadeuszowi Łepkowskiemu w sześćdziesiątą rocznicę urodzin i czterdziestolecie pracy przyjaciele, koledzy, uczniowie*, ed. by Marcin Kula (Warsaw: PWN, 1989), pp. 146–53

Sapori, Armando, 'Gli Italiani in Polonia fino a tutto il Quattrocento', in *Studi di storia economica*, vol. III (Florence: Sansoni, 1967), pp. 149–76

——, *Le marchand italien au Moyen Age* (Paris: Colin, 1952)

——, 'Storia interna della compagnia mercantile dei Peruzzi', in *Studi di storia economica*, vol. II (Florence: Sansoni, 1957), pp. 653–91

Schenk, Hans, *Nürnberg und Prag: Ein Beitrag zur Geschichte der Handelsbeziehungen im 14. und 15. Jahrhundert* (Wiesbaden: Harrasowitz, 1969)

Scholz-Babisch, Marie, 'Oberdeutscher Handel mit dem deutschen und polnischen Osten nach Geschäftsbriefen von 1444', *Zeitschrift des Vereins für Geschichte Schlesiens*, 64 (1930), 56–74

Simsch, Adelheid, 'Die Handelsbeziehungen zwischen Posen und Nuernberg im 15 und 16 Jahrhundert', in *Der Aussenhandel Ostmitteleuropas (1450–1650): Die ostmitteleuropäischen Volkswirtschaften in ihren Beziehungen zu Mitteleuropa*, ed. by Ingomar Bog (Cologne: Böhlau Verlag, 1971), pp. 139–46

Simson, Paul, *Geschichte der Stadt Danzig*, vol. I (Danzig: Verlag von U. W. Kafemann, 1913)

Słoń, Marek, 'Początki osady walońskiej i kościoła Św. Maurycego we Wrocławia', in *Dzieje parafii św. Maurycego na Przedmieściu Oławskim we Wrocławiu: Od początków osady walońskiej – poprzez czas Festung Breslau – do współczesności*, ed. by Rościsław Żerelik (Wrocław: Wydawnictwo Gajt, 2007), pp. 11–20

——, 'Szpital jako centrum kultu miejskiego', in *Ecclesia et civitas: Kościół i życie religijne w mieście średniowiecznym*, ed. by Halina Manikowska and Hanna Zaremska (Warsaw: IH PAN, 2002), pp. 361–73

——, 'Szpitale lwowskie w wiekach średnich', *Przegląd Historyczny*, 85.3 (1994), 221–37

——, *Szpitale średniowiecznego Wrocławia* (Warsaw: IH PAN, 2000)

Sowina, Urszula, 'The Relations of the Town of Kraków and its Patriciate with the Ruler and the Wawel Court from the Thirteenth to the First Half of the Sixteenth C.', in *La court et la ville dans l'Europe au Moyen Âge et des tempes modernes*, ed. by Léonard Courbon and Denis Menjot (Turnhout: Brepols, 2015), pp. 225–36

Starzyński, Marcin, *Krakowa rada miejska w średniowieczu* (Kraków: Societas Vistulana, 2010)

——, 'Najstarszy dokument hebrajski na ziemiach polskich (1485) i jego tłumaczenia', *Roczniki Historyczne*, 83 (2017), 187–202

Stopka, Krzysztof, 'Kultura religijna Ormian polskich (Struktura i stosunki kościelno-publiczne)', in *Animarum cultura: Studia nad kulturą religijną na ziemiach polskich w średniowieczu*, vol. 1, ed. by Halina Manikowska and Wojciech Brojer (Warsaw: IH PAN, 2008) pp. 229–70

——, *Ormianie w Polsce dawnej i dzisiejszej* (Kraków: Księgarnia Akademicka, 2000)

Stromer, Wolfgang von, 'Der kaiserliche Kaufmann — Wirtschaftspolitik unter Karl IV.', in *Kaiser Karl IV.: Staatsman und Mäzen*, ed. by Ferdinand Seibt (Munich: Prestel, 1978), pp. 63–73

——, 'Nürnberg–Breslauer Wirtschaftsbeziehungen im Spätmittelalter', *Jahrbuch für fränkische Landesforschung*, 34–35 (1974–1975), 1079–1100

——, *Die Nürnberger Handelsgesellschafft Gruber–Podmer–Stromer im 15. Jahrhundert* (Nürnberg: Selbstverlag des Vereins für Geschichte der Stadt Nürnberg, 1963)

——, 'Nürnberger Unternehmer im Karpatenraum: Ein oberdeutsches Buntmetall-Oligopol 1396–1412', *Kwartalnik Historii Kultury Materialnej*, 16.4 (1968), 641–62

——, 'Wirtschaft unter den Luxemburgen', in *Nürnberg — Geschichte einer europaeischen Stadt*, ed. by Gerhard Pfeiffer (Munich: Beck, 1971), pp. 92–100

Suchodolska, Ewa, 'Dzieje polityczne (połowa XIII–połowa XIV w.)', in *Dzieje Mazowsza*, vol. 1, ed. by Henryk Samsonowicz (Pułtusk: Akademia Humanistyczna im. A. Gieysztora, 2006), pp. 213–56

Szacherska, Stella M., 'Złoty wiek miasta (1495–1580)', in *Dzieje Płocka*, ed. by Aleksander Gieysztor (Płock: Towarzystwo Naukowe Płockie, 1978), pp. 126–80

Székely, György, 'Wallons et Italiens en Europe Centrale aux XIe–XVIe siècles', *Annales Universitatis Scientiarum Budapestensis*, 6 (1964), 3–71

Ślaski, Kazimierz, and Benedykt Zientara, *Historia Pomorza*, vol. I.2 (Poznań: Wydawnictwo Poznańskie, 1972)

Tandecki, Janusz, 'Rozkwit toruńskiego ośrodka handlowego i produkcyjnego w latach 1350–1411', in *Historia Torunia*, vol. 1, ed. by Marian Biskup (Toruń: Wydawnictwo TN w Toruniu, 1999), pp. 167–220

Tichomirov, Michail N., *Drevnjaja Moskva (XIII–XV vv)* (Moscow: Izdat. MGU, 1948)

——, *Rosja średniowieczna na szlakach międzynarodowych*, trans. by Jan Jarco (Warszawa: IW PAX, 1976)

Trajdos, Tadeusz, 'Dobroczyńcy mendykantów średniowiecznego Lwowa', in *Społeczeństwo Polski średniowiecznej*, vol. VIII, ed. by Stefan K. Kuczyński (Warszawa: IH PAN, 1999), pp. 219–54

Warschauer, Adolf, 'Einleitung', in *Stadtbuch von Posen*, ed. by Adolf Warschauer (Posen: Eigenthum der Gesellschaft, 1892), pp. 5–198

Weber, Max, *Economy and Society: An Outline of an Interpretive Sociology*, ed. by Gunther Roth and Claus Wittich (Berkeley: University of California Press, 1978)

Wendt, Heinrich, *Schlesien und der Orient: Ein geschichtlicher Rückblick* (Breslau: Hirt, 1916)

Wenta, Jarosław, 'List Awinioński w dziejopisarstwie pomorskim i polskim połowy XIV wieku', *Przegląd Historyczny*, 73.3–4 (1982), 275–81

Wiesiołowski, Jacek, 'Kultura i społeczeństwo w późnym średniowieczu', in *Dzieje Poznania*, vol. I, ed. by Jerzy Topolski (Warsaw: PWN, 1988), pp. 310–69

——, *Socjotopografia późnośredniowiecznego Poznania* (Poznań: Wydawnictwo PTPN, 1997)

——, 'Środowiska kościelne i kultura', in *Kultura Polski średniowiecznej (XIV–XV w.)*, ed. by Bronisław Geremek (Warsaw: Semper, 1997), pp. 256–307

——, 'Życie codzienne ludności: Kultura materialna', in *Dzieje Poznania*, vol. I, ed. by Jerzy Topolski (Warsaw: PWN, 1988), pp. 285–309

Witzendorff-Rehdiger, Hans-Jürgen von, 'Herkunft und Verbleib Breslauer Ratsfamilien im Mittelalter: Eine genealogische Studie', *Jahrbuch der schlesischen Friedrich-Wilhelms-Universität zu Breslau*, 3 (1958), 111–36

Wójcik, Marek L., 'Klęski elementarne w średniowiecznym Wrocławiu. I. Pożary i zarazy', *Rocznik Wrocławski*, 6 (2000), 27–39

Wyrozumska, Bożena, 'Czy Jan Olbracht wygnał Żydów z Krakowa?', *Rocznik Krakowski*, 59 (1993), 5–11

——, 'Nieznany dokument Kazimierza Wielkiego', *Krakowski Rocznik Archiwalny*, 10 (2001), 191–95

——, 'Wstęp' in *Ormianie w średniowiecznym Krakowie: Wypisy źródłowe*, ed. by Bożenna Wyrozumska (Kraków: Towarzystwo Miłośników Historii i Zabytków Krakowa, 2003), pp. 5–8

——, 'Wstęp', in *Żydzi w średniowiecznym Krakowie: Wypisy źródłowe z ksiąg miejskich krakowskich*, ed. Bożenna Wyrozumska (Kraków: PAU, 1995), pp. 7–11

Wyrozumski, Jerzy, *Dzieje Krakowa*, I: *Kraków do schyłku wieków średnich* (Kraków: Wydawnictwo Literackie, 1992)

——, *Kazimierz Wielki* (Wrocław: Zakład Narodowy im. Ossolińskich, 1986)

——, *Państwowa gospodarka solna w Polsce do schyłku XIV wieku* (Kraków: PWN, 1968)

Zaremska, Hanna, 'Statut Bolesława Pobożnego dla Żydów: Uwagi w sprawie genezy', *Roczniki Dziejów Społecznych i Gospodarczych*, 54 (2004), 107–33

——, 'Zmowa śląskich Żydów', in *Źródło: Teksty o kulturze średniowiecza ofiarowane Bronisławowi Geremkowi*, ed. by Wojciech Brojer (Warsaw: IH PAN, 2003), pp. 135–62

——, *Żydzi w średniowiecznej Europie Środkowej: w Czechach, Polsce i na Węgrzech* (Poznań: PTPN, 2005)

——, *Żydzi w średniowiecznej Polsce: Gmina krakowska* (Warsaw: Instytut Historii PAN, 2011)

Zbierski, Andrzej, and Kazimierz Jasiński, 'Gdańsk w okresie panowania królów polskich i książąt pomorskich', in *Historia Gdańska*, vol. I, ed. by Edmund Cieślak (Gdańsk: Wydawnictwo Morskie, 1985), pp. 71–336

Zhuk, Ihor, 'The Architecture of Lviv from the Thirteenth to the Twentieth Century', in *Lviv: A City in the Crosscurrents of Culture*, ed. by John Czaplicka (Cambridge, MA: Ukrainina Research Institute–Harvard University, 2005), pp. 95–130

Ziątkowski, Leszek, *Dzieje Żydów we Wrocławiu* (Wrocław: Wydawnictwo Dolnośląskie, 2000)

Zientara, Benedykt, 'Walloons in Silesia in the 12th and 13th Centuries', *Quaestiones Medii Aevi*, 2 (1981), 127–50

Żebrowski, Tadeusz, 'Stolica książąt mazowieckich i płockich w latach 1138–1495', in *Dzieje Płocka*, ed. by Aleksander Gieysztor (Płock: Towarzystwo Naukowe Płockie, 1978), pp. 74–125

ANDRZEJ PLESZCZYŃSKI

Ethnic-Economic Relations within the Cities of Lublin, Zamość, and Lviv in the Sixteenth to Nineteenth Centuries

In the previous chapter, Grzegorz Myśliwski pointed out the key role of everyday economic relations in shaping long-term cooperation between various ethnic groups living in the medieval cities of the Kingdom of Poland. Was this phenomenon similar in the modern period? Then, in addition to the existing religious and cultural differences, new phenomena appeared in the cities of the Kingdom of Poland: the denominational divisions of Western Christianity and violent political changes which were also related to ethnic and religious differences (Turkish, Russian, and Swedish expansion).

Introduction

The idea of the research presented here is to compare the most important parameters of the socioeconomic and ethnic situation that existed in three eastern-central European cities, that is, in Lublin, Zamość, and Lviv between the sixteenth and the nineteenth centuries. The purpose of this comparison is to look at the evolution of the ethnic, economic, and inter-ethnic relations within these cities, in the context of external political and economic changes that occurred from the late Middle Ages until the beginning of the so-called industrial epoch which started in former Poland, and in the region of eastern-central Europe, shortly before the mid-nineteenth century.[1]

---

1 Brenner, 'Economic Backwardness in Eastern Europe'; Bidekeux and Jeffries, *A History of Eastern Europe*, pp. 160–64.

Andrzej Pleszczyński • (apleszczynski@gmail.com) is a Professor of Medieval History, Marie Curie-Skłodowska University, Lublin. His main research interests are the early and high medieval history of central and eastern Europe, German–Polish relations during the Middle Ages, and medieval chronicles.

Inter-Ethnic Relations and the Functioning of Multi-Ethnic Societies: Cohesion in Multi-Ethnic Societies in Europe from c. 1000 to the Present, II, ed. by Przemysław Wiszewski, EER 18 (Turnhout: Brepols, 2022), pp. 209–226

BREPOLS ❧ PUBLISHERS   10.1484/M.EER-EB.5.132152

This is an open access chapter made available under a cc by-nc 4.0 International License.

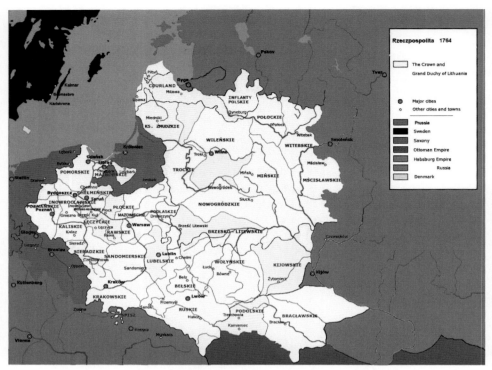

Map 8.1. Polish-Lithuanian Commonwealth in 1764. Source: <https://commons.wikimedia.org/wiki/File:Polish-Lithuanian_Commonwealth_in_1764.PNG>. Mathiasrex, Maciej Szczepańczyk, based on layers of Halibutt, CC BY-SA 3.0.

These above-mentioned urban centres were chosen as the subject for research for several reasons. The key point is their location on the major trade route which connected the Black Sea region with Poland and the countries of central Europe.[2] The second reason is the fact that they were somehow representative, during the period under discussion, for analysing the economic, ethnic, and social phenomena that also occurred in the other cities in the territory of the former Polish-Lithuanian Commonwealth, if not all the region of eastern-central Europe.[3]

Let us look more carefully at these three cities. Lublin was located in an ethnically Polish territory and was the property of the king. Lviv also belonged to the monarch,

---

2   Bogucka and Samsonowicz, *Dzieje miast*, pp. 181–83; Cieślak, Gawarecki, and Stankowa, *Lublin w dokumencie 1317–1967*, pp. 52–53; Charewiczowa, *Handel średniowiecznego Lwowa*, pp. 31–34; Frick, 'Lviv', pp. 568–69.

3   Miller, *Urban Societies in East-Central Europe*, pp. 7–19. The term 'central and eastern Europe' is quite imprecise and at the same time controversial; generally on the question, see e.g. Kłoczowski, ed., *Central Europe between East and West*; also Halecki, *The Limits and Divisions*; Okey, 'Central Europe/Eastern Europe'.

but was situated in the Ruthenian area. Zamość was a private city, which lay in an ethnically mixed region, on the border of regions dominated by the Polish population to the west and Ruthenian to the east.[4] All these cities from their foundation have been inhabited by people of different origins.[5]

Now it is time to justify the chronological confines of our investigation. The upper chronological boundary of the research was defined as the beginning of the nineteenth century because this period constituted, to a certain extent, the threshold of the pre-industrial age, which fundamentally changed economic, social, and ethnic relations in all the major cities of the region.[6] In order to ensure the coherence of the research, it must be limited to periods with a similar socioeconomic situation.

Our discussion has to be rather of a general nature, because the subject is broad and complex. Several phenomena which interested us are unclear because the available sources are incomplete as a result of the damage incurred through war which the city archives have suffered since the mid-seventeenth century. Therefore, we only have, often randomly kept, local government and tax documentation, inventories of municipal properties, and finally court files regarding economic matters.[7] This means that we can only write with limited certainty about some matters of interest. In essence, however, the profession of the historian — although they have more or less partial information at their disposal — consists of making statements on the basis of the available sources, irrespective of their quantity and quality.

Moving on to the question of the comparison of the changes in the population and the potential ethnic composition of the cities that we are interested in between the sixteenth and early nineteenth centuries, and having highlighted the most important points, let us note that we only have relatively complete and certain demographic and economic data for the end of the period under study. As far as earlier times are concerned, the data is estimated and based on information from the aforementioned economic and tax sources.

We start our considerations with Lublin which we will focus on the most. The phenomena observed in Zamość, and especially the ones in Lviv, which was in comparison to the former a true metropolis, will provide the contrast needed to draw out some generalizations.

---

4 Szczygieł, 'Zamość w czasach staropolskich'.
5 In general, cities whose economy is based on long-distance trade have always been multi-ethnic. In the east of Europe, this factor was reinforced by the fact that the idea of a city was imported from the West, and initially the people who organized towns and cities were mostly foreigners.
6 Kochanowicz, 'The Polish Economy and the Evolution of Dependency'; see also Snyder, *The Reconstruction of Nations*, pp. 3–4.
7 Siemieński, *Przewodnik po archiwach polskich*, p. 28; and the collection of studies *Stan badań nad wielokulturowym dziedzictwem dawnej Rzeczypospolitej*; Tomczak, *Zarys dziejów archiwów polskich*; Trojanowska, 'Źródła do dziejów Żydów lubelskich'.

Lublin

Lublin at the beginning of the nineteenth century had only about ten thousand residents. Most of them, around 70 per cent, were Poles.[8] Because in those times and areas religion was seen to be the same as nationality,[9] almost all of them were Catholics; only a small group within them — up to 2 per cent — were Greek Catholics. An unspecified percentage (estimated to be at most 3 per cent) of the people referred to as Poles were Protestants — almost all of them came from assimilated German families. The rest of the population was mainly Jewish — about 30 per cent.[10] The ethnic image of the city was complemented by the small group of Orthodox Christians; this faith at that time equated to a declaration of belonging to the Ruthenian ethnic group, sometimes only to the Russian one.[11]

Now let us move back in time over a century earlier to the end of the seventeenth. Then the population of Lublin was only about five thousand residents. Archival data does not allow for a more accurate approximation of ethnic composition. Based mainly on the data of religious institutions and the aforementioned religious beliefs, it is assumed that 25–30 per cent of the population were Jews, up to 5 per cent Protestants, mainly Germans, but there were also people of Scots, English, and Dutch origin.[12] The share of permanently resident Orthodox Christian populations was not recorded, while there were a similar percentage of Greek Catholics as the later period. Catholics or Poles accounted for about 65–70 per cent of the total population.[13]

The situation in the sixteenth century looks slightly different. The city had then more inhabitants than at the beginning of the nineteenth century — about eleven thousand.[14] It is estimated that more than half of them were Catholics, mainly Poles. It must be remembered, however, that many of the ancestors of merchants and craftsmen families living in Lublin and identified as Poles came from abroad, mostly from Germany, but also from Italy, the Netherlands, Scotland, and even from France.[15] Only newcomers from the West, and especially Protestants, maintained their ethnic distinctiveness. Catholic migrants were assimilated very quickly.[16] There is even an early record of this phenomenon. King Casimir the Great sold out the office, revenues,

---

8 Mencel, 'Lublin przedkapitalistyczny', pp. 199–204.
9 Vasiliauskas, 'The Practice of Citizenship among the Lithuanian Nobility'.
10 The rich history of Lublin Jews is documented in Balaban, *Die Judenstadt von Lublin*; Kuwałek and Wyskok, *Lublin — Jerozolima Królestwa Polskiego*; briefly Kopciowski, 'Outline History of the Jews in Lublin'.
11 On the complications of defining nationality in the former Polish-Lithuanian Commonwealth, see Dini, 'Views on Languages and Polyglossia'; Plokhy, *The Origins of the Slavic Nations*; Biely, *The Chronicle of the White Russia*.
12 Krawczyk, 'Szkoci w Lublinie i Lubelskiem w XVII wieku'; see also Bajer, *Scots in the Polish-Lithuanian Commonwealth*, p. 563 (see Lublin in Index of Places).
13 Stankowa, 'Zmierzch znaczenia Lublina'; Gmiterek, 'Lublin w stuleciach XVII i XVIII'.
14 Miller, *Urban Societies in East-Central Europe*, p. 27.
15 Szewczyk, *Ludność Lublina w latach 1583–1650*; Szczygieł, 'Złoty wiek miasta'.
16 Szewczyk, *Ludność Lublina w latach 1583–1650*, pp. 13–14.

ETHNIC-ECONOMIC RELATIONS WITHIN THE CITIES OF LUBLIN, ZAMOŚĆ, AND LVIV   213

and estates of a hereditary vogt of Lublin to 'burgher [originated] from Mainz' (*civis de Moguntia*), but the form of the buyer's name was already Polish — Franczko.[17]

During the sixteenth century, about 15 per cent of Lublin residents were Protestants; many of them were referred to as Germans, although that was cultural rather than an ethnic identification, and among those alleged Germans one can find western Europeans from various countries, especially Scots.[18] Moreover, at that time, many of the city's inhabitants of Polish origin were more or less open to the Reformation.[19] Therefore, the declared Christian denomination of Lublin inhabitants did not have to correspond to their ethnic origin at that time. The population of Lublin Jews is estimated at about 10 per cent, up to 15 per cent, the rest were Orthodox Ruthenians (up to 5 per cent), Italians, Armenians, and others.[20]

The coexistence of these different nationalities did not go smoothly. Conflicts were interwoven with economic and religious reasons. But the sources from the sixteenth century do not yet contain any references which would allow us to document ethnic violence in the city.[21] We only know about conflicts which were based on economic and social grounds.[22] The early modern era is the only period in which the sources confirm the existence of economic cooperation between Christian citizens living within the city fortifications and the Jews settled outside city walls in the suburb called in Polish 'Podzamcze' (below the castle).[23] But later the situation changed.

Seventeenth-century documents only refer to the cooperation of Jews with Church institutions and the nobility who had their residences nearby the city.[24] In contrast, the Christian burghers were in a state of permanent conflict with the Jews, which was interrupted only briefly by the wars that heavily devastated the whole of the Polish-Lithuanian Commonwealth that started in 1648 and ended in 1660.[25] During this period Lublin and its suburbs were threatened many times by enemies. During the year 1655 the Moscow-Cossack troops besieged Lublin. Although the city was not captured, the suburbs, especially Podzamcze, were completely destroyed. The Cossacks slaughtered all the Jews who had fallen into their hands, which amounted

---

17 Hoff, *Lublins Gründungshandfesten*, pp. 16–17; Bogucka and Samsonowicz, *Dzieje miast*, p. 467.

18 Bogucka and Samsonowicz, *Dzieje miast*, p. 59.

19 Kossowski, *Protestantyzm w Lublinie i lubelskiem*; Tworek, *Zbór lubelski i jego rola w ruchu ariańskim*.

20 Tworek, 'Rozkwit miasta: Renesans'; Szczygieł, 'Lokacja miasta na prawie niemieckim'; Wojciechowski, 'Gmina żydowska w Lublinie w XVI wieku'; Miller, *Urban Societies in East-Central Europe*, p. 50.

21 There are even testimonies about a certain amount of cooperation and attempts to achieve agreement and compromise; see Szczygieł, 'Ugoda Żydów lubelskich z gminą miejską'.

22 Szczygieł, *Konflikty społeczne w Lublinie*.

23 Kuwałkowie and Kuwałkowie, 'Żydzi i chrześcijanie w Lublinie'; Trojanowska, 'Źródła do dziejów Żydów lubelskich', pp. 8–9.

24 Kuwałkowie and Kuwałkowie, 'Żydzi i chrześcijanie w Lublinie', pp. 22–23; Hundert, 'Identity Formation in the Polish-Lithuanian Commonwealth', pp. 132–33, 140.

25 Glaser and Sysyn, 'Chronology of Mayor Events', pp. xiii–xix; also Kohut, 'The Khmelnytsky Uprising, the Image of Jews'; Frost, *After the Deluge*.

214 ANDRZEJ PLESZCZYŃSKI

to several thousand and included refugees from other areas of the country.[26] For several years, the ban on Jews on settling within the walls of the city, *De non tolerandis Judeis*,[27] issued over a century earlier by the Polish king Sigismund the Old at the request of the townspeople who feared Jewish competition, was not observed.[28] It seems that the Christian city elite realized then that the lack of a strong Jewish community living before the mid-seventeenth century in the completely destroyed and depopulated suburb of Podzamcze was a serious detriment to the economy of the entire city.[29] However, around 1670 complaints appeared in the court that the Jews were not only living in the city but also trading there.[30]

The accusations against the Jews of ritual murder in Lublin were more than a century old and were mainly inspired by local Jesuits.[31] At the same time, there were regular complaints by members of the Jewish population of Podzamcze about attacks carried out by Christians, mainly Jesuit college students, assisted by urban hoodlums.[32] The aforementioned events were the result of the increasingly fierce rivalry and conflicts between the Catholic and Jewish and Protestant populations living in Lublin, documented from the end of the sixteenth century. The domination of the Catholics in the city — and the general change in the attitude of the Polish elite towards Protestantism[33] — meant that successive Polish monarchs issued more-or-less strict regulations on the supporters of the Reformation which limited the freedom of the Protestant cult in Lublin.[34] From the second half of the seventeenth century, after a series of invasions by the Orthodox (Cossacks) and Protestant (Swedish and Transylvanian) armies, the situation in the city was highly unfavourable for both the supporters of the Reformation and Orthodoxy. The apogee of religious bigotry and persecutions of followers of Christian denominations other than Catholicism and

---

26 Balaban, *Die Judenstadt von Lublin*, pp. 42–49; Kuwałkowie and Kuwałkowie, 'Żydzi i chrześcijanie w Lublinie', p. 23.

27 Kuwałkowie and Kuwałkowie, 'Żydzi i chrześcijanie w Lublinie', p. 10. For more on this topic, see Piechotka and Piechotka, *Oppidum Judaeorum*, pp. 36–48; Miller, *Urban Societies in East-Central Europe*, pp. 93–94, 99. Jews also obtained the privilege of banning Christians from settling in their neighbourhood: Miller, *Urban Societies in East-Central Europe*, p. 100; see also Pogonowski, *Jews in Poland*, pp. 59–86.

28 Kuwałkowie and Kuwałkowie, 'Żydzi i chrześcijanie w Lublinie', p. 25.

29 The destruction of the Podzamcze suburb made Christian merchants impoverished, because wealthier foreign merchants, Jewish and Christian, deprived of the support of their former trading partners from Podzamcze, chose fairs other than those in Lublin.

30 Kuwałkowie and Kuwałkowie, 'Żydzi i chrześcijanie w Lublinie', pp. 24–28.

31 In the Lublin Jesuit church were buried the remains of a child murdered in 1598 allegedly by Jews in Świniary (northern Lublin): Guldon and Wijaczka, *Procesy o mordy rytualne w Polsce*, p. 92; see also Balaban, *Die Judenstadt von Lublin*, pp. 31–33, 50–62; Kuwałkowie and Kuwałkowie, 'Żydzi i chrześcijanie w Lublinie', p. 25; Węgrzynek, 'Czarna legenda' Żydów, pp. 118–19 (the case from 1598 and the accusation of murdering a boy did not concern Lublin Jews, but the sentence was to be carried out at the Lublin synagogue).

32 Kuwałkowie and Kuwałkowie, 'Żydzi i chrześcijanie w Lublinie', p. 28.

33 Ptaśnik, *Miasta i mieszczaństwo*, pp. 295–96; Tollet, 'Religious Existence and Competition'.

34 Cieślak, Gawarecki, and Stankowa, *Lublin w dokumencie 1317–1967*, p. 68 (King Stefan Batory's decree against the Arians), pp. 71–72 (King Sigismund III's decree against Protestants in general).

ETHNIC-ECONOMIC RELATIONS WITHIN THE CITIES OF LUBLIN, ZAMOŚĆ, AND LVIV   215

of Jews, as in the entire Polish-Lithuanian Commonwealth, occurred during the
Third Northern War (1700–1721), the period of the political and economic crisis
of the state.[35]

Zamość

Zamość was a completely different type of town than Lublin. It was built from scratch
by Jan Zamoyski in 1580. According to the intentions of the great magnate, Zamość
was supposed to be a fortress and an ideal city with the founder's family residence.[36]
Since Zamoyski had studied in Italy for a long time (he was even the rector of the
law department of the University of Padua),[37] the work of constructing the city was
entrusted by him to the architect of Padua, Bernardo Morando.[38] During the city's
construction, many Italians and Germans were recruited. They later received plots in
the city and became part of its bourgeoisie, and because they were usually Catholics
they assimilated quickly with the Polish population.[39] Jan Zamoyski established an
academy at the time of the creation of the city. Thanks to the fact that he was one of
the richest magnates of the Polish-Lithuanian Commonwealth, he could afford to
bring scholars from many western European countries to this school. Some of them
settled in Zamość permanently. Zamoyski had also done a great deal to get merchants
from different countries to come to his city.[40]

In opposition to Lublin, already at very beginning, during the construction of the
city, Jews (both Ashkenazi and Sephardic)[41] were allowed (initially even about 10
per cent of the inhabitants of Zamość) to settle within and build a synagogue there.[42]
The Armenians who were fairly numerous (up to about 5 per cent) had their own
church, which was inside the city walls.[43] The situation of the Armenians and Jews
in the city was definitely better than in any Polish royal town. They had extensive
autonomy and their own separate judiciary. Armenians in particular were cherished
by the Zamoyski family: some of them even became mayors of Zamość, and they
were constantly members of the city council.[44]

---

35 Jezierski and Leszczyńska, *Historia gospodarcza Polski*, pp. 63–64; see also Frost, *The Northern Wars*.
36 Iskrzycki, *Dzieje Zamościa i południowej Lubelszczyzny*, pp. 7–15.
37 Leśniewski, *Jan Zamoyski — hetman i polityk*, pp. 11–15; Ptaśnik, *Miasta i mieszczaństwo*, p. 461.
38 Szczygieł, 'Ruch budowlany w Zamościu w XVII wieku'.
39 Iskrzycki, *Dzieje Zamościa i południowej Lubelszczyzny*, p. 11.
40 Klementowski, 'Udział profesorów Akademii Zamojskiej w sądownictwie miasta'; and also
     Mierzwa, 'William Bruce, profesor Akademii Zamojskiej'; Iskrzycki, *Dzieje Zamościa i południowej
     Lubelszczyzny*, p. 12; Feduszka, 'Szkoci i Anglicy w Zamościu', p. 61.
41 Piechotka and Piechotka, *Landscape with Menorah*, pp. 69–70; Bilewicz, 'Frenkowie'.
42 Morgenstern, 'O osadnictwie Żydów w Zamościu'; Miller, *Urban Societies in East-Central Europe*,
     p. 95.
43 Zakrzewska-Dubasowa, 'Ormianie zamojscy', pp. 30–33; Maksoudian, 'Armenian Communities in
     Eastern Europe', pp. 62–66.
44 Zakrzewska-Dubasowa, 'Ormianie zamojscy', pp. 59–61; see also Matwijowski, 'Uprawnienia stanowe
     Ormian'; Fidecka, *Kamienice ormiańskie w Zamościu*.

216 ANDRZEJ PLESZCZYŃSKI

Fifty years after its creation, shortly before the middle of the seventeenth century, the city had about four thousand inhabitants. Also later, during the second half of the seventeenth century and the time of crisis that occurred because of the Third Northern War, the number of people living in Zamość was similar.[45] However, the ethnic structure of the city had changed. The Armenians and other ethnic, Christian minorities had almost disappeared, while the proportion of Poles and Jews in the city rose, with the second ethnicity reaching about 25 per cent at the middle of eighteenth century; almost all of the rest of the inhabitants were Polish. A century later the total number of inhabitants of Zamość increased to about eight thousand. Circa 35 per cent of them were Jews, the rest declared themselves to be Poles, and the other ethnicities had disappeared.[46]

Lviv

Lviv, which was the second largest city in the Polish-Lithuanian Commonwealth after Gdańsk, already at the end of sixteenth century had thirty thousand residents.[47] The population of the city was definitely multinational, although from the late Middle Ages the Polish language dominated. Usually even citizens of foreign descent were willingly admitted to the Polish nationality while cultivating their own original ethnic heritage, language, customs, and religion.[48]

Since 1361 the city had had an Armenian archbishopric (since 1630 in union with Rome),[49] bringing together the largest Armenian diaspora in those days in Europe.[50] The Latin archbishopric and the Orthodox bishopric were also located in Lviv: the former since 1412 and the latter from 1539. The Orthodox bishop had jurisdiction over not only the Ruthenians but also the Vlachs.[51] In the city, however, in the modern period the Catholics were always in the majority. They mostly identified with the Poles — although their ethnic origin was far more varied than in Lublin. They came mainly from Germany, but also from Italy, Hungary, and other western and central European countries.[52]

---

45 Szczygieł, 'Zamość w czasach staropolskich', pp. 110–15.
46 Ćwik, 'Zamość pod zaborami'.
47 Hrytsak, 'Lviv'; Bogucka and Samsonowicz, *Dzieje miast*, p. 470; Miller, *Urban Societies in East-Central Europe*, p. 27.
48 Gąsiorowski, 'Tatarzy we Lwowie w XIII–XVIII wieku'.
49 Dziedzic, 'Czas próby i determinacji'; Panossian, *The Armenians*, p. 83.
50 Maksoudian, 'Armenian Communities in Eastern Europe', pp. 62–69; Cowe, 'Medieval Armenian Literary and Cultural Trends', pp. 301, 321, 323; Kapral, *Urzędnicy miasta Lwowa*, pp. 245–46 (part IV — the Armenian self-government).
51 Czołowski, *Historja Lwowa*, pp. 18–19. Particularly interesting is the person of Konstanyn Korniakt (αωνσταντίνος Κορνιακτός, Konstantinos Korniaktos), a Greek merchant from Crete, a zealous follower of the Orthodox Church who, after becoming a citizen of Lviv, not only eagerly contributed to the Orthodox community but also financed the so-called Wallachian church: Malinowski, *Where East Meets West*, p. 222.
52 Isajewycz, 'Społeczeństwa Lwowa i Krakowa'.

There is no data on the proportions of the different ethnic groups in the city population. Only in the case of Jews is it estimated that they accounted for about 20–25 per cent of the total population in the whole modern period, and this number did not change significantly. What is important is that the Jews were allowed to locate their homes within the fortifications of Lviv.[53]

There has never been a serious religious or ethnic disturbance in the city that was connected with open violence. The attack on the Jewish quarter and the pogrom there, led by students of the Jesuit college in 1664, was a rather isolated phenomenon.[54] There were, of course, numerous conflicts between the dominant layer of the Polonized patriciate and other nationalities, especially Ruthenian merchants and artisans,[55] partly also Armenian,[56] but they were not accompanied by any serious riots.

It is characteristic that when Lviv was under serious threat, even exhausted after a long siege, the municipal authorities refused to hand over the city's Jews to the Cossacks as a precondition for the cancellation of the siege.[57]

It is worth noting here the special feature of the siege of Lviv from 1672 by a powerful Turkish-Cossack army. Poland was at that time in deep political crisis, and the city was left to face its enemies alone. Therefore after a few weeks of siege the citizens had to pay a tribute. Because such a large sum could not be collected right away, the municipal authority sent hostages to the Turks — four Poles, two Armenians, and two Jews.[58] These figures seem to portray to some extent the proportions of the ethnic composition of the then political elite of the city and their solidarity in this dangerous situation. The lack of Ruthenians in this composition — although they were a significant component of the inhabitants of Lviv — had a number of reasons. Here only one can be noted with a risk of too large a simplification. Namely, that the Ruthenians were generally — although there were also richer merchants among them — the poorest ethnic group in Lviv and they were not members of the patricianship.[59] Therefore they were not required to provide hostages.

---

53 Within the city fortifications, richer Jews had their own separate quarter, poorer Jews lived in the suburbs and in *jurydykas*: Isajewycz, 'Społeczeństwa Lwowa i Krakowa', p. 69; Bałaban, *Żydzi lwowscy*; Miller, *Urban Societies in East-Central Europe*, p. 92; Piechotka and Piechotka, *Landscape with Menorah*, p. 59; Krachkovska, 'The Jewish Community of Lviv'.

54 Relatively late, only in 1728, there was one accusation of ritual murder, and from 1759 we have reports of a dispute in which the Jews were accused by the Franciscans. The king's intervention prevented the outbreak of violence; see Manekin, 'L'viv'; also Czołowski, '*Mord rytualny*'. However, there were sharp social conflicts, just like in other cities in the region; see e.g. Hul, 'Przywódcy pospólstwa miasta Lwowa'.

55 In fact, the Ruthenians were second-class citizens in the city until the 1830s: Ptaśnik, *Miasta i mieszczaństwo*, pp. 331–40; Charewiczowa, *Handel średniowiecznego Lwowa*, pp. 109–20; see also Łoziński, *Patrycjat i mieszczaństwo lwowskie*, pp. 307–52.

56 Ptaśnik, *Miasta i mieszczaństwo*, pp. 333–40; Łoziński, *Patrycjat i mieszczaństwo lwowskie*, pp. 265–306.

57 Borek, 'Lwów w diariuszach i pamiętnikach', p. 50; Korcz, *Zarys dziejów Lwowa*, p. 40.

58 Józefowicz, *Kronika miasta Lwowa*, p. 320.

59 Ptaśnik, *Miasta i mieszczaństwo*, pp. 331–39; Isajewycz, 'Społeczeństwa Lwowa i Krakowa', p. 72.

Conclusions

Now it is time to summarize our information and to consider why some phenomena occurred in one city but not in another. We can note that in Lublin and Zamość, after the period of optimum demographic development, which existed from the mid-sixteenth century to the beginning of the seventeenth century, there was a dramatic decline in the number of inhabitants. It was so significant that the number of inhabitants in these cities did not recover until the beginning of the nineteenth century.

The demographic decrease was accompanied by the change in the nature of trade and urban production. The mass bartering of locally produced merchandise which was of average or poor quality declined. This was connected with the fall in urban production and commerce. Only merchants and craftsmen who provided the social elites with imported luxury goods and supplied religious centres maintained their importance.[60] Trade in luxury goods produced in the East was monopolized by the Jews, displacing the Armenians and other Christian merchants.[61] The percentage of the Jewish population in the cities was steadily increasing.[62] This fact would be even more visible if we leave the city walls of royal cities and look outside the strictly controlled urban areas, beyond the power of the municipal law. The so-called *jurydyki*, the areas of legal enclaves belonging to noblemen or Church institutions, were located there.[63] The proportion of Jews in the number of inhabitants of *jurydyki* was mostly bigger than in normal suburbs, especially after the mid-seventeenth century. It is clear that the owners of these private satellite towns, which profited from the cooperation with cities but did not pay any taxes to cities' treasuries, preferred the Jewish population as residents instead of Christians. This situation occurred even when the owner of the town was a Church institution — a collegiate church or a monastery.[64] Only the owners of private cities, in our case Zamość, were able to protect their own interests and, in order to efficiently control their income, prevented the creation of *jurydyki* and the dispersal of trade centres beyond the city walls. They also diligently made sure that there were no ethnic conflicts in the city, especially anti-Jewish riots.[65]

In the time of economic and political crisis in the seventeenth century the ethnic diversity of urban communities diminished. During this century the Jewish population in the entire Polish-Lithuanian Commonwealth was becoming unified. The Ashkenazi Jews had greater advantages, although they were not necessarily wealthier than the Sephardic Jews. However, in early modern Poland they were becoming more and more numerous until at the end of the eighteenth century they had erased almost

---

60 Bownik, *Kupiectwo lubelskie 1317–1959*, pp. 53–55; Horn, 'Rola gospodarcza Żydów w Polsce'.

61 Ptaśnik, *Miasta i mieszczaństwo*, p. 104; Petrovsky-Shtern, *The Golden Age of Shtetl*, pp. 93–94.

62 Bogucka and Samsonowicz, *Dzieje miast*, pp. 470 ff.; Bogucka, 'The Jews in Polish Cities', pp. 51 ff.; Łoziński, *Patrycjat i mieszczaństwo lwowskie*, pp. 192 ff.; Bałaban, *Żydzi lwowscy*, pp. 231–58, 332–60.

63 Mazurkiewicz, *Jurydyki lubelskie*, pp. 52–54; Bogucka and Samsonowicz, *Dzieje miast*, pp. 494–96; see also Šiaučiūnaitė-Verbickienė, 'The Jewish Living Space', pp. 20–21; Lukowski, *Liberty's Folly*, pp. 76–79; Miller, *Urban Societies in East-Central Europe*, pp. 57–61.

64 Piechotka and Piechotka, *Landscape with Menorah*, p. 104.

65 Teter, *Jews and Heretics in Catholic Poland*, pp. 25–32; Mahler, 'Żydzi w dawnej Polsce'.

ETHNIC-ECONOMIC RELATIONS WITHIN THE CITIES OF LUBLIN, ZAMOŚĆ, AND LVIV 219

completely the Sephardic Jews.[66] The same process of unification was observed in Lublin and Zamość among the Christian population: western Europeans, even Protestants, soon became Polonized, just like the Greek Catholics or sometimes even Orthodox.[67] It seems as if in times of trouble and when threatened from various angles people wanted to shelter in a larger and stronger group.

The serious cause of the observed phenomena was the legislation introduced as the result of the Brest Union of Catholic and Orthodox Churches in the Polish-Lithuanian Commonwealth (1596), supported by King Sigismund III Vasa, that in fact forced the surrender of the Orthodox Church to the jurisdiction of Rome.[68] Although the severity of the repression directed against the Orthodox declined considerably in several decades after the union, the seeds of the previously unknown religious conflict had been sown by then. This, in turn, not only seriously contributed to the destruction of the Polish-Lithuanian state, but also played an enormous role in the changes in cities. After all, the role of the Brest Union is well known as an important cause of the outbreak of Cossack uprisings.[69]

These, as we know, seriously undermined the economic and social position of the Polonized, small and medium nobility of the eastern territories of the Polish-Lithuanian Commonwealth. They were the main consumers of urban goods there. However, the Cossack rebellions were directed not only against Catholic noblemen, but also against the Jewish population.[70] The slaughter of Jews by the Cossacks caused a Jewish exodus to the larger cities that could offer them shelter. This process, in turn, prompted the opposition of Catholics, who were afraid of losing their dominant position in cities and of competition in crafts and trade. This in turn led to a rising tide of anti-Jewish violence in royal towns,[71] which ricocheted and also touched both Protestant and Orthodox communities causing either their escape or unification with the Polish people.

The phenomenon of open violence directed towards the people of other religions did not occur in Zamość. It was the private city, under strict control of the Zamoyski family. But we can observe a similar fact in Lviv which belonged to the king. The city was a real phenomenon, a unique microcosm, where people of different origins and religion lived side by side, while preserving their separate customs, but also cultivating local patriotism.[72] In this case, the matter is very complex and not easy

---

66 Bilewicz, 'Frenkowie', p. 31; Shatzky, 'Sephardic Jews in Poland'; see also Dubnow, *History of the Jews in Russia and Poland*, pp. 262–65; Ptaśnik, *Miasta i mieszczaństwo*, pp. 355–56 (some anti-Semitic overtones here).

67 Ptaśnik, *Miasta i mieszczaństwo*, p. 350. This process lasted until the end of the eighteenth century. A century later it happened that in rich families with Ruthenian origins, for a long time Polonized, they tended to return to their former nationality. Sometimes such decisions divided families, even siblings — see e.g. the case of the Szeptycki family: Korolevsky, *Metropolitan Andrew*.

68 Tollet, 'Religious Existence and Competition', pp. 76–82.

69 Chodynicki, *Kościół prawosławny a Rzeczpospolita Polska*, pp. 320–22, 414–20.

70 Piechotka and Piechotka, *Landscape with Menorah*, pp. 89–90; see also Glaser, 'The Heirs of Tul'chyn'; see also Kohut, 'The Khmelnytsky Uprising, the Image of Jews'.

71 Tollet, 'Religious Existence and Competition', pp. 82–87.

72 Czaplicka, 'Lemberh, Leopolis, Lwów, Lviv'.

to explain. Although I know this may be considered a great simplification, I will risk the view that the cause of such a great solidarity between many various ethnic groups was caused by the constant outside threats against the city since it was situated near a restless border. Lviv since the Middle Ages had been exposed to Tatar invasions; in the seventeenth century there were also Cossacks, Turks, Swedish, and Russian troops which were wreaking havoc across all of central Europe. It was also not without significance, especially against the background of the very poor standing of cities in the entire region of central and eastern Europe since the seventeenth century, that Lviv, located on a lucrative trade route, was relatively rich, and compromise and cooperation turned out to be beneficial for all ethnicities living in the city.

The phenomena presented above indicate a gradual decline in the ethnic diversity in cities threatened by the economic and political crises of the seventeenth century. The same crisis could easily provoke inter-ethnic conflicts within towns. Sometimes strict control over townsmen's lives by the owner prevented conflicts between ethnic groups. However, belonging to a numerous, wealthy, and privileged ethnic group was a more certain source of personal security. These large ethnic groups rarely chose to stand up against each other, because their members had too much to lose and the outcome of a dispute was unpredictable to them. The situation of the largest city, Lviv, turns out to be particularly interesting. The city had the greatest ethnic diversity among the cities studied, and at the same time its citizens operated in the most difficult political conditions. However, cooperation between different ethnic and religious groups is much more frequent than conflicts. Apparently, it was cooperation, not conflict, that optimized the residents' profits from living in a dangerous environment, but one that gave hope for a relatively prosperous life, even if the price was to live and cooperate peacefully with 'Others'.

Works Cited

Secondary Studies

Bajer, Peter Paul, *Scots in the Polish-Lithuanian Commonwealth, 16th–18th Centuries: The Formation and Disappearance of an Ethnic Group* (Leiden: Brill, 2012)

Balaban, Majer, *Die Judenstadt von Lublin* (Lublin: Ośrodek 'Brama Grodzka' – Teatr NN, 2012; originally published Berlin: Jüdischer Verlag, 1919)

Balaban, Majer, *Żydzi lwowscy na przełomie xvigo i xviigo wieku* (Lwów: Fundusz Konkursowy im. Hip. Wawelberga, 1906)

Bidekeux, Robert, and Ian Jeffries, *A History of Eastern Europe: Crisis and Change* (New York: Routledge, 2007)

Biely, Ales, *The Chronicle of the White Russia: An Essay on the History of One Geographical Name* (Minsk: Encyclopedix, 2000)

Bilewicz, Aleksandra, 'Frenkowie: Kim byli lwowscy i zamojscy Sefardyjczycy?', in *Żydzi w Zamościu i na Zamojszczyźnie: Historia – kultura – literatura*, ed. by W. Litwin, M. Szabłowska-Zaremba, and S. J. Żurek (Lublin: Towarzystwo Naukowe KUL, 2012), pp. 31–44

Bogucka, Maria, 'The Jews in Polish Cities', in *Studies in the History of the Jews in Old Poland in Honor of Jacob Goldberg*, ed. by Adam Teller, Scripta Hierosolymitana, 38 (Jerusalem: Magnes Press, Hebrew University, 1998), pp. 51–57

Bogucka, Maria, and Henryk Samsonowicz, *Dzieje miast i mieszczaństwa w Polsce przedrozbiorowej* (Wrocław: Zakład Narodowy im. Ossolińskich, 1986)

Borek, Piotr, 'Lwów w diariuszach i pamiętnikach XVII wieku', in *Lwów: Miasto-społeczeństwo-kultura*, vol. IV, ed. by K. Karolczak (Kraków: Wydawnictwo Naukowe Wyższej Szkoły Pedagogicznej, 2002), pp. 43–63

Bownik, Zygmunt, *Kupiectwo lubelskie 1317–1959* (Lublin: Wojewódzkie Zrzeszenie Prywatnego Handlu i Usług, 1960)

Brenner, Robert, 'Economic Backwardness in Eastern Europe in Light of Developments in the West', in *The Origins of Backwardness in Eastern Europe: Economics and Politics from the Middle Ages until the Early Twentieth Century*, ed. by Daniel Chirot (Berkeley: University of California Press, 1991), pp. 15–52

Charewiczowa, Łucja, *Handel średniowiecznego Lwowa* (Lwów: Wydawnictwo Zakładu Narodowego imienia Ossolińskich, 1925)

Chodynicki, Kazimierz, *Kościół prawosławny a Rzeczpospolita Polska: Zarys historyczny 1370–1632* (Warsaw: Skład Główny Kasa imienia Mianowskiego – Instytut Popierania Nauk, 1934)

Cieślak, Franciszek, Henryk Gawarecki, and Maria Stankowa, *Lublin w dokumencie 1317–1967* (Lublin: Wydawnictwo Lubelskie, 1976)

Cowe, Peter, 'Medieval Armenian Literary and Cultural Trends (Twelfth–Seventeenth Centuries)', in *The Armenian People from Ancient to Modern Times*, ed. by Richard G. Hovannisian, vol. I: *The Dynastic Periods: From Antiquity to the Fourteenth Century* (Los Angeles: Palgrave Macmillan, 1997), pp. 293–326

Ćwik, Władysław, 'Zamość pod zaborami', in *Czterysta lat Zamościa*, ed. by Jerzy Kowalczyk (Wrocław: Ossolineum, 1983), pp. 129–43

Czaplicka, John, 'Lemberh, Leopolis, Lwów, Lviv: A City in the Crosscurrents of European Culture', in 'Lviv: A City in the Crosscurrents of Culture', ed. by John Czaplicka, special issue, *Harvard Ukrainian Studies*, 24 (2000), 13–46

Czołowski, Aleksander, *Historja Lwowa: Od założenia do roku 1600, (Lwów w obrazach 1)* (Lwów: Koło T. S. L. im. Adama Asnyka we Lwowie, 1925)

——, '*Mord rytualny': Epizod z przeszłości Lwowa* (Lwów: Aleksander Czołowski, 1899)

Dini, Pietro U., 'Views on Languages and Polyglossia in the Grand Duchy of Lithuania according to Johannes Stobnica's *Epitoma Europe* (1512)', in *Speculum Slaviae Orientalis: Muscovy, Ruthenia and Lithuania in the Late Middle Ages*, ed. by Vyacheslav V. Ivanov and Julia Verkholantsev, UCLA Slavic Studies, n.s., 4 (Moscow: Novoe Izdatel'stvo, 2005), pp. 36–42

Dubnow, Shimon Meyerovich, *History of the Jews in Russia and Poland*, I: *From the Beginning until the Death of Alexander I (1825)* (Philadelphia: Jewish Publication Society of America, 1916)

Dziedzic, Stanisław, 'Czas próby i determinacji: O utrwaleniu unii polskiego Kościoła ormiańskiego ze Stolicą Apostolską', in *Lwów: Miasto, społeczeństwo, kultura. Studia z dziejów Lwowa*, vol. II, ed. by Henryk W. Żaliński and Kazimierz Karolczak (Kraków: Wydawnictwo Naukowe Wyższej Szkoły Pedagogicznej, 1998), pp. 47–57

Feduszka, Jacek, 'Szkoci i Anglicy w Zamościu w XVI–XVIII wieku', *Czasy Nowożytne*, 22 (2009), 51–61

Fidecka, Urszula, *Kamienice ormiańskie w Zamościu* (Zamość: Muzeum Okręgowa w Zamościu, 1985)

Frick, David, 'Lviv', in *Europe 1450 to 1780: Encyclopedia of the Early Modern World*, ed. by Jonathan Dewald, vol. III (New York: Thomson Gale Charles Scribner's Sohn, 2004), pp. 568–69

Frost, Robert, *After the Deluge: Polish-Lithuania and the Second Northern War, 1655–1660* (Cambridge: Cambridge University Press, 2004)

——, *The Northern Wars: War, State and Society in Northeastern Europe, 1558–1721* (Harlow: Addison Wesley, 2000)

Gąsiorowski, Stefan, 'Tatarzy we Lwowie w XIII–XVIII wieku: Przyczynek do badań', in *Lwów: Miasto-społeczeństwo-kultura*, IX: *Życie codzienne miasta*, ed. by Kazimierz Karolczak and Łukasz Tomasz Sroka (Kraków: Wydawnictwo Naukowe Uniwersytetu Pedagogicznego Kraków, 2014), pp. 13–22

Glaser, Amelia, and Frank E. Sysyn, 'Chronology of Mayor Events Associated with the Khmelnytsky Uprising and the Depiction of Bohdan Khmelnytsky (Introduction)', in *Stories of Khmelnytsky: Competing Literary Legacies of the 1648 Ukrainian Cossack Uprising*, ed. by Amelia M. Glaser (Stanford: Stanford University Press, 2015), pp. xiii–xix

Glaser, Amelia M., 'The Heirs of Tul'chyn: A Modernist Reappraisal of Historical Narrative', in *Stories of Khmelnytsky: Competing Literary Legacies of the 1648 Ukrainian Cossack Uprising*, ed. by Amelia M. Glaser (Stanford: Stanford University Press, 2015), pp. 127–38

Gmiterek, Henryk, 'Lublin w stuleciach XVII i XVIII', in *Lublin: Dzieje miasta*, I: *Od VI do końca XVIII wieku*, ed. by Ryszard Szczygieł, Henryk Gmiterek, and Piotr Dymmel (Lublin: Wydawnictwo Tylda, 2008), pp. 91–128

Guldon, Zenon, and Jacek Wijaczka, *Procesy o mordy rytualne w Polsce w XVI–XVIII wieku* (Kielce: Wydawnictwo DCF, 1995)

Halecki, Oscar, *The Limits and Divisions of European History* (New York: Sheed & Ward, 1950)

Hoff, Erwin, *Lublins Gründungshandfesten zu deutschem Recht 1317/1342: Mit Beiträgen zur Schrift- und Siegelentwicklung unter den letzten Piasten in Polen* (Krakau: Burgverlag Krakau GmbH, 1942)

Horn, M., 'Rola gospodarcza Żydów w Polsce do końca XVIII wieku', in *Żydzi wśród chrześcijan w dobie szlacheckiej Rzeczypospolitej*, ed. by Waldemar Kowalski and Jadwiga Muszyńska (Kielce: Wydawnictwo Wyższej Szkoły Pedagogicznej w Kielcach, 1996), pp. 17–30

Hrytsak, Yaroslav, 'Lviv: A Multicultural History through the Centuries', in 'Lviv: A City in the Crosscurrents of Culture', ed. by John Czaplicka, special issue, *Harvard Ukrainian Studies*, 24 (2000), 47–75

Hul, Olga, 'Przywódcy pospólstwa miasta Lwowa czasie wystąpień przeciwko radzie miejskiej w latach 1576–1577', *Annales Universitatis Mariae Curie-Skłodowska, Sectio F: Historia*, 70 (2015), 75–97

ETHNIC-ECONOMIC RELATIONS WITHIN THE CITIES OF LUBLIN, ZAMOŚĆ, AND LVIV   223

Hundert, Gershon David, 'Identity Formation in the Polish-Lithuanian Commonwealth', in *Citizenship and Identity in a Multinational Commonwealth: Poland-Lithuania in Context, 1550–1772*, ed. by Karin Friedrich and Barbara M. Pendzich, Studies in Central European Histories, 46 (Leiden: Brill, 2009), pp. 131–47

Isajewycz, Jarosław, 'Społeczeństwa Lwowa i Krakowa: Różne ujęcia, różne tradycje', in *Kraków i Lwów w cywilizacji europejskiej*, ed. by Jacek Purchla (Kraków: Międzynarodowe Centrum Kultury, 2003), pp. 63–74

Iskrzycki, Artur, *Dzieje Zamościa i południowej Lubelszczyzny* (Lublin: Muzeum Lubelskie, 1956)

Jezierski, Andrzej, and Cecylia Leszczyńska, *Historia gospodarcza Polski* (Warsaw: Wydawnictwie Key Text, 2003)

Józefowicz, Jan Tomasz, *Kronika miasta Lwowa od roku 1634 do 1690* (Lwów: Wojciech Maniecki, 1854)

Kapral, Myron, *Urzędnicy miasta Lwowa w XIII–XVIII wieku* (Toruń: Wydawnictwo Adam Marszałek, 2008)

Klementowski, Marian Lech, 'Udział profesorów Akademii Zamojskiej w sądownictwie miasta i ordynacji w XVI–XVIII wieku', in *W kręgu akademickiego Zamościa: Materiały z międzynarodowej konferencji na temat Akademia Zamojska na tle praktyki edukacyjnej w Europie Środkowo-Wschodniej (koniec XVI–koniec XVIII wieku), Lublin-Zamość, 11–13 maja 1995*, ed. by Henryk Gmiterek (Lublin: Wydawnictwo UMCS, 1996), pp. 143–59

Kłoczowski, Jerzy, ed., *Central Europe between East and West* (Lublin: Instytut Europy Środkowo-Wschodniej, 2005)

Kochanowicz, Jacek, 'The Polish Economy and the Evolution of Dependency', in *The Origins of Backwardness in Eastern Europe: Economics and Politics from the Middle Ages until the Early Twentieth Century*, ed. by Daniel Chirot (Berkeley: University of California Press, 1991), pp. 92–130

Kohut, Zenon E., 'The Khmelnytsky Uprising, the Image of Jews, and the Shaping Ukrainian Historical Memory', *Jewish History*, 17.2 (2003), 141–63

Kopciowski, Adam, 'Outline History of the Jews in Lublin', in *The Jews in Lublin – the Jews in Lviv: Places-Memory-Present*, ed. by Joanna Zętar, Elżbieta Żurek, and Sławomir Jacek Żurek (Lublin: Publishing House of Catholic University of Lublin, 2006), pp. 13–20

Korcz, Władysław, *Zarys dziejów Lwowa* (Zielona Góra: Zachodnie Centrum Organizacji, 1994)

Korolevsky, Cyril, *Metropolitan Andrew (1865–1944)*, ed. and trans. by Serge Keleher (Lviv: Stauropegion, 1993)

Kossowski, Aleksander, *Protestantyzm w Lublinie i lubelskiem w XVI–XVII w.* (Lublin: Składnica główna Dom Książki Polskiej; Warsaw: Towarzystwo Przyjaciół Nauk, 1933)

Krachkovska, Anna, 'The Jewish Community of Lviv from the 16th to the 18th Century: The Territory and the Legal Status', in *The Jews in Lublin — the Jews in Lviv: Places-Memory-Present*, ed. by Joanna Zętar, Elżbieta Żurek, and Sławomir Jacek Żurek (Lublin: Publishing House of Catholic University of Lublin, 2006), pp. 33–37

Krawczyk, Antoni, 'Szkoci w Lublinie i Lubelskiem w XVII wieku', *Rocznik Lubelski*, 35 (2009), 77–86

Kuwałek, Robert, and Wiesław Wyskok, *Lublin — Jerozolima Królestwa Polskiego* (Lublin: Stowarzyszenie Dialog i Współpraca, 2001)

Kuwałkowie, Anna, and Robert Kuwałkowie, 'Żydzi i chrześcijanie w Lublinie w XVI i XVII wieku: Przyczynek do dziejów Żydów w Lublinie w okresie staropolskim', in *Żydzi w Lublinie: Materiały do dziejów społeczności żydowskiej Lublina*, ed. by Tadeusz Radzik, vol. II (Lublin: Wydawnictwo UMCS, 1998), pp. 9–32

Leśniewski, Sławomir, *Jan Zamoyski — hetman i polityk* (Warsaw: Bellona, 2008)

Łoziński, Władysław, *Patrycjat i mieszczaństwo lwowskie w XVI i XVII wieku* (Lwów: Księgarnia H. Altenberga, 1902)

Lukowski, Jerzy Tadeusz, *Liberty's Folly: The Polish-Lithuanian Commonwealth in the Eighteenth Century* (London: Routledge, 1991)

Mahler, Rafał, 'Żydzi w dawnej Polsce w świetle liczb. Struktura demograficzna I społeczno-ekonomiczna Żydów w Koronie w XVIII wieku', *Przeszłość demograficzna Polski*, 1 (1967), 131–80

Maksoudian, Krikor, 'Armenian Communities in Eastern Europe', in *The Armenian People from Ancient to Modern Times*, ed. by Richard G. Hovannisian, vol. II: *Foreign Dominion to Statehood: The Fifteenth Century to the Twentieth Century* (Los Angeles: Palgrave Macmillan, 1997), pp. 51–89

Malinowski, Jerzy, *Where East Meets West: Portrait of Personages of the Polish–Lithuanian Commonwealth, 1576–1763* (Warsaw: National Museum in Warsaw, 1993)

Manekin, Rachel, 'L'viv', in *Encyclopedia of Jews in Eastern Europe* <http://www. yivoencyclopedia.org/article.aspx/Lviv> [accessed 22 August 2017]

Matwijowski, Krystyn, 'Uprawnienia stanowe Ormian', in *Studia z dziejów Rzeczypospolitej szlacheckiej*, ed. by Krystyn Matwijowski and Zbigniew Wójcik (Wrocław: Wydawnictwo Uniwersytetu Wrocławskiego, 1988), pp. 241–47

Mazurkiewicz, Józef, *Jurydyki lubelskie* (Wrocław: Zakład Narodowy im. Ossolińskich, 1956)

Mencel, Tadeusz, 'Lublin przedkapitalistyczny', in *Dzieje Lublina: Próba syntezy*, ed. by Józef Mazurkiewicz and others, vol. I (Lublin: Wydawnictwo Lubelskie, 1965), pp. 199–217

Mierzwa, Edward Alfred, 'William Bruce, profesor Akademii Zamojskiej i agent handlowy The Eastland Company', in *W kręgu akademickiego Zamościa: Materiały z międzynarodowej konferencji na temat Akademia Zamojska na tle praktyki edukacyjnej w Europie Środkowo-Wschodniej (koniec XVI–koniec XVIII wieku), Lublin-Zamość, 11–13 maja 1995*, ed. by Henryk Gmiterek (Lublin: Wydawnictwo UMCS, 1996), pp. 207–23

Miller, Jaroslav, *Urban Societies in East-Central Europe, 1500–1700* (Aldershot: Routledge, 2008)

Morgenstern, J., 'O osadnictwie Żydów w Zamościu na przełomie XVI i XVII wieku', *Biuletyn Żydowskiego Instytutu Historycznego*, 43–44 (1962), 3–17

Okey, Robin, 'Central Europe/Eastern Europe: Behind the Definitions', *Past & Present*, 137.1 (1992), 102–33

Panossian, Razmik, *The Armenians: From Kings and Priests to Merchants and Commissars* (London: Columbia University Press, 2006)

Petrovsky-Shtern, Yohanan, *The Golden Age of Shtetl: A New History of Jewish Life in East Europe* (Princeton, NJ: Princeton University Press, 2014)

Piechotka, Maria, and Kazimierz Piechotka, *Landscape with Menorah: Jews in the Towns and Cities of the Former Rzeczpospolita of Poland and Lithuania*, trans. by Krzysztof Z. Cieszkowski (Warsaw: Salix alba Press, 2015)

——, *Oppidum Judaeorum: Żydzi w przestrzeni miejskiej dawnej Rzeczypospolitej* (Warsaw: Wydawnictwo Krupski i S-ka, 2004)

Plokhy, Serhii, *The Origins of the Slavic Nations: Premodern Identities in Russia, Ukraine, and Belarus* (Cambridge: Cambridge University Press, 2006)

Pogonowski, Iwo Cyprian, *Jews in Poland: A Documentary History* (New York: Hippocrene Books, 1993)

Ptaśnik, Jan, *Miasta i mieszczaństwo w dawnej Polsce* (Kraków: Nakład Gebethnera i Wolfa, 1934)

Shatzky, Y., 'Sephardic Jews in Poland', in *Zamość: Memorial Book*, ed. by Mordechai Wolf Bernstein (Mahwah, NJ: Jacob Solomon Berger, 2004), pp. 38–47

Šiaučiūnaitė-Verbickienė, Jurgita, 'The Jewish Living Space in the Grand Duchy of Lithuania: Tendencies and Way of its Transformation', in *Jewish Space in Central and Eastern Europe: Day-to-Day History*, ed. by Jurgita Šiaučiūnaitė-Verbickienė and Larissa Lempertienė (Cambridge: Cambridge Scholars Publishing, 2009), pp. 7–26

Siemieński, Józef, *Przewodnik po archiwach polskich*, vol. 1: *Archiwa dawnej Rzeczypospolitej* (Warsaw: Wydawnictwa Archiwów Państwowych, 1933)

Snyder, Timothy, *The Reconstruction of Nations: Poland, Ukraine, Lithuania, Belarus, 1569–1999* (New Haven: Yale University Press, 2003)

Stan badań nad wielokulturowym dziedzictwem dawnej Rzeczypospolitej, vols I–XIV (Białystok: Instytut Badań nad Dziedzictwem Kulturowym Europy, 2010–2021)

Stankowa, Maria, 'Zmierzch znaczenia Lublina: Upadek (1648–1764)', in *Dzieje Lublina: Próba syntezy*, ed. by Józef Mazurkiewicz and others, vol. 1 (Lublin: Wydawnictwo Lubelskie, 1965), pp. 123–48

Szczygieł, Ryszard, *Konflikty społeczne w Lublinie w pierwszej połowie XVI wieku* (Warsaw: Wydawnictwo Naukowe PWN, 1977)

——, 'Lokacja miasta na prawie niemieckim i jego rozwój do końca XVI wieku', in *Lublin: Dzieje miasta*, I: *Od VI do końca XVIII wieku*, ed. by Ryszard Szczygieł, Henryk Gmiterek, and Piotr Dymmel (Lublin: Wydawnictwo Tylda, 2008), pp. 23–55

——, 'Ruch budowlany w Zamościu w XVII wieku', in *Zamość miasto idealne: Studia z dziejów rozwoju przestrzennego i architektury*, ed. by J. Kowalczyk (Lublin: Wydawnictwo Lubelskie, 1980), pp. 103–19

——, 'Ugoda Żydów lubelskich z gminą miejską w sprawie udziału w życiu gospodarczym miasta z 1555 roku', in *Żydzi wśród chrześcijan w dobie szlacheckiej Rzeczypospolitej*, ed. by Waldemar Kowalski and Jadwiga Muszyńska (Kielce: Wydawnictwo Wyższej Szkoły Pedagogicznej w Kielcach, 1996), pp. 43–50

——, 'Zamość w czasach staropolskich: Zagadnienia gospodarczo-społeczne', in *Czterysta lat Zamościa*, ed. by Jerzy Kowalczyk (Wrocław: Ossolineum, 1983), pp. 95–116

——, 'Złoty wiek miasta', in *Lublin: Dzieje miasta*, I: *Od VI do końca XVIII wieku*, ed. by Ryszard Szczygieł, Henryk Gmiterek, and Piotr Dymmel (Lublin: Wydawnictwo Tylda, 2008), pp. 56–89

Szewczyk, Roman, *Ludność Lublina w latach 1583–1650* (Lublin: Towarzystwo Naukowe KUL, 1947)

Teter, Magda, *Jews and Heretics in Catholic Poland: A Beleaguered Church in the Post-Reformation Era* (Cambridge: Cambridge University Press, 2006)

Tollet, D., 'Religious Existence and Competition in the Polish-Lithuanian Commonwealth c. 1600', in *Religious Existence and Cultural Exchange in Europe, 1400–1700*, ed. by Istaván György Tóth and Heinz Schilling, Cultural Exchange in Early Modern Europe, 1 (Cambridge: Cambridge University Press, 2006–2007), pp. 42–55

Tomczak, Andrzej, *Zarys dziejów archiwów polskich*, I: *Do wybuchu I wojny światowej* (Toruń: Uniwersytet Mikołaja Kopernika, 1974)

Trojanowska, Maria, 'Źródła do dziejów Żydów lubelskich w XVI–XVIII wieku w zasobie Archiwum Państwowego w Lublinie', in *Żydzi w Lublinie: Materiały do dziejów społeczności żydowskiego Lublina*, ed. by Tadeusz Radzik, vol. I (Lublin: Wydawnictwo UMCS, 1995), pp. 7–12

Tworek, Stanisław, 'Rozkwit miasta: Renesans', in *Dzieje Lublina: Próba syntezy*, ed. by Józef Mazurkiewicz and others, vol. I (Lublin: Wydawnictwo Lubelskie, 1965), pp. 80–112

——, *Zbór lubelski i jego rola w ruchu ariańskim w Polsce w XVI i XVII wieku* (Lublin: Wydawnictwo Lubelskie, 1966)

Vasiliauskas, Artūras, 'The Practice of Citizenship among the Lithuanian Nobility, ca. 1580–1630', in *Citizenship and Identity in a Multinational Commonwealth: Poland-Lithuania in Context, 1550–1772*, ed. by Karin Friedrich and Barbara M. Pendzich, Studies in Central European Histories, 46 (Leiden: Brill, 2009), pp. 71–102

Węgrzynek, Hanna, *'Czarna legenda' Żydów: Procesy o rzekome mordy rytualne w dawnej Polsce* (Warsaw: Bellona, 1995)

Wojciechowski, S., 'Gmina żydowska w Lublinie w XVI wieku', *Biuletyn Żydowskiego Instytutu Historycznego*, 2.4 (1952), 204–30

Zakrzewska-Dubasowa, Mirosława, 'Ormianie zamojscy i ich rola w wymianie kulturalnej i handlowej między Polską a Wschodem' (unpublished Habilitationsschrift, Uniwersytet Marii Curie-Skłodowskiej Lublin, 1965)

COSMIN POPA-GORJANU

Economic and Social Aspects of Multi-Ethnic Transylvania during the Thirteenth and Fourteenth Centuries

The authors of the chapters on the history of Silesia and the Kingdom of Poland emphasized the role of legal, economic, and cultural relations initiated by members of various ethnic groups that guaranteed the maintenance of the internal stability of multi-ethnic societies based on everyday cooperation. In the case of the lands of the Crown of Hungary, the royal authorities played a much greater role than initiatives of individual ethnic groups in shaping inter-ethnic relations. In this chapter, we want to assess what influence the decisions of the Hungarian kings had on the formation of the multi-ethnic community of Transylvania and the shaping of relations between individual groups.

Introduction

Transylvania was the easternmost region conquered and incorporated into the kingdom of Hungary during a lengthy process which started in the eleventh century. Its internal development during the eleventh and twelfth centuries is only partly known due to the paucity of the written sources. However, from the thirteenth century, the sources improve, where an increasing number of charters supply better glimpses into the whereabouts of an evolving society, characterized by the plurality of ethnic groups that came to live within it and a dynamic process of social and economic change. From a geographical point of view, medieval Transylvania refers to a territory in the central part of Romania that is nestled within the Carpathian Mountains, bordered by the Apuseni Mountains to the west, the Southern Carpathians to the south and the Eastern Carpathians in the east. The areas of the Banat, Crişana, and Maramureş,

---

Cosmin Popa-Gorjanu • (cosminpg@uab.ro) is Associate Professor in Medieval Romanian History at the 1 Decembrie 1918 University of Alba Iulia, Romania. He has published on the history of medieval nobility, regional identities, and medieval Transylvanian history.

Inter-Ethnic Relations and the Functioning of Multi-Ethnic Societies: Cohesion in Multi-Ethnic Societies in Europe from c. 1000 to the Present, II, ed. by Przemysław Wiszewski, EER 18 (Turnhout: Brepols, 2022), pp. 227–248

BREPOLS ❧ PUBLISHERS   10.1484/M.EER-EB.5.132153

This is an open access chapter made available under a cc by-nc 4.0 International License.

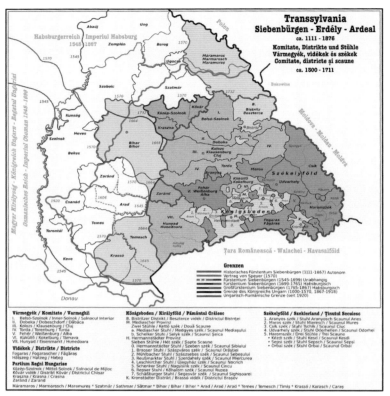

Map 9.1. Administrative division of Transylvania, c. 1111–1867. Source: https://commons.wikimedia.org/wiki/File:Siebenb%C3%BCrgen_1300-1867.jpg. DietG, CC BY-SA 3.0.

which are sometimes regarded as parts of the modern perception of Transylvania, did not belong to the administrative unit of medieval Transylvania. There is one important aspect regarding Transylvania that should be mentioned at the outset, namely the emergence during the twelfth and thirteenth centuries of three distinct administrative territorial blocks within it. These were the area of the seven noble counties, covering the northern, central, and western parts of the region (with some enclaves within the Saxon and Szekler territories), those of the Saxon colonization, located mainly in the southern part of the province and in the north-east, and those of the Szekler colonization which covered the easternmost part of the province, bordering the Eastern Carpathians. This image of a tripartite organization of the territory of Transylvania was reflected in the division of authority between the royal dignitaries governing this area in the thirteenth century, with the Voivode of Transylvania, a member of the royal council, governing the area of the seven counties, the Count of the Saxons who oversaw the area of the Saxons from southern Transylvania, and the Count of the Szeklers, whose jurisdiction extended over the eastern part of the province, running from Maramureş in the north to Braşov in the south, and who governed both the

Szeklers and Saxons living in this territory. The attempt to identify the mechanisms of building cohesion between these is dependent on a dynamic image of smaller or larger groups seeking to promote their own interests and succeeding to obtain the favour of the king in order to advance their social, economic, and political interests. The following is a discussion of various social and economic trends identifiable in records regarding the exploitation and distribution of salt, litigation among the members of the early castral system, and the privileges solicited by the various groups of royal guests, the nobles, Romanians, and Szeklers.

Ethnic names were used in the primary sources to refer to various population groups in Transylvania from the late twelfth century. The importance of ethnicity in the thirteenth and fourteenth centuries needs to be assessed. Viewed retrospectively, from the twenty-first century, it appears as a period in which apparently multi-ethnicity was not particularly problematic. On the contrary, the settlement of various ethnic groups was stimulated through a policy of attracting immigrants from western Europe into the kingdom. The results of this policy turned Transylvania into a region inhabited by diverse ethnic groups such as Romanians, Hungarians, Germans, and others. One of the questions that came about in the 'Cuius Regio' project,[1] was why Transylvania did not evolve into a melting pot. How was it possible that three major ethnic groups continued to coexist in the region in spite of some assimilation processes? Some of the answers could be offered by the level of institutional, social, and economic development of the age, and the reduced capacity of the medieval state or other forces to impose rules and systems capable of absorbing different ethnic groups within a uniform society. In this essay I will focus on some of the documents which shed light on specific groups and moments; these documents help us to understand the diversity and complexity of some social and economic aspects and their evolution. Given the context of the primary sources, some groups are much better illuminated than others; nevertheless, I am trying to avoid the unbalanced and biased view that is tempting when comparing groups with different economic and social statuses.

The image that is formed from the scanty primary sources is that of a rural society, consisting of people who were recorded according to the services which they provided; they were assigned various obligations and tasks within the archaic castle system that developed during the first two centuries of existence of the Kingdom of Hungary.[2] The records of the first half of the thirteenth century reflected categories and forms of social and economic organization from that early stage and, at the same time, changes and evolutions which resulted from the emergence of privileged groups within that society, who swept away much of the former system and created the framework of social and economic evolution for the

---

1 'Cuius Regio: An Analysis of the Cohesive and Disruptive Forces Destining the Attachment of (Groups of) People to and the Cohesion within Regions as a Historical Phenomenon', director Dick E. H. De Boer, collaborative research project supported through the European Science Foundation (EUROCORECODE).

2 For descriptions of the organization of services provided by the rural population in the tenth and eleventh centuries in Bohemia, Poland, and Hungary, see Krzemieńska and Třeštik, 'Wirtschaftliche Grundlagen', pp. 16–18; Engel, *The Realm of Saint Stephen*, pp. 74–76.

following centuries. The consolidation of the category of lay landowners, called by the generic term *nobiles*, took place through the massive transfer of material resources from the control of the king and royal officials to private landowners. The large-scale donation of royal land with or without population to laymen set in motion a long process of internal colonization led by these landowners who sought to increase their gains from landownership. Large swathes of inhabited or uninhabited territories came under the control of this group of landowners whose entrepreneurial skills led to the formation of villages or the rearrangement of inhabited territory. While their dominant political and social positions have long been recognized in the historical literature, their role in terms of economic development has not been emphasized enough. It is true that the perception of the nobility as a *parasitical* category who survived much longer as a result of their historical importance partly explains why this stage of its efforts did not receive much attention. The erosion of the royal domain by large donations was identified as the process which generated the extensive use of written instruments, which allows historians to get a glimpse into that society. The other important line of evolution was the consolidation of the groups of royal guests (*hospites*), whose conditions, rights, and obligations started to be recorded in charters of privileges. Thus, the dynamics of transformation are identifiable through the examination of the charters of privileges obtained by the winners of the struggle for change, namely the nobility and the *hospites*. While these sources give precise details about rights, obligations, and indeed advantages of the privileged ones, they indirectly offer some information about those who were not favourites, namely the groups which predated the emergence of the nobility and the arrival of the guests and their evolution in parallel with those of the luckier groups.

The first task is to explain what the premises of social evolution were and what happened with the groups that came to coexist in this region. The standard descriptions of the organization of the Kingdom of Hungary during the first two centuries of its existence indicate the administrative structure consisting of royal counties headed by the *comites* (*ispánok* in Hungarian), royal representatives who were appointed by the king and carrying out administrative, fiscal, military, and judicial responsibilities.[3] The population of these counties consisted of several groups. The *iobagiones castri* were directly connected with the castral system, rendered in English *castle warriors*, and *castrenses*, or *castle folk*. The first group provided military services while the *castrenses* were the inhabitants of the castle area who were obliged to provide food supplies and labour services to the castle. Both groups were semi-free, since their status involved hereditary obligations which tied them to their place. There was an upper layer, consisting of royal dignitaries, descendants of the tribal chieftains, or foreign knights who entered the service of the king. There were also some groups of semi-free population, the so-called *conditionarii*, the rural population who owed the king specialized services, and a similar group called *udvornici*. Normative sources and charter evidence from the eleventh and twelfth centuries indicated the categories of

---

3 Engel, *The Realm of Saint Stephen*, pp. 72–73.

free and unfree population.[4] The unfree population consisted of hereditary slaves, who were either prisoners of war or locals sold into slavery after being convicted of crimes.

There are very few direct sources which document the Transylvanian social structure in the eleventh and twelfth centuries. It is possible to discern the earlier situation through the interpretation of extant sources from the thirteenth century onwards; these sources reflect some of the groups in existence at the time they were recorded. The information offered by a couple of documents referring to royal revenues from salt exploitation and distribution allows some assessment of early social and economic aspects. The inhabitants of Transylvania, belonging to different groups, began to solicit and to obtain records that help us envisage their economic and social statuses from the beginning of the thirteenth century.

Transylvanian Salt in the Early Records

Transylvania is a region rich in salt reserves. The exploitation of this mineral in the region goes back at least as far as the Bronze Age and possibly to the Neolithic.[5] Thus, salt extraction continued from prehistory to the period of Roman rule in Dacia (c. AD 106–270), and then through the periods of Avar and later Bulgarian domination in Transylvania.[6] The conquest of the region and its inclusion into the Hungarian kingdom had brought these resources under the control of the monarchy. The proportion of royal revenues from salt distribution can be estimated by some later documents.[7] The earliest record of the salt extracted in the region dates from 1075, when King Géza I donated the revenue from the royal portion from the toll of salt mines from Turda to the monastery of Hronský Beňadik.[8] In 1138, King Bela II donated thirty 'mansiones' (farms) from Transylvania who owed dues in salt to the monastery of Dömös.[9] They owed 24,000 blocks of salt, a quantity that could be transported six times a year with two ships by transporters from Sahtu, a village located outside

---

4 Engel, *The Realm of Saint Stephen*, pp. 69–72.
5 Cavruc and Chiricescu, eds, *Sarea, Timpul și Omul*, pp. 37–49.
6 Madgearu, 'Salt Trade and Warfare', pp. 107–09.
7 Romhányi, 'Salt Mining and Trade'.
8 *Documente privind istoria României. Veacul XI, XII și XIII C. Transilvania*, ed. by Ionașcu and others, p. 1. The foundation charter was interpolated in the thirteenth century, but the mention of the donation of the royal revenue from salt was not criticized. 'Ultra silvam <ad castrum, quod vocatur Turda>, dedi tributum salinarum, in loco, qui dicitur hungarice Aranas, latine autem Aureus, scilicet medietatem regie partis', *Diplomata Hungariae Antiquissima*, ed. by Györffy, pp. 212, 217–18.
9 *Documente privind istoria României. Veacul XI, XII și XIII C. Transilvania*, ed. by Ionașcu and others, p. 356. *Erdélyi Okmánytár*, I, ed. by Jakó, p. 125. 'In Ultrasilvanis partibus sunt mansiones, que sal dare debent, scilicet XXIIII[or] milia salis. Nomina autem mansionum sunt: Wosas, Martin, Kinis, Besedi, Senin, Sokol, Lesin, Ginon, Fuglidi, Boch, Kosu, Himudi, Satadi, Uza, Eulegen, Vir, Emis, Viuscy, Halisa, Ellu, Wendi, Ogsan, Cesti, Orsci, Sounik, Simeon, Wasil, Isaac, Vtos, Cima'.

Transsylvania. The same document also gives the names of the salt transporters.[10] The same charter also mentioned the obligations of other inhabitants of Transylvania, who had to pay annually twenty martens, a bear hide, and one bison horn.[11]

In 1165, King Stephen III donated to the Abbey of St Margaret from Meseş the tax on salt paid at that toll. Salt carriers passing through the Meseş gate from Transylvania to Hungary had to give to the monastery one block for each carriage loaded with the royal salt.[12] In 1184, the king's revenue from Transylvania was estimated to be 16,000 marks from salt and 15,000 marks from the foreign guests living in this province.[13] Those involved in the cutting of salt appeared in the written records much later, during the late thirteenth century. However, at that time, they were *hospites*. Several urban communities developed close to the salt mines in Turda, Dej, Ocna Dejului, Cojocna, and Ocna Sibiului.[14] The kings of Hungary granted to the *hospites* the right of self-administration, to elect their own judges, and to use their own customs in the administration of justice; they were exempted from the jurisdiction of the Voivode of Transylvania and county and salt chamber officials.

A few examples can illustrate this development in the case of two urban communities, those of Dej and Ocna Dejului. After their earlier charters of liberties, issued by Kings Béla IV and Stephen V, had been destroyed during the invasions of the Tatars, during the reign of Ladislas IV, the 'hospites' of Ocna Dejului received a confirmation of their privileges following the model of Buda, Esztergom, and Satu Mare privileges.[15] In 1261, the junior King Stephen confirmed the charter issued by Voivode Erney between 1252 and 1260 to the 'hospites' in Dej.[16] The charter was subsequently confirmed in 1279 by King Ladislas IV, in 1283 by Voivode Apor, and in 1284 by Voivode Roland.[17] In 1290, King Ladislas IV confirmed in a new charter the exemption from the taxation of salt extracted for their own use by the 'hospites' of Dej, by any officials, either the voivode, the Count of Inner Szolnok, or the salt chamberer.[18] In 1291, King Andrew III confirmed all previous charters of the 'hospites' of Dej.[19] In 1320, King Charles of Anjou granted a new charter of liberties to the

---

10 *Documente privind istoria României. Veacul XI, XII şi XIII C. Transilvania*, ed. by Ionaşcu and others, p. 356, 'Subu, Mihali, Uwanus, Halaldi, Maradek, Gucur, Ceuse, Forcos, Embel, Michael, Silev, Vosos, Sima, Numarek, Bise, Pedur, Wendeg, Tuda, Kewereg, Niundi, Sumpu, Custi, Aianduk, Nicolus, Buken'.

11 *Documente privind istoria României. Veacul XI, XII şi XIII C. Transilvania*, ed. by Ionaşcu and others, p. 3; *Erdélyi Okmánytár*, I, ed. by Jakó, p. 125, 'In Ultrasilvanis partibus sunt homines, qui debent per annum dare XXti martures, C corrigias et unam pellem ursinam et 1 cornu bubalinum'.

12 *Documente privind istoria României. Veacul XI, XII şi XIII C. Transilvania*, ed. by Ionaşcu and others, p. 4.

13 *Documente privind istoria României. Veacul XI, XII şi XIII C. Transilvania*, ed. by Ionaşcu and others, p. 10.

14 In 1291, King Andrew III confirmed the charters of liberties of the *hospites* of Turda, which were destroyed in the Tartar attacks. They were granted the liberties of the *hospites* in Ocna Dejului, Sic, and Cojocna (*Documente privind istoria României. Veacul XI, XII şi XIII C. Transilvania*, ed. by Ionaşcu and others, pp. 181–82).

15 *Urkundenbuch*, I, ed. by Zimmermann and Werner, pp. 169–70.

16 *Urkundenbuch*, I, ed. by Zimmermann and Werner, pp. 85–86.

17 *Urkundenbuch*, I, ed. by Zimmermann and Werner, pp. 140, 146–47.

18 *Urkundenbuch*, I, ed. by Zimmermann and Werner, p. 166.

19 *Urkundenbuch*, I, ed. by Zimmermann and Werner, pp. 180–81.

communities in Dej and Ocna Dejului. He gave special protection to any free person that would come to settle in these royal cities, promising that these new citizens will enjoy all the liberties of city dwellers.[20] The charter forbade any royal officials or nobles to impede people who wanted to settle in the cities. The charter declared that Saxons, Hungarians, and people of other status could freely settle in those royal cities ('sive Saxones sive Hungari sive alterius conditionis homines cuiuscumque'). Mixed ethnic communities were not uncommon in Transylvania or other areas of Hungary; however, one should also note that some Saxon cities in the region were not as open to the settlement of non-Saxons within their walls.

Castrenses, iobagiones castri, servi, dusinici exequiales

The dynamics of social change in the thirteenth century can be traced in charters recording pious donations to churches involving not only goods or landed properties, but also people. Changes were also underway as concerns the population of royal castles. The castle folk, namely people living in villages attached to royal castles, could be assigned by the king to provide services to churches. Thus, for example, in 1227 the king gave four 'mansiones' (farms) from 'Oranas Vinc' (today, Unirea, Alba County), inhabited by the 'castrenses' Bicca, Nel, and two others to the archbishopric of Esztergom.[21] To what extent did they preserve their status as *castrenses* after such assignment? Even though they might have maintained the memory of their original status, interaction with the representatives of their new lords and the practice of providing services and dues might have contributed to the adoption of a new identity, namely that of tenant peasants of the Church.

During the first decades of the thirteenth century, *castrenses* from various castle domains challenged the status of other villagers, claiming that these belonged to their rank. The phenomenon seems to point to the transfer of some castle folk onto the estates of the nobles. The register of Oradea recorded several cases of litigation involving *castrenses* accusing other villagers of having a similar status. The defendants rejected the accusations by claiming free status. Similar litigation about status appeared amongst the castle warriors, with individuals claiming to belong to the elite layer of the castle warriors, namely the so-called 'liberi Sancti Regis' (royal freemen). Upon hearing such status claims, county counts ('curialis comes') assigned the litigating

---

20 *Urkundenbuch*, I, ed. by Zimmermann and Werner, p. 346, 'quod quicumque liberae conditionis homines ad civitates nostras Deeswar et Deesakna vocatas causa commorandi venire voluerint sive Saxones sive Hungari sive alterius conditionis homines cuiuscumque, libere veniant et secure commorentur in eisdem sub nostra protectione speciali eademque libertate gaudeant et fruantur, quae per praedecessores reges regni Hungariae et per nos mediantibus signis et instrumentis nostris eisdem est concessa et in quibus ceteri civitatenses nostri commorantur'.

21 *Erdélyi Okmánytár*, I, ed. by Jakó, p. 167; *Documente privind istoria României. Veacul XI, XII și XIII C. Transilvania*, ed. by Ionaşcu and others, p. 230; *Documente privitore*, ed. by Hurmuzaki, pp. 105–06. The four *castrenses* were to serve the church according to its privilege ('secundum suam libertate servirent').

parties a bailiff ('pristaldus') and sent them to trial by hot iron, a procedure carried out at the chapter of Oradea.[22] A representative of the parties engaged in litigation had to carry the hot iron. The notices recorded in Oradea presented briefly the actors in the litigation, the issue at stake, and the outcome of the procedure. Several cases of this kind were recorded in the Oradea register, but here I refer to two cases from the area of Transylvania.

In 1214, the 'castrenses' from Ban, a village belonging to Crasna castle, supported by the centurion Tumpa, accused Iecur, son of Redea, Sol and Boutun, sons of Sacicu, and Syteci, son of Babuci, that they were also 'concives eorum' (their fellow-citizen).[23] On the contrary, the defendants asserted that they were freemen and of Ruthenian ethnicity. They brought as their defender a certain Chedur, also of Ruthenian stock and tenant peasant of a certain Barnaba.[24] Chedur supported their claims of freedom, saying that they were his relatives. Then Chedur proved their claim by carrying the hot iron.[25] This is one of the few instances where the indication of ethnicity was mentioned in a case about social status. Free status and Ruthenian descent were asserted by the defendants. Why did they think that Ruthenian descent was a convincing argument of their free status? While various hypothetical answers could be imagined, a definite answer to this question cannot be offered without supplementary evidence. The fact that Chedur was a tenant peasant of Barnaba signals one of the new paths that were wide open during the thirteenth century, namely the dissolution of the royal domains and the transformation of *castrenses* into tenant peasants of the Church or lay landowners. Freemen could also choose to live in a village donated to or owned by a lay landowner.

Another instance of a case of litigation concerning disputed status was recorded in the same year. It was started by the castle warriors of Dăbâca fortress. When the Count of Dăbâca was inspecting his troops, Hereust, a castle warrior, stood in the line of the *iobagiones Sancti regis*. Two of the warriors pushed him out from their ranks saying that he did not belong to that category. Commander Keuerug and the castle warrior, Kereu, supported this position. At Oradea, however, the two accusers dropped the case and recognized that they had accused Hereust unjustly.[26]

A special category was that of slaves assigned to churches for memorial services. The sources referred to them as *dusunuc*. This example is from the area of Bihor County, outside Transylvania, but is illustrative for the formation of the category of tenant peasants of the Church. A certain Tecus, son of the artisan Dennis ('artifex'), who opened the grave of St Ladislas, was granted perpetual freedom with all his

---

22 For uses of trial by hot iron in medieval Europe, see Bartlett, *Trial by Fire and Water*, pp. 25–33.

23 *Regestrum varadinense*, ed. by Karácsony and Borovszky, p. 180.

24 *Regestrum varadinense*, ed. by Karácsony and Borovszky, p. 180, 'Illi autem dixerunt, se esse liberos et genere Ruthenos, et adduxerunt defensorem libertatis suae, nomine Chedur, genere Ruthenum, ioubagionem Barnabae, qui dicens illos cognatos suos esse, tenuit libertatem eorum'.

25 *Documente privind istoria României. Veacul XI, XII și XIII C. Transilvania*, ed. by Ionașcu and others, pp. 59–60.

26 *Documente privind istoria României. Veacul XI, XII și XIII C. Transilvania*, ed. by Ionașcu and others, pp. 60–61.

ECONOMIC AND SOCIAL ASPECTS OF MULTI-ETHNIC TRANSYLVANIA

descendants by King Bela III. In his turn, Tecus granted his slave, Urug, as 'dusinicum exequialem', with all his male descendants, to the church in 'Beseneu' (near Oradea) where he was to serve each year one funerary commemoration with two liturgies ('missas'). Urug had the obligation to give to the church one sheep, thirty loaves of bread, one goose, one hen, and two barrels of beer, and, according to his servile status, he owed the priest the tithe, two 'cubulos frugum suarum et unam gallinam'.[27]

The examples described illustrate the social categories that existed within the castle system, namely *castrenses* and *iobagiones castri*, and also outside it, on the estates belonging to lay landowners. Freemen could choose to live on private landed properties, paying rents to landowners for the plots of land they cultivated but preserving their free status, that is, the possibility of moving wherever they wished after paying their dues. Slaves were assigned by their masters to serve churches for memorial purposes, just as the king himself could assign some of the *castrenses* to the Church. In time, such groups came to form the category of tenant peasants. As we saw, Chedur was already 'iobagio' of a lay landowner. At that time, *iobagio regis* indicated a royal dignitary, just as *iobagio castri* referred to the military elite of the castle system, and the same word came to be used for the tenant peasants. This early social structure and its categories underwent significant changes during the thirteenth century. One of the driving factors of the changes was the formation and consolidation of the category of lay landowners, recognized legally as the nobility. Its members benefitted from the erosion of the royal domain through the expansion of their estates and the control of the population living in their territories. Parallel to this, there was another development, namely that of the guests of the king.

Royal Guests, Saxons

The arrival of Western colonists in Hungary had begun already in the eleventh century. Several waves of Western settlers came to various parts of the kingdom, including Transylvania.[28] In this region, one of the earliest groups to be settled was that which received small territories near Alba Iulia and Orăștie. This first group was followed by others who arrived around the mid-twelfth century and settled in the area of Sibiu and in the north-eastern parts of the province, in the areas of Rodna and Bistrița. No settlement charters are preserved. However, we can get a glimpse of the social and economic conditions of the guests by examining the rights recorded in their charters from the thirteenth century.

In 1206, King Andrew II confirmed the privileges of the 'primi hospites regni' (first guests of the kingdom), the Saxons living in the Transylvanian villages of Cricău, Romos, and Ighiu. These were the descendants of an earlier wave of immigrants who had settled near Alba Iulia probably at the turn of the eleventh century or during the

---

27 *Regestrum varadinense*, ed. by Karácsony and Borovszky, p. 288.
28 A general survey of the process, with its stages, directions, and effects on the economic development in Kubinyi and Laszlovszky, 'Demographic Issues of Late Medieval Hungary', pp. 60–63.

first half of the twelfth century.[29] During the thirteenth century, the three, and then only two, communities of guests were very active in defending their various rights, as suggested by the several charters received from the kings of Hungary. In 1206, their privileges consisted in the exemption from the jurisdiction of any judges, from providing hospitality ('descensus') to the voivode, from the payment of the customary taxes of other Saxons, and from the obligation of guarding the borders. However, they were obliged to attend campaigns outside the kingdom when the king participated in person. They were exempted from the payment of taxes on vineyards planted by themselves and from tithes or tolls ('decimarum et tributorum') on pigs or cattle pasturing in their free forest.[30] In 1225, King Andrew II granted to the Saxons of Cricău and Ighiu an exemption from paying any toll fees when they purchased or sold wines, when transporting it on water or dry land.[31] In 1238, King Béla IV confirmed to the two communities the territory that was granted by his predecessors. He also gave the Saxons from Cricău and Ighiu the right to elect their own 'villicum', who was to pass judgement on the litigation of the inhabitants according to Saxon customs. Litigation with non-Saxons was to be judged by the voivode in person and not by his 'vicejudex'. They were exempted from all taxation, and the voivodes were forbidden from demanding billeting in their settlements. The privilege maintained the obligation to provide 'descensus' to the king. The two communities were to send to the king's banner two soldiers equipped in chainmail, with two saddled horses, and two tents. These soldiers were to fight under the king's banner and to get accommodation with the king' soldiers and not in the quarters of his barons. The exemption from wine tax was maintained.[32]

In 1266, Stephen, junior king and duke of Transylvania, responded to the complaints of the guests from Cricău and Ighiu that the continuous demands of billeting ('descensus') from the Voivode of Transylvania had caused them losses. They complained about the deputy voivode, who had forced them to attend his judicial court even when they litigated among themselves. Despite their privileges, they were forced to provide labour services. Thus, the king forbade voivodes from demanding billeting from them except in emergency cases, when the voivode had to act to protect the region. In that case, since he provided protection, the guests were expected to host him gladly and generously. They could not be forced to bring their cases to the court of the voivode when litigating among themselves. Only when they litigated with outsiders could the voivode act as judge. The deputy voivode was forbidden to judge any of their cases. Because the communities complained that they had insufficient land, the king donated them deserted land belonging to Alba fortress, Gyvmurd.[33] In spite of the high number of privilege charters requested and

---

29 Nägler, *Aşezarea*, pp. 129–31. An interesting view of the process of colonization of the Saxons was that sketched out by Weber, 'An Introduction to the Study of Saxon Settlement', pp. 52–54.

30 *Urkundenbuch*, I, ed. by Zimmermann and Werner, pp. 9–10.

31 *Urkundenbuch*, I, ed. by Zimmermann and Werner, p. 43, 'quod de vino primorum hospitum nostrorum Saxonum videlicet de Karako et Capundorph nec de vendentibus nec de ementibus tributum aliquod aliquis audeat recipere'.

32 *Urkundenbuch*, I, ed. by Zimmermann and Werner, pp. 66–68.

33 *Urkundenbuch*, I, ed. by Zimmermann and Werner, pp. 97–98.

obtained by the two communities, they remained vulnerable to abuses committed by the voivode or the deputy voivode. Perhaps their small size explains partially why these thriving communities of guests suffered setbacks in the fourteenth century and by the fifteenth century had become tenants of the bishops of Transylvania.[34]

The Teutonic Order in Transylvania

Although the presence of the Teutonic knights in south-eastern Transylvania was short, lasting only from 1211 to 1225, the records connected to them shed light on some aspects of the society and economy in the south-eastern part of the province at that time.[35] In 1222, King Andrew II confirmed the privileges granted to the Teutonic knights originally invited to the Bârsa area in 1211 to fight the Cumans who controlled the territories east of the Carpathian Mountains.[36] They were granted permission to build stone fortifications and cities. Like other privileged groups in Transylvania, they were exempted from the obligation to host the voivode and from the payment of free deniers and 'pondera' and any other payments, could elect and appoint their own judge, and could trade salt on six barges on the Mureş and Olt Rivers. The knights could transport salt while navigating towards the west and could bring other goods while navigating eastwards to Transylvania. They were granted enough salt from the mines for their twelve barges. They were also exempt from the payment of any toll fees when transiting the 'terra Siculorum' and 'terra Blacorum'.[37] The inhabitants of Bârsa district were subordinated to the knights. However, the king forbade any inhabitant or guests of the kingdom to settle in the area granted to the Teutonic knights. After the order was expelled by King Andrew II in 1225, the land became a royal domain. According to Thomas Nägler, German colonists had settled in fifteen localities on the territory of what became Braşov district.[38]

The Saxons from Southern Transylvania (*Andreanum*, 1224)

One of the strongest communities of royal guests was that settled around the mid-twelfth century in southern Transylvania, around Sibiu. Evidence about the ecclesiastical organization of the Transylvanian Germans from the late twelfth century already signalled the strength of the colonists invited by King Géza II and anticipated the role that Sibiu was to play in the future political structuring of the Transylvanian

---

34 Sălăgean, 'Cricău', pp. 58–60.
35 Nägler, *Aşezarea*, pp. 148–57. A recent analysis of the records regarding the Teutonic knights in Transylvania in Posán, 'A Német'.
36 *Urkundenbuch*, I, ed. by Zimmermann and Werner, pp. 11–12, 'quondam terram Borza nominee, ultra silvas versus Cumanos'.
37 *Urkundenbuch*, I, ed. by Zimmermann and Werner, pp. 18–19, 'nullum tributum debeant persolvere nec populi eorum, cum transierint pet terram Siculorm aut per terram Blacorum'.
38 Nägler, *Aşezarea*, p. 157.

Saxons.[39] We get a better insight into the range of rights and privileges enjoyed by this community through the charter of privileges called *Andreanum* or the *Golden Bull of Saxons*.[40] In 1224, King Andrew II confirmed the privileges of the 'hospites Teutonici' (Germans) from Transylvania, who had complained that they had lost the liberties granted to them by King Géza II and became so impoverished that they were unable to render their customary services to the king. The confirmation of those liberties agreed that all colonists settled from Orăştie to Baraolt, including those living on the land of the Szeklers from Sepsi and Drăuşeni, would be under the jurisdiction of the Count of Sibiu. The Count of Sibiu was obliged to appoint officials recruited among the inhabitants only. The inhabitants were free to elect as officials those whom they thought fit. Venality of office was forbidden. They owed the king a lump sum of five hundred silver marks per year. No landowner was to be exempt from contributing to the royal revenue unless they had a special royal privilege. The royal guests were to provide five hundred soldiers in the external royal campaigns, if the king took the field in person. Additionally, the king confirmed their old privilege of getting supplies of salt at no cost, for eight days, at the feasts of St George, King St Stephen, and St Martin. The king forbade toll keepers from impeding them when they go or return. The forest and the waters were to be used freely, by both the poor as well as the rich. The settlers also obtained the right to reject any donation of villages or 'predia' (land estate) to any royal servants, who were forbidden from requesting such donations from the king. Saxon traders could travel free of any toll taxes throughout the kingdom.[41] In case the king went on a campaign in their area of settlement, they were only obliged to provide him with billeting ('descensus') three times. If the voivode needed to camp in their territory, they would give him billeting once at his arrival and once more at his departure. They also received the right to use the forest of Pechenegs and Romanians and the waters together with the Pechenegs and Romanians, without owing any service in compensation for this right.[42] This provision sheds light on the relationship between the royal guests and their neighbours, living in areas covered by forests and along valleys of rivers. By royal decision, the Saxons of Sibiu were to use the resources of the territory controlled by Romanians and Pechenegs in common with them and without any obligation in exchange. This charter and its provisions became one of the central documents for the rallying of various communities of guests which were not included in the geographic limits indicated in it. Before the mid-thirteenth century, the set of rights stipulated in the *Andreanum* came to be referred to as the customs of Sibiu province and were indicated as a model for later charters of privileges granted to other communities of guests in Transylvania.[43]

---

39 Nägler, *Aşezarea*, pp. 136–41.
40 *Urkundenbuch*, I, ed. by Zimmermann and Werner, pp. 34–35.
41 *Urkundenbuch*, I, ed. by Zimmermann and Werner, pp. 34–35.
42 *Urkundenbuch*, I, ed. by Zimmermann and Werner, p. 35, 'Praeter vero supra dicta silvam Blacorum et Bissenorum cum aquis usus communes exercendo cum praedictis scilicet Blacis et Bissenis eisdem contulimus, ut praefata gaudentes libertate nulli inde servire teneantur'.
43 Câmpeanu, 'Consideraţii', p. 35.

ECONOMIC AND SOCIAL ASPECTS OF MULTI-ETHNIC TRANSYLVANIA   239

In 1248, Lawrence, voivode of Transylvania, granted to the communities of German guests from Vințu de Jos and Vurpăr (Burgberg) exemptions for the use of woods, pastures, and waters according to those enjoyed by the inhabitants of the Sibiu count.[44] Their privilege fixed the amount of silver owed by each household (three 'pondera'). Those who possessed cattle had to pay 1.5 'pondera', and those having no cattle just one. The fees for the *naves* navigating on Mureș River were one quarter of a mark of silver for 'kerep', and for the 'olch' type ship only half of that fee. The voivode granted them free passage on both sides of the river. They were also assigned to provide 'descensus' to the voivode two times, in case the official came to their region.

Saxon Knights

The Saxon knights were among the guests settled in southern Transylvania. In 1206, King Andrew II donated to his knight Johan Latinus the domain Cwezfey. He was a royal guest, but unlike other *hospites*, who were cultivators, miners, or craftsmen, his status was that of a member of the military elite and the privileges granted to him were exceptional.[45] No local official could judge him; only the king and the palatine could do so. All his immobile acquisitions (houses, landed properties, vineyards, mills, and any other possessions) that he would acquire in the future were guaranteed by the king. He and his men were free and exempt from paying any tolls when they travelled for commercial purposes.[46] In 1231, the sons of John Latinus, Corrard and Daniel (called 'milites nostros Saxones'), were rewarded for their services by King Béla IV, who gave them an exemption from the taxation of their villages.[47] The tax collectors were forbidden to access the villages. They were to pay a lump sum of three gold quarters each year at Christmas. The knights could use the sums owed to the king to cover their own expenses when they went to the royal army. For their four knightly villages they were to pay three golden quarters each year, at Christmas. Furthermore, their villagers were exempt from providing any services.

During the last decades of the thirteenth century, an upper echelon of Saxon landowners emerged from within the milieu of royal guests. Most probably they

---

44 *Urkundenbuch*, I, ed. by Zimmermann and Werner, p. 77, 'fidelibus suis Teutonicis in Wynch et in Burgberg commorantibus […] omnem per omnia libertatem videlicet in silvis, pascuis et aquis, sine quorum aminiculo temporaliter vita humana non ducitur, quam habent provinciales comitatus Scybiniensis, duximus indulgendam'.

45 Johannes Latinus received a first grant in 1204, from King Emeric, who rewarded him for his services by being exempt from the jurisdiction of the Transylvanian Saxons and granted the privilege of conversation in the royal palace and exemption from taxation, *Urkundenbuch*, I, ed. by Zimmermann and Werner, pp. 7–8.

46 *Urkundenbuch*, I, ed. by Zimmermann and Werner, p. 8: 'Johan Latini hospitis fidelis nostri militis servitiorum merita fideliter et efficaciter nobis impensa considerantes'.

47 *Urkundenbuch*, I, ed. by Zimmermann and Werner, pp. 54–55 'scilicet villam Albae ecclesiae, villam Homuspotoc, villam Sarpotoc, villam Latinam necnon et populos eorundem de villa Oplid ab omni collecta absolvimus, nec nostris collectoribus nec populis Scibiniensibus collectam persolvant'.

were the descendants of the leaders of the colonists from the twelfth century who had enjoyed some economic advantages and traditionally led their villages. In the royal decree from 1290, the Transylvanian Saxons holding *predia* (land estates) and behaving like noblemen ('Saxones Transilvani predia tenentes et more nobilium se gerentes') were mentioned as enjoying the same rights and having the same obligations as the nobles of the kingdom ('nobiles regni').[48] At the beginning of the fourteenth century, with the change of the ruling dynasty, the Saxons approached King Charles Robert, who confirmed the *Andreanum* in 1317, thereby precluding the development of the Saxon landowners as nobility. Afterwards, the Saxons could own villages, but only outside the royal land.

In the fourteenth and fifteenth centuries, some Saxon settlers chose to settle in villages belonging to noblemen in the counties. According to the calculations proposed by Thomas Nägler, 149 Saxon villages were located in the territory of counties, on lands belonging to noblemen or the Church. This is a surprisingly high number, if we compare it with the 198 villages located on royal land in Transylvania. According to the same historian, in the thirteenth century, the conditions offered by noblemen who sought to develop the exploitation of their landed properties were not as unappealing as those of the later centuries, which facilitated their attempts to attract Saxons as well as Hungarian or Romanian tenants.[49] Thus, while an important number of Saxons were free peasants, those living on noble land were tenant peasants. The structure of the Saxons included also craftsmen, counts (*Greb*), and nobles.[50]

Nobility and Ethnicity

One of the factors in the emergence of the nobility as a category defined by collective privileges and legally recognized rights was the policy of King Andrew II (1204–1235) called *novae institutiones*. This policy, which aimed to recruit servants for the king, led to the transfer of royal castles and lands, through permanent donation, to private landowners.[51] The main beneficiaries of this policy were the so-called 'servientes regis' (royal servants). These royal servants succeeded in obtaining from King Andrew II a confirmation of a set of rights in the so-called Golden Bull charter

---

48 *Decreta*, I, trans. and ed. by Bak and others, p. 45, 'Item si aliqua potentis extrinseca ad invadendum regnum nostrum venerit, aut aliqua pars vel provincia regni ab obedientia regis vel potentia regni se abstraxerit aut alienare aliquo modo voluerit, nobiles regni nostri et Saxones Transilvani predia tenentes et more nobilium se gerentes nobis astare et adiuvare nos tenebuntur'. Further stipulations regarding the military obligations and rights of the nobility of the realm and the Transylvanian Saxons were added. Thus, they were not to be compelled by any barons to go on campaigns without pay or without the king and were exempt from royal taxation. Article XIV, concerning the payment of tithes, used the formula 'quilibet nobilis sive Saxo de numero nobilium' (*Decreta*, I, trans. and ed. by Bak and others, p. 46). There appeared no distinction between the nobles and the nobly living Saxons as concerned rights and obligations; nevertheless, the Saxons were not yet considered identical with the nobility.

49 Nägler, *Aşezarea*, pp. 221–24.

50 Nägler, *Aşezarea*, p. 223.

51 Engel, *The Realm of Saint Stephen*, pp. 91–93.

ECONOMIC AND SOCIAL ASPECTS OF MULTI-ETHNIC TRANSYLVANIA   241

of 1222, a document that later contributed to the consolidation of the legal status of the Hungarian nobility. During the next decades, the system of administration based on royal castles, castle warriors ('jobagiones castri'), and castle folk gradually disappeared. The former elite of the castral system either became members of the body of royal servants or sank into the ranks of the peasantry. In Transylvania, the nobility consisted mainly of Hungarian-speaking families, yet in the long run, it remained accessible to upwardly mobile individuals, such as the Romanian *knezes*, Saxons, or Szeklers willing to acquire the noble privileges. One of the conditions was that of owning land. Although this regional group was composed from families who traced their ancestry back to the chieftains of the conquering Magyars, before the foundation of the Kingdom of Hungary, most of them were relatively recent.

The rise of the Transylvanian nobility can be examined at individual level through the fragmentary evidence of royal donations of landed properties to various individuals. According to Marius Diaconescu, eleven noble kindreds (out of about 180) owned landed properties in Transylvania before the Mongol invasion, and for five more the moment when they became landowners in the region is not known. Two more kindreds or branches of kindred arrived in the second half of the thirteenth century.[52] Based on the interpretation of evidence about landed properties of medium size (that is, roughly from four to eight villages), he suggested that a couple of dozen landowning families from the fourteenth century might have been descended from royal *servientes*. But as Diaconescu admitted, none of the documents referred to them as *servientes* and their descent from such royal servants remains a supposition.[53] As concerned the fate of the castle warriors, although direct evidence is absent, the same author supposed that lesser noble families holding one or two villages were probably descended from members of that category who were ennobled sometime towards the end of the thirteenth century.[54] The nobility also gained new members from the other two ethnic groups resident in Transylvania. This category descended partially from the leaders of the Saxon settlers, called *graven* or *comites*, who received land donations from the king. Some of them continued to live among the Saxons, while others gradually built matrimonial connections with noble families and established themselves as nobles. Diaconescu traced the genealogies of about twenty Saxon families who owned land in the fourteenth century.[55]

In fact, by 1288–1291, the documents mentioned the community called 'universitas nobilium partium Transilvanarum' (community of Transylvania noblemen), thus

---

52 Diaconescu, *Structura*, pp. 37–38.
53 Diaconescu, *Structura*, pp. 42–44. In 1204, Johannes Latinus, who lived among the Transylvanian 'Teuthonicos' (Germans), was rewarded for his service ('servitium') which he provided to King Emericus. He was to be judged only by the king and the judge of the 'filios iobagionum nostrorum' (*Urkundenbuch*, I, ed. by Zimmermann and Werner, p. 42). In 1206, Johannes was called 'hospitis fidelis nostri militis', while in 1231, his sons, Daniel and Corrardus, were called 'fideles et dilectos milites Saxones Vltrasiluanos' (*Urkundenbuch*, I, ed. by Zimmermann and Werner, p. 54). Thus, while they provided military service and received exemptions that were like those granted to *servientes*, they were not called as such.
54 Diaconescu, *Structura*, p. 49.
55 Diaconescu, *Structura*, pp. 52–55.

recognizing the existence of the estate of nobility in the province.[56] A specification of the royal decree issued in 1290 forbade Voivodes of Transylvania to request 'descensus' from the local nobility. Although this right was already stipulated in the Golden Bull of 1222, it seems that the voivodes disregarded it and taxed the Transylvanian nobles. In my previous research on the development of regional identity in Transylvania, I focused on the collective activities of the nobility of this region during the fourteenth century.[57] That research gave me the opportunity to examine the collective privileges requested and granted to this group from 1324 to 1367, by Kings Charles Robert of Anjou and his son, Louis the Great, or the Voivode of Transylvania, Thomas Szécsényi. In 1324, for example, King Charles Robert rewarded the military support provided by the noblemen from Transylvania in his campaign against the rebellious Saxons by granting the nobles the exemption from providing *descensus* to the voivode and from paying taxes in money and dues in food.[58] A particularly significant charter was that conceded by Voivode Thomas Szécsényi, in 1342; it recognized the jurisdiction of Transylvanian nobles over their tenant peasants in all crimes except homicide, arson, and robbery, which belonged to the competence of the count (*ispán*).[59] The nobility became the dominant category at the level of the seven counties of medieval Transylvania.

The Romanians

The Romanians appeared in the earliest written sources for Transylvania at the beginning of the thirteenth century, but the details regarding their social and economic standing are meagre for much of the thirteenth century. No comparable charters of privileges like those granted to the communities of guests or those given to the nobles seem to have ever been given to them. Several sources indicated that they lived in the proximity of the Saxon colonists, the Szeklers, and Pechenegs in the southern parts of Transylvania at the beginning of the thirteenth century. In 1223, King Andrew II confirmed the donation of Cisnădie by Master Gocelinus to the Cistercian Monastery Cârța. On that occasion the king also confirmed another donation he had made to the monastery, namely a land taken from the Romanians living in the Făgăraş area ('terrram [...] exemptam de Ballacis').[60]

---

56 Sălăgean, *Transilvania*, pp. 218–22.
57 Popa-Gorjanu, 'The Nobility as Bearers of Regional Identity', pp. 46–58.
58 *Documente privind istoria României. Veacul XIV C. Transilvania*, ed. by Ionaşcu, pp. 137–38; Budapest, MNL, DL 40487, 'Quod ex parte universorum nobilium seu Regalium seruientium de terra Transilwana [...] nobis humiliter suplicatum ut de victualibus, exactionibus, fertonum ac descensibus Baronum specialiter woiwode Transilvanum quibus ad modum aggravabantur, ipsis totum ea relaxandum de benignitate Regia gratam facere dignaremur'.
59 Popa-Gorjanu, 'The Nobility as Bearers of Regional Identity', pp. 51–53.
60 *Urkundenbuch*, I, ed. by Zimmermann and Werner, pp. 27–28: 'item etiam confirmamus in praesenti privilegio terram quam prius eidem monasterio contuleramus exemptam de Blaccis pro remedio animae nostare ac per fidelem ac dilectum nostrum Benedictum tunc temporis vaivodam assignari facientes'; for Cârța monastery see Bencze, 'The Monastery of Cârța'.

ECONOMIC AND SOCIAL ASPECTS OF MULTI-ETHNIC TRANSYLVANIA 243

The earliest mention of taxes collected from the Romanians by the King of Hungary dates to 1234. The document is a letter from Pope Gregory IX which instructs King Béla to make the Romanians (*Walathi*) accept the authority of the Roman Catholic bishop of the Cumans and give to the prelate a share of the revenues the king collected from them. The pope referred to Romanians living east of the Carpathian Mountains, who were reluctant to accept the jurisdiction of the Roman Catholic prelate. Another aspect of an otherwise little-known phenomenon was the report that many Hungarians, Germans, and Catholics from Hungary went to live with the Romanians, and became one people with them and took ecclesiastical sacraments from the 'false Greek bishops'.[61] If the information was true, that would amount to an insight into a phenomenon of the aggregation of a multi-ethnic society that seemed to be sufficiently successful to cause concern to the pope.

In 1256 and 1262, King Béla IV confirmed the privileges of the Archbishop of Esztergom, which included among others the right to collect the tithes from royal revenues, including those collected from the Szeklers and Romanians. The customary tax of Szeklers was the *signatura bovum*, while Romanians were usually paying *quinquagesima ovium* and tithes from other animals.[62] In 1357, King Louis of Anjou relinquished the royal revenue from the fiftieth paid by the Romanians living in the villages of the Losonczi nobles in Transylvania.[63] During the fourteenth and fifteenth centuries, the monarchs granted to various landowners the right to collect and to keep the fiftieth from their tenants, but this tax continued to be seen as royal revenue.[64]

In the second half of the thirteenth century, some Romanians living on the royal domains moved to estates owned by lay landowners or ecclesiastical lords. This was the case which is illustrated by a privilege from 1293, granted by King Andrew III to Alexander, son of Gurk of Akos kindred, who was given permission to gather and settle Romanians on his hereditary estates near the Mureş River, at Ilia, Gurasada, and Feneş, in Hunedoara/Hunyad county.[65] Alexander was thus rewarded for his

---

61 *Vetera Monumenta*, ed. by Theiner, p. 131, 'quidam populi, qui Walathi vocantur, existent, qui etsi censeantur nomine christiano, sub una tamen fide varios ritus habentes et mores, illa committunt, qui huic sunt nomini inimica. Nam Romanam ecclesiam contempnentes non a venerabili frare nostro [...] Episcopo Cumanorum, qui locis diocesanus existit, sed a quibusdam pseudoepiscopis Grecorum ritum tenentibus universa recipiunt ecclesiastica sacramenta, et nonulli de Regno Ungariae, tam Ungari, quam Theutonici et alii orthodoxi, morandi causa cum ipsis transeunt ad eosdem, et sic cum eis, quia populus unus facti cum eisdem Walathis, eo contrempto, premissa recipiunt sacramenta, in grave orthodoxorum scandalum et derogationem non modicum fidei christiane'.

62 *Urkundenbuch*, I, ed. by Zimmermann and Werner, pp. 80, 87, 'similiter in decimis percipiendis regalium proventuum ex parte Siculorum et Olacorum, in pecudibus, pecoribus et animalibus quibuslibet, exceptis terragiis Saxonum, sed ex parte Olacorum etiam ubique et a quocumque provenientium, in regno Hungarie persolvi consuetorum'.

63 *Documenta Romaniae Historica* , ed. by Pascu and others, p. 154, 'proventus nostros quinquagesimales de possessionibus et Olachiis ipsorum, in partibus Transsiluanis constitutibus et existentibus'.

64 Doboşi, *Datul oilor*, pp. 26–44.

65 Budapest, MNL, DL 50545, 'concedimus ut ad quasdam terras suas hereditarias Elye, Zad et Fenes vocatas Olacos possit aggregare ac aggregatos retinere omnem collectam ac debitum eorundem Olacorum predicto Alexandro relinquentes'.

service in various campaigns and especially that against Duke Albert of Austria. The king ceded to Alexander not only the right to attract inhabitants in his villages, but also the taxes that Romanians customarily paid to the king. In the same year, King Andrew III confirmed an earlier donation of King Ladislas IV allowing the chapter of Alba Iulia to settle sixty Romanian families on their estates at Aiud and Filesd.[66] Although the king had previously ordered all Romanians who had moved on noble domains to return to the royal estate Scekes, he nevertheless allowed the chapter to retain the sixty Romanian families, as allowed by King Ladislas IV.[67] The king confirmed that the Romanian 'mansiones' (farms) were exempted from the payment of the customary dues owed by Romanians, such as the fiftieth, tithes, or other taxes.[68] This was not a privilege granted to Romanians, but to the chapter, which was to collect those revenues for its own use. During the fourteenth century, the number of mentions of noble owned villages with mixed populations — Hungarian, Romanian, or Saxon — increased.

The status of Romanians varied according to the areas in which they lived. They lived in villages led by chieftains called *knezes*. The *knezes* might have been elected at an early stage, but after the mid-fourteenth century, when information about their situation is available, that office was already hereditary. The *knez* led his men, collected the dues owed by the villagers, maintained order, and performed military services on behalf of the royal castles. In the areas of dense Romanian presence, such as Hațeg, Făgăraș, in southern Transylvania, and in the adjacent regions of Zarand, Banat, and Maramureș, *knezes* were led by a military leader holding the office of voivode. The voivodes were *knezes* elected by their peers and should not be confused with the Voivode of Transylvania, who was a royal dignitary appointed by the monarch. Records from the fourteenth century in various parts of the Kingdom of Hungary testified to the prevalence of these two institutions in Romanian communities. This organizational structure was not created by the kings of Hungary, who simply recognized the rights of lordship of *knezes* by issuing individual charters like those granting noble properties, except that the charters granted *keneziatus* rights to various *knezes*.

The area of Hațeg, a lowland area in south-western Transylvania, on the northern rim of the Southern Carpathians, presented an interesting laboratory for historical analysis of the process of political incorporation and social adaptation of a traditional

---

66 'Istud est transcriptum priuilegi [*sic!*] Andree Regis super relaxatione quinquagesimarum et decimarum Olahalium', Budapest, MNL, DL 31059, contemporary note on the back of the charter.

67 *Urkundenbuch*, I, ed. by Zimmermann and Werner, p. 195; Budapest, MNL, DL 31059, 'Quod cum nos constricti suscepti Regiminis aculeis, habito consilio omnium barronum nostrorum nobiscum assidencium, universos Olacos in possessionibus nobilium vel quorumlibet aliorum residentes, ad predium nostrum Regale Scekes vocatum ordinassemus reuocari, reduci et etiam compelli redire inuitos, si forte nostre in hac parte non acquiesscerent parere iussioni'.

68 *Urkundenbuch*, I, ed. by Zimmermann and Werner, pp. 195–96, 'quod nullus collector seu executor regalis decimae seu quinquagesimae vel collectarum quarumlibet pro tempore constitutus Olacos ipsius capituli in terris suis superius comprehensis residentes usque numerum praefixum audeat molestare, nec quinquagesimam, decimam seu exactionem aliam quamlibet exigere praesumat ab eisdem'.

society into the institutional framework of the Kingdom of Hungary.[69] Before the mid-thirteenth century, the area of Hațeg was the northern part of a Romanian voivodate stretching across both sides of the Carpathians. In 1247, King Béla IV decided to give the territory of 'terra Zeurini' (Severin/Szörény, today known as Oltenia) to the Hospitaller knights who were expected to assist the king in the struggle against the Tatars.[70] By this agreement, the king separated Hațeg from the voivodate, keeping it under royal control. Although the agreement was not fulfilled, it sheds light on the otherwise obscure political, social, and economic structures in the territory of the future principality of Wallachia in 1247. In the 1270s a royal castle was erected in the centre of the Hațeg area and a few communities of 'hospites' developed within an area where Romanians seemed to be the majority of the population.[71] Romanian *knezes* were slow in adopting the methods of proving ownership of their *knezates* with royal charters, and their reliance on traditional oral knowledge of the local community became problematic around the mid-fourteenth century, when the Angevin kings tried to enforce a justice system based on the use of written documents in litigation over landed properties.[72] A few litigation cases from the area of Hațeg and Hunedoara involving Romanians reveal the differences between the Romanian customary law, deriving property rights from the work of clearing woods or establishing settlements, and the official law which gave precedence to the possession of written documents. As Maria Holban has demonstrated, after the royal decree of 1351, Romanian *knezes* in Transylvania and the Banat began to adapt to the requirements of the official law and requested official charters for the villages they owned.[73] Some of these *knezes* who owned villages on the domains of the royal fortresses continued their efforts to achieve equal status with the nobility and acquire noble status. The process continued well into the first half of the fifteenth century.

Conclusions

Transylvania witnessed a wide range of changes during the thirteenth century. From its initial social and economic structure, based on the royal counties with their military groups and service populations (*servientes, udvornici*), to the gradual emergence and development of estates of lay landowners and the settlement of various groups of western colonists endowed with privileges there was significant change. Given these developments, the structure could not remain harmonious or cohesive. Differences in status and in economic potential were bound to appear between various groups. The privatization of parts of the royal domain through donations of land made to

---

69 Several Romanian medievalists have contributed to the archaeological and historical investigation of the society of this region in the Middle Ages: Radu Popa, Adrian Andrei Rusu, Ioan-Aurel Pop, Ioan Drăgan.

70 On the Hospitaller knights, see Hunyadi, 'Military Religious Orders', pp. 117–18.

71 Popa, *La începuturile*, pp. 72–74.

72 Popa, *La începuturile*, pp. 190–91.

73 Holban, 'Deposedări', pp. 157–58.

royal supporters consolidated the group of nobles, known as *servientes regis* for much of the thirteenth century and rendering the former military elite, *iobagiones castri*, obsolete. While in Transylvania such *servientes* were not mentioned, there are many charters of ennoblement that illustrate the transfer of lands belonging to the domain of royal castles into the hands of nobles who supported the monarch. By the end of the thirteenth century, the *iobagiones castri* started to vanish from the written records as a distinct group. Former *castrenses*, libertines, or other groups became tenant peasants on noble estates and came to be collectively known as *iobagiones*. Some other groups, such as the Szeklers and Romanians, whose presence in certain areas was signalled in various sources, remained out of the limelight for long periods of time.

Szeklers were recognized as one of the privileged groups in Transylvania, inhabiting a distinct territory in the eastern part of the province and using their own customs in the administration of their affairs under the supervision of a royal dignitary, *comes Siculorum*. Romanians never acquired collective privileges comparable to those of the nobility or the royal guests. In fact, what is known about their conditions comes from privileges granted to other groups, such as the Saxons, the Teutonic order, or the Church. By the fourteenth century, many Romanian *knezes* and voivodes lived in villages belonging to lay or ecclesiastical landowners. Although they enjoyed a somewhat elevated status, they became intermediaries between their landlords and their villagers. Romanians who lived on the still-extant royal domains in the districts of royal fortresses had a different status and more prospects of upward mobility. The fact that the kings did not give away lands in the border areas, such as Hațeg district, meant that *knezes* under the authority of a royal fortress could turn their *knezates* into noble properties, by earning merit through military service and receiving them from the king as noble properties, completely separated from the jurisdiction of the royal castle. The process of the formation of the Romanian nobility from the former *knezes* was documented for a period of almost one hundred years, lasting approximately from the mid-fourteenth to the mid-fifteenth century.

The unevenness in the status of various groups suggests that mechanisms of growth favoured certain groups. The royal guests (*hospites*) were in fact the group that benefitted in the greatest measure from royal generosity and protection. The fact that they brought with them more advanced technologies and contributed to the economic development of the region is indisputable. They are credited with the introduction of the heavy plough and advanced agricultural and mining techniques superior to the subsistence agriculture practised before their arrival. Groups of guests of variable sizes received charters of privileges. They received not only suitable lands for economic activities but also extensive rights of self-administration, judicial autonomy, and exemptions from taxation and tolls, in exchange for providing military services for the king. Clearly the information that we receive from statutory evidence creates an image of inequality within a society separated into privileged and unprivileged groups. When we read about exemptions from taxes, custom fees, or *descensus*, we note that some communities received support for their development from the monarchs, but were similar measures applied indiscriminately to other communities? There are no such signs. It would probably be unwarranted to suppose that the monarchy, one of the principal factors which influenced the direction of social and economic development in the province, was concerned about maintaining harmony among various groups of subjects. The imbalance between the number of

ECONOMIC AND SOCIAL ASPECTS OF MULTI-ETHNIC TRANSYLVANIA

collective privileges preserved by royal guests' communities or the nobility and other local communities remains one of the main obstacles in assessing to what extent a mechanism for the building of cohesion within this society was at work in the thirteenth century.

Works Cited

Manuscripts and Archival Sources

Budapest, Magyar Nemzeti Levéltár, Diplomátikai Levéltár (DL)

Primary Sources

Decreta Regni Mediaevalis Hungariae, I: *1000–1301*, 2nd rev. edn, trans. and ed. by János M. Bak, Pál Engel, György Bónis, and James Ross-Sweeney (Idyllwild, CA: Charles Schlacks, Jr., 1999)

Diplomata Hungariae Antiquissima: Accedunt epistolae et acta ad historiam Hungariae pertinentia, vol. I,, ed. by Gregorius Györffy (Budapest: in aedibus Academiae Scientiarium Hungaricae, 1992)

Documenta Romaniae Historica C. Transilvania, ed. by Ștefan Pascu, Ioan Dani, Aurel Răduțiu, Viorica Pervain, Konrad G. Gündisch, and Sabin Belu, vol. XI: *1356–1360* (Bucharest: Editura Academiei R. S. România, 1981)

Documente privind istoria României. Veacul XI, XII și XIII C. Transilvania, ed. by Ion Ionașcu, L. Lăzărescu-Ionescu, Barbu Câmpina, Eugen Stănescu, David Prodan, and Mihail Roller (Bucharest: Editura Academiei R. P. Române, 1951)

Documente privind istoria României. Veacul XIV C. Transilvania, II: *1321–1330*, ed. by Ion Ionașcu (Bucharest: Editura Academiei R.P. Române, 1953)

Documente privitore la istoria Românilor, I: *1199–1345*, ed. by Eudoxiu Hurmuzaki (Bucharest: Socec, 1887)

Erdélyi Okmánytár: Oklevelek, levelek, és más írásos emlékek Erdély történetéhez, I: *1023–1300*, ed. by Zsigmond Jakó (Budapest: Akadémiai Kiadó, 1997)

Regestrum varadinense examinum ferri candentis ordine chronologico digestum, descripta effigie editionis a. 1550, ed. by János Karácsony and Samu Borovszky (Budapest: Hornyánszky Viktor, 1903)

Urkundenbuch zur Geschichte der Deutschen in Siebenbürgen, I: *1191 bis 1342*, ed. by Franz Zimmermann and Carl Werner (Hermannstadt (Sibiu): Franz Michaelis, 1892)

Vetera Monumenta Historica Hungariam Sacram Illustrantia, ed. by Augustin Theiner, vol. I (Rome: Typis Vaticanis, 1859)

Secondary Studies

Bartlett, Robert, *Trial by Fire and Water: The Medieval Judicial Ordeal* (Oxford: Clarendon Press, 1986)

Bencze, Ünige, 'The Monastery of Cârța: Between the Cistercian Ideal and Local Realities', *Studia Universitatis Babeș-Bolyai — Historia*, special issue (2013), 17–30

Câmpeanu, Liviu, 'Considerații administrative-juridice asupra celor două scaune (Mediaș și Șeica Mare) în evul mediu', *Anuarul Institutului de Istorie 'A.D. Xenopol'*, 48 (2011), 35–40

Cavruc, Valeriu, and Andrea Chiricescu, eds, *Sarea, Timpul și Omul* (Sfântu Gheorghe: Editura Angustia, 2006)

Diaconescu, Marius, *Structura nobilimii din Transilvania în epoca agevină* (Cluj-Napoca: Mega, 2013)

Doboși, Alexandru, *Datul oilor (Quinguagesima ovium): Un capitol din istoria economică a românilor din Transilvania* (Bucharest: Academia Română, 1937)

Engel, Pál, *The Realm of Saint Stephen: A History of Medieval Hungary, 895–1526* (London: I. B. Tauris Publishers, 2001)

Holban, Maria, 'Deposedări și judecăți în Hațeg pe vremea Angevinilor', *Studii Revistă de Istorie*, 13.5 (1960), 147–64

Hunyadi, Zsolt, 'Military Religious Orders and the Mongols around Mid-13th Century', in *Competing Narratives between Nomadic People and their Sedentary Neighbours: Papers of the 7th International Conference on the Medieval History of the Eurasian Steppe, Nov. 9–12, 2018, Shanghai University, China*, ed. by Chen Hao (Szeged: University of Szeged, 2019), pp. 111–23

Krzemieńska, Barbara, and Dušan Třeštik, 'Wirtschaftliche Grundlagen des frümittelalterlichen Staates in Mitteleuropa (Böhmen, Polen, Ungrarn im 10.–11. Jahrhundert)', *Acta Poloniae Historica*, 40 (1979), 5–31

Kubinyi, András, and József Laszlovszky, 'Demographic Issues of Late Medieval Hungary: Population, Ethnic Groups, Economic Activity', in *The Economy of Medieval Hungary*, ed. by József Laszlovszky, Balázs Nagy, Péter Szabó, and András Vadas (Leiden: Brill, 2018), pp. 48–64

Madgearu, Alexandru, 'Salt Trade and Warfare: The Rise of the Romanian-Slavic Military Organization in Early Medieval Transylvania', in *East Central and Eastern Europe in the Early Middle Ages*, ed. by Florin Curta (Ann Arbor: University of Michigan Press, 2005), pp. 103–20

Nägler, Thomas, *Așezarea sașilor în Transilvania* (Bucharest: Kriterion, 1992)

Popa, Radu, *La începuturile evului mediu românesc: Țara Hațegului* (Bucharest: Editura Științifică și Enciclopedică, 1988)

Popa-Gorjanu, Cosmin, 'The Nobility as Bearers of Regional Identity in Fourteenth Century Transylvania', *Annales Universitatis Apulensis, Series Historica*, 16.2 (2012), 41–58

Posán, László, 'A Német Lovagrend megítélese Magyarországon II: András korában', *Történelmi Szemle*, 58.3 (2016), 465–74

Romhányi, Beatrix, 'Salt Mining and Trade in Hungary before the Mongol Invasion', in *The Economy of Medieval Hungary*, ed. by József Laszlovszky, Balázs Nagy, Péter Szabó, and András Vadas (Leiden: Brill, 2018), pp. 184–204

Sălăgean, Tudor, 'Cricău—un sat din comitatul Alba în secolele XIII–XIV', *Apulum*, 43.1 (2006), 51–61

——, *Transilvania în a doua jumătate a secolului al XIII-lea: Afirmarea regimului congregațional* (Cluj-Napoca: Centrul de Studii Transilvane, 2003)

Weber, Eugen, 'An Introduction to the Study of Saxon Settlement in Transylvania during the Middle Ages', *Medieval Studies*, 18 (1956), pp. 50–60

DANIEL BAGI

The Dracula and the Others

The Multi-Ethnic Character of the Hungarian Political Elite until the Fifteenth Century

The example of the medieval history of Transylvania shows that the kings of Hungary were very pragmatic in the way they sought to regulate inter-ethnic relations in their kingdom. Their main goal was to maintain the dominant political position in the region by supporting or weakening appropriate ethnic groups. Their activity in relation to the highest political elites of the kingdom, including the royal court, was similar. From the very beginning, the medieval rulers of Hungary attached great importance to the cultural and civilizational benefits of the presence of knights and nobles from various ethnic communities at their court. Over time, the kings gained specific political benefits from the creation of a wealthy group of incomers who were dependant on the ruler and unconnected to the Hungarian local elites. Such a policy, however, only meant a limited effort to build a multi-ethnic state elite. Eventually, the newcomers maintained the status as clients of a particular king; consequently, they did not come into close contact with members of their own ethnic group outside the milieu of the royal court.

Early Days: King St Stephen and *Libellus de institutione morum*

The medieval Kingdom of Hungary was from the very beginnings of its history a multi-ethnic polity.[1] One of the earliest proofs for this assertion is to be found in the

---

1 Kristó, 'Oroszok az Árpád-kori Magyarországon'; Györffy, *A magyarság keleti elemei*; Berend, *At the Gate of Christendom*.

Daniel Bagi • (bagidani@gmail.com) is Professor of History of Eastern and Central Europe at the University of Budapest. His main research interests are the medieval history of eastern-central Europe, especially of Hungary, and the historiography of the high medieval period.

Inter-Ethnic Relations and the Functioning of Multi-Ethnic Societies: Cohesion in Multi-Ethnic Societies in Europe from c. 1000 to the Present, II, ed. by Przemysław Wiszewski, EER 18 (Turnhout: Brepols, 2022), pp. 249–262

BREPOLS ✿ PUBLISHERS   10.1484/M.EER-EB.5.132154

This is an open access chapter made available under a cc by-nc 4.0 International License.

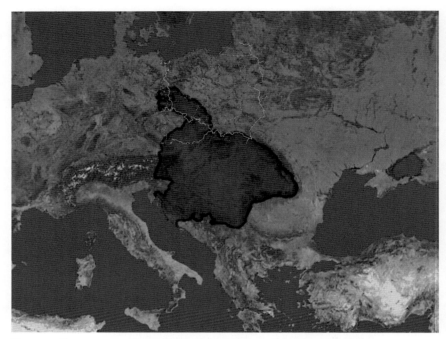

Map 10.1. Hungary 1490. Source: <https://commons.wikimedia.org/wiki/File:Hungary_1490_(PL2018).png>. CC BY-SA 4.0.

so-called *Libellus de institutione morum* of King St Stephen to his son, Prince Emery, which is also called *Admonitions*.[2] The *Admonitions* must have been written in the second decade of the eleventh century, before Emery's death,[3] and as a narrative text, it is one of the latest Carolingian *Specula regia* (King's mirrors) preserved in Europe. The text differs, however, from the customary style of ninth- to tenth-century Carolingian *Specula*. The *Admonitions* urges the future ruler to keep the usual royal virtues, but with supposition that the whole royal power comes from the relationship of the ruler to the 'decors of the royal palace', the bishops, the noblemen, the royal council, and the incoming guests, who are called *hospites* in the text.[4] The last textual passage of this part of the king's *Admonitions*, which relates that 'kingdoms of one language and of one custom are weak and feeble',[5] caused a lot of discussion among scholars. As

---

2 *Libellus de institutione morum*, pp. 613–27.
3 See Szűcs, 'Szent István intelmei', pp. 271–89.
4 Szűcs, 'Szent István intelmei', p. 278.
5 *Libellus de institutione morum*, p. 625: 'Nam unius lingue uniusque moris regnum inbecille et fragile est. Propterea iubeo te fili mi, ut bona voluntate illos nutrias, et honeste teneas, ut tecum libentius degant, quam alicubi habitent. Si enim tu destruere, quod ego edificavi, aut dissipare quod congregavi studueris, sine dubio maximum detrimentum tuum patietur regnum. Quod ne fiat, tuum quottidie auge regnum, ut tua corona ab hominibus habeatur augusta'.

THE DRACULA AND THE OTHERS   251

many of them argued, the text contains a clear confirmation of the multilingual and multi-ethnic characteristics of the early Arpadian monarchy. Following them, until the present day there are journalists who have argued in political debates for the existence of a *minority policy* of the kings of the Arpadian dynasty from the thirteenth century onwards.[6] Others, such as K. Guoth, who died tragically young, asserted that this chapter of the *Libellus* is proof of its later origin, because guests especially from Germany only came to Hungary at the earliest in the thirteenth century.[7]

However, Elemér Mályusz and later Jenő Szűcs have demonstrated that the *Admonitions* follows the formal and contextual requirements of the ninth- to tenth-century literary and political customs.[8] The term 'regnum' (kingdom) mentioned in this sentence does not mean directly the whole sociopolitical organism or polity nor the country in its political sense, but rather the royal court and power. The newcomers or guests were members of the intellectual and military elites, bishops and knights invited by the king, who — as the text of the *Admonitions* suggests — brought 'documenta et arma' (charters and weaponry); this means knowledge and military force in the service of the ruler.[9] Therefore the *Libellus de institutione morum* provides evidence for the multinational character of Hungary as far as the royal court and the ecclesiastical positions are concerned. A similar situation can be observed everywhere in eleventh-century eastern-central Europe, where in the new kingdoms, ecclesiastical and military dignitaries of foreign origins were frequently mentioned. But in this specific context it shows something else: the full integration of many foreign ethnic newcomers in the king's service.

More specific information about foreigners can be found in one of the earliest letters written by Fulbert of Chartres to Bonipert, the bishop of Pécs. Here, Fulbert confirms to his friend that he has complied with his request to obtain a copy of Priscian's *Grammatica* for the church school in Pécs.[10] Besides serving as evidence of the earliest phase of the school at Pécs, the letter also provides information about Bonipert himself, who — like many of his fellow bishops in central Europe during the first half of the eleventh century — came from France.[11] But not only were the ecclesiastical elite groups 'hired' from foreign European regions, but the knights themselves were too. The German noblemen Hont and Pázmány helped King St Stephen to overwhelm his competitor, Koppány, in 997, as is known from the

---

6   For the first example, see Szekfű, 'Még egyszer középkori kissebségeinkről'.
7   Guoth, 'Egy forrás két történetszemlélet tükrében'.
8   Mályusz, 'Az egynyelvű ország', pp. 55–56; Szűcs, 'Szent István intelmei', p. 286.
9   *Libellus de institutione morum*, pp. 624–25: 'Roma vero usque hodie esset ancilla, nisi Eneades fecissent illam liberam. Sicut enim ex diversis partibus et provinciis veniunt hospites, ita diversas linguas et consuetudines, diversaque documenta et arma secum ducunt, que omnia regna ornant et magnificant aulam et perterritant exterorum arrogantiam.ita diversas linguas et consuetudines, diversaque documenta et arma secum ducunt'.
10 *Diplomata Hungariae Antiquissima*, no. 18, p. 104.
11 On Bonipert, see Fedeles and Koszta, *Pécs (Fünfkirchen)*, pp. 43–46; on the content of the letter, see especially p. 44.

foundation charter of the Benedictine abbey of Pannonhalma.[12] The two knights were richly rewarded by the king: Hont's and his clan name survives in the name of the county of Hont, which still exists today. Pázmány became the ancestor of the famous *gens* Pázmány, whose members played a significant role in the medieval history of Hungary.[13] These two particular examples confirm that although the elite groups were described in the sources with the modern term 'foreigners', their ethnicity was of little or no significance for the royal court in comparison to personal bonds, *fidelitas*,[14] and their Christian faith.

Kings from the House of Anjou

The first proof of the distinction between domestic and foreign elite groups is the initial illumination of the so-called *Chronicon Pictum Vindobonense*.[15] This elegantly decorated chronicle is one of the texts which conveys the *Hungarian Chronicle Composition* compiled by the Anjou dynasty. It must have been written around 1358. The text itself is complicated in character, since it contains practically all the narratives written about the Hungarian royal court since the middle or the end of the eleventh century.[16] But the illuminations were prepared in the fourteenth century to spread the political and philosophical ideals of the ruling dynasty.[17] In the illumination in question (Figure 10.1), King Louis I the Great is shown among the Hungarian elites, who are dressed differently. One group, standing to the heraldic right of the king, is wearing Western-style clothes, while the others, standing to the king's left, are depicted in oriental dress.[18]

The interpretation of this illumination has caused a lot of debate among scholars.[19] The most credible explanation is that the two differently dressed groups represent the ancient and traditional Hungarian elites from the late Arpadian age (on the king's left) and the newcomers, who had been invited to the court of the Angevins from abroad, mainly from western Europe (on the king's right).[20] The illumination, of course, has, first of all, an allegorical meaning. The kings from the House of Anjou were the first rulers in the history of Hungary who tried to modernize the kingdom; they introduced reforms based on western European administrative practices.[21]

---

12 *Diplomata Hungariae Antiquissima*, no. 5/II. po. 39: 'asdtantibus ducibus videlicet Poznano, Cuntio, Orzio'. According to the *Hungarian Chronicle Composition* Hont and Pázmány belonged to the highest military ranks in Hungary. See *Chronici Hungarici compositio saeculi XIV*, c. 64, p. 313: 'ibique [scil. Stephanus] ad custodiam corporalis salutis suae duos principes Hunt et Pazman constituit'.
13 See Veszprémy, 'Hont', p. 267; Veszprémy, 'Szent István felövezéséről'.
14 On fidelity, see Bagi, *Divisio Regni*, pp. 168–98.
15 See *Képes Krónika*.
16 See Kornél Szovák in *Képes Krónika*, p. 224.
17 Marosi, *Kép és hasonmás*.
18 *Képes Krónika*.
19 See for example Bak, 'Harcosok vagy ősök?'.
20 Marosi, *Kép és hasonmás*, pp. 124–25.
21 Engel, *The Realm of Saint Stephen*, pp. 141–42.

Figure 10.1. First page of Vienna Illuminated Chronicle / *Chronicon Pictum Vindobonense* / *Képes Krónika*. Source: Wikimedia Commons, <https://commons.wikimedia.org/wiki/File:K%C3%A9pes_Kr%C3%B3nika_1360.jpg>. Image in the public domain.

However, they were also the first ones who had to acknowledge and accept that royal policy would face resistance from members of the traditional legal communities. Those communities, depicted as oriental 'ancients', had earned their privileges and rights from the Arpadian kings, the predecessors of the Anjou dynasty who were by then on the Hungarian throne, and were trying to preserve them against royal policy during the fourteenth century.

But as well as the allegorical interpretation, this illumination is also evidence of the changes within the ethnic make-up of the Hungarian elites. During the long reign of the Anjou kings, besides the old noble families, who supported the new dynasty during the struggles for the throne between 1301 and 1310,[22] among newly emerging clans of Hungarian origin we can find a lot of newcomers from various parts of Europe.[23] One of the most significant examples is a noble family of Italian origin — the Drugeths.[24] They came to Hungary with Carl I of Anjou and had eminent careers at the Hungarian court. Philip and John, two of the three Drugeth brothers, achieved the highest royal dignity: they became palatines.[25] But it was not only Italian noblemen who enriched the Angevin court. Carl I of Anjou was married to Elisabeth of Poland, the daughter of the King Władysław I the Elbow-High of Poland.[26] Therefore, during the entire Anjou period in Hungarian history we can find Polish noblemen among the members of the royal court. The two most important representatives of this group were undoubtedly Duke Władysław of Opole and Ścibor of Ściborzyce; the former had a lot of important positions in the political hierarchy of the Kingdom of Hungary. After being *comes* of several counties, he achieved the highest position amongst the courtly offices: he became royal palatine and played a significant role in the takeover of power in Cracow by Louis the Great in 1370.[27] Ścibor of Ściborzyce belonged to the latest elite of the Anjou court, but his career had begun during Sigismund of Luxemburg's reign.[28]

To conclude, it should be asserted that the lay and ecclesiastical elites of the medieval Kingdom of Hungary were international in character until the end of the fourteenth century. They looked, if we can overemphasize a little, like the board of a modern supranational company. The internationalization not only affected the highest ranks: even the provincial cathedral chapters consisted of more and more canons of foreign provenance.[29] However, ethnicity and ethnic diversity did not play a significant role in the selection for an office. The fidelity and loyalty to the king sealed by the estates and goods donated by a king guaranteed peace and order better than our contemporary, generic concepts of how societies functioned.

---

22 Zsoldos, 'Hűséges oligarchák', pp. 347–54.

23 Engel, 'Nagy Lajos bárói'.

24 See generally Engel, 'Druget', p. 174; Zsoldos, 'A Druget-vagyon születése', pp. 63–65.

25 Engel, *Középkori magyar adattár*, p. 225.

26 Dąbrowski, *Elżbieta Łokietówna*; recently Marzec, *Pod rządami nieobecnego monarchy*, p. 34; Bagi, *Az Anjouk Krakkóban*, p. 26.

27 Pór, *Opuli László herceg*; Sroka, *Książę Władysław Opolczyk na Węgrzech*.

28 See Dvořaková, *Rytier a jeho kráľ*.

29 Fedeles, *Die personelle Zusammensetzung des Domkapitels*, p. 245.

Late Medieval Changes

The situation started to change after the extinction of the Hungarian branch of the Anjou dynasty in 1387. After Queen Maria of Anjou (1382–1387) died suddenly, her husband, Sigismund of Luxemburg, was elected King of Hungary.[30] His legal status was, however, different from his predecessors. The Anjou rulers regarded themselves as successors of the blood of the Holy Kings,[31] that is, the Arpads. But with their extinction, the bloodline of the prime dynasty was broken. Sigismund was regarded as a new, indeed foreign, ruler, who had to be elected by the Hungarian elites.[32] The early years of Sigismund's rule were filled with conflicts. The groups of the political elites, who elected him, were united in diverse alliances, the so-called leagues, against both the king and each other. The situation escalated after the Battle of Nicopolis in 1396, which ended with the defeat of the Hungarian army and meant a loss of face for the king who was the main commander during the battle.[33] Worse still, in 1403 Sigmund was captured and arrested by the leagues of barons and had to negotiate his political future with them.[34]

The conflict was solved by disbanding all the leagues in the country and by creating a new one under the king's auspices. It incorporated both the aristocrats and the king and his men. This new corporation was called the Dragon Order, a special social group created by the ruler himself,[35] which served as a pool for all future aides of the king.[36] If the Hungarian elites during the Anjou age looked like the multi-ethnic board of an international company, Sigismund's Dragon Order surpassed its limits significantly. The Dragon Order was dedicated to ensuring peace in the country between the elite groups and the ruler himself. Among the first generation of members, we can find barons and noblemen of two diverse origins. Some of them originated from the late Angevin Hungarian elite, whilst others belonged to the new *amici* of the king. Although the romantic historiography and some national Marxist authors tried to make a distinction between the native Hungarians and foreigners within Sigismund's elite,[37] the situation was much more complicated. With regard to their ethnic origin, we can find a very diverse and multicoloured picture.

One of the most influential members of the Order was John of Garai (Garai János), the son of the late palatine Nicolaus of Garai. The ethnic roots of the family must have been in Croatia, but at the beginning of the fifteenth century it belonged to one of

---

30 On Sigismund's reign, see generally Mályusz, *Kaiser Sigismund in Ungarn*.
31 Pór and Schönherr, *Az Anjou ház és örökösei*, pp. 3–4.
32 Mályusz, *Kaiser Sigismund in Ungarn*, p. 34.
33 Pálosfalvi, *Nikápolytól Mohácsig*, pp. 12–17.
34 Mályusz, *Kaiser Sigismund in Ungarn*, pp. 39–54. See furthermore Engel, *Királyi hatalom és arisztokrácia*.
35 For the creation and existence of social groups in the Middle Ages, see Althoff, *Verwandte, Freunde und Getreue*.
36 Mályusz, *Kaiser Sigismund in Ungarn*, p. 56.
37 Pór and Schönherr, *Az Anjou ház és örökösei*, p. 347.

the most eminent late Arpadian noble clans (Dorozsma).[38] John of Garai's family was primarily one of the notorious enemies of the new king. Indeed, he was a member of the group who had captured Sigismund in 1401. Peter of Perényi also belonged to the same kind of noblemen. His family's rise to prominence had taken place in the late Arpadian period, but unlike John of Garai, he was, even before 1403, one of Sigismund's friends. On the other hand, we can find a lot of the Order members who did not have Hungarian origins or past. One of them, Herrmann of Cilli, was an old friend of Sigismund.[39] He had saved the king's life in the Battle of Nicopolis in 1396, and he played until 1456 an important role in the political life of Hungary. Indeed, he became the king's father-in-law, as Sigismund married Barbara, his daughter.[40] We also find among the Order members Philippo Scolari and Stibor of Stiboric. Scolari is commonly known as Pipo of Ozora. Pipo of Ozora was of Italian origin, and his career began in the last years of the Anjou dynasty in Hungary.[41] He was one of the closest allies of the king, and one whose religiosity has been well known since his lifetime.[42] Stibor of Stiboric has already been mentioned: he came from Poland, and his career had started during the reign of the Anjous.

To make a partial summary at this point, we can assert that contrary to some opinions represented in the earlier historiography, the divisions within the Hungarian elite were not caused by the ethnic origin of its members, but by their political choices — against or for the king. The Dragon Order tried to bridge this confrontation, uniting both the friends and enemies of the king in the same corporation. Focusing attention on the multi-ethnic composition of the Hungarian elites in the fifteenth century, it is worth pondering, who — as a group — were the 'foreigners' that played an important role in politics, and whether we can notice changes in their place of origin.

When analysing the composition of the Hungarian barons who influenced royal politics during Sigismund's reign, we have to note that primarily they came from the Westernized regions of the Kingdom of Hungary. This was partially the result of the political reality of the Anjou period (ruling the territories of Poland and Italy), and partly that of Sigismund's political choices, such as his warm acceptance of migrants and aristocrats from Styria, where the counts of Cille came from. It also mirrored the geopolitical position of Hungary. But as time went by, the political interests of both the king and Hungarians changed, and this caused a change in the provenience of the elite too. The change in the political interests of Hungary was determined first of all by the emergence of the Ottoman Empire, which at the beginning of the fifteenth century had already reached the Balkans and become a neighbour of Hungary. The new challenge from the south-east increased the importance of the countries located between the Ottoman Empire and Hungary: Moldavia, Wallachia, Bosnia, and Serbia. The changed situation influenced both military activities undertaken during the fifteenth century (creating a double defensive line on the south-eastern

---

38 Wertner, *A magyar nemzetségek a a XIV*, pp. 57–59; Engel, 'Druget', p. 229.
39 On his life, see Engel, 'Zsigmond bárói'.
40 Fößel, 'Barbaravon Cilli'; Dvořaková, *Barbara von Cilli*.
41 Prajda, 'The Florentine Scolari Family'.
42 Fedeles and Prajda, '"Olyan vallásosan, szokásaiban és életmódjában olyan mértéktartóan élt"'.

border of the country) and the process of change in the ethnic composition of the Hungarian elites. On the one hand, from Sigismund's reign on we can observe the appearance of newcomers, partially of foreign origin, who started serving the king primarily in lower positions, but with time achieved promotion to the top echelons of a courtly career. On the other hand, the changes affected the highest strata of the elite.

One of the most spectacular examples of the first group of newcomers is the family of the Hunyadis.[43] János Hunyadi was probably of foreign origin: his father came from Walachia and started serving Sigismund after 1409. János Hunyadi himself had been born in Kolozsvár/Klausenburg/Cluj, and he rose up the royal court from office to office during Sigismund's reign, until he obtained important political and military positions after 1453. Based upon his political connections, his son, Mátyás Hunyadi, would reach the royal throne.[44] We must add that the rapid and successful career of this newcomer family could never have come about without János Hunyadi's family relations with other clans in a similar aristocratic position. His wife, Elisabeth of Szilágyi, came from a comparable newcomer family but of Hungarian origin.

More interesting are the changes in the class of the most influential barons. From the third decade of the fifteenth century among them appeared aristocrats from southern countries: the despot of Serbia, Georg of Brankovic,[45] and the dukes of Wallachia, Vlad Tepes and his son of the same name. Brankovic was the nephew of Stefan Lazarevic, the former Serbian duke who was one of King Sigismund's oldest allies, and he possessed a lot of domains in Hungary. Brankovic inherited not only the throne of Serbia from his uncle, but also his possessions in Hungary, and when the Ottomans occupied Serbia in 1439, he escaped to Hungary. He was one of the key figures in the peace negotiations with the Ottomans in 1444 before the Battle of Varna, where the Polish and Hungarian king Władysław I (in Poland, III Warneńczyk) was killed.[46] The sultan offered ten years of peace to Hungary and promised to give back Brankovic's Serbian castles and possessions. Brankovic as one of the most influential political actors in Hungary convinced János Hunyadi to support this idea: in return, Hunyadi might have obtained Brankovic's possessions located in Hungary, which would not have been essential for the Serbian ruler after he had got back his ancient domains. The case shows clearly how particular interests and ethnic affiliation could influence historic events. The tragic finale of the operation is commonly known. The papal legate, Giuliano Cesarini, talked King Władysław into ambushing the Ottomans, who — we need to add — had met the terms of the peace treaty correctly. King Władysław never came back from the battlefield. Brankovic got back his possessions for a while, but went over to the Ottomans. Hunyadi was the only one who gained from the conflict, since he obtained Brankovic's domains. Duke Brankovic's case provides proof both for the modification of the elite in Hungary and for the weaknesses of the durability of the new friendships among the new members of the Hungarian elite.

---

43 Kovács, 'A Hunyadi család'; Pálosfalvi, *A Hunyadiak kora 1437–1490*.
44 Hoensch, *Mathias Corvinus*; Kubinyi, *Mátyás király*.
45 Pálosfalvi, 'A Brankovicsok a középkori magyar királyságban'.
46 Engel, 'A szegedi eskü és a váradi béke'.

If Brankovic was an unreliable friend of the kings of Hungary, their relationship with the dukes of Wallachia was even more dubious. Due to the increasing Ottoman expansion in the Balkans, the duchy of Wallachia had become since the third decade of the fifteenth century one of the most important new allies of Hungary. Vlad Tepes II (1436–1447) was the first Wallachian ruler who had been involved in the social network of the Hungarian king, since in 1431 he had become a member of the Dragon Order. The title and the friendship with the rulers of Hungary was transferred to his son, Vlad Tepes III, called the Dracula (1448–1476). The cognomen, which became famous worldwide from the twentieth century onwards, meant first of all dragon and devil, and indicated membership in the Dragon Order. Michel Beheim, one of the most important German writers of the fifteenth century, recorded the first story about the cruelty of the duke.[47] His description of Vlad Tepes III spread in Europe,[48] and Bram Stoker's nineteenth-century novel *Dracula* was based on this image,[49] which became the basis for the diverse Dracula movies of the twentieth century. While Stoker's story is a real belletrist fiction, based upon the information gained from Ármi Vámbéry, the famous Hungarian orientalist, who met Stoker in London and explained to him the story of Vlad Tepes, in reality, both father and son represented a new kind of late medieval south-eastern European ruler. They were balanced between the Ottoman Empire and the Kingdom of Hungary, trying to survive between the two major powers. Vlad Tepes III must have had an uncertain relationship with the Hungarian king Mathias Corvinus. On the one hand, he betrayed the Hungarian king and was captured by him. The significance of this affair is even shown by one poem by the famous humanist and bishop of Pécs, Janus Pannonius. The duke was simply called a tyrant,[50] and due to the fact that this epigram was written for Mathias Corvinus, we have no reason to doubt that he had lost the favour of the Hungarian ruler. On the other hand, there is a fragment in a charter issued for a house sold in Pécs from 1489. The house was named Drakulyaháza in this charter,[51] which might indicate that Vlad Tepes had a domicile there with his second wife, Justina Szilágyi, who was related to the Hungarian king.[52] If this information is correct, we would have to accept that the Walachian ruler was even taken into the royal family.

Conclusions

To sum up: the Kingdom of Hungary was from the beginnings of its history a multi-ethnic society, and as everywhere in the eastern-central European states, even the political and ecclesiastical elites were recruited from different parts of Europe. But during the eleventh to thirteenth centuries, ethnicity did not play a significant role in political

---

47 Beheim, 'Von ainem wutrich der hies Trakle waida von der Walachei', pp. 285–316. See Salgó, 'Drakula története és a korabeli sajtó'.

48 Bohn, Einax, and Rohdewald, 'Vlad der Pfähler als historische Reizfigur'.

49 Stoker, *Dracula*.

50 Pannonius, 'De captivitate Dragulae Waiwodae Transalpini', v. 1: 'captus fert vincula tyrannus'.

51 See Slov. Národ. Archív, Archives of Révay Family, Diplomas, No U587.

52 To this question, see Fedeles, 'Drawlyahaza'.

activities and the choices of foreigners during their stay in the kingdom. They integrated with the local elites and supported their hosts — kings or ecclesiastical institutions — regardless of their own ethnic identity. Changes in the role played by foreigners can be observed right after the extinction of the Arpads, but the radical shift came during the reign of Sigismund of Luxemburg. The king himself was a foreigner, and to ensure a peaceful reign, he created a new group of elites, involving new and mostly foreign people. Their ethnic composition represented both the royal political interests and its changes during the fifteenth century. The changes can be observed especially after the threat of Ottoman invasion had increased in the second half of the fifteenth century. In that moment the ethnic character of the foreigners changed. Instead of nobles and aristocrats of western (Italy, Germany, Austria) or northern (Poland) origin, a new network of royal friends appears, who came mostly from south-eastern Europe.

Works Cited

Manuscripts and Archival Sources

Bratislava, Slovenský Národný Archív, Central Archives of the Révay Family, Diplomas, No U587 (online: Magyar Nemzeti Levéltár (Hungarian National Archives), Fényképgyűjtemény (Photo collection), no. 260135, <https://archives.hungaricana. hu/hu/charters/226443/>

Primary Sources

Beheim, Michel, 'Von ainem wutrich der hies Trakle waida von der Walachei', in *Die Gedichte des Michel Beheim: Nach der Heidelberger Hs. cpg 334 unter Heranziehung der Heilderberger Hs cpg 312 und der Münchener Hs cgm 291 sowie sämtlicher Teilhandschriften,* I: *Gedichte Nr. 1–147,* ed. by Hans Gille and Ingeborg Spriewald (Berlin: Akademie Verlag, 1968), pp. 285–316
Chronici Hungarici compositio saeculi XIV, ed. by Alexander Domanovszky, Scriptores Rerum Hungaricarum I, edendo operi praefuit Emericus Szentpétery (Budapest: Budapest Academie Litterarum Typographia Universitatis, 1938)
Diplomata Hungariae Antiquissima: Accedunt epistolae et acta ad historiam Hungariae pertinentia, vol. I, ed. by Gregorius Györffy (Budapest: in aedibus Academiae Scientiarium Hungaricae, 1992)
Képes Krónika, trans. by János Bollók, commentary by Kornél Szovák and László Veszprémy, study and bibliography collected by Kornél Szovák (Budapest: Osiris, 2004), <https://web.archive.org/web/20120304111134/http://konyv-e.hu/pdf/ Chronica_Picta.pdf> [accessed 7 December 2019]
Libellus de institutione morum, ed. by Iosephus Balogh, Scriptores Rerum Hungaricarum I, edendo operi praefuit Emericus Szentpétery, vol. II (Budapest: Budapest Academie Litterarum Typographia Universitatis, 1938)
Pannonius, Janus, 'De captivitate Dragulae Waiwodae Transalpini', in *Jani Pannonii opera omnia,* ed. by Sándor V. Kovács (Budapest: Tankönyvkiadó, 1987), no. 372

Secondary Studies

Althoff, Gerd, *Verwandte, Freunde und Getreue: Zum politischen Stellenwert der Gruppenbildungen im frühen Mittelalter* (Darmstadt: Wissenschaftliche Buchgesellschaft, 1990)

Bagi, Daniel, *Az Anjouk Krakkóban: Nagy Lajos lengyelországi uralmának belpolitikai kérdései* (Pécs: Kronosz Kiadó, 2014)

——, *Divisio Regni: The Territorial Divisions, Power Struggles, and Dynastic Historiography of the Árpáds of 11th- and Early 12th-Century Hungary, with Comparative Studies of the Piasts of Poland and the Přemyslids of Bohemia* (Budapest: Research Centre for the Humanities, 2020)

Bak, János M., 'Harcosok vagy ősök? Még egyszer a képes krónika címlapjáról', *BUKSZ — Budapesti Könyvszemle*, 10 (1998), 65–66

Berend, Nora, *At the Gate of Christendom: Jews, Muslims and 'Pagans' in Medieval Hungary, c. 1000–1300* (Cambridge: Cambridge University Press, 2000)

Bohn, Thomas M., Rayk Einax, and Stefan Rohdewald, 'Vlad der Pfähler als historische Reizfigur', in *Vlad der Pfähler — Dracula. Tyrann oder Volkstribun?*, ed. by Thomas M. Bohn, Rayk Einax, and Stefan Rohdewald (Wiesbaden: Harrassowitz Verlag, 2017), pp. 9–20

Dąbrowski, Jan, *Elżbieta Łokietówna* (Kraków: Akademia Umiejętności, Drukarnia Uniwersytetu Jagiellońskiego, 1914)

Dvořaková, Daniela, *Barbara von Cilli: Die schwarze Königin (1392–1451). Die Lebensgeschichte einer ungarischen, römisch-deutschen und böhmischen Königin* (Frankfurt: Peter Lang Verlag, 2017)

——, *Rytier a jeho kráľ: Stibor zo Stiboríc a Žigmund Luxemburský. Sonda do života stredovekého šľachtica s osobitým zreteľom na územie Slovenska* (Bratislava: Rak, 2003)

Engel, Pál, 'Druget', in *Korai Magyar Történeti Lexikon*, ed. by Gyula Kristó (Budapest: Akadémiai Kiadó, 1996), p. 176

——, *Királyi hatalom és arisztokrácia viszonya a Zsigmond-korban (1387–1437)* (Budapest: Akadémiai Kiadó, 1977)

——, *Középkori magyar adattár: Magyarország világi archontológiája 1301–1457* (Budapest: Arcanum, 2001)

——, 'Nagy Lajos bárói', *Történelmi Szemle*, 28.3 (1985), 393–413

——, *The Realm of St Stephen: A History of Hungary, 895–1526* (London: Bloomsbury, 2005)

——, 'A szegedi eskü és a váradi béke: Adalék az 1444. év eseménytörténetéhez', in *Mályusz Elemér Emlékkönyv*, ed. by Éva H. Balázs, Erik Fügedi, and Ferenc Maksay (Budapest: Akadémiai Kiadó, 1984), pp. 77–96

——, 'Zsigmond bárói', in *Művészet Zsigmond király korában*, ed. by László Beke and others, vol. I: *Tanulmányok* (Budapest: Müvészettörténeti Kutató Csoport, 1987), pp. 114–19

Fedeles, Tamás, 'Drawlyahaza', in *Fons, skepsis, lex: Ünnepi tanulmányok a 70 esztendős Makk Ferenc tiszteletére*, ed. by Tibor Almási and others (Szeged: SZTE Történeti Segédtudományok Tanszék, Szegedi Középkorász Műhely, 2010), pp. 107–14

——, *Die personelle Zusammensetzung des Domkapitels zu Fünfkirchen im Spätmittelalter (1354–1526)* (Regensburg: Verlag Ungarisches Institut, 2012)

Fedeles, Tamás, and László Koszta, *Pécs (Fünfkirchen): Das Bistum und die Bischofsstadt im Mittelalter* (Vienna: Institut für Ungarische Geschichtsforschung, 2011)

Fedeles, Tamás, and Katalin Prajda, '"Olyan vallásosan, szokásaiban és életmódjában olyan mértéktartóan élt", Adalékok Filippo Scolari és családja vallásosságához', *Történelmi Szemle*, 56.3 (2014), 357–82

Fößel, Amalie, 'Barbaravon Cilli: Ihre frühen Jahre als Gemahlin Sigismunds und ungarische Königin', in *Sigismund von Luxemburg — ein Kaiser in Europa. Tagungsband des internationalen historischen und kunsthistorischen Kongresses in Luxemburg, 8.–10. Juni 2005*, ed. by Michel Pauly and François Reinert (Mainz am Rhein: P. von Zabern, 2006), pp. 95–112

Guoth, Kálmán, 'Egy forrás két történetszemlélet tükrében', *Századok*, 76 (1942), 43–64

Györffy, György, *A magyarság keleti elemei* (Budapest: Gondolat Kiadó, 1990)

Hoensch, Jörg K., *Mathias Corvinus: Diplomat, Feldherr und Mäzen* (Graz: Styria, 1998)

Kovács, Péter E., 'A Hunyadi család', in *Hunyadi Mátyás: Emlékkönyv Mátyás király halálának 500. Évfordulójára*, ed. by Gyula Rázsó and László V. Molnár (Budapest: Zrínyi Kiadó, 1990), pp. 29–51

Kristó, Gyula, 'Oroszok az Árpád-kori Magyarországon', in *Tanulmányok az Árpád-korról* (Budapest: Magvető Könyvkiadó, 1983), pp. 191–207

Kubinyi, András, *Mátyás király* (Budapest: Vince, 2001)

Mályusz, Elemér, 'Az egynyelvű ország', in *Klió szolgálatában: Válogatott történelmi tanulmányok* (Budapest: MTA Történettudományi Intézet, 2003), pp. 53–72

——, *Kaiser Sigismund in Ungarn 1387–1437* (Budapest: Akadémiai Kiadó, 1990)

Marosi, Ernő, *Kép és hasonmás: Művészet és valóság a 14–15. századi Magyarországon* (Budapest: Akadémiai Kiadó, 1995)

Marzec, Andrzej, *Pod rządami nieobecnego monarchy: Królestwo polskie 1370–1382* (Kraków: Societas Vistulana, 2017)

Pálosfalvi, Tamás, 'A Brankovicsok a középkori magyar királyságban: Szerb, magyar, török érdekharcok a 15. Században', *Historia*, 32 (2010), 6–9

——, *A Hunyadiak kora 1437–1490* (Budapest: Kossuth, 2009)

——, *Nikápolytól Mohácsig* (Budapest: Zrínyi, 2005)

Pór, Antal, *Opuli László herceg: Magyarország nádorispánja* (Budapest: Magyar Tudományos Akadémia, 1909)

Pór, Antal, and Gyula Schönherr, *Az Anjou ház és örökösei (1301–1439)*, A magyar nemzet története, 3 (Budapest: Athenaeum részvénytársulat betűivel, 1895)

Prajda, Katalin, 'The Florentine Scolari Family', *Journal of Early Modern History*, 14 (2010), 513–33

Salgó, Ágnes W., 'Drakula története és a korabeli sajtó', *Világtörténet*, 32 (2010), 28–37

Sroka, Stanisław A., *Książę Władysław Opolczyk na Węgrzech: Studium z dziejów stosunkówe polsko-węgierskich w XIV wieku* (Kraków: Wydawnictwo PiT, 1996)

Stoker, Bram, *Dracula* (Westminster: Archibald Constable and Company, 1897)

Szekfű, Gyula, 'Még egyszer középkori kissebségeinkről', *Magyar Szemle*, 39 (1940), 169–77

Szűcs, Jenő, 'Szent István intelmei: Az első magyarországi államelméleti mű', in *Szent István és az államalapítás*, ed. by László Veszprémy (Budapest: Osiris Kiadó, 2002)

Veszprémy, László, 'Hont', in *Korai Magyar Történeti Lexikon*, ed. by Gyula Kristó (Budapest: Akadémiai Kiadó, 1996), pp. 267–68

———, 'Szent István felövezéséről', *Hadtörténeti Közlemények*, 36 (1989), 3–13

Wertner, Mór, *A magyar nemzetségek a a XIV. század közepéig*, vols I–II (Temesvár: Magyar Tudományos Akadémia, 1891–1892)

Zsoldos, Attila, 'A Druget-vagyon születése', in *Művészet és mesterség: Tisztelgő kötet R. Várkonyi Ágnes emlékére*, vols I–II (Budapest: L'Harmattan, 2016), pp. 63–85

———, 'Hűséges oligarchák', in *A történettudomány szolgálatában: Tanulmányok a 70 éves Gecsényi Lajos tiszteletére*, ed. by Magdolna Baráth and Antal Molnár (Budapest: Magyar Nemzeti Levéltár, 2012), pp. 347–56

MONIKA RAMONAITĖ

The Medical Marketplace as a Way of Communicating beyond Religion

Non-Christian Medical Practitioners in the Society of the Grand Duchy of Lithuania

Moving from central Europe to the east, in the following chapters we enter the history of the Grand Duchy of Lithuania (GDL). It was a special political organization which had linked together many ethnic and religious communities since the late Middle Ages. The supreme authority of the Grand Duke of Lithuania was often associated with the dignity of the King of Poland from 1385, and always between 1569 and 1795. The influence of the grand duke on life in the principality was strong until the end of the fifteenth century, but it was weakened in the modern period. The vast territory of the state was inhabited by dozens of diverse ethnic communities. There were a lot of tensions and even conflicts between all of them, although they found ways to cooperate in daily and economic life. To what extent were the unique cultural and economic conditions that forced daily cooperation between different ethnic and religious groups responsible for this state of affairs?

In this chapter, we will look at a specific type of relationship between members of distinct ethnic and religious groups. Maintaining health is one of the basic human needs. It is closely related to the need to be open to the interference of another human being. The doctor is both a guarantee of the patient's safety and a potential threat to his life. The patient has to trust the doctor at a critical moment in his life. Was it, then, in an exceptional situation common in everyday life, and at the same time having the character of a borderline situation, that people were able to overcome potential fears of the 'Other', of people from other ethnic and religious communities? In this chapter, I focus on non-Christians (Jews and Karaites), who provided medical services to Christians, their position within the medical marketplace in the GDL, as well as society's attitude towards them. The aims of this research are to determine

Monika Ramonaitė • (ramonaitem@gmail.com) is Director of Vilnius University Museum and lecturer at the Medicine faculty of Vilnius University. Her research is focused on the history of medicine, science, and education in the Grand Duchy of Lithuania and eastern Europe.

Inter-Ethnic Relations and the Functioning of Multi-Ethnic Societies: Cohesion in Multi-Ethnic Societies in Europe from c. 1000 to the Present, II, ed. by Przemysław Wiszewski, EER 18 (Turnhout: Brepols, 2022), pp. 263–290

BREPOLS ❧ PUBLISHERS   10.1484/M.EER-EB.5.132155

This is an open access chapter made available under a cc by-nc 4.0 International License.

Map 11.1. The Lithuanian State in the thirteenth–fifteenth centuries. Source: <https://commons.wikimedia.org/wiki/File:Lithuanian_state_in_13-15th_centuries.png>. CC BY-SA 2.5.

the educational and occupational opportunities for Jewish and Karaite medical practitioners in this Christian environment. Furthermore, I will attempt to ascertain how important the religious aspects were when Christians in the GDL evaluated and chose non-Christian medical services.

Introduction

The term *medical marketplace* has been used for over thirty years. At the beginning it was used in Anglophone texts, related to the healthcare history of England. This term was defined as the commercializing of medical services, healthcare, and medical practitioners' diversity, which used to be regulated by legal, economic, and sociocultural factors.[1] Soon it was used in research on the history of healthcare in other Western countries, such as Italy, France, the Netherlands, as well as in German cities.[2]

The term *medical marketplace* has not been used in Poland and the GDL in research relating to the history of medicine. I will refer to the Harold Cook thesis, which states that a medical marketplace forms only after a variety of different medical practitioners emerge.[3] As a result, I define the medical marketplace as a plurality of medical services, which included legal or regulated medical practitioners and various illegal unqualified healers, their relationships and interactions. This definition also includes medical service supply and demand in specific areas of countries.

Katherine Park in her research about early modern medicine in Florence has found that the medical marketplace was highly influenced by non-economic phenomena, such as the sociocultural environment, informal personal relationships, religious beliefs, and personal values.[4] Health itself used to be one of the most important and fragile values, which was believed to be dependent on God's will. Usually, patients would establish personal relationships with doctors as clientele, and trust between them was important. In Christian Europe, selecting the right healing methods and medical services was strongly connected with religious self-consciousness. For instance, the Church would allow you only a certain set of healing methods. As an example, all kinds of magic were forbidden, and also only certain personnel would be allowed. Nonetheless, under extreme health circumstances, even the Church's laws and public opinion were quite often ignored.

But in this article, I focus on non-Christians (Jews and Karaites), who were providing medical services to Christians, their position within the medical marketplace in the GDL as well as society's attitude towards them. The aims of this research are to determine the educational and occupational opportunities for Jewish and Karaite medical practitioners in this Christian environment. Furthermore, I will attempt to

---

1 On this topic, see more in Jenner and Wallis, 'The Medical Marketplace'.
2 Gentilcore, *Healers and Healing*; Cook, *The Decline of the Old Medical Regime*; Park, *Doctors and Medicine*; Ramsey, *Professional and Popular Medicine*.
3 Cook, *The Decline of the Old Medical Regime*.
4 Park, *Doctors and Medicine*.

266 MONIKA RAMONAITĖ

ascertain how important the religious aspects were when evaluating and choosing non-Christian medical services.

Scholars have already drawn attention to the existence of Jewish and Karaite medical practices in the Polish-Lithuanian Commonwealth's society. However, nobody so far has tried to research non-Christian medical practitioners as a single group in the general GDL and Polish medical marketplace; this is what I seek to undertake here. In the context of this study, it should be noted that M. Kizilov examines in his article Jewish and Karaite medical personnel and their relationships with the court of the Polish king Jan Sobieski.[5] I. N. Gath in his article challenged M. Kizilov and revealed that there were possibilities for the Karaites to gain a medical degree and work as physicians.[6] M. Horn's and M. Bersohn's studies are valuable because of the large amount of biographical data for Jewish doctors from the sixteenth to the eighteenth centuries.[7]

Various sources were used to study Jewish doctors and their services in the GDL society. Jewish medical practitioners were mentioned in legal sources, such as Jewish privileges or court cases.[8] Jewish medics and their salaries were recorded in accessions and account books of estates.[9] The evaluation of Jewish medical practitioners who worked in the Grand Duchy of Lithuania and Poland was possible thanks to memories recorded in traveller journals, usually created by medical doctors and noblemen.[10] Hence, the books of the medical doctor S. Sleszkowski pointed out the fierce religious arguments against the Jewish physician.[11]

I will start with a presentation of the GDL medical marketplace and its specific characteristics. Later, the features of non-Christian medical personnel will be defined as well as their position within the GDL medical marketplace. Lastly, I will describe how non-Christian services were evaluated and according to which criteria by the GDL society.

The GDL Medical Marketplace: Formation and Features

The formation of a tripartite ensemble of medicine practitioners was the main factor that led to the formation of the medical market in various European countries.[12] From the beginning of the thirteenth century groups of practitioners were divided into

---

5 Kizilov, 'Karaite Joseph Ezra Dubitskii and King John III Sobieski'.

6 Gath, 'The Elusive Karaite Doctor Joseph Ezra Dubitski'.

7 Horn, 'Medycy nadworni władców'; Bersohn, *Słownik biograficzny uczonych Żydów Polskich*.

8 *Akty izdavajemyje / Акты издаваемые*, XVIII, b. 299, p. 347; Lelis, 'Medicinos pagalba Lietuvoje', pp. 121–22; Lietuvos valstybės istorijos archyvas, F. 443, ap. 2, b. 79, l. 364–423^V, b. 80, l. 606–36^V; *Russko-Jevriejskij arhiv / Русско-еврейский архив*, II, no. 137, p. 87; no. 167, p. 113.

9 *Dokumenty Moskovskogo arhiva / Документы Московского архива*, pp. 207–08; Lietuvos mokslų akademijos, Vrublevskių biblioteka, F. 37, b. 888, l. 5: *Russko-Jevriejskij arhiv / Русско-еврейский архив*, II, no. 137, p. 87; no. 167, p. 113.

10 Connor, *The History of Poland*, II, Letter IX, pp. 81, 87, 88; *Georgo Forsterio laiskai*; Byševska, *1786 metų kelionės į Vilnių dienoraštis*; 'Dyaryusz życia Ignacego Łopacińskiego'.

11 Śleszkowski, *Jasne dowody*.

12 Cook, *The Decline of the Old Medical Regime*.

physicians or medical doctors, surgeons, and apothecaries. This tripartite ensemble was recognized and separated from other professionals with several legal regulations.[13]

The activity and legitimacy of medical doctors was defined by the diploma that was given after their thesis defence at university.[14] Surgery was treated as a practical craft, and therefore a large number of surgical procedures were passed on to the barber-surgeons.[15] Their legal status was defined by the regulations and rules of their guild.[16] In order to become a fully competent barber-surgeon, it was necessary to pass exams in human anatomy and knowledge of medical treatments. These exams were usually regulated by the senior guild members and medical doctors with a university degree.[17] Guild membership guaranteed an opportunity to practice surgery.[18] They treated a variety of injuries, wounds, skin conditions, and venereal diseases.

The third type of medical assistant was pharmacists. They became the only official supplier of medicinal materials and drugs that were produced and sold in their own public pharmacies.[19] There were two ways that pharmacy shops were legalized across Europe. The first, popular in France, was when pharmacists and medical doctors were united into guilds, which were regulated by their own statutes.[20] Secondly, the German type was when pharmacists' rights were regulated by a city government's privileges and special provisions made for all pharmacy shops.[21] Such regulations were enforced in Poland, and later in the GDL as well.[22]

During the thirteenth–fifteenth centuries, medical doctors, barber-surgeons, and pharmacists became the most valued and mostly unique legal medical personnel in various European countries. The core of professional medical practitioners was surrounded by the medical marginals. They were composed of different groups of healers who operated within the core despite not having formal training or corporate status. They differed by their activities' evaluation and regulation, as well as their relationship to well-established practitioners depending on country or region.[23]

There were various medical practitioners beyond the professional legal medical establishment boundaries, but they could be divided into two main groups: folk or popular medicine practitioners, and self-educated healers or empiricists. Folk medicine practitioners used to use a variety of traditional healing methods transferred through the generations very often by word of mouth or practical experiences.[24] In one or another form this medicine was widespread, especially in the countryside, where

---

13 Gentilcore, *Medical Charlatanism*; Jenner and Wallis, 'The Medical Marketplace', p. 4; Ralley, 'Medical Economies', p. 25.
14 Lebrun, *Jak dawniej leczono*, p. 21; Talbot, 'Medical Education', p. 83.
15 Talbot, 'Medical Education', p. 80; Wallis, ed., *Medieval Medicine*, pp. 131, 315.
16 Sokół, *Historia gdańskiego cechu chirurgów*, pp. 46–37.
17 Wallis, ed., *Medieval Medicine*, pp. 281–82.
18 Porter, *The Greatest Benefit to Mankind*, p. 277.
19 Kremers and Urdang, *History of Pharmacy*, pp. 33, 58, 70.
20 Kremers and Urdang, *History of Pharmacy*, pp. 56, 67–68.
21 Kremers and Urdang, *History of Pharmacy*, pp. 85–86.
22 Sokół, *Medycyna w Gdańsku*, p. 116.
23 Cook, *Matters of Exchange*.
24 Grmek, 'The History of Medical Education in Russia', p. 303.

professional medical practitioners were scarce. Also, traditional medicine was often practised among relatives, friends, or neighbours.[25] Western European historians interpret high use of traditional medicine in the medical marketplace in various ways. First of all, this was mostly because traditional types of medical practitioners did not charge for their services; instead often a simple grateful gift was enough.[26] In the cities, these services increased the diversity of medical services.

However, I will not analyse how traditional medical practitioners belonged to the medical marketplace. Traditional medicine itself was firstly based on religious beliefs and traditions; therefore, it was fairly reserved and used only within a certain society's boundaries, mostly within groups of the same religion or creed. But in this article, I will focus on building interconnections through treatment practices between different religious and ethnic groups in traditional society.

Secondly there was the medical marginal group, which could be called a commercial services supplier, who did not belong to the tripartite ensemble medical model due to a lack of education or education in different fields. Self-educated healers or empiricists usually gained money from their invented treatments that consisted of a combination of folk medicine and academic medicine learned from books or through practical activities. They used to learn from medical doctors, books, or through watching other doctors and practising.[27] Such empirical healers often only used a single method or operation, especially those not performed by legal medical practitioners. For example, some might specialize as hernia healers which were quite dangerous surgical operations that many barber-surgeons were too scared to perform because the patient could die and they would then lose their good reputation.[28]

All these doctors usually travelled a lot for work, and they often had nicknames. Their practical ways of healing, treatment, popularity, and demands for their services mainly depended on the particular requirements of each country as well as their interactions with legal medical practitioners and local government, and public opinion about their services. Unregulated medical healers' 'success story' usually depended not only on the results of their treatment, but also on the special shows they used to prepare and perform to advertise themselves and encourage gossip to be spread.[29] The ratio between the tripartite ensembles and unprofessional medics in society, the different ways they interpreted their services, and public opinion about them were the reasons for differences either in some certain societies or regionally in the medical marketplace. In different countries their evaluation and spread differed, which was a reason why the medical marketplace became more competitive, particularly as a result of the great diversity of medical practitioners.[30]

---

25 Porter, *The Greatest Benefit to Mankind*, pp. 31, 39.
26 Ralley, 'Medical Economies', p. 25; Gentilcore, 'Was There a "Popular Medicine"?'.
27 Gentilcore, 'Was There a "Popular Medicine"?', pp. 151–54; Wallis, ed., *Medieval Medicine*, p. 335.
28 Porter, *The Greatest Benefit to Mankind*, p. 278; Rublack, 'Pregnancy, Childbirth and Female Body', p. 90.
29 Lebrun, *Jak dawniej leczono*, p. 25; Gentilcore, 'Charlatans, Mountebanks and Other Similar People', p. 299; Gentilcore, *Medical Charlatanism*, pp. 254, 255.
30 Gentilcore, 'Charlatans, the Regulated Marketplace and the Treatment of Venereal Disease', p. 69; Wallis, ed., *Medieval Medicine*, p. 313.

In western Europe, where the cities were economically strong and large and also the plurality and number of medical practitioners was high, their activities were tightly regulated by local authorities. In Italy, Britain, France, and Germany, the universities and the owners of cities used to initiate the establishment of special medical college or *protomedicus* institutions, which regulated medical practitioners' activities.[31] Medical colleges consisted of several respected and educated medical doctors from that city. All local as well as foreign medical doctors had to obtain a licence to practice from this institution. The medical college supervised the activities of barber-surgeons and pharmacists; they also sought to regulate and license some unskilled medical practitioners such as midwives, stone removers, and oculists.[32] The institution also collected medical practitioners' taxes for the cities and imposed fines on unofficial practitioners who had worked without authorization.[33] The *protomedicus* was a one-person institution — the official city physician. He had similar functions as the medical colleges. The *protomedicus* regulated the city's medical practitioners' activities, took care to protect the city's inhabitants from the plague, and ensured that inhabitants followed the instructions to guard against plague.[34]

D. Gentilcore pointed out that giving the medical college and the *protomedicus* authority over elite medical doctors had a major impact on the hostile assessment and the negative image of non-professional medical services in wider society. The elite medical practitioners were the main critics of non-professionals and fiercely opposed the inadequacy of empirics' treatment methods. However, during the sixteenth to eighteenth centuries non-professional medicine remained widely used throughout the whole of Europe.[35]

What's more, medical colleges had to give licences to those non-professional physicians who paid taxes and were allowed by the city authorities to operate in the city: for example, oculists or sometimes traditional sellers and producers of only specific balsams or drugs that were popular and considered effective. They were fully legalized and even respected in some societies despite the fact that they did not belong to the tripartite ensemble of medicine practitioners.

With respect to the GDL, the very first practitioners who represented the tripartite ensemble of medical doctors, barber-surgeons, and pharmacists only began to work at the turn of the sixteenth century in this country. The main reason for their emergence in this country was associated with the rebirth of the duke's court after a long break and the consequent spread of innovation from it.

In 1492 Alexander became the duke of the GDL, after a break of half a century; he was the first ruler who resided in the GDL permanently. After the death of Vytautas the Great, the grand duke of Lithuania in 1430, there was only one ruler

---

31 Cook, *The Decline of the Old Medical Regime*; O'Malley, 'Medical Education', p. 92; Gentilcore, 'Charlatans, the Regulated Marketplace and the Treatment of Venereal Disease', p. 58.
32 Ralley, 'Medical Economies', p. 32.
33 Cook, *The Decline of the Old Medical Regime*.
34 Gentilcore, 'Charlatans, the Regulated Marketplace and the Treatment of Venereal Disease', p. 67; Gentilcore, '"All that Pertains to Medicine"'.
35 Gentilcore, 'Charlatans, Mountebanks and Other Similar People', p. 306.

for the GDL and Poland, who usually resided in Kraków. There were some working medical doctors, pharmacists, and barber-surgeons from Poland in the environment of Alexander's court.[36] In the very beginning of the sixteenth century, Western types of medicine practitioners began to serve GDL nobles and the gentry, and later they spread to the wider range of the social stratum. The important factor which led to the increasing demand and necessity for European medical services was the increase in noblemen's educational trips to western Europe, where they became familiar with medical practices and medical science there.[37]

In 1509, the first guild of barber-surgeons was established in Vilnius, the GDL capital, and after that in other major cities too. It seems that in the GDL barber-surgeons were organized according to the statutes of the Gdańsk city barber-surgeons' guild.[38] Guild members only received a permit to treat patients after they passed the exam which was organized and supervised by medical doctors. In the beginning of the sixteenth century, the first public pharmacies were established in the GDL, which supplied drugs and medicinal materials for towns in the GDL. During 1510–1522, the first public pharmacy was founded in Vilnius.[39] At this time more foreign medical doctors began to practise in the GDL too.

Soon after the first western European medical practitioners began to work in the country, a clear division between the legitimacy of various types of personnel activities and public opinion about their activities began to emerge in the territory of the GDL. The legal medical practitioners became easily recognized and highly valued in the society of the GDL. Meanwhile, all the other healers were increasingly starting to be treated as medical marginals who were illegal, and even potentially dangerous because of their harmful treatments.[40]

Compared with other European countries, especially with those where faculties of medicine were strong, for example, in Italian cities or France, the GDL had very few medical doctors during the period between the sixteenth and eighteenth centuries; for example, during the sixteenth century there were about ninety medical doctors who practised in the Grand Duchy of Lithuania.[41]

However, medical doctors were highly respected and valued in the GDL, as a result of their education, necessity, and the authority they possessed. Usually, they practised on the ruler or the nobility's estates; this was attractive because of the good salaries that were offered and the opportunities to get financial sponsorship for publishing their works and studying abroad. Moreover, medical doctors were

---

36 Lietuvos didžiojo, pp. 88–95.
37 Lietuvos Didžiosios Kunigaikštystės, pp. 191–92, 203–06; Connor, The History of Poland, ii, Letter IX, p. 81; Vaišnoravičius, Kelionė po Europą, pp. 79–80.
38 Sokół, Historia gdańskiego cechu chirurgów, pp. 37–46; Akty cechów wileńskich, no. 4, pp. 7–9, no. 41, pp. 48–49.
39 Ragauskienė, 'Vaistininkai xvi a. Vilniujes', p. 36.
40 Gąsiorowski, Zbiór wiadomości, p. 180; 'Sukčius', in Lietuvos Didžiosios Kunigaikštystės, p. 54; Gentilcore, Medical Charlatanism, pp. 254, 255; Ramonaitė, 'Vakarų Europos medicinos', pp. 26–28.
41 Ramonaitė, 'Vakarų Europos medicinos', p. 22; Ruderman, Jewish Thought and Scientific Discovery, p. 205.

THE MEDICAL MARKETPLACE AS A WAY OF COMMUNICATING BEYOND RELIGION   271

often exempt from taxes and enjoyed property privileges as a reward for their good service.[42] A small number of medical doctors were practising in the largest cities of the GDL and in Vilnius. For this reason, as well as the high cost of their services, some social classes or citizens could not use them at all.[43]

Guilds of barber-surgeons as well as the public pharmacies were established in the main cities and towns, and it looks as if their services were available for a wider range of people in the GDL. Until 1772 there were public pharmacies in the seventeen most important cities and towns of the GDL, which officially supplied drugs and medical material not only for doctors but also for those who tried to heal themselves.[44] Barber-surgeons mostly treated injuries; they undertook so-called external medicine, like treating skin conditions, venereal disease, pulling teeth, as well as performing bloodletting — the most popular procedure for the healing of various internal diseases.[45] However, the guilds of the barber-surgeons were established only in the main centres of the GDL, and officially trained and qualified barber-surgeons weren't available in the smaller towns and villages and provincial areas, nor were remedies from city pharmacies.[46] To sum up, the core medical practitioners who belonged to the tripartite medical model became recognized, valued, and also desirable in the GDL. On the other hand, they were only available to a small part of the entire GDL community, who had these specialists on their estates or who lived in the biggest cities of the country and were able to buy these services.

The small number of legal medical practitioners, such as medical doctors and barber-surgeons, and also the extremely high prices of the medical services were the main factors that meant that the so-called non-professional irregular practitioners of medicine were popular and served the largest part of the GDL society. First of all, the services of traditional folk medicine were widely used, especially in the provincial areas of the GDL: small towns, estates, and villages, far from the main country centres and major cities.[47] Folk medicine was used by both Christian and non-Christian parts of the GDL society in their own communities.[48] As mentioned before, this type of medicine was not commercial.

Nonetheless, in the GDL the boundary between the people who were trying to make a living out of medicine and the people belonging to the tripartite ensemble was very

---

42   Grutinio Pilsnensi, *Medicus dogmaticus*; *Lietuvos Metrika (1440–1523)*, 10-oji užrašymų knyga, no. 103, p. 100; *Lietuvos Metrika (1524–1529)*, 14-oji užrašymų knyga, b. 147–50, pp. 125, 126; *Lietuvos Metrika (1528–1538)*, 15-oji užrašymų knyga, b. 58, pp. 98–99; *Lietuvos Metrika (1499–1514)*, 8-oji užrašymų knyga, no. 555, p. 405.

43   *Georgo Forsterio laiskai*, no. 33, pp. 136–37; Connor, *The History of Poland*, II, Letter IX, p. 81; Frankas, *Atsiminimai apie Vilnių*, p. 63.

44   Ramonaitė, 'Vakarų Europos medicinos', p. 25.

45   *Akty izdavajemyje / Акты издаваемые*, XVIII, no. 749, p. 29; XXI, b. 197, pp. 156–57; XXVI, no. 19, p. 11.

46   1545 m. *Kauno magistrato aktų knyga*, f. 7, b. 13840, no. 509, l. 63; 1583 m. *Kauno magistrato aktų knyga*, b. 13850, no. 559, l. 308.

47   Ramonaitė, 'Vakarų Europos medicinos', pp. 25–26.

48   Miškinienė, *Seniausi Lietuvos totorių rankraščiai*, pp. 83, 85; Muchowski, *Folk Literature of the Polish-Lithuanian Karaites*.

blurred and rather unclear. One of the reasons for this was, as we have mentioned already, the limited availability of tripartite ensemble medical practitioners in most of the GDL.

The other, most important reason was that whilst the tripartite ensemble model was adopted from other European countries and became popular in the GDL, the status of the legal practitioners was never finalized because of the failure to develop a medical college and *protomedicus* institute. Nevertheless, some of the medical services' legalizing methods had been copied from western Europe. The strictest rules were defined for public pharmacy shops and its pharmacists' legal status. The privileges given by cities clearly defined professional possibilities, duties, rights, and in some cases supervision institutes.[49] In the big cities of the GDL, barber-surgeons had their rights and duties and education clearly defined in their guild statutes.[50] In cities, where strong guilds were located, illegal barber-surgeons' activities could end up in long court trial processes. A perfect example would be a never-ending fight between barber-surgeons and the *łaziebnicy* in Vilnius, which took over two hundred years. The *łaziebnicy* were trying to take over the functions of the barber-surgeons who repeatedly complained about it to the government.[51]

However, even in the guild statutes of Vilnius, it was stated that their activities and education should be supervised by medical doctors; yet it is not clear how it was done in practice, and the references do not specify this. Nonetheless, the work of the barber-surgeons' guilds was focusing only around the main centres. It seems that most barber-surgeons, especially those who worked in provincial towns, had not been trained at the guilds or had never been examined on their medical knowledge as was stipulated in the guilds' statutes and so on.

Moreover, during the sixteenth to eighteenth centuries in the GDL there was neither any academic institution where medical subjects could be taught nor any nearby college of medicine, where the supervision of medical doctors' practice could be undertaken and their qualifications checked. It seems that even some moderate medical doctors, sometimes even without necessary education, were welcomed in this country, firstly because of the huge lack of medical service, and secondly because of the high prestige the title 'medical doctor' imparted to marginal medics.[52] Because of this lack of clarity, a niche appeared for non-professional and self-taught medical doctors. In the eighteenth century, this provoked criticism, mainly because these medical doctors lacked education, medicine was being sold by whomever, and there were very few barber-surgeons and proper medical doctors. Similar criticisms were expressed for the whole Commonwealth.[53]

---

49 1659 m. 'Boguslavo Radvilos privilegija suteikta Jonui Brezynai'; see Hačeba, 'Seniausios Lietuvoje vaistinės', pp. 12–13.

50 *Akty cechów wileńskich*, no. 4, pp. 7–9, no. 41, pp. 48–49.

51 *Akty cechów wileńskich*, no. 41, pp. 48–49.

52 *Georgo Forsterio laiskai*, no. 32, p. 132; *Akty izdavajemyje / Акты издаваемые*, XXVIII, b. 32, p. 22; Connor, *The History of Poland*, II.2, pp. 87–88.

53 Nowosielska, 'Multi Medici, multa funera'; Connor, *The History of Poland*, II.2, pp. 89–90.

Non-Christian Medical Practitioners' Place and Activities in the GDL Medical Marketplace

The sixteenth- to eighteenth-century sources from the GDL mention non-Christian practitioners who practised medicine beyond their own traditional society's boundaries. Such practitioners were mostly Jews. It is also known that there were a few Karaites. One of the traditional GDL non-Christian groups — the Tatars — has not been found within the field. However, there is still a possibility that there might have been Tatars involved; as will be noted later in this article, criticism against non-believers' medical practitioners was also applied to Tatars, although only generally.[54]

All medical practitioners — Jews and Karaites — were not a homogeneous group because of their social status, education, attitude towards their activities, and recognition. During the sixteenth to eighteenth centuries, these non-Christian medical practitioners are mentioned as medical doctors, as barber-surgeons, and starting from the second half of the eighteenth century as feldsher. At first sight, such definitions show that these non-Christians belonged to the tripartite ensemble personnel. Despite this, during this time period non-Christians had different social status, as well as different opportunities for obtaining education and for undertaking professional and economic activities in particular areas. These factors raise doubts about whether all the non-Christians could have belonged to the tripartite ensemble model of medical professionals and raise the question of whether they were characterized using such definitions. Therefore, this article will focus on Jewish and Karaite medical practitioners as a group and will analyse whether these factors had any influence on their activities, and what exact status Jewish and Karaite practitioners had in the GDL.

At the beginning of the sixteenth century, various GDL sources mention people of Jewish background described as *doktor, doctor medicinae, доктор, medicus,* or *phisicus.*[55] These terms, in the background of Christian medical practitioners, firstly meant the people who had a doctor's degree or at least a master's from a university and also had an opportunity to make a living out of medicine.[56] Meanwhile, Jewish rights (Karaite as well) to study in various European universities were highly restricted until the end of the eighteenth century.[57] As a result, it seems logical to question what were the particular reasons for Jewish and Karaite medical practitioners being called doctors, and what was their exact education.

---

54 Śleszkowski, *Jasne dowody*, p. 1.

55 *Źródła biograficzno-bibliograficzne*, pp. 118, 214, 216; 'Munus Servitoriatus Medicini Regij Infideli Peter Samson datur', in *Źródła biograficzno-bibliograficzne*, p. 594; 'Libertatio Isaac Iudaei phisici de Hispania', in *Źródła biograficzno-bibliograficzne*, p. 305.

56 O'Malley, 'Medical Education', p. 102; 1556 m. 'Jurgiui Petkūnui suteiktas medicinos ir filosofijos daktaro diplomas', Lietuvos mokslų akademijos, Vrublevskių biblioteka, RS, f. 6, b. 90.

57 Joshu Jacob Frank was the first Jewish student who gained a degree at Vilnius University in 1793: Г. Аграновский, 'Первые студенты-литваки в российских вузах', *Lechaim*, August 2013, <https://lechaim.ru/ARHIV/256/agranovskiy.htm>.

This question was partly answered by historians such as B. D. Ruderman and J. M. Efron.[58] Their work regarding the questionable Jewish education found that Jews actually had opportunities to obtain university education in medical science and law in a few universities in Europe during this time period.[59] At the beginning of the fifteenth century the University of Padua, located in the Venetian Republic, was the first to start accepting Jews for medical studies. Until the first half of the eighteenth century not only for Jews, but also for the rest of Europe this university was the most attractive and popular place to study medical science.[60] A little later, after Padua began to allow Jews to study, other Italian universities followed, such as Naples, Ferrara, Perugia, and Pavia.[61] In the seventeenth century the University of Leiden started to accept Jews, and it became very popular amongst Jews thereafter.[62] German cities in Germany, such as Halle and Konigsberg, as well as the Netherlands started to admit Jews from the first half of the eighteenth century.[63]

However, the availability of these universities to Jewish students was limited. For example, Jews were required to pay higher tuition fees and additional taxes during their studies, and the conditions for obtaining a degree were more complicated for them.[64] Therefore, they needed to have enough financial resources to study at university and also to live abroad. For this reason, only a relatively small number of Jews could afford studies in these universities. For example, in 1517–1619, several thousand medical students graduated from Padua, but only eighty of them were Jews, while in 1619–1721 only 149 were Jews.[65]

The Jews who decided to study at university had to be prepared for spiritual, moral, and social challenges as well. They were not allowed to join student corporations and nations. For example, the Padua Polish nation, which encompassed all students from the Polish-Lithuanian Commonwealth, even had a special letter to defend their right not to accept to their nation Jewish students.[66] In Italian cities, Jews who studied at the universities had to live apart from all Christian students, mostly in the local Jewish ghetto.[67] Jewish youth who came from traditional and closed eastern European communities were not culturally, socially, and linguistically prepared for studying at university.[68] On the other hand, studying at European universities enabled Jews to become more familiar with the culture of science and natural science studies. It had long been impossible in the eastern European closed traditional Jewish communities, which had mainly focused on in-depth religious

---

58 Ruderman, *Jewish Thought and Scientific Discovery*, p. 10; Efron, *Medicine and the German Jews*.
59 Ruderman, *Jewish Thought and Scientific Discovery*, pp. 28, 29, 42.
60 Ruderman, *Jewish Thought and Scientific Discovery*, p. 100.
61 Ruderman, *Jewish Thought and Scientific Discovery*, p. 103; Gath, 'The Elusive Karaite Doctor Joseph Ezra Dubitski', p. 9.
62 Collins, 'Jewish Medical Students and Graduates'.
63 Partyka, 'Żydowscy lekarze', pp. 134, 135; Efron, *Medicine and the German Jews*, pp. 28–29, 42.
64 Ruderman, *Jewish Thought and Scientific Discovery*, pp. 106, 110; Warchał, 'Żydzi polscy', p. 58.
65 Warchał, 'Żydzi polscy', p. 57.
66 Warchał, 'Żydzi polscy', p. 58.
67 Warchał, 'Żydzi polscy', p. 58.
68 Ruderman, *Jewish Thought and Scientific Discovery*, p. 109; Maimon, *An Autobiography*, pp. 188–89.

THE MEDICAL MARKETPLACE AS A WAY OF COMMUNICATING BEYOND RELIGION 275

studies. The Jews who went to study became familiar with scientific culture; they also became emancipated, more secularized, and often distanced from their traditional native community. After their studies, they rarely wanted to return to their homeland and tended to choose the way of life and career of a travelling scientist in foreign countries.[69] To be more precise, this could have been related to the fact that such a lifestyle was common to all medical doctors who graduated from European universities. It was common practice for medical doctors to change their place of residence every few years, to travel and look for material for their research and of course for better customers and salaries. Salamon from Kalvaria, from the second part of the sixteenth century, was one of the first Jewish medical doctors from the GDL who chose a traveller lifestyle. He worked for a while in the Duchy of Moscow. A historiographic tradition said that he was a doctor at the court of Ivan the Terrible, from which he later had to escape.[70]

During the sixteenth to eighteenth centuries, it is possible to capture attempts by the GDL Jews to rebuild their identity. Moche Marcuze, who lived in the eighteenth century, was renowned as an Enlightenment physician and was a Jewish Haskala activist, who paid a lot attention to midwifery and healthcare. At one stage of his life, he practised in the Commonwealth and there wrote and published one of the first medical books in Yiddish.[71] Publicly, he said that he came from Prussia and from there reached the Commonwealth. However, Efron has found matriculation documents that show that Moche Marcuze indeed came from Słonim in the GDL. In 1766 he came from this town to Konigsberg and enrolled in medicine studies at the university there.[72] We can only guess why he did not want to disclose his own origins, even after he had returned to the Commonwealth. Perhaps, after studying, he felt as if he represented German Jewish scholars and did not want to be identified with any traditional-religious community, or maybe he thought that being a Jew from German lands would be more credible. It may also be that foreignness was seen as adding value to his treatments, and giving him exclusivity and exoticism, which led to Jewish doctors being in demand among Christian customers.[73]

Perhaps this was one of the main reasons why the Jewish medical doctors who were most successful in the GDL were strangers. Usually they were invited to this country by the nobles who travelled in Europe, as well as the ruler's court.[74] The rulers competed for famous and highly successful Jewish medical doctors. The very famous physician Amatus Lusitanus from Portugal (1511–1568), after graduating from the University of Ferrara, spent a lot of time studying and commenting on the works of antique authors and provided interesting observations on blood circulation. This

---

69 Maimon, *An Autobiography*, p. 104.
70 *Źródła biograficzno-bibliograficzne*, p. 930; Bersohn, *Słownik biograficzny uczonych Żydów Polskich*.
71 Nevin, *More Meanderings*, pp. 157, 158.
72 Efron, *Medicine and the German Jews*, p. 79.
73 Aikin and Enfield, *General Biographies*, p. 222.
74 Connor, *The History of Poland*, II, Letter IX, p. 81; *Źródła biograficzno-bibliograficzne*, p. 930; Warchał, 'Żydzi polscy', p. 52; *Georgo Forsterio laiskai*, p. 182.

scholar, despite being invited and persuaded to come, refused to come to work for the Polish and Lithuanian ruler Sigismund and chose another client.[75]

The first notable Jew who worked in a Polish ruler's court was Izaok from Spain. He came to Kraków in the second half of the fifteenth century.[76] He was a doctor for the King of Poland and Grand Duke of Lithuania Casimir IV Jagiellon and later served all his sons: John Albrecht, Alexander, and Sigismund. They gave him numerous privileges such as an exemption from taxes and other exceptional rights compared to other local Jews.[77] Izaok, a medical doctor, had acquired a huge amount of trust from the ruler's court and functioned not only as a doctor, but also as a diplomat. He would quite often travel as a messenger to the Tatar khan.[78] Sigismund the Old also had a few Jewish doctors working for his family. These Jews would become fairly important in other matters as well. They included Efraim Fiszel and his son Moise Fishel, who finished his education in around 1520 and came back to Kraków.[79] At that time, their family was rich and well known amongst local Jewish society. He was invited to work at the ruler's court in the following year. During his service, he acquired quite a few privileges and protections from the ruler. These privileges included lower taxes and exceptional rights compared to other Jews.[80]

Another Jew worth noting is Scelom Szymon Aszkenazy, who originated from eastern Europe as we can deduce from his name. One version says he came from Venice to Poland together with Queen Bona as her personal doctor, whereas another version claims he was working for King Sigismund August, though a little later — 1559–1564. From his court Scelom left for Turkey, where he became a personal doctor of vizier Achmed Sokoll. Szymon Aszkenazy travelled and undertook various Turkish messenger diplomatic functions. He started appearing in the Commonwealth context again once Henry III of France was elected as a ruler.[81] In the court of Sigismund August, a dozen different medical doctors were working at once. A Jew who came from Spain, Salamon Kalachora, was one of the most well known. He obtained his education in Italy, was actively communicating with scientists and intellectuals of that time, and came to the court in around 1560. The duke granted him a servitor service and gave him exactly the same rights as other Christian doctors working for him were given.[82]

At the end of the seventeenth century, the duke of the Commonwealth, John Sobieski, had a few non-Christian medical doctors in his court.[83] Jonas Casal, from Italy, was the head of all the duke's medical personnel. B. O'Connor, an Englishman who worked for a while in the court of the Sobieskis, noticed that this particular Jew

---

75 Horn, 'Medycy nadworni władców', p. 16; Aikin and Enfield, *General Biographies*, p. 222.
76 Privileges in *Źródła biograficzno-bibliograficzne*, p. 930.
77 Horn, 'Medycy nadworni władców', p. 4.
78 Bersohn, *Słownik biograficzny uczonych Żydów Polskich*.
79 Horn, 'Medycy nadworni władców', pp. 8, 16.
80 *Źródła biograficzno-bibliograficzne*, pp. 217–18.
81 Warchał, 'Żydzi polscy', p. 52.
82 Horn, 'Medycy nadworni władców', p. 19; *Źródła biograficzno-bibliograficzne*, p. 939.
83 Connor, *The History of Poland*, I, pp. 199, 1698.

THE MEDICAL MARKETPLACE AS A WAY OF COMMUNICATING BEYOND RELIGION   277

was especially respected for once curing the disease *plica polonica*, which was thought to be incurable.[84] Jonas Casal had a great deal of authority in the court and was really close to the family of the ruler. The queen, Maria Kazimierza, was particularly fond of him, and she invited him to join a closed group of the queen's literati.

The most famous foreign Jew who had been working for the GDL was Joseph Solomon Delmendigo. Originally from Crete, he was a typical universal travelling scientist of the seventeenth century.[85] Like a true representative of the world of science of that time period, he was interested in many fields: he had been taught astronomy in Padua by Galileo; here he also acquired a doctor's degree in medicine; he was also into mathematics and, furthermore, was famous in Europe for his interest in Kabala and alchemy. After his studies he travelled the world gathering practical scientific experience as well as theoretical knowledge, also trying to get financial support for his scientific research.[86] From 1620 he worked for the Radziwiłł family in Birżai-Dubingiai for a couple of years.[87]

There were very few local Jews from the GDL or Poland who had obtained degrees at a university and had come back to their native country. Most likely this was due to the high costs of the education itself, travelling to western Europe, and living there. During the sixteenth to eighteenth centuries there were only five Jews who certainly came from the GDL and studied in Padua.[88] One of them was Aaron Gordon, who went to the University of Padua in 1692 and graduated after three years. It is, however, worth mentioning that according to historians he received a licence of a surgeon rather than a medical doctor.[89] After his studies, this individual came back to Vilnius and became a practitioner, even a legendary Jewish doctor of Vilnius.[90] Another example, Leiba Gordon, who was identified as a member of Aaron Gordon's family, graduated from the University of Padua in 1729. In the historiography he is presented as a brother of Aaron, although it is doubtful as there was almost thirty years between their dates studying in Padua. Leiba, while studying in Padua, did not hide his admiration towards a favourite, but controversial, Kabala specialist and mystic, Moshe Chaim Luzzatto, about whom he was writing letters to rabbis in Vilnius.[91] In 1732 Jakutiel Gordon obtained a doctor's degree in philosophy and medicine. He was born in Vilnius, a son of Leon. The other two Jews from the GDL who studied in Padua were Joseph Jelnevicz from Vilnius, who obtained a doctor's degree in philosophy and medicine in 1697, as did Jacob Wallech from Grodno in 1722.[92]

---

84 Kizilov, 'Karaite Joseph Ezra Dubitskii and King John III Sobieski', p. 52; Connor, *The History of Poland*, II, Letter IX, p. 95.
85 Ruderman, *Jewish Thought and Scientific Discovery*, p. x; Efron, *Medicine and the German Jews*, pp. 39–40.
86 Patai, *The Jewish Alchemists*, pp. 401–03; Ruderman, *Jewish Thought and Scientific Discovery*, p. x.
87 Patai, *The Jewish Alchemists*, pp. 401–03.
88 For data of Jews in Padua, see Warchał, 'Żydzi polscy', pp. 68–72.
89 Warchał, 'Żydzi polscy', p. 68; Zinberg, *A History of Jewish Literature*, p. 142.
90 Warchał, 'Żydzi polscy', pp. 69, 72.
91 Zinberg, *A History of Jewish Literature*, p. 182.
92 Warchał, 'Żydzi polscy', pp. 69, 72.

278   MONIKA RAMONAITĖ

From the eighteenth century onwards, students from Poland and Lithuania, Jews included, started to choose universities in Germany more. This was most likely due to the shorter distance and cheaper living and studying costs. Konigsberg and Halle were the most popular choices amongst the German universities.[93] For example, in 1758 Abraham Meyer, who came from the Commonwealth, acquired his doctor's degree with a dissertation on his research on the *plica polonica* disease which presented its situation in Lithuania and Poland and the possible methods for curing it. This particular disease received a lot of attention from the medical doctors of the GDL and was believed to be incurable until the mid-nineteenth century.[94]

At the end of the eighteenth century, George Forster, a natural scientist working in Vilnius, mentioned that two out of four Jews serving Vilnius city had received degrees in Konigsberg.[95] Moreover, J. Storm, who undertook research on the Jews of Konigsberg, noted that some foreign Jews, in order to avoid various limitations regarding commercial activities, would register themselves as students at the Albertina (University of Konigsberg); however, they would not study and would simply continue to develop their businesses.[96]

A very small number of Jewish medical practitioners had a status as medical doctors with university degrees. Quite a notable proportion of Jews and Karaites were called *doktor, medicus, lekarz,* or *докторъ* by their clients and other medical doctors. Nonetheless, there is no evidence of their education and the qualifications they might have acquired.[97] One such example was Karaite Abraham ben Josziahu from Troky, who is believed to have become a personal doctor of Jan Kazimierz.[98] Furthermore, according to Gath, there was another Karaite, Ezra son of Nisan (1596–1666), who certainly was a medical practitioner, although there is no information about his education. These medical practitioners were widespread in the GDL area and were called medical doctors because of their practical knowledge of medicine. Salamon Maimon (1753–1800), who was living nearby Grodno, illustrated the methods of how such knowledge was obtained. In his autobiography, he wrote that his father discussed with one Jewish doctor who, truly speaking, had never studied at a university; however, he obtained all of his medical knowledge from one of his doctors he served and through reading medical books in Polish. He was, nonetheless, quite a good medical practitioner and was successful in the field.[99] Salamon Maimon also tried to become a doctor in a similar way. He had read two medical books, which had information on how to recognize certain diseases and the methods of curing them, and Maimon

---

93   Storm, 'Culture and Exchange', pp. 139, 183, 191.
94   Meyr, *Dissertatio.*
95   *Georgo Forsterio laiskai*, p. 91.
96   Storm, 'Culture and Exchange', pp. 183, 191.
97   *Dokumenty Moskovskogo arhiva / Документы Московского архива*, pp. 207–08, 209; Lietuvos valstybės istorijos archyvas, F. 443, ap. 2, b. 79, l. 364–423ᵛ, b. 80, l. 606–36ᵛ; Lietuvos mokslų akademijos, Vrublevskių biblioteka, F. 37, b. 888, l. 5: 'Minimas žydas doktor 1702 Faivišas'; *Russko-Jevriejskij arhiv / Русско-еврейский архив*, II, no. 137, p. 87; no. 167, p. 113.
98   Bersohn, *Słownik biograficzny uczonych Żydów Polskich.*
99   Maimonas, *Gyvenimo istorija*, p. 48.

THE MEDICAL MARKETPLACE AS A WAY OF COMMUNICATING BEYOND RELIGION   279

straightaway put his knowledge into practice with a large amount of enthusiasm.[100] However, he soon realized that just being ambitious with that amount of knowledge was not enough; thus he left for Germany. Nevertheless, such self-taught doctors were common in the GDL, and their services were popular.

In the GDL, non-Christian barber-surgeons were much more common than the medical doctors. This profession was popular with Jews and Karaites; they were called *chirurgus, barber,* or *cyrulik*.[101]

In the GDL and other European countries a distinctive feature of barber-surgeons was that they, just like other craftsmen, belonged to a regulated guild. Their learning process used to take place inside the guild. As mentioned before, barber-surgeons' guilds were located in the main centres of the GDL. In cities, where guilds were strong, their members strictly controlled who could be a barber-surgeon. This is best illustrated by the aforementioned example of the dispute between the Vilnius barber-surgeons and the *łaziebnicy* which lasted for over two hundred years, and the main fight was over the possibility of performing exactly the same functions.[102] Meanwhile, Jews were not generally allowed to become members of craft guilds for Christians, or to practise their craft on or offer their services to Christians.[103] Despite this, Jewish barber-surgeons became well known for their services throughout the GDL during the seventeenth and eighteenth centuries. In the earlier historiography which researched economic relationships between Jews and Christians, it was noted that Jews managed to overcome the guild organizations and practised their crafts mainly because of the weaknesses of many GDL guilds.[104] In some private towns they belonged to general guilds and followed their rules except for Christian traditions. For example, the regulations of the private towns of Biržai and Kėdainiai stated that all Jews could take part in a craft's guilds together with Christians in the seventeenth century.[105]

In other areas Jews would do a barber-surgeon's job ignoring the guilds or simply when in some part of a city or a town where there were not any other Christians able to offer a similar service.[106] For example, in 1679 the community of Minsk gave privileges to Jews, who were allowed to practise their craft in the city without paying any guild taxes. These crafts included barber-surgeons, since there were no other specialists there at that particular time.[107] Since Jews were not members of

---

100 Maimonas, *Gyvenimo istorija*, pp. 98–99.
101 Lietuvos valstybės istorijos archyvas, F. 525, ap. 8, b. 1485, l. 62ᵛ; F. 443, ap. 2, b. 79, l. 364–423ᵛ, b. 80, l. 606–36ᵛ; *Akty izdavajemyje / Акты издаваемые*, XVIII, no. 749, p. 29; *Akty izdavajemyje / Акты издаваемые*, XXI, b. 197, pp. 156–57; *Akty izdavajemyje / Акты издаваемые*, XXVI, no. 19, p. 11; Lietuvos valstybinis istorijos archyvas, F. 694, ap. 1, no. 3493, b. 65.
102 *Akty cechów wileńskich*, no. 4, pp. 7–9, no. 41, pp. 48–49.
103 Šiaučiūnaitė-Verbickienė, *Žydai Lietuvos Didžiosios*, pp. 154–55.
104 Šiaučiūnaitė-Verbickienė, *Žydai Lietuvos Didžiosios*.
105 *Akty cechów wileńskich*, no. 4, pp. 7–9, no. 41, pp. 48–49; *Akty izdavajemyje / Акты издаваемые*, I, no. IV, p. 253, no. XVIII, p. 309.
106 Šiaučiūnaitė-Verbickienė, *Žydai Lietuvos Didžiosios*, p. 158; *Dokumenty Moskovskogo arhiva / Документы Московского архива*, pp. 205–15.
107 *Akty izdavajemyje / Акты издаваемые*, XIX, b. 74.

guilds, their education is questionable. Very likely, just like other craftsmen, they obtained their knowledge through services for their teachers. Furthermore, it might be assumed that Jews with such crafts, just like Christians, had started their activities before the first guilds' establishment and before their rules were adjusted for the tripartite ensemble in western European medical practices. This could be because guilds needed some certain number of craftsmen and a competitive environment. The first Jewish barber-surgeon, born in Kaunas, is mentioned in 1492 in the background of the expulsion of Jews from the GDL;[108] meanwhile the first guild in Vilnius was only established in 1509.

Jewish barber-surgeons had become usual in the everyday life of the GDL over time. It had become typical to find a Jewish barber-surgeon with a good position within the medical personnel of the rulers and various other dukes' courts. Samuel Bar Meszulam is one such example; he had worked for Sigismund the Old and Sigismund Augustus. Samuel came from Italy to Poland and had worked there from 1530.[109] In 1545 he left for Lithuania and became a personal surgeon of Sigismund Augustus; however, after his father's health became worse, Samuel returned to Kraków, where he was granted property and various other privileges.[110] Jewish surgeons worked in Nyasvizh Radziwiłłs' courts and other cities under their control.[111]

Jewish barber-surgeons mostly worked in smaller cities and towns, which had no barber-surgeons' guilds. For instance, nearby Grodno there was a famous Jewish surgeon working who was hurt by the drunken duke Karol Stanisław Radziwiłł with his own tools while trying to let his blood.[112] Nearby Mstislavl, I. Lopacinski was hurt and a barber-surgeon of the same town, the Jew Morda, helped him.[113] During the second half of the eighteenth century, Jewish barber-surgeons and old female herbalists became the well-recognized first choice for medical help in the small GDL towns and parishes.[114] Around that same time a new category of medical practitioner arose, feldshers, who were usually Jews. This term comes from Prussia, and its first meaning is a person who was responsible for the health of an army in a field.[115] It looks like this term started being used at the end of the eighteenth century; it implied someone with broader functions than a barber-surgeon, who was consulted regarding various treatment questions and applied various treatment techniques. Such functions can be analysed from the following example. In 1782 during the visit of Kaunas deaner it was declared that there were five feldsher Lutherans in the city. Almost all of them claimed to be medical doctors. Whereas there were also four Christian feldsher, and they would undertake medical activities following the example of the Lutherans. Beyond the River Neris Jewish barber-surgeons treated people with all kinds of

---

108 *Lietuvos Metrika (1499–1514), 8-oji užrašymų knyga*, no. 403, p. 303.
109 Horn, 'Medycy nadworni władców', p. 7.
110 *Źródła biograficzno-bibliograficzne*, p. 939.
111 Warsaw, Archiwum Główne Akt Dawnych, AR XXI, b. D94, C117.
112 Maimonas, *Gyvenimo istorija*, p. 79.
113 'Dyaryusz życia Ignacego Łopacińskiego'.
114 *Pabaisko dekanato vizitacija*, pp. 83, 153, 199, 211, 306.
115 Efron, *Medicine and the German Jews*, p. 86.

THE MEDICAL MARKETPLACE AS A WAY OF COMMUNICATING BEYOND RELIGION   281

diseases without consulting with doctors.[116] Between 1765 and 1793 in the book of income and expenses for the estate of Salantai, various expenses for medicine are mentioned. On 31 December 1778 a Jewish feldsher was visiting who was looking after the washerwoman Barbara. Later the feldsher Dawid was invited to treat her throat. Such an example demonstrates not only broader functions of a typical Jewish barber-surgeon, but also the understanding of a feldsher. This term started to mean a medical practitioner with basic medical knowledge or an unqualified medical practitioner.

All in all, it can be claimed that amongst the medical practitioners of the GDL, Jewish medical practitioners, who were called medical doctors and barber-surgeons, had also found their place. Some of them were indeed qualified and belonged to the tripartite ensemble medical core. There were medical doctors with university degrees. Additionally, there were also Jewish barber-surgeons, who were first understood to be craftsmen developing their skills and knowledge according to guild rules. They had become the norm and were seen every day in places which had no guild organizations. The other group had no proper medical education and were called doctors or barbers because of the functions they performed, which later gave rise to the term *feldsher* that in turn gave a definition to an unqualified medical practitioner.

Jewish Medical Practitioners' Evaluation within GDL Society

In western Europe Jewish medical practitioners used to be evaluated differently. On the one hand, their practice became popular and widely used in Europe. On the other hand, in 1555, during the peak of the Reformation movement, Pope Paul IV announced the bull *Cum nimis absurdum*. This bull, as well as stipulating many limitations for Jews, declared that Jews were prohibited from treating Christians. In 1581 this prohibition was repeated once again, though in reality this law was not followed. On top of that, in the Republic of Venice, where the University of Padua was located, Jews were not granted licences which would allow them to treat and work amongst Christians.[117] Additionally, in many European countries Christians themselves received a lot of criticism for using Jewish medical practitioners' services and were also given warnings about the inappropriateness of Jews' services because of their religion. They were told that they were risking the loss of salvation for their soul if they continued using Jewish services.[118] Jewish medical services which were offered to Christians would quite often become a target for anti-Judaism texts. During this time period, Sebastian Sleszkowski (1576–1648) was the one who opposed the Jews across the whole Commonwealth the most. He was a medical doctor and after 1621 served for a while in the court of Sigismund Vasa.[119] Sleszkowski was famous

16 *Vyskupo*, p. 91.
17 Bamji, *Medical Care*, p. 9.
18 Warchał, 'Żydzi polscy', p. 58.
19 Gąsiorowski, *Zbiór wiadomości*, p. 133.

for his anti-Judaism books, which were opposed to Jewish traditions, religion, and connections with Christians as well as, according to him, a very defective and harmful medical practice. The first of them *Odkrycie zdrad, złośliwych ceremonii, tajemnych rad, praktyk szkodliwych Rzeczypospolitej żydowskich*, came out in 1621. In this volume's introduction he called out to the burgomasters of the twelve largest Commonwealth cities, as well as those in Vilnius, and warned them to counsel against the harmful Jewish activities. The Jews themselves he calls the source of problems and misfortune in the Commonwealth. A lot of criticism focused on the Jewish medical practitioners, who were, according to him, greedy and overcharged for their services.[120] What is more, they purposely poison their patients who had different religious beliefs, because, according to Sleszkowski, Jews are told to do so by their religion.[121] This claim about Jewish medical practitioners' harmfulness was further developed in a book published two years later: *Jasne dowody o doktorach żydowskich, że nie tylko duszę.* This book was purposely directed against two of his rival medical practitioners, the Jews Aaron from Lublin and Jacob from Bełżyc, doctor of Sigismund Vasa.[122] The fact that the book was widely read is demonstrated by the fact that it was republished twice.[123] In this particular book Sleszkowski is trying to prove how dangerous Jewish medical practice was. Sleszkowski used religious aspects and knowledge of Jewish beliefs and traditions, which he interpreted in his own way. Even though Sleszkowski was a medical doctor, there is very little in his book about how professional or unprofessional Jewish medical practitioners were. The book's main statement was that in the Talmud Jews were instructed to kill the Christians.[124] For this reason Jewish doctors, who posed as Christians, purposely treat them wrongly, and Christian pharmacists cooperate with them purely out of greediness. Their purpose is to ruin the health of Christians and take over their assets. They are doing this in a very subtle way so that even the city government cannot detect and punish it. He also claims that Jews learn medical science themselves and do poisonous spells rather than proper treatment.[125] According to the author, the Jews hate Jesus Christ, which is why Jewish treatment methods cannot be applied to Christians, and God is not helping those who are using Jewish services and they are risking the loss of their salvation.[126] In his earlier volume, Sleszkowski claims that with the help of his book he wanted to show Christians that they have to use doctors of the same religion, because these Jewish Beelzebubs will steal the health not only of your body, but also of your soul.[127]

In one part of the book Sleszkowski pays a lot of attention to the myth of ritual murders. He discusses tools and circumstances in which Jews seemingly kill Christians

---

120 Śleszkowski, *Odkrycie*, fols 2, 5ʳ, 2ʳ.
121 Śleszkowski, *Odkrycie*, fols 2, 2ʳ, 3ʳ⁻ᵛ, 5ʳ.
122 Gąsiorowski, *Zbiór wiadomości*, p. 133.
123 Published in 1649 and in 1758.
124 Śleszkowski, *Jasne dowody*, pp. 2, 3, 5–6.
125 Śleszkowski, *Jasne dowody*, pp. 7, 8, 12.
126 Śleszkowski, *Jasne dowody*; Śleszkowski, *Odkrycie*, fol. 4ʳ.
127 Śleszkowski, *Odkrycie*, fol. 4ʳ.

and use their blood.[128] Hence, in the whole of Europe as well as in the GDL, there were some Christian fears, related to the practices of Jews, concerning the myth of ritual murders. They were told that Jews tortured Christians and even killed them in order to take their blood for their own religious rituals. Interestingly, while Sleszkowski was a medical professional, he does not connect barber-surgeons' practices with ritual murder at all. Moreover, in cases of ritual murder in the GDL, there are no Jewish barber-surgeons or other medical practitioners who were directly accused of such practices with Christian bodies and blood.[129] Even bearing in mind that there were versions where Christian blood was needed not only for rituals, but for magic and traditional medicine.[130] This might show that there were different trains of thought when it came to the Jews as a religious group and the Jews as medical practitioners from whom you bought medical services. The fact that medical services in the GDL were separated from religious matters is well illustrated by an event which is described by the scribe of the GDL treasurer I. Lopacinski in his diary. After he was seriously wounded, he was treated by a well-known barber-surgeon of Mstislavl, the Jew Morda, another Jew, Majer, and a Jesuit pharmacist, Eimond.[131] The aforementioned two books by Sleszkowski were probably the most well-known across the whole Commonwealth of this type of texts directed against Jewish medical practitioners. Sleszkowski's arguments against the practitioners were generally classical anti-Judaism statements, which had as the main idea that Jews harm Christians and are trying to make them poor and eventually extinct. Similar statements against the Jews have not been found. At the end of the eighteenth century, a different position is described by Bernard Connor, a medical doctor from the United Kingdom. In *The History of Poland*, he claims: 'For your Lordship must understand that in Poland, particularly at Court, Religion is no Objection against any Person, especially a Physician'.[132] Actually, Jewish medical practitioners were not attacked anymore for religious reasons; however, they were criticized for their unprofessional services and inappropriate education.

Jewish medical doctors who were educated, especially the ones serving the ruler, were generally viewed positively by their clients and had no special status at court. For instance, Jonas Casal was the first doctor well respected in the court, even though according to Bernard Connor he was overrated and did not have the latest medical knowledge compared with other court doctors. The Jewish medical practitioners who were working for the king of the court used to be rewarded with privileges and a salary equal to Christian medical personnel. In 1768 Stanisław August Poniatowski rewarded his doctor Peter Samson with a servitor privilege, which claims he has all the necessary medical knowledge and experience and that is why he got such rights and freedom just like other medical practitioners working in the court.[133]

---

128 Śleszkowski, *Odkrycie*, fol. 3ᵛ.

129 For data on the GDL ritual murder cases and defendants, see Šiaučiūnaitė-Verbickienė, *Žydai Lietuvos Didžiosios*, pp. 368–73.

130 Węgrzynek, 'Praktyki medyczne'; Tokarska-Bakir, *Legendy o krwi*.

131 'Dyaryusz życia Ignacego Łopacińskiego'.

132 Connor, *The History of Poland*, I, p. 199.

133 *Źródła biograficzno-bibliograficzne*, p. 594.

The evaluation of other non-professional Jewish medical practitioners differed. On the one hand, their services were widely used in the GDL, especially in the smaller towns, which had very few medical personnel. On the other hand, their services were criticized for being amateur and unprofessional.[134] In the already mentioned income and expenses book of Salantai a tendency can be seen that the personnel of an estate are treated by local Jewish feldshers and doctors. Meanwhile, for the owner the major medical doctors from Klaipėda and Gargždai were invited, who were probably more expensive and more knowledgeable with better qualifications. As it can be seen from the diseases, Jewish medical practitioners would usually treat somewhat simpler diseases or illnesses, while in the case of a more serious and difficult illness such as jaundice, breast tumour, or eye inflammation, professional doctors would come in to help.[135] Despite that, one could always choose cheaper and locally available Jewish services, which the court owners thought were not very professional. The more educated and noble people did not trust the Jewish medical practitioners' services that much, and that is demonstrated by the example of L. Byszewska. In 1786 when she was travelling to Vilnius, she met an old Jew from Łańcut, who introduced himself as a doctor. L. Byszewska explains that she asked the Jew to show his licence and the medicines which he used to treat people. The doctor doesn't have them, and the lady decided that the Jew's medical practice kills sick people rather than helps them.[136] Interestingly, this example shows some sort of breakpoint between the educated people in the Commonwealth. Byszewska asks the doctor to show her his licence, which allows him to practise medical craft and proves his qualification. Within the background of the Commonwealth it is a new feature which was introduced during the Enlightenment period; it sought to bring attention to health protection and the importance of medical education.

During the sixteenth to eighteenth centuries, Jewish medical practitioners were mostly criticized by professional medical doctors. Unlike S. Sleszkowski, criticism by other medical doctors was first directed against such medical practitioners' unprofessionalism and not their religion. Christian Friedrich Schulze, who spent eight years in the GDL, released his book of observations about this country in 1754. Schulze writes in his book that just about anyone can sell medicine in Lithuania. He gave an example of a nobleman buying a depletive powder from a Jew, which left the noblemen with terrible diarrhoea and stomach ache after drinking the medicine. Even though the patient was seriously treated, he died a few days after.[137] At the end of the eighteenth century, George Forster, who had worked in Vilnius, and also Jozef Frank, who started practising there at the beginning of the nineteenth century, described a sad capital's situation, pointing to unsatisfactory services given by the Jewish practitioners.[138] George Forster, while considering his own career as a doctor,

---

134 Węglorz, *Zdrowie, choroba*, p. 225.
135 Węglorz, *Zdrowie, choroba*, pp. 420–37.
136 Byševska, *1786 metų kelionės į Vilnių dienoraštis*, p. 62.
137 Schulze, *Kurze Nachricht*, p. 68.
138 *Georgo Forsterio laiskai*, p. 136, no. 33.

THE MEDICAL MARKETPLACE AS A WAY OF COMMUNICATING BEYOND RELIGION   285

writes: 'both Jews Dr Leboscius and Dr Polonus determine prices for their visits so unmercifully and sent so many people to rest in peace and so poorly know their field that they were asked for help only when there was nothing else to do'.[139] This opinion of professional doctors who had worked in the GDL demonstrates Gentilcore's and Cook's point that medical doctors thought of themselves as an elite who were the only legal practitioners of medicine. They always stressed their special status and professionalism, and despised and criticized the self-taught empiricists, whom they called charlatans and marginals. Real clients of these unprofessional practitioners never called them charlatans and always evaluated them by what they actually did — barber-surgeons, pharmacists, medical doctors.[140] In the case of the GDL, it is clear that some parts of this non-professional market were taken by Jewish and Karaite medical practitioners who lacked proper qualifications. There was clearly a tendency for the elite and educated people as well as medical doctors of the Commonwealth to associate the Jewish medical practitioners with unprofessional and marginal medicine.

Conclusions

It could be claimed that within the GDL the Jewish medical doctors with a university degree could get a well-paid position and even become personal doctors of the ruler. While working for the ruler they would receive financial exemptions and other privileges, as well as similar rights as Christian medical doctors working alongside them.

Other medical practitioners, who were not professionals, during the sixteenth to eighteenth centuries, became important and well known for their medical help, especially in its provincial country areas. Criticism towards them was mostly expressed by medical doctors and the GDL's noble class. In almost all cases they would stress their unprofessionalism and lack of knowledge of medicine. They were generally related to other self-taught empiricists without putting much emphasis on their ethnic origin. But there were exceptions to this rule. A well-known case is the book by S. Sleszkowski, in which Jewish medical practitioners were heavily criticized for religious reasons. By applying anti-Judaism arguments, the author claims that in the Talmud Jewish medical practitioners were instructed to make the Christians poor and eventually drive them to extinction. The book was quite popular and was reprinted twice.

Despite this, evidence of the criticism and the rejection of Jewish medical practitioners' services because of religious prejudices could not be found. Juridical cases of accusations of deliberate harm to the health and life of a client by a Jewish medical doctor were not discovered during this research. Therefore, we can draw the conclusion that in the medical marketplace of the GDL religious issues had very little effect, whereas the

---

139 *Georgo Forsterio laiskai*, p. 136, no. 33.

140 Gentilcore, 'Charlatans, the Regulated Marketplace and the Treatment of Venereal Disease', pp. 67, 69; Gentilcore, 'Charlatans, Mountebanks and Other Similar People', p. 298; Cook, *The Decline of the Old Medical Regime*.

most important criteria for choosing the right medical services was their availability. The Jews adapted themselves to the medical marketplace of the GDL and offered their services mostly in those places where other medical practitioners were absent or where there were very few of them. That is why at the end of the eighteenth century, a Jew — feldsher, doctor, or barber-surgeon — became the symbol of a non-professional but rather popular first option for medical help in the various regions of the GDL.

Works Cited

Manuscripts and Archival Sources

Lietuvos mokslų akademijos, Vrublevskių biblioteka, F. 37, b. 888, l. 5; RS, f. 6, b. 90
Lietuvos valstybės istorijos archyvas, F. 443, ap. 2, b. 79; F. 433, ap. 2, b. 80; F. 525, ap. 8, b. 1485; F. 694, ap. 1, no. 3493, b. 65
Vilnius, Library of the University of Vilnius, *Kauno magistrato aktų knyga*, in RS, f. 7, b. 13840, no. 442, l. 63., f. 7, b. 13840, no. 509, l. 63; VUB RS, b. 13850, no. 559, l. 308
Warsaw, Archiwum Główne Akt Dawnych, AR XXI, b. D94, C117

Primary Sources

Aikin, John, and William Enfield, *General Biographies or Lives*, vol. 1 (London: G. G. and J. Robinson, 1799)
Akty cechów wileńskich, ed. by Henryk Łowmiański, Maria Łowmiańska, and Stanisław Kościałkowski, vol. 1 (1st edn: Wilno: [n.pub.], 1939; 2nd edn: Poznań: Wydawnictwo Poznańskie, 2007)
Akty izdavajemyje Bilienskoju komissieju dlia razbora drievnih aktov / Акты издаваемые Виленскою комиссіею для разбора древнихъ актовъ, XVIII: *Akty o kopnyh sudah / Акты о копныхъ судах* (Vilna: Tipografija A. G. Syrkina, 1891); XIX: *Akty, otnosyashchiyesya k istorii byvshey Kholmskoy yepaskhii / Акты, относящиеся к исторіи бывшей Холмской епасхии* (Vilna: Tipografija A. G. Syrkina, 1892); XXI: *Akty Grodnienskago zemskago suda / Акты Гродненскаго земскаго суда* (Vilna: Tipografija A. G. Syrkina, 1894); XXVI: *Akty Upitskovo grodskovo suda / Акты Упитскаго гродскаго суда* (Vilna: Tipografija A. G. Syrkina, 1899); XXVIII: *Akty o yevreyakh / Акты о евреях* (Vilna: Tipografija 'Russkiy Pochin', 1901)
Byševska, Liudvika, *1786 metų kelionės į Vilnių dienoraštis*, ed. by Vydas Dolinskas, Piotras Jacekas Jamskis, and Eva Manikovska, trans. Vyturys Jarutis and Beata Piasecka, introd. by Eva Manikovska (Vilnius: UAB 'Standartų spaustuvė', 2008)
Connor, Bernard, *The History of Poland in Several Letters to Persons of Quality, Giving an Account of the Antient and Present State of that Kingdom, Historical, Geographical, Physical, Political and Ecclesiastical …* , ed. by John Savage, vols I–II (London: printed by J.D. for Dan Brown … and A. Roper, 1698)
Dokumenty Moskovskogo arhiva Ministerstva juticii / Документы Московского архива Министерства юстиции, ed. by M. Dovnar-Zapolskij, vol. 1 (Moscow: Tovariszczestvo tipografii A. I. Mamontova, 1897)

THE MEDICAL MARKETPLACE AS A WAY OF COMMUNICATING BEYOND RELIGION   287

'Dyaryusz życia Ignacego Łopacińskiego pisarza skarb. W.K. Lit., brata rodzonego
  wojewody Brzeskiego', *Biblioteka Warszawa*, 3 (1855), 400–425
Frankas, Jozefas, *Atsiminimai apie Vilnių*, trans. by Genovaitė Dručkutė (Vilnius: Mintis,
  2009)
Gąsiorowski, Ludwik, *Zbiór wiadomości do historyi sztuki lekarskiej w Polsce od czasów
  najdawniejszych, aż do najnowszych*, vol. II (Poznań: Jan Konstanty Żupański, 1853)
Georgo Forsterio laiškai iš Vilniaus, trans. by Jonas Kilius, ed. by Jonas Grigonis, Jonas
  Kubilius, Vytautas Merkys, Arnoldas Piročkinas, and Algirdas Šidlauskas (Vilnius:
  Mokslas, 1988)
Grutinio Pilsnensi, Andrea, *Medicus dogmaticus* (Cracoviae: Officina Andreae Petricouij,
  1598)
Hačeba, J., 'Seniausios Lietuvoje vaistinės', *Farmacijos žinios*, no. 11 (1933), 12–13
Lietuvos Metrika (1440–1523), 10-oji Užrašymų knyga, ed. by E. Banionis and A. Baliulis
  (Vilnius: Mokslo ir enciklopedijų leidykla, 1997)
Lietuvos Metrika (1499–1514), 8-oji užrašymų knyga, ed. by Algirdas Baliulis (Vilnius:
  Mokslo ir enciklopedijų leidykla, 1995)
Lietuvos Metrika (1524–1529), 14-oji užrašymų knyga, ed. by L. Karalius and D. Antanavičius
  (Vilnius: Lietuvos istorijos instituto leidykla, 2008)
Lietuvos Metrika (1528–1538), 15-oji užrašymų knyga, ed. by Artūras Dubonis (Vilnius: Žara,
  2002)
Lietuvos didžiojo kunigaikščio Aleksandro Jogailaičio dvaro sąskaitų knygos, ed. by
  Antanavičius Darius and Petrauskas Rimvydas (Vilnius: Pilių Tyrimo Centras Lietuvos
  Pilys, 2007)
*Lietuvos Didžiosios Kunigaikštystės kasdieninis gyvenimas: Lietuvos istorijos skaitinių
  chrestomatija*, ed. by Algirdas Baliulis and Elmantas Meilus (Vilnius: Vilniaus Dailės
  akademijos leidykla, 2001)
Maimon, Solomon, *An Autobiography*, trans. by John Clark Murray (Urbana: University of
  Illinois Press, 2001)
Maimonas, Saliamonas, *Gyvenimo istorija*, trans. by Vita Gaigalaitė (Vilnius: Lietuvių
  literatūros ir tautosakos institutas, 2004)
Meyr, Abraham, *Dissertatio Inavgvralis Medica Sistens Theoriam Ac Therapiam Plicae
  Polonicae / Qvam ... In Academia Regia Fridericiana, ... Pro Gradv Doctoris Svmmisqve
  In Medicina Honoribvs Et Priviligiis Doctoralibvs Rite Impetrandis, D. XIV. Avgvst.
  MDCCLVIII. Ervditorvm Censvrae Exhibvit Avctor ... Polono-Brodensis, Gente Ivdaevs*
  (Halae Magdeburgicae: Vesterus, 1758)
Miškinienė, Galina, *Seniausi Lietuvos totorių rankraščiai: Grafika. Transliteracija. Vertimas.
  Tekstų struktūra ir turinys* (Vilnius: Vilniaus universiteto leidykla, 2001)
Muchowski, Piotr, *Folk Literature of the Polish-Lithuanian Karaites: Abkowicz 3 Manuscript,
  Part 2* (Paris: Editions Suger Press, 2013)
*Pabaisko dekanato vizitacija 1782–1784 m. atlikta Vilniaus vyskupo Ignoto Jokūbo Masalskio
  parėdymu*, ed. by Algirdas Antanas Baliulis, Lietuvių Katalikų Mokslo Akademija,
  Lietuvos istorijos šaltiniai, 9 (Vilnius: Kataliku Akademija, 2010)
*Russko-Jevriejskij arhiv: Dokumenty I materiały dlia istorii jevriejev / Русско-еврейский архив:
  документы и материалы для истории евреев*, ed. by Siergiej Aleksandrovicz Bierszadskij,
  Сергей Александрович Бершадский, 1–2 (St Petersburg, 1882–1900)

Schulze, Christian Friedrich, *Kurze Nachricht einiger besonderer Zufälle, sowohl einheimischer als anderer Kranckheiten, welche in dem Königreich Pohlen, insonderheit aber in dem Gros-Herzogthum Lithauen pflegen wahrgenommen zu werden* (Dresden: Friedrich Hekel, 1754)

Śleszkowski, Sebastian, *Jasne dowody o doktorach żydowskich, że nie tylko dusze, ale i ciało w niebezpieczeństwo zginienia wiecznego wdają, którzy Żydów, Tatarów i innych niewiernych przeciwko zakazaniu Kościoła świętego Powszechnego za Lekarzów używają, abo radą, perswazją, zaleceniem, promocją, abo jakimkolwiek innym sposobem do tego powodem są, aby ich drudzy używał* (Kraków: [n.pub.], 1623, 1758)

——, *Odkrycie zdrad, złośliwych ceremonii, tajemnych rad, praktyk szkodliwych Rzeczypospolitej żydowskich* (Braniewo: [n.pub.], 1621)

Vaišnoravičius, Kazmieras Jonas, *Kelionė po Europą su jaunuoju kunigaikščiu Ostrogiškiu. 1667–1669 metų dienoraštis*, trans. by Birutė Mikalonienė and Eglė Patiejūnienė (Vilnius: Lietuvių literatūros ir tautosakos institutas, 2009)

Vyskupo Ignoto Jokūbo Masalskio Kauno dekanato vizitacija 1782 m., ed. by Vytautas Jogėla, Fontes Historiae Lituaniae, 6 (Vilnius: Katalikų akademija, 2001)

Warchał, Jan, 'Żydzi polscy na uniwersytecie padewskim', *Kwartalnik poświęcony badaniu Żydów w Polsce*, 1.3 (1913), 37–72

Źródła biograficzno-bibliograficzne do dziejów medycyny w dawnej Polsce, ed. by Franciszek Giedroyć (Warsaw: Druk K. Kowalewskiego, 1911)

Secondary Studies

Bamji, Alex, *Medical Care in Early Modern Venice*, Economic History Working Papers, 188 (London: London School of Economics, 2014)

Bersohn, Mathias, *Słownik biograficzny uczonych Żydów Polskich XVI, XVII i XVIII wieku* (Warsaw: Druk[arnia] Piotra Laskauera i S-ki, 1905)

Collins, Kenneth, 'Jewish Medical Students and Graduates at the Universities of Padua and Leiden: 1617–1740', *Rambam Maimonides Medical Journal*, 4.1 (2013), <https://www.ncbi.nlm.nih.gov/pmc/articles/PMC3678911/>

Cook, Harold J., *The Decline of the Old Medical Regime in Stuart London* (Ithaca, NY: Cornell University Press, 1986)

——, *Matters of Exchange: Commerce, Medicine, and Science in the Dutch Golden Age* (New Haven: Yale University Press, 2007)

Efron, John M., *Medicine and the German Jews: A History* (New Haven: Yale University Press, 2001)

Gath, Isak, 'The Elusive Karaite Doctor Joseph Ezra Dubitski, the "Sobiski Hours" and the Myth of the Polish-Lithuanian Karaite Physicians', *Karaite Archives*, 3 (2015), 5–36

Gentilcore, David, '"All that Pertains to Medicine": *Protomedici* and *Protomedicati* in Early Modern Italy', *Medical History*, 38.2 (1994), 121–42

——, 'Charlatans, Mountebanks and Other Similar People: The Regulation and Role of Itinerant Practitioners in Early Modern Italy', *Social History*, 20.3 (1995), 297–314

——, 'Charlatans, the Regulated Marketplace and the Treatment of Venereal Disease in Italy', in *Sins of the Flesh: Responding to Sexual Disease in Early Modern Europe*, ed. by Kevin Siena (Toronto: Centre for Reformation and Renaissance Studies, 2005), pp. 57–80

———, *Healers and Healing in Early Modern Italy* (Manchester: Manchester University Press, 1998)

———, *Medical Charlatanism in the Early Modern Italy* (Oxford: Oxford University Press, 2006)

———, 'Was There a "Popular Medicine" in Early Modern Europe?', *Folklore*, 115.2 (2004), 151–66

Grmek, M. D., 'The History of Medical Education in Russia', in *The History of Medical Education: An International Symposium Held February 5–9, 1968*, ed. by C. D. O'Malley (Los Angeles: University of California Press, 1970), pp. 303–28

Horn, Maurycy, 'Medycy nadworni władców polsko-litewskich w latach 1506–1572 (ze szczególnym uwzględnieniem lekarzy i chirurgów żydowskich)', *Biuletyn Żydowskiego Instytutu Historycznego w Polsce*, 1(149) (1989), 3–23

Jenner, Mark S. R., and Patrick Wallis, 'The Medical Marketplace', in *Medicine and the Market in England and its Colonies, c. 1450–c. 1850*, ed. by Mark S. R. Jenner and Patrick Wallis (New York: Palgrave Macmillan, 2007), pp. 1–24

Kizilov, Mikhail, 'Karaite Joseph Ezra Dubitskii and King John III Sobieski: On Jewish Physicians, Christianity, and a Fifteenth-Century Illuminated Manuscript from Windsor Castle', *East European Jewish Affairs*, 38.1 (2008), 45–64

Kremers, Edward, and George Urdang, *History of Pharmacy* (Madison, WI: American Institute of the History of Pharmacy, 1986)

Lebrun, François, *Jak dawniej leczono: Lekarze, święci i czarodzieje w XVII i XVIII wieku*, trans. by Z. Podgórska-Klawe (Warsaw: Oficyna Wydawnicza Volumen, 1997)

Lelis, Jonas, 'Medicinos pagalba Lietuvoje iki XIX a. pradžios', in *Iš mokslų istorijos Lietuvoje*, vol. 1 (Vilnius: Valstybinė politinės ir mokslinės literatūros leidykla, 1960), pp. 118–24

Nevin, Michael, *More Meanderings in Medical History* (Bloomington: iUniverse, 2012)

Nowosielska, Elżbieta, 'Multi Medici, multa funera: Negatywny wizerunek lekarza w XVII–XVIII w.', *Kwartalnik Historii Kultury Materialnej*, 62.3 (2014), 379–88

O'Malley, C. D, 'Medical Education during the Renaissance', in *The History of Medical Education: An International Symposium Held February 5–9, 1968*, ed. by C. D. O'Malley (Los Angeles: University of California Press, 1970), pp. 89–104

Park, Katharine, *Doctors and Medicine in Early Modern Florence* (Princeton, NJ: Princeton University Press, 2014)

Partyka, Wiesław, 'Żydowscy lekarze i cyrulicy w Ordynacji Zamojskiej w XVII–XVIII wieku', *Kwartalnik Historii Żydow / Jewish History Quarterly*, 226 (2008), 133–43

Patai, Raphael, *The Jewish Alchemists: A History and Source Book* (Princeton, NJ: Princeton University Press, 1996)

Porter, Roy, *The Greatest Benefit to Mankind: A Medical History of Humanity from Antiquity to the Present* (London: W. W. Norton & Company, 1999)

Ragauskienė, Raimonda, 'Vaistininkai XVI a. Vilniuje', *Vilniaus istorijos metraštis*, 1 (2007), 29–54

Ralley, Robert, 'Medical Economies in Fifteenth Century England', in *Medicine and the Market in England and its Colonies, c. 1450–c. 1850*, ed. by Mark S. R. Jenner and Patrick Wallis (New York: Palgrave Macmillan, 2007), pp. 24–46

Ramonaitė, Monika, 'Vakarų Europos medicinos paslaugų teikimo modelis ir jo pritaikymas Lietuvos Didžiojoje Kunigaikštystėje XVI–XVIII a.', *Lietuvos Istorijos studijos*, 38 (2016), 9–31

Ramsey, Matthew, *Professional and Popular Medicine in France 1770–1830: The Social World of Medical Practice* (Cambridge: Cambridge University Press, 1988)

Rublack, Ulinka, 'Pregnancy, Childbirth and Female Body in Early Modern Germany', *Past & Present*, 150.1 (1996), 84–110

Ruderman, David B., *Jewish Thought and Scientific Discovery in Early Modern Europe* (New Haven: Yale University Press, 1995)

Sokół, Stanisław, *Historia gdańskiego cechu chirurgów, 1454–1820* (Wrocław: Zakład Narodowy im. Ossolińskich, 1957)

——, *Medycyna w Gdańsku w dobie odrodzenia* (Wrocław-Warszawa: Zakład Narodowy im. Ossolińskich, 1960)

Storm, J., 'Culture and Exchange: The Jews of Königsberg, 1700–1820' (Washington University in St Louis: Washington University Open Scholarship All Theses and Dissertations (ETDs))

Šiaučiūnaitė-Verbickienė, Jurgita, *Žydai Lietuvos Didžiosios kunigaikštystės visuomenėje* (Vilnius: Žara, 2009)

Talbot, Charles, 'Medical Education in the Middle Ages', in *The History of Medical Education: An International Symposium Held February 5–9, 1968*, ed. by C. D. O'Malley (Los Angeles: University of California Press, 1970), pp. 73–88

Tokarska-Bakir, Joanna, *Legendy o krwi: Antropologia przesądu* (Warsaw: W.A.B., 2008)

Wallis, Faith, ed., *Medieval Medicine: A Reader* (Toronto: Toronto University Press, 2010)

Węglorz, Jakub, *Zdrowie, choroba i lecznictwo w społeczeństwie Rzeczypospolitej XVI–XVIII wieku* (Toruń: Wydawinctwo Adam Marszałek, 2015)

Węgrzynek, Hanna, 'Praktyki medyczne we wczesnonowożytnej Polsce i ich wpływ na funkcjonowanie oskarżeń o mord rytualny', *Czasy Nowożytne*, 25 (2012), 85–114

Zinberg, Israel, *A History of Jewish Literature* (New York: Press of Case Western Reserve University, 1975)

DOVILĖ TROSKOVAITĖ

Towns as Areas of Ethnic Communication and Competition

*The Case of Karaites in Trakai/Troki and Vilnius/Wilno/
Vilna in the Seventeenth to Twentieth Centuries*

In one of the previous chapters, Grzegorz Myśliwski showed how various ethnicities coexisted within the boundaries of the city of Kraków. He focused on strategies of cooperation and rivalry between ethnic groups which tried to keep or strengthen their ethnic identities without emphasizing the close connection with the space in which they lived. But territory is not only a space with certain boundaries. It may also be an area inhabited by a particular ethnic group different than the state's dominant society, which sees this particular territory (region, town, etc.) as their own space, where they experience, express, and embed their unique identity. The group identifies themselves with this place and sees it as their homeland, no matter its actual political belonging. The notion of belonging to a certain territory and vice versa is a core element of modern national identity of most ethnic groups and nations. Therefore in this chapter I will examine the use of territorial arguments in the ideological struggle between Jewish groups, which led to the formation of modern nationalism in one of them — the Polish Lithuanian Karaites. I will use the concept of territorialization, as elaborated by Giorgio Shani,[1] and examine how it works among non-dominant groups in the Christian society of eastern Europe. I will argue that the dominant society has an important role in the territorialization of certain areas by non-dominant groups, even though this territorialization is symbolic and ideologized.

---

1 Shani, 'The Territorialization of Identity'.

Dovilė Troskovaitė • (dovile.troskovaite@gmail.com) is an assistant in the Faculty of History at Vilnius University. Her field of research focuses mainly on the history of east European Karaites and their relations with Rabbinite Jews.

Inter-Ethnic Relations and the Functioning of Multi-Ethnic Societies: Cohesion in Multi-Ethnic Societies in Europe from c. 1000 to the Present, II, ed. by Przemysław Wiszewski, EER 18 (Turnhout: Brepols, 2022), pp. 291–307

BREPOLS ❧ PUBLISHERS   10.1484/M.EER-EB.5.132156

This is an open access chapter made available under a cc by-nc 4.0 International License.

Introduction

The Jews are usually seen in the historiography as an easily migrating group, and their relationship with a certain territory, except that of the Holy Land, is seldom discussed, especially in ideological contexts. There are studies about their coexistence in Christian societies, their legal and social status,[2] relations with noblemen and certain states or rulers,[3] but not much is known about their ideological and cultural relations with the territory in which they lived. In this context, the works of Bernard Weinryb are of high importance, where the author analysed the arrival legends that were common in European Jewish communities.[4] I will focus on the case of the Karaites and their relations with the particular towns that belonged to the Grand Duchy of Lithuania (later, the north-western region of the Russian Empire, Poland, and again Lithuania), that of Vilnius/Wilno/Vilna[5] and Trakai/Troki, their role in the formation of a modern national Karaite identity, its connection with Jewish self-perceptions, and the role of Polish society in this process. The thesis of the chapter is closely connected with the main subject of the volume: How did an ethnic minority maintain and strengthen its identity living within the network of social relations with the politically and demographically dominant ethnicities? How did the Karaites manage to define and secure 'their' place on Earth — not only metaphorically — and to save themselves from the disastrous consequences of their long-lasting inconsistency with the interests of the dominant ethnicities in their territory?

Trakai/Troki in the National Narrative of Lithuanian Karaites

The discussion of the settlement of Trakai/Troki focuses on two main groups: the dominant Christian society and the Jewish community, which was divided into two parts — the Rabbinic Jews, who were a considerably larger part of the community, and the Karaite Jews, who, despite their small number, were very active in communicating with both Rabbinic Jews and the Christians. Both Jewish communities tried to solve mutual disagreements by involving the government and local courts to solve matters. In this communicative scheme, Christian society, as the dominant one with power concentrated in their hands, were the intermediaries between both Jewish communities.

The first and the most long-lasting conflict between the two was for the right to reside in the small town of Trakai/Troki, about twenty kilometres away from the capital Vilna. Trakai/Troki is the first known settlement of Karaites in the Grand Duchy of Lithuania (GDL). The discussion of the circumstances of their arrival is

---

2 Verbickienė, *Žydai Lietuvos Didžiosios Kunigaikštystės visuomenėje*.
3 Rosman, *The Lords' Jews*.
4 Weinryb, 'The Beginnings of East'.
5 In this paper I will use the name Vilna through the whole paper to stress its importance in the Jewish environment, to which the Karaite community also belonged.

still ongoing in the historiography, but it is clear that soon after the establishment of the community the town became the administrative and religious centre of the Karaites. Despite the facts that the Karaites were constantly migrating and forming small temporal communities mainly in the northern part of the country and that the economic situation in Trakai/Troki was often very poor, especially after 1665 when it was devastated by the war, this town was constantly inhabited by the Karaites and it never lost its importance as the administrative centre of all the Karaites of the duchy (at least officially).[6]

As early as 1646 the Trakai/Troki Karaite community gained a privilege from the Polish king Wladislaw IV Waza which prohibited Rabbinite Jews from settling in the town (reconfirmed several times in the nineteenth century).[7] At first it was only a means of regulating economic relations between the two groups, but later in the nineteenth century it became an ideological tool that helped the Karaites to form their own ethno-national identity.

From being a purely economic issue in the seventeenth and eighteenth centuries, it was later transformed into an ideological fight for a territory, which did not belong to these communities but through virtual territorialization became an imagined homeland for the Lithuanian Karaites. I will use the term 'territorialization', which is usually used to describe an act of organizing as a territory, like it was used by Giorgio Shani in his paper on the territorialization of Sikh identity.[8] Even though the Karaites could not have any territorial claims physically, they needed to have them at least symbolically. This was necessary for their ethnic national identity, which was formed by the adaptation of emerging national sentiments among ethnic groups in the Russian Empire. In the fourth decade of the nineteenth century, the Crimean Karaites began to search for their history under pressure from the Russian authorities. In the north-western part of the empire this process began a decade later but had the same reasoning — the Trakai/Troki Karaites had made a claim to have a better social and economic status than that of the Rabbinite Jews. This process of separation, motivated by the search for better financial prospects and prestige in the dominant society, led to a consistent separation from Jewishness — from the people of Erets Israel. If Israel was not the homeland the Karaites wanted to associate themselves with, they needed a territory to replace it. Growing secularization in the community at the end of the nineteenth century did not require them to relate it to their religious tradition. Rather on the contrary, the notion of a separate ethnicity required other qualities from that of the territory: as in the case of other forming nationalisms in eastern Europe (Lithuanian, Polish), the priority was given for the

---

6 The preconditions for such an image of the city were formed in 1441 when Karaites of Trakai/Troki were granted the Magdeburg law, which gave the Karaite settlement an exceptional status in the GDL.
7 *Lietuvos magdeburginių miestų privilegijos ir aktai.*
8 'Central to this nationalist narrative is the territorialisation of Sikh socio-political identity in the homeland of the Punjab. As early as 1946, the SGPC committed itself to the "goal of a Sikh state" and therefore, the territorialisation of the Sikh qaum. The Sikh people needed a state of their own to "preserve the main Sikh shrines, Sikh social practices, Sikh self-respect and pride, Sikh sovereignty and the future prosperity of the Sikh people"': Shani, 'The Territorialization of Identity', p. 13.

antiquity of the community, its long and glorious history. On the other hand, it was also characteristic of the early Jewish historiography in the region. The case of Trakai/Troki shows how the claims of a historical homeland were embodied in the Polish-Lithuanian Karaite community.

It was not only the privilege of 1646 issued by Wladislaw IV Waza which prohibited Rabbinite Jews from settling in the town of Trakai/Troki. The Lithuanian Vaad (Jewish self-governing institution) also issued regulations, securing the Karaite right to dwell in the town and keeping the Rabbinites away from it. At the time the prohibition was issued, Trakai/Troki was a small, economically undeveloped place, and the regulation of the Jewish population prevented them from harsh competition in carrying out business. The Karaites were successful in ensuring that the prohibition against Rabbinites living in Trakai/Troki lasted for nearly three hundred years, until the nineteenth century. The resolution of the Governing Senate, issued in 1829, shows that the Karaites managed to 'prove their exceptional right to settle in Trakai/Troki and to carry out business, which is not allowed for Rabbinites'.[9] It was argued that taking into account the fact that the privileges, granted by the Polish kings starting from 1646 (when the prohibition against the Rabbinites was first issued) up until the privilege of 1776, had always existed and were never cancelled, their existence would be approved.[10] However, the Jewish legal and social situation in the nineteenth century was very different than that of the past. The so-called Jewish Statute, issued in 1804, prohibited Jews from living in villages. Consequently they began to migrate to nearby towns, and Trakai/Troki, which previously had not been a very attractive place for Rabbinites to settle, became their point of destination; taking into account the existence of the Pale of Settlement and the growing Jewish population, there was not much they could choose from.[11] The contradiction between the prohibition against Rabbinites settling in Trakai/Troki, issued by the Governing Senate in the third decade of the nineteenth century, and the provisions of the statute, encouraging Jews to move to the towns, had to be resolved by the Vilnius Supreme Court, which had to announce its decision to the Ministry of Internal Affairs and Department of Spiritual Affairs of Believers of Other Faiths.[12] No matter its decision, the Governing Senate confirmed this prohibition again in 1835, probably because of the release of a new Jewish statute in the same year.[13] The decision stated that Rabbinite Jews had to abandon the town of Trakai/Troki in one year, those who had owned some property in five years, and those who have contracts after the end of them.[14] There were fewer than two hundred

---

9 A right granted to Karaites to live and trade in Trakai/Troki, *Sbornik starinnych gramot*, p. 251 (6 September 1829).

10 *Sbornik starinnych gramot*, p. 252.

11 The Pale of Settlement was established by the law of the Russian Empire and functioned between 1791 and 1917 in the western territory of the state, where permanent residency by Jews was allowed. It was forbidden for Jews to live in the empire outside this territory.

12 *Sbornik starinnych gramot*, p. 252.

13 The Jewish legal status was confirmed on 13 April 1835, *Sbornik starinnych gramot*, p. 354.

14 *Sbornik starinnych gramot*, pp. 354–55.

Rabbinite Jews living in Trakai/Troki at that time (and around six hundred Karaites).[15] Interestingly, such a small case was designated to the Governing Senate, one of the highest administrative and legislative bodies in the empire. It is obvious that for both the Karaites and the government the case was not just about making the Rabbinites leave Trakai/Troki. For the Karaite community, it was a chance to demonstrate their power and prestige, while for the government it was one of many ways of solving the Jewish question: they saw the Karaites as better Jews, who did not have features attributed to the Rabbinites and recognized as evil by the dominant society, the government, and the Orthodox Church: adherence to Talmud or distinct dressing. The Karaites didn't speak Yiddish in everyday life, which was called *jargon*, and what was most important, they were not associated with deicide like the Rabbinite Jews. By securing a privileged position for the Karaites, the government demonstrated to the Rabbinites what they could expect by 'showing their willingness to change themselves'. However, the measures set up by the Governing Senate probably did not work, because after one year it was repeated once again and approved by the Ministry of Internal Affairs and the emperor.[16]

It seems that the competition for dominance in the town had to be over in the middle of the nineteenth century. Due to the efforts of Christian burghers and the Vilna civil gubernator Pochvistjev, who were seeking the return of the Rabbinites, the question of permitting them to live in the town of Trakai/Troki was re-examined once again.[17] The leaders of the Karaite community continued to defend their position seeking to, as they declared, protect themselves from persecution for their religion (!) and misfortunes that appeared together with the Rabbinites.[18] This time, the decision was favourable for the Rabbinites: in 1862 they were allowed to live in Trakai/Troki.[19] At the very end of the nineteenth century, there were 377 Karaites and 1112 Rabbinites living in Trakai/Troki.

It seems that this last decision on the right to dwell in Trakai/Troki had settled the matter and finished the discussion between those two communities. However, the exceptional right for the Karaites to live in Trakai/Troki (though abolished in 1862) remained important for the Karaites in an ideological context, especially when the Karaites were trying to rethink their history at the beginning of the twentieth century. In the national historical narrative of the Karaites, Trakai/Troki became an important argument which proved their long historical past; it also became a territory of their own, which they managed to take over, at least symbolically, and incorporate in their historical narrative as the local homeland of the Karaites. The importance of Trakai/Troki and the notion of belonging to this place for centuries were demonstrated in an article by an unknown author, published in 1911 in the Karaite journal *Karaite Life* (Rus. *Karaimskaya zhizn*). It was printed as a reaction to an article in the Jewish

---

15   Author unknown, 'Iz istorii Trokskich karaimov', p. 29.
16   Repeated permission for Jews to live in Trakai/Troki, *Sbornik starinnych gramot*, p. 394 (1836).
17   Vilnius, Lietuvos valstybės istorijos archyvas (hereafter, LVIA), F. 378 BS, ap. 1847, b. 436, l. 137–41.
18   LVIA, F. 378 BS, ap. 1847, b. 436, l. 148–56.
19   LVIA, F. 378 BS, ap. 1847, b. 436, l. 216.

journal *Jewish Antiquity* (Rus. *Evereiskaya starina*), where a (Jewish) author discussed the development of the right of Rabbinites to settle in Trakai/Troki.[20] The Karaite author claimed to reconstruct the 'real' or correct picture of Karaite relations with the Rabbinite regarding this question. I will not go into an in-depth analysis of the content of this article, which lists the privileges of the Karaites to live in Trakai/Troki and prohibitions against the Rabbinites to do so, ending up with the aforementioned decision of 1862, which was conducive to Rabbinite Jews. Most importantly in this article, the Karaite author tries to stress the antiquity of the Karaite community in Trakai/Troki and the longevity of the tradition forbidding the Rabbinites from dwelling there, which had been recently discontinued. The fact that such a text appeared in the Karaite press fifty years after the judgement shows that the symbolic struggle with the Rabbinites for an ideological takeover of the place was still going on, even without an active participation of the Rabbinites in it.

Together with the efforts to get legislative confirmation of their monopolist right to live in Trakai/Troki, the Karaites used other means to demonstrate that the town belonged to them. At the beginning of the twentieth century, the glorification of Trakai/Troki as a cradle of the Polish-Lithuanian Karaites flourished with the appearance of secular Karaite poetry. Szymon Kobecki (1865–1933), Szymon Firkowicz (1897–1982), Michał Tynfowicz (1912–1974), and some other less-known amateurs devoted their lines to depict the beauty of their homeland, which, however, was limited to the town of Trakai/Troki and its surroundings. This proves only that the Karaites did associate the beginning of their history with this town, and it was both their personal homeland and the homeland of their nation, as they had called themselves at that time.

The question may arise, why did the Lithuanian Karaites not associate themselves with the territory of Crimea, from which they claimed to be brought to the Grand Duchy of Lithuania and settled in Trakai/Troki? Indeed, with the activities of Seraja Szapszał (1873–1961) — the communal and spiritual leader of the Polish Karaites in the interwar period — especially from the fourth decade of the twentieth century, Crimea started to be presented as a cradle of the eastern European Karaites, who claimed to be the descendants of the Chazzars. S. Szapszał managed to combine those two places into one narrative, providing a concept of two homelands — the Crimea was associated with the beginning of all east European Karaites, whereas Trakai/Troki remained a local cradle of Polish Karaites. Elaboration of this narrative weakened the importance of Trakai/Troki, and local Karaite authors even tried to combine those two places in their poems.[21]

Nonetheless, although the Karaites did not manage to preserve their exceptional right to dwell in Trakai/Troki, they gained, at least symbolically, a territory, which began to be associated exclusively with their community. They could create a virtual homeland, which they lost by separating themselves from the people of Israel. The land of Palestine, which for centuries was their lost homeland, became less and less home-like as long as the Karaites were trying to dissociate themselves from all other

---

20 Author unknown, 'Iz istorii Trokskich karaimov', p. 24.
21 Troskovaitė, 'Lenkijos ir Lietuvos karaimų savivokos formavimas', pp. 167–91.

Jews. Alongside this, the prohibition against Jews settling in Trakai/Troki had another no less important meaning: it meant the higher status and the better image of the Karaites in the eyes of the dominant society in comparison with those of the Rabbinite Jews. We can presume that the growing prestige of Trakai/Troki Karaites, even if it comes to a small number of people in a tiny little place like Trakai/Troki, could strengthen their sense of separateness from Jewishness and a notion of their separate ethnic identity.

Through the mediation of a particular town, the Karaite community managed to draw identity boundaries between them and the 'Others' — the Rabbinite Jews. The imperial government (including local and state authorities) by repeatedly issuing this prohibition let the Karaites exploit Trakai/Troki as a virtual homeland for their community and strengthened the formation of their national identity. It can be argued that it was also because of the successful symbolic occupation of Trakai/Troki that the Karaites managed to create a form of nationalism. This was based on the same elements as that of the regional nationalisms of the Poles and Lithuanians — the common origin and language, and the territory, which in the case of the Polish-Lithuanian Karaites was the small town of Trakai/Troki, where they claimed to have lived for centuries and presented themselves as the first autochthonous inhabitants.

The Role of the State in Territorializing Vilna and the Formation of it as the Centre of the Modern Karaite Community

The case of Vilna was completely different from that of Trakai/Troki. Vilna started its history as an increasingly attractive cultural and economic centre, as the letters of the Lithuanian Grand Duke Gediminas (1275–1342), which were sent from Vilna in the fourteenth century, demonstrate; he invited all peoples who were involved in crafts and trades to come and dwell in the city. It became a focal point for the migration of different ethnic and confessional groups and from the very beginning was everybody's city — that is, every ethnic or religious group, be it Poles, Jews, Old Believers, or other, had an image of their own Vilna. It may seem that for the Karaites, who established themselves in the neighbourhood of Vilna at the beginning of the fifteenth century, it could have been a potentially perfect area for the development of their economic activities and cultural life, especially in the seventeenth century and later, when Trakai/Troki ceased to be an attractive place for the Karaites to live and communal migration to other cities of the Grand Duchy of Lithuania began. But contrary to what might be expected, they chose to migrate northward to the private towns of the magnates Radziwiłłs (Lit. Radvilos) — Birże (1602/1603) and Nowemiasto (1658), and the surrounding areas of Poswol and Poniewież (1676). Vilna did not become a desirable place for Karaite migration until the beginning of the twentieth century even though it was comparatively close to their maternal place of residence (Trakai/Troki), which was also a capital of the Grand Duchy of Lithuania. It seems that the community appeared in Vilna in the nineteenth century, but it was rather small — in 1869 there were fifty-seven Karaites in the city. However, in the early twentieth century the community grew considerably to approximately a hundred Karaite families.[22]

Modernity brought Karaites with a different attitude to the former capital city of the Grand Duchy of Lithuania. After 1919 Vilna became a part of Poland, and this political shift coincided with the growing Karaite interest in it. The emergence of Vilna as the centre of the secular ethnic Karaite community began in the second decade of the twentieth century, with the appearance of communal printing and other cultural activities there. At that time, the Karaites in Vilna already had an established community — they maintained a prayer house and a communal building in Zwierzyniec (Liet. Žvėrynas),[23] and were building a synagogue (*kenesa*) in the area. For that purpose, donations were gathered from the Karaites of Vilna and other places. In 1914 the building was erected, but the interior was not finished until 1923.[24] The community was growing and in the interwar period consisted of about 120–250 persons.[25] Already in the 1920s the city became the most significant Karaite community in Poland — the concentration of educated and active intellectuals, who often occupied themselves in trade, manufacturing, engineering, law, etc.,[26] and were ready to use part of their income for communal purposes, brought the Vilna community to the leading position among Polish Karaites, especially in relation to Poland's governing institutions.

Undoubtedly, the role of the governing institutions, both local and state, played a significant role in the territorialization of Vilna by the local Karaite community. The Polish government understood that the ethnic diversity of the state's borderlands was an obstacle to its cultural and mental inclusion into the state and the promotion of the loyalty of its inhabitants to the Polish government. Here the interests of certain minorities and the government met — such groups as the Karaites and Muslim Tatars, who never dominated in this city, gained support, both financial and legal, from the government, who encouraged them to establish their cultural centre in Vilna and helped in this way to territorialize it.

However, the Polish Ministry of Religious Affairs and Public Education (Pol. Ministerstwo Wyznań Religijnych i Oświecenia Publicznego), responsible for the state's policy towards religious minorities, did not realize at first what benefit such a small group like the Karaites might bring to the state. In a reply to an unknown curator on 5 February 1925, the ministry comments on the letter sent by the Halicz Karaite leader Jan Grzegorzewski, asking for financial support to the community, that

---

22 Cohen-Mushlin and others, eds, *Synagogues in Lithuania*, p. 242.
23 Cohen-Mushlin and others, eds, *Synagogues in Lithuania*, p. 242; *Karaimskoje slovo*, the reverse of the title page.
24 *Karaimskoje slovo*, p. 23.
25 Different numbers are indicated in the sources and historiography — a report on a Karaite communal meeting gives the number of 120–30 Karaites living in Vilna in 1927 (see Vilnius, Lietuvos centrinis valstybės archyvas (hereafter, LCVA), F. 51, ap. 4, b. 79, l. 14), while the publication *Karaimi Wileńscy w okresie międzywojennym*, p. 20, gives a number of 250.
26 For example, in the meeting of the Vilna Karaite community on 13 March 1927, the community's board (*zarząd*) was elected. It included the president, lawyer Izaak Zajączkowski, the vice-president, Lieutenant-colonel Noe Robaczewski, citizen Jozef Lopatto, and railway official Emanuel Aronowicz. Letter to Vilna *wojewoda*, LCVA, F. 51, ap. 4, b. 79, l. 70.

TOWNS AS AREAS OF ETHNIC COMMUNICATION AND COMPETITION   299

there is no real reason [to allocate funds] because the Karaite nation is very small and does not demonstrate any signs of Polish patriotism, which could justify exceptional exclusiveness [of them].[27]

On the other hand, the Ministry of Foreign Affairs had a different opinion and more far-sighted insight, saying that

a favourable treatment of the needs of the Karaites can bring great benefits to the Polish state. Although they are small in number, Karaites may be small but real executors of loyal deeds on the benefit to the state in the territory of Kresy.[28]

In the long run, this position, expressed by the ministry, would gain more and more importance in the mutual relations between the Karaites and the Polish state. The positive attitude to the Karaites, demonstrated by state institutions, mainly meant support to the Vilna community, which was recognized as representative of all Polish Karaites. It was mainly due to the fact that it was the only institutionalized Karaite community in Poland in early 1920,[29] when the mutual communication began. The fact that the Karaites were associated with Vilna by the Polish authorities is illustrated by the plans of the Ministry of Religious Affairs to establish a Department of Oriental Languages, History, and Culture at the Stefan Batory University in Vilna, arguing that the Polish Oriental communities — Karaites and Tatars — were concentrated there.[30] Needless to say, such a policy had a positive impact on the territorialization of Vilna by the local Karaite community.

As in the case of Troki, the state institutions played an important role in the ability of a particular minority group to appropriate a certain territory and begin to be associated with it. The Vilna Karaites gained the support of both local and state authorities in territorializing the city in exchange for loyalty, demonstrated by this community, to the Polish state. Even the last chapter of the law on the Karaite legal position in the state states that this law must be adopted taking into account, among other reasons, the loyalty demonstrated by the Karaites to the Polish state.[31]

The Territorialization of Vilnius: A New Ideological Centre of Modern Karaites and their National Ideology

If in the aforementioned case of Trakai/Troki, the ideological and cultural fight took place among Karaites and Rabbinite Jews, even if without the intensive participation of the latter, Vilna turned into a centre of collision within the Karaite community between

---

27 A letter to a curator, 5 February 1925, Warsaw, Archiwum Akt Nowych, Ministry of Religious Affairs and Public Education (hereafter, ANN, MSRIOP), syg. 1461, l. 87.
28 ANN, MSRIOP, syg. 1461, l. 87. *Kresy* is the Polish term describing the eastern borderlands of the Polish-Lithuanian Commonwealth and then interwar Poland.
29 ANN, MSRIOP, syg. 1461, l. 255–56.
30 The minutes of the general Karaite meeting, 11 June 1927, LCVA, F. 51, ap. 4, b. 79, l. 30ᵛ.
31 Law of Polish Karaite Legal status, ANN, MSRIOP, syg. 1463, l. 449.

religious orthodoxy on the one hand, presented by one of the Vilna Karaite leaders, Eliasz Jutkiewicz, and the advocates of modern ethnic Karaite identity, dissociated with the tradition of Judaism, led by macenate Izaak Zajączkowski, on the other.[32]

Sometimes the conflict turned into harsh discussions between the representatives of these ideological groups, such as in the elections of Karaite delegates to the general assembly of Polish Karaites, which had to elect the chief Karaite *hacham* in 1927. The voting for the assembly was rather a formality as the elected delegates of a particular community had to present the collective opinion of the group in question, while the real election battle took place in local Karaite settlements. The discussions around the elections of *hacham*, the role and tasks of this institution, the possible candidates, and the appointment of the electors represented the collision of these two ideologies within Karaite communities, especially that of Vilna. The success of any of these groups could have led to the territorialization of Vilna and the ideological dominance over other Karaite settlements.

The vivid example of the ideological fight for domination in Vilna was reflected by a clerk (reporter) of Vilna, Voivode R. Wulc.[33] In his report, Wulc gave a short summary of the meeting, concentrating on the general atmosphere and dissenting opinions among Karaites, concerning the institution of *hacham*, its responsibilities, possible candidates, and qualifications needed. It must be noted that the institution of *hacham* was quite new, established in the Russian Empire in 1837 as the highest official within the Tauria Karaite Spiritual Board.[34] The Karaites of Lutsk, Vilna, Trakai/ Troki, and other settlements within the territory of the empire were subordinated to this institution and its leader. However, in 1869 a similar institution was established in Trakai/Troki,[35] which, though, had been active before that date, and the Karaites from the north-western region were subjected to it. However, I do not possess data about the election of the Trakai/Troki *hacham* in the period under discussion. It may have happened that the Trakai/Troki *hazzan* was occupying this position, and in this case the election of *hacham* in 1927 was a new experience for the Karaite communities under consideration. Getting back to the Wulc report, being an outsider among the Karaites, he had brought several important insights, with which he characterized both groups. Firstly, he referred to two clearly identifiable groups.[36] The first, as was already mentioned, guided by I. Zajączkowski, consisted mainly of young Karaites, described by the author as linked to the state ('jest bardziej [...] państwową'), meaning probably loyalty to the state and integrational notions, and considering position of the *hacham* as a political figure and secular communal leader. I. Zajączkowski, as the leader of this group and the candidate in the election of the delegate from the Vilna community to the general assembly of Polish Karaites, had openly declared in this meeting that he would vote for S. Szapszał. The second group identified by Wulc consisted of elder,

---

32 Report (date not indicated), LCVA, F. 51, ap. 4, b. 79, l. 41; also LCVA, F. 53, ap. 23, b. 726, l. 55.
33 LCVA, F. 51, ap. 4, b. 79, l. 41. Voivode is the Polish government representative responsible for government of a voivodship, the basic territorial unit of the interwar state.
34 The legal status of Tauria Karaite clergymen, *Sbornik starinnych gramot*, p. 401 (3 March 1837).
35 Bairašauskaitė, 'Apibrėžimo ir tapatumo kolizija', p. 31.
36 In the source: 'podział obecnych na dwie grupy dał się odrazu zauważyć', LCVA, F. 51, ap. 4, b. 79, l. 41.

religious, and orthodox Karaites, led by Eliasz Jutkiewicz and Vilna *hacham* (*sic!*) Feliks Małecki.[37] This group would have preferred to have the *hacham* as a religious leader and authority within the community, which was understood, as Wulc had noted, as a national minority ('mniejszość narodowa'), or a Karaite minority ('mniejszość karaimska').[38] Though it is not clear what was the meaning of these perceptions, it may present a cautious position of these Karaites, aiming to preserve clear cultural and, more important, religious boundaries as a minority, separating them from the rest of Polish society. Attributing the term *hacham* to Feliks Małecki shows the use of this term according to the tradition of Judaism, where the term describes a wise and highly educated person, usually in religious matters, a sage.[39] Naturally, it did not correspond to the understanding of this position among the adherents of the first group, led by I. Zajączkowski.

The meeting described brought conflict between these two groups: as was mentioned, I. Zajączkowski openly supported Szapszał's candidacy to the position of Polish Karaite *hacham*, whereas E. Jutkiewicz spoke up for a certain compromise and suggested having Szapszał as a secular communal leader and establishing a religious position for F. Małecki.[40] Wulc sees this as a political manoeuvre, seeking to attract part of the votes of I. Zajączkowski's supporters. However, this initiative failed after I. Zajączkowski was elected as a representative of the Vilna community. Responding to this, F. Małecki refused to work together with the future *hacham*, who was not a religious leader and canon connoisseur; two members of the revision committee, responsible for legitimate elections, resigned from their positions supporting F. Małecki and E. Jutkiewicz.[41]

In October 1927 in the general meeting of the Trakai/Troki Karaite community, a delegate to a general assembly of Polish Karaites was elected as well. The elected Emil Kobecki, a director of the Supreme Chamber of State Control (Pol. Naczelna Izba Kontroli Państwa) and his substitute Józef Zajączkowski, director of a bank, were obliged to represent the local community's vote in the election of the Karaite *hacham*. The president of the Vilna Karaite community, I. Zajączkowski, publicly announced that E. Kobecki would give his vote for the candidature of S. Szapszał to the position of Polish Karaite *hacham*.[42] As we can see, I. Zajączkowski was active in promoting Szapszał's candidature to the position of Polish *hacham* in both Trakai/Troki and Vilna communities, and in both cases was successful to secure two votes from their representatives in favour of Szapszał during the coming elections. However, this seems to be against the regulations of elections which were accepted by the representatives

---

37 LCVA, F. 51, ap. 4, b. 79, l. 41.
38 LCVA, F. 51, ap. 4, b. 79, l. 41.
39 See *Thesaurus Dictionary*.
40 LCVA, F. 51, ap. 4, b. 79, l. 41.
41 LCVA, F. 51, ap. 4, b. 79, l. 41.
42 'Mr Zajączkowski had declared that Mr Kobecki [...] will give his vote [in favour of] Mr Szapszał in the general Karaite assembly electing the *hacham* of all Karaite communities in the territory of Poland', LCVA, F. 51, ap. 4, b. 79, l. 46.

of all Polish Karaite communities at the general meeting in Halicz on 11–12 June 1927, which stated that each delegate gives his vote individually in secret ballot.[43]

The ideological advantage of the supporters of Szapszał was clearly noticeable during the election assembly and the ballot itself as he was the only candidate to vote for. It meant that intensive propaganda, carried out among Karaite communities by I. Zajączkowski, helped the Vilna community to expand their ideology and power among all the Karaite settlements and began its entrenchment in Poland's Karaite communities. From the moment of the election of Szapszał to the position of chief Karaite leader, and the setting up of the *hacham* institution in Vilna, it meant that ideologically Vilna was territorialized as the centre of the new secular ethnic Karaite identity and that the opposing part of the community, led by orthodox religious leaders, was pushed away to the periphery of communal life. However, it seems that this ideological split remained in existence during the whole interwar period, though the group of modernists were constantly gaining more financial and cultural power among Karaites and were better represented in the dominant society.[44]

By analysing the minutes of the Vilna Karaite meetings, we can trace the moment when the balance of ideological powers had changed. Back in 1926 and before, both I. Zajączkowski and E. Jutkiewicz were taking leading positions in the Vilna Karaite communal administration: in that year E. Jutkiewicz was elected to the administrative board by forty votes, while I. Zajączkowski received twenty-five.[45] The first was nominated as president, the second as vice-president of the community.[46] We may presume that E. Jutkiewicz was seen as a communal leader by the Karaites, especially in the circles closely related to the *kenesa*. He was constantly trying to keep the religious leaders and officials (*gabbaim* and *shamashim*) within the administration of the Vilna Karaite community, including by giving them positions as honorary officials, as in the communal meeting on 9 October 1923, when E. Jutkiewicz proposed to include the *gabbaim* of the community in the Administration of Vilna Karaite Association, granting them a right to vote.[47] However, on 13 March 1927, just before the elections of the *hacham*, harsh discussions took place on the election of the community's administration in the meeting of Vilna Karaites. E. Jutkiewicz questioned the procedure, and after the second round of voting, he remained unelected to any official position in the community.[48] This change, however, does not mean that E. Jutkiewicz was completely pushed aside from the communal life of Vilna Karaites — he continued to be an active member, especially concerning the financial issues of the Karaites. However, on the eve of *hacham* elections he was not able to participate in decision making as he had before.

---

43 Annex to the minutes of the meeting, No. 2, LCVA, F. 51, ap. 4, b. 79, l. 32.
44 Troskovaitė, 'Lenkijos ir Lietuvos karaimų savivokos formavimas', ch. II.
45 Minutes of Vilna Karaite meeting, 7 January 1926, in *Karaimi Wileńscy w okresie międzywojennym*, pp. 45–46.
46 Minutes of Vilna Karaite meeting, 23 January 1926, in *Karaimi Wileńscy w okresie międzywojennym*, pp. 42–43.
47 Minutes of the meeting of Vilna Karaite religious community, 9 October 1923, in *Karaimi Wileńscy w okresie międzywojennym*, pp. 29–37.
48 Minutes of the meeting of Vilna Karaite religious community, 13 March 1927, in *Karaimi Wileńscy w okresie międzywojennym*, pp. 52–55.

The Society of Lovers of Karaite History and Literature as a Means of the Territorialization of Vilna: The Creation of a Centre of National Karaite Identity

The idea of establishing a Society of Lovers of Karaite History and Literature (Towarzystwo Miłośników Historii I Literatury Karaimskiej)[49] and promoting its activities was already a second stage of the entrenchment of secular national ethnic Karaite identity and at the same time the territorialization of Vilna as its centre. The idea came to S. Szapszał in 1931, and in April 1932 the first organizational meeting of the society took place in Vilna, in the house of the Vilna Karaite community. It seems that ideologically, organizationally, and structurally the society was organized like the Vilna Karaite community — a general meeting of all members, administration, and the Revision Committee operated there.[50] Consequently, as most of the members of this society were of Karaite origin, they were also active in the Vilna community. Not surprisingly, on 24 April 1932 in the first organizational meeting of the society, two candidates were nominated to the position of president — the already well-known I. Zajączkowski and E. Jutkiewicz. The latter withdrew from the election, so I. Zajączkowski occupied this position, holding at the same time the analogous position in the Vilna Karaite community.[51] However, it is important that the idea of this society was to expand its activities (and promoted ideology) to the whole territory of Poland and to attract representatives of Karaite settlements in Halicz, Luck, and Trakai/Troki to join its activities, which they did.[52] The society was also directed at the strengthening of Karaite national identity — the term *nation* was attributed to Karaites already in the first meeting of the society in April 1932.[53] The content of this identity was revealed in Szapszał's speech, dedicated to the establishment of the society — he had stressed the importance of 'our past, our history […] language, […] and ethnography [of] our *nation*'.[54] It was a new stage in communal life and its self-perception — the already existing Karaite journal *Karaite Thought* (Pol. *Myśl Karaimska*)[55] was perceived as a platform for Karaites to 'get acquainted with ourselves and to introduce to our countrymen our tiny

---

49 The idea of the establishment of this society probably belongs to S. Szapszał, but the organizational work was done by Eliasz Jutkiewicz, who began this initiative in December 1931, informing Karaite settlements in Trakai/Troki, Łuck, Halicz, and Warszaw, and presented the project of the statute; see *Karaimi Wileńscy w okresie międzywojennym*, p. 136, n. 3. For more on the society, see Gąsiorowski, 'Towarzystwo Miłośników Historii i Literatury Karaimskiej'.

50 Statut Towarzystwa Miłośników Historii i Literatury Karaimskiej: *Karaimi Wileńscy w okresie międzywojennym*, Annex, pp. 198–201.

51 The minutes of the first organizational meeting of the Society of Lovers of Karaite History and Literature, 24 April 1932, *Karaimi Wileńscy w okresie międzywojennym*, p. 137.

52 *Karaimi Wileńscy w okresie międzywojennym*, p. 137.

53 *Karaimi Wileńscy w okresie międzywojennym*, p. 138.

54 The minutes of the first organizational meeting of the Society of Lovers of Karaite History and Literature, 24 April 1932, *Karaimi Wileńscy w okresie międzywojennym*, Annex, pp. 142–43.

55 *Myśl karaimska* was a scientific, literary, and social journal devoted to the Karaite community in Poland, published in Polish, with insertions in Tiurkic (Karaite), from 1924 to 1947.

nation'.[56] Probably this was one of the reasons why after the establishment of the society, the journal became a part of it.[57] The elaboration and representation of secular modern national self-identity was a shift in the community's development, which required other strategies and activities than the maintenance of religious self-perception perceived by most of the Karaites at the beginning of the century. However, this new trend within the community was very successful: Vilna became associated with the modern Karaite community. On 16–17 May 1932, the Second Congress of Orientalists took place in Vilna, instead of previously considered Lviv/Lwów, because 'Vilna is the centre of our Karaite and Tatar [communities] and has beautiful Oriental traditions'.[58] It seems that the ideological power and influence of the society was constantly growing. As the minutes of its meetings shows, the number of its members was significant — they were attended by up to one hundred individuals, which mean that the organization managed to attract many Karaites but also people of other origin.[59] Such well-attended meetings usually were academic in nature, presenting lectures on different topics of Karaite history, language, and culture. They were often presented by Karaites themselves, like S. Szapszał, A. Zajączkowski, and others. Most of them were later published in the journal *Karaite Thought*, in this way reaching an even broader audience.[60]

The activities of the society involved, though to a lesser extent, E. Jutkiewicz as well. Being an adherent of the religious and traditional side of the Vilna Karaite community, he became involved in the cultural mainstream of the society's activities, promoting, in this way, the national Karaite identity as well. It may well be true that he had mitigated his position because the group of enthusiasts of modern ethnic national Karaite identity was constantly growing and gaining more and more power among Karaites and support from dominant society, be it governmental powers, scholars, or other groups. It may also be true that such people as E. Jutkiewicz tried to balance his position by making a compromise between religious and ethnic national identity. For example, on 22 April 1935, E. Jutkiewicz announced a proposition to use the Tiurkic (Karaite) language in the meetings of the society instead of Polish and to strengthen the teaching of their mother tongue among Karaite youth and adults.[61] Another reason for the moderate position

---

56 Pol. 'poznawanie siebie samych I zaznajamianie naszych wspólziomków z tem, czem jest nasz skromny naród', The minutes of the first organizational meeting of the Society of Lovers of Karaite History and Literature, 24 April 1932, *Karaimi Wileńscy w okresie międzywojennym*, Annex, p. 143.

57 The minutes of the first organizational meeting of the Society of Lovers of Karaite History and Literature, 24 April 1932, *Karaimi Wileńscy w okresie międzywojennym*, p. 136.

58 Pol. 'Wilno jest ośrodkiem naszych Karaimów i Tatarów i że posiada piękne tradycje orientalistyczne', Vilnius, Lietuvos mokslų akademijos biblioteka, Rankraščių skyrius (hereafter, LMAB, RS), F. 143–947, l. 10, 12, quoted from *Karaimi Wileńscy w okresie międzywojennym*, p. 144, n. 12.

59 On 15 October 1932 (58 attendees), on 2 April 1933 (about 100), on 9 December 1933 (71), on 13 October 1934 (about 100), 18 April 1938 (68). See *Karaimi Wileńscy w okresie międzywojennym*, pp. 151, 154, 157, 160, 184.

60 See, for instance, the minutes of the meeting on 13 October 1934, *Karaimi Wileńscy w okresie międzywojennym*, pp. 160–61.

61 The minutes of the first organizational meeting of the Society of Lovers of Karaite History and Literature, 22 April 1935, *Karaimi Wileńscy w okresie międzywojennym*, p. 166.

demonstrated by Jutkiewicz may have been growing anti-Semitic notions in Europe and in Poland, which could have affected the growing imbalance between traditionalists and modernists among Karaites. For example, Samuel Bobowicz in his letter to S. Szapszał, sent on the eve of the Second World War, flatly stated that 'during the ages we were marked with blackness of Jewishness [...] we have to turn away from Jewishness once and for all so that all nations would recognize this'.[62] Clearly, such a position was influenced by the fear of the Nazi ideology and politics. Though S. Bobowicz lived abroad and was not a member either of Vilna or of any other Polish Karaite community, it may well be true that such notions existed among the local Karaites as well.

During about twenty years of intensive Karaite activities in Vilna, the city began to be associated with this community as their administrative and cultural centre. It was shaped by a range of communal organizations and certain landmarks that indicated how the city (also) belonged to the Karaites. The local Karaites managed to create a complete territorialized community, where the central role was played by the society, the journal *Karaite Thought*, and the institution of Polish Karaite *hacham* — the most important communal, political, and cultural figure for Polish Karaites. The city's territory was marked by the erection of the Vilna *kenesa*,[63] which was the community's religious centre but also served as a monument for modern ethnic Karaite identity: a clear indication of such intention is the Karaite coat of arms, put as the main symbol of their identity on its dome peak.

The first half of the twentieth century marked a golden age for Polish Karaites, and this important period of time became associated with the city of Vilna and activities that were taking place among local Karaites. At that time, the Karaites were associated with Vilna as much as they were with Trakai/Troki, with only a time distinction between two: the first was associated with the establishment of the Karaites in Poland, its historical past, and the second with its contemporary flourishing and revival of Karaite culture. However, in the course of time, neither in the Soviet period nor later, Vilnius did not became a part of the Karaite historical narrative: when the independence of Lithuania was declared in 1990, the Vilna period began to be remembered as the place of cultural flourishing by the Karaite community, but the place itself was not actualized and not included in the plot of Karaite historical legend.

Conclusions

The twentieth century dramatically changed the role of Vilna in the Karaite community, which finally became an actual communal centre, leaving the Trakai/Troki residence aside and changing its dominance as the religious and cultural centre of Lithuanian

---

62 Letter from S. Bobowicz to S. Szapszał, 1938, LMAB, RS, F. 143, b. 182, l. 2.
63 Its erection began in 1911 under the architect Michail Prozorov. In two years the walls were built and the roof was finished, but further works were interrupted by World War I. Work was restarted in 1921, and after two years it was opened for the Karaites.

and Polish Karaites. It was in the twentieth century when Trakai/Troki entrenched its image as the historical homeland of local Karaites, but at the same time it lost its importance as an actual centre of the community. In other words, it became a virtual and ideologically elaborate image of a homeland, rather than an actual focal point of their lives. With the emergence of the Karaite community in Vilna in the beginning of the twentieth century, the need to lay down roots in the city's environment grew stronger. Cultural activities, the birth of national self-identity, and the growing ideological power of its adherents made the Karaites more visible in the environment of Vilna, which was mainly dominated by Jews and Poles. It became a centre for Polish Karaites administratively, culturally, and ideologically because of the creation of the institution of the *hacham*, the establishment of the journal *Karaite Thought* and the Society of Lovers of Karaite History and Literature, and other activities, which created, maintained, and promoted a Karaite national identity. However, these intensive activities brought the Karaites to a paradoxical situation: Vilna became a Karaite cultural centre and a place of formation of the community's modern national self-identity largely thanks to cooperation with state authorities and avoiding conflicts with other ethnic communities. But despite its importance to contemporary Karaite leaders, Vilna was never included in the plot of their historical narrative, which was formed around images of the Crimea and Trakai/Troki: the first understood as a cradle of eastern European Karaites, and the second as a local derivation of what can be called a historical homeland.[64]

Works Cited

Manuscripts and Archival Sources

Vilnius, Lietuvos mokslų akademijos biblioteka, Rankraščių skyrius, F. 143–947; syg. 143, b. 182
Vilnius, Lietuvos centrinis valstybės archyvas, F. 51, ap. 4, b. 79; F. 53, ap. 23, b. 726
Vilnius, Lietuvos valstybės istorijos archyvas, F. 378 BS, ap. 1847, b. 436
Warsaw, Archiwum Akt Nowych, Ministry of Religious Affairs and Public Education, syg. 1461, 1663

Primary Sources

Author unknown, 'Iz istorii Trokskich karaimov', *Karaimskai'a zhizn'*, 2 (1911), 24–30
Karaimi Wileńscy w okresie międzywojennym: Protokoły z posiedzeń organizacji karaimskich, ed. by Urszula Wróblewska (Białystok: Wydawnictwo Uniwersyteckie Trans Humana, 2015)
Karaimskoje slovo, 7–8 (1914)
Lietuvos magdeburginių miestų privilegijos ir aktai, vol. VI, ed. by Algirdas Baliulis (Vilnius: LII leidykla, 2008)

---

64 On the historical narrative of Lithuanian Karaites, please see Troskovaitė, 'Is There Only One Homeland?'.

Sbornik starinnych gramot i uzakonenii Rosijskoi imperii: Kasatelno prav i sostoi'ani'a rusko-podannych Karaimov, ed. by Zaria Abramovich Firkovich (St Petersburg: Leschtukovskaia Parovaia Skoropietschatnia P.O. Iablonskavo, 1890)
Thesaurus Dictionary, <https://www.thefreedictionary.com/Hacham> [accessed 9 December 2019]

Secondary Studies

Bairašauskaitė, Tamara, 'Apibrėžimo ir tapatumo kolizija: Lietuvos karaimų socialinio statuso klausimu XIX amžiaus pirmojoje pusėje', *Lituanistica*, 65.1 (2006), 24–37

Cohen-Mushlin, Aliza, Sergey Kravtsov, Vladimir Levin, Giedre Mickūnaitė, and Jurigta Šiaučiūnaitė-Verbickienė, eds, *Synagogues in Lithuania: A Catalogue N–Ž* (Vilna: Vilniaus dailes akademijos leidykla, 2012)

Gąsiorowski, Stefan, 'Towarzystwo Miłośników Historii i Literatury Karaimskiej w Wilnie i jego członkowie w latach 1932–1939', in *Karaj kiuńlari Dziedzictwo Narodu Karaimskiego we współczesnej Europie*, ed. by Mariola Abkowicz and Henryk Jankowski (Wrocław: Bitik. Karaimska Oficyna Wydawnicza, 2004), pp. 71–83

Rosman, Moshe J., *The Lords' Jews: Magnate–Jewish Relations in the Polish-Lithuanian Commonwealth during the Eighteenth Century* (Cambridge, MA: Harvard University Press, 1991)

Shani, Giorgio, 'The Territorialization of Identity: Sikh Nationalism in the Diaspora', *Studies in Ethnicity and Nationalism*, 2.1 (2002), 11–19

Troskovaitė, Dovilė, 'Is There Only One Homeland? The Forming Image of Troki (Trakai) and Crimea in the Self-Identity of the Karaites in the 19th–20th c.', *Tiurkų istorija ir kultūra Lietuvoje, specialus Lietuvos istorijos studijų leidinys*, 11 (2014), 288–398

——, 'Lenkijos ir Lietuvos karaimų savivokos formavimas XIX a. vid. – XX a. pirmoje pusėje: tarp atsiskyrimo ir prisitaikymo' (Formation of Polish and Lithuanian Karaite identity in the 19th–20th centuries: Between separation and adaptation) (unpublished doctoral thesis, Lithuanian Institute of History and Klaipeda University, 2014)

Verbickienė, Jurgita, *Žydai Lietuvos Didžiosios Kunigaikštystės visuomenėje: Sambūvio aspektai* (Vilnius: Žara, 2009)

Weinryb, Bernard, 'The Beginnings of East — European Jewry in Legend and Historiography', in *Studies and Essays in Honour of Abraham A. Neuman*, ed. by Meir Ben-Horin, Bernard Weinryb, and Solomon Zeitlin (Philadelphia: Brill for Dropsie College, 1962), pp. 445–502

JURGITA ŠIAUČIŪNAITĖ-VERBICKIENĖ

A Gift or 'Poklon dla Pana' as One of the Ways of Building Social Cohesion

The Case of the Vilnius Jewish Community in the Second Half of the Eighteenth Century

The strategies for shaping relations between minorities analysed in the previous chapter indicated the desire to use ties with the dominant ethnic group in order to ensure a safe position in a multi-ethnic society, also in opposition to other minorities. Obtaining favourable relations with the dominant ethnic group in the political community, especially its elite, was of key importance for the minorities living in the Grand Duchy of Lithuania (GDL). Therefore, in this chapter, I would like to present one of the communication mechanisms for establishing and strengthening this type of relationship between the Jewish community and the Christian elite in the GDL.

Introduction

In this chapter, I would like to deal with communication between social groups understood primarily not as information transfer but as bonding and persuading practice with strong pragmatic character. No matter which historical period is discussed, gifts — which are the main object of analysis here — always have a pleasant and favourable effect on the ones who receive them. In the social structure of the eighteenth century and earlier, pleasant, favourably disposing, or loyalty-showing gifts were a common way of maintaining good relationships and communication that also facilitated the overcoming of some everyday issues. In this chapter based on the case of the Vilnius Jewish community, I would like to draw attention to the symbolic and social meaning of practices which have not been widely explored, but which were very common in early modern societies. The subject of analysis is the giving of gifts as an act of communication which bridged the gaps between specific social groups in the GDL and in the same moment was also a means of building cohesion within

Jurgita Šiaučiūnaitė-Verbickienė • (jurgita.verbickiene@if.vu.lt) is a Professor of History in the Faculty of History at Vilnius University. She has published on the sociocultural history of non-Christian groups in the Grand Duchy of Lithuania.

Inter-Ethnic Relations and the Functioning of Multi-Ethnic Societies: Cohesion in Multi-Ethnic Societies in Europe from c. 1000 to the Present, II, ed. by Przemysław Wiszewski, EER 18 (Turnhout: Brepols, 2022), pp. 309–320

BREPOLS ✠ PUBLISHERS   10.1484/M.EER-EB.5.132157

This is an open access chapter made available under a cc by-nc 4.0 International License.

its multi-ethnic society. The main source for this research is an archival manuscript in Polish — an account and description of the revenue and expenditure of the Vilnius kahal, which contains records from 23 June 1787 to 17 March 1788. The main questions discussed below concern communication strategies and the pragmatic ends of these acts performed by the Vilnius Jewish elite: What kind of gifts did the Jewish community give, and what circle of recipients was this practice intended for? What strategies did the Vilnius kahal use in the planning of gift giving, and which aims in context of building cohesion were meant to be achieved?

Historical Context

Due to the fundamental state-initiated changes in community administration, the period following the year 1764 when the convocation Sejm of Warsaw adopted the constitution 'Jewish poll tax' (Pol. *Pogłówne Żydowskie*)[1] was important in the lives of the Jews of the Polish-Lithuanian Commonwealth. I have in mind the liquidation or limitation of functions of the Vaads of Poland (formed as a joint Polish Crown and Grand Duchy of Lithuania self-government institution of Jews in 1583) and Lithuania (as a separate body operating from 1623, Heb. *Vaad Medinat Lita*),[2] the reform of taxation of the Jews, the first general census of the Jews (which took place in 1764–1765), as well as the process of accounting and the repayment of the debts of the bankrupt community.

In the historiography, the beginning of the indebtedness of the Jews in the Polish-Lithuanian Commonwealth is linked to the turn of the sixteenth and seventeenth century or the early seventeenth century.[3] These processes were the result of social and economic causes, as a result of which the Jewish communities,[4] who traditionally were lenders, became not only borrowers but also incurred heavy debts. The accurate date of this fundamental turning point that reduced the Jews into an insolvent community cannot be determined due to an absence of sources. It is very likely these were parallel processes in both the GDL and Poland.[5] The financial situation of the Jewish community and its potential lenders was further complicated by the period of intensive wars and hardship that has left its mark in the history of the Polish-Lithuanian Commonwealth under the name of the *Deluge*. Sigismund III Vasa, king of the Polish-Lithuanian Commonwealth from 1587 to 1632, had claims to the Swedish throne after his father's death and involved the commonwealth in a prolonged war against Sweden to gain control over the province of Livonia. Soon a

---

1 Constitution for Grand Duchy of Lithuania: *Volumina Legum*, pp. 26–29.
2 Changes in the organization of the Jewish self-government after the dissolution of the Vaads are discussed by Michałowska-Mycielska, *Sejm Żydów Litewskich (1623–1764)*, pp. 289–96.
3 Leszczyński, *Sejm Zydów Korony, 1623–1764*, p. 143; Kalik, 'Patterns of Contacts', p. 103.
4 Private indebtedness is not the subject of this article and is in itself a separate fascinating topic for research.
5 For more about the Jewish debt situation in the Polish-Lithuania Commonwealth, see Kalik, 'Patterns of Contacts'.

war against Moscow spread, during which the troops of Tsar Aleksei Mikhailovich of Moscow occupied Vilnius as the capital of the GDL (1655–1662). As if that was not enough, in 1657 Vilnius was ravaged by a devastating epidemic of plague. According to Israeli researcher Mordechai Nadav, the financial situation of the Lithuanian Jewish community markedly deteriorated around 1700 when it ran short of funds for debt repayments and taxes. In 1700, the community of Vilnius along with other chief communities was a defendant in a number of cases concerning overdue debts heard at the Lithuanian Tribunal (the highest appeal court in the Grand Duchy).[6] The situation was aggravated by the Northern War (1700–1721): for at least a dozen years of the eighteenth century, communication between communities was disrupted and the connection between chief communities and smaller ones coordinated by then did not exist. It is natural that with increasing demands on the treasury during the war, an ever-rising poll tax was imposed on the Jews.[7]

The written sources originating from the GDL show that both the Jewish community of Vilnius and the Lithuanian Vaad found themselves in a rather complicated financial situation by the middle of the seventeenth century. Considerable amounts of money borrowed more than a hundred years prior from Wojciech Cieciszewski, rector of the Jesuit Vilnius Academy (1646–1649), were recognized as overdue debts of the Jews of Vilnius when their debts were calculated in the late eighteenth century.[8] The Lithuanian Vaad was incapable of collecting the ever-rising poll tax, and in 1655 in Selcy its representatives were considering how to pay the increased poll tax and complained that there was nobody to borrow money from as they used to do earlier ('meanwhile [...] we have no one to borrow from like in earlier years, everything has to be covered by collecting [money] from the population').[9] Roman Rybarski, who analysed the functioning of the treasury of the Polish-Lithuanian Commonwealth in the seventeenth century, paid attention to the fact that in the second half of the century the Jews of the GDL used to delay paying the poll tax or paid it in instalments.[10] The examination of the indebtedness of the Lithuanian Vaad until its liquidation in 1764 carried out by Anna Michałowska-Mycielska suggests that its financial situation was rather difficult in as early as the middle of the seventeenth century and was gradually becoming worse.[11] At that time, the lenders of the Lithuanian Vaad included individual Jewish communities, private individuals (Jews both from the GDL and from Poland; a large number of lenders came from the city of Lublin and

---

6 Nadav, *The Jews of Pinsk, 1506 to 1880*, p. 270.
7 Nadav, *The Jews of Pinsk, 1506 to 1880*, p. 271.
8 Lietuvos valstybės istorijos archyvas (Lithuanian State Historical Archives; hereafter, LVIA), collection 11, index 1, file 1040, p. 27.
9 Dubnow, ed., *Pinkas ha-Medina*, no. 504.
10 Rybarski, *Skarb i pieniądz za Jana Kazimierza, Michała Korybuta i Jana III*, pp. 232–33. The author gives an example that illustrates the payment of the poll tax in 1677: when the Lithuanian Vaad paid to the treasury about 3000 *złoty* of the 20,000 *złoty* payable, a transfer for part of the money — about 10,000 *złoty* — was submitted. It is not known whether it was paid and how the remaining amount of that year's poll tax was paid.
11 Michałowska-Mycielska, *Sejm Żydów Litewskich (1623–1764)*, pp. 244–34.

its surroundings, which, according to the author, can be explained by loan contracts concluded at the time of the famous Lublin fairs), as well as the Christian nobles, religious orders, or individual clergymen.

The data discussed shows that at the level of Jewish self-government and its most influential communities, the situation was rather complex in the second half of the seventeenth century, and borrowing in order to pay the taxes imposed by the state had developed into something of a habit. It has been calculated that the poll tax made up about half of all the expenditure of the Polish Vaad,[12] and it is very likely that a similar proportion might have also been the case in the GDL.[13] Before 1764, that is, the launch of the process of the calculation and clearance of Jewish debts supervised by the Treasury Commission, the state did not take any interest in the revenue and expenditure of kahals or Vaads and did not control it. The payment and management of state and community taxes was treated as a manifestation of the independence of Jewish self-government at both the local and the state levels. To the state, fiscal relations with a community centralized at the duchy level must have also been more convenient than dealing with separate regional and local groups. The state started taking some interest in the debts of the Jews only in the second half of the eighteenth century, when, according to the calculations of Ignacy Schiper, the debts of Polish and Lithuanian Vaads exceeded 2,450,000 *złoty*.[14] The debts of the Jews of the GDL were not that huge:[15] their overall indebtedness could have reached about 1,000,000 *złoty*.[16]

Despite the measures applied by the state, the repayment of Jewish debts to the clergy, fraternities of religious orders, and private individuals — mostly the nobles and magnates — was too slow. Twenty-eight years after the state had triggered steps to control and monitor not only the taxation of the Jews in the state but also the process of the repayment of the community debts, the Four Year Sejm returned to the consideration of the issue so relevant to the nobility and landowners with full force. The Sejm was looking for ways to stabilize the unmanageable situation, because

---

12 Leszczyński, *Sejm Żydów Korony, 1623–1764*, p. 137.

13 It should necessarily be borne in mind that in the context of communal revenue-expenditure the poll tax was just one regular type of expense, yet the money collected from various communal taxes was not sufficient to pay it.

14 Schiper, 'Wewnętrzna Organizacja Żydów w daw. Rzeczpospolitej', p. 107.

15 Anishchenko, *Cherta osedlosti*, p. 19; Schiper, 'Zniesienie autonomji centralnej i ziemskiej w 1764 r.', p. 107.

16 On the basis of other authors and the document 'Uniwersał Komisyi skarbowej' (1764) that he had seen himself, Ignacy Schiper claims that the debts of the kahals of the Grand Duchy of Lithuania were as follows: Vilnius – 722,800 *złoty*, Brest – 222,720 *złoty*, Hrodna – 386,571 *złoty*, Pinsk – 309,140 *złoty*. Schiper does not provide any comment on whether the analysed document mentioned the debts of yet another influential community, that of Slutsk (see Schiper, 'Podatotnoye oblozhenie evreev', p. 281). It should be noted that very likely Schiper resorted to a document that indicated approximate debts, because at least in the Grand Duchy of Lithuania decisions regarding the sizes of identified debts were adopted only in 1766. Mordechai Nadav mentions that a debt of the Pinsk community of the same amount was recorded in 1768 (Nadav, *The Jews of Pinsk, 1506 to 1880*, p. 272). The latter date seems to be the most credible.

the Jews' debts were being repaid to their creditors too slowly and the process of borrowing, although forbidden, did not stop.[17]

Before the Jewish census of 1764–1765 and the declaration of the insolvency and bankruptcy of the Jewish communities, the state did not interfere with the administration of revenue and expenditure or financial accounting in the Jewish communities. On the one hand, in this context the Treasury Commission implemented control of an internal documentation of the Jewish community. A period of indebtedness, when the incomes and outcomes of the Jewish communities were under the control of the Treasury Commission, is very specific for research on the social behaviour of the leaders of the Jewish communities. The main challenge was to concentrate all of the income of the Jewish communities into debt repayment. On the other hand, the Jews tried to find ways to survive in such a financially complicated situation and to create a circle of patrons. In this chapter I would like to focus on gifts as one of the solutions they tried to apply to strengthen their links with the surrounding society and secure resources for debt payments. There are not a lot of sources and examples for analysis of this sensitive topic, especially because it is quite difficult to separate bribes (as tools for receiving exceptional possibilities or benefits) from gifts for patrons. The latter were chosen mostly as ways to create long-lasting patronage or the support of influential people.

Sources for the Accounting of Revenue and Expenditure of the Vilnius Community

A number of important sources were produced against the backdrop of the above-mentioned complicated historical circumstances and found their way into the body of documents from the Treasury Commission of the GDL. Their content allows us to reconstruct the revenue and expenditure of the bankrupt kahal of Vilnius, the expediency of and expectations for their usage. Later in this chapter I would like to focus on the analysis of several financial accounting documents of the Vilnius kahal produced at the end of the eighteenth century. They were all in Polish as per the requirement of the state, in order for its officials to be able to control the financial flows of the Jewish communities. All of these documents except one had an identical structure: the content begins with the accounting of each month's revenue, which is followed by accounted expenditure. An identical principle for preparing accounting documents allows us to compare the data given in them. In two of the sources analysed, the kahal's revenue and expenditure information was partially duplicated. One of them is a detailed revenue account (report) of the income of thirteen months from 1 September 1790 to 1 October 1791,[18] and the second is a ledger of the community's

---

17 Few projects to resolve the problem of the indebtedness were proposed during the Four Year Sejm, and the position and suggestions in this case were presented by both nobles and Jews as well: *Materiały do Dziejów Sejmu Czteroletniego*, nos 10, 76, etc.

18 LVIA, Senieji aktai (Old acts; hereafter, SA), collection 3757.

costs and receipts covering the period from 1 March to 1 September 1791.[19] The larger part of the community's receipts recorded in these accounting documents show various *korobka* (box) taxes and the minimal expenditure of just a few typical kinds:[20] for the *shtadlan* (a community's trustee in charge of managing affairs with state authorities, town administration, or individuals), for the maintenance of the hospital, and so-called *extra expensa* which are not set out in detail.

The kahal's revenue and expenditure report for the calendar year of 1790–1791 shows receipts from ten *korobka* taxes. In the majority of cases these are taxes on essential goods related to the traditional lifestyle that could not be bought outside the community: kosher food, ritual supplies, and original communal or family rituals. The official status of these accounting documents is verified by the signature of Antoni Kiersowski, who was the supervisor of the kahal's revenue, or, in Polish, *Dozorca prowentów kahalnych*. A comparison of the above-mentioned data with those from the chronologically earlier ledger of revenue and expenditure of the Vilnius community containing records from 23 June 1787 to 17 March 1788 will reveal obvious differences.[21] It is this document that raises questions regarding its purpose and especially the nature of the accounted expenditure and the allocation of the funds of the indebted community. The balance of the kahal's revenue and expenditure accounted in this ledger is negative: the expenditure exceeded income by over 2000 *złoty*. Meanwhile, the revenue recorded in other official documents used to exceed expenditure, and there used to be a sufficient amount of cash in the communal money box. Another peculiarity of the third ledger was the absence of the signature of the supervisor of the kahal's revenue, an official appointed by the Treasury Commission. These circumstances and the extraordinary nature of the expenditure accounted in the ledger raise well-founded suspicions that this ledger might have been used for the accounting of the community's unofficial expenditure, despite the fact that, like the other two accounting documents, it was compiled at the time when the state was keeping a close eye on the expenditure of the Jewish community in order to optimize the process of debt repayment. A possible purpose of this ledger — recording the community's illegal expenditure — does not offer answers to two relevant questions: first, why this seemingly internal document was kept in Polish (if it was prepared for the kahal's use only, it would be more relevant to write it in Hebrew and not care about its translation), and, second, under what circumstances it found its way, along with official documents, to the archival fund of the Treasury Commission. Although in its content this ledger differs from other surviving accounting documents of the Vilnius kahal, it also bears similarities with other eighteenth-century accounting sources of kahals that are known to historians.

---

19 LVIA, SA, collection 3960.

20 *Korobka* are taxes collected inside the Jewish community and under community regulation from different goods and services; the closest match are excise taxes. The well-known name of this tax in the historiography is *koropka* as well. *Korobka* was established in the seventeenth century to assist individual communities to pay their debts.

21 LVIA, SA, collection 3757.

It should be noted that researchers have spotted only a few of them so far. Gershon Hundert analysed the documents of revenue and expenditure of the Jewish community of the private town of Opatów,[22] which inconsistently recorded the kahal's monetary flows from 1728 to 1784. Jacob Goldberg and Adam Wein published expenditure accounts (1785–1789) recorded in the *Pinkasim* of the Działoczyn kahal.[23] These two documents of the communities of the Polish towns are chronologically close to the analysed sources of accounts of the Vilnius kahal. What links these documents is that a part of the accounted expenditure of the communities were allocated to gifts to influential or useful individuals. But in two of the three surviving accounting documents of the Vilnius kahal of the second half of the eighteenth century this item of expenditure was either attributed to *extra expensa* or not accounted at all.

Gifts and Social Cohesion Building

No matter which historical period is discussed, gifts always have a pleasant and favourable effect on those who receive them. In the social structure of the eighteenth century and earlier, pleasant, favourably disposing, or loyalty-showing gifts were a common way of maintaining good relationships and of facilitating ways to overcome everyday issues. On the other hand, a gift was also appreciated as a recognition of the power or influence of a particular individual. Therefore, gifts from a Jewish community as a means of making contact with the Christian part of society were not an exception. The phenomenon of gifts as the means of communication and as an instrument for influencing early modern society has not been a theme which has been widely addressed in the historiography. It is not even quite clear in what way the functions of a gift and its impact on the receiver differed from a bribe, which is a similar phenomenon but with negative connotations. The research presented based on the Vilnius kahal case allows us to suggest one possible difference. Gifts were not always expensive goods, but they were periodically given with the expectation of building long-lasting, good relations and confidence between the parties involved. Gifts helped to create and maintain a positive attitude on the part of the powerful individual towards the gift-giver which might be used by the latter when they needed assistance. And then this relationship was supplemented with bribes given in the expectation that they could change a complicated situation into a more favourable one for the giver. Gifts were not exceptional but fairly common instruments of social behaviour which helped to stabilize social order and cement ties between clients and mighty protectors or patrons.

The Jewish community used gifts to achieve their required goals or to win favours in earlier times, too, and this can be seen in the decisions of the Lithuanian Vaad.[24] It

---

22 Hundert, *The Jews in a Polish Private Town*.
23 Goldberg and Wein, 'Księga kahału w Działoszynie z drugiej połowy XVIII w.'.
24 In the *Pinkas* of the Lithuanian Vaad there were decisions about the collecting of money for gifts and bribes, as well as the decisions concerning the amount of money dedicated for gifts in different situations and for members of different positions in society. See more in Dubnow, ed., *Pinkas ha-Medina*.

should be pointed out that kahals of both Vilnius and Działoczyn used to give only material gifts and did not try to achieve their aims with cash.[25] In the case of Opatów, this cannot be firmly confirmed due to the specific nature of the source, but the same trend seems to prevail there as well.[26]

The meaning imparted onto the gift and its significance are quite accurately and subtly conveyed by the definition 'a gift to the master/lord', or *poklon dlia pana* in Polish,[27] used in the sources. As can be seen from the gifts made by the Vilnius kahal, the objects considered to be gifts do not coincide with our understanding of what might be luxury objects (as we might expect such gifts to be) such as works of art, weapons, pedigree horses, or expensive household appliances. The gifts bestowed by the Vilnius kahal were very practical, for everyday use, without much variety, and in the majority of cases were easily accessible in the local market.

The nature of the gifts allows them to be divided into three groups. The largest group consisted of goods for everyday use — meat, fish, vodka, candles, or firewood.[28] Gifts in the second group were intended for a narrower circle of recipients and included luxury food products — lemons, coffee, and sugar.[29] Mentions of more refined gifts suggest conscious differentiation of them in connection with social position and stronger influence of their recipients. Such presents were most often received by representatives of the clergy:[30] the nuncio, Bishop Jerzy Tyszkiewicz of Vilnius, judicial priests, or Franciscan monks. As can be seen from late eighteenth-century accounting documents of the Vilnius Jewish community, only on rare occasions were these luxury foods given to laymen, as for example, to commissar or Mister Kruszensky,[31] whose position remains unknown up until today. A similar trend can be observed in Opatów, where exotic fruits and coffee were given as gifts exclusively to the clergy and dignitaries.[32] The third and the smallest group of gifts consisted of the coverage of travel and accommodation expenses for individuals who were influential or useful under certain circumstances.[33]

The nature of the gifts suggests that the kahal of Vilnius made practical gifts that predominantly satisfied the routine daily needs of the recipients such as food and/ or candles, or firewood during the cold seasons of the year. The most essential items such as candles and firewood were the gifts most frequently given to officials, private individuals, army officers, or for the needs of the Vilnius castle.[34] However, contrary to making a gift of food, in this case the seasonal nature of the gift is observed: during

---

25 Goldberg and Wein, 'Księga kahału w Działoszynie z drugiej połowy XVIII w.' and LVIA, SA, folder 3755.
26 Hundert, *The Jews in a Polish Private Town*, pp. 98–104.
27 For example, LVIA, SA, collection 3755, p. 12^v.
28 LVIA, SA, collection 3755, pp. 13, 15, 15^v, 18, 23^v, and others.
29 LVIA, SA, collection 3755, pp. 12^v, 13, and others.
30 LVIA, SA, collection 3755, p. 13^v.
31 LVIA, SA, collection 3755, p. 12^v.
32 Hundert, *The Jews in a Polish Private Town*, p. 101.
33 LVIA, SA, collection 3755. For example, the Vilnius kahal covered the travel expenses of *podstarosta* (p. 13^v) or paid transportation wain for commissars of the Treasury Commission (p. 13).
34 LVIA, SA, collection 3755, pp. 13, 14, 14^v, 15, and others.

the cold periods of the year candles were a popular gift, while the first records of expenditure incurred on firewood were made in autumn months.[35] In the accounting documents of the Vilnius kahal of the eight months of 1787 and 1788 covered, expenses for gifts are recorded in detail and tidily, with indications of gift recipients' surnames or their jobs. With the exception of several entries pointing to a set of expenses incurred due to the *sejmik* (local parliament of nobles), the welcoming of the voivode, or a wholesale purchase of food for gifts, these expenses were payments to Shlom *Kramnik* (salesman) for the coffee, lemons, and sugar supplied to the kahal;[36] acquisitions of large amounts of vodka were also intended 'na poklon dlia panow'.

Hundert, who analysed the expenditures of the Opatów community, noticed that among the recipients of the kahal's gifts there was a group of individuals whose favour was sought every year and expenses were made to that effect. This group was quite numerous, about twenty-five people.[37] Such circumstances suggest that gifts used to be resorted to not only for the management of daily matters, but also for securing communal safety in a residential environment. Another trend singled out by Hundert was occasional gifts that were more extensively made on the eve of Easter and Christmas.[38]

The documents of expenditure over nine months (June 1787–March 1788) of the Vilnius kahal do not reflect this trend of bestowing gifts by the Opatów community. There was no campaign of giving gifts before Christmas in Vilnius, and Easter was simply outside the accounting period. However, the ledger of revenue and expenditure of the Vilnius kahal shows the expenses that the community incurred due to the local parliament (*sejmik*) in 1788. Interestingly, the gifts bestowed during the *sejmik* did not differ from ordinary gifts.[39] The most popular gift was meat.[40] Expenses of the Vilnius community for gifts rose dramatically during the time of the *sejmik*: in one week they amounted to 45 per cent of the community's total expenses minus salaries regularly paid to the community's employees.[41] In comparison, even during those weeks when expenses for gifts exceeded the ordinary amounts, they did not account for more than 20 per cent of the kahal's weekly expenditure. After the deduction of state taxes, the Opatów community used to spend between 8 and 15 per cent of its annual expenditure on average,[42] but this data was true before 1769. The Vilnius community was functioning in a society laden with additional tensions caused by the prolonged debt repayment and the control of communal spending.

---

35 In sources the number of inscriptions about expenses for candles and firewood increase from the eleventh week of the calendar year, approximately from the end of June, and shows preparation for the beginning of the cold season.

36 LVIA, SA, collection 3755, p. 13.

37 Hundert, *The Jews in a Polish Private Town*, pp. 100–103.

38 Hundert, *The Jews in a Polish Private Town*, p. 101.

39 LVIA, SA, collection 3755, p. 24. This group of expenses was fixed on a separate line 'na expens czasu seimików' (expenses during the *sejmik*) and totalled 198 *złoty*.

40 LVIA, SA, collection 3755, pp. 22–24.

41 LVIA, SA, collection 3755, list of incurred costs in weeks 31–34 of the year.

42 Hundert, *The Jews in a Polish Private Town*, p. 100, data based on table 6.4.

The Vilnius community made gifts to influential public officials, army officers, bishops and other high officials of the Catholic Church, fraternities of religious orders, and certain individuals who were apparently useful for the kahal under certain circumstances. Regarding the frequency of gift-making, their recipients can be divided into three groups: (1) individuals who received gifts of about the same size every week, (2) individuals who received gifts periodically several times a year, and (3) individuals who received a gift once during the accounting period. Interestingly, the first group included public servants directly involved in the control of the Jewish community and its financial accounting. One of them was the sub-prefect (Pol. *podstarosta*). He not only received a salary from the Jewish community for the control of its financial flows, but also enjoyed, on a weekly basis, meat or fish for which the kahal would spend a set amount of money. Curiously, the accounting of expenditure of many weeks opens with the accounting of food intended for the sub-prefect: this item of expenditure was even entered as 'the sub-prefect's share' (Pol. *porciy*).[43] The sub-prefect periodically received candles, and was gratified with luxurious exotic gifts of lemons and coffee. Every week gifts of products for daily consumption were made to the castle and the army garrison. Periodic gifts — on several occasions during the accounting period — were made to the Bishop of Vilnius, the vice-voivode, some officials of the court of law, the captain of Vilnius castle, and some private individuals. The positions of the above-mentioned individuals indicate that the community was not maintaining regular contacts with them, yet their favourable attitude and support for Jews were indispensable. Correspondingly, loyalty and recognition were demonstrated on a regular basis. There was no connection between the gifts and certain political events, shifts in the public mood, or religious feasts. Even bestowing of one-off gifts should be linked with strengthening communal interests during a specific period, like the *sejmik*. It should be noted that compared with periodical or regular gifts, these gifts were not allocated in sizeable amounts. It would be 'some meat' or *fliaha vodka* (a flask of vodka). Unfortunately, nothing is known of the purpose of 193 *złoty* that were entered in the documents as *sejmik* expenses.[44]

Conclusions

The historical data discussed here shows that the Jewish communities in Vilnius and Opatów had a clear-cut gift-making strategy and were consistent in it. They sought to maintain regular contacts with influential and useful individuals directly involved with the community and to periodically gratify potentially useful or generally powerful members of the public. Gifts were given year after year to a defined group of useful individuals.

It seems that even the formation of the circle of recipients of relatively inexpensive gifts that satisfied the daily needs of the recipients had its own logic: the optimization

---

43 LVIA, SA, collection 3755, pp. 14, 14ᵛ, 15, and others.
44 LVIA, SA, collection 3755, p. 24.

of expenditure needed for this sort of gift made it possible to regularly remind a useful person of a trusting community that recognized his influence. Apparently, this effect would not have been achieved with a one-off yet very expensive luxury gift of limited use. Aside from other reasons, such a choice might have been dictated by society's material well-being and the local tradition of gift-making. Another obvious pattern of gift-making of the Vilnius Jewish community was that gifts were given simultaneously to a noble or an influential official and to his environment. For instance, prior to the arrival of the voivode in Vilnius, gifts were given to the vice-voivode, the voivode's marshal, and the voivode's servants.[45] Upon arrival in the capital, the voivode would also be gratified with personal gifts. A similar strategy in gift-making is observed in the Vilnius community's relations with other individuals and their servants. Following such gift-making practice, a favourable opinion about this specific community was formed not only in an influential individual but also in his environment, which was capable of shaping the patron's opinion or decisions.

Gifts were a universal, time-tested instrument for the long-lasting building of social cohesion. It was suitable for overcoming religious and ethnic differences within society by strengthening the relationship of specific groups with state officials and influential private individuals. They were a way to improve relations with a society that was not always favourably disposed towards the Jews. Most important in the context of gift-making was the choice of the most appropriate tactic and strategic planning of the gift-giving process. At the end of the eighteenth century the indebted Vilnius Jewish community operated along the lines of measures that had proven their effect, thus closing the gap between the dominant, Christian, Lithuanian, Rus', and Polish part of society on the one hand and Jews on the other.

Works Cited

Manuscripts and Archival Sources

Vilnius, Lietuvos valstybės istorijos archyvas (Lithuanian State Historical Archives), Senieji aktai (Old acts), collection 11, index 1, file 1040; collections 3755, 3757, 3960

Primary Sources

Materiały do Dziejów Sejmu Czteroletniego, vol. VI, ed. by Artur Eisenbach, Jerzy Michalski, Emanuel Rostworowski, and Janusz Woliński (Wrocław: Zakład Narodowy im. Ossolińskich – Wydaw. Polskiej Akademii Nauk, 1969)
Prawa, Konstytucye y Przywileie Królestwa Polskiego, y Wielkiego Xięstwa Litewskiego, y wszystkich Prowincyi należących na walnych seymiech koronnych od seymu Wiślickiego roku Pańskiego 1347 aż do ostatniego seymu uchwalone. Volumina Legum, vol. VII, 2nd edn (St Petersburg: Nakładem i drukiem Jozafata Ohryzki, 1860)

---

45 LVIA, SA, collection 3755, pp. 22$^\text{v}$–23.

Secondary Studies

Anishchenko, Evgeniy, *Cherta osedlosti: Belarusskaia̅ sinagoga v tsarstvovanie Ekateriny II* (Minsk: Art-Feks, 1998)

Dubnow, Simon, ed., *Pinkas ha-Medina o pinkas waad ha-kehilot ha-raszijot be-medinat Lita: Obłastnoj pinkos Waada gławnych jewriejskich obszczin Litwy*, trans. by Irena Tuwim, vol. I (St Petersburg: Tipo-lit. Ĭ. Lur´e, 1909)

Goldberg, Jacob, and Adam Wein, 'Księga kahału w Działoszynie z drugiej połowy XVIII w.', *Biuletyn Żydowskiego Instytutu Historycznego*, 56 (1965), 59–79

Hundert, Gershon, *The Jews in a Polish Private Town: The Case of Opatów in the Eighteenth Century* (Baltimore: Johns Hopkins University Press, 1991)

Kalik, Judith, 'Patterns of Contacts between the Catholic Church and the Jews in the Polish-Lithuanian Commonwealth: The Jewish Debts', in *Studies in the History of the Jews in Old Poland in Honor of Jacob Goldberg*, ed. by Adam Teller, Scripta Hierosolymitana, 38 (Jerusalem: Magnes Press, Hebrew University, 1998), pp. 102–22

Leszczyński, Anatol, *Sejm Żydów Korony, 1623–1764* (Warsaw: Żydowski Instytut Historyczny, 1994)

Michałowska-Mycielska, Anna, *Sejm Żydów Litewskich (1623–1764)* (Warsaw: Dialog, 2014)

Nadav, Mordechai, *The Jews of Pinsk, 1506 to 1880*, ed. by Mark Mirsky and Moshe Rosman (Stanford: Stanford University Press, 2008)

Rybarski, Roman, *Skarb i pieniądz za Jana Kazimierza, Michała Korybuta i Jana III* (Warsaw: Nakładem Towarzystwa Naukowego Warszawskiego, 1939)

Schiper, Ignacy, 'Podatnoye oblozhenie evreev', in *Istoria evreiskogo naroda*, XI: *Istoria evreev v Rossii* (Moscow: Izdanie t-va Mir, 1914), pp. 300–334

——, 'Wewnętrzna Organizacja Żydów w daw. Rzeczpospolitej', in *Żydzi w Polsce odrodzonej: Działalność społeczna, gospodarcza, oświatowa i kulturalna*, ed. by Ignacy Schiper, Aryeh Tartakower, and Aleksander Hafftka, vol. I (Warsaw: Wydawnictwo 'Żydzi w Polsce odrodzonej', 1923), pp. 81–111

ENDRE SASHALMI

Façades of a Multi-Ethnic Empire

Presenting and Publicizing the Coronation of the 'All-Russian Emperor', Alexander III (1883)

The present study intends to show the various scenarios that aimed to achieve the integration of different ethnic groups; these were scenarios which represent the so-called vertical model of integration where a given ethnos takes a dominant position over minority groups in a manner that can be called asymmetric. The coronation of Alexander III in 1883 offers an exceptionally relevant case to show how a key event in the history of a multinational empire could serve this purpose with the use of written and visual sources (propagandistic, iconographic as well as legal ones) employed by the government to convey the following message: although the Russian Empire was a multi-ethnic state, the Russian nationality was to play not only the dominant but also the unifying role, therefore providing the cohesion of the empire. Orthodox faith as the marker of Russianness figured prominently in these scenarios, and subsequent governmental measures, such as the introduction of the Russian language as a compulsory subject in primary schools in 1885, were clearly conceived in the spirit of a top-down asymmetric integration policy.

Introduction

Alexander III came to the throne in 1881, after the assassination of his father, Alexander II. Because of the many previous failed attempts on the life of Tsar Alexander II, the new tsar saw his father's reign as a period when the traditional values of Orthodox Russia, including the unquestionable respect for the tsar, were not only jeopardized but rather gone due to his father's liberal reforms. Alexander III firmly believed that his father's fate was the result of his liberal policy; therefore, he saw the preservation of unchanged autocracy as the pillar of social and political stability — a belief inculcated into him by Pobedonostsev, his tutor and chief procurator of the Holy

---

Endre Sashalmi • (endresashalmi@gmail.com) is Professor of History at the University of Pécs and specializes in the history of seventeenth- to eighteenth-century Russia.

Inter-Ethnic Relations and the Functioning of Multi-Ethnic Societies: Cohesion in Multi-Ethnic Societies in Europe from c. 1000 to the Present, II, ed. by Przemysław Wiszewski, EER 18 (Turnhout: Brepols, 2022), pp. 321–338

BREPOLS ❧ PUBLISHERS   10.1484/M.EER-EB.5.132158

This is an open access chapter made available under a cc by-nc 4.0 International License.

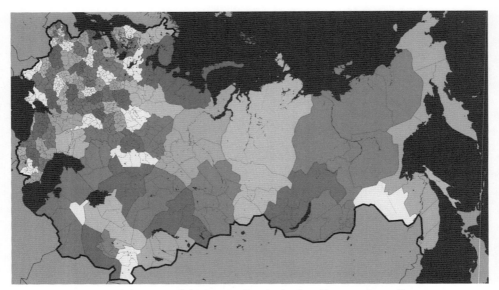

Map 14.1. Subdivisions of the Russian Empire in 1897. Source: <https://commons.wikimedia.org/wiki/File:Subdivisions_of_the_Russian_Empire_in_1897_(governorate_level,_uyezd_level_and_localities).svg>. CC BY-SA 4.0.

Synod.[1] Alexander III's manifesto in 1881 made it clear that the golden thread of his reign would be precisely to *preserve* 'the power and justice of *autocratic* authority [...] from any pretensions to it'.[2]

The purpose of preserving autocratic power led to a marked emphasis on *Russianness*, which partly meant a turn to Russia's history of the pre-Petrine period, and also to *Russification* — to use these debated terms which I try to describe, and reconstruct from sources, rather than define, later on.[3] Therefore, it can be said that the assassination proved to be a turning point in the history of the Russian Empire as a multi-ethnic and multinational and, hence, multicultural state. As Richard Wortman stated in his groundbreaking work:

> Two overarching myths, a European and a National myth framed the presentation of political power in Russia from Peter the Great to the abdication of Nicholas II [...]. Only with the assassination of Alexander II in 1881 did the

---

1 Tolmachev, *Aleksandr III i ego vremia*, p. 191; Wcislo, *Reforming Rural Russia*, p. 61.
2 Wcislo, *Reforming Rural Russia*, p. 61.
3 For a theoretical and practical discussion of these issues, see Miller, *The Romanov Empire and Nationalism*, ch. 2: 'Russification or Russifications?', pp. 45–65. The English term *Russification*, in fact, cannot make clear the difference which was reflected in nineteenth-century Russian terminology: i.e. the distinction between *obrusit'* (to make Russian), and *obruset'* (to become Russian). Miller, *The Romanov Empire and Nationalism*, p. 50.

emperor and his advisers introduced a myth to preserve absolute power that emphasized the monarch's national character.[4]

Before giving an impression what 'national character' means in the context of Russian history, it is necessary to clarify a certain terminological confusion. As was noted by Geoffrey Hosking (and many others before him), there are two words in the Russian language, namely *russkii* and *rossiiskii*, which are translated into English (and also into Hungarian, for example) with one word only, that is, *Russian*. The two words, however, reflect that 'there are two kinds of Russianness'.[5] The first one is 'connected with the people, the language',[6] the customs, we may also add, the *Russian soul*. It derives from the word *Rus'*, and it has an ethnic connotation. The other word is connected 'with the territory, the multinational empire', the state, and comes from the word *Rossiia*.[7] In the seventeenth century *Rossiia* became the official designation of the territories absorbed by Muscovy. Besides *Rossiia* we also encounter the term *Rossiiskoe gosudarstvo*, which in the seventeenth-century context can be translated as the 'Russian realm'; this term is in use even today but with the modern meaning, the *Russian state*. It was also from the adjective *rossiiskii* that the new title of Peter the Great, *Vserossiiskii Imperator* (All-Russian Emperor), and hence the new official designation of the state, *Vserossiiskaia Imperiia* (All-Russian Empire), was derived in 1721. In these cases, the adjective did not refer to ethnicity at all. 'All-Russian', indeed, meant one's belonging to the empire either as *a subject*, regardless of ethnic or religious affiliation, or its *ruler*, as the adjective *vserossiiskii* was present on the coins of the tsars, Alexander III included: 'All-Russian Emperor and Autocrat' being the full official title of the ruler. Therefore, the adjective *vserossiiskii* referred to the multi-ethnic character of the empire.

The turn to the Muscovite past as a marker of Russianness, in the sense of the Russian national character, expressed by the adjective *russkii*, was to be reflected in many ways. Some signs were more obvious than others: after some years the change became visible in the new, Muscovite style of church architecture, which was termed the *Russian style*, and was based on the model of the church called in popular parlance the Church of Basil the Blessed, located in the Red Square in Moscow. But there were other visible markers of the Muscovite past from the very beginning, such as the standard bearded portrait of the tsar, as Muscovite tsars before Peter had grown a beard as a marker of Orthodoxy. As late as 1904 a government decree still defined

---

4 Wortman, *Scenarios of Power*, p. 6. The term *absolute power* should be changed into *autocratic power* to understand the crucial difference between Western absolute monarchies that had existed previously in Europe, and the Russian political system! There is no space to go into details here, but it must be noted that *absolute power* did not mean legally unlimited power, so it did not involve the idea that the ruler was completely above all laws whatsoever, while this was a *conditio sine qua non* of autocracy as it was clearly stated in the Fundamental Laws of the Russian Empire in 1832. For the problem of *absolute monarchy* — autocracy, see my article '"God Is High up, the Tsar Is Faw Away"', pp. 138–41, and especially my recent book, *Russian Notions of Power and State*, pp. 252–71, 431–36.

5 Hosking, *Russia*, p. xix.

6 Hosking, *Russia*, p. xix.

7 Hosking, *Russia*, p. xix.

people of Russian origin in religious terms, stating that subjects counted as Russian nationality should only be those who professed the Orthodox faith, therefore being Russian and being Orthodox went together.[8] This was the case despite the fact that from the 1880s onwards the basis of distinction between Russians and non-Russians was moving from the category known as *inovertsy*, that is, 'peoples of other faith' (that is non-Orthodox), to *inorodtsy* (i.e. 'other born').[9] Consequently, Russianness, in the sense of national character, was inevitably linked to Orthodoxy, but from the 1880s on, the Russian language also became increasingly important in this respect. In 1885 Russian language as a compulsory subject was introduced in primary schools. All these mean that the 'very concepts of nation and nationality [...] were largely absent in Imperial Russia, at least until the later nineteenth century'.[10]

As for the rituals which emphasized Russian national character, and which had the greatest impact on the population of the empire due to its media coverage, the complex ceremony of Alexander III's coronation, which came rather late, two years after his accession to the throne, was no doubt crucial. The importance of Russian coronations in general is elucidated by Wortman in the following manner:

> A Russian coronation not only consecrated the Russian emperor, but also made known the image he intended to embody as a monarch, setting forth what might be described as the symbolic program for his reign.[11]

This is the message I have in mind when I use the term *presenting the coronation*. Closely related to this issue are the means of spreading, that is, publicizing the message. I will concentrate precisely on these topics by examining those contemporary written and visual sources connected to Alexander III's coronation which could reach a wider stratum of the population: these sources reflect not only that which I tried to subsume under the Russian national character but also the multi-ethnic character of the tsar's empire. This latter element, however, was to be more of a façade, as we shall see, because Alexander III wanted to be much more a Russian Orthodox tsar (*russkii tsar'*) than an 'All-Russian Emperor' (*Vserossiiskii Imperator*).

This complex phenomenon just described was most visible, in my view, in the presence and the role played by the representatives of different ethnic groups during the coronation festivals, and their representation in visual sources and texts related to the coronation.

As the empire expanded, the participation of exotic representatives of the different national and ethnic groups at the coronation increased. These were most colourful and expressive under Alexander III and Nicholas II, yet it was they

---

8 Weeks, *Nation and State in Late Imperial Russia*, p. 8.
9 Kappeler, *The Russian Empire*, p. 169. The explanation of these categories is given in Kappeler's glossary. *inorodtsy*: 'Created in 1822 for the non-sedentary ethnic groups of Siberia, the term was subsequently applied to other ethnic groups in the Asiatic parts of Russia, and to the Jews. 2. From the middle of the nineteenth century a pejorative term for all non-Russians in the tsarist empire'.
10 Weeks, 'Managing Empire', p. 27.
11 Wortman, *Visual Texts, Ceremonial Texts, Texts of Exploration*, p. 277.

FAÇADES OF A MULTI-ETHNIC EMPIRE   325

who increasingly emphasized the Russian (russkoe) as opposed to All-Russian (rossiiskoe) character of the empire.[12]

Immediate Effects of Alexander II's Assassination

Before turning to the main subject itself, it must be pointed out that there was an immediate effect of Alexander II's assassination which cannot be left unmentioned in the context of multi-ethnicity and multiculturalism: namely the riots that broke out against the Jewish population of the empire. The anti-Jewish hysteria which resulted in the pogroms of 1881–1882 was a clear sign that a turning point had occurred. From the perspective of the non-Jewish population, the 'anti-Jewish outbreaks have attained a character of an epidemic', as was written in the Russian journal *Golos* (Voice) in 1882.[13] It is not my aim to deal with this topic at all, as it has been well researched, but it must be mentioned that the phenomenon was also a turning point from the point of view of the Jewish population, in the sense that they no longer regarded integration and assimilation as a feasible solution.[14]

In the context of multiculturalism, it also has to be pointed out that the hysteria was partly the product of what we can call seasonal high religious tensions. It resulted from the accidental coincidence of the time of the Jewish Passover (which began on 14 April that year) with the Orthodox Easter.[15] While the Jews were feasting, commemorating their liberation by God from Egyptian slavery, the Orthodox Christians commemorated the Crucifixion and, at the same time, were still mourning the violent death of their tsar (1 March).[16] Religious tension was even furthered by the fact that the violent death of the tsar was conceived of and publicized in religious terms; the assassinated tsar was hailed as a Christ-like person: 'in the popular mind the slaying of the tsar was immediately elevated to a second Crucifixion'.[17] From this there was just one step to treating the celebrating Jews as scapegoats responsible for the murder of the tsar, nurtured by the application of the most widespread and most ancient charge against the Jews present from the Middle Ages on: namely that they were the Christ-killers. Whatever other factors played their part in the emerging accusation that it was the Jews whose conspiracy murdered Tsar Alexander II, it can be stated that this was a widely held belief, which is confirmed by contemporary foreign accounts of Russia.[18]

---

12 Rieber, *The Struggle for the Eurasian Borderlands*, p. 110.
13 Klier, *Russians, Jews, and the Pogroms of 1881–1882*, p. 17.
14 Nathans, *Beyond the Pale*, p. 9.
15 Nathans, *Beyond the Pale*, p. 186.
16 Nathans, *Beyond the Pale*, p. 186.
17 Flier, 'The Church of the Savior on the Blood', pp. 30–32. That was partly the reason why the dedication of the church to be built on the spot where Alexander II was mortally wounded became the 'Saviour on the Blood'. Flier, 'The Church of the Savior on the Blood', p. 30.
18 Lowe, *Alexander III of Russia*, pp. 206–07.

Predominance of the Russian Nationality and the Multi-Ethnic Character of the Emperor's Subjects: The Role and Image of Township Elders during the Coronation of Alexander III (1883)

> **Predominance** of the **Russian nationality** (Preobladanie Russkoi narodnosti), the **Supremacy of Orthodoxy, Autocracy** united with People's local self-government.[19]
>
> Alexander III's 'politico-theological trinity' was 'autocracy, orthodoxy, national homogeneity'.[20]

These two statements chosen as mottos, uttered by V. V. Komarov, a Russian journalist supporting Russification, on the one hand, and a British journalist, Charles Lowe (the Berlin correspondent of the *Times*), on the other, are eloquent, in my view, as they reflect the official government policy commencing from 1881 on. Both statements echoed the triad formulated by Uvarov in 1833 as the guiding principles in education: orthodoxy, autocracy, peoplehood (*narodnost'*). But whereas *narodnost'* for Uvarov simply meant the devotion of the tsar's subjects to orthodoxy and autocracy, from 1881 on this term was clearly to have a meaning very different from the one it had conveyed before 1881, as until Alexander III's accession it was not associated with the concept of *nationality*, and Russianness in the ethnic sense.

The imperial coat of arms of 1882 is a good point of departure to study the problem identified in the first part of the title of this chapter, because it can be considered as foreshadowing the turn of the tide in terms of nationalist policy which became manifest in presenting and publicizing the coronation. The 1882 coat of arms, which was a modified version of the one introduced in 1857, reflected the European and Asiatic character of the empire — most probably that was the aim of Alexander II in 1857 when a new imperial coat of arms was made. If one takes a look at these two coats of arms, striking is the parallel use of European types of crowns and Muscovite head regalia ornamenting the shields — not only the Monomakh cap used for the inauguration of the tsars until Peter the Great, but also the other personal caps of sixteenth- to seventeenth-century tsars modelled on that. The placement of the given head regalia and crowns was not accidental at all: their order corresponded to the order of the multiple titles of the All-Russian Emperor, and with the exception of the one representing the Great Duchy of Finland, these regalia were real, existing objects.[21] The sheer fact that the coat of arms of the empire was changed in 1882, that is, before the coronation, should make us think about its possible causes. What could

---

19 Quoted from A. Stepanov, 'Komarov Vissarion Vissarionovich', *Russkaia natsionlal'naia filosfiia.* <http://www.hrono.ru/biograf/bio_k/komarov_vv.html> [accessed 29 November 2016]. By the expression, 'local self-government', he meant the Slavophile ideal of *village communities*.

20 Lowe, *Alexander III of Russia*, p. 204.

21 Pchelov, *Rossiiskii gosudarstvennyi gerb*, p. 62.

FAÇADES OF A MULTI-ETHNIC EMPIRE

be the reason behind the change of the compositional frame of such an important state symbol?

The 1857 coat of arms has a *U* shape with the Great Russian coat of arms (the mounted lancer) in the centre of the curve. It is reminiscent of a banner, that is, a flag used in churches, while the 1882 version has the shape of a circle.[22] The composition of the 1882 version emphasizes much more the centrality of the Great Russian coat of arms,[23] which is surrounded by the other coats of arms: hence the composition, in my view, implies the central role of the Great Russian nationality. Concerning the iconographic message of the 1882 version, I share the opinion of Pchelov, one of the specialists on the subject. In his view the

> composition of the coat of arms rested on the symbolic expression of the idea of unification of lands under the single sceptre of the Russian monarch (*rossiiskogo monarkha*) but the coat of arms of the imperial dynasty stood at the base of the whole composition, underlining thereby that the unity was forged by the dynasty and the figure of the emperor.[24]

As far as I know, hitherto the 1882 coat of arms has not been placed into the general context of Russian nationalism.

Turning our attention to the coronations, it must be noted that from the time of Catherine the Great, Russia's rulers were proud of having the greatest number of ethnic groups in their empire. The imperial sublime projected not only an image of an empire of vast reaches, but also that of the empire that comprised a multitude and variety of peoples. This latter phenomenon Victor Zhivov has described as 'an ethnographic myth of empire'.[25] The attitude towards exotic people, and generally towards ethnicities other than Russians, varied from ruler to ruler in the nineteenth century during the coronations, which is well described by Richard Wortman.[26] The presence of exotic peoples at the coronations represented the 'civilizing mission' of the Russian emperors. To be sure, Jews were denied the possibility to represent themselves as one of the ethnic and religious groups of the empire.

The British journalist Lowe, whose words have been quoted as a motto, published a lengthy book on Alexander III's reign in 1895, just one year after the tsar's death. He wrote the following statement concerning the choices of the Russian government in 1881. The statement is all the more important because it places Russian government policy in a European perspective in constitutional terms, which inevitably had serious implications for the issues of ethnicity and multiculturalism.

> He [Alexander III] had three alternatives before him: either to maintain the status quo; or to move in the same direction as Austria — i.e., towards decentralisation; or, finally, to nationalize the Empire at the expense of the subject races, and in

---

22 Pchelov, *Rossiiskii gosudarstvennyi gerb*, p. 69.
23 Pchelov, *Rossiiskii gosudarstvennyi gerb*, p. 69.
24 Pchelov, *Rossiiskii gosudarstvennyi gerb*, p. 69.
25 Quoted in Wortman, *Visual Texts, Ceremonial Texts, Texts of Exploration*, p. 47.
26 Wortman, *Visual Texts, Ceremonial Texts, Texts of Exploration*, pp. 47–70.

favour of the most important — the 'Great Russians'. He chose the third of these and his watchword became: 'Russia for the Russians'.[27]

As we noted earlier:

> As the empire expanded, the participation of exotic representatives of the different national and ethnic groups at the coronation increased. These were most colourful and expressive under Alexander III and Nicholas II, yet it was they who increasingly emphasized the Russian ('russkoe') as opposed to All-Russian ('rossiiskoe') character of the empire.[28]

Indeed, from 1883 on there was a sharp turn of attitude:

> The coronation descriptions no longer expressed admiration for the Eastern representatives in the entry procession [...]. A coronation volume published by the Pan-Slavist Vissarion Komarov expressed sentiments of national superiority and colonial disdain.[29]

Wortman briefly described the phenomenon referring partly to Komarov's account, but there are still important issues in Komarov's lengthy book, no doubt the most detailed record of the chain of events comprising the coronation and its aftermath. Komarov was one of the seven Russian journalists who occupied coveted places in the cathedral during the 1883 coronation ritual itself, and besides writing a whole book on the event (which is one of my main sources) he gave the most detailed popular account of events in his daily issued cheap Pan-Slavist journal: both enjoyed government sponsorship and backing.[30]

For the occasion of the coronation representatives from the common people living in the different governorships of the Russian Empire were selected; these men were called 'township elders' (*volostnye starshiny*) and were invited by the authorities to Moscow to witness the coronation as it had happened in 1856. They became part of the coronation scenario which was a very elaborate chain of consecutive events.

The contrast between the role and the image of the exotic people participating at the coronation procession, and that of the so-called township elders who came from various ethnicities, is striking. The names of these latter people were given, and they were predominantly Russian(ized) names, which did not mean, of course, that they all were Orthodox, and some names ostensibly refer to Muslims.

The positive image of the township elders vis-à-vis the Asiatic ethnic groups was emphasized in many ways during the 1883 coronation. Both groups participated in the

---

27 Lowe, *Alexander III of Russia*, p. 183. For the most recent evaluation of nationalist policies in the Austro-Hungarian Empire in the late nineteenth century, see Pieter Judson's remark: 'By the beginning of the twentieth century ideologies of nationalism and of empire increasingly depended on each other for coherence. Far from constituting opposed or binary concepts and political projects (as they are usually considered to be) "nationhood" and "empire" both depended on each other for their explanatory coherence'. Judson, *The Habsburg Empire*, p. 333.

28 Rieber, *The Struggle for the Eurasian Borderlands*, p. 110.

29 Wortman, *Visual Texts, Ceremonial Texts, Texts of Exploration*, p. 64.

30 Wortman, *Scenarios of Power*, p. 213.

FAÇADES OF A MULTI-ETHNIC EMPIRE 329

coronation procession, but whereas the exotic people were disdained and ridiculed by Komarov in his book, the important role attributed to the township elders was made evident to all by the fact that twelve of these elders could witness the coronation ceremony itself in the Assumption Cathedral.[31] The only ethnic delegation present in the cathedral were solely the representatives of Finland! Komarov gives detailed information concerning the township elders whose main role came some days after the coronation, when the imperial couple received the greeting of the various groups of the society.

That day, the imperial couple stood in front of the throne in the Andreev Hall and received the greetings of the guards, the army and fleet, the civil servants, and finally the 'township elders' (*volostnye starshiny*). Not only the ceremony itself but also the wording of its description is of great importance for us, that is, the way it was communicated to the public by Komarov, because they both reflect the official concept of the Russian nationality's dominance in a multi-ethnic empire:

> the township elders [...] were present in Moscow from all corners of Russia (*Rossiia*). The most interesting of the greetings that day was, of course, that of the township elders, gathered one by one from each and every district. Altogether there were 619 township elders present. All the township elders in Moscow were placed under the authority of Prince Nikolai Nikolaevich Khovanskii, by the minister of internal affairs. They were wonderfully housed in the German street in a building which previously used to be a factory; they were provided with all things necessary, treated excellently, and Prince N. N. Khovanskii took care of them with such an attention which earned him the greatest honour. The township elders' behaviour was exemplary.[32]

Then, in an alphabetical order of the names of the provinces, the township elders were ushered to the imperial couple by a nobleman from the given governorship where they came from. As the township elders were approaching the imperial couple in groups, according to the above order, the province was named by the minister of internal affairs, and he introduced the delegates to the imperial couple; in case of an absence of such an usher-nobleman, the elders were introduced by Prince Khovanskii. Komarov goes on:

> Meanwhile the township elders presented to Their Majesties bread and salt (*khleb-sol'*), almost exclusively on silver plates, or holy icons [...]. When the township elders were passing — these elected ones of the common Russian folk (*vybornye prostogo russkogo Naroda*) — all [others around] said that 'Here goes Russia' (*Rossiia*).[33]

The wording is crucial as *Russia* (*Rossiia*) was identified with the Russian folk!

Then the list of provinces with their gifts follows (in alphabetical order) but without giving the complete survey of all the provinces. The province of Astrakhan

---

31 Wortman, *Scenarios of Power*, p. 220.
32 Komarov, *V pamiat' sviashchennogo koronovaniia gosudaria*, pp. 297–98.
33 Komarov, *V pamiat' sviashchennogo koronovaniia gosudaria*, p. 298.

is mentioned four times in the list with gifts from its different districts, while in the case of the Polish territories under Russian rule it is just written: 'From the peasants of the ten provinces of the Polish Kingdom a big silver plate was presented'.[34] The usual pattern of the list follows this scheme: after the name of the province comes the name of that district (*uezd*) within the province where the person presenting the gift came from, and the given person is identified by his name. The gifts, as Komarov stated, were almost exclusively bread and salt (*khleb-sol'*) on silver plates and icons, but with a few exceptions the plates and the icons were not specified. A notable exception in the case of the icons is the remark that 'the orthodox peasants from the Lublin, Sedelsk, Suvalsk provinces presented an icon of the saint and pious prince Aleksandr Nevskii',[35] which is important because he was the patron saint of the emperor. From the Irkutsk province the gift presented was not only the usual plate, but in addition to that, forty expensive sable furs, the specialty of Siberia, were given to the imperial couple.[36] In one case it is mentioned that a refined silver plate bore the coat of arms of the district's towns, and the map of the district was also represented.[37]

The gifts presented to the imperial couple, or rather to the tsar and tsaritsa as the gifts conveyed this message, were highly symbolic objects. They were not the special objects characteristic of the given region, with the exception of the furs from Siberia, but symbolically standardized gifts. Since bread (*khleb*) and salt (*sol'*) reflected the main occupations of the Russian peasantry, farming and gathering (as the salt was the crucial preservative), they had very important symbolic meaning: their importance is shown by the fact that the words taken together, '*khleb-sol*' ('breadandsalt'), acquired the meaning of 'hospitality' in the Russian language.[38] The phrase became part of the court ceremonial of Muscovite tsars. When the tsar wanted to invite someone to dine with him, he said: 'you will now eat bread and salt with me'.[39]

The other group of gifts, that is, the icons, presented by these representatives likewise reflected the Russian national (*russkii*) character, as the core of this identity was Orthodox faith.[40] A further proof of the statement that the gifts were highly symbolic of Russianness is the detail given by Komarov as the very last item on the list of gifts:

> One of the descendants of Ivan Susanin presented Their Imperial Majesties bread and salt on a simple wooden but refined plate with a following inscription carved in it: 'To the most pious Tsar, Alexander III and to Mariia Fedorovna Tsaritsa […]; the descendants of Ivan Susanin'.[41]

---

34 Komarov, *V pamiat' sviashchennogo koronovaniia gosudaria*, pp. 298–99.

35 Komarov, *V pamiat' sviashchennogo koronovaniia gosudaria*, p. 299.

36 Komarov, *V pamiat' sviashchennogo koronovaniia gosudaria*, p. 298.

37 Komarov, *V pamiat' sviashchennogo koronovaniia gosudaria*, p. 298.

38 Smith and Christian, *Bread and Salt*, pp. 5, 65.

39 Smith and Christian, *Bread and Salt*, p. 119.

40 I agree with Weeks that 'the role of the Orthodox religion (Pravoslavie) for Russian identity cannot be overstated'. Weeks, 'Managing Empire', p. 27.

41 Komarov, *V pamiat' sviashchennogo koronovaniia gosudaria*, p. 299.

FAÇADES OF A MULTI-ETHNIC EMPIRE   331

Komarov also noted in another of his reports on the coronation that this peasant was one of the twelve peasants who were allowed to be present in the church during the rite of coronation. This detail is all the more important because at the coronation Glinka's 'A Life for the Tsar' was played, the theme of which was the heroic deed of Ivan Susanin, who, according to the story, saved the life of the first Romanov tsar.

It is not an accident that among the gifts of the representatives of the many ethnicities this fact deserved special attention, as no other reference from the Muscovite past to the Orthodox faith and loyalty to the tsar could be more straightforward and proving the close bond between the common people and the tsar, and consequently Russian Orthodoxy, than the figure of Ivan Susanin — especially after the violent death of Alexander II. Ivan Susanin was a simple peasant, as the legends go, who sacrificed his life in 1613 to save the newly elected Romanov tsar, Mikhail, and therefore Orthodox Russia, when the Catholic Poles allegedly intended to capture Mikhail. He deceived the Polish troops and led them into a swamp where they could not find the way out and where they perished. His legendary figure became the symbol of unchallenged peasant loyalty to the tsar as he was tortured to death by the invaders.

Komarov also describes the emperor's lunch with the township elders, which is the most crucial part for us and confirms my conclusion regarding the significance of the gifts. In describing the event Komarov mentions: 'For some reasons, only the representatives from Finland were not invited'.[42] This detail is also important, given the fact that only the delegation of Finland was allowed to enter the cathedral for the coronation. Therefore, the absence of Finland's representatives in the 'ethnic banquet' is striking. In my view it clearly reflects the detachment of Finland as an entity from the other parts of the Russian Empire, as in Finland the tsar, in principle, was a constitutional ruler, though many of the Finnish privileges were mutilated after Alexander III's accession. Komarov also notes that for the Caucasian region and Siberia there was just one representative for each territory.[43] Then Komarov draws the conclusion:

> This way, in the persons of these township elders, no doubt, the people from all corners of the Russian land (*Russkoi zemli*) gathered. No doubt, here were the representatives of all tribes and peoples/nationalities (*plemen i narodov*) who make up the composition of the empire. Here it could also be seen clearly that the mass of Russian peoples/nation (*massa Russkogo naroda*) is so great, that the other peoples/nationalities ('*narody*') comprise only a negligibly small part, sticking to the Russian mass (*russkoi masse*), and that these peoples/nationalities ('*narody*') in a moral sense (*v nravstvennom znachenii*) have been absorbed long ago by the all-encompassing spiritual world of the Russian nation (*dukhovnym mirom Russkogo naroda*).[44]

---

42 Komarov, *V pamiat' sviashchennogo koronovaniia gosudaria*, p. 348.
43 Komarov, *V pamiat' sviashchennogo koronovaniia gosudaria*, p. 348.
44 Komarov, *V pamiat' sviashchennogo koronovaniia gosudaria*, p. 348. This was the (desired) process expressed by Russian term *obruset'*, i.e. to 'become Russian' spontaneously.

This wording reflects the 'Herrenvolk' concept, and the quotation marks used two times referring to 'narody', together with the content of the passage, would even point to the questioning of their separate existence, clearly having in mind the 'civilizing mission' attributed to the Russian nationality in the empire. That this claim is well founded is confirmed by the rest of the passage:

> Those who conceive Russia (*poniatie o Rossii*) in the sense that it is the conglomerate of peoples/nationalities (*konglomerat narodov*), they act without understanding the issue, or with aims hostile to the state (*vrazhebnym gosudarstvu*). In Russia (*V Rossii*) there is but one nation — the Russian nation (*russkii narod*). One Ruler — the Russian Tsar (*Russkii Tsar'*). Everything that is left is attached to the Russian building (*k russkomu zdaniiu*) and to the foot of the Russian throne, as the nests of swallows are stuck to the pentroofs of enormous houses.[45]

So, Lowe got the point right when he stated: *Russia was for the Russians*. The very last sentence reflects visually the same spirit expressed in the new Russian imperial coat of arms of 1882, but the house here is, of course, not just the empire, but at the same time, the House of the Romanovs. It is interesting to compare the attitude reflected in the just mentioned sources with contemporary population data. According to the 1897 population survey of the Russian Empire, 'the peasant estate numbered of 53.4 million, or 86 percent of the total population of Russia'.[46] Out of these the ethnic Russian peasants are estimated at 43.2 million and the non-Russian peasants 6.2 million: the remaining 4 million were 'members of other ethnic groups who had been assimilated to the Russian speaking majority'.[47]

And Komarov's conclusion on the role of the township elders is as follows:

> Therefore, there is not the slightest doubt that the gathering of township elders was of great significance, and besides, it was the first gathering from all places of the empire in its present borders and measures.[48]

Komarov therefore gives the names of all participants at the lunch. In his description of the lunch, he uses the words *narodnost'*, *natsional'nost'*, meaning 'nationality', in referring to the people present, which justifies the translation of *narod* as *nationality*. He mentions of the township elders that as they were seated around the tables, 'it was impossible to identify their nationality (*natsional'nost'*) on the basis of clothing and faces'.[49] And referring to the lunch cards depicting the tsar's banquet, he adds that the cards had images with the 'different nationalities (*raznye narodnosti*) inhabiting Russia (*Rossiiu*), and the view of Moscow'.[50] Indeed the terms used for national

---

45 Komarov, *V pamiat' sviashchennogo koronovaniia gosudaria*, p. 348. This is the concept to make every nationality Russian, i.e. *obrusit'*.

46 Moon, *The Russian Peasantry*, p. 19.

47 Moon, *The Russian Peasantry*, pp. 15, 19.

48 Komarov, *V pamiat' sviashchennogo koronovaniia gosudaria*, p. 348. Township elders were present, in fact, at Alexander II's coronation in 1856, but probably not on such a large scale as in 1883.

49 Komarov, *V pamiat' sviashchennogo koronovaniia gosudaria*, p. 360.

50 Komarov, *V pamiat' sviashchennogo koronovaniia gosudaria*, pp. 351–52.

FAÇADES OF A MULTI-ETHNIC EMPIRE 333

or ethnic groups were imprecise in the late Russian Empire: 'ethnic communities went by the terms *narod, narodnost', natsional'nost'* all of which were more or less synonymous. *Plemia* signified both the tribe and the nation'.[51]

Old Believers as a Target Group of Russian National Cohesion

In my opinion a further fact pointing to the policy that Orthodoxy was seen as a crucial part of Russianness by the government, and the intention to create the unity of Great Russians on a religious basis, was the removal of several restrictions and prohibitions (on the occasion of the 1883 coronation) which earlier had been imposed on Old Believers. Komarov gives the detailed list of these new regulations.[52] Besides allowing them to practice their rites with few restrictions, they were given important civil rights by the government. The first group of privileges provided them with the right to 'carry out communal prayer, fulfil spiritual rites, and conduct worship to God according to their rites both in private homes and equally in buildings specially designated for that function'.[53] The most important exceptions were that they had no right to public procession — which most probably can be explained with the aim of precluding a possible uproar from the established Church or the common believers — and the appearance of their places of worship were not to look like churches of the established Church.[54] As for civil rights, henceforward they were entitled to passports, they could freely engage in trade and crafts,[55] and they could even be elected as township elders, though in this case the deputy had to be an orthodox belonging to the state Church.[56] The places of worship were vital to Old Believers (and sectarians), and the 1883 laws 'dramatically expanded their freedom to practice their faith unmolested and allowed them for the first time to have their own buildings specially designated for that function'.[57]

These measures, at the same time, were in direct contrast to the restrictive decrees placed on Jews in 1882 (May Laws). Benjamin Nathans raises the necessity of comparing the legal status of Jews in Russia with those groups of the empire who also suffered from legal discrimination and mentions the Old Believers.[58] He regrets the lack of research in this field but strangely enough does not refer in this respect to the 1883 laws concerning Old Believers. I think one can plausibly claim that the purpose of the legislation on Old Believers obviously was to strengthen the cohesion of Russian Orthodox people regardless of whether they belonged to the established Church or to the various groups of the Old Believers (except the castrated ones). The

---

51 Karjahärm, 'Terminology Pertaining to Ethnic Relations', p. 30.
52 Komarov, *V pamiat' sviashchennogo koronovaniia gosudaria*, pp. 186–87.
53 Translation is from Breyfolge, 'Prayer and the Politics of Space', p. 227.
54 Komarov, *V pamiat' sviashchennogo koronovaniia gosudaria*, p. 186.
55 Komarov, *V pamiat' sviashchennogo koronovaniia gosudaria*, pp. 186, 187.
56 Komarov, *V pamiat' sviashchennogo koronovaniia gosudaria*, p. 186.
57 Breyfolge, 'Prayer and the Politics of Space', p. 227.
58 Nathans, *Beyond the Pale*, p. 319.

issue hitherto has not been interpreted from this angle. Not even the most recent monographs on Old Believers in English make this point. One author treats the 1883 laws as one of the 'smaller concessions given in times of political instability'.[59] Another one just mentions these laws as the culmination of a process that began in the early 1860s.[60]

In my view, the granting of almost equal rights to the Old Believers cannot be separated from the nationalist turn and the strengthening of the Orthodox foundations of autocratic power that entered a new phase in 1881. But a prelude to this may be considered the move of Nicholas I in 1839, although from a completely opposite angle. This year witnessed the final dissolution and incorporation of the Uniate Church in the Russian Orthodox Church in the territory of the Russian Empire.[61] (Only the small diocese of Chełm in the Kingdom of Poland escaped this fate.)[62] And the elimination of the Uniate Church was very much in line with the ideology formulated by Uvarov (in 1833).

Returning to the issue of the Old Believers, by 1883 the regime was stable, and the concessions given to the Old Believers were substantial, as we have seen. Therefore, political instability as a cause of quasi-emancipation can be excluded. To treat the 1883 quasi-emancipation as a culmination of the process that began under Alexander II's reign is also problematic as Alexander III's policy was rather conservative. Similarly, the Old Believers were 'the most conservative and traditional part of the Great Russian population'.[63] In some areas they even constituted from 5 to 12 per cent of the total population.[64] Although it is true that the peaceful sects of Old Believers very often represented economically flourishing groups, the aim of the legislation, especially considering its timing, 3 May 1883, that is, less than two weeks before the coronation, was more of a sign of a general pardon than a political move based on economic considerations.

The quasi-emancipation of Old Believers in 1883 is all the more striking when we consider what opinion Pobedonostsev, the procurator of the Holy Synod, held of them. In the 1860s he still maintained that the Old Believers 'were more dangerous than revolutionaries'![65] This statement will not sound strange considering the fact that the Old Believers had long refused to pray for the tsar, but Orthodoxy was seen as a crucial factor of political loyalty. The first line of the Russian anthem ('God Save the Tsar'), appearing on the 1883 coronation jetons and in a *lubok*[66] (see this problem later on) issued on the occasion of the coronation, fits into this picture very well! Therefore, the most plausible explanation of the 1883 laws is the aim of strengthening the cohesion of the Russian Orthodox people. In a sense it can even be treated

---

59 Marsden, *The Crisis of Religious Toleration in Imperial Russia*, p. 252, n 29.
60 Werth, *The Tsar's Foreign Faiths*, p. 148.
61 Kappeler, *The Russian Empire*, p. 84.
62 Dunn, *The Catholic Church and Russia*, p. 52.
63 Zenkovsky, 'The Russian Church Schism', p. 152.
64 For the geographical distribution and percentage of Old Believers in the Russian Empire, see Sidorov, *Orthodoxy and Difference*, pp. 60–70.
65 Zenkovsky, 'The Russian Church Schism', p. 152.
66 Russian name for popular print.

FAÇADES OF A MULTI-ETHNIC EMPIRE   335

as a form of administrative Russification, considering that the 1904 government decree that we have referred to defined people of Russian origin in religious terms! Namely, subjects counted as Russian nationals could only be those who professed the Orthodox faith, and the decree specifically mentioned those who belonged to the official Orthodox Church as well as Old Believers.

The strengthening of the cohesion of Russian Orthodox people, at the same time, had to do a lot with the phenomenon that I call 'the beard issue'. If the beard was very important for an ordinary Orthodox, it was much more so for the Old Believers! And in this respect Emperor Alexander III followed the custom of Muscovite tsars. Perhaps no other visible symbol of the new reign was more straightforward than the beard, which can be understood in the context of the well-known Petrine reform: compulsory shaving became an emblematic act of Peter the Great's reign, the sign of Westernization. Not only officials and officers, but also rank and file soldiers as well as town-dwellers had the obligation to shave with the exception of the clergy and peasantry. Alexander III's new bearded image was clearly a sign that the tsar associated himself with the Russian Orthodox tradition, as shaving had been considered by male Orthodox believers as the distortion of the Christ-like image of man.

During the Russo-Turkish war of 1877–1878, Russian soldiers were allowed not to shave. At that time the future Alexander III also stopped shaving his face 'in order to show his patriotic loyalty to these men but also to eventually present himself in the mould of a medieval Russian knight (bogatyr')'.[67] This new image became much more than a personal habit. Alexander III's beard 'was soon seen as a symbol of national strength and old Muscovite strength and virility'.[68] By the time coins with the bearded portrait of Alexander III appeared in 1883, the imperial guards had already been allowed to have beards as a result of a decree passed soon after Alexander's accession. Formerly the beard 'connoted peasants and clergy, the backward and uncouth elements of Russia, revolutionaries and Jews'.[69] And we must add: especially Old Believers!

The bearded portrait of Alexander appears on the coronation coin, that is, the one-rouble silver coin of Alexander III. On this coronation coin, besides autocratic power (expressed by the regalia and the inscription 'By the Grace of God Alexander III All-Russian Emperor and Autocrat'), the other message was Russianness, conveyed by the bearded portrait of the tsar. The appearance of the ruler's portrait on coinage is all the more striking because after the reign of Emperor Paul I (1796–1801) there was a clear tendency in the nineteenth century for the rulers' portraits to disappear from coins. The twenty-five silver 'kopek' denomination which was minted from the reign of Alexander I (1801–1825) contained no portrait of the ruler until 1885, but afterwards the portrait became a standard.[70] In the case of the one-rouble silver coin there is no portrait of the ruler in power after 1831, though during the reign of

67 Jahn, '"Us": Russians on Russianness', p. 63.
68 Jahn, '"Us": Russians on Russianness', p. 63.
69 Wortman, *Scenarios of Power*, p. 192.
70 Orlov, *Monety Rossii, 1700–1917*, p. 132. This and the following conclusions are drawn on the basis of data given in Orlov's catalogue.

Nicholas I (1825–1855) large quantities were minted with the portrait of his brother, Alexander I. Nevertheless, the number of one-rouble silver coins without rulers' portraits is greater.[71] Beginning from 1883 there is a marked change when 279,143 one-rouble silver coronation coins were minted with the tsar's portrait.[72] And altogether a bit over seven million one-rouble silver coins were minted during the rest of Alexander III's reign with his portrait on them![73] Probably no other medium could compete with this regarding ruler visibility and fostering Russian nationalism (because of the national significance of the beard) and winning over some Old Believers. 'That the monarch wore a beard transformed him into a national symbol.'[74]

Conclusion

The widespread popularization of Alexander III's coronation in images and texts, that is, in popular prints, newspapers, drawings, and even in official edicts, etc., taken as a whole, promoted the Russian national sentiment, and at the same time expressed the very image that the 'monarch was God's living deputy on earth, a living icon, a source of protection and redemption.'[75]

A *lubok* depicting the coronation and giving the impression of an *icon* because of its scattered scenes, clearly reflects this spirit, the 'divine right of the Russian emperor'. On the top of the image rays of the sun are breaking through the gloomy clouds separating them into two parts. Above the rays there is an inscription, 'God save the Tsar', which was the first line of Russia's anthem. Below that inscription, on the very top of a mandorla-like, that is, an almond-like, framing which is posed between Heaven and Earth, rests the Great Imperial Crown of Russia and the sceptre on a cushion, and in the mandorla stands the figure of Alexander III in his coronation mantle. A reversed *V*-shaped curtain hanging on the sceptre can be seen behind the tsar, and it frames his figure as if enlightening him. Below the mandorla there is a ribbon with the inscription: 'All-Russian [Emperor]'. In the centre of the lower register and on the flanks, we have people of various ethnic groups wearing different clothes.

The ideological message is clear: divine grace is expressed by the rays of the sun which comes through the clouds (the iconographic representation of heaven) and illuminates the Russian imperial crown as well as the inscription. The tsar is crowned from the Heavens, and he is even depicted as an intercessor or mediator between God and the people, which, in fact, he was according to the Orthodox Church. (The mandorla was typically used in icons with the figure of Christ.) At the same time, the image also laid emphasis on the multi-ethnic character of the tsar's empire by

---

71 Orlov, *Monety Rossii, 1700–1917*, pp. 188–92.
72 Orlov, *Monety Rossii, 1700–1917*, p. 194.
73 But after 1883 on the reverse was the double-headed eagle.
74 Wortman, *Scenarios of Power*, p. 192.
75 Tarasov, *Framing Russian Art*, p. 252.

representing various ethnic groups, but this phenomenon was clearly subordinated to the principles of Russian nationalism of which the Orthodox faith was the core element.

Works Cited

Primary Sources

Komarov, V. V., *V pamiat' sviashchennogo koronovaniia gosudaria imperatora Alexandra III i gosudaryni imperatitsy Marii Fedorovny* (St Petersburg, 1883) <http://dlib.rsl.ru/viewer/01003547868#?page=7> [accessed 2 November 2016]
Lowe, Charles, *Alexander III of Russia* (New York: Macmillan and Co., 1895) <https://archive.org/details/alexanderiiirusooolowegoog> [accessed 2 November 2016]
Orlov, A. P., *Monety Rossii, 1700–1917* (Moscow: IPKA 'Pablisiti', IKF 'Konstantin', 1994)

Secondary Studies

Breyfolge, Nicholas B., 'Prayer and the Politics of Space: Molokan Church Building, Tsarist Law, and the Quest for a Public Sphere in Late Imperial Russia', in *Sacred Stories: Religion and Spirituality in Modern Russia*, ed. by M. D. Steinberg and H. J. Coleman (Bloomington: Indiana University Press, 2007), pp. 222–52
Dunn, Denis J., *The Catholic Church and Russia: Popes, Patriarchs, Tsars, Commissars* (London: Routledge, 2017)
Flier, M. S., 'The Church of the Savior on the Blood: Projection, Rejection, Resurrection', in *Christianity and the Eastern Slavs*, II: *Russian Culture in Modern Times*, ed. by R. P. Hughes and I. Paperno (Berkeley: University of California Press, 1994), pp. 25–48
Hosking, Geoffrey, *Russia: People and Empire, 1552–1917* (Cambridge, MA: Harvard University Press, 1998)
Jahn, Hubertus F., '"Us": Russians on Russianness', in *National Identity in Russian Culture*, ed. by Simon Franklin and Emma Widdis (Cambridge: Cambridge University Press, 2006), pp. 53–73
Judson, Pieter, *The Habsburg Empire: A New History* (Cambridge, MA: Harvard University Press, 2016)
Kappeler, Andreas, *The Russian Empire: A Multi-ethnic History*, trans. by Alfred Clayton (London: Routledge, 2014)
Karjahärm, Toomas, 'Terminology Pertaining to Ethnic Relations as Used in Late Imperial Russia', *Acta Historica Tallinnensia*, 15 (2010), 24–50
Klier, John Doyle, *Russians, Jews, and the Pogroms of 1881–1882* (Cambridge: Cambridge University Press, 2011)
Marsden, Thomas, *The Crisis of Religious Toleration in Imperial Russia: Bybikov's System for the Old Believers, 1941–1855* (Oxford: Oxford University Press, 2015)
Miller, Alexei, *The Romanov Empire and Nationalism: Essays in Methodology of Historical Research* (Budapest: Central European University Press, 2008)
Moon, David, *The Russian Peasantry, 1600–1930: The World the Peasants Made* (London: Routledge, 1999)

Nathans, Benjamin, *Beyond the Pale: The Jewish Encounter with Late Imperial Russia* (Berkeley: University of California Press, 2004)

Pchelov, Evgeniy V., *Rossiiskii gosudarstvennyi gerb: Kompozitsiia, stilistika i semantika v istoricheskom kontekste* (Moscow: Rossiiskii gosudarstvennyi gumanitarnyi universitet, 2005)

Rieber, Alfred, *The Struggle for the Eurasian Borderlands: From the Rise of Early Modern Empires to the End of the First World War* (Cambridge: Cambridge University Press, 2014)

Sashalmi, Endre, '"God Is High up, the Tsar Is Faw Away": The Nature of Polity and Political Culture in 17th–Century Russia. A Comparative View', in *Empowering Interactions: Political Cultures and the Emergence of the State in Europe 1300–1900*, ed. by Wim Blockmans, André Holenstein, and Jon Mathieu in collaboration with Daniel Schläppi (Aldershot: Ashgate, 2009), pp. 131–48

——, *Russian Notions of Power and State in a European Perspective, 1462–1725: Assessing the Significance of Peter's Reign* (Boston, Academic Studies Press, 2022)

Sidorov, Dmitri, *Orthodoxy and Difference: Essays in Geography of Russian Orthodox Church(es) in the 20th Century* (San Jose: Pickwick Publications, 2001)

Smith, R. E. F., and David Christian, *Bread and Salt: The Social and Economic History of Food and Drink in Russia* (Cambridge: Cambridge University Press, 1985)

Tarasov, Oleg, *Framing Russian Art: From Early Icons to Malevich* (London: Reaktion Books, 2007)

Tolmachev, E., *Aleksandr III i ego vremia* (Moscow: Terra, 2007)

Wcislo, Francis William, *Reforming Rural Russia: State, Local Society, National Politics 1855–1914* (Princeton, NJ: Princeton University Press, 2014)

Weeks, Theodore R., 'Managing Empire: Tsarist Nationalist Policy', in *The Cambridge History of Russia*, ed. by Dominic Lieven, vol. II: *Imperial Russia, 1689–1917* (Cambridge: Cambridge University Press, 2006), pp. 27–44

——, *Nation and State in Late Imperial Russia: Nationalism and Russification on the Western Frontier, 1863–1914* (DeKalb: Northern Illinois University Press, 1996)

Werth, Paul W., *The Tsar's Foreign Faiths: Toleration and the Fate of Religious Freedom in Imperial Russia* (Oxford: Oxford University Press, 2014)

Wortman, Richard S., *Scenarios of Power: Myth and Ceremony in Russian Monarchy. From Alexander II to the Abdication of Nicholas II*, vol. II (Princeton, NJ: Princeton University Press, 2000)

——, *Visual Texts, Ceremonial Texts, Texts of Exploration: Collected Articles on the Representation of Russian Monarchy* (Boston: Academic Studies Press, 2014)

Zenkovsky, Serge, 'The Russian Church Schism', in *Readings in Russian Civilization: Russia before Peter the Great*, ed. by Thomas Riha, vol. I, 2nd rev. edn (Chicago: University of Chicago Press, 1969), pp. 141–53

JOANNA WOJDON

Polish American Parishes of the Nineteenth to Twenty-First Centuries and their Role in Shaping Polish American Identity and Status

The studies by Troskovaitė and Šiaučiūnaitė-Verbickienė, presented earlier, indicated activities which enabled ethnic minorities to function in modern societies dominated politically and economically by another ethnic group. This chapter returns to the issue, but from a twentieth-century perspective. In this period, it was typical to maintain separate ethnic identities and to search for communication tools that would simultaneously establish and maintain favourable relations with the dominant ethnos. This study shows that this trend has only partially held up in modern democratic societies. However, efforts to assimilate the minority and create a possibly homogeneous community play a greater role than before.

Introduction

The first permanent Polish settlement in the United States was Panna Maria in Texas, which was established by a group of immigrants from Upper Silesia. The group was recruited by Father Leopold Moczygemba. The first event in the history of the Polish American community as a group was a Christmas Eve service held in Panna Maria in 1854. Soon a church was built (Figure 15.1) and a parish formally established, which has been continuously functioning to this day.[1]

The Church thus appears as an organizer of migration and the settlement process. The priest is the spiritual leader of the rural community and organizes other aspects

1 Brożek, *Polacy w Teksasie.*

Joanna Wojdon • (joanna.wojdon@uwr.edu.pl) is Professor of History at the Historical Institute, University of Wrocław, and the head of the Department of Methodology of Teaching History and Civic Education. Her research interests include the history of the Polish American ethnic group and public history.

Inter-Ethnic Relations and the Functioning of Multi-Ethnic Societies: Cohesion in Multi-Ethnic Societies in Europe from c. 1000 to the Present, II, ed. by Przemysław Wiszewski, EER 18 (Turnhout: Brepols, 2022), pp. 339–355

BREPOLS ❧ PUBLISHERS   10.1484/M.EER-EB.5.132159

This is an open access chapter made available under a cc by-nc 4.0 International License.

Figure 15.1. Immaculate Conception Church in Panna Maria, Texas. Photo by Krzysztof Wojdon (2018).

POLISH AMERICAN PARISHES OF THE NINETEENTH TO TWENTY-FIRST CENTURIES   341

of its life, with the ethnic parish becoming the basic organizational unit. A permanent sign of the Polish group's presence is the church building. Later it was atypical that priests organized migration, which was guided by its own mechanisms. However, there is no doubt that a steady stream of newcomers from Poland augmented the Catholic Church in the United States, and that membership of the Catholic Church was an important element of Polish ethnic group identification.

The religiosity of the Polish American community and the phenomenon of Polish parishes have already been the subject of many studies. In 2017, the Catholic University of Lublin began a project to draw up an inventory of Polish parishes in the United States; this is a task that requires a research team and years of work.[2] This chapter has different objectives. It does not seek to reconstruct the history of one or more parishes, but rather to examine the role of Polish parishes in strengthening the sense of community, shaping the identity, and building the status of the Polish ethnic group in the United States within the context of building social cohesion on the one hand and, on the other, breaking it down. There are four key aspects to this dichotomy: (1) how parishes contributed to the building of cohesion and (2) how they gave rise to divisions within the Polish ethnic group; (3) how they separated the Polish community from and (4) how they brought it closer to mainstream American society. At the same time, it is important to note that the roles of parishes have changed over time as Polonia (the name used in Poland and in the Polish American community for the people of Polish descent living abroad) itself and American society and the Church, American and universally, have been negotiated and changed, often vis-à-vis the process of migration and adaptation of newcomers. Those processes, as in the earlier periods and in different places, did not always proceed smoothly or without tensions and conflicts.

The activities of both priests and lay members of the parishes illustrate the multitude of options available to shape and reshape one's social identity, usually in the course of negotiating it through various layers (ethnic, religious, political, moral) and with various stakeholders. And indeed, as in other historical contexts, in the United States of America of the nineteenth and twentieth centuries, the network of dependencies between different ethnic groups was used by political actors, as well as within the Catholic Church.

Parishes

The parish in Panna Maria, Texas, was a typical territorial parish, which encompassed a new settlement founded by Polish immigrants. However, this was not a typical model for the Polish ethnic group. Most of the later Polish parishes were not territorial but national in character. Here, the Poles used the pattern developed in the American Catholic Church with regard to the German and Italian ethnic groups.[3] National

---

2 'Ruszył projekt "Parafie i kościoły polskie w Stanach Zjednoczonych"'.
3 Juliani, 'Italian Americans and their Religious Experience'.

parishes were created at the initiative of immigrants within the regular American territorial parishes with the local bishop's approval. They included representatives of a particular ethnic group living in the area. There could be several national parishes within a single territorial parish. At the same time, a national parish could have faithful coming from more than one territorial parish.

After arriving in the United States in the nineteenth century, immigrants from Poland usually began by attending services held in existing parishes, territorial or national, established by previously settled groups. In his now-classic essay, Will Herberg argued that immigrants on their arrival in the United States were characterized by greater religiosity compared both with their pre-departure state and with those already settled in the United States.[4] Religious practices met their spiritual needs and were also something known and homely. Services conducted in Latin were a familiar ritual in a sea of everyday foreign life that immigrants had to contend with. However, sermons were preached in local languages — English in territorial parishes, Italian, German, Czech, or another language in national parishes. As Charles Hirschman writes, the parish was a bridge between the Old and New Worlds. The aspiration to attend services in one's own language and have 'one's own' priest was the main driver for creating national parishes.[5]

National parishes also allowed the unhindered cultivation of traditional religious rituals, often alien to other ethnic groups. In the case of the Poles, it was, for example, Holy Mass at Christmas Eve, blessing food for Easter, or Marian devotions.[6] Over the years, some of these rituals have been abandoned, but others have become part of Polish American culture and have been maintained by subsequent generations, even if those who celebrate them have become Americanized and no longer participate in the life of national parishes.[7]

Another factor pushing towards national parishes was the desire to implement their own projects, taking into account their own needs and Polish traditions. This need grew as immigrants solidified into the local community and the local labour market.[8] Existing national parishes tended to pursue the goals of the groups who had created them, while territorial parishes were dominated — as was the entire American Church hierarchy — by the Irish, who showed little understanding of ethnic issues and were notorious for their dislike of new immigrants.[9]

It should be remembered that at least until the middle of the twentieth century, the Catholic Church in the United States did not have a good reputation and had to fight for its position.[10] Protestant-dominated American society was not characterized by religious tolerance, and Catholics were even viewed with suspicion; they were

---

4 Herberg, *Protestant — Catholic — Jew*, cited in Hirschman, 'The Role of Religion', p. 1208. Cf. Smith, 'Religion and Ethnicity in America'.
5 Hirschman, 'The Role of Religion', p. 1223.
6 Chrobot, 'Typologies of Polish American Parishes', p. 91.
7 Cf. Erdmans, *The Grasinski Girls*.
8 On the origins of Polish parishes, see, inter alia, Walaszek, 'Kościół, etniczność, demokratyzacja'.
9 This resentment towards Italians is discussed in Juliani, 'Italian Americans and their Religious Experience' and Vecoli, 'Prelates and Peasants', among others.
10 Hirschman, 'The Role of Religion', p. 1222.

POLISH AMERICAN PARISHES OF THE NINETEENTH TO TWENTY-FIRST CENTURIES   343

suspected of having a dual loyalty — with priority to the Vatican — and of seeking to create 'a [church] state within the [American] state'. If the Church hierarchy wanted to prove the fallacy of such reasoning, it had to emphasize the 'Americanness' of its subordinate institutions rather than support national distinctions. The ill-treatment in the Church complained about by Americans of Polish descent was therefore not necessarily due to a particular dislike that the 'Aryans' had for Poles, but to the efforts of the ecclesiastical hierarchy to improve the position of the Church in the American sociopolitical system — although it is questionable whether this justified discrimination against the Polish and other non-Irish ethnic groups.[11]

However, for both ideological and pragmatic (including economic) reasons, the Church hierarchy was keen to ensure that immigrants retained their faith and attachment to Catholicism, rather than become diluted in the Protestant sea.[12] National parishes, where life was lived in the native language, among people with similar backgrounds and experiences, performed this function better than American territorial parishes. As Hirschman writes, 'the bonds of faith are reinforced when a religious community can provide non-spiritual fellowship and practical assistance for the many problems that immigrants face'.[13] From the point of view of the American Church, this was an important argument in favour of creating national parishes.

Successive immigrants from the Polish lands came to the already established Polish world and, as it were, naturally joined the existing Polish parishes; at the same time, they confirmed the need for and guaranteed the continuity of their existence. The Polish parishes provided religious, moral, and practical support to compatriots who felt lost at the beginning of their emigration adventure. They performed many different functions, not only religious (although these should not be forgotten either). As Leonard Chrobot writes, national parishes in the nineteenth and early twentieth centuries were 'a combination of the village parish, the emerging American territorial parish, and a community service agency'.[14]

The parish was the first place to care for the newcomers. There they could find out what to do and how to do it when they arrived in America, where to look for a job, enrol their children in school, or take out an insurance policy. As they settled into the Polish community, the newcomers became involved in various activities organized in the area, of which there were many.

Various groups and associations, both religious and secular in nature, were active in the parishes — from rosary circles and altar boys to local structures of ethnic insurance providers. This richness can be seen, for example, in the jubilee books, where, on the occasion of round anniversaries, the groups active in the parish are listed — sometimes even dozens.[15] Some Polish organizations were based on a parish

---

11   Cf. Buczek, 'Polish American Priests and the American Catholic Hierarchy'.
12   Cf. Juliani, 'Italian Americans and their Religious Experience'.
13   Hirschman, 'The Role of Religion', p. 1229.
14   Chrobot, 'Typologies of Polish American Parishes', pp. 89–90.
15   Leś, *Kościół w procesie asymilacji Polonii amerykańskiej*, p. 193, writes about the seventy organizations that functioned at Chicago's St Hyacinth's parish from its inception in 1894 until 1977, with about fifty of them being created in the first twenty-five years.

structure. For example, the Polish Roman Catholic Union (founded in 1873), one of the oldest and largest Polish American fraternal organizations, adopted the parish as its basic organizational unit.[16] Parish choirs formed the backbone of the Singers' Union of America.[17] Established in 1944, the Polish American Congress is an umbrella organization bringing together other Polish American organizations. Parishes can be members alongside lay organizations.[18]

All these groups carried out a rich variety of organizational and social activities. They held parties, afternoon tea, and balls, organized collections to help Poles back home or workshops on drawing Easter eggs or making traditional Christmas tree decorations. The parishes were the focus of organized Polonia life. It has not always been an idyllic life, with conflicts sometimes even leading to the secession of a group of believers and creating a new parish.[19] The engagement of the parishioners in frictions and tensions confirms the vital role that parishes played in the life of Polonia.

Parishes carried out charitable activities, both on an ad hoc basis (e.g. collecting food and clothing, including the ones to be shipped to Poland) and on a systematic basis, such as operating orphanages and nursing homes. Such institutions testify to the fact that the Polonia cared for the preservation of the Polish identity of the younger generation, as well as for Polish-language care for the sick or elderly, who were generally less Americanized than the younger generations. The magnificent buildings constructed for these activities have left a lasting mark on the places where they were built. The activities are reflected, for example, in the surviving collections of photographs from St Josaphat Parish in Milwaukee.[20]

Parochial schools played an important role in maintaining Polish identity and, at the same time, in facilitating entry into American society. They were the basis of education for the younger generation of ethnic groups until the Great Depression of the 1930s. On the one hand, they made life easier for children brought up in Polish neighbourhoods who did not know English. On the other hand, they were to protect them from the bad influence of the Protestant public school. Sending children to such schools was the fulfilment of both religious and national duties.[21] As late as 1966, 73 per cent of Polish American children had received some form of education in a parochial school.[22] It is, therefore, safe to say that parochial schools played a crucial role in shaping the identity of successive generations of the Polish American community.

Gradually the English language permeated the parochial schools more and more. This happened as a result of both steps taken by the American authorities and the changing nature of the Polish community itself. In the interwar period, the authorities,

---

16 Radziłowski, *The Eagle and the Cross.*
17 Blejwas, *Choral Patriotism.*
18 Wojdon, *White and Red Umbrella.*
19 Numerous examples of conflict are given by Walaszek, 'Kościół, etniczność, demokratyzacja'.
20 Kwasniewski Photographs.
21 Praszałowicz, *Amerykańska etniczna szkoła parafialna.*
22 The research of A. Greeley and P. Rossi is cited by Pula, 'Polish-American Catholicism', p. 6.

POLISH AMERICAN PARISHES OF THE NINETEENTH TO TWENTY-FIRST CENTURIES   345

in pursuit of their *melting pot* policy, began to require schools to meet certain standards, including recognizing an education acquired in a parochial school on condition that instruction was provided in English.[23] In turn, Polonia was becoming more and more entrenched in America. The restoration of Poland's independence in 1918 did not bring the wave of re-emigration that had initially been expected. The perspective of staying in the United States permanently changed the language priorities of Polish youth. Natural assimilation processes were taking place.

The teaching of the Polish language (for those who wished) moved to Saturday schools and included pupils who attended either parochial or public schools during the week. Parochial schools sometimes lent their premises for this purpose but were not always directly involved in the teaching process. Their staff also became increasingly Americanized, even if they had Polish roots.[24]

By the second half of the twentieth century, parochial schools were all-American institutions.[25] Some enjoyed a prestige that allowed them to survive even after the liquidation of the parish from which they originated, although they are no longer ethnic schools but American Catholic public schools. The size of their buildings and other former parish buildings remains a material testimony to how important Polish American parishes used to be.[26]

Churches

Founding churches was traditionally — in the Polish lands — the privilege of the upper classes of society, as ordinary peasants could not afford such activities. In America, wages allowed common immigrants to engage in activities reserved in their country of origin for the nobility and aristocracy. The Polish American churches, therefore, ennobled the emigrants. They were an object of pride, even if the costs involved required considerable sacrifice.[27]

The magnificent buildings testified to the piety and economic strength of the Polish group in relation to the host society: the American Protestant majority as well as other Catholic ethnic groups. They could have been used as an argument in competition for influence, including over the American Catholic Church.

The church buildings, as well as the accompanying parish houses, schools, orphanages, etc., continue to arouse appreciation and amazement among outsiders both for their monumentalism, the style known as the Polish Cathedral Style, and for the fact that ordinary workers, who constituted the majority of Polonia, were able and willing to fund them. They testify to the economic success of Polish immigrants in the United States, to their generosity — skilfully inspired, driven, and controlled

---

23 Buczek, 'Polish American Priests and the American Catholic Hierarchy'.
24 Leś, *Kościół w procesie asymilacji Polonii amerykańskiej*, p. 193.
25 Praszałowicz, 'Polish American Sisterhoods', p. 52.
26 Praszałowicz, 'The Cultural Changes of Polish-American Parochial Schools'; Sibiga, *Kształcenie polonistyczne*.
27 Walaszek, 'Kościół, etniczność, demokratyzacja', pp. 27–28.

by the Polish clergy (A. Walaszek writes, for example, about the practice of selling tickets for Masses or for confessions by Polish parish priests[28]) — and also to their settling in America. After all, temporary migrants would not spend so much money on investments in the country they were about to leave to return home.

The parish buildings were intended to make immigrants' mark and to create something lasting that would also serve future generations. This has proved illusory. With the rise of their material status and position in American society after World War II, the Polish community joined the all-American trend and began moving en masse from their traditional urban neighbourhoods to the suburbs. In turn, African Americans and Hispanics, often also of the Catholic faith, settled in Polonia's former places of residence. They became the new parishioners of Polish parishes and caretakers of former Polish churches. For example, the monumental Basilica of St Josaphat in Milwaukee now stands in the heart of a Mexican neighbourhood, and at St Stanislaus Kostka parish in Chicago, Masses are celebrated in English, Polish, and Spanish.[29] Parishes were thus changing their ethnic character.

Sometimes the consequences of the migration of the Polish community were even more profound, for with the Polish population moving out, parishes lost the economic basis of their existence. There was a lack of funds to maintain the huge buildings, which were in decline. For some time yet, at least some churches attracted their former parishioners to Sunday and holiday services, forming what Robert Zecker called 'streetcar parishes'.[30] The Polish Americans would return to their old places to meet their parents or friends, and do some shopping in a Polish shop or have a Polish dinner in a restaurant.[31] With time, these pilgrimages disappeared too; ethnic shops and businesses collapsed without their daily (and not only festive) clientele, so the list of reasons to visit these places further dwindled. In the former Chicago 'Polish Downtown', where in its heyday there were two large parishes within a mile of each other, including the parish of St Stanislaus Kostka, reputed to be the most populous parish in the world with forty thousand worshippers, the Holy Trinity Church (Figure 15.2) is today looked after by the Polish Catholic Mission — that is, priests delegated and supported from Poland, not by the local Polish American community.[32]

Some other Polish churches were not so fortunate. Danuta Piątkowska lists dozens of New York churches, once serving exclusively or mainly the Polish community, that have ceased to exist at all.[33] A similar phenomenon can be observed in Chicago.

During the urban renewal of the 1950s and 1960s, some churches were demolished along with the Polonia neighbourhoods they served, and the land was used for

---

28 Walaszek, 'Kościół, etniczność, demokratyzacja', p. 33.
29 St Stanislaus Kostka Parish, <http://ststanschurch.org> [accessed 15 January 2018].
30 Zecker, *Streetcar Parishes*.
31 Pula, *Polish Americans*, p. 125.
32 Trójcowo Chicago, <www.trojcowo.com> [accessed 30 December 2017].
33 Piątkowska, *Polskie kościoły*.

Figure 15.2. Holy Trinity Church in Chicago. Photo by Krzysztof Wojdon (2014).

highway construction or, as a little later in Detroit, to enlarge an automobile factory site. The people of Polonia tried to protest, but generally without success.[34] Exceptions include Chicago, where, thanks to the efforts of the Polish community, the Kennedy motorway was routed so that St Stanislaus Kostka Church survived.[35]

In recent years, the troubles of Polish parishes have been compounded by the financial problems of the American Catholic Church, including those related to the payment of compensation to victims of paedophile priests. In search of funds (or savings), church authorities reached for the assets of Polish parishes. They meticulously analysed which ones were loss-making (or which properties could be sold for a significant profit), and desacralized former Polish churches to raise funds from the sale of land and buildings. Thus, their downfall was sealed.

Meanwhile, the Polish community, moving into the suburbs or the southern states, became involved in the Catholic parishes there. Admittedly, in most cases it has no longer made an effort to build new churches and uses less impressive buildings. However, Polish religious traditions are still maintained, various groups are active in parishes, Masses are celebrated in Polish — by priests of Polonia or Polish origin.[36]

---

34 Wylie, *Poletown*.
35 Moreno, 'Stanislaus Kostka Church Celebrates 150 Years'.
36 Chrobot, 'Typologies of Polish American Parishes', among others, writes about these transformations.

Priests and their Status in the Community and beyond

The position of the priest, especially the parish priest — as the example of Fr Moczygemba of Panna Maria shows — was sometimes a leading one. Priests were the leaders of the local elite, including the economic elite. The crucial role of the religious orders — especially the Resurrectionist priests and the Felician Sisters[37] — in Polish parochial schools cannot be overlooked. They formed the core of the teaching staff. Priests and nuns were active in research, especially in a study into the past of Polonia.[38] There are over 1200 priests in the database of significant figures in Polish American life, based on *Who Is Who in Polish America* by Rev. Francis Bolek.[39]

Priests took on political roles.[40] It was not unusual for them to hold positions in Polish organizations. As John Radziłowski writes:

> understanding the PRCUA [Polish Roman Catholic Union of America] means understanding the Polonia community from which it developed, the key parish of St Stanislaus Kostka, and the Congregation of the Resurrection, which played a vital role in the history of both.[41]

In fact, virtually every Polish community organization had (and still has) its own chaplain. His duties included leading prayers during the meetings of the board or organizational ceremonies.

A good priest had great power and enjoyed great authority. Even in the second half of the twentieth century, the press in the People's Republic of Poland noted that the position of Polish American priests resembled the state known in the Polish lands in the nineteenth century and before. And the fact that the authorities of the Polish People's Republic appreciated the position of priests among the Polish community is evidenced by the selection process to which clergy members leaving for work in the United States were subjected to in Poland. Only representatives of certain religious orders could apply for a passport (orders that happened to protest against the policy of the communist authorities were deprived of this privilege), and before leaving, they had to have an interview with representatives of the security apparatus and were subjected to surveillance in the United States.[42]

Despite this harassment, the flow of Polish priests to the United States never stopped, even though, with time, priests who came from the Polish community itself were educated. It was not a quick or trouble-free process, as entering the path of preparation for the priesthood in the United States usually meant accelerated

---

37 Walaszek, 'Kościół, etniczność, demokratyzacja', pp. 23–27; Praszałowicz, 'Polish American Sisterhoods'.

38 Jaroszyńska-Kirchmann, 'The Polish American Historical Association'; Bukowczyk, '"Harness for Posterity the Values of a Nation"'.

39 My own calculations based on 'Pinkowski Files: Database of American Polonia', <http://www.poles.org/db/> [accessed 30 December 2017].

40 Cf. Buczek, *Last of the Titans*.

41 Radziłowski, *The Eagle and the Cross*, p. 35.

42 Zamiatała, 'Duszpasterstwo polonijne'; Zamiatała, 'Władza komunistyczna'.

POLISH AMERICAN PARISHES OF THE NINETEENTH TO TWENTY-FIRST CENTURIES   349

Americanization and contradicted the postulated role of priests as guardians and promoters of Polishness. Polonia attempted to establish a Polish seminary — in Detroit in 1885 on the initiative of Father Józef Dąbrowski. In 1909, the school complex he created was moved to a specially purchased site in Orchard Lake, Michigan.[43] It was also the location for Polish pastoral work and an archive and museum centre. There has always been the problem of directing Orchard Lake graduates and other Polish priests to Polish parishes. In the twentieth century, many times — and not only in Detroit — the Polish community reported cases of priests who did not know the Polish language at all being assigned to Polish parishes, while priests of Polish origin were sent to completely non-Polish parishes.[44]

The position of the Polish clergy in the American Church hierarchy was rather low. For many years, priests of Polish origin had been denied access to the upper echelons of the Church hierarchy.[45] The first American bishop of Polish origin was Paweł Rhode, who was appointed auxiliary bishop of the Archdiocese of Chicago in 1908.[46] Only after World War II were there slightly more nominations, but they were still disproportionate to the number of American Catholics of Polish descent.[47] Cardinal John Król became president of the United States Conference of Catholic Bishops (Bishop of Cleveland in 1953, Archbishop of Philadelphia in 1961, Cardinal in 1967), which could be seen as a symbolic act of recognition of the position of the Polish community, but the appointment was more evidence of Król's own prominence than of the significantly growing influence of the Polish ethnic group on the American Church, especially since the bishops, even of Polish origin, were primarily concerned with the Church and not with the Polish community, which sometimes felt let down by this. Even the election of Cardinal Karol Wojtyła as pope in 1978, although it contributed to a decisive improvement in the position of Americans of Polish descent in American society,[48] did not mean an end to the problems of Polonia within the structures of the American Catholic Church.

In the second half of the twentieth century, the frustration of the Polish community at being undervalued by the American ecclesiastical hierarchy was expressed, for example, by events in Detroit in the 1970s, where leading Polish community organizations called for a boycott of fundraising for the archdiocese, believing that little of the money raised was then used to meet the needs of the Polish community. The archdiocesan authorities invited the Polish activists to talk, and the open conflict was resolved, but the situation remained tense in subsequent years.[49]

The Polish American community has been notorious for being more willing to donate to the Church than to other causes. In connection with subsequent investments

---

43 Renkiewicz, *For God, Country and Polonia*.
44 Wojdon, *White and Red Umbrella*, pp. 199–200.
45 Walaszek, 'Kościół, etniczność, demokratyzacja', pp. 58–62.
46 Pienkos, 'Rhode, Paul Peter'.
47 Galush, 'Religious Life'; Wojdon, *White and Red Umbrella*, pp. 150–51.
48 Jozefski, 'The Role of Polish and American Identities', pp. 49–50.
49 Wytrwal, *Behold!*, pp. 569–71. Cf. similar problems with school collections in the Diocese of Pittsburgh in the 1920s. Buczek, 'Polish American Priests and the American Catholic Hierarchy'.

and the need to maintain parish facilities, priests imposed numerous tributes and obligations on parishioners. They were very successful at this (as evidenced by the scope and size of parish buildings/facilities, including schools, orphanages, hospitals, rectories, churches, chapels, etc.). Some parishes followed the Protestant model, with the parishioners deciding to establish a separate parish and building a church, to which they contributed, and then hiring a priest whose services they paid for with their own contributions. They, therefore, expected to have a say in the staffing of the parish priest's post and a decisive voice on further investment and other parish matters. The Church authorities did not share this vision. Against the background of the staffing of the rectory and various economic problems — when priests incurred debts on behalf of the parish or carried out their own plans — parishioners rebelled, sometimes even leading to violence. Adam Walaszek describes the years-long conflicts in which Polish priests were involved.[50]

The most serious conflict over the management of ethnic parishes occurred at the turn of the twentieth century and involved Rev. Franciszek Hodur of a Polish parish in Scranton, Pennsylvania. Father Hodur tried to assert his rights even at the Vatican, and when that failed, he radicalized his postulates, demanding, among other things, liturgy in the Polish language, more decentralized management of parishes, and the abolition of celibacy for priests. As a result, he seceded and established the Polish National Catholic Church, which soon developed into hundreds of parishes, independent of the 'Roman' Church. Father Hodur himself was in turn ordained as a bishop in the Catholic Church of the Union of Utrecht.[51]

The *national* character of the Polish National Catholic Church lost its importance after the Second Vatican Council, when national languages entered the liturgy of the Catholic Church, and the Polish community succeeded in their demands, by writing appropriate petitions to the local bishops, to include the Polish language in Polish parishes, in addition to English. The PNCC parishes are now shrinking, and ideologically the church is closer to the Catholic Church than to Protestants, for example, on the ordination of women, same-sex marriages, and attitudes to abortion. In 1958, the size of the PNCC was estimated at 270,000 believers in 162 parishes; in 2008, it was estimated at 25,000 in 122 parishes.[52] At the beginning of the twenty-first century — despite all the difficulties — there were about eight hundred Polish parishes within the Roman Catholic Church in the United States.[53]

Conclusions

Leonard Chrobot distinguished five types of Polish parishes in the United States in the twenty-first century. The first one — run by the Polish Catholic Mission — is

---

50 Walaszek, 'Kościół, etniczność, demokratyzacja'; Kuzniewski, *Faith and Fatherland*.
51 Kubiak, *Polski Narodowy Kościół Katolicki*.
52 Jozefski, 'The Role of Polish and American Identities'.
53 Chrobot, 'Typologies of Polish American Parishes', p. 84.

POLISH AMERICAN PARISHES OF THE NINETEENTH TO TWENTY-FIRST CENTURIES   351

aimed at newcomers from Poland (for a short or long stay) and is conducted entirely in Polish by immigrant priests from Poland. The second — in well-functioning Polish American communities — combines Polish- and English-speaking pastoral ministry. The former is mainly aimed at the elderly and the latter at the younger parishioners. As Fr Chrobot pointed out, however, there are shortages in the ranks of Polish-speaking priests brought up in the United States. The third type of Polish parish exists in areas where the Polish community has moved away but still comes to worship. Parishes of the fourth type are those threatened with extinction. Finally, the fifth type is the former Polish parishes, which no longer exist because, for example, the whole district, including the church, was demolished or the faithful moved away, and the church was desacralized for lack of funds for its maintenance.[54]

From the very beginning, not all Polish parishes were the same. This was influenced, among other things, by the character of the parishioners, the peculiarities of the place where they settled, including the American environment, and the personality of the pastor. Polish churches have functioned and continue to function differently in Chicago, where nearly a million Americans of Polish descent are the dominant ethnic group; differently in New York, where, despite its similar size, the Polish community is one of many groups; still differently in small New England towns with a high percentage of people of Polish descent or among contemporary Polish retirees in Florida. Prominent Polish pastors included Father Wincenty Barzyński of Chicago, Father Jan Pitass and Father Feliks Burant of St Stanislaus the Bishop and Martyr Parish in New York, Father Lucyan Bójnowski of New Britain (Connecticut), not to mention Father Hodur.

Some highlight the contemporary crisis of Polish parishes in the United States.[55] They link it to the progressive Americanization of the Polish community — and with it, its dispersal and incorporation into regular territorial American parishes — as well as to secularization, which has been observable since the 1960s, although the Polish community is regarded as one of the ethnic groups that has resisted it the longest. They also point to the assimilationist policy of the American Church hierarchy and the Church in general, including Polish parishes.[56] However, based on my own experience of living in the United States, I am quite far from sharing this pessimism.

Polish parishes can be seen as a unifying factor for Polonia as a group, but also as a means of separating it from WASPs, and as a guardian and marker of identity — the model of the Polish-Catholic (i.e. presuming that being Polish implied being Catholic) was doing very well overseas. Parishes thus defined the distinctiveness of the Polish group, situating it within other European Catholic groups. Polish churches and parishes served the spiritual needs of the ever-growing Polish community as much as they were an expression of its status — both towards relatives and friends back home

54 Chrobot, 'Typologies of Polish American Parishes'.
55 Grondelski, 'Polish American Parishes'.
56 Woźnicki, 'Kościół Katolicki w Stanach Zjednoczonych'.

and towards American society. Polish church tradition maintained distinctiveness and identity while facilitating entry into American society.[57]

One of the classic theories of Americanization is that immigrants become Americans by being ethnic Americans, that is, they first join an existing ethnic group and through it enter (they or their descendants) American society.[58] Ethnic parishes would thus, according to this model, be a transitional stage on the way to the full integration of the faithful into the structures of the American Catholic Church.

Polonia was no exception. As Hirschman writes, among the first steps of new immigrants in the United States is to join religious structures because they give a sense of familiarity, community, belonging, order, and harmony in a new, foreign world. And if it turns out that such structures do not exist, they need to be created. In his view, this applies not only to Catholic structures, but also to those of other denominations and religions.[59] The Polish community followed in the footsteps of the trail blazed by the Irish, Italian, and German groups — which could sometimes make things easier and sometimes make things more difficult, when groups that did not want to share their hard-won position stood in the way of the plans and ambitions of Americans of Polish descent.

Nor were conflicts within parishes unusual — personal, economic, and sometimes ideological. Involvement in the life of the ethnic church sometimes resulted in divisions within the Polish group, the extreme result of which was the creation of the Polish National Catholic Church. But also, within it, the parish became the basic organizational unit and the centre of its activities.

The role of parishes in the lives of Polish Catholics and other American Catholics is evidenced by the fact that members of these communities were not asked *What neighbourhood do you live in?* but *What parish are you from?* — as in Eileen McMahon's book on Irish Americans.[60] In the Polish dialect, the Polish neighborhoods in large cities took the names of the parishes: Jackowo (the parish of St Jacek, i.e. St Hyacinth), Trójcowo (from Święta Trójca — Holy Trinity), or Stanisławowo (St Stanislaus).

Parishes organized Polish life, provided care, a sense of belonging, and opportunities for self-fulfilment, played other important functions, and maintained religious and ethnic identity and created opportunities for its expression. They were the forge of the elites and the engine of social advancement. Many Polish careers began there, both as individuals and as groups (e.g. religious orders). Parishes also provided status vis-à-vis other American ethnic groups, including Catholics. They provided a framework for cooperation and complicity in the American Catholic Church and thus brought the Polish Americans into the mainstream American society.

---

57 Similarly, McMahon, *What Parish Are You From?*, writes about Irish parishes: 'On the one hand, the parish retarded Irish assimilation, yet, on the other hand, it also facilitated assimilation. By promoting family stability, education and even economic mobility, the parish was a model for successful adaptation to a new world environment' (Kindle edition).

58 Handlin, *The Uprooted*.

59 Hirschman, 'The Role of Religion', pp. 1208–10.

60 McMahon, *What Parish Are You From?*

Parishes also preserved the bond with the ancestral homeland, organized aid for Poland (also for Polish parishes), and thus became a marker of the immigrants' status in relation to their places of origin, a testimony to their success in America.

Works Cited

Primary Sources

Kwasniewski, Roman B. J., Photographs, University of Wisconsin-Milwaukee Manuscript Collection 19

Moreno, Nereida, 'Stanislaus Kostka Church Celebrates 150 Years', <https://www.chicagotribune.com/news/ct-chicago-church-150-years-saint-stanislaus-kostka-parish-met-20170423-story.html> [accessed 30 December 2017]

'Pinkowski Files: Database of American Polonia', <http://www.poles.org/db/> [accessed 30 December 2017]

'Ruszył projekt "Parafie i kościoły polskie w Stanach Zjednoczonych"', <http://www.mkidn.gov.pl/pages/posts/ruszyl-projekt-bdquoparafie-i-koscioly-polskie-w-stanach-zjednoczonychrdquo-6770.php> [accessed 15 January 2018]

St Stanislaus Kostka Parish, <http://ststanschurch.org> [accessed 15 January 2018]

Trójcowo Chicago, <www.trojcowo.com> [accessed 30 December 2017]

Secondary Studies

Blejwas, Stanislaus, *Choral Patriotism: The Polish Singers Alliance of America, 1888–1998* (Rochester: University of Rochester Press, 2005)

Brożek, Andrzej, *Polacy w Teksasie* (Opole: Instytut Śląski, 1972)

Buczek, Daniel, *Last of the Titans: Monsignor-Colonel Alphonse A. Skoniecki of Massachusetts* (Sterling Heights: Society of Christ in America, 1986)

———, 'Polish American Priests and the American Catholic Hierarchy: A View from the Twenties', *Polish American Studies*, 33.1 (1976), 34–43

Bukowczyk, John, '"Harness for Posterity the Values of a Nation" — Fifty Years of the Polish American Historical Association and Polish American Studies', *Polish American Studies*, 50.2 (1993), 5–100

Chrobot, Leonard, 'Typologies of Polish American Parishes: Changing Pastoral Structures and Methods', *Polish American Studies*, 58.2 (2001), 83–94

Erdmans, Mary, *The Grasinski Girls: The Choices They Had and the Choices They Made* (Athens: Ohio University Press, 2004)

Galush, William, 'Religious Life', in *The Polish American Encyclopedia*, ed. by J. Pula (Jefferson: MacFarland, 2011), p. 443

Grondelski, John, 'Polish American Parishes in the United States: Reflection on their Future, on the Basis of New Jersey's Experience', *Studia Migracyjne — Przegląd Polonijny*, 36.2 (2010), 105–22

Handlin, Oscar, *The Uprooted: The Epic Story of the Great Migrations that Made the American People*, 2nd edn (Philadelphia: University of Pennsylvania Press, 1973)

Herberg, Will, *Protestant — Catholic — Jew: An Essay in American Religious Sociology* (Chicago: Chicago University Press, 1960)

Hirschman, Charles, 'The Role of Religion in the Origins and Adaptation of Immigrant Groups in the United States', *International Migration Review*, 38.3 (2004), 1206–33

Jaroszyńska-Kirchmann, Anna, 'The Polish American Historical Association: Looking Back, Looking Forward', *Polish American Studies*, 65.1 (2008), 57–76

Jozefski, Jeffrey, 'The Role of Polish and American Identities in the Future of the Polish National Catholic Church', *Polish American Studies*, 65.2 (2008), 27–52

Juliani, Richard, 'Italian Americans and their Religious Experience', in *The Routledge History of Italian Americans*, ed. by William J. Connel and Stanislao Pugliese (New York: Routledge, 2018), pp. 193–211

Kubiak, Hieronim, *Polski Narodowy Kościół Katolicki w Stanach Zjednoczonych Ameryki w latach 1897–1985: Jego społeczne uwarunkowania i społeczne funkcje* (Wrocław: Ossolineum, 1970)

Kuzniewski, Anthony, *Faith and Fatherland: The Polish Church War in Wisconsin, 1896–1918* (Notre Dame: University of Notre Dame Press, 1980)

Leś, Barbara, *Kościół w procesie asymilacji Polonii amerykańskiej: Przemiany funkcji polonijnych instytucji i organizacji religijnych w środowisku Polonii chicagowskiej* (Wrocław: Ossolineum, 1981)

McMahon, Eileen, *What Parish Are You From? A Chicago Irish Community and Race Relations* (Lexington: University of Kentucky Press, 1995)

Piątkowska, Danuta, *Polskie kościoły w Nowym Jorku* (Nowy Jork: Wydawnictwo Świętego Krzyża, 2002)

Pienkos, Donald, 'Rhode, Paul Peter', in *The Polish American Encyclopedia*, ed. by J. Pula (Jefferson: MacFarland, 2011), p. 452

Praszałowicz, Dorota, *Amerykańska etniczna szkoła parafialna: Studium porównawcze trzech wybranych odmian instytucji* (Wrocław: Ossolineum, 1986)

———, 'The Cultural Changes of Polish-American Parochial Schools in Milwaukee, 1866–1988', *Journal of American Ethnic History*, 13.4 (1994), 23–45

———, 'Polish American Sisterhoods: The Americanization Process', *U.S. Catholic Historian*, 27.3 (2009), 45–57

Pula, James, 'Polish-American Catholicism: A Case Study in Cultural Determinism', *U.S. Catholic Historian*, 27.3 (2009), 1–19

———, *Polish Americans: An Ethnic Community* (New York: Twayne Publishers, 1990)

Radziłowski, John, *The Eagle and the Cross: A History of the Polish Roman Catholic Union of America, 1873–2000* (Boulder: Columbia University Press, 2003)

Renkiewicz, Frank, *For God, Country and Polonia: One Hundred Years of the Orchard Lake Schools* (Orchard Lake: Center for Polish Studies, 1985)

Sibiga, Zygmunt, *Kształcenie polonistyczne dzieci i młodzieży w szkołach polonijnych Stanów Zjednoczonych Ameryki Północnej* (Rzeszów: Wydawnictwo WSP, 1994)

Smith, Timothy, 'Religion and Ethnicity in America', *American Historical Review*, 83.5 (1978), 1155–85

Vecoli, Rudolph, 'Prelates and Peasants: Italian Immigrants and the Catholic Church', *Journal of Social History*, 2.3 (1969), 217–68

Walaszek, Adam, 'Kościół, etniczność, demokratyzacja — parafie polonijne w USA (1854–1930)', *Studia Migracyjne — Przegląd Polonijny*, 41.1 (2015), 5–66

Wojdon, Joanna, *White and Red Umbrella: The Polish American Congress in the Cold War Era, 1944–1988* (Reno, NV: Helena History Press, 2015)

Woźnicki, Andrzej, 'Kościół Katolicki w Stanach Zjednoczonych wobec spraw duszpasterstwa migracyjnego', *Studia Polonijne*, 4 (1981), 113–24

Wylie, Jeanie, *Poletown: Community Betrayed* (Urbana: University of Illinois Press, 1989)

Wytrwal, Joseph, *Behold! The Polish-Americans* (Detroit: Endurance, 1977)

Zamiatała, Dominik, 'Duszpasterstwo polonijne w polityce władz wyznaniowych PRL wobec Polonii w latach siedemdziesiątych', *Studia Polonijne*, 27 (2006), 7–23

———, 'Władza komunistyczna wobec duszpasterstwa polonijnego prowadzonego przez zakony męskie', *Studia Polonijne*, 33 (2012), 27–55

Zecker, Robert, *Streetcar Parishes: Slovak Immigrants Build their Nonlocal Communities* (Selinsgrove: Susquehanna University Press, 2010)

PRZEMYSŁAW WISZEWSKI

Concluding Remarks

Inter-Ethnic Cooperation — Fluid Networks of Everyday Practices

In the studies presented in this book, one is struck by the correlation between ethnic groups undertaking activities that strengthen their relations with other ethnos within a single political community and the creation of stories that explain the meaning of these activities while maintaining the ethnic distinctiveness of the cooperating groups (**Wiszewski**, **Bagi**, **Gallinari**). As the past was inextricably linked here with the present, so too was the everyday cooperation between ethnically distinct groups who sought to strengthen their own identity in relation to a shared past. And what was the most important element of these stories from my point of view was the fact that through these narratives communities sought to negotiate, analyse, strengthen, and transfer to younger generations mechanisms for cooperation. These processes of teaching/learning cooperation throughout time and space can be observed, but almost without exception they are created within a given political society and by its specific social groups or institutions. Cooperation was required in order for these groups to grow or just to survive in hostile surroundings (**Myśliwski**, **Troskovaitė**, **Ramonaitė**). Wherever there has been an increase in external factors that impacted on local history (the papacy, royal power), the tendency to polarize communities and concentrate the majority towards ideas relevant to the dominant political actors and against minorities is evident (**Pinto Costa and Lencart**, **Bonet Donato**). At the same time, where political pressure on inter-group relations was decreasing, and the availability of resources (knowledge, means of production, military power) was limited, cooperation between groups in conflict, in theory, was increasingly important. Also, cooperation between groups was crucial in areas as sensitive as concern for health and the participation of the elites in disregarding the ethnic origins of their members for political power and opportunities to benefit from the income generated by communities (**Ramonaitė**, **Brufal-Sucarrat**). Both political games on a supra-regional scale and local economic and political conditions meant

Przemysław Wiszewski • (przemyslaw.wiszewski@uwr.edu.pl) is a Professor of Medieval and Early Modern History at the Historical Institute, University of Wrocław, with special interest in the medieval and early modern history of social relations, values structures within medieval societies, and regional history.

Inter-Ethnic Relations and the Functioning of Multi-Ethnic Societies: Cohesion in Multi-Ethnic Societies in Europe from c. 1000 to the Present, II, ed. by Przemysław Wiszewski, EER 18 (Turnhout: Brepols, 2022), pp. 357–361

BREPOLS ❧ PUBLISHERS 10.1484/M.EER-EB.5.132160

This is an open access chapter made available under a cc by-nc 4.0 International License.

that nowhere were the connections between the specific interests of various groups fixed in a single, unchanging way for decades and centuries. They were constantly updated in correlation with changing conditions (**Barros**, **Bagi**, **Popa-Gorjanu**). In everyday life, cooperation was more natural, brought more profits, and needed less effort than a conflict between ethnically various groups within one political society. In local society one had to deal with a diversity of neighbours on a daily basis with the help of local law and customs. Repetition of inter-ethnic, profitable economic or cultural contacts became in time a habit. A habit promoted in turn repeatability of behaviour, and that caused a lack of detailed analysis of cultural differences, in general — a domestication of an 'Other' without blurring borderlines between 'we' and 'them'. Time and everyday profits played a crucial role in the process of establishing peaceful cooperation based on mutual benefits, though not always of the same kind (i.e. protection for special services or goods, **Ramonaitė**, **Šiaučiūnaitė-Verbickienė**).

The different approach to inter-ethnic relations on a supra-regional and local scale is interestingly reflected in the chapters on the urban situation. This is where cooperation between different ethnic groups engaged in the same profession (trade, crafts) who competed in demanding, rather limited markets comes into focus. Here, too, we can see the variety of laws to which different groups within a single urban community were subject. It is striking that the most remarkable propensity for cooperation can be observed where a more significant number of ethnic groups perform specialized functions in the economic and social ecosystems of cities (**Myśliwski**, **Pleszczyński**). Even when one ethnic group is politically dominant, the others maintain their distinctions and participate in shaping urban policies. One cannot, of course, speak of an idyll. Aggression and exclusion when fighting over scarce resources also occur in cities. The desire of minority ethnic groups to assert their position and identity by defining 'their' homelands within the boundaries of a political organization and with the help of the dominant ethnic group was also present. This was accompanied by attempts to exclude other minority ethnic groups from the geographical and political space of ideological 'homelands' (conflict between Karaites and Rabbinic Jews, **Troskovaitė**). It does not seem obvious, but in troubled, multi-ethnic relations within political organizations, religious dissimilarities or similarities were of less importance than networks of stable political and economic alliances between majority and minority groups. Although the constellation of these alliances changed, their aims were always the same — to stabilize through the law and through daily habits relations between members of these groups that complemented each other. In very ethnically diverse communities, supporting each other by ethnic groups with their diverse skills, knowledge, and contacts with the surrounding world has been and is of key importance for maintaining cooperation that is beneficial for all.

Finally, using the example of the political activity of a minority group (Lithuanian Jews) and the dominant elite (the court of the Russian tsars) in the modern period, the researchers discuss the key topic of communication in power relationships for multi-ethnic societies. How were diverse societies' approaches to cooperation shaped? What are the mechanisms of transmission that ensured the information retained its meaning? In the case of grassroots activities initiated by minority groups, there is a desire to symbolically accentuate the unique ties between an ethnic group that accepted

CONCLUDING REMARKS 359

its inferior status and the dominant political actors in the region (**Šiaučiūnaitė-Verbickienė**). At the same time, in the multi-ethnic Russian Empire, the diversity of ethnos subjected to the tsar's rule was consciously accentuated. However, it leaves no doubt that ethnic Russians are the dominant group (**Sashalmi**). The inherent characteristics of communication within multi-ethnic communities was not due to linguistic diversity. More important than developing language skills was shaping the principles of cooperation between ethnic groups based on the adoption of a set of common values. Acceptance of these values opened up the possibility for daily negotiations between members of various ethnic groups regarding the manner and scope of cooperation. Cultural differences were then relegated to the background.

Despite the passage of time, one can see the common elements of human behaviour. A minority community strove on the one hand to build identity nodes, physical spaces, and social institutions that reinforced the distinctiveness of their group in a multi-ethnic society. On the other hand, these key institutions for the group's identity were progressively used to integrate its members into mainstream society's culture and social life (**Gallinari**, **Ramonaitė**, **Wojdon**). Preserving ethnic identity and building a political community need not lead to conflict unless it is in the interests of the key actors in the political game. But that will be the main subject of the last volume of the project.

At the same time, the analyses presented above point to two distinctly different ways of building cooperation in multi-ethnic communities. One is based on building a vertical structure in which the most important goal of the members of a given ethnos is to play the role of a dominant group over minority groups.[1] In this model, a politically dominant group, most often identifying itself with a unifying vision of its past and culture, subordinates other communities also defined by ethnicity (**Sashalmi**). It is also possible that politically dominant individuals and institutions create a new, dominant, privileged ethnic group. Its acceptance is initially strictly dependent on the support of the institutions which create favourable conditions for it. Over time, this group can become independent while remaining a dominant element in society (**Bonet Donato**, **Popa-Gorjanu**). Minority groups, on the other hand, try to secure a privileged relationship with the politically dominant group in order to survive and strengthen its identity within a political community (**Barros**, **Bagi**, **Šiaučiūnaitė-Verbickienė**). But the same minorities, at the same time, tried to define their own space, a unique place in the space of the political entity in which they had come to live (**Troskovaitė**). The dynamics of the relationships between dominant and underprivileged groups which developed in this way did not lead to conflict as long as it was sufficiently multilateral. Numerous and relatively strong with their consciously built relationships, both vertical (with the dominant group) and horizontal (among themselves), groups that were subordinated to the dominant ethnicity were not forced to abandon their identity (**Myśliwski**, **Pleszczyński**). Indeed, such a process could have been too costly for the dominant community. Only

---

1 Nora Berend, 'Real and Perceived Minority Influences in Medieval Society: Introduction', *Journal of Medieval History*, 45.3 (2019), 277–84 at', pp. 280–81.

when the number and diversity of subordinated groups was decreasing, or when the relations between them — horizontal and vertical — were becoming less important for the ruling elites, could the forced incorporation of ethnic minorities into the dominant community or their removal outside the community occur (**Wiszewski**).

Alongside these relationships based on a model of domination and dependence, there were very important horizontal relationships. They were established between groups which cooperated with each other in daily activities, and guaranteed them an equal position in their political community. There were also mutual material benefits that facilitated survival and development (**Barros, Wiszewski, Gallinari, Brufal-Sucarrat, Ramonaitė**). The two types of relations did not contradict each other; on the contrary, most often — as indicated above — they complemented each other, creating a dynamic model of social balance (**Wiszewski, Gallinari, Bagi, Myśliwski, Pleszczyński**). It was even resistant to political crises, as long as the elites in power did not want to exploit the possibility for ethnic conflict for their own benefit at any given moment (**Gallinari**).

The daily cooperation of members of different ethnic groups within a single political community has not been idyllic in the European past. The threat of a conflict arising from the lack of acceptance of the 'Other' has always been present. Usually, however, the benefits of cooperation outweighed the benefits of conflict. The decisive role was played by the continuous experience of a concrete profit from the presence of 'Others' in the immediate environment, from using their unique skills and qualities. The law, enforced by the political authorities, played a key role in calculating the benefits of cooperation. It defined a framework for cooperation that would be safe for all and gave the possibility of cultivating a specific ethnic identity by minorities themselves. The latter was necessary for ensuring a sense of security for members of ethnic minorities in the face of the uncertainty of daily participation in changing political or economic relations. The latter required constant negotiation with their fellow participants, who were often from other ethnic groups, about the principles of mutual relations as set out by the law. The counterweight to this experience of *fluid everyday* was stable belonging to a specific ethnic group, a particular communicative community which referred back to common, unchanging cultural codes derived from the past. The dynamic relationship between the variable and stabilizing components of everyday social relations gave the multi-ethnic political community a great deal of flexibility, the ability to creatively respond to new challenges, and at the same time guaranteed a stable structure, which supplied a dependable framework for everyday life.

Everyday interactions between members of various ethnic groups, constantly building a sense of the benefits derived from participation, and finally emphasizing their compliance with the generally applicable law, built up the cohesion and resistance to the external threats faced by diverse communities. Less resilient, paradoxically, these communities were affected by the internal use of ethnic identity as an argument in political struggles. The benefits of inter-ethnic cooperation were obvious, but required constant attention and the commitment of the parties involved in the relationship. It did not take much effort for politicians to present the permanent features of a given ethnic identity as threatening to others, and then disseminate that knowledge while invoking the same trait in different contexts. And what is simple and does not require any effort has been and is a desirable tool in a political game which leads to conflicts that only strengthen the politicians who initiated them. But the issue of the activity of political players in the context of inter-ethnic relations in a community will be addressed in the final volume of our series.

Index

Afonso I Henriques the Conqueror, king of Portugal: 110
Afonso III the Boulonnais, king of Portugal: 81
Afonso IV the Brave, king of Portugal: 81–83, 90
Afonso V the African, king of Portugal: 83, 85, 88
Agalbors, daughter of Ponc de Cervera, wife of Ramon Berenguer IV: 117, 119
Agramunt: 35, 36
Alagón, Leonardo de: 134
Alba Iulia: 244
Alexander I, tsar: 336
Alexander II, tsar: 24, 321–23, 325–26, 331
Alexander III, tsar: 24, 321–36
Alexander Jagiellon, king of Poland: 182–83
Alfonso I, king of Aragon: 119
Alfonso II the Chaste, king of Aragon: 12, 31–34, 50, 51
Alfonso IV, king of Aragon: 120
Alfonso V, king of Aragon: 132
Algarve: 74, 107
Almohads: 49
Almoravids: 57–71
Andalusians: 57–67, 70–71
Andrew II, king of Hungary: 235–42
Andrew III, king of Hungary: 243–45
Armenians: 18, 164, 167, 169, 174, 176–77, 181–83, 185–86, 190–93, 195–96, 213, 215–18

Balear Islands: 46, 118
Barisone I, judge of Arborea: 115, 117–19
Barnim I, duke of Szczecin: 164, 170
Bela II, king of Hungary: 231

Bela IV, king of Hungary: 236, 239, 243
Bohemians: 177–78, 196
Bolesław I the Pious, duke of Greater Poland: 164
Bolesław I the Tall, duke of Silesia: 145, 151
Bolesław II Rogatka, duke of Silesia: 148, 150, 152
Bonaventura of Arborea, daughter of judge Hugh II of Arborea: 120
Brzeg, town in Silesia: 152–53

Caffa: 168
Cagliari: 16–17, 117, 124, 126, 129, 132, 134, 135
Callixtus II, pope: 42
Callixtus III, pope: 108, 109
Carl I Robert of Anjou, king of Hungary: 254
Casimir III, duke of Pomerania: 171
Casimir III the Great, king of Poland: 163–65, 167, 188, 212
Casimir IV Jagiellon, king of Poland: 165, 172, 194, 276
castrenses: 233, 235, 246
Catalans: 13–14, 125
Celestine III, pope: 104
Ceuta: 109, 110
Charles Robert d'Anjou, king of Hungary : 240, 242
Clement III, pope: 36
Chronicle of Polish Dukes: 150
Chronicon Pictum Vindobonense: 252–54
Cologne: 166
Constantinople: 107
Crusades: 37–38, 41–43, 99–100
Cubello, Leonardo: 132
Czechs: 146

364 INDEX

Deeds of the counts of Barcelona: 43
Dej: 232–33
Dinis (Denis), king of Portugal: 81
Dragon Order: 255–56, 258
Doria, Brancaleone: 130–31, 135
Duarte (Edward) the Philosopher King, king of Portugal: 83
Dutchmen: 212

Elisabeth of Poland, daughter of the Władysław the Elbow–High, queen of Hungary: 254
Emery, son of s. Stephen, king of Hungary: 250
Englishmen: 212
Estonians: 11
Eugene III, pope: 49

Fara, Juan Francisco: 127
Finland: 329, 331
Florence: 163, 176, 181
Frederick I Barbarossa: 119
Frisians: 162
Fulgineo, Federico de, Dominican friar: 125–26

Galli Anonymi Cronicae et gesta ducum sive principuum Polonarum: 162
Garai, family: 255–56
Gdańsk: 161–62, 166, 169, 170–73, 176–77, 179, 181, 184, 186, 188, 190–92, 195–96, 270
Genoa: 46, 119, 125, 163, 167, 169
Georg of Brankovic, despot of Serbia: 257–58
Germans: 17–18, 19, 145–46, 153, 162, 164, 167–68, 170, 173, 175–76, 180–84, 186–87, 189, 191–92, 195–96, 212–13, 215, 228–29, 233, 235–40, 242–43, 251–52
Géza I, king of Hungary: 231
Géza II, king of Hungary: 237
Granada: 101, 107
Gregory VII, pope: 117
Gregory IX, pope: 243
Guinea: 107

Henryk I, duke of Jawor: 150
Henryk I the Bearded, duke of Silesia: 145, 151
Henryk II the Pious, duke of Silesia: 148
Henryk III the White, duke of Silesia: 149, 152
Henryk IV Probus, duke of Silesia: 150, 164
The Henryków Book: 145–46
Holy Land: 107, 108
Hospitallers: 49, 109
hospites: 230, 232, 235, 246
Hugh de Cervera, viscount of Bas: 119
Hugh II, judge of Arborea: 115, 123, 125, 128, 130
Hugh III, judge of Arborea: 130–31, 135
Hungarians: 19, 20, 229, 233, 240, 241, 243
Hunyadis, family: 257

Iglesias, town on Sardinia: 126
iobagiones: 230, 234–35, 246
Irishmen: 342
Italians: 18, 125, 128, 161, 167–69, 172–73, 176–77, 179, 181, 183–87, 189, 191–93, 196, 213, 215, 254, 256, 341, 342, 352,

James II, king of Aragon: 120, 125
Jews: 12, 15, 18, 21–23, 73–92, 111, 162, 164–69, 171–72, 174–76, 178, 181, 182, 186–89, 191–96, 212–15, 217–19, 265–66, 273–86, 292–93, 297–98, 309–19, 325, 333, 336, 358
João de Xira, friar: 110
João I, king of Portugal: 81, 85, 108
João II, king of Portugal: 84, 90
John, prince of Arborea: 121–23
John III Sobieski, king of Poland: 276–77

Karaites: 21, 22, 168, 265–66, 273–75, 278–79, 285, 291–305, 358
Kaunas: 279–80
Knezes: 241, 243–46
Kołobrzeg: 162

Konrad I, duke of Silesia: 149
Kraków: 162–67, 169, 173–78, 181–96, 270, 276, 280,

languages
   German: 144, 148, 150, 174
   Latin: 144, 148, 174
   Polish: 146, 148, 174, 344–46
   Tiurkic (Karaite): 304
Lateran, Fourth Council: 76–77, 80
law
   German: 144, 146–47, 151–52, 163
   Polish: 144, 146–47, 151
Leo X, pope: 102, 109
Leonor of Arborea, daughter of Marianus IV: 130–31, 135
Liber de institutione morum: 250–
Lisbon: 74, 83, 85–87, 92, 110
Lleida: 14, 35, 36, 46, 49, 57, 60–71
Louis the Great of Anjou, king of Hungary: 242–43, 252, 254
Lubiąż, Cistercian abbey: 145
Lublin: 18, 188, 210–16, 219, 282, 311–12, 330
Lviv: 18, 19, 161, 165–69, 174–78, 181–86, 190, 192–93, 195, 210–11, 216–20

Majorca: 118
Majorcans: 125
Manuel I, king of Portugal: 74, 90, 101, 109
Maria, daughter of judge Hugh II of Arborea: 120–21
Marianus I, judge of Arborea: 116
Marianus IV, judge of Arborea: 120–23, 128, 130–31, 135
Marianus V, judge of Arborea: 131
Marrakesh: 57, 59, 60
Masovians: 164
Matthias Corvinus, king of Hungary: 258
Mestwin II, duke of Pomerelia: 171
Milicz: 147
Moldova: 167
Moncada, Pere de: 122
Moncada, Sibilla de, wife of John of Arborea: 122

Moscow: 323
Muslims: 14–16, 27, 33, 36, 37, 39–50, 60–71, 73–92, 100–01, 105, 110, 111, 164, 328

Neapolitans: 125
Nicholas I, tsar: 334, 336
Nicolàs Carròs of Arborea: 134
Nicopolis, battle of: 255, 256
Nuremberg: 163–64, 172, 187

Ocna Dejului: 233–34
Old Believers: 333–36
Opatów: 315–18
Oradea: 232–33
Order of Avis: 99, 100, 104, 108, 109
Order of Calatrava: 50, 99, 104, 108
Order of Christ: 103, 104, 108, 109, 110
Order of St James: 104, 108
Order of St John: 99, 104, 109
Oristano: 130
Ourique, battle of: 110

Padua: 273–74, 277
Panna Maria, Texas: 339, 341
Paul II, pope: 108
Pechenegs: 238
Pedro I, king of Portugal: 78, 80
Pere de Exerica, natural son of Alfonso IV, king of Aragon: 120
Peter, son of judge Hugh II of Arborea: 120
Peter I, judge of Arborea: 119
Peter III, judge of Arborea: 120
Peter IV, king of Aragon: 121–23, 129
Peter II the Catholic, king of Aragon: 31
Pisa: 117, 120, 124, 126, 128, 133
Płock: 161–62, 169–70, 174, 178, 181–83, 187–89, 191, 195, 196
Poles: 17–18, 145, 153, 167, 171–73, 177–78, 183–84, 186–88, 192, 195–96, 212, 254, 343–44, 346, 352
Pomeranians: 171, 172, 179, 196
Poznań: 165, 169
Prussians: 163, 171
Przemysł I, duke of Greater Poland: 149

Radvila, family: see Radziwiłł
Radziwiłł, family: 277, 280, 297
Ramon Berenguer III, count of Barcelona: 32, 41, 42, 43
Ramon Berenguer IV, count of Barcelona: 12, 31, 33–34, 38, 40–49, 51, 63, 65, 67, 117–19
Red Ruthenia: 164, 166, 195
Rhodes Island: 100, 107
Romanians: 19, 229, 238, 240–45
Russians: 24, 323–
Ruthenians: 11, 161–62, 164, 169, 177–79, 181, 187, 196, 213, 216–17, 234

Sassari: 132
Saxons: see Germans
Scots: 212–13
Seville: 59
Sibiu: 237–39
Sicilians: 125
Sigismund of Luxemburg, emperor, king of Bohemia and Hungary: 20, 255, 257, 259
Sigismund I the Old, king of Poland: 165, 183, 214, 276, 280
Sigismund August, king of Poland: 276, 280
Sleszkowski, Sebastian: 281–84
Stephen, saint, king of Hungary: 250, 251–52
Stephen III, king of Hungary: 232
Stephen V, king of Hungary: 236
Szczecin: 161–63, 170–71, 173, 179, 181, 186, 189, 191, 192, 196
Szeklers: 228–29, 241, 246
Środa Śląska: 147–48

Tagus River: 74
Tallin: 11
Tatars: 164, 168, 298, 304
Terragona: 41–42
Templars: 44–45, 47, 49, 66
Teutonic Order: 171–72, 190, 237
Tortosa: 35, 36, 43, 46–47, 49, 57, 60–61
Trakai: 22, 292–97, 299–302, 304–05

Transylvania: 167
Turda, salt mines: 231
Turks: 102, 108, 110

Urban II, pope: 39
Urgell, county of: 30
Usatges of Ramon Berenguer IV, count of Barcelona: 31–34, 50

Valencia: 49, 60–61, 71
Varengians: 162
Venice: 163
Vienne, Council of: 77, 84
Villano, archbishop of Pisa: 118
Villanova, town on Sardinia: 128, 133
Vilna: see Vilnius
Vilnius: 22, 23, 270–71, 277–78, 280, 284, 292–93, 297–305, 309–19
Vlachs: 216
Vlad Tepes II, duke of Wallachia: 257–58
Vlad Tepes III the Dracula, duke of Wallachia: 257–58

Wallachia, principality: 245, 256, 258
Walloons: 163, 166–67, 177, 179, 185
Wieliczka, salt mines: 176
William of Montpellier: 45, 48
Władysław, archbishop of Salzburg, duke of Silesia: 152
Władysław of Opole, duke: 254
Władysław the Posthumous, king of Bohemia: 165
Władysław I the Elbow-High, king of Poland: 163, 254
Władysław I (III Warneńczyk), king of Hungary and Poland: 257
Władysław II the Exile: 151
Władysław II Jagiełło, king of Poland: 165
Wolin: 162
Wrocław: 152–53, 161, 164–68, 173, 175–76, 179, 181–82, 184–85, 187, 189–96

Zamość: 18, 211, 215–16
Zaragoza: 14, 57, 60–61
Zurara, Gomes Eanes de: 109, 110

Early European Research

All volumes in this series are evaluated by an Editorial Board, strictly on academic grounds, based on reports prepared by referees who have been commissioned by virtue of their specialism in the appropriate field. The Board ensures that the screening is done independently and without conflicts of interest. The definitive texts supplied by authors are also subject to review by the Board before being approved for publication. Further, the volumes are copyedited to conform to the publisher's stylebook and to the best international academic standards in the field.

Titles in Series

Sociability and its Discontents: Civil Society, Social Capital, and their Alternatives in Late Medieval and Early Modern Europe, ed. by Nicholas Eckstein and Nicholas Terpstra (2009)

Diseases of the Imagination and Imaginary Disease in the Early Modern Period, ed. by Yasmin Haskell (2011)

Giovanni Tarantino, *Republicanism, Sinophilia, and Historical Writing: Thomas Gordon (c. 1691–1750) and his 'History of England'* (2012)

Writing Royal Entries in Early Modern Europe, ed. by Marie-Claude Canova-Green, Jean Andrews, and Marie-France Wagner (2013)

Friendship and Social Networks in Scandinavia c.1000–1800, ed. by Jón Viðar Sigurðsson and Thomas Småberg (2013)

Identities in Early Modern English Writing: Religion, Gender, Nation, ed. by Lorna Fitzsimmons (2014)

Fama and her Sisters: Gossip and Rumour in Early Modern Europe, ed. by Heather Kerr and Claire Walker (2015)

Understanding Emotions in Early Europe, ed. by Michael Champion and Andrew Lynch (2015)

Raphaële Garrod, *Cosmographical Novelties in French Renaissance Prose (1550–1630): Dialectic and Discovery* (2016)

Languages of Power in Italy (1300–1600), ed. by Daniel Bornstein, Laura Gaffuri, and Brian Jeffrey Maxson (2017)

Performing Emotions in Early Europe, ed by Philippa Maddern, Joanne McEwan, and Anne M. Scott (2018)

Women and Credit in Pre-Industrial Europe, ed. by Elise M. Dermineur (2018)

Emotion and Medieval Textual Media, ed. by Mary C. Flannery (2019)

Luxury and the Ethics of Greed in Early Modern Italy, ed. by Catherine Kovesi (2019)

Memories in Multi-Ethnic Societies: Cohesion in Multi-Ethnic Societies in Europe from c. 1000 to the Present, I, ed. by Przemysław Wiszewski (2020)

Historiography and the Shaping of Regional Identity in Europe: Regions in Clio's Looking Glass, ed. by Dick E. H. de Boer and Luís Adão da Fonseca (2020)

Wojtek Jezierski, *Risk, Emotions, and Hospitality in the Christianization of the Baltic Rim, 1000–1300* (2022)

In Preparation

Private Life and Privacy in the Early Modern Low Countries, ed. by Michaël Green and Ineke Huysman

Legal Norms and Political Action in Multi-Ethnic Societies: Cohesion in Multi-Ethnic Societies in Europe from c. 1000 to the Present, III, ed. by Przemyslaw Wiszewski